The Many Colors of Hinduism

The Many Colors of Hinduism

A Thematic-Historical Introduction

CARL OLSON

RUTGERS UNIVERSITY PRESS
NEW BRUNSWICK, NEW JERSEY, AND LONDON

LIBRARY OF CONGRESS CATALOGING-IN-PUBLICATION DATA

Olson, Carl.
The many colors of Hinduism : a thematic-historical introduction / Carl Olson.
p. cm.
Includes bibliographical references and index.
ISBN-13: 978-0-8135-4067-2 (hardcover : alk. paper)
ISBN-13: 978-0-8135-4068-9 (pbk. : alk. paper)
1. Hinduism. 2. Hinduism–History. I. Title.
BL1202.O68 2007
294.5—dc22 2006032346

A British Cataloging-in-Publication record for this book is available from the British Library.

Manufactured in the United States of America

This book is dedicated to
Professor Julius Lipner,
a man with a heart as big as he is.

CONTENTS

PART III
Issues in Modern and Contemporary Hinduism

PREFACE

This book is intended as an introduction to the Hindu religious tradition for college undergraduate courses. I am convinced that writing such a book is impossible. But I would like to share what little I have learned teaching this course for more than twenty-five years. Many traditional texts on Hinduism tend to stress its classical religious tradition with its emphasis on the Brahmin textual tradition and practices, and they tend to neglect the practices of lower castes. Prior texts on Hinduism have also tended to ignore completely, or sorely neglect, the role and voices of women within the culture. Likewise, previous introductory texts have neglected the importance of the religiosity of common folk living in villages throughout India. There has also been a tendency in books of this type to overlook devotion to the deity Rāma and the Sant tradition of north India. Moreover, previous books on Hinduism have stressed the importance of texts, making sacred scripture or religious texts normative for the study of the religion. Those emphasizing textual evidence tend to forget about the oral nature of the culture from ancient times to the present. This introduction seeks to overcome some of the shortcomings of prior introductory studies of Hinduism and to present a more balanced account of this rich religious tradition, without claiming to cover everything.

In addition to giving more attention to the religious practices of lower-caste Indians, the role of women in the culture, and the religious life of village folk, this text introduces students to various themes of the Hindu way of life through the utilization of important cultural metaphors, symbols, and narratives. The intention in following this approach is to enable students to enter empathetically into the religion and to appreciate the rich unity and diversity of Indian culture. Since it is difficult to make generalizations about Hinduism that will be true for the whole of it, a thematic/historical approach will contribute to a student's comprehension of its many competing and even contradictory aspects. This study will not stress the classical tradition at the expense of the more current religious ways of life, but it will rather attempt to balance them.

This thematic/historical approach is supported and informed by certain presuppositions and pre-understandings on the part of the author. A fundamental presupposition is that "Hinduism" is a construct of scholars to provide a label for Indian religiosity in its multitudinous variety. The vast majority of the people of India have simply practiced their religion throughout the centuries without making it into an "ism." It is even possible to argue that there is no entity called Hinduism in historical time and place. I tend to agree with the Indian historian Romila Thapar, who claims that there are many "Hinduisms." Even though the term "Hinduism" is used to describe an enormously complex configuration of religious traditions and practices and originates in the imagination of intellectuals, this does not necessarily mean that we must discard the term. I agree with the Indologist Alf Hiltebeitel when he writes, "In Hinduism, we are faced with a deep and diverse tradition, one that cannot be expected to rethink the name it wants to call itself, no matter how recent the name may be." The term "Hinduism" will be discussed more fully in the first chapter.

I confess that I approach the subject as an outsider. Nonetheless, the book is based on textual evidence and the voices of Indian insiders. I have also relied on the fieldwork of anthropologists in close contact with insiders, voices of Indian thinkers, and some of my own personal experiences. As an outsider, I have attempted to immerse myself in India's rich history, literature, and culture in order to enjoy empathetically the various manifestations of Hinduism. It is my sincere hope that readers will recognize that this book was a labor of love and not an attempt simply to reveal the strange elements of the religious culture for the prurient interest of other outsiders. An outsider studying and interpreting a specific religious tradition offers another perspective that is neither inferior nor superior to that of the insider. It is just a different perspective, in which the insider would be able to recognize his or her tradition, assuming that the outsider is successful. The use of metaphor and narrative in this study is intended to evoke a dialogical understanding and not a confrontation between insider and outsider. It is important to let Hindus tell their stories and for outsiders to listen and learn. By its grounding in Indian culture, the narrative approach does potentially less harm, it uses a method that is friendlier to another culture, it is an approach that is actually used by the culture being studied, and it reduces the imposition of outside categories that might distort the subject.

Along these lines, the complexity of Hinduism (for lack of a better term) can be captured best by a suitable metaphor. Julius Lipner adopts the metaphor of the banyan tree—a single tree with many branches that grow into the soil—in order to convey the sense of a unity within the context of a wide diversity. Metaphors have the ability to express notions that ordinary language cannot convey adequately. Since Lipner has already appropriated the banyan tree, I shall adopt the metaphor of the rainbow, which I think is equally effective. The rainbow metaphor captures the variety and many colors of Hinduism over the centuries. The colorful saris of young girls and women throughout India, who color the life of Indian culture every day, inspire this metaphor. Another source of inspiration is the stalls outside of temples that sell the colorful garlands of flowers that one can purchase to offer to the deities within the temple or simply wear around one's neck. A wheel symbolizing the *dharma* (doctrine, teaching, law, or custom) would also have been a good choice for a metaphor, although the rainbow perhaps better suggests the vast variety, unity, and richness of the religious culture.

There are many people to thank in a book of this nature. The most obvious group is scholars of broad and more specialized studies of Hinduism from whom I have learned much. Many of these scholars are cited in the footnotes of the chapters. I am very appreciative of the generosity and graciousness of the many different people of India who have allowed me into their homes and temples. Thanks, too, to my colleagues Glenn Holland and Eric Boynton for their wonderful teaching and companionship. Thanks also to former Dean LaLloyd Michaels and President Richard Cook for giving me the Teacher-Scholar Chair in the Humanities at Allegheny College, which gave me the opportunity to begin this book.

Outside of the academic world La Lloyd, Lefty, Casey, and old gimpy have shared some enjoyable and dialogical walks in the woods of Pennsylvania. Appreciation goes to Holly and Marlon for their creative powers, and to Kelly for continuing her education in a field in which she will be able to help others. Julius Lipner of Cambridge University shared some of his own scholarship with me, Anindita Lipner shared her warm and gracious hospitality, and the atmosphere of Clare Hall and its wonderful folks gave me the impetus to begin this project. The ducks on the River Cam provided some quiet moments for reflection. I need to thank Mike Myers of Washington State University for being a fun companion in India and John Koller of RPI for playing the role of temple guru.

I appreciate the faith and enthusiasm that former editor David Myers at Rutgers University Press gave to this project. And I also appreciate the continued encouragement and help given to me by the successive editors Kristi Long and Adi Hovav and the very professional staff at the press. Although I am sorry to learn of Kristi's departure from the press for an adventure in Scotland, the press will be in good hands under the leadership of Adi Hovav. Before an actor or actress goes on stage or steps before a camera on a movie set, he or she needs a make-up artist to make him or her look photogenic. In a venture of this sort, the make-up artist is the copyeditor, who was in this instance Margaret Case. I appreciate her efforts to make this text more readable and for giving me the illusion of being photogenic for a larger public.

It is my hope that some day in the not too distant future that my grandson Benicio will be able to read what Professor Grandpa composed, learn from it, and come to appreciate the complex religious culture of India. The little guy has brought much joy to our life, and it will be interesting to watch his development from an apparently postmodern and deconstructive young man into someone who is, one hopes, less skeptical about life. And for long-suffering Peggy, thanks for being there. Finally, I need to thank the many wonderful students that I have had the privilege to teach over the past few decades for inspiring me to improve.

I have tried to adhere to the correct transliteration of terms and diacritical marks, although for the convenience of students I have made some exceptions that will be evident in the body of the text, with Westernized spellings for such names as Krishna with which most readers are more familiar. Foreign terms are defined or explained within the body of the text. This approach removes the need for a glossary, and saves pages and trees.

PART I

The Nature of Hinduism

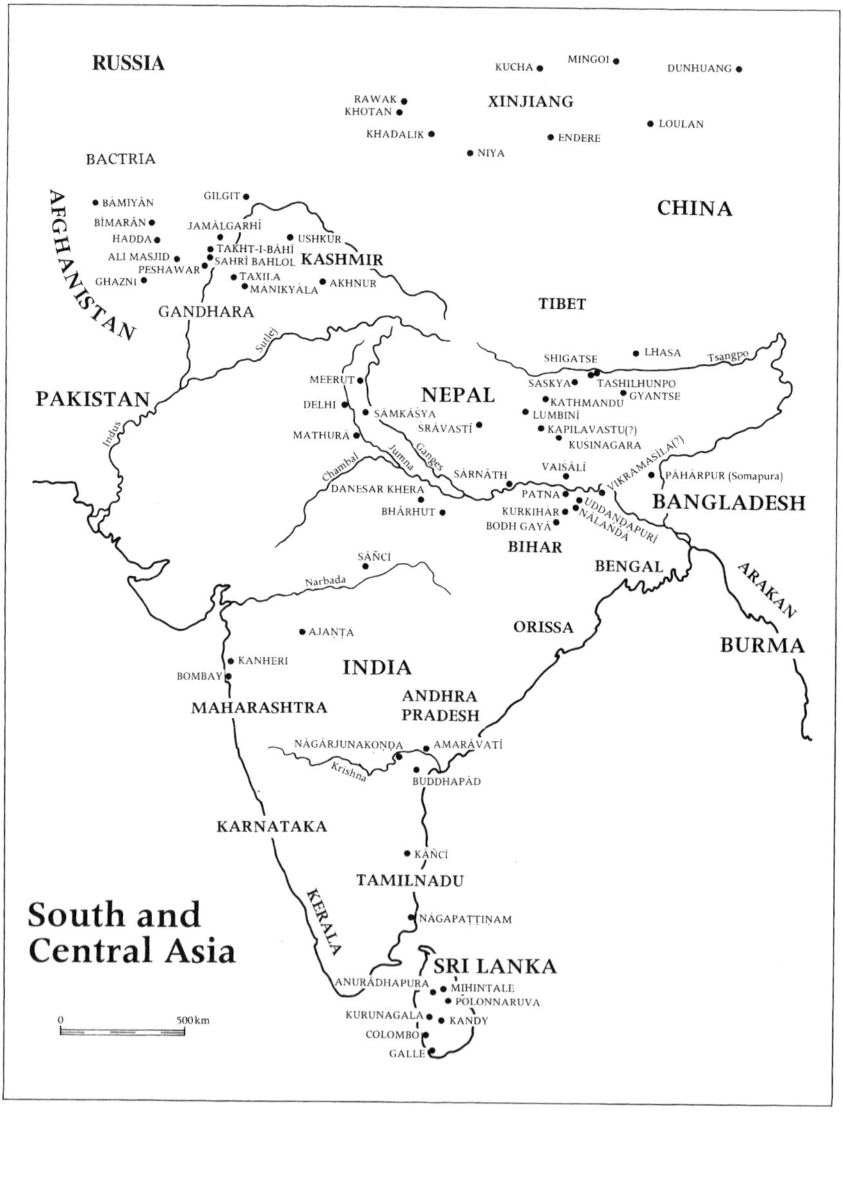

South and Central Asia

1

A Journey to Mother India

Traveling to India from a small town in western Pennsylvania is both an adventure and an arduous chore. It is a long trip, and may involve booking a hotel in London to catch a connecting flight the next day for the second half of the trip to the subcontinent. If you fly to the airport at Chennai (formerly Madras) in the southern part of the country, for instance, after arriving and passing through customs, you can jump into the taxi of an eager driver, who races at high speed to take you to your hotel, continually zigzagging his vehicle through traffic as you hang on for dear life. Looking out of the window of the speeding taxi, you pass a twenty-foot neon sign for the Gaṇeśa gas station on your right, and you see a sign for a Gaṇeśa grocery store on your left, which are both named for the popular elephant-headed deity and son of the great god Śiva. On the meridian strip divining the four-lane highway, you notice lounging cows watching the traffic pass by. You also see buses jam-packed with human bodies. How can personal purity regulations be observed under such circumstances, when people are packed together like sardines in a can? You also see colorfully dressed young girls, presumably on their way to school, and others on the rear seat of a motorbike being driven by an adult male. As vehicles pass your taxi on the left, you notice from the back seat that directly in front of the taxi, fifty yards down the highway, there is a cow looking directly at your vehicle and blocking the driving lane. The driver slams on his brakes, but he does not honk his horn, which you will discover is unusual because drivers in the city operate their vehicles with one foot on the accelerator and one hand on the horn. The driver stops before hitting the cow, which is still looking directly at the taxi. The driver waits for the other cars to pass, and then he drives around the cow without uttering a profanity at the bovine. This represents more than an attempt to protect his vehicle from damage. Certainly, the action of the driver demonstrates a respect for a living creature. He does not worship the animal. He simply goes around the cow. This is clearly a different kind of place; it is not better or worse than your place of origin—it is just different. But it is different in a way that raises your level of curiosity.

The cow wandering on the four-lane highway is emblematic of the difference from the rural area from which you came, which is home to many cows, where they are confined to pasture lands and controlled by a fence made of barbed wire or wood. The wandering cow that my taxi driver was careful not to hit or curse at represents a symbol of his country, much as the bald eagle is a symbol for your country. Although in the twentieth-century Mahatma Gandhi advocated reverence for the cow as he struggled to lead his country from the yoke of colonialism, the Indian reverence for the cow is much more ancient.

If one goes back to the most ancient body of literature in Indian history, called the Vedas, it is possible to find evidence for the sanctity of the cow. The Vedas suggest the economic value of the cow to ancient Indians because of its valuable products, which are eventually identified as five specific items: milk, urine (used as a disinfectant and cleaning agent because of its high ammonia content), butter, ghee (clarified butter), and dung (used, dried, as a fuel in rural India). The number of cows a person owned determined a person's wealth.[1] Because of their connection to wealth, cows were attractive booty during war, and they were desirable fees for ritual services rendered by priests. The cow served as a metaphor for fecundity, maternity, well-being, and beauty. As odd as it might sound, it was considered flattering for a woman to be compared to a cow during the vedic period (RV 10.95.6). It was also considered an honor for a woman's motherly nature to be compared to that of a cow (RV 4.45.2). The feminine, passive cow was a counterpart to the masculine, aggressive stallion. The phallus and seed of the horse and their counterparts, the udder and milk of a cow, symbolically expressed the opposition of these two culturally important animals.[2]

According to a narrative in the Vedas (RV 3.31), Indra, a warrior deity, frees captive cows from a cave, and he allows them to roam freely. By freeing the cows from the darkness of the cave, Indra transforms them into symbols of light. Within the vivid imagination of vedic poets, the cow also became connected to the life-giving powers of the cosmic waters.[3] Because of influence from the doctrine of nonviolence (*ahiṃsā*) that originated with Jainism and Buddhism around the sixth century B.C.E., the cow became a symbol of the earth goddess and the unity of life. Gradually, cows were exempted as a source of food and revered as special animals. Eventually, they became symbolic of Mother India.

As one travels around India, more than just free-roaming cows strike one as unexpected; a visitor also encounters a wide diversity in customs, religion, languages, geography, climate, and culture. On a tour of India, one encounters the impressive Himalayan mountain range in the north, the deserts of the west, the rich soil of the relatively flat central valleys or the hilly central plateaus, and the more tropical climate of the southern part of the country. On such a journey around the country, it is possible to encounter people speaking any of fourteen major languages, each with numerous local variations. Some of these languages are Indo-Aryan, while others are indigenous Dravidian languages of the south; there are also many tribal languages. In addition to a wide variety of religious practice, it is also possible to encounter many different ways of thought, such as materialism, monism, dualism, pluralism, and idealism. Some schools of thought stress empirical ways of knowing, whereas others emphasize intuition associated with the practice of meditation. Some of these patterns of thought have been influenced by foreign modes of thinking because of the migration of groups, trade, and martial conquest from such diverse groups as Persians, Greeks, Muslims, and Westerners.

Mother India offers a visitor a smorgasbord of thought, and this wide variety means that there is no single valid position or truth. There are, however, a variety of different perspectives that provide partial glimpses of truths, even though particular schools of thought might claim to offer a full view of reality. With this wide variety of thought, it is permissible for a person to think or believe virtually anything. Liberal tolerance of thought is countered by a cultural intolerance of socially deviant behavior, which is discussed more fully in chapter 4.

Hindu and Hinduism

Before there was a geographical term to distinguish "India" from other locations in Asia, there were references in the ancient vedic texts to a river called Sindhu (RV 5.53.9). This term also designated the inhabitants and territory around the Indus area located in the northwest part of the subcontinent. When the Persians commanded by Darius I invaded this region around the fifth century B.C.E., they used the term for the river Sindhu, transformed it into the Persian word *hind*, which becomes *al-hind* in Arabic, and they referred to all the indigenous people by this term. With the invasion of the northwest region by Alexander the Great in the third century B.C.E., the Greeks referred to the Sindhu River as Indos and used the term Indikoi to refer to its inhabitants, which gives us the terms India and Indian.[4] Therefore, the derivation of the terms "India" and "Indian" are of foreign origin.

As Muslims entered the Indus valley in the eighth century, the term "Hindu" was used to differentiate natives and foreigners. By the fifteenth century, the term is used by Śrīvara, a Śaiva historian, to distinguish indigenous people from Muslims. During the same century, the devotional poet Kabīr appropriated the term to distinguish between Hindus and Turuṣkas (Muslims).[5] But such usage of the term should not be construed to suggest that "Hinduism" was a uniform system of religion. The term is also used in the following century in Sanskrit and Bengali sources to distinguish Hindus from foreigners or Muslims.[6] By the end of the eighteenth century, the British adopt the term "Hindoo" or "Hindu" to designate the people of "Hindustan." In addition, Portuguese and British colonialists also called Indians "Gentoos," meaning "gentile" or "heathen."[7] Conversely, Indians used the term *mleccha* (barbarian, impure) to refer to foreigners. Some native writers used the term "Hindu," and it became more broadly accepted during the nineteenth century. By this period, native inhabitants were seeking to establish their own national identity to counter the oppressive condition of colonial domination by outsiders. Indigenous Indians did not use the term, however, for specifically religious reasons.

The term "Hindu" is not a term used historically by the people of India to describe themselves. The people of India are more likely to describe their identity by a specific caste or community. The religious implications of the term "Hinduism" originate with the so-called Orientalists and their scholarly work, with its Judaeo-Christian presuppositions.[8] Thus, although the term "Hindu" owes its origin to Persian sources, Hinduism is an abstraction inspired by scholars from the West, according to some scholars. But this is only part of the story. Natives recognized a cultural and political advantage to having their own recognized religion similar to Christianity, Judaism, or Islam. The better-educated, higher-caste members of Indian society pushed the Sanskritic textual and priestly version of a constructed Hinduism over any local or tribal forms, giving a student of the subject an ahistorical abstraction that is still used to interpret India's religious history. With the emergence of a monolithic Hinduism shaped by Western orientalists and assisted by native pundits during the colonial period, the heterogeneous aspects of a complex tradition was simplified and distorted in "a monolithic and monolinear fashion."[9] This constructed Hinduism came to be considered a world religion alongside other such entities. This invented 'Hinduism,' originating in the studies of Oriental scholars and embraced by some members of the upper strata of Indian society, was also accompanied by the growth of a nationalist consciousness during the nineteenth century.[10] During the nineteenth century, Vinayak Damodar Savarkar advocated the term Hindutva (Hinduness) for political reasons. Savarkar envisioned Hindutva as a sociocultural category with the intention of unifying the various disparate groups that inhabited the subcontinent. Originally differentiated from religious Hinduism, Hindutva functioned as a political ideological slogan within the context of colonial domination. Thereby, Hindutva became a magnet around which conservative Indian political forces could unite as a political movement and a religious force. This scenario seems to suggest that external and internal political thinking shaped Hinduism. Thus it is incorrect to view Hinduism simply as a British invention for several reasons: British colonial power was not absolute over the entire subcontinent, Hindu agency and creativity must be taken into account, and it would be inaccurate and disruptive to claim that Hinduism was foreign to India prior to the arrival of the British.[11]

Does this mean that Hinduism is a useless term? Does the term refer to a cultural reality? Should we get rid of the term and find a substitute? According to the scholar Heinrich von Stietencron, Hinduism is not a coherent system and thus not a religion. Hinduism is rather a geographically defined group of religions that are distinct from each other, but they are related in geographical, historical, socioeconomic, and political ways. These various religions have influenced each other continuously, and they have jointly made contributions to a common culture.[12] Therefore, Hinduism is a plural entity and not a single unified tradition. This position implies that the term "Hinduism" is not a very useful term based on the reality of a multiplicity of religions included within a single designated term.

Within the context of the pluralistic nature of Hinduism, another scholar, Brian K. Smith, attempts to use the authority of the Vedas as a way to determine who is a Hindu. In other words, any person who accepts the sacred Vedas as a revealed body of literature can be accepted as a Hindu.[13] A critic of this assertion counters that there is no common religion—because there are many different paths, doctrines, philosophies, or traditions, using the Vedas as a measure of Hinduism is inadequate.[14] Against the argument that the pluralistic nature of Hinduism renders the term meaningless, it is also possible to view individual cults and sects as cognitive systems or socioreligious institutions that are not necessarily different religions. Underlying the apparent pluralism, there is common social consensus that the different cults and sects are interchangeable and characterized by an underlying identity.[15]

Even if one recognizes the problems associated with the term "Hinduism" and acknowledges that it is a term constructed to some extent by outsiders to Indian culture, there are still scholars who think that the term is worth retaining. Julius Lipner, for example, thinks that is a useful construct to the extent that it refers to the general features of Indian culture instead of a single religion. The Sanskrit equivalent of "Hindu", as we have said, is *hindutva* or *hinduta*. Such a term suggests a particular way of being in the world or, more specifically, a distinctive type of mentality that is paradoxical:

> It is a paradoxicality that rises from an insightful aversion to dogmatism in articulating the findings of reason and experience, and from the nurtured desire to inject a healthy dose of relativism in our perception of things. It represents a paen to the liberative workings of myth rather than to the absolutising dictates of doctrine (though there is plenty of doctrinal consolidation in Hinduism), to spontaneity and unpredictability in our relationships with the divine, to the necessarily ineffable in our studied graspings of reality. As such this paradoxicality is an affirmation of the mature realization of the fact of change, of the bewildering aspect of life's endless metamorphoses, of the ubiquitous porosity of boundaries, rather than a recoiling from the robust challenges of life. It evinces an increasingly tried and trusted readiness to encounter the world head-on, rather than some retreat into the seductive embrace of prevarication.[16]

The retention of the term "Hindu" is practical so long as it is used to refer to the culture in a nonessential manner that would turn it into a static essence. Lipner views "Hinduism" as a term that conveys a sense of family resemblance: "Hinduism is an acceptable abbreviation for a family of culturally similar traditions."[17] The scholar Richard, King gives some reasons for keeping the term "Hinduism": It is a useful term for general purposes on the introductory level; religious movements have arisen from the nineteenth century that approximately corresponded to the term as conceived by Orientalists; and it is also possible to retain the term with the qualification that it represents a pluralistic phenomenon. King advocates a non-essentialist approach that does not seek to define the essence of something as vague as "Hinduism," and he wants to call attention to the ruptures and discontinuities of the tradition.

Since this book is an introduction to the subject, I will retain the term "Hinduism" and acknowledge that it is an umbrella term for a wide variety of practice and thought. It might be useful to recognize that a pluralistic entity such as Hinduism represents many paths to salvation that ordinary people practice without giving it a name. In other words, Hinduism is something that people on the subcontinent of India and other locations simply do. These practitioners do not necessarily think about whether it represents a unity or a multiplicity, or what a practitioner should call it. For centuries, inhabitants of the Indian subcontinent followed a religious path without giving it a name. Since contemporary Indians use the term to characterize their way of being religious and to distinguish themselves from members of other religions, the use of the term "Hinduism" neither distorts their way of life nor negatively superimposes a totally foreign category upon them. At the same time, it is possible to acknowledge the limitations of the term and refrain from asserting that it possesses an essence that transcends almost three thousand years of history.

It is possible to grasp the differences between Hinduism and other religions by reviewing some of its general characteristics. Hinduism is polytheistic, with threads of monotheism in various sectarian traditions. The preeminent Indologist Max Müller (1823–1900) referred to this phenomenon as henotheism—the worship of one god without denying the existence of other gods.[18] Axel Michaels gives three reasons for the inadequacy of Müller's term. First, there can be no polytheism without henotheism. Second, to restrict henotheist variants to only particular divine beings is unjustified, because it is possible to discover the diffusion of numerous deities and prominent regional gods.[19] Third, henotheism cannot grasp the complex connections related to inclusive ways of devotion between god and believer. Müller's critic wants to substitute the word "equitheism" for henotheism. The term "equitheism" should be used with caution, because it suggests the equality of all divine beings, and does not convey the uniqueness related to devotion associated with an individual's personal deity.

Unlike Christianity and Islam, Hinduism does not owe its origin to a single founder, and it does not have a specific date of origin. There is no unified all-Indian religious organization such as a church. There is no single holy text (although many texts are considered sacred), or any single doctrine or symbol that is considered authoritative for everyone. Without a founder, universal organization, or authoritative text, Hinduism lacks a binding religious authority. There is no holy center for the whole of India, as Mecca is for Islam or Rome for Roman Catholicism. Instead there are seven sacred cities in India, many religious leaders, a multitude of texts, and many doctrines and symbols. If a student of Hinduism were to be given an assignment to devise a motto for the religion, a possible candidate might be: More is better. Unlike the ethnic monotheism found in Judaism and Islam, Hinduism does not draw a sharp distinction between divine and human beings. This suggests that it is possible for gods to become humans and for human beings to become gods.

With its multitude of gods and goddesses, its many sectarian movements, schools of thought, temples, sacred locations, and different beliefs and practices, Hinduism is a model of a religion that stands in sharp opposition to Western notions of what constitutes a religion. This distinction is further evident by the association of Hinduism with the caste social system. Hindu society is structured horizontally into castes, just as it is divided vertically into religious sects of various kinds. The wide variety of beliefs from which a person can choose stands in sharp contrast to the more rigid social system and its generally non-negotiable norms of acceptable behavior. These features imply that Hinduism does not represent orthodoxy as much as it stands for an orthopraxis. In other words, a Hindu possesses freedom of belief, but a person is more circumscribed with respect to correct behavior.[20] The freedom of thought, however, means that heresy is practically impossible, although some schools of thought would claim that denying the revelatory nature of the sacred Vedas, as, for instance, Buddhism does, represents a form of heresy.

Search for Origins

The search for the origins of Indian culture begins with two ancient civilizations: the Indus Valley culture (flourished from 2500 B.C.E. to about 1500 B.C.E.) and Aryan culture (which developed during the second millennium B.C.E.). Due to the socially constructed nature of the notion "Aryan" and its lack of a basis in biology, it is probably more accurate to refer to "Indo-Aryan-speaking peoples." Scholars have proposed two general theories to explain the relationship between these two cultures. According to one account, the Indus Valley civilization declined, and it was replaced by the Aryan culture that originated with an Indo-European people that gradually migrated into the subcontinent of India. As these Indo-Europeans settled in the fertile, northern plains, they replaced the dying Indus Valley civilization. From the perspective of a competing theory, Indo-Aryan culture developed out of that of the Indus Valley civilization. There were no northern invaders or migrants, and there was no disruption in Indian culture. This second theory portrays a continuity from the ancient past to the present time.

The Indus Valley civilization is also known more commonly as the Harappa culture, with the former referring to the major river and the latter designation derived from one of its major towns. The other major town, about 350 miles away, was Mohenjo Daro (Mound of the Dead). Radiocarbon dating has established the existence of these towns at around 2750 B.C.E. Under the direction of Sir John Marshall (1876–1958), who was director general of the Archaeological Survey of India, excavations began in the 1920s at Mohenjo Daro, while D. R. Sahni excavated at Harappa. The archaeologists unearthed sites that demonstrated an impressive urban culture for over 40,000 inhabitants, who enjoyed an advanced standard of living for the time. A sophisticated drainage system, internal toilets, garbage chutes, uniform building bricks, and uniform urban planning suggested a high standard of living. Besides storehouses for grain, there were many homes built according to a similar architectural plan around a central courtyard, with water and drainage systems connected to a sewer system located in the street. The civilization developed its own writing system, known as the Indus Valley script, which has not yet been deciphered. Obviously, the unlocking of the script would reveal important information about the culture.

The cities were carefully planned with a large residential area, parallel streets, houses built at right angles to the streets, access lanes that were perpendicular to the streets, and a citadel, which probably served some civic and/or religious purpose. At the Mohenjo Daro site, a huge pool (measuring 39 by 23 by 10 feet deep) with adjoining rooms and porticos suggests the importance of bathing. An adjacent well was used to fill the pool. There was also technology in place to drain the pool. The pool may have served a need for purification, possibly connected to the performance of ritual. Archaeologists have also excavated brick platforms and apparent fire altars within buildings possibly used for worship.

There were many terracotta female figurines unearthed that suggest possible goddess images, whereas some unearthed stones possess a phallic character. These findings suggest the importance of fertility and reproduction for humans, domestic animals, and plants. In addition to this type of evidence, archaeologists also discovered seals depicting humans, domestic and wild animals, and plants. The most famous seal depicts a figure seated in a yoga type of posture surrounded by various animals such as deer, rhinoceros, elephant, and buffalo. The seated figure wears a hat with what appears to be two horns. This figure has been called the Paśupati (Lord of Creatures) seal, which some scholars have identified as a prototype of the later deity Śiva. If one connects this figure with the phallic-shaped stones discovered, it is possible that the stones may have represented aniconic representations of the Paśupati figure. There are also some seals with an apparent spirit emerging from a pipal tree, with worshipers standing before it holding small plants. Some seals depict a horned person emerging from the same type of tree, with seven long-braided figures standing before it, which could have been priestly or holy men.

Between 1800 and 1700 B.C.E., there was a sudden decline of the Indus Valley civilization. Scholars have conjectured about a combination of reasons related to flooding, drought, military invasion, or devastating epidemic. Because of a lack of evidence of large-scale massacres, some scholars reject attributing the decline to raids of marauders, and they adhere to great changes in environmental conditions.[21]

According to one theory, the Indo-Aryans (meaning noble or honorable) migrated into the Indus Valley area of northwest India from central Asia by traveling through the mountain passes of Afghanistan around 1500 B.C.E. It is the opinion of some scholars that some of the immigrants traveled into Iran, because of the affinities between the Iranian religion of the Avesta and the Aryan religion of the Vedas. Other Aryan groups migrated west into Europe. Due to a lack of archaeological evidence for a massive invasion, it is very likely that Indo-Aryan speakers gradually migrated from Indo-Iranian borderlands and Afghanistan, and did not arrive in a sudden massive invasion.[22] By 1000 B.C.E., the Indian immigrants reached the region of the Ganges River, and their culture continued to spread to the Deccan and later into other parts of southern India. According to this theory, the Aryans conquered the indigenous people, who were descendants of the Indus Valley civilization and spoke a Dravidian language. The Indo-European language of the invaders eventually evolved into Sanskrit, which was to become the classical and learned language of India. The absence of the horse in archaeological evidence from Harappan civilization is used to support the argument of scholars that Aryan immigrants succeeded the indigenous people; they clam that the horse was unknown to the original inhabitants and was introduced by invaders.[23] A critic finds the horse evidence ambiguous because the lack of horses in the archeological remains could also be indicative of the animals' elite status and rarity.[24] Another possibility is that horses were unimportant from ritual or functional perspectives to the civilization, and thus were not represented in what has survived. What is clear is that the horse and chariot were eventually introduced from central Asia, and the animal became common in the second millennium B.C.E.[25]

An alternative viewpoint represents what could be called a cultural transformation argument. According to this thesis, Indo-Aryan culture is an outgrowth of the Indus Valley civilization. This argument rejects any immigration from outside of India. The Indus Valley culture was instead the foundation from which the Aryan or vedic culture developed. This thesis is supported by evidence suggesting continuities between painted grey ware associated with Indo-Aryan culture and the indigenous cultures of the region. Moreover, there is no archaeological evidence to substantiate migrations into India.

Another possibility is a modified migration theory. According to this theory, Indo-Aryan immigrants entered northern India, but they did not disrupt the Indus Valley civilization, although they did adopt certain elements of this preexisting, settled, continuous culture. At the same time, the indigenous Dravidian culture absorbed features of the Indo-Aryan culture. While this mutual cultural influence was occurring over a long period of time, the Indo-Aryans became the dominant culture.[26]

Other evidence that undermines the idea that vedic culture grew out of the Indus culture is technological. Although iron is known in later vedic literature and is traditionally associated with the Indo-Aryans, there is no evidence of smelted iron artifacts in Indus Valley cities. This does not mean that iron ore and items may not some day be unearthed at Harappa locations, so the iron evidence is not full proof. It is possible, however, that the Indo-Aryan nomads coexisted with more settled urban societies that then learned the new comers' technology.[27]

Survey of Indian Literature

Leading a pastoral and wandering lifestyle at first, the Indo-Aryan immigrants (assuming they were such) included gifted poets who created oral poems that were passed on from generation to generation by a disciplined and intricate method of memorization. Many of these are hymns of praise to gods and leaders. These hymns are called the Vedas, which means sacred knowledge. The Vedas are known as *śruti*, a term that means "what is revealed". Their revealed status set them apart, and each poem became fixed by elaborate systems of recitation at an early period, which made the possibilities of alterations to the poems by later poets or redactors more unlikely. This revealed literature is distinguished from later literature called *smṛti*, which is "something remembered." According to internal evidence, the Vedas originated in northern India and spread to the Punjab and more eastern regions between 1500 B.C.E. and to around 400 B.C.E. vedic schools, which were called Śākhā (branch), evolved to control the transmission of texts. These schools reflected adherence to particular texts, and they created an interpretive body of literature.

Vedic literature contains four collections: Rig, Sāma, Yajur, and Atharva. Each of these collections is subdivided into four sections: Saṃhita (*mantra* or sacred formula collections), Brāhmaṇa (theological and ritual commentary), Āraṇyaka (forest or wilderness texts), and Upaniṣad (speculative and secret philosophical texts). These four parts are also considered śruti (revealed). It is possible for a learned person to comment upon them, but they are not to be questioned. The Vedas represent the ancient sacred scripture of Hinduism, but this scripture is not conceived as a body of writing. Instead, the sacred scripture is something that has been heard and orally transmitted from one generation to another.

The *Rig Veda* is the oldest collection of verses; it consists of hymns that are addressed to deities and recited by priests in rituals. The *Rig Veda* contains 1,028 hymns, arranged in ten books or, more precisely, circles (*maṇḍlas*). Books 2 to 7 are called the family collections because they were preserved within families or groups that memorized them and transmitted them. The family books are arranged from the shortest (2) to the longest book (7). Book 8 contains several more diminutive family collections. A later collection of hymns is contained in book 9, which consists of hymns recited during the Soma ritual, whereas book 10 and part of book 1 are the latest additions to the vedic corpus. Adhering to numerical principles, the books are arranged according to "author" (family or clan), deity, and meter. In addition, the hymns to deities are arranged according to length with the longest at the beginning of the book. If hymns are equal in length, the hymn with a longer meter is placed first.

It is highly likely that the *Rig Veda* predates the introduction and common use of iron, which would push its origin prior to about 1200 B.C.E. Many of the poets that created and transmitted the poems belonged to the Angirasa and Kāṇva clans, who treated these poems as private property of the clans.[28] The Vedas reflect the worldview of the priestly class with respect to religion, ritual, society, and values. In this sense, it gives a reader a one-dimensional view of ancient Indian religiosity.

In contrast to the *Rig Veda*, the *Sāma Veda* consists of extracted material from the *Rig Veda*, with the exception of 75 verses. The contents of the collection are called *sāmans* (chants)—they are stanzas recited during the Soma rite, and they represent the earliest form of preserved music in India. The verses are modified as the chanting priests perform them. The *Sāma Veda* consists of two parts: an actual text (*arcika*) and the melodies (*gāna*).

The *Yajur Veda* mostly consists of mantras (sacred formulas) that are repeated and used in rituals. These mantras accompany ritual actions of the priest. The mantras are arranged according to ritual usage and not numerically. Besides the new and full-moon offerings, the *Yajur Veda* also includes collections for the Soma rite that function as paradigms for other rituals. There are two branches of the *Yajur Veda*: *Black Yajur Veda* and *White Yajur Veda*. The former is a mixture of verses and expository prose, whereas the latter branch contains only mantras. The *White Yajur Veda* is also known as the Vājasaneyi Saṃhitā, of which there are two recensions: Mādhyaṃdina and the Kāṇva. There are three major versions of the *Black Yajur Veda*.

The *Atharva Veda* is a collection of hymns concerned with magical rites intended to heal the medically afflicted. It also includes poems about destructive sorcery. In addition, there are some speculative hymns, others concerned with the rites of passage, and two appendixes. There is internal, textual evidence that the *Atharva Veda* was not embraced in the early historical period, because the *Rig Veda* refers to itself as threefold (19.9.9): verses (*ṛcs*), sacrificial formulae (*yajuses*), and chants (*sāmans*), or it is called the threefold knowledge (*trayī vidyā*, AB 5.32–33). The emphasis on the number three suggests that the fourth veda or *Atharva Veda* took time to be accepted as equal to the other Vedas; this development probably dates to the sūtra literature (ŚŚS 16.2.9) around 200 B.C.E.–200 C.E. Overall, the four Vedas are liturgical texts because of their importance in various rituals.

The various rules and explanations of rituals are provided by the various Brāhmaṇas, which consist of priestly discourse on the rituals. These texts speculate about the wider cosmic significance of particular rituals: their origin, purpose, and meaning. Generally, the Brāhmaṇas associated with the *Black Yajur Veda*, such as the *Taittirīya Brāhmaṇa*, are considered the historically oldest, whereas the White Yajur Veda is connected to the *Śatapatha Brāhmaṇa* (which also appears in two recensions called the White and the Black). Each of the Brāhmaṇas represents a different priestly tradition, demonstrates internal differences, and rests on different authoritative figures. The *Aitareya* and *Kauṣītaki Brāhmaṇas* are associated with the *Rig Veda*. The former text is devoted to the Soma sacrifice, whereas the letter text is concerned with construction of the sacred fire, daily morning and evening oblations, new and full-moon rituals, and the four monthly sacrifices. The *Pañcaviṃśa* and *Jaiminīya Brāhmaṇas* are attached to the *Sāma Veda*, and the *Gopatha Brāhmaṇa* is associated with the *Atharva Veda*.

Closely associated with the various Brāhmaṇa texts are numerous Upaniṣads, which are considered secret texts that are often in the form of a dialogue or sometimes a debate. The Upaniṣads evolved from the Āraṇyakas (forest texts), and it is difficult to find a sharp distinction between the two genres. The oldest Upaniṣads are the *Bṛhadāraṇyaka* and *Chāndogya*, which are followed by the *Aitareya*, *Taittirīya*, and *Kauṣītaka*. The next group of Upaniṣads are the following, in probable order of composition: *Kena*, *Īśa*, *Kaṭha*, *Śvetāśvatara*, *Praśna*, *Muṇḍaka*, *Mahānārayana*, *Māṇḍūkya*, and *Maitrī*. The Upaniṣads will be discussed more fully in chapter 3. Some of these texts were composed over a long period of time. The Upaniṣads are also not a homogenous body of literature, because the texts often sharply differ from each other, with such positions as monism and theism opposing each other.

In order to study and use the four Vedas in ritual, practitioners must also use the six limbs of the Vedas that are intended to support, protect, and implement them in a ritual context. The six limbs, called *vedāngas*, can be conceived as auxiliary sciences necessary for the study of the texts. The first limb is called the *śikṣa*, which provides instruction for precise pronunciation of the texts and deals with phonetics in general. The second limb is *kalpa*, which gives details of the rituals. The *vyākaraṇa* is concerned with grammar, whereas the *nirukta* focuses on etymology of words and analysis of semantic structure. *Chandas* specializes in the details of verse meters. Finally, *jyotiṣa* is concerned with issues related to astronomy and astrology, because it is essential to know precisely the most auspicious times for the performance of rituals in order to be in harmony with cosmic forces. Moreover, the sacrificial cult gave impetus to mathematical knowledge and basic geometry. Such knowledge was necessary for calculation associated with the sacrificial arena, manufacture of bricks, and construction of altars for the sacrifices.[29]

Indian culture was arguably the first to subject its language to careful scrutiny. Before the end of the fourth century B.C.E., the grammarian Pāṇini's analysis of the Sanskrit language appeared in his *Aṣṭādhyāyī* (Eight Chapters). Patañjali's *Mahābhāṣya* (Great Commentary) on language was composed in the second century B.C.E. Initially, the Sanskrit language was limited to use by an elite. It became, however, more widespread as various rulers adopted it as their official language. This development resulted in the distinction between Sanskrit language and culture and regional languages and their cultures.[30]

As has been said, the four Vedas and their four sections are traditionally considered revealed (*śruti*) literature, whereas the other major literary category is a body of works called smṛti (that which is remembered). Smṛti represents traditional wisdom that is remembered by wise individuals. Although memory can be individual or collective, smṛti implies a group experience of remembrance that guides it at the present moment, enables a group to recapture its past, and recall valuable lessons. Memory can enable one to hear and understand the message of what was revealed, but what is remembered does have fallible human authors, whereas there is no human author of what is revealed. The following types of literature fall into the category of smṛti: the Dharma Sūtras (approximate dates of composition

600–200 B.C.E.), the epic *Mahābhārata* (composed between 300 B.C.E. and 300 C.E.), the epic *Rāmāyaṇa* (composed between 200 B.C.E. and 200 C.E.), and the Purāṇas, which began to be composed around 400 C.E. These bodies of literature will be discussed more fully in later chapters.

Historical Overview of the Classical Period (c. 300 B.C.E.–700 C.E.)

Any historical survey of Indian history needs to acknowledge the tentative nature of any claims to historical accuracy because of the lack of evidence in many instances. Scholars of Indian cultural history encounter a lack of historical sources, an incomplete literary record, and a dearth of stone inscriptions. Thus there are many controversial points of Indian history that are debated by scholars, as evident in the previous discussion about its origins; scholars do agree that many documents have been lost, and what has survived tends to reflect the life of the social elite. Therefore, the historical narrative presented in the following paragraphs is only presented as a possible reading of the Indian past and should not be accepted as an exact representation of the history of India. Rather than attempt to invent a history of India that would fit prior preconceptions of the culture, it is best to assume the position of a skeptical reader, retain an open mind, and be prepared to change your opinion with the arrival of new evidence.

From around 1000 to 300 B.C.E., the Indo-Aryans' gradually expanded their control over north India. In the process, they assimilated and integrated their culture with that of the indigenous people. The style of pottery called painted grey ware indicates that by 1000 B.C.E. the Indo-Aryans had mastered the art of iron metallurgy, which contributed to their military success and their ability to cultivate more land. Even though the Indo-Aryans suffered from internal intertribal and clan conflicts, they gradually created settlements that provided geographical identity for a clan or a confederacy of clans; after they took possession of a territory they often named it after the ruling clan. In order to maintain the possession of a territory, a political organization was necessary, which led to the development of chiefdoms and eventually kingdoms in the north and, in addition, the emergence of towns.

The first genuine Indian empire was that of the Mauryan Dynasty (322–183 B.C.E.). It was founded by a low-caste individual named Chandragupta (r. 322–298 B.C.E.), who freed India from Macedonian rule, while also politically uniting a large part of the continent. Around 305 B.C.E., Chandragupta defeated the Greek general Seleucus Nicator, who was forced to relinquish parts of Afghanistan. With a peace sealed by a matrimonial alliance, Seleucus sent an ambassador, Megasthenes, to reside at the Mauryan court. This ambassador wrote a book on India entitled *Indika* that has not survived, although references to this work by other authors provide a partial glimpse of its contents.

There were several significant changes ushered into Indian culture by Chandragupta. He established, for instance, a central administration with the aid of his adviser Kauṭilya, reputed author of the political treatise entitled the *Arthaśāstra*

(Treatise on Polity), to govern his vast and diverse empire. His imperial vision placed the king at the center of power, assisted by a council, decentralized administration, and numerous spies. A growing agrarian economy afforded the dynasty a firm economic basis, while political unification provided security. These developments created a favorable environment for the expansion of various craft guilds, towns, trade, and an evolution toward an urban culture. Chandragupta's son Bindusāra (298–273 B.C.E.) and his offspring the famous Aśoka (269–232 B.C.E.) expanded the geographical domain of the dynasty.

The Mauryans advocated religious tolerance, and supported both orthodox Hindu and heterodox religious movements. A good example of this spirit is evident on the Twelfth Rock edict of Aśoka, which appeals for religious tolerance for all sects. Even though Aśoka converted to Buddhism late in his life, his *dharma* (law) did not advocate an exclusively Buddhist perspective; it was rather generally consistent with the moral persuasion and social responsibility common to all sects. The dynasty donated caves for the purpose of housing monks, and they also financed the construction of monasteries and memorial mounds (*stūpas*). In addition, the dynasty sponsored vedic sacrifices, although vedic priests felt threatened and did not hold the dynasty in the highest regard.

The stable environment created by the dynasty enabled ascetic movements such as the Ājivakas to thrive and Jainism to establish itself among the commercial class. The Jains advocated non-injury (*ahiṃsā*) to all living things and encouraged frugality. There is even a legend that Chandragupta became a Jain monk after abdicating his throne and that he fasted unto death like a Jain ascetic. The truth of this legend is uncertain. During this period, the schism between the Śvetāmbara and Digambara sects of Jainism occurred, over a disagreement about whether or not ascetics should wander naked.

Buddhism spread rapidly during this period, and it enjoyed the support of Aśoka, who converted to the religion after his conquest of Kalinga and his remorse for the bloody carnage caused by the war. There is a legend that he became a Buddhist monk, although he more likely lived for a period of time among the Buddhist brotherhood. This period also witnessed the development of various Buddhist schools. During Aśoka's reign, it is alleged that the third Buddhist council was held around 250 B.C.E. at Pataliputra. Aśoka's son Mahendra is given credit by tradition for converting the island of Sri Lanka to Buddhism.

In addition to the success of heterodox religious movements during the Mauryan Dynasty, two Hindu devotional sects were slowly developing that were to dominate the later historical periods: the Greek ambassador Megasthenes provided evidence of the worship of Śiva and Vāsudeva-Krishna, a deity of the Bhāgavata religion.

After the death of Aśoka, a political decline began that culminated in the assassination of Bṛhadratha, the final Mauryan ruler, by his commander-in-chief Puṣyamitra Śuṅga, who founded the subsequent Śuṅga Dynasty. This resembled a loose feudal kingdom with the king surrounded by vassal states of various sizes.

There has been considerable scholarly debate about the reasons for the decline of the Mauryan Dynasty. They involved social, economic, and administrative, factors, combined with outside military pressure. Whatever the precise reasons for the decline, it would be many centuries before another empire would be established. The history of post-Mauryan India is a long story of struggles of one state with others for regional dominance.

In this post-Mauryan era of political fragmentation, the northwestern borders of India experienced a series of invasions initially led by Bactrian Greeks, who dominated the Punjab. These Greco-Bactrian kingdoms did not survive long. King Menander (Milinda) ruled from Śākala; he is a major figure in a Buddhist book entitled the *Questions of Milinda*. The Parthians occupied Bactria early in the second half of the second century B.C.E. The Scythians (known as Śakas in India) also invaded the region, and they were among the first group of central Asian nomads to enter the South Asian subcontinent. Next came the Pallavas at the end of the first century B.C.E., who were in turn conquered by the Yüeh-chih. This region finally came under the rule of Kaniṣka (possibly 78–144 C.E.), whose control extended into Central Asia. Besides being revered as a patron of Buddhism, Kaniṣka surrounded himself with artists, poets, and musicians. Aśvaghoṣa, a Sanskrit poet-dramatist who composed a biography of the Buddha, was an important member of his court. Kaniṣka, a convert to Buddhism, hosted the Fourth Council of Buddhism in Kashmir. During his rule, the Gandhāra school of art flourished under the influence of art of the Roman Empire. The Kushan Empire endured for a century beyond the death of Kaniṣka, when Sassanians originating from the west overthrew it.

During the first century C.E., there were three major kingdoms in the Dravidian south of India: Cōḻa (Coromandel Coast), Kerala (Malabār), and Pāṇḍyaṉ (southern tip of peninsula). Each of these kingdoms competed with the others for political influence in the region. In the second century, southern Indians invaded Sri Lanka. These ancient Tamil kingdoms were vulnerable to conquest by a new power, the Pallavas, who became entrenched in the southern region by 325 C.E. During the first century B.C.E in the western Deccan, the Satavahanas established a Dynasty, which is often called the Andhra Dynasty. A king named Satakarni ruled around 50 B.C.E with a commitment to military expansion. In order to legitimate their rule, the new kings performed vedic sacrifices. But the Vakatakas eventually succeeded them, and dominated the northern Deccan.

The instability of rapidly rising and falling dynasties was countered to some extent by the stability provided by trade. Merchants and artisans become more prominent as urban cultures developed and trade increased. The minting of coins provided a more uniform method of exchange and accounting, and it provided impetus for long-distance trade. This radical departure from prior economic practices also witnessed the beginnings of guilds (*shreni*), which fixed rules of work and addressed issues of quality and price of products. Significant developments in grammar, mathematics, astronomy, literature, philosophy, and religion did not occur before the Gupta Dynasty (320–540 C.E.).

The rise to power of Chandragupta, who was the founder of the dynasty, was aided by his marriage to the princess Kumāradevī of the Licchavi tribe. Comprising most of Bihār and portions of Bengal and Awadh, the kingdom established by Chandragupta was entrusted to and expanded by his son Samudragupta (c. 335–376 C.E.), who defeated nine kings of northern India and was also a poet and a musician. Chandragupta II (c. 376–415), another patron of literature and the arts, secured the western border of India, giving the dynasty control over northern India. The Gupta Dynasty never attained, however, the centralized control exhibited by the Mauryan Empire. During this period, Mahāyāna Buddhism and devotional Hinduism developed, along with the legal codes. During the reign of Chandragupta II, the dramatist and poet Kālidāsa resided at court; he was famous for two great epic poems entitled *Kumārasambhava* and *Raghuvamṣa*. He also composed the lyrical poem *Meghadūta* and the drama *Śakuntalā*.

During the reigns of Kumāragupta (c. 415–454) and Skandagupta (c. 454–467), the dynasty was threatened by an invasion of the Hūṇas. Kumāragupta struck gold coins that depicted a six-headed, ten-armed war god Kārtikeya, who was seated on a peacock. This divine figure was the king's symbol of power. Skandagupta expended considerable effort and wealth, which drained his treasury and weakened his empire.

During the Gupta Dynasty, Jainism and Buddhism began to decline because of a lack of royal patronage, although they still continued to be vigorous religious forces. Migrating to the west and south of the country, Jainism continued to retain support among the commercial class. There was an internal change within Jainism exhibited by the Second Council at Valabhī (c. 512 or 525), at which the Jain canon was arranged. During this period, popular worship was directed to the images of Jain saints. There were important literary activities among the Buddhists, as evident in the contributions of the monk Buddhaghoṣa, the brothers Asaṇga and Vasubandhu of the Yogācāra school, and the logician Dignāga. Mahāyāna monks and scriptures were capturing the imagination of other monks and nuns, whereas ordinary people appeared to respond positively to the assertion that anyone could become a *bodhisattva* (enlightened being), whose primary duty was to save all beings from the cycle of suffering. The historical Buddha became embodied as the eternal truth in the doctrine of the *trikāya* (three bodies), which gave an intellectual foundation to a devotional form of the religion. Chinese pilgrims testified to the worship of bodhisattvas such as Avalokiteśvara (personification of compassion), Mañjuśrī (personification of wisdom), the goddess Tārā, and the veneration of *stūpa*s (memorial mounds).

During the period, heterodox religious movements such as Buddhism and Jainism lost considerable popular support to sectarian Hinduism, in part due to royal patronage and the wide popular appeal of devotionalism. The Gupta Dynasty identified itself particularly with Vaiṣṇavism by adopting the bird Garuḍa, a vehicle of the deity Viṣṇu, as its royal emblem, using the Boar (Varāha) incarnation (*avatāra*) as a symbol of royal power, and by referring to themselves on coins as worshipers of Viṣṇu.

Even though the Guptas favored theistic Hinduism, they also continued to adhere to the ancient vedic religion. Samudragupta revived, for instance, the horse sacrifice. The Vedas continued to be viewed as the infallible, sacred, and eternal revelation. Nonetheless, the powerful appeal and hold of the ancient texts, rites, and deities was losing ground to the newer devotional movements.

Having been given legitimacy as a state religion by the Guptas, theistic Hinduism flourished as evident in the growth of temple construction and the production of two classes of texts (collections of myths about deities) Purāṇas and Āgamas (collections of texts expounding doctrines). The performance of *pūjā* (worship) in temples and homes gradually transformed sacrifice, and it became the preferred act of religious expression for many Hindus, with its focus on images of the theistic deities. In addition, pilgrimages to holy locations and bathing in sacred rivers gained popularity and significance. Another important development was the emergence of Śakti cults, which were based on indigenous and aboriginal beliefs and were influenced by tantric notions and practices, which will be discussed in later chapters. The wives and consorts of the major theistic deities became more important. Śrī Lakṣmī, the wife of Viṣṇu, appeared on more dynastic coins. Expectations were raised that the king would embody and execute within the kingdom the goddess's qualities of beauty, prosperity, and good fortune. In addition, the androgynous form of Śiva was engraved on Gupta seals. Therefore, the Guptas enhanced the establishment of the dominant form of Hindu religiosity for many centuries.

The creative impetus provided by the Gupta Dynasty can also be witnessed in science and the arts. Āryabhaṭa was the first astronomer to calculate pi, to determine the length of the solar year, to argue the spherical nature of the earth and that it rotated on its axis, and to explain how eclipses originate. Bharata's *Nāṭyaśāstra*, a treatise on dance, drama, and poetry, was composed during this period. Important literary works by Bhāravi, Magha, and Bhavabhūti, and Śūdraka's *The Little Clay Cart* provide glimpses of urban life. Viśākhadatta wrote a play entitled *Mudrarākṣasa* about the overthrow of a king by the Mauryans, and he also recounted Chandragupta II's rise to power in *Devī-candra-gupta*. Finally, the narratives of the *Pañcatantra* (thought to be a source for Aesop's *Fables*) were intended to educate a young prince in the lessons of statecraft. In addition to these developments in literature, Bhāmaha developed literary criticism.

Gupta power was eroded by the Hūṇas, a branch of the White Huns or Hephthalites from central Asia, and the Hūṇa leader eventually gained control over the northern region and parts of central India. The Gupta Empire ended around 540 C.E., breaking up into smaller kingdoms, which represented a return to an earlier pattern of political fragmentation. About a century and a half later, Harṣa successfully countered the Hūṇas. Gaining control over northern India,

Harṣa ascended the throne in 606 and reigned for forty-one years by creating a feudal structure that maintained social stability; he also loved philosophy and literature, and he even wrote three dramas. He patronized the poet, his friend Bāṇabhaṭṭa, who composed a work chronicling the king's rise to power entitled the *Harṣacarita* (The Life of Harṣa), which was the first biography of a king and inaugurated a new genre of literature. The Chinese Buddhist pilgrim Hsüan Tsang enjoyed an honored position at court during the period of 630–644, and he described his experiences in India in written form as well as returning to China with Buddhist scriptures. Harṣa died without leaving heirs, and his empire fell apart after his death. Succeeding centuries present a scenario of endemic warfare between rival dynasties until the invasion of Muslims.

After the collapse of the Harṣa empire, regional centers of power emerged. These kingdoms included the Pālas (770–1125) in the east, the Gurjara-Pratīhāras (600–1100) in the west and north, the Rāṣṭrakūṭas (752–973) in the southwest, the Cāḷukyas in the Deccan region (600–1100), and the Pallavas in the south (600–700). Although smaller kingdoms were dependent upon the larger kingdoms, the vassal lords were allowed to retain their symbols of sovereignty. These vassal lords acknowledged their dependent status by swearing oaths and performing appropriate duties to a remote, exalted, and even defied great king, who legitimized his status and gained allegiance of the populace by sponsoring the building of magnificent temples. The Pallava king Narasiṃha-varman II built, for instance, the shore temple at Mahabalipuram and a temple now called Kailāsanātha at Kāñcīpuram, whereas Dantidurga helped Nandi-varman capture Kāñcīpuram, an act commemorated by building the Vaikuntha Perumal temple in the city. Dantidurga was succeeded by Krishna I, who became famous for supporting the rock-cut temple at Ellora, called the Kailāsa temple.

The political regionalism characteristic of the period after Harṣa accompanied a religious regionalism, with the emergence of various devotional sectarian movements that often incorporated elements of local cults and divine beings. Some of these local deities became associated with a deity such as Viṣṇu, for instance, by becoming one of his many incarnations. The devotional fervor of the new religiosity was expressed in regional languages. This period also witnessed the spread of Tantrism. Important literary works included Bhāravi's *Kirātārjūniya*, inspired by a theme from the epic *Mahābhārata*, and Daṇḍin's *Daśakumāracarita* (The Tale of the Ten Princes). Two Tamil epic poems also dated to this general period are entitled the *Cilappatikāram* (Story of the Anklet) and *Maṇimēkalai*, by Cīttalai Cāttaṉār, about the daughter of a courtesan who becomes a Buddhist nun.

Historical Overview of the Medieval Period (c. 700 C.E.–1800 C.E.)

Beginning around 711 C.E., Muslim settlements appeared on the western coast of India. There were also small colonies of Muslims in southern Punjab that preceded the Afghan raiders led by Mahmud of Ghazni (971–1030), who was called the "Sword of Islam," through the Khyber Pass in 997. Mahmud's raids resulted in the smashing of temple idols and widespread looting. Before he died, Mahmud annexed the Punjab. His reign represented the initial wave of Turko-Afghan Muslims to invade north India. Mahmud lured al-Birunī, an historian, astronomer, physician, and philosopher, and the great Persian poet Firdausī to his court in Ghazni. At this time, features of Indian culture such as its numerical system, astronomy, and its decimal system also influenced Muslims.

Eventually, Qutb-ud-din Aybak proclaimed himself sultan of Delhi in 1206 and started the Mamluk (slave) Dynasty. This transformed north India from a "Land of War" into a "Land of Submission" in Muslim terminology, in which Hindus assumed the status of *dhimmis* (protected peoples of the book under Muslim rule). The Delhi Sultanate and later Mughal Empire did not adversely affect the daily life of Hindus, whose status as tolerated and protected unbelievers was secure. The majority of Hindus were indifferent to their new rulers because they could practice their religion, were not deprived of their land and belongings, and simply paid taxes to a new ruler. Hindus served as clerks in the government, and Hindu kings ruled within their domains under Muslim suzerainty. The spirit of brotherhood embodied within the Muslim faith made it impossible for Muslims to find anything positive about the caste system. Nonetheless, Muslims and Hindus intermingled over a course of time, although Islam always remained a foreign religion from the perspective of the upper social classes of Hindu society. In addition, Muslim rule was conceived by some Indians as the dawning of the chaos associated with *adharma* (unrighteousness).[31]

The Khaljis inaugurated the second Muslim dynasty in 1290, whereas the Tughlugs established the third Muslim dynasty around 1300 in Delhi. Ibn Battūta, a Muslim world traveler, served as chief judge at the court for a time in the latter dynasty. In 1336, a new Hindu kingdom arose in the southern Deccan with its capital called Vijāyanagar (City of Victory) led by Harihāra I (r. 1336–1357). While the Muslims controlled the north, this empire controlled areas such as Mysore, Madras, and Kerala.

During the Sultanate period (c. 1200–1500), Muslim Sufism established itself when three mystical orders—Chishtī, Suhrawardī, and Firdausī—migrated into northern India. Some Sufi masters wrote biographies of their spiritual journeys, such as *The Morals of the Heart* by the poet Amīr Hasan Sijzī and the collection of letters addressed to a disciple by Shaikh Sharaf ud-din Yahyā of Manīr. During this period, Sufism was heavily influenced by Ibn 'Arabī's pantheistic doctrines. It emphasized love of God and uniting with God in a mystical union. Sufi mystics thus gave the appearance of sharing religious sensibilities with some Hindus, for during this period there were Hindu figures such as Kabīr (b. 1398), Nānak (b. 1469), and Caitanya (b. 1485) who condemned the caste system, rituals, and idolatry. Kabīr taught that Allah and Rāma were names for the same deity, whereas Nānak contributed to the development of Sikhism using both Hindu and Muslim elements. Such religious figures gave the impression of accommodating Islam from the perspective of orthodox Hindus.

Around 1517, the Turkish leader Babur appeared from Afghanistan and established the beginnings of the Mughal Dynasty, which included Turkish and Mongol elements, although Turkish influence was predominant. Fifty miles from Delhi on April 21, 1526, Babur defeated a numerically superior army by using more skillful battle maneuvers. The following year he defeated a Rajput army that was no match for the Mughal cavalry. Babur was known as a solider-statesman with the sensibilities of a poet, a man of good taste and humor.

After the passing of Babur, the next important Muslim figure was his grandson Akbar (1542–1605), an illiterate man who was predisposed toward mysticism and was a lover of animals and nature. At the battle of Panipat on November 5, 1556, Akbar became lord of north India; he instituted many humane changes by abolishing the practice of enslaving prisoners of war and their families, did not coerce people to convert to Islam, and abolished the pilgrimage and poll taxes. By means of marriage, war, incorporating Rajput chiefs into the service of the empire, granting local autonomy, and developing a strong system of administration, he gained many Hindu rulers' allegiance and loyal service. Around 1575, Akbar had a profound mystical experience, which motivated him to institute religious discussions at court between different groups. Such a tolerant attitude motivated orthodox Muslims to lead a revolt against his rule in 1580, which was crushed by the following year. Akbar promoted an eclectic cult heavily influenced by Zoroastrianism, which was centered on him as a semidivine being. But he also commissioned translations of Indian texts such as the *Atharva Veda*, *Rāmāyaṇa*, and *Mahābhārata*. He prohibited the killing of cows, refrained from eating meat on certain days, and celebrated Hindu festivals. His long reign of forty-nine years came to an end when Akbar was fatally poisoned by his son Salim, who adopted the name Jahangir (World Seizer).

Known for his drinking and cruelty, Jahangir (r. 1605–1627) extended the Muslim empire. He married a Persian named Nur Jahan (Light of the World) in 1611. He placed his son Khurran in command of the army in 1613, and renaming his son Shah Jahan (Emperor of the World). Shah Jahan (r. 1628–1657) possessed a refined artistic sense for architecture, as evident in such structures built during his reign as the Taj Mahal (a tomb for his wife Mumtaz), the Delhi Fort, and the Jama Masjid. He was overthrown and imprisoned by his son Aurangzēb (r. 1658–1707), who also destroyed other relations who might claim the throne. Aurangzēb ascended the throne as Alamgir (World Conqueror), and terminated the era of religious tolerance. A pious and orthodox Sunni Muslim, he insisted that Islamic law be enforced by public censors, outlawed Hindu religious festivals, did not permit the building or repairs of Hindu temples, and re-imposed the poll tax on Hindus. In addition to being a ruthless leader who expanded the empire, Aurangzeb became an ascetic and sage later in his life. After his death in 1707, the Mughal Empire slowly began to decline because of a combination of factors that included interregional religious wars, court incompetence, greed, factionalism, and invasions of the northeastern part of the empire. Its last remnants were overthrown by the British in 1857.

An excellent example of religious opposition to Aurangzēb was that of the Sikhs. Ironically, Aurangzeb helped to unite the Sikhs when he beheaded the ninth Guru Tegh Bahadur in 1675 for refusing to convert to Islam. The Sikh successor, Guru Gobind, transformed the sect into a militant religious body called the Army of the Pure (Khalsa), and changed their names from Sikhs (Disciples) to the martial Singhs (Lions), who became holy warriors not afraid to face martyrdom in battle. Gobind prohibited alcohol and tobacco, and he eschewed idolatry and caste. But he added meat to the Sikh diet, and he promoted a holy book called the *Granth Sahib*.

Hindu opposition to Mughal rule also emerged, for instance, in Maharashtra, led by Śivaji Bhonsle (1627–1680), who was crowned Catrapati ('Lord of the Universe'). He has been called the father of the Maratha nation and recognized as the founder of Indian guerrilla warfare. He fought for self-rule and full religious freedom. During his lifetime, people believed that he was a reincarnation of the deity Śiva.

The long Muslim dominance of north India had begun with the violent destruction of Hindu idols and temples; Muslims, professing faith in a singular God, holy book, and prophet, could not accept the heterogeneity of the Hindu religious way of life. Eventually, Muslims and Hindus settled down to a tolerable coexistence, though the latter deeply resented their subordinate status. The Muslim influence on Indian culture is evident in music, dance, painting, and architecture. Administrative structures and establishment of new trade routes and practices endured for a long time, with Persian serving as the official language of government. Although Islamic law was used only in limited cases, all Hindus were obliged to pay taxes to the Muslim rulers. The most profound religious influence exerted by Muslims upon Hindus was made by Sufi saints and their simple message of love of God and neighbor, no discrimination, and advocacy of a classless society that appealed to Hindus from the lower socioeconomic level of Indian society. Hindus responded to Islam by forming religious sects such as those established by Caitanya (d. 1533), Tulsīdās (d. 1623), and Dādū (d.1603). Hindu religious leaders such as Tukārām (d. 1649) glorified Hinduism and its historical past.

While the Muslims controlled northern India, Western Europeans were enticed to India in the late fifteenth century by spices, which were needed to make meats palatable and to sweeten wines and ales, and by the prospect of making huge profits in trading them. In 1498, Vasco de Gama of Portugal led a tiny fleet to the port of Calicut located on the Malabar Coast, seeking spices and Christian converts. Not only did he find Syrian Christians already there, but his country also enjoyed a lucrative spice monopoly for decades until the British defeated the Spanish armada in 1588. On December 31, 1600, Queen Elizabeth granted a royal charter to a company of London adventurers. This group, led by Thomas Smythe, represented the initial version of the East India Company. The British fortified factory warehouses, and hired and trained Indian sepoys (police) to protect forts, which evolved into private company armies. The company did not allow proselytizing by Christians because it did not want to offend inhabitants. The company did, however, exploit a cheap labor supply. The British became entrenched in the Bengal region after Robert Clive led forces to victory at Plassey in 1757, which secured the region for the company.

Historical Overview of the Modern Period (c. 1800 and after)

Because of corruption within the East India Company, the British Parliament passed laws to regulate it. Warren Hastings was appointed the first governor-general (1772–1785) of the East India Company, and he administratively integrated the company by eliminating the middleman *nawabs*, for instance, and having all revenue flow to Calcutta. He also gave peasants better information about their property rights and indebtedness. He left his post after learning about the India Act of 1784, which replaced the company's Court of Directors with a Board of Control. After essentially saving the company, his corruption led to his trial for high crimes.

Cornwallis (1738–1805), who became governor-general of Bengal and commander-in-chief of its army, replaced Hastings. Cornwallis's defeat in the American Revolutionary War did not shake his confidence in the conviction that the British are the best-qualified people to govern others. A war against Tipū Sultān led to the acquisition of the Malabar Coast in 1792 for the British. Before he left India in 1792, Cornwallis instituted a Code of Forty-Eight Regulations, which set standards for the services, courts, and revenue collection. During this time, the company gained a monopoly on salt and officially regulated a monopoly on the production and sale of opium, which enjoyed huge sales in China.

Sir John Shore ruled the company for five years. Richard Colley Wellesley (1761–1842), who established an environment of aristocratic arrogance, followed Shore in 1798. In addition to increasing the territory protected by the company, Wellesley and his brother Sir Arthur Wellesley, called the Iron Duke of Wellington, defeated and killed Tipū Sultān on May 4, 1799. For his arbitrary and violent behavior, his Board of Directors censured Richard Wellesley.

The year 1813 brought the end of the ban on missionary work, even though members of the East India Company feared that this would cause social disruption among the indigenous people. Missionaries representing various churches began arriving in India to save, from their perspective, benighted heathens. The missionaries did not enjoy great success; many of their converts came from the lower strata of Indian society, and their economic neediness and motivation to convert resulted in what were popularly called "rice Christians." Bringing what they sincerely and self-righteously believed to be the light and truth of the Christian message to those in need of salvation, evangelical Christians were convinced that their faith represented the highest form of religion from a religiously evolutionary perspective, an attitude that also convinced them that Indian religious beliefs, institutions, and practices invited deconstruction and replacement by Christian values, religion, and civilization.[32] Using derogatory terms such as "pagan," "barbarian," "ignorant," and "superstitious" to categorize the people that they encountered, missionaries made Indians feel inferior, and they depicted the Indian lifestyle as lurid, harsh, and spiritually benighted. The ridicule, mockery, and disgust directed toward Indians by missionaries were not totally compensated for by their pity and compassion toward their potential converts, even though missionaries made useful social contributions by establishing schools, orphanages, and hospitals. The evangelicals were appalled by the worship of idols because of the Hebraic command not to create and worship images depicting divine beings. The iconoclastic attitudes of missionaries toward Hindu idolatry must be understood within the context of anti-Catholicism at home in England.[33] Because missionaries, who were focused on converting Indians in order to save them, and their work upset the social status quo among Hindus, there developed a tension between the zealous missionaries and the British company officials who were concerned with social stability. The tension would never be resolved.

The later eighteenth century was a period during which Westerners began to seriously study Indian culture. Sir William Jones (1746–1794) founded the Asiatic Society of Bengal in 1784, because he could foresee benefits for Indians of learning about their culture. Horace Hayman Wilson produced the first Sanskrit-English dictionary; Wilson also opposed making English the language of India. Charles Wilkins (1749–1836) was the first person to translate the *Bhagavad Gītā* into English from Sanskrit. Moreover, Thomas Colebrooke (1765–1837) published *Essays on the Religion and Philosophy of the Hindus*, which successfully introduced the European public to Indian thought.

The context of the work of these scholars and missionaries was shaped to a great extent by elaborations on Charles Darwin's theory of evolution, whereby societies, like animals, were understood within an evolutionary pattern. This implied that there were societies, such as the British, that have a duty to educate foreign societies perceived to be lower on the evolutionary social ladder. The evolution of societies was accompanied by a belief in progress, exemplified by John Stuart Mill's essay entitled *On Liberty* (1859). The general acceptance of the notions of evolution and progress combined with the scientific practice of classifying and comparing new data. The methods of classification and comparison were used by British officials to gather data pertaining to caste, religion, and race within the context of collecting census data. And around the mid-nineteenth century, racial superiority, which was grounded in the comparative method, became a feature of British nationalism.[34]

By the mid-nineteenth century, there was an emphasis on unification of government and modernization of technology. Company leaders devised and instituted a doctrine of lapse, which justified tearing up treaties made with Indian princes and stealing their states. This practice was also applied to pensioners' titles and pensions awarded as compensation for the prior seizure of lands. The process of modernization involved the building of railroads, which enabled the company to rapidly transport troops and allowed the authorities to reduce their garrisons. Indian cities were linked with the electric telegraph, which was initiated by Dr. William O'Shaughnessey in Bengal in 1851 and supported by the Marquess of Dalhousie (r. 1848–1856), who served as governor-general and vigorously advocated public works projects. In 1837, a postal service act was passed to unite the subcontinent. The creation of a postal service provided a stimulus to learning, literacy, and literature among Indians.[35]

This progress was interrupted by the Mutiny of 1857, which was directly connected to introduction of the new breech-loading Enfield rifle and its cartridges reportedly smeared with animal fat and lard. The authorities instructed sepoys to bite off the tip of the cartridge before inserting it into the open breech, to get the best possible result. Muslims and Hindus perceived something sinister about the cartridges, believing them to be purposely smeared with pig and cow fat in order to defile the users and force their conversion to Christianity. The perceived insidious missionary plot led to a mutiny that was ignited at Meerut on May 9, 1857. After revolting against British officers, the sepoys marched to Delhi, where they triggered a revolt that caused a loss of British control over much of north India. Later Indian nationalists would interpret this movement as the first war of independence. The Mutiny of 1857 shocked the British, but they remained confident that their rule would continue to endure into the future because of their ardent faith in progress and a perception that Hinduism and Islam were static and incapable of change.[36]

The Mutiny of 1857 motivated the British Parliament to pass the Government of India Act, which essentially transferred all rights of the East India Company to the crown. This legislation initiated a new approach to India by rejecting the doctrine of lapse and wooing Indian princes, who were promised the restoration of all prior treaties. Missionaries were instructed to reduce their attempts to convert the populace; they responded by focusing more on educational work.

During the nineteenth century, Hindus responded to British political control and cultural criticism by missionaries by initiating reform and revival movements. Rammohan Roy (1772–1833), called the father of the Hindu Renaissance, was employed in the revenue department of the East India Company. He studied and was inspired by ancient Indian texts such as the Upaniṣads. In 1815, he started holding regular meetings with Bengali friends to discuss theology and philosophy. He founded the Brahmo Samāj (Society of Brahma) in 1829 to give these meetings a more formal structure. A later organization called the Ārya Samāj was founded by Dayānanda Sarasvatī (1824–1883) to stimulate a Hindu revival by returning to the Vedas. Over time, this organization inspired nationalistic political action.

In addition to political changes, there were also important economic changes caused by events beyond the borders of India. The Industrial Revolution produced, for instance, profound changes in England and India because technological advances enabled British factories to produce cheaper cloth than that made in India. Since their cloth was undersold by foreign competition, countless Indian spinners, weavers, and other handicraftsmen found themselves without work. Many of these people returned to farming to earn their living, whereas people in England flocked to urban areas to be near textile factories.

In response to the predominance of British economic, military, and political power in India, Indian nationalist aspirations began to be expressed by means of verbal protest, acts of violence, civil disobedience, and nonviolence. The reaction to British hegemony was led by individuals such as Mahadev Govind Ranade (1842–1901), who founded the All People's Association (Poona Sarvajanik Sabha), and Gopal Krishna Gokhale (1866–1915), who was a disciple of Ranade. These men developed a brand of nationalism that insisted that Indians must take responsibility for reforming their own society. Hailed as the Lokamanya (Revered by the People), B. G. Tilak (1856–1920) was a major cultural revolutionary nationalist before Gandhi. Inspired like Gandhi by the message of the *Bhagavad Gītā*, Tilak published a commentary on the text in which he advocated working in the world for the benefit of others without desire for the fruits of one's actions and toward one's spiritual destiny. Using the text as a manual for action, Tilak argued that violence in a just cause was permissible, whereas renunciation of the world was both a sign of personal weakness and an unpatriotic act. Another radical revolutionary was Aurobindo Ghose (1872–1950), who retired from politics after having a profound religious experience while serving a jail sentence for violent political activity, to devote the rest of his life to religion and writing as Sri Aurobindo. As important as these figures were within the Indian context, no single person compared to Mohandas K. Gandhi in international stature; his life can be used to focus attention on events shaping Indian history in the twentieth century.

Advocate of Nonviolence

Although Gandhi was an extremely shy and insecure person as a young man, he evolved into a charismatic figure who came to stand alone and serve as an inspiration to others as an apostle of nonviolent resistance against colonialism and against armed conflict as a solution to political problems. His charisma was not related to his speaking ability. Rather it was connected to the ascetic persona that he adopted and embodied during his adult life—that of a holy man seeking enlightenment.[37] The profound esteem in which others held him is exemplified by his title Mahatma (Great Soul) and the affectionate name of Bapu (father).

Gandhi, youngest of six children, was born on October 2, 1869, to Karamchand and Putali Bhai Gandhi, members of the Modh Bania caste, originally a middle-ranking social group of grocers in the western state of Gujarat. He conceived of his own education as a series of experiments. After an unsuccessful tenure studying at Samaldas College in Bombay, Gandhi went to England to study law, a voyage that made him an outcaste due to the prohibition against foreign travel by his caste group. Gandhi later related in his autobiography his problems in England, with Western customs, his homesickness, his frugal lifestyle, and his experiments with his diet. During this period, Gandhi read the Hebrew Bible, which did not make a great impression upon him, and the New Testament, to which he had a positive reaction. The book that exerted, the greatest influence on him at this time, however, was the *Bhagavad Gītā*. Gandhi met Madame Blavatsky and Mrs. Annie Besant of the Theosophical Society, and he read some of their books, which stimulated him to read other books on Hinduism; these dispelled any notion that it was a religion overwhelmed with superstition, and strengthened his aversion to atheism. At a later date the work of Tolstoy entitled *The Kingdom of God Is within You* and John Ruskin's work *Unto This Last* were to make a lasting impression upon Gandhi's thought. From within Indian culture, Hindu devotional practices, hearing stories from the epic *Rāmāyaṇa*, the piety of his mother, and the Jain doctrine of nonviolence (*ahiṃsā*) all influenced Gandhi.

After the conclusion of his studies in England, Gandhi returned to India, where he learned of the death of his beloved mother. He began his legal career, which eventually led to a job in South Africa. After he moved to South Africa in 1893, Gandhi was able to overcome his shyness, gained self-confidence, developed his social and political philosophy, and engaged in political and social action. Gandhi became aware of certain restrictions on his compatriots, and after he experienced discrimination personally, he was motivated to form an association of Indians in the city of Pretoria in order to inform the authorities about their hardships. When a bill to deprive Indians of their right to elect members of the Natal legislative assembly was being considered, Gandhi submitted a petition protesting the change and sent copies of the petition to different newspapers. After becoming a champion of indentured laborers, Gandhi also led a protest that resulted in a small victory against the poll tax of the Natal government. In 1894, Gandhi played an instrumental part in establishing the Natal Indian Congress, a movement whose purpose was to promote good will among the European and Indian communities, to keep Indians at home informed, to educate African Indians about their homeland, and to improve moral, social, economic, and political circumstances for all Indians in South Africa. In 1896, Gandhi returned to India, where he wrote a pamphlet that became known as the "Green Pamphlet" because of the color of its cover, about the situation in South Africa.

When Gandhi then returned to South Africa, the white authorities accused him of condemning them in India and falsely charged him with smuggling workers into the country, but the local press later exonerated him. A fundamental struggle during this period occurred over the Black Act of 1906, which the Transvaal legislature passed in order to require all Indians wishing to reside or trade in the colony to register. After a campaign by the Indians against registration, Gandhi and J. C. Smuts, minister responsible for Asian questions, agreed that Indians would voluntarily register because compulsory registration was a form of social degradation. Due to a misunderstanding among the parties, the law was not repealed until 1911. During this period of his life, Gandhi wrote a work of political theory entitled *Hind Swaraj* (Indian Home Rule) that was originally published in the magazine *Indian Opinion* in late 1909 and issued in 1910 as a booklet. This work, which was proscribed in India, was written as a dialogue between an editor, through whom Gandhi spoke, and a reader about the detrimental effects of modern civilization on India.

After a trip to England, Gandhi and his family decided to return to India in 1913; there he volunteered his services for ambulance work during World War I, much as he did previously during the Boer War in South Africa. During 1915, Gandhi established the Satyagraha Ashram in Ahmedabad. During 1916, Gandhi worked to abolish the system of indentured labor in India. The following year he became involved with educational issues, and he was also elected the president of the Gujarat Sabha in 1917.

Gandhi aided in the abolition of tenant farming that legally bound a person to plant three of every twenty parts of his land with indigo for his landlord, in the so-called Indigo Incident of 1917; he assisted laborers to gain arbitration in the Mill-hands Case; and a widespread crop failure lead to the Kheda Satyagraha that resulted in a suspension of taxes for poor farmers. Gandhi was able to demonstrate his political skills for the first time on an all-India issue in the Khilafat Incident, protesting the internment of two Muslim brothers for their Pan-Islamic and pro-Turkish sympathies and journalism. Gandhi's efforts earned him a mass Muslim following.

A major source of tension between the Indians and the British was created by the passage of the Rowlatt Bills (1918) to enable the government to fight terrorism. The Indian public interpreted these bills as proof of British intentions to retain imperial rule. In response to these bills, Gandhi created a new organization called the Satyagraha Sabha, and he called for a *hartal*, a traditional expression of mourning that entailed refraining from work. The government kept Gandhi within the confines of the Bombay Presidency to avoid trouble. When Gandhi was removed from a train, this action was widely publicized as an arrest, precipitating violence that culminated with martial law being declared in Amritsar and the killing of 400 unarmed civilians and numerous casualties at Jallianwalla Bagh by British-led troops. These incidents of violence devastated Gandhi, and he engaged in a three-day fast of personal penitence, admitting that he had made a mistake calling for a hartal when people did not know how to obey the law and act from an informed sense of social duty. Although the hartal was unsuccessful, Gandhi was thrust into the public conscience as an all-India public figure.

When the British treated General Dyer, a central figure in the massacre at Jallianwalla Bagh, as a hero, and mishandled the fate of Muslim members of the Khilafat movement after World War I, Gandhi became convinced that he must more actively oppose British rule; he began to refer to it as satanic and thought that it was his moral duty to work for its termination. Along with campaigning for the Khilafat cause, Gandhi advocated wide noncooperation with the British in 1919, and the following year he became president of the Home Rule League, an event that extricated him from isolation from political institutions and motivated him to travel throughout India to publicize his program during 1921. He was forced to abandon his campaign of civil disobedience after twenty-two policemen were massacred in the Uttar Pradesh region in February of 1922. During the following month, Gandhi was arrested and pleaded guilty to inciting disaffection toward the government, for which he was sentenced to six years imprisonment after he requested the judge to impose on him the severest penalty. He was released early and unconditionally in January 1924 in order to have an emergency operation for appendicitis. In response to increasing communal riots and religious intolerance in 1924, Gandhi vowed to fast and live only on water. This form of personal penance and plea for unity by Gandhi motivated Motilal Nehru to organize a Unity Conference in Delhi on September 26, 1924, which adopted a resolution primarily drafted by Gandhi that deplored communal dissension. By 1925, Gandhi began to devote his attention to the cause of *khadi* (homespun cloth), the spinning and weaving of *svadeshi* (nonimported) clothes to help India become more self-sufficient, and serve as a means to teach organization and discipline, function to break down barriers of caste and education, and to shape the masses for the self-control required of genuine *satyagrahis* (nonviolent protesters). Gandhi's emphasis on spinning and weaving represented what he called a "constructive program." Gandhi hoped to bring leaders into closer touch with ordinary people and to enhance the dignity of work in the minds of intellectuals. British administrators had emphasized the importance of the prestige of place and power, and Gandhi turned this around by "making ignominy and pain the hallmarks of a new and greater esteem according to the logic of nationalism."[38]

During the 1930s, civil disobedience served in the quest for legitimacy by the Congress Party as it sought to position itself to negotiate the future of India with the British. The most notable new form of *satyagraha* (nonviolent protest), which included civil disobedience, took the publicly announced form of marching 241 miles from the city of Ahmedabad, beginning on March 12, 1930, to the coast of Bombay to make salt, which was a commodity required by every Indian. Salt production was a heavily taxed government monopoly. Because it was illegal for anyone else to manufacture it, Gandhi's action was intended to call attention to this injustice by marching to the ocean and making salt there. For this action, Gandhi was again jailed.

The viceroy, Lord Irwin, who hoped to reach an agreement that would reconcile the opponents, released Gandhi from jail on January 25, 1931. The talks between Gandhi and Irwin resulted in a pact on March 15, 1931, that ended civil disobedience and the boycott of British goods; the government recognized the svadeshi movement, and Gandhi agreed to attend the next Round Table Conference on British-Indian relations in London. At this session of the Round Table Conference, Gandhi introduced issues of social reform by insisting that he represented the Untouchables, claiming they were Hindus (although many higher-caste Indians did not recognize them as such). The conference was an unsuccessful event. A week after he returned to India, Gandhi was arrested, on January 4, 1932, by the rigidly conservative government of Lord Willingdon, who decided to take a tougher position by outlawing the Congress organization. During September 1932, Gandhi launched a fast-unto-death in response to the announcement about a voting scheme to be incorporated in India's new constitution that allowed for separate elections of various indigenous social and religions groups, which he felt would sow discord among Indians. While imprisoned in Yeravda jail in Bombay, Gandhi and the Untouchable leader B. R. Ambedkar came to an agreement about the proportion of representation by the depressed classes. After the Hindu Leaders Conference meeting in Bombay on September 25 agreed that no Hindu should be classified as an Untouchable by virtue of his or her birth, Gandhi broke his fast on September 26, drinking a glass of orange juice given to him by his wife. After 1937, Gandhi withdrew from politics and administration to pursue his utopian vision of nonviolence and *svaraj* (home rule) through work centered in the village of Sevagram in central India. He also wrote a paper called the *Harijan* (Children of God), which is what he named the Untouchables.

With the advent of World War II, Gandhi's public role and India's political life were profoundly altered. On October 17, 1940, Gandhi initiated his individual satyagraha campaign by sending his foremost disciple, Vinoba Bhave, revered as India's "walking saint," to proclaim his resolve to nonviolently resist the war effort. The final great satyagraha campaign was the Quit India movement, which was in part a response to the failed mission of Sir Stafford Cripps, who came with an offer of full dominion status for an Indian union along with the proviso that any province or state could decide not to join the union, and that British rule would remain unchanged until the end of the war. The Quit India campaign was interpreted by the British government as a form of sedition in wartime, and it responded sternly by arresting all leaders. The campaign assumed a un-Gandhian form by becoming violent and destructive. While Gandhi was imprisoned at the Aga Khan's palace, in Poona, his wife Kasturbhai died on February 22, 1944, and he was finally released on May 6, 1944, after a severe attack of malaria. Gandhi met in September with Muhammad Ali Jinnah, leader of the Muslim League, but their talks broke down when the Muslim leader insisted on the creation of Pakistan as an absolute prerequisite to independence, whereas Gandhi refused to discuss Pakistan until the British granted self-rule.

After India's independence in 1947, Gandhi lamented the division of India and the communal carnage (between Hindus and Muslims) that resulted during the period from 1946 to 1947. During the irruption of communal violence, Gandhi toured numerous villages in Bengal, and in September of 1947 he again fasted, attempting to restore sanity to the residents of Calcutta. For Hindu extremists, Gandhi became a symbol of "anti-Brahmanism" because he continued to preach nonviolence instead of hatred of Muslims.[39] After the violence died down, leaders pledged to prevent further violence. While he was greeting numerous people on January 30, 1948, on his way to a prayer meeting in the garden of Birla House in Delhi, a young Hindu named Naturam V. Godse fired three shots at point-blank range into Gandhi, who slumped to the ground uttering as his last words the name of Rām, his personal deity. The assassin was a member of a conservative paramilitary group called the Rashtriya Svayamsevak Sangh (National Organization of Volunteers). The death of

Gandhi marked the passing of the most charismatic figure of the Indian movement for independence and India's single most recognizable international persona. After his death, anti-Brahmin riots swept major cities, the perpetrator was convicted and hanged, and the RSS was outlawed.

After the country won independence from Great Britain, Jawaharlal Nehru (1889–1964), a close associated of Mahatma Gandhi in the struggle for freedom, was appointed the first prime minister of the democratic country. During his years of leadership, Nehru kept his daughter Indira close by his side, and he essentially groomed her to replace him in the future. The mature Nehru's vision of the future included a single world guided by socialist humanism. Nehru was suspicious of religion, and he thought that it needed to be subdued before it destroyed the Indian people.[40] Nehru was also suspicious of Marxism because of its authoritarianism, which was contrary to his preference for individual freedom; he wanted to create a nation that was democratic, secular, and socialist on an Indian pattern.

During Nehru's era, several major campaigns were initiated to battle problems of peasant backwardness and rural poverty. Vinoba Bhave traveled India by foot, for instance, to ask landowners to adopt him as their son and grant him a gift of land, with the intention of turning the land over to landless laborers. Bhave collected over a million acres. He later followed this campaign by asking for gifts of a village and human life. By 1966, Nehru's five-year economic plans had catapulted his country to the world's seventh-ranked most industrially advanced country. Nehru attempted to lead nonaligned Afro-Asian nations with his foreign policy of neutralism and its emphasis on national independence and anticolonialism. But the Chinese invasion in 1962 and the spread of provincial linguistic agitation caused problems for Nehru.

After signing an agreement of peace, friendship, and cooperation with Pakistan, Nehru died suddenly of cardiac arrest in 1966. A collective leadership led by Prime Minister Lal Bahadur Shastri (1904–1966) guided the country. When Shastri also died, the Congress Party leaders threw their support behind Indira Gandhi, daughter of Nehru. She encountered labor strikes, food riots, and linguistic and religious separatist agitation in the Punjab as Sikhs demanded a separate state.

In July of 1969, Indira Gandhi proposed the nationalization of India's banks together with limits on personal income, private property, and corporate profits. She also instituted a program of land reform. The old guard of the Congress Party attempted to remove her from her leadership role, but she rallied a majority of party members to form a new party, called Congress Party (I). Mrs. Gandhi's new party enjoyed a stunning victory in the general election of 1971. During the same year, she signed a twenty-year treaty with the Soviet Union, and she helped to liberate Bangladesh from Pakistan. In 1974, India became a nuclear power. By the middle of the decade, events took a turn for the worse. Mrs. Gandhi proclaimed a state of national emergency on June 26, 1975, which suspended all civil rights, imposed control of the press, and banned opposition political parties; air flights over Delhi were canceled, and the military was placed on alert. A Twenty-Point

Program of economic reforms was unveiled a week later. Finally, on January 18, 1977, Mrs. Gandhi invoked emergency rule.

During the Emergency of the mid 1970s, Mrs. Gandhi sought to create a personality cult by prominently displaying her picture and sayings on streets, on buses, at thoroughfares, in shop windows, and in other public places. Indira study circles were organized at universities, a new collection of her speeches was circulated, she was proclaimed the guardian of law and order, and the populace was urged to support her Twenty-Point Program. Numerous documentary films were made to promote her and her program. She tended to assume a guise larger than the party, government, or prime minister. The Congress Party (I) contributed to this cult with its campaign slogan in 1975: "Indira is India, and India is Indira." This slogan was set to music in the party's song "Indira Hindustan Ban Gai" (Indira has become India). It was now official: Indira and India were nondual.

Nonetheless, her restriction on freedoms led to her defeat in general elections by Morarji Desai's Janata Morcha party. After Desai's government could not reach any consensus about social and economic problems, however, Mrs. Gandhi returned to power in 1980. That same year her son Sanjay, who was being groomed as her political heir, was killed in a plane crash.

Even though many Indians suffered hardships and indignities during the Emergency, many others welcomed the order that the Emergency brought in its wake. Ved Mehta quoted an Indian woman who approved of it and added: "Everyone says that she is Goddess Durga, that she has Goddess Durga's shakti (energy and power) and no one can cross her without being smitten by it."[41] This identification of Mrs. Gandhi with Durgā, a goddess of violence and destruction, was confirmed by other people, such as a painter commissioned to do a series of portraits of her, who painted a triptych of Mrs. Gandhi as Durgā.[42] A popular poster depicted Mrs. Gandhi receiving inspiration and energy from Durgā. And a cover of *Femina* magazine, a feminist Indian publication, once depicted Mrs. Gandhi with multiple arms holding not only the various weapons of Durgā but also food. Such a magazine cover demonstrated both the terrible aspect of the goddess-politician and her life-giving powers. Mrs. Gandhi's deified status in the minds of some Indians did not protect her from meeting a tragic end.

In early 1984, Jarnail Singh Bhindranwale (1947–1984), a previously unknown young Sikh fundamentalist, initiated violent action for national autonomy for Punjab. He led a group of followers that seized control of the Golden Temple and its so-called Immortal Tower in Amritsar. After Mrs. Gandhi imposed martial law throughout the region, Indian troops stormed the Golden Temple, an action that led to the death of thousands of Sikhs and more than a hundred soldiers. Less than half a year later two Sikh guards assassinated Mrs. Gandhi. Her murder sparked a violent response by mobs of Hindus, who rampaged through the streets of cities killing Sikhs and setting fire to property owned by them.

After the tragic death of Mrs. Gandhi, her political party rallied around her son Rajiv, an Indian Airlines pilot. Although Rajiv proved to be a popular leader, he abandoned the socialist path of Nehru and his mother by cutting income and inheritance taxes. While on a tour of the south, Rajiv was killed by a female suicide Tamil Tiger bomber in Madras on May 2, 1991. The Tamil Tigers were fighting for an independent state in northern Sri Lanka. The assassination of Rajiv Gandhi was a response to the Indian government's suppression of the independence movement on the island nation.

The decade of the 1990s in India witnessed to a Hindu fundamentalist reaction against the secular republic initiated by Nehru. At the beginning of the decade, orthodox Hindus began to call for the destruction of a sixteenth-century mosque (Babri Masjid) originally erected by Mughal emperor Babur in Ayodhyā. Hindus believed that this mosque had been constructed over a temple commemorating the birthplace of the deity Rāma. They wanted to replace the mosque with a temple to their deity. In October 1990, The fundamentalist leader L. K. Advani mounted a golden chariot to travel several hundred miles to the site. Thousands of his devout followers dragged and pushed the chariot to Ayodhyā. Holy men and priests blessed millions of sacred bricks for the rebuilding of the temple. Even though Advani was arrested, a large mob destroyed the massive mosque on December 6, 1992. These same types of conservative religious forces gained great influence over the government during the decade, worked to eclipse the secular tendencies of Nehru, and, many feared, would confirm Nehru's worst fears about religion.

The early twentieth-century writer V. D. Savarkar served as the modern inspiration for Hindu fundamentalism with his book *Essentials of Hindutva* written in 1922, in which he defined elements of Hindu nationalism and what it means to be a Hindu in particular. A Hindu was defined as an inhabitant of Hindustan who holds his or her land holy and considers it the location of his or her ancestors. Hindu deities and the blood of Hindu martyrs sanctified this land, he wrote. Hindus are not only those who love the holy land but they also represent a nation and a race that share a common origin and blood. Muslims, even though they may have been born in India, are excluded from this group, whereas Jains are considered Hindus—even though they do not practice Hinduism and do not believe in the Vedas as divinely revealed literature—because, it is said, they belong to a common Hindu culture. The common denominator for this Hindu culture is the Sanskrit language, and the two epics—*Rāmāyaṇa* and *Mahābhārata*—function as the basis of the culture. Savarkar envisioned a return of the god Rāma, a conqueror and world ruler, to Ayodhyā to usher in the birth of the Hindu nation that would culminate in a fusion of nationhood, territory, language, race, and civilization.

Savarkar's work inspired Hindu fundamentalist political parties such as the Bharatiya Janata Party (BJP), its allied organization the Vishva Hindu Parishad (VHP), and other organizations. Such organizations claim to be nonsectarian, not associated with any specific sectarian doctrine; they are missionary, pan-Hindu mass movements, social reformists, seeking to unite various sects, and to spread Hindu ethical and spiritual values. Some of the groups advocate a particular text such as the *Bhagavad Gītā*, image worship at home, and regular temple attendance as necessary activities. Nehru's advocacy of secularism, more recent fears about globalization, the growth of liberalism of the national economy, and increasing demands by lower-caste groups for economic and political party have given impetus to a tide of religious enthusiasm and fanaticism that in its early days had been directly associated with Gandhi's assassination by member of the Rashtriya Swayamsevak Sangh (RSS).

Founded by Keshav Baliram Hedgewar in 1925 on a day marking Rāma's slaying of the demon Rāvaṇa, the Rashtriya Swayamsevak Sangh (National Organization of Volunteers) was created to protect and promote nationalism, religion, and culture in response to Muslim political mobilization. Seeking to eradicate differences among Indians and encouraging them to acknowledge their past glory, the organization's constitution intends to promote a spirit of self-sacrifice and discipline and to reinvigorate Hindu society, while combining nationalism with the essence of being a Hindu. This type of organization and others similar to it in spirit oppose conversion to nonindigenous religious traditions, advocate cow protection, and promote teaching about Hindu culture, which are issues that reflect ethnic, sociopolitical, and nationalistic concerns.

Such representative groups of Hindu fundamentalism share common features that include conservative and separatist sentiments with radicalism. These conservative groups believe that they possess a monopoly on the truth, view the world as divided between insiders and outsiders, believe in a common destiny that includes a utopian future, and are united against evil. These kinds of foundational features also includes some functional elements, such as an experience of radical conversion, commitment to revival of cultural vitality, and observance of a strict separatism.[43]

Preview of Book

The remainder of this study of Hinduism is designed to concentrate on central themes in the religious tradition. The metaphor of fire is used to discuss ancient vedic religion, and the swan is used as a way to relate the upaniṣadic texts and life of the renouncer. This is followed by a discussion of major cultural notions related to dharma, the social system, family life, and rites of passage. The notion of experience enables chapter 5 to examine the practice of yoga and the nondualism of Advaita Vedānta. The sensual nature of Hinduism is covered in chapter 6 by reviewing the roles of seeing, hearing, touching, smelling, and tasting within Indian culture. Chapters 7–9 concentrate on various aspects of the Vaiṣṇava religious traditions by utilizing themes such as embodiment, divine play, madness, eroticism, and righteous kingship to discuss the divine beings Viṣṇu, Krishna, and Rāma and the devotional movements that they inspired. Chapter 9 discusses both Rāma and the Untouchables, who are both under represented in most introductory texts. The themes of dance, asceticism, and androgyny help one to grasp the significance of Śiva and the various sectarian movements associated with this deity. What I have called the "feminine thread" covers the topics of goddesses, the role of women in Indian culture, and female holy figures in chapter 11 based on the many fine studies of these themes that have appeared over the past two decades. The inclusion of a discussion about the cultural role of women will also provide more balance to this work and enable us to examine different religious phenomena. The important themes of desire and androgyny help us to understand Tantric Hinduism in Chapter 12. Chapter 13 examines the domain of village Hinduism; this chapter is intended to provide some further balance to the book by examining the way ordinary people within northern and southern villages practice Hinduism. Finally, this book looks at Indian reform movements that began in the eighteenth century and continue into the twenty-first century.

2

Tongues of Fire of the Vedic Sacrificial Cult

Fire is bright, warm, wonderful, and an awesome power. It is probably incorrect to claim that humans invented fire; it is more likely that fire revealed itself to humans as the aftermath of a lighting strike, in an experience analogous to revelation. Humans attempted to domesticate this ambivalent power, to harness it for good purposes. The ambivalence of fire is evident in its dreaded and destructive power when it cannot be controlled and its simultaneous ability not only to warm but also be a means of purification and transformation. If it becomes uncontrollable, it can destroy humans, animals, dwellings, and forests. When humans control fire it can transform raw flesh or vegetation into something cooked and eatable. Within the ritual context of the fire sacrifice, fire enables, by means of its inherent transformative capacity, to send food to the gods in return for rain, which human beings need to grow crops in order to survive and continue sacrificing to the divine beings.

This scenario suggests why and how fire plays an important role in Indian culture, where it assumes a variety of literary and religious usages. In some contexts, the destructive nature of fire is stressed. There is also metaphorical use of fire in connection with the fire of passion and procreation. Fire is also considered a basic element, one of those that construct all that exists. In the religious sphere, there is the fire of ritual and the internal yogic fire that consumes the seeds of actions by the fire of knowledge. Within the ancient vedic religious context, fire is called the messenger of the gods, a divine being named Agni, the eater of offerings, the means of conveying the oblations to the gods; it is also a means of purifying and consecrating people, things, and areas, and it drives away evil spirits.

This chapter borrows the metaphor of fire, to discuss its importance at a formative historical period of Indian culture, in order to grasp the centrality of the priestly sacrificial system. The metaphor of fire can also function as a tool to investigate the ancient vedic worldview: its divine pantheon, the theory of sacrifice and practitioners of it, the symbolism of the sacrifice and its connection to the worldview, the nature of selected sacrifices, and the eschatology of the vedic period. The metaphor of fire operated, with other vedic features, to inspire and to ground the later historical development of Hinduism in what came to be perceived as a prestigious, divisively revealed and sanctioned cultural foundation. It is not unusual for later movements within Hinduism to seek religious confirmation and authenticity by claiming to conform to or represent the true spirit of the Vedas.

Domestic Fire

In addition to its importance in the complex sacrificial cult, fire played an important religious role in everyday life. In ancient India, during the time of marriage a new couple would have a fire installed in their household, and it was the duty of a householder to keep this domestic fire alive. If it went out, the householder had to rekindle it by a process of friction using fire-sticks, a process often described in sexual language, which was intended in part to stress the importance of sexual congress and need for offspring within the context of domestic life for a couple. The domestic fire defines the unity of a household, and it is related to the inhabitants of a home in both a personal and ambivalent way. On the one hand, the fire is dangerous and unpredictable, and it is also considered the creative self of a person, but with a destructive potential.[1] The domestic fire manifests an intricate and intimate web of relationships between the householder, the fire, animals, and other family members. The hearth fire thus unifies the various parts of a typical home. The personal nature of the fire is also evident when it is called the son of the male head of household, because he controls and gives birth to it. This father-son relationship is reversed when the householder dies, because the fire (son) is used to ignite the funeral pyre of the deceased, who is reborn at that time by the fire.[2] In this scenario, the former son (fire) gives birth to his father (deceased householder).

In addition to maintaining the fire, a householder must not lose it, or mix it with another fire. Any violation of domestic fire etiquette can cause the fire, a self-willed element, to transgress its place of confinement and threaten the well-being of its owner. The inherent hostile tension of fire is especially true of the sacrificial fire, which wants to consume the flesh of the sacrificer, but the flesh of an animal substitute must annually placate it.[3] Therefore, fire is both a friend that carries the burnt oblation to the gods and a potentially destructive enemy. Because of its central place within the home of ancient Indians, the fire served as a permanent witness of domestic life, and a married couple was encouraged to worship it for protection.[4] Even though fire was considered ambivalent and dangerous, it functioned as a mediator, protector, physician, and preserver of medicine. Most important, fire assumed the form of the divine being Agni, and played a major role in the sacrificial cult of ancient Indians and in their attempt to achieve power and other benefits through the sacrifice.

In addition to representing the domestic fire and having close proximity to human beings, the god Agni is a perfect example of the ancient belief in the connection between a name and power. The name Agni is a mode of being in which the name, character, functions, and way of life are intimately linked in either a divine or human being. In short, Agni is identical to the fire. Knowing this divine name is important because it enables the knower and reciter of the name to gain command of it.[5] This ability of humans does not detract from the power of Agni. As the possessor of power (*sahas*), Agni can resist or restrain other divine or human beings by means of the autonomous nature of the power that he possesses or of which he partakes.[6] This power sustains heaven, earth, mountains, plains, waters, and the sun (RV 8.15.2). This is equivalent to claiming that it is built into the nature of reality. Not only do divine beings use it but humans also attempt to tap into it. Humans attempt to utilize this power by engaging in sacrifice, a violent, dangerous, and ambivalent process.

Creative Conflict

The practitioners of ancient vedic religion struggled to survive in an uncertain and hostile world. This social reality is sometimes captured in the violence of its mythology. At the beginning of cosmic time, there was a tremendous conflict between two antithetical groups: Ādityas (that is, coming from the mother goddess Aditi) and Dānavas (that is, descendents of Dānu). The latter group appears as serpents or boars, and the demonic serpent named Vṛtra, who symbolizes the ground and potency of existence, is their leader. This demonic being contains the possibilities of all life. In ancient Indian mythology, the Dānavas operate to bind, restrain, hold in check, cover over, or enclose the cosmic waters and the sun, which serves as the embryo of the cosmic waters. They thus represent inertia and destruction, and thus come to symbolize death. In contrast, the Ādityas, who are associated with the cosmic order (*ṛta*, RV 8.25.3), take the appearance of humans or birds, and the deity Varuṇa leads them. They are described as dwelling in the lap of their mother Aditi, who is called the great mother, is devoid of definite physical features, and is identified with the earth. Aditi is a power that is opposed to all limitations and thus represents freedom, while her sons the Ādityas are associated with celestial light, source of life, and stand against evil and darkness. This group operates on the surface of the earth, and they represent expansion, release, development, and growth. Their overall goal is creation, and they thus symbolize immortal life. In summary, the Dānavas stand for nonbeing, whereas the Ādityas represent being. These groups are the two antithetical and contending forces in the universe: death and life.

The tension in the natures of the two groups leads to an inevitable conflict when the demonic Vṛtra, encloses the champion of the Ādityas, Varuṇa, as well as Agni, god of fire, and Soma, deified immortal elixir. This event signals a return to chaos. To counter this dreadful event, the Ādityas arrange for the birth of the warrior god Indra with the purpose of destroying Vṛtra. After he is born, Indra exacts a promise from the gods: if he defeats Vṛtra, he will become their king. After the gods agree to this arrangement—they have no viable choices—an eagle gives Indra three vats of Soma (intoxicating liquid) to drink, to enhance his power. A great, violent, and bloody cosmic struggle ensues between the two major antagonists. Finally, Indra splits open Vṛtra's head, and the cosmic waters are released. It is said that Vṛtra's fatal wound inflicted by Indra created room (*lokam*, RV 10.104.10) for the world and life. This means that Indra's violent act separates being (*sat*) from nonbeing (*asat*). Furthermore, nonbeing is converted into being, an act that also establishes the cosmic law (*ṛta*). This violent act transforms Indra into Viśvakarman, the All-Maker. In this creation narrative it is possible to recognize the transformation of chaos into cosmos or order.

After the creative act of Indra, Varuṇa is freed and begins to organize everything. There is a bit of irony involved in Varuṇa's activity because his major characteristic involves fettering or ensnaring others after he has experienced the indignity of being ensnared himself. Varuṇa prescribes the laws by which the cosmos should operate, and he becomes the guardian of the cosmic law (*ṛta*). Finally, human beings are created to support the divine beings.

As impressive, heroic, creative, and defining as Indra's act proves to be, it nonetheless possesses serious flaws. A fundamental flaw is that evil is not totally extinguished, because *rākṣasas* (demons) lurk below the earth by day, and they emerge at night to ensnare humans. If the continued existence of demonic beings is the negative aspect of Indra's flawed work from the perspective of humans, it is a positive outcome from the viewpoint of the divine beings. Why? Humans would have no incentive to serve, worship, and sacrifice to the gods if evil had been completely eliminated. Without evil, the gods would perish because of a lack of daily sacrifices.

The Indra-Vṛtra myth conveys an important message about human existence during the vedic period, which is that life is a continuous struggle between the forces of existence and nonexistence. The victory between these forces as symbolized in the myth is not a victory that humans can win once and forever. Human existence is radically contingent and uncertain, because there is the constant danger of the cosmos and order collapsing into nothingness. Therefore, the cosmos and life must be continually sustained and renewed.

Vedic Worldview

The gargantuan struggle between Indra and the demonic Vṛtra establishes order out of chaos. The creation myth presupposes that humans cannot live for any length of time in a condition of chaos. The primary intelligent order guiding the universe is *ṛta* (literally "the course of things"). The term *ṛta* is derived from a Sanskrit root meaning "to go," which implies proceeding straight, regularly, or along a fixed course. It is possible that the regularity of the sun and stars, the passing of the seasons, and the alternation of day and night evoked the notion of a consistent pattern, rhythm, and structure of the world to vedic poets. Hence, ṛta is the law, unity, or rightness that underlies the orderliness of the cosmos.

This underlying structure is more fundamental than the divine beings, who are also subject to its norms. The dynamic unifying ṛta directs the emergence, dissolution, and reemergence of life. In addition, it gives to each thing and event its own structure and nature. A tiger or an elephant has a structure and nature, for instance, that accords with the ṛta. If ṛta did not exist, there would be chaos instead of order in the universe, and there would be immorality and disorder on the social level of existence. The reason that the vedic sacrifice works is because of ṛta. In fact, the sacrifice is the ritual correspondence to ṛta on earth. By following this fundamental law, human beings become established in truth (*satya*), because the cosmic law is directly connected to truth and what is real. Moreover, humans who sacrifice properly achieve a fuller and more harmonious life, because one lives in concert with the fundamental energies and rhythms of life.

The order (*ṛta*) of the vedic cosmos consists of a triple-structured world (*loka*): sky, atmosphere, and earth (AV 12.3.20).[7] The sky is considered masculine and the earth is feminine. This male-female structure is reflected in vedic hymns that depict the sky raining down upon the earth and fertilizing her (RV 5.83.4). The atmosphere is the liminal space between the other two. The threefold vedic world also consists of a basic cosmic dichotomy between being (*sat*) and nonbeing (*asat*). The former sphere is where gods and human live; it consists of the earth's surface, the sky, and the intermediate space of the atmosphere. This threefold region is characterized by light, warmth, and moisture, and is subject to the universal cosmic law (*ṛta*). If the cosmic law is followed, the result is life, growth, prosperity, and order. The sphere of nonbeing is located below the earth, and it is inhabited by demons. It is characterized by cold, darkness, drought, and a lack of cosmic law, and is obviously the sphere of death and decay. Thus vedic poets discover themselves subject to a basic cosmic dichotomy between being and nonbeing. The mythological struggle between Indra and Vṛtra reflects this basic conviction. Nonetheless, vedic poets are convinced that the world is meaningful, a unified structure, an interconnected totality, whereas nonbeing represents a constant threat into which being can fall, if the cosmic law and its concomitant sacrificial cult are not faithfully followed and practiced.

Divine Hierarchy

The fundamental dichotomy between being and nonbeing is reflected in the supernatural realm, because the gods signify being and the demons denote nonbeing. The Sanskrit term for god is *deva*, which means "shining" or "auspicious." The gods shine, whereas demons do not give light. The term for demon is *asura*, which means "lord" and "powerful." These creatures of power can be either benevolent or malevolent.

There is not a wide gap between gods and human beings. There are, however, characteristics that are possessed by the divine beings that distinguish them from humans. The gods float effortlessly above the ground when visiting earth, no dust clings to their garments or skin, their eyes are wide open, they do not blink their eyes, and finally they cast no shadows.

In addition to embodying the tension between the gods and demons, it is possible that the members and actions of the pantheon itself reflect conflict and friction between different ethnic groups, clans, and families that emphasize certain divine figures at the expense of others, although there is no way to verify such a social conflict. Along with social tensions, the changes among deities reflect the continual influx of new ideas and a creative tension with preexisting notions.[8] Deities enjoying well-defined characters in the earlier vedic period eventually give way to more ill-defined figures at a later historical period. Moreover, vedic deities that personified natural phenomena could not become transformed into sectarian gods, as did Viṣṇu and Rudra (Śiva), because they were already clearly defined.[9] The vague natures of Viṣṇu and Rudra during the vedic period enabled later seers to attribute new feats and characteristics to these deities as they developed into major sectarian figures that are well known today.

The vedic divine pantheon is populated by over 3,003 divine beings, according to some poets. But there are also passages that refer to 303, 33, 3, or first one divine being (RV 3.9.9; 3.6.9; ŚB 4.5.7.2). This polytheism is not as confusing as it might seem; the divine hierarchy corresponds to the three spheres of the world (*loka*). The gods are not, however, confined solely to a specific level of the cosmos; some deities are active in all three spheres. But deities are more active in certain spheres of the cosmos than they are in other regions. The sky is dominated by Dyaus, who is father of heaven, the sun deity Sūrya, Viṣṇu, and deities associated with cosmic order such as Varuṇa, Mitra, and the other Ādityas. The major figures in the atmosphere are Indra, Vāyu or wind, and Rudra, who will evolve into Śiva. The earth is dominated by Soma, Agni, who is the god of fire, and various goddesses. These various gods and goddesses symbolize various powers of life and nature. Soma is a pressed juice that functions as a hallucinatory drink of immortality, and thus symbolizes ecstasy, transcendence, and illumination. The deity Vāc symbolizes the power of speech, Dyaus signifies the powers of heaven, Pṛthivī represents the earth, and the Maruts are storm gods that denote the power of nature.

The divine beings are also grouped according to the social structure of ancient India. The highest Brahmin caste corresponds to the creative deity Brahmā, who is the source of the other deities (BĀU 1.4.11–15), and the fire deity Agni. Another priestly deity is Bṛhaspati, lord of prayer, who possesses a bowstring that is identified with the cosmic law. The deities of the warrior caste are Indra, Varuṇa, Soma, Rudra, and Yama (god of the dead). The Vasus, Rudras, Ādityas, Viśva Devas, and Maruts represent the Vaiśyas, which is the third-highest caste. Finally, the fourth caste (Śūdra) is associated in vedic classification with Pūṣan (prosperity), a son of the mother Aditi who is closely associated with the sun as the source of life. The four castes and deities associated with Agni and the Brahmins are related to certain powers such as *tejas* (splendor, heat, light), and the quality of courage is connected to Indra and the warrior caste. This system of classification reflects a logic that equates sacrificial deities with the priestly caste and heroic gods with the warrior caste.[10] Thus the social system of classification directly reflects the cosmic order (*ṛta*).

Despite the implications of the Indra-Vṛtra creation myth, the gods and goddess are not, strictly speaking, creators. They function rather as artisans to form a thing from preexisting matter, to oversee what is already there, and to be lords of the world. An excellent example of the divine artisan is Tvaṣṭṛ; who is considered the chief architect and fashioner of the gods. Saraṇyū is the impetuous daughter of Tvaṣṭṛ; she hurried into creation, married (RV 10.17.1) Vivasvat, the Radiant, and gave birth to twins named Yama and Yamī. Saraṇyū also gave birth to the Aśvins, harbingers of the morning dawn. They are solar deities described as golden in appearance and dress, riding in a golden chariot (RV 7.7.28–29). Their name implies an association with horses (*aśva*). They are fond of honey (RV 1.47), and they are also known as the divine physicians, with an ability to heal the decrepit and blind (RV 1.122.8).

The most obvious solar deity is Sūrya, the sun, who is considered an aid to vision. When he lights the world his brightness makes people happy. He is imagined riding on a golden chariot drawn by horses (RV 1.21.3). Because he supports the sky, he is called its pillar (RV 4.13.5). In close proximity to Sūrya there is the pretty daughter of the sky called Uṣas (Dawn). She is described paradoxically as both old and very young (RV 3.61.1). Dressed in red robes, she rides on golden horses, and she frustrates the dark forces of the night and their attempt to perpetuate evil on earth.

During the early vedic period, Varuṇa operates as the guardian of the cosmic order, before being eclipsed in importance by Indra. The name of Varuṇa is derived from a Sanskrit root that means "to cover." In this respect, Varuṇa is the coverer or encompasser; he is the god who envelops like darkness, or he covers with his bonds. Thus he is imagined metaphorically to bind humans with his noose. He is described in later literature with two aspects—a terrible one and a benevolent one (MS 3.9.6). Spies on earth assist him (RV 1.25.3). Since nothing can be kept secret from him, he becomes feared as the punisher. His vedic association with the night and punisher of transgressions contributes to his later evolution into a sinister god associated with what is malformed, ugly, and decrepit. He is the guardian of the cosmic law (*ṛta*), and his constant companion in the Vedas is Mitra. When they appear together they express day and night, darkness and light. In later literature, Varuṇa also becomes the lord of water and is associated with snakes. He eventually disappears as an important deity.

The Indra-Vṛtra myth manifests the heroic exploits of the major vedic deity Indra and his close association with the Soma liquid and its invigorating powers, which enable him to overpower the demon. Indra is depicted riding on a bull, a symbol of masculine sexual power, which points to the god's connection to fertility. As a phallic deity, Indra stands opposed to ascetics, who practice celibacy. When ascetics practice their spiritual discipline they heat the throne of Indra. When the god becomes uncomfortable he often sends a celestial nymph (*apsaras*) to annoy, distract, or sexually seduce the ascetic. Indra's weapon, the thunderbolt (*vajra*), which he uses to destroy demons, emphasizes his phallic nature. Indra's killing of the demon symbolically represents the destruction of the old cosmic order and the eternal renewal of the cosmos by violent destruction.

The secret of Indra's creative cosmic acts and demon destruction is his *māyā*, which is a notion related to wisdom and extraordinary or supernatural power. At a later date, the term comes to mean illusion, unreality, trick, or deception. An excellent example of Indra using his māyā (illusory, deceptive power) is its use against a demoness named Long-Tongue (JB 1.161–63). This demoness licked up the Soma in all directions. Indra could not capture her, and he ordered that everyone stop performing Soma sacrifices until he could stop the demoness. Indra chose a handsome young man named Sumitra to flirt with her and to deceive her. Sumitra (Good Friend) comes right to the point and proposes that they have sex. The demoness does not think that they could have sexual relations because Sumitra possesses only a single penis, whereas she possesses multiple vaginas on every limb of her body. The young man returns to Indra for help with this conundrum. Indra solves the problem by creating multiple penises for Sumitra, and he returns to the demoness, who is overjoyed to see how amply he is equipped. As they lie together, the handsome young man becomes stuck in the demoness and pins her down. She responds that she thought that he was a good friend, as his name suggests, but Sumitra replies that he is only a good friend to a deserving person. While the demoness is incapacitated, Indra arrives and kills her with his thunderbolt.

Closely associated with Indra during the vedic period is Viṣṇu, who helps Indra destroy Vṛtra by giving him knowledge. In the Vedas, Viṣṇu is famous for his three steps that traverse the earth, sky, and the beyond. He is a minor deity in the vedic period, but he is a god of great potential, who will eclipse the vedic deities with the exception of Rudra, who evolves into Śiva.

The name of Rudra is derived from a root that means to weep or howl. In one version, he weeps because he was born without a name. Rudra possesses an ambiguous nature, because he is a creator and destroyer, possesses an shining exterior and a dark interior, and is a god of the storm and of healing herbs; he is terrible and formidable, but he is also auspicious and mild. He is a protector of cattle, and he is called a bull, but he also maintains an intimate relation with demonic beings.

As the sacrificial cult gained importance during the later vedic period, gods such as Agni and Soma became more important. That there are over two hundred hymns dedicated to Agni in the Vedas is indicative of his importance. He serves as a mediator between divine beings and humans, who encounter each other at the sacrificial altar. Agni acts to lead the gods to the sacrifice, and he takes the sacrificial offerings of humans to the gods. Agni is born every morning in the sky as the sun, whereas he is also manifested as lightning in the atmosphere, and he assumes the form of fire on earth, thus operating significantly on each of the levels of the triple world (*loka*). Even though he is known as an unscrupulous seducer of women and an adulterer, Agni is also a symbol of the renewal of all things and the interrelatedness of all things. While on earth, he is considered a friend of humans, which is represented by the fire maintained by the laity in their homes.

According to the Śatapaṭha Brāhmaṇa (6.1.1.5), the deity Prajāpati is identified with the fire altar. The necessity of constructing the fire altar is related to the aftermath of Prajāpati's creative action, because he relaxes after creating the universe and its inhabitants, which causes him to disintegrate when his vital breaths depart his body. Agni agrees to restore him by building the fire altar. This scenario contributes to explaining the reason for Prajāpati's name, which suggests a god of offspring. It is possible that Prajāpati is a deity that played an important role as a popular folk deity, and poets and ritualists incorporated him into the sacrificial cult with new functions and qualities.[11] The actions of Agni are reenacted in the performance of the complex rite of building the fireplace (*agnicayana*) and the piling of five layers of bricks to form the body of Prajāpati, who plays a very important role in the ritualistic texts, along with Soma.

To be distinguished from an ordinary alcoholic drink (*surā*), Soma is the deified drink of immortality, while it gives strength and long life to the gods and humans. This elixir of immortality is both fire and water, which is born in heaven and guarded by demonic powers. Transported by an eagle, Indra steals the elixir for humans and gods (RV 4.26.1–6). It is called the king of plants, and it possesses a very important place in the sacrificial cult. By drinking Soma, a person partakes of divinity or immortality, which is described as "having gone to the light" (RV 8.48.3). Moreover, it enables one to discover mysterious worlds and achieve deeds beyond one's natural power.

Sacrifice and Power

According to the *Rig Veda* (10.81–82), Viśvakarma (All-Maker), who is the lord of speech or *brahman* (a power innate to a word), creates by the power of the sacrifice. In this hymn, everything that exists is created by means of the sacrifice. The sacrifice is more than the origin of the cosmos, because it also accounts for the unity and diversity in the universe. In a profound sense, the sacrifice is built into the order of things, and it makes it possible to move from one order of reality to another. In fact, the sacrifice controls everything, implying that to know the sacrifice is to know and control the inner workings of the universe. Because of its all-encompassing nature, the ancient vedic sacrifice becomes an explanatory model for the structure of the cosmos and all human actions.[12]

There is a physical and a mental aspect of the sacrifice. The former aspect encompasses the actions of the priests and sacrificer. The priests make certain that the sacrifice is performed correctly and without interruption once it begins. The mental aspect of the sacrifice represents the internal attitude of the sacrificer, which must correspond to the external action. The mental part of the sacrifice involves thinking about and reciting sacred formulas (*mantras*) that embody within their sound a power both to express the truth and to bring it into reality.

By reciting mantras associated with a particular deity, the reciter can form a mental vision of the deity. The mantra is powerful because it is grounded in truth (*ṛta, satyā*), is guided by the method of *viniyoga*, operating in accord with certain interpretive principles based on an associative mode of thought. When the priests recites mantras during a sacrifice, their nonsensical utterances weave together the various aspects of the rite like a thread weaving together two pieces of fabric. By using Sanskrit ("well-formed") mantras, the priests believe that they are reproducing in sound the very structure of reality, because of their conviction about the correspondence between sound and reality. It is believed that the mantra must be verbally pronounced to be powerful. The pronunciation of the mantra is a performative act, which means that it makes something happen. In this case it gives impetus to the power inherent within the mantra and sets it in motion.[13] Together with their conviction of the power of mantra, it is also important for the participants to trust in the automatic result of the sacrifice.

The essential link between the physical and mental aspects of the sacrifice is *tapas* (heat), which is a natural power built into the structure of reality. Tapas is a creative, destructive, and purifying power. By means of tapas, one becomes invincible and is able to reach the highest point in the cosmos (RV 10.154.2). Through tapas, a person can gain poetic inspiration (RV 8.59.6), strength, and most important, by practicing it one is not reborn or conquers death (RV 10.183.1). Therefore, tapas enables one to lift oneself from the normal human condition. A person can also expect to gain secret wisdom and contact with the gods by practicing tapas, which is an active process and product of that very activity.

In addition to its ability to bestow gifts and powers upon someone, tapas also plays an important role in cosmogonic contexts as the force behind creation. According to a vedic creation hymn (RV 10.129.3), one learns that before the creative action everything was water, symbolizing the primordial chaos. Within an all-encompassing darkness, it was impossible to distinguish night from day, and vice versa. The life force was enclosed in emptiness, but it was born through the power of tapas, which was a creative incubating heat contained within it. In another hymn (RV 10.190.1), the creative warmth of tapas gives birth to truth and order. These examples inform us that heat not only represents the force behind creation itself but also ubiquitously permeates every aspect of creation, much as threads hold a garment together. In the Brāhmaṇa texts, the divine being Prajāpati desired to reproduce himself because he was alone. He practiced tapas, became heated, and produced waters from himself (ŚB 6.1.3.1). In another episode, while creating, Prajāpati was overpowered by death, and he practiced tapas in order to rid himself of evil, which resulted in the creation of stars from the pores of his body (ŚB 10.4.4.1–2). This type of narrative suggests that the gods use tapas to fashion the cosmos. Moreover, it is a power that precedes the gods in origin, although they are able to use this universal force of heat.

Within the sacrificial sphere, tapas plays an important role. Before the Soma sacrifice, the sacrificer and his wife are required to perform an initiation rite, which includes tapas as an essential part of the consecration (AB 2.1.4.7). By means of tapas, the sacrificer becomes purified, sheds his body, assumes a divine form, and symbolically attains the realm of the gods, where he, as a god, can perform the sacrifice. Tapas is, moreover, conceptually associated with fire in the sense that they share creative warmth.

In addition to tapas, another mysterious and hidden power is brahman, which is credited with holding together the universe. This mysterious power that is embodied within words is revealed to vedic seers. It is credited with causing things to increase, gives prosperity, bestows strength, and animates things (RV 2.12.14). By seeing and knowing brahman, wise men can perform ritual dramas in order to align their action within the world with divine models of behavior.[14] In the ritual texts, it is identical with fire (ŚB 1.3.3.19), speech (ŚB 2.1.4.10), and sacrifice (ŚB 3.1.4.15), whereas the *Kauṣītaki Upaniṣad* (1.7) identifies it with the sacred Vedas. It is historically common for brahman to be associated with what is imperishable, immovable, firm—a fundamental and sustaining principle on which, in Indian literature, everything rests.[15] Hence, it is the basis, support, or ultimate ground of all existence.

Major Sacrificial Performers

The vedic sacrifice became more complex over time. In response to this growing elaboration and complexity, priestly training became more specialized. Concurrent with this growing priestly specialization and ritual complexity, those gods more directly associated with the sacrificial cult grew in stature, from the perspective of vedic priests. Agni is a primary example of a god retaining significance for ritual specialists. In a priestly family collection of vedic hymns, Agni becomes all the gods (RV 5.3.11). Another such priestly deity is Prajāpati, who rises to prominence in the ritual texts of the Brāhmaṇas. It is said that he is the first to perform sacrifice, which makes him the first victim to be offered (ŚB 11.1.8.2–4). This primordial sacrificial action on his part identifies him directly with the sacrifice. By giving himself to the gods as a sacrificial victim, he creates a duplicate of himself in the form of the sacrifice. This ritual action enables him to redeem his life from the gods. This origin myth possesses important implications for the sacrificer.

Because the patron of a particular sacrifice is the sacrificer (*yajamāna*), this means worshiping on his own behalf, which enables him to repay a debt. Every man is both affected by debt and defined by it. Each person owes an essential debt to death. When a man offers a sacrifice, he purchases himself back from death (ŚB 3.6.2.16). Moreover, when performing a sacrifice, a male householder becomes a cooker of the sacrificial offering to the gods. By becoming a sacrificial cooker, the householder cooks the world in the sense of maintaining the sacrifice and the world by his actions, and he sharply distinguishes himself from the non-cookers in vedic society such as unmarried students and wandering ascetics, who are forbidden to light a fire to cook their meals.[16]

Although the sacrificer arranges for a sacrifice to be performed by hiring the priests and paying for it, his actions are minimal. It is more correct to say that the sacrificer attends the rite, while the priests do the work. The sacrificer, however, reaps the spiritual benefits, whereas the priests do not receive any such benefits, with the exception of gifts for their services from their patron, the sacrificer. In contrast to the patron, the wife of the sacrificer has an active part; this includes an act of gazing. The wife gazes, for instance, on the water vessel before its contents are poured over the animal victim (BŚS 20.28), purifies the breaths of the animal (KŚS 6.6.2), or she touches the breaths of the animal with water (ŚB 3.8.2.4). The limited actions of the sacrificer and his wife are dramatically different from the crucial role of the priests. If they make errors, cause accidents, or are guilty of oversights, they can harm the sacrificer and drain away any value of the rite for the patron. In order to protect the sacrificer and the rite, priests can correct their mistakes by expiations (*prāyaścitti*) that are intended to ensure a favorable result of the rite.

Each of the priests is responsible for specific ritual duties and represents a particular body of vedic literature. The *hotṛ* priest is responsible for pouring the oblations. He operates as the chief reciter and priest, and it is his duty to recite passages from the Rig Veda. He is the priest that provides brahman (truth power) to the sacrifice, which makes it effective. The hotṛ is directly connected to the fire because he is said to be the human counterpart of the divine fire.[17] In addition, the hotṛ and sacrificer are identified by the ritual texts, where both of them are said to represent the self of the sacrifice (ŚB 9.5.2.16).

Other priestly functionaries include the *udgātar*, *adhvaryu*, and *agnidh*. The udgātar priest sings songs from the *Sāma Veda* for their pleasing and powerful sound. The adhvaryu priest repeats verses from the *Yajur Veda*, and he performs the majority of the ritual actions, such as preparation of the ground, offering of oblations, and care and manipulation of implements; and he cooks the oblations. He could be considered the manual operator of the sacrifice. The agnidh priest helps the adhvaryu care for the fires and assists with the cleaning up after the conclusion of the sacrifice.

The brahman priest is the overseer of the entire sacrifice, and he represents the *Atharva Veda*. Sitting in the center of the sacred area, he remains mostly silent throughout the ceremony. This silence is deceptive, because it is considered half of the sacrifice. How is this possible? The two tracks of the sacrifice are speech and mind. The brahman priest's job is the latter track. The silence of the brahman presupposes that speech disperses power when verbally expressed, whereas silence concentrates the power of speech and keeps it intact.[18] It is his function to correct any errors made by the other performers. In this way, he functions to safeguard the sacrifice (which is considered to be a dangerous power to be handled with great caution), the patron, and ultimately the entire cosmos. In a metaphorical sense, the silent brahman priest is a healer of any wounds inflicted upon the sacrifice by means of inadvertent mistakes.

Even though a sacrificer initiates a sacrifice by requesting that it be performed, hires the priests to complete the rite, and pays for it, the role of the various Vedic priests means that the sacrificer does not approach the sacred directly and alone. The various priests serve as intermediaries between the sacrificer and the divine beings. The priests prevent the sacrificer from committing fatal errors that could potentially unleash destructive powers. By operating as intermediaries, the priests stand on the threshold between the sacred and profane, and they represent both realms at the same time. Nonetheless, by means of the power inherent within a sacrifice, the sacrificer travels to the world of the gods.

The theme of journey is closely associated with the sacrifice because the sacrificer goes to and returns from the realm of the gods, a journey symbolically associated with the death and rebirth of the sacrificer in the sacrifice. By his journey, the sacrificer unites with the world of the gods to whom the sacrifice is directed (ŚB 2.6.4.8). The unity achieved between the sacrificer and divine beings is sometimes expressed as the former becoming "food" of the gods (ŚB 3.6.3.19). Even though the sacrifice involves a journey to another world, the sacrificer must still return to this world because the gods do not want humans to reside in their world (ŚB 3.1.4.3). When the sacrificer returns to the phenomenal world he reenters it transformed by his journey.

Sacrificial Plot and Its Symbolism

During the vedic period, no temples existed in India. All public sacrifices were performed outdoors, on the bare earth. Before the sacrifice could occur, it was necessary to determine a propitious time, because not all times are equally favorable. In order to determine the most opportune time, the services of an astrologer were utilized.

Because the sacrificial rites required an accurate knowledge of the months, seasons, and year, ancient vedic astronomy (*jyotiṣa*) assisted priests to determine the correct positions of the sun and moon, which was accomplished with the circle of the twenty-seven star-groups (*nakṣatras*) of the zodiac—a system that was to later become obsolete when information from other cultures arrived in India. Nonetheless, each of the multiple star-groups were related to a particular month and corresponded to a deity from the vedic pantheon; Agni, for example, was associated with the initial star-group in the month of Kārttika. Astronomic accuracy was essential because there was a coeval relationship between the calendar and the sacrificial system, based on the belief that a year was identical with the sacrifice, and a complete cycle of seasons measured the year by the sun and the month by lunar means.

Once the most auspicious time is determined, the site of the sacrifice is consecrated by priests and transformed into holy ground by the establishment of fires, which are also identified with Agni, god of fire. The basic ground plan consists of three altars that symbolically represent a miniature cosmos. The connecting link between the three altars is the god Agni, by virtue of the fire on the altars.

Agni's presence on the three altars unites the entire sacrifice and the three-tiered world (*loka*) of the vedic worldview.

An essential feature of a vedic sacrifice is directional orientation. The ritual texts elaborately describe mapping of the sacrificial plot, the arrangement of materials, and the way for participants to orientate themselves. The east, which is considered the quarter of the gods (ŚB 3.1.1.2), is the most auspicious direction and serves as the basic direction of the sacrifice. Just as the sun rises each morning in the eastern direction, the sacrificial actions begin in this direction (GG 4.2.22). The north is also considered auspicious, and it is identified as the region of humans (ŚB 3.1.1.7), whereas the south is considered the inauspicious direction of departed ancestors. The south is also the direction of Yama (lord of the dead), while the southwest is the region of Nirṛti, a dreadful goddess of decay and death (ŚB 7.2.1.8). In order to be in harmony with these various directions and perform the rite correctly, the sacrifice is carefully choreographed with the sacrificer and priests performing their movements in synch with the proper directions of the compass.

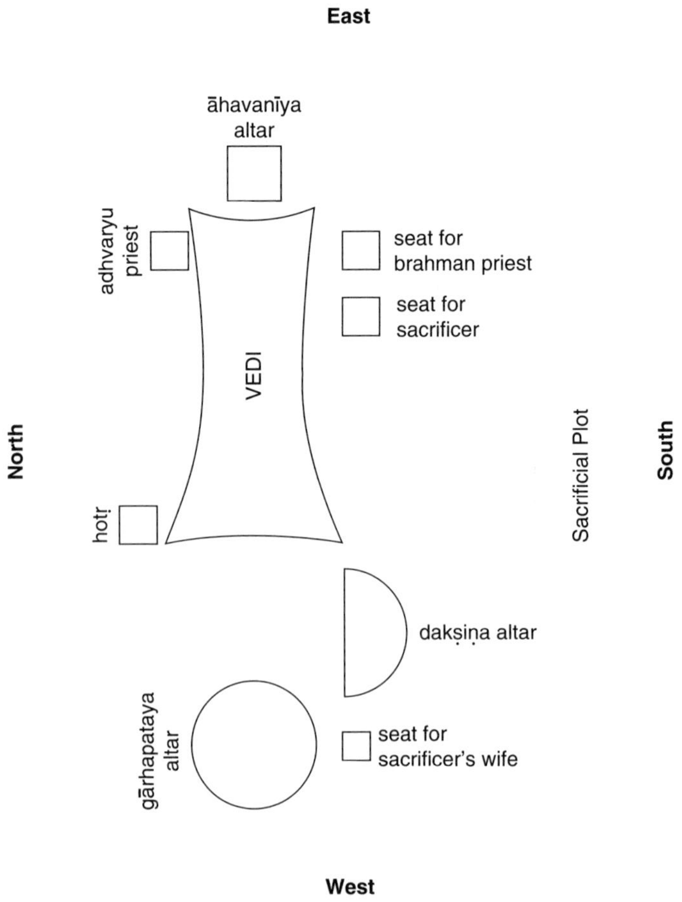

With the sacrificial plot directed toward the east, the *gārhapatya* fire, to the west, refers to the head of the household. Its altar is round and symbolically represents the earth, and is the altar at which food for the sacrifice is prepared. The *āhavanīya* fire is located in the direction of the rising sun, and it is the fire of offering, with a square shaped altar, which signifies the four-directional sky. The third fire is the *dakṣinā*, which is located in the southern direction, associated with death. This altar is semicircular, and it represents the atmosphere between earth and sky, whose purpose is to ward off evil spirits or demons and to receive offerings to departed ancestors. Within this miniature cosmos, there is an additional feature called the *vedi*, which is a ritually insulated grass-lined pit covered by sacred *kuśa* grass and shaped approximately like an hourglass. This shape resembles the torso of a woman, symbolizing the sacrificer's wife, and beyond her it points to the earth with whom the sacrificer unites.[19] During the ceremony, priests place the oblations and sacrificial utensils on the vedi to preserve their sanctity and power. The pit is also intended as a place for the gods to sit as honored guests who are entertained by sacred hymns and songs and offered food in the form of oblations. Each offering can be made to either a specifically named deity or to a group of divine beings.

External to the sacred sacrificial plot is the *yūpa* (sacrificial stake) to which an animal is tied and killed before being offered to the gods. When the victim is tied to the yūpa this act physically binds the victim with the sacrificer, and thereby equates the yūpa with the sacrificer and victim.[20] The yūpa manifests a triple structure that corresponds to the triple structure of the cosmos (TS 6.3.4.3; ŚB 3.7.1.2.5). It also functions as a cosmic ladder that enables the gods to descend to earth, and it enables the sacrificer to ascend to heaven. As the sacrificer symbolically ascends this cosmic ladder, the lower part of the yūpa gives him power over earthly things, the middle section gives him power over things of the sky, and the upper part of the stake gives him power over heavenly things. Because the yūpa also symbolizes the sacrificer, he symbolically ascends himself. Overall, the yūpa symbolizes a universal pillar. This *axis mundi* (center of the world) is a sacred place, which constitutes a break in the homogeneity of ordinary space. This break is symbolized by an opening by which passage from one cosmic region to another is made possible in terms of either ascent or descent.[21] Because it is possible to locate the world around this cosmic axis, the yūpa symbolically represents the center of the cosmos.

Vedic Animal Sacrifice

Vedic priests distinguished between two types of sacrifice: domestic (*gṛhya*) and public (*śrauta*). The former type was designed for the god of a household, and it used a single fire. The public or solemn rites used three fires, and they were for the broader welfare of the kingdom or world. The origin of the three fires can be traced to the *Rig Veda* (1.15.4), where Agni is invited to sit down in three places. The sacrifices performed with three fires are called śrauta (solemn) because they were concerned with śruti (revelation). The central physical focus of a vedic rite was the fire, as may be clear by now. The *agnihotra* (fire offering) was performed twice daily, in the early morning and evening. The evening agnihotra must begin before sunset, and the morning rite must commence before the sun rises (KŚS 4.13.2). Ideally, a householder should perform it every day.

Another distinction made by vedic ritual specialists is based on the type of offerings. Sacrifices that consist of offerings of vegetable and dairy products are called *haviryajñas*, whereas oblations of Soma are called *somayajñas* (Soma sacrifices). Besides the agnihotra (fire offering), the new and full-moon sacrifice (*darśapūrṇamāsa*) is another example of a haviryajñas sacrifice, which is conducted every two weeks. This ritual serves as the model for another class of ritual known as *iṣṭis*, which refers to the pouring of an oblation into the sacrificial fire of vegetable and/or animal substances. More precisely, iṣṭis is the preparation and offering of a sacrificial cake. In the case of the full-moon offering, it is a sacrificial cake for Agni and Soma, whereas the new-moon offering involves a cake for Agni and Indra. Other rites within this group are the four monthly sacrifices (*cāturmāsyas*). Being performed every four months, the four monthly sacrifices represent seasonal rites: *vaiśvadeva* is performed in the spring, *varuṇapraghāsa* is executed in the rainy season, autumn is the time for the *sākamedha*, and the *āgrayaṇa* represents a first-fruits sacrifice offered at harvest time. In contrast to these examples, the *agniṣṭoma* (praise of Agni) is the model for Soma sacrifices. This rite derives its name from the praise offered to Agni, god of fire, or because the final chant is addressed to him.[22] The Soma is pressed and offered on a single day in a sequence of three pressings that occur in the early morning, midday, and evening. Another Soma sacrificial classification refers to rites that take two to twelve days to perform and those that take more than twelve days.

There are also optional ceremonies associated with a Soma sacrifice. A good example is the *agnicayana* (piling up bricks for the fire altar), in which five victims are immolated, one of them theoretically a man. The heads of the victims are combined with the first bricks in a ceremony that imitates the reconstruction of the world by Prajāpati. Among the five layers of bricks, the second and fourth layers represent a different pattern from the other three layers. The altar requires bricks of several shapes (such as, triangular, oblong, and square), and each brick possesses a distinctive name. As each brick is placed on the others, a mantra is recited.[23] The entire altar consists of 10,800 bricks piled in five courses. Sometimes the altar is created in the form of a bird, which symbolizes the sacrificer's ascent to heaven.

Vedic priests do not randomly select any animal to sacrifice, because every effort is made to match the animal victim with the deity whom the sacrifice is intended to reach. This practice is called *bandhu* (connection), and it is made between parts of the day and the cardinal directions, between space and time, between society and the seasons, and between the worlds and parts of the day. A basic similarity revolves, for instance, around color. Because of their own color, the Aśvins are offered a reddish-white male goat, which implies an identity between the victim and deity. If a sacrifice is directed to Prajāpati, the animal is ideally hornless, dark gray, and uncastrated. The ultimate victim, however, is the sacrificer, because every sacrifice is a form of self-sacrifice, as evident in the *Aitareya Brāhmaṇa* (2.11), which identifies the sacrificer directly with the victim. This suggests that the sacrificer offers himself to the gods, even though the animal victim acts as his substitute. The victim redeems the sacrificer, extends his life, and helps him to gain immortality (ŚB 11.7.1.2–3).

Scholars tend to agree that all sacrifice involves violence—actual or symbolic—because a victim must be killed. Certainly, violence and death characterize early vedic sacrifice, although it is possible to witness in the texts a movement toward a more nonviolent form of sacrifice. Directions to avoid looking directly at the animal as it is being killed and the use of euphemisms such as saying that the victim is quieted instead of killed provide suggestions of this trend. Moreover, life and immortality are bestowed upon the victim when it is sprinkled with water and given vital breaths.[24] As the priests moved toward a symbolically nonviolent sacrifice, they became more obsessed with ritual precision and anxiety about committing errors. Because of such concerns, the vedic priests attempted to create a closed system that they could control and direct by means of ritual.[25] The priests also attempted to minimize the danger associated with sacrifice. If the path of sacrifice can serve as a vehicle to transport a person to heaven, the path is described as narrow because success or failure is tenuous and indisputable (ŚB 2.3.4.37). Therefore, sacrifice can be considered as occurring within a constant context of anxiety. Within such a system, priests intend for the ritual to produce results automatically. Although the process of bringing about the results is hidden from empirical perception, the results could be objectively perceived in the form of cattle, health, male progeny, long life, or any other intended result.

Although all sacrifice involves some form of violence, there is no rite in which this is more evident than in the *paśubandha* (animal sacrifice), which should be performed every six months or once a year throughout one's life. A vedic animal sacrifice consists of three components: consecration, invocation-immolation, and communion-purification. The consecration phase involves transforming the sacrificial area and individual sacrificer from profane to sacred. The establishment of fires consecrates the area chosen for the sacrifice, whereas the sacrificer experiences an initiatory purification (*dīkṣā*), which prepares him for the offering. The initiation ceremony implies that the sacrificer must become holy and be reborn a divine being in order to have contact with the gods. The initiation involves constructing a specially built hut in which the sacrificer will be placed. The purification process includes shaving the sacrificer and having his nails cut (TS 1.2.1), taking a bath of purification after which he dons new garments (ĀpŚS 6.15ff.), being anointed and dressed in the skin of a black antelope (ĀpŚS 10.8.11), having his head veiled, and clenching his fist (ĀpŚS 10.11.2). This scenario suggests that the sacrificer reverts to the state of a fetus, an observation reinforced when he fasts and consumes only milk. He is instructed to refrain from contact with men of impure castes and women, he is forbidden to answer any questions, and he must not be touched

(ĀpŚS 10.11.7ff.). At the beginning of the preliminary Soma ceremony, he unclenches his fist and unveils himself, which suggests rebirth as a deity or as a sacred being.

The second phase of invocation-immolation begins with a bath, after which the sacrificial victim is taken into the sacrificial area, various libations are offered, the animal is addressed, and laudatory epithets are heaped upon it. The victim's feet are directed to the north, while its head faces west (KŚS 6.5.15). The animal is also exhorted to keep calm. Meanwhile, a priest asks a god's permission to use the animal, because the animal is considered the property of the gods (ĀpŚS 7.12.6). The permission serves a dual purpose: it acknowledges the sacred character of the victim, and the victim must be persuaded to allow itself to be sacrificed peaceably, which is done for the welfare of human beings. If the victim does not give permission to be killed, there is a fear that it could return as a demonic spirit to take revenge on members of society. Thus, the spirit within the animal that will be liberated by the sacrifice must be conciliated.

The victim is bound to a stake (*yūpa*), and a priest invites the sacrificer to approach the victim. This sacrificial stake is considered the first victim, because a tree must be cut down to procure it. Its position at the margins of the sacrificial plot is indicative of its serving as a boundary between the village (cosmos) and the forest (chaos).[26] Because of its function within the sacrificial plot, the yūpa is a symbol of death and violence. It is aptly identified in the *Taittirīya Saṃhitā* (2.1.5.7) with the *vajra* (thunderbolt of Indra). Both being associated with violence and death, it is possible to draw a connection between the yūpa and the thunderbolt, and with impalement and piercing.[27]

The victim is given sacred water to drink and is anointed with butter, a sacred substance because of its association with the cow (ĀpŚS 7.13.4). The priest circumambulates the victim three times, which is symbolically equivalent to Agni surrounding the victim, consecrating it, and setting it apart. The priests make excuses for the victim's death, and the ritual performers, moreover, lament the death. It is common practice to strangle the victim, who is reborn by its death. The *śamitra* (slaughterer, literally "quieter") holds the animal's mouth shut firmly to stop its breathing, or he strangles the animal to death with a rope or sacred noose (KŚS 6.5.17–18). Without shedding blood, the victim dies, and this fact is announced by the śamitra. The victim serves as an intermediary through whom communication is established between humans and gods, and the sacrifice also works to unite all the participants.

The final phase of the animal sacrifice is communion-purification. The animal is cut open, and the omentum, a part rich in fat, is extracted and cooked (ŚB 3.8.2.16–20). The omentum is compared to a white seed that regenerates the sacrificer, assists him attain heaven, and confers immortality upon him (AB 2.14). The sacrificer is repeating precisely what the gods did after the offering of omentum at the beginning of time. The sacrificer consumes part of the victim, and he assimilates to himself the characteristics of the victim. Then the priests and gods are given their share.

Giving shares of the victim presupposes heating its bodily parts over various fires. Heating transforms the raw "stuff" into acceptable ritual offerings, because the gods accept only cooked food. The act of cooking emphasizes the subordinate position of humans to divine beings, because the former can only eat after the gods are satisified.[28] It is only after the conclusion of the cooking process that the victim's parts are ready for distribution to divine and human ritual participants for consumption, which again is indicative of the importance of fire.

A concluding purification is necessary because the participants have acquired a sacred character, which isolates them from the profane world. Their sacred character represents a danger to members of society, to which they will be returning. Therefore, purification is essential to remove their dangerous sacred character; this is accomplished by washing their hands (ĀpŚS 26.16.ff.). Finally, the remains of the sacrifice are destroyed, and the blood of the victim is poured out for consumption by demons.

After the sacrifice is concluded, the sacrificer dispenses gifts (*dakṣiṇā*) to the priests, which creates a binding force between the parties (RV 8.79.5). The gifts are also productive in the sense that the act of giving enables the sacrificer to disperse himself throughout the universe and thereby enter into a procreative union with the elements of the sacrificial universe. Moreover, there is a close connection between gift and faith (*śraddhā*) that manifests a mutual trust between the god and his devotees.[29] The merit of the gift itself is tied to the mental attitude of the giver, the manner in which the gift is acquired, the worthiness of the giver and recipient, and the humble way in which it is given to another.[30]

Human Sacrifice

According to a late vedic hymn called the *Puruṣasūkta* (RV 10.90), the gods create the cosmos and everything within it from the body of a primordial male giant by dismembering it. The giant man's mouth became the Brahmin caste, his arms were made into the warrior, his thighs formed the worker, and his feet gave birth to the servant. The hymn establishes the social hierarchy from a priestly viewpoint. The cosmic victim that is immolated by the gods is identified with the sacrifice. In this way, the sacrifice can be understood as a primordial act of creative violence performed by the gods at the beginning of time. The ritual action of the gods or of humans constructs reality instead of simply symbolizing it. The sacrifice of the cosmic man suggests additionally the integration of all the parts of reality and the constitution of the real.

This vedic hymn also forms a paradigm for the enigmatic human sacrifice (*puruṣamedha*). This rite is enigmatic because scholars differ over several issues related to the rite, such as whether or not ancient Indians really sacrificed human beings, and its relationship to the horse sacrifice.[31] Although there are dissident voices, the best evidence seems to suggest that the human sacrifice is modeled on the ancient horse sacrifice (*aśvamedha*), and it is a symbolic rite, as it is depicted in the texts, which leaves open the possibility that human victims were used before the oral tradition was transformed into texts.[32] There is probably no way to know for certain if actual human victims were sacrificed, but the influence of the symbolic nature of the sacrifice can be discovered in ascetic disciplines and excessive devotional practices of later periods, which makes it useful to consider this form of sacrifice as part of the cultural setting for later religious expressions.

As in the horse sacrifice, which will be discussed in a later chapter, a human victim is released for a year to wander; all his desires are gratified except for sexual pleasure, which may reflect a fear about losing spiritual and physical potency. The human victim is guarded in the same manner as the horse. The first wife of the person sponsoring the sacrifice lies down near the human victim, a scenario similar to that of the horse sacrifice, and they are both covered with a cloth (ŚŚS 16.12.7–8). Then, a theological discussion occurs among the priests (ŚŚS 16.13.16). It is said that by performing the human sacrifice, the sacrificer reaches everything that he cannot attain by means of the horse sacrifice.[33]

The human sacrifice is a five-day event, and each day is equivalent to a different season of the year and part of the cosmos (ŚB 13.6.1.10). The number five is not merely an expression of an indeterminate plurality but of a totality, which corresponds to the entire world collectively.[34] The sacrificial texts also state that the sacrifice takes forty days to perform, which enables one to obtain, respectively, the terrestrial world, air, sky, and four regions of the universe (ŚB 13.6.1.3). In other words, one attains everything within the cosmos. It is possible to grasp this point by knowing that the primordial man is both the sacrifice and the sacrificial victim, while he also represents the totality of the spatio-temporal universe.[35]

The brahman priest, who is seated to the right of the victim, praises him with the sixteen-versed hymn, because everything consists of sixteen parts, which is an extra element added to a total composed of fifteen parts (ŚB 13.6.2.12). The sixteenth part not only exceeds, but it also encompasses the preceding fifteen-partite totality.[36] When the wife of the sacrificer lies down near the human victim, this action signifies a symbolic copulation, which symbolizes a rite of fertility, renewal, and continuance of cosmic generative forces, with the sacrificer attempting to secure a place in the rhythm of the cosmos.[37]

In addition to its cosmic significance, the human sacrifice possesses social importance by virtue of its ability to unite the different social groups. This unity involves a union of each participant with the gods, a uniting of the participants among themselves, and the wandering victim who unites the entire country, because the victim brings the territory traversed in touch with a sacred power (ŚŚS 16.10.9). The human victim, who is a living representative of the cosmic Puruṣa, is akin to the navel of the cosmic man, which is a symbolic mark of the cord that links generations and is symbolic of the continuity of society.

From an ontological perspective, the human sacrifice pleases the gods, which induces them to grant the sacrificer all his desires, enables him to surpass all beings, and obtain power and courage (ŚB 13.6.2.11). The texts assert that the sacrificer is healed by the recited hymns and becomes free through the oblation (ŚŚS 16.3.3). The sacrificer's being is transformed into a deity, which is reminiscent of the cosmic Puruṣa, the origin of all created things. This is the flow of life of the sacrifice, which represents an infinite series of births and deaths forming a circle without end.[38] Finally, the cosmic, social, and ontological elements of the human sacrifice are merged with the recital of the *Puruṣasūkta* (10.90) during the rite. This repeated recital of the cosmogonic myth assures the continuity of the cosmos, society, and human existence. The human sacrifice is an imitation of the creation hymn (10.90), which serves as its sacred prototype. This feature of the rite is indicative of the inseparable nature of myth and ritual in vedic religion and how they interpenetrate each other. The primordial human sacrifice depicted in the hymn is recalled and reenacted in the human sacrifice, which means that it is a reenactment of the creation of the cosmos by means of sacrificial action, a type of action that is intended to regulate the struggle between being and nonbeing witnessed in the Indra-Vṛtra myth.

Within an uncertain, anxious, and dangerous context of life and death, various kinds of vedic ritual are intended to allow the ritualist to gain the upper hand over the forces of death. Vedic seers think that by a regular sequence of rites, it is possible to control these negative forces and maintain harmony within the triple sphere of being. The periodic fire sacrifice is an excellent example of such ritual action. Because the fire sacrifice is identical with the creation of the universe, the performance of this rite works to create and maintain the universe. This scenario presupposes that over time everything grows old or wears out, and needs to be periodically renewed or recreated. Therefore, without the performance of the fire sacrifice, the universe would disintegrate and human life would be terminated.

Vedic Eschatology

Eschatology is a technical term for the doctrine of last things or what happens at the end of time. Vedic eschatology begins with Yama, who is the first mortal to die and enter the other world (AV 18.3.13). Because of his preeminent position, Yama becomes the lord of the dead, and the guardian of the southern direction. During the vedic period, he is considered a benevolent figure, and people pray to him for such things as happiness, long life, and immortality. For the dead, Yama provides food and shelter, whereas he gives longevity to the living. In the Brāhmaṇas, Yama is called death or the ender, and he is closely associated with time (*kāla*). This does not mean that he is a deity of death; he is better understood as a god of the dead.[39]

Yama is also closely connected with two female figures: Nirṛti and Yamī. The former is described as dark, and she is called evil because of her association with pain, decrepitude, decay, and death (ŚB 7.2.1.3). She is said to bind an offender with a sturdy rope (AV 6.63.1, 2). According to a late vedic hymn, Yamī sexually desires her brother Yama, but he refuses her suggestion for a sexual encounter because of their family relationship (RV 10.8). She proceeds to become a malignant force.

In the later epic literature (300 B.C.E.–300 C.E.), Yama is called the *dharmarāja*, which refers to his roles as the great legislator and judge (Mbh 1.66.30). Before passing judgment on a person, he weights the person's heart, serving as the moral supervisor of the cosmos and dispenser of justice. He retains his association, however, with death in the epic literature.

The average vedic Indian fears death, and prays for a full period of life, which is equated with a hundred years. In short, death is regarded as evil and life as happy. Since in the *Rig Veda* there is no reference to a soul in the true sense, what happens to a person after death? After death, a person becomes a shadowy double of the former living person. This suggests that it is the personality that survives after death. The dead are destined to journey to either of two places. The first is called the path of the gods (*devayāna*), which is the fate of those individuals who have led a good life. The second possibility is the path of the fathers (*pitṛyāna*), which is identified as the abode of the dead. This place is located under the earth, and it is the destination of those who also performed evil deeds. Yama is depicted as reigning over the joyless place of the fathers; it is identified with this god's realm in the southern direction by a Brāhmaṇal text (TB 1.3.10.5). By traveling the preferable path of the gods, a person obtains long life and materialistic pleasure. The extent of pleasure is often determined by the merit earned by performing sacrifices on earth and the gifts given to priests for their services.

Later texts refer to re-death (*punarmṛtyu*), which is a second death in the future life. It is not strictly speaking the notion of rebirth of later Hinduism. It does involve, however, passing to another realm after death, although it does not include a permanent condition for the deceased. In other words, it implies that life in heaven must end. The *Śatapatha Brāhmaṇa* (10.4.3.10) draws a distinction between those born after death to a condition of immortality and those born only to die again after an indeterminate period in the other realm. The fire sacrifice is stated to provide release from repeated death (ŚB 2.3.3.9), and a person who builds a fire altar is enabled to conquer recurring death (ŚB 10.1.4.14). Furthermore, an offering of libations of cups of liquor (*surā*) on the southern altar wards off recurring death for a sacrificer's ancestors (ŚB 12.9.3.12). It is possible that the notion of re-death planted a seed for the later development of the notion of rebirth. An early Upaniṣad text (BĀU 1.2.7; 1.5.2) responds to the notion of repeated death by teaching that a certain kind of knowledge can get rid of it.

Vedic eschatology does not explicitly include a notion of hell, although there is a place described as realm of darkness and punishment (RV 7.104.3, 17), and the *Atharva Veda* (5.19.3) refers to sinners sitting in flowing blood and eating their hair. The *Rig Veda* (4.5.5) refers to evil people going to a deep place, and it also informs its reader that Indra and Soma hurl evildoers into a pit, which is a bottomless darkness from which no one returns (RV 7.104.3). This vagueness and lack of attention to the possible pains experienced in hell is, however, clarified by the story in the Brāhmaṇical literature (JB 42–44.15.234–248; ŚB 11.6.1) of the descent into hell of Bhṛgu, who receives a vision of hell and its horrors. The lord of hell is described as a black man with yellow eyes, holding a staff, and flanked by two women attendants. The epic literature reintroduces Yama into hell, where he is described as fearsome and surrounded by countless diseases (Mbh 3.221.9). He is also described as a dark figure with red eyes, holding a noose, and with a fierce appearance (Mbh 3.281.16). Finally, Yama is described as a voracious monster that swallows people (Mbh 7.85.18), which is indicative of his development from the less threatening vedic figure.

In contrast to hell, the notion of heaven is slightly more developed, and it is described as a place of light and happiness (RV 10.14.16). Forbidden to evildoers, heaven represents the realm of the pious (RV 10.17.4). The *Atharva Veda* (4.34.5–6) describes eating and drinking, family reunions, eternal light, cooling breezes, soft music, sexual enjoyment, joy, and flowing streams of milk, Soma, honey, and wine. Social distinctions based on wealth or class are absent in heaven, and there is no sickness, old age, or deformity. The destination of the dead is not definitively defined in the Vedas, because there are several other possible fates: a new body (RV 10.16), revival after death (RV 10.58), rebirth (RV 10.16), or dispersal among various elements of the world (RV 10.16.3). The notion of a postmortem judgment does not appear until the later Brāhmaṇa texts. The various ambiguous eschatological notions discussed continue to evolve and are more fully developed by the time of devotional sectarian movements, and hell is connected to the metaphor of color with its different shades of red, blue, and yellow flames.

Concluding Comments

The phenomenon of fire serves as an informative metaphor for vedic culture. For members of vedic culture, fire could be a friend or a destructive enemy. Within the domestic context, fire evokes notions of peace, comfort, and tranquillity, even though there lurks the ever-present danger that it will get out of control and destroy a home. The sacrificial fire suggests, metaphorically, violence and death, but it also implies transformation from raw to cooked, from disorder to order, and from chaos to cosmos.

The many forms of fire (*agni*) give vedic poets insight (*dhi*) into the mysteries of the universe. The light of fire enables the poets to see the hidden truths of ṛta (cosmic law), brahman (truth power), and tapas (heat). It also inspires the poet to see the sacred, the harmony, and the unity within the universe and beyond the diversity of it. The inspired poets express their discoveries in a sacred language. The truth that they discover enables them to align themselves with divine forces such as fire.

Even though there is embodied within fire a hostile tension, it is still part of the order of the cosmic law (*ṛta*). As a part of the cosmic law, it creates the world, it unites the various spheres of the world as symbolized by the three sacrificial altars, it joins together gods and humans, and provides a social bond among members of vedic society. By cooking the flesh of the victim, it unites the sacrificer with a substance transformed into something holy. And it transforms the raw flesh into cooked, edible, and thus civilized food to be consumed by the sacrificer, priests, and divine beings, which thereby unite all the participants.

In this respect fire is similar to the cosmic Puruṣa, which functions to explain the unity and diversity of everything and their relationship to each other. And like the Puruṣa, fire provides a means of moving from one order of reality to another. The puruṣamedha (human sacrifice) and the fire sacrifice control the real. Knowing the secret of these rituals does not merely mean to know the sacrifices; it is also to control the universe, because knowledge of something gives one control of it.

The power of fire in the form of heat (*tapas*) is built into the very structure of the natural world. This heat (*tapas*) unites the physical and mental aspects of the sacrifice. It is also a creative power that makes life possible, and it is a power that human beings can use for their benefit in their everyday life. As evident with the Indra-Vṛtra creation myth, warmth represents life. Finally, fire symbolizes and introduces a bright reddish color into the colorful rainbow that will eventually become Hinduism.

3

The Swan, World Renunciation, and Upaniṣads

The swan is a beautiful bird with wide wings that came to symbolize those figures that renounced the world and sought to fly above it on their religious quest for ultimate reality. Ancient Indian literature manifests many symbolic associations between the swan (*haṃsa*) and such phenomena as the sun (RV 1.163.6), light (RV 4.40.5), and heat (*tapas*) of the sun and fire (RV 10.114.1). Other passages connect the swan with speech and spells (RV 10.177.1–2), the law (RV 9.48.4), and the truth (RV 10.55.6). The swan is also associated with Agni (RV 1.65.50; 10.125) and other vedic deities. These kinds of connections are continued in the ritualistic Brāhmaṇa literature and the Upaniṣads at a later date.

Although the association between the swan and light, heat, and sun is continued in upaniṣadic texts, a significant change occurs when it comes to symbolize the immortal self within the individual.[1] According to probably the oldest upaniṣadic text, the swan (*haṃsa*) is identified as a bird of passage, whereas the historically later Maitrāyana Upaniṣad (6.8; 7.7) makes the additional claim that it is pure, eternal, lustrous, invisible, and neither good nor evil. The *Kuṇḍika Upaniṣad* (5.2) makes a connection between the *ātman* (self) and the solar swan, while the *Śvetāśvatara Upaniṣad* (6.15; 3.17) makes similar types of association between the swan and the immortal self.

The swan is an ambiguous bird because it can both swim on the surface of the water and fly through the sky. Because the swan is equally comfortable in the water and in the sky, it suggests a liminal figure, much like the wandering renouncer.[2] The free-wandering swan resides on land, water, or in the air by moving aimlessly as it desires, unconcerned with establishing a fixed abode or finding a sacred center in which to live. The swan is also ambiguous in a second sense—it is associated with low-lying land and water, and it is also connected to height. The connection of the swan with the vehicle (*vāhana*) of the god Brahmā in later epic and purāṇic literature is well known. What is less well known is the belief that the swan exceeded all birds in the height of their flight, according to the epic *Rāmāyaṇa* (4.58.24–27).

This suggests that the swan is also symbolic of the transcendence of the earth, yet is immanent on the earth and functions as a love messenger, for instance, in the romantic story of Nala and Damayantī in the epic *Mahābhārata* (3.50–78).

Besides its twofold ambiguous nature, Indian writers have attributed to the swan certain powers such as swiftness of flight, the ability to separate milk from water, a graceful style of walking, a lovely voice, and high moral virtues. Some writers have contrasted, for instance, the magnanimous swan with the malicious crow and hypocritical heron.[3] The *Tejobindu Upaniṣad* (3–4) sets similar high moral standards by adding to these moral standards freedom from worldly attachments, the senses, duality, egoism, and family ties. When the swan is associated with the renouncer it also suggests the notions of purity, spirituality, absolute freedom, and transcendence. The *Jābāla Upaniṣad* (6) refers to the unmanifested nature of the highest swan (*paramahaṃsa*), who is the renouncer that gives up all symbols of his former way of life such as the hair-tuft, sacred thread, possessions, and body. Appearing to resemble madmen, though not insane, the renouncer returns to a birth-like condition where he possesses nothing and lives in a state of freedom with a pure mind. By living in uninhabited places, the renouncer can devote his energy to meditation on the higher self and rid himself of the evil effects of karmic resides, much like the high-flying swan. Within this chapter, the swan functions as a metaphor for the world renouncer as we discuss some fundamental notions such as rebirth, karma, and soul that are traditionally identified with Hinduism. The teachers of the early Upaniṣads do not advocate renunciation of the world although later Upaniṣads refer to the importance of renunciation. The term "Upaniṣads" refers to a wide collection of sacred texts that Hindus believe to be revealed (*śruti*) literature. The elements of the term are suggestive, because it is composed of the root verb meaning "to sit" (*sad*), and the adverbs "down" (*ni*) and "near" (*upa*). More precisely and concretely, the term implies a student sitting down near a teacher to receive instruction in a secret teaching. This suggests that the teaching method is personal, relational, dialogical, and secret. The special emphasis on the secret nature of instruction is evident when it is stated that teaching takes place in the forest, which is a place apart from society. There are numerous teachers mentioned in the texts, and some of them are women—the Upaniṣads are not the product of a single mind. This intellectually corporate enterprise is contained in some 108 Upaniṣadi texts, although there are only thirteen major texts. Some of the later texts manifest a sectarian nature that reflects devotion to either Śiva or Viṣṇu. The Upaniṣads are called Vedānta, which means that they represent the end or culmination of the Vedas. To call the texts Vedānta also means that they enclose the deepest secrets of the Vedas.

Origins of Renunciation

It is difficult to determine the precise origins of renunciation. The Sanskrit term for renunciation (*saṃnyāsa*) does not become a common term until around the third and second centuries B.C.E.[4] The early use of the term refers to the act of discarding an unwanted item. It eventually denotes the rite of initiation into renunciation, and it evolves around the third to fourth centuries C.E. to refer to the lifestyle manifested by the world renouncer in the fourth stage of life.

According to one group of scholars, renunciation and its ascetic lifestyle is not indigenous to the world of upaniṣadic thought. Early renouncers, around the second century B.C.E., are outside the vedic mainstream because their goals and values are contrary to those of the vedic priesthood.[5] Overtime, the priests gradually accepted the values, new teachings, and meditative and ascetic practices of the renouncers. From an alternative perspective, some people lost confidence in the power of the sacrifice to achieve their goals. The renouncer, who represented a model of a new source of power, replaced the priest as a powerful figure, because his acquired powers gave him dominance over others, the ability to ascend to and converse with the gods, and the power to work miracles and other wonders. Although their actual numbers were never great, the ascetic values and practices of the renouncers were gradually absorbed into the vedic religious culture.

It is highly likely that both internal and external influences shaped the way of the renouncer. It is possible to find ascetic elements within the vedic sacrificial cult and the life of a student that influenced the values and practices,[6] but there are also features in the lifestyle of the precursors of the classical renouncer that indicate external influences. Such features as unusual attire, bodily dirt (for example, actual filthiness and matted hair), and bizarre behavior represent possible external influences. Diverse ethnic groups with different religious beliefs and practices probably influenced Aryan classes that were not part of and even opposed to the way of religion of the early vedic period. Different groups of holy wandering beggars, who often formed around a charismatic leader, such as followers of the Buddha, would form a sect that adhered to the teaching of the leader. It was not uncommon for one group to merge with another, which placed a value on proselytizing and enhanced the prestige of the leader by winning converts. In addition to these developments, there were probably economic factors that played a part in the development of renunciation.[7] It is also possible that social, political, climatic, or historical factors that are lost in time played a part.

It is possible to find examples of a religious skepticism embodied within the Vedas that probably contributed to the development of the practice of world renunciation. A vedic poet wants to know who can say that they have seen the god Indra (RV 8.89). Another poet relates that some people admit that god exists, whereas others claim that god does not exist because they have not seen the deity. Other vedic poets reflect their search for an ultimate first principle of the universe. Different poets identified this fundamental principle with Vāc (Holy Utterance, RV 10.125), Viśvakarma (All-Maker, RV 10.81), Puruṣa (Cosmic Self, RV 10.90), or Bṛhaspati (Lord of the Holy Word, RV 10.17.1). The search for the single principle of the universe motivated a quest for knowledge that would give the knower power. Within the context of ancient Indian culture, it is common to find one thing identified with another item on often very slender grounds. To make the assertion that "the cow is breath" represents an attempt to control an animal like a cow by controlling one's breath. This principle of identification is extended more broadly in order to gain a kind of power by means of knowledge. This path of thinking is dependent upon a basic presupposition: If a person can know the one principle of the universe, one can control everything. Renouncers are committed seekers trying to acquire such power. The sages depicted in the Upaniṣadic texts come to the almost unanimous consensus that this principle is Brahman, which is a term that means to make firm, strong, solid, to expand, or to promote. The most ancient sense of the term is the power immanent in the words, verses, and formulas of the Vedas. Because a spoken word possesses a strange power in ancient India, it is believed to contain within itself the essence of whatever it denoted. This means that a person who knows the word not only possesses knowledge about it but can also control that which is identical to the word.

The Quest for the Real

An early upaniṣadic sage pleads to be led to the real, to freedom from darkness, and from death to immortality (BĀU 1.3.28). The journey begins by turning inward and examining one's inner self. The upaniṣadic sages Yājñavalkya and Uddālaka represent different early viewpoints about the self, mechanism of release, and goal. Some later Upaniṣads manifest a theistic perspective. Although the *Śvetāśvatara Upaniṣad* is concerned with release from the cycle of rebirth, its prescribed path to release is theistic, because liberation is due to knowledge of a personal deity and not an impersonal Brahman. In addition, there is a role for the grace of god in the teachings of this text (3.20; 6.21). In the discussion that follows, this chapter will offer a nondualistic interpretation of the Upaniṣads without claiming that it is the only possible or correct way to read the texts, which are the products of diverse minds at different moments of Indian history.

The secret of the Upaniṣads is difficult to discern because it cannot be known by sense perception. This is illustrated by the encounter between a student named Śvetaketu and his teacher Uddālaka, when the former asks for instruction about ultimate reality (ChU 6.12.1–3). In order to make his point, the teacher instructs the student to bring a fig. The teacher directs the student to cut it open and look at the fine seeds inside of the fruit. Then the teacher instructs the student to divide a seed, and tell the teacher what he sees. When the student replies that he perceives nothing, the teacher takes the opportunity to tell him that from that very essence a large tree grows. From this foundation, the teacher asserts that a fine essence is also the soul (*ātman*) of the world. The teacher concludes by stating '*tat tvam asi*' (that you are). In other words, the student is identical to the underlying essence of the world, even though he cannot perceive it with his senses.

Next, Uddālaka teaches his student that reality is all-penetrating and all-pervading (ChU 6.13.1–3). The teacher instructs his student to place salt in a container of water and leave it over night. The student is then asked to taste the water from three different parts of the container and to report how it tastes to his instructor. The teacher draws the analogy that salty water is like reality in the sense that it is all-penetrating and all-pervading.

It is difficult to see, know, teach, and think about this reality. Nonetheless, other teachers of the Upaniṣads defined the self as self-luminous and timeless, not subject to birth and death, spaceless, eternal, unchanging, and without origin. The assertion made by Uddālaka to his student "that you are" points to the identity of the self and ultimate reality. This means to assert that the ātman (immortal self) is identical to Brahman. How is this basic identity possible? The demonstrative pronoun "that" represents the pure consciousness that is the ground of Brahman, whereas the personal pronoun "you" is the pure consciousness that underlies a human being. Since the pure consciousness of Brahman and the self are identical, there is a complete identity between them. If this is the case, what is the problem? The answer is ignorance (*avidyā*). The self (*ātman*) is like, for instance, a pond of pure water with a dark film on its surface. The pure water is always there just beneath the dark and obstructing surface. In order to see the pure water, an aspirant must remove the dark film (that is, ignorance), which hides the pure water.

With respect to the nature of the self, this analogy is not far fetched, because the self is depicted as being concealed by five sheaths in the *Taittirīya Upaniṣad* (2.3.3–9). It is possible to picture the five sheaths as five concentric circles that coincide with the grosser exterior to the subtler interior. The physical body is the most gross and exterior sheath. The following four sheaths are the breath (*prāṇa*), mind (*manas*) and senses, consciousness (*vijñāna*), and finally bliss (*ānanda*). Upaniṣadic sages conceive of these sheaths as a covering of ignorance. The message is for a student to get beyond the outer coverings to the real self, which is blissful in nature. In the majority of the Upaniṣads, the path to bliss is attained by a way of knowledge (*vidyā*), which is the exact opposite of the ordinary way that we live. The goal is expressed in the following way: The self that realizes Brahman through knowing becomes Brahman.

According to the sages of the Upaniṣads, everyone is theoretically capable of becoming an enlightened being. But it is necessary for a seeker of truth to realize one's true self, which can only occur by means of one's own efforts. The truth about reality is, for instance, like a precious jewel that one wears around one's neck. When one forgets about the jewel and thinks it is lost, one rushes around frantically trying to find it, and suffers grief imagining that it is lost forever. Upon a chance encounter, the distraught person meets another person who points to the jewel around one's neck. What has changed? The simple answer is that nothing has really changed, with the exception of one's ignorance.

When one discovers the self, does this mean that one can now define it? The answer is an ambiguous yes and no. This can be illustrated with three characters within a mythical context (ChU 8.7–12). The narrative portrays the god Prajāpati instructing the deity Indra and the demon Virocana in a sequence of lessons about the self. Initially, Prajāpati tells his two students that the self is identical with the embodied self (*jīva*) during the condition of wakefulness. The demon Virocana is satisfied and returns to the demons with the answer, but Indra is unsatisfied with the response, because, if the self is identical with the body, the self would also be subject to fear, old age, and death just like the physical body. When Indra returns for further instruction, Prajāpati informs the curious god that the real self is identical with the self in the condition of dreaming. Again, Indra is not satisfied, because then, although the self might not suffer from the limitations and characteristics of the body, it still remains subject to the shortcomings of the mind. Consequently, the self is not free from fear and pain, which leaves Indra inquiring further. Although dreams occur within the body of the dreamer, it does not follow that they are unreal. The dreamer constructs his or her own universe while dreaming and eventually destroys it. If we recall the basic dichotomy of the vedic worldview, the dreamer witnesses both being (*sat*) and nonbeing (*asat*).[8] The next teaching from Prajāpati is the following: The real self is identical with the self in the condition of deep sleep. Again, Indra is not satisfied because in deep sleep one is conscious of nothing. Within deep sleep, there is no consciousness of oneself or external objects. In short, deep sleep is a transient condition. With Indra becoming frustrated about ever reaching the genuine teaching, Prajāpati finally teaches him the ultimate truth. The previous teachings were merely a series of tests of the student. Prajāpati now teaches that the essential self (*ātman*) is not identical with bodily consciousness, dream consciousness, or deep sleep; the self is of the nature of self-consciousness (*cit*).

What does this mythical narrative tell us about the nature of the self? We can draw the conclusion that the self is free from all the limitations common to the body and mind. The self is neither subject, nor object, nor act. It is neither knower, nor known, nor the knowing. It is eternal. And it can be defined as sat (being), cit (consciousness), and ānanda (bliss). This fundamental definition means that the self transcends the states of wakefulness, dream, and deep sleep. This is the reason why the self is called the fourth (*turīya*), which is another way of indicating that it is pure consciousness. The *Maitri Upaniṣad* (7.II.7) identifies, for instance, the "fourth" with the highest state of consciousness. Ultimately, this experience cannot be expressed or captured in words. Language is adequate to express dualistic—subject and object—kinds of experience, but it is insufficient to express nondualistic experience that is devoid of inside and outside distinctions. The realization that the self is being, consciousness, and bliss serves as a means to liberate one self from the phenomenal world. This is analogous to knowing the true nature of the desert. When you know its true nature you do not run after the illusory water of the mirage.

We have noted that many of the upaniṣadic sages identify the self (*ātman*) with the universal principle Brahman. Since they are identical, Brahman can also be defined positively as being, consciousness, and bliss. By asserting that Brahman is being, a sage is expressing his conviction that it negates all empirical being. This means that Brahman alone is real. It is also implies that Brahman could not have originated from anything else. In fact, Brahman comprises both being (*sat*) and nonbeing (*asat*). To assert that Brahman is consciousness means that it is neither the agent of knowing nor an object of knowledge. Pure consciousness is the ground of all distinctions and the very core of being. The notion of ānanda (bliss) introduces a principle of value into the positive definition of Brahman. Because bliss is something that is unconditionally valuable, the only genuine value resides in the nondual Brahman. Moreover, to know Brahman is to know it as blissful. The definition of being, consciousness, and bliss is about all that can be positively affirmed about it.

The sages tend to prefer a negative way of talking about Brahman. When it is stated that Brahman is *neti, neti* (not this, not that), this means that it is basically indefinable (BĀU 2.3.6). This implies that Brahman is without qualities, indescribable, impersonal, and nonrelational. To claim that it is impersonal means that it exceeds both the finite and the infinite. It does not have qualities like a deity, and a person cannot have a personal relationship, with it, as with a deity. Brahman is beyond the limitations of any deity. It is nonrelational in the sense that it is beyond all relations, and it is yet paradoxically the ground that sustains all relations. Moreover, Brahman is indescribable in the sense that human conceptual forms cannot exhaust it. If this is the case, the best procedure for a sage to follow is silence or the use of symbols.

Sages often point to Brahman by using the symbolic mantra OM. This sacred mantra (formula) can be transcribed as AUM. According to the *Māṇḍūkya Upaniṣad* (3–5), each of the three letters is symbolically significant in the following way: A equals waking conscious, U is equivalent to dream consciousness, and M represents deep-sleep consciousness. Because the mantra culminates in silence, this last aspect is called the fourth (*turīya*). The fourth represents totality, unity, and Brahman. The fourth is beyond empirical relations. It represents the culmination of phenomenal existence, and it is nondual. The fourth serves as the ground from which sounds comes forth. After the mantra is uttered, it eventually disappears, and only the silence remains. This silence is metaphorically Brahman.

The Human Situation

A basic presupposition of thinking reflected in the Upaniṣads is that human beings are subject to time and causation. In ancient India, time (*kāla*) is identified with the god Prajāpati (AV 19.53–54). Time serves as a cosmogonic force—it is born simultaneously with the sun, according to the *Maitri Upaniṣad* (6.14–16). The sun, which is the source and support of all living things, is also identified with Brahman, and time is by extension identified with Brahman. On the cosmic level, time is a power that brings about the evolution and involution of the entire universe.

From the human perspective, time is a mysterious and unpredictable agent of birth and death. Time is conceived as cyclical, with a beginning and end that are inconceivable. Time is described as all-inclusive and rolling on endlessly. It is generally conceived to be destructive. The mouths of time (*kāla*) are identified with the six seasons, which swallow up creatures. According to the *Maitri Upaniṣad* (6.15), time cooks all creatures, which suggests that creatures are ripened by the passage of time in order to make them fit to be swallowed by death. Other metaphorical ways of viewing time is the conception of time as a noose that binds one and tightens, as one grows older, or time is like a winged horse, which carries away all creatures. Finally, time is like a wheel, which revolves ceaselessly.

In the Indian religious imagination, time is closely connected with rebirth (*samsāra*), which literally means the act of going about, wandering through, or passing through a series of conditions. In short, it represents the cycle of birth and death. In the early Upaniṣads, there are two theories that attempt to account for the origin of rebirth. In the theory of the five fires (BĀU 6.2), the cremation of a body at death is a sacrifice. When the body is cremated the faith of the individual ascends to heaven, and the gods offer it as sacrificial fires. It changes to Soma, then to rain, food, seed, embryo, and it then receives a new mode of being. This early theory is developed further in the *Muṇḍaka Upaniṣad* (1.2) where sacrificial actions, charity, and asceticism play essential roles. These features help the deceased pass into the smoke from the cremation fire and eventually to the moon. There the deceased becomes food, and gods feed upon it. It continues to evolve into space, rain, and plants, which are consumed by humans, turned into semen, passed to women, and are born. Another text refers to the two paths after death: the bright path or way of the gods, which is open for those who practice penance and faith, and the dark path or way of the fathers, which is available to gift-giving, ethical individuals (ChU 5.3–10). Those following the second path eventually return to the cycle of human existence. In this second type of theory, action (*karma*) is the controlling force of rebirth.

It is important to be aware that the immortal soul is like a rider on a vehicle, which is identified with the body. When the soul arrives at the end of its journey, at death, the soul leaves the body and transmigrates to another body. This is metaphorically expressed by comparing the soul to a caterpillar, which passes from one blade of grass to another (BĀU 4.4.2–6). Because the soul is immortal, it does not vanish at the death of the body. The theory implies that the world is in a state of perpetual flux. From another perspective, rebirth (*samsāra*) can be conceived as a kind of energy, such as an electrical current. What determines the rebirth of a soul? This depends on the actions (*karma*) of the soul in a previous life. Thus it is probably more accurate to conceive of rebirth as a bundle of forces fluctuating within an electromagnetic field with good and bad deeds acting as the positive and negative charges.

The notion of karma is derived from a Sanskrit root that means "to make," and it also implies work, action, rite, or performance. In the *Rig Veda*, karma means especially sacrificial action. From this vedic usage, it evolves into the law of cause and effect. In this way, karma represents the cause of rebirth (*samsāra*) in the historically earliest *Bṛhadāraṇyaka Upaniṣad* (4.4.3). Karma operates in the physical spheres as a universal law to which everything is subject, and it also functions in the moral sphere as a personal law. Basically, karma means that all actions have inevitable moral consequences. Therefore, one becomes good by good action and bad by bad action (BĀU 3.2.13). If one avoids evil actions and performs only positive actions, no bad karma is accumulated. According to the *Chāndogya Upaniṣad* (5.10.7), good conduct leads to a good rebirth in the body of a human being with upper-caste status, whereas evil deeds lead to a bad rebirth in the body of a dog, pig, insect, or lower caste.

Whatever action an individual performs creates a karmic residue, which is either meritorious or unmeritorious. The resulting residue depends on the quality of the act. Upon the death of the body, an individual's inactivated karmic residues pass to a new body, and karma determines the appropriate type of body. Karmic residues operate in a new body to determine three things: the kind of body (that is; human, insect, or mammal), the length of life under normal circumstances, and the affective tone of experiences (that is; pleasant or painful) that an individual will have after rebirth.

There are basically three types of karmic residues: previous residues that will maturate in one's present lifetime, those that will mature in another life, and those that will be produced in the present life and will also mature in this lifetime. It is helpful to imagine karmic residues like an arrow in flight. The metaphorical arrow of karmic residues will continue until its energy is exhausted, or unless something obstructs it such as premature death due to violence. Such a scenario suggests that an individual can shape his or her personal destiny and create one's identity. Therefore, one is both free and responsible for what one does and who one becomes. During one's current life, virtuous deeds can influence inherited past karma and reduce it. But past and present karma cannot be completely eradicated; it serves as an external visible sign to everyone of past deeds that are currently invisible.[9] The entire cyclical pattern of karma and rebirth (*samsāra*) appears to a person as *māyā* (unreal, illusory).

In early vedic literature, māyā denotes the power of a god or demon to produce an illusory effect, to change form, and to appear in deceptive ways to humans or divine beings. When applied to the world, māyā is preferably translated as unreal because the world is temporal and constantly changing. At the very least, māyā emphatically implies that what seems to be real is confusing and not as certain and concrete as it appears. Māyā also suggests that people are ordinarily deceived about what they know, because māyā limits their ability to know with certainty. The illusion maker is Brahman, who projects this illusory world. Humans find themselves confined within this illusory world, according to the *Śvetāśvatara Upaniṣad* (4.9–10). If ultimate reality is singular, the manifold differences of experience, which seem real, do not constitute this one reality. Moreover, the differences of experience and diversity are only appearances and nothing substantial (BĀU 4.4.19–20). This position presupposes that which possesses form is unreal, whereas that which possesses no form is real. As we have noted, the only reality is Brahman, although the world can be grasped as a self-manifestation of the creative energy of Brahman.

This makes the world dependent upon Brahman, who alone is absolute or independent reality. Therefore, everything beside Brahman is relative and dependent, which suggests that the world as it appears to human beings is māyā (unreal). The narrative of the three blind men illustrates these points. Three blind men are placed at different points of an elephant, and they are asked to describe the elephant. The first blind man feels the tail of the elephant, and he reports that it is like a rope. Feeling the side of the large pachyderm, the second blind man states that it is like a wall. Finally, the last blind man, after feeling the trunk of the elephant, claims that it is like a tree. The three blind men are metaphors for all human beings who cannot see things as they really are in fact or in their wholeness.

Two Upaniṣad texts offer warnings to people in the world. The *Kaṭha Upaniṣad* (2.4) warns people not to find reality and certainty in the unrealities and uncertainties of the world. The *Chāndogya Upaniṣad* (8.3.1–3) gives a slightly different slant when it affirms that there is a covering of untruth that hides the truth from humans, just as the surface of the earth hides a golden treasure from prying eyes. If māyā obscures human vision, as illustrated by the metaphor of the three blind men, the reason that the real nature of the world is hidden from us is ultimately due to ignorance, which is also implied by the metaphor.

The *Kaṭha Upaniṣad* (2.1–5) compares those living in the midst of ignorance as deluded blind men being led by a man who is himself blind. This metaphor suggests that ignorance (*avidyā*) signifies an entire attitude toward life—an attitude that mistakes the relative or the things of this world as the real or absolute. It is this erroneous notion that is the cause of bondage within the world. It is like wearing eyeglasses with distorted lenses and getting an incorrect view of the world. When the correct lenses are placed in the glass frames, it is possible to see the world as we should. When we attempt to perceive the world through distorted lenses we see everything dualistically. It is the ignorant mind that superimposes a world of duality upon what one perceives. This false way of grasping the world means that we miss the fact that reality is nondual. False knowledge is important because it leads to further rebirth. The goal of the aspirant is to overcome false knowledge (*avidyā*) and to attain release from ignorance and rebirth that is fueled by ignorance.

This state of release is *mokṣa* or *mukti* (liberation, freedom). How is this goal achieved? It comes by intuitively realizing Brahman, because one who knows Brahman becomes Brahman. Therefore, release (*mokṣa*) consists in knowledge of Brahman, but ultimate reality is not affected by this knowledge. From a metaphorical perspective, a person's goal is not to see many trees, but it is rather to see the entire forest. In other words, one's goal is to see the all in Brahman. And if Brahman is the sole reality, one becomes aware of the only real thing by coming to know it.

If knowledge of Brahman is the key to liberation, what is the condition of a liberated person after this awareness dawns? Such a person possesses no desires and knows everything. Once Brahman is realized there is nothing more to desire and nothing more worth knowing. According to the *Maitri Upaniṣad* (7.6), the aware person does not see death, sickness, distress, and sees only the all. A liberated person is also free from the effects of karma. Like a reed in a fire, a knower's karma is consumed. The knower becomes like a leaf of a lotus flower to which no water (*karma*) can cling. Once the state of mokṣa (liberation) is achieved, the flow of time ceases, which puts an end to the process of rebirth.

It would be a mistake to assume that release is easy. In order to arrive at one's destination, an aspirant for liberation follows a rigorous path.

The Way of the World Renouncer

The sage Aṇgiras teaches the path of the renouncer to a householder in the *Muṇḍaka Upaniṣad* (3.1.5). The path includes the following steps: truth (*satya*), student life of chastity (*brahmacārya*), austerity (*tapas*), and knowledge (*jñāna*). The *Maitri Upaniṣad* (4.4) records the sage Śākāyanya specifying knowledge (*vidyā*), austerity (*tapas*), and meditation. From these sketchy outlines, it is possible to conclude that the path is basically an ascetic lifestyle. This is confirmed by the historically later *Āruṇi Upaniṣad*, which begins with a narrative about a young man disturbed by the effects of karma. The youthful Āruṇi asks the deity Prajāpati for a method to avoid the effects of karma. The deity responds that he must renounce his family, other social relations, hair tuft (a symbol of socioreligious lineage), sacred thread, performing sacrifice, vedic studies, the seven higher and lower worlds, and the universe. When renouncing the world, an individual should only take a staff, an upper garment, and loincloth, and give up everything else.

As evident in the previous chapter, the notion of tapas means literally heat. Tapas can refer to the natural heat of the sun or a fire. It also denotes a natural heat associated with biological conception, embryonic maturation, and birth. In addition to the heat associated with sexual desire, tapas also indicates a hatching heat, much like that of a hen as she sits on her eggs. In the Upaniṣads, it refers to the heat generated by asceticism, which is a nonnatural heat. Hence, tapas kindles the inner fire of illumination. And those that practice it achieve immortality, according to the *Muṇḍaka Upaniṣad* (1.2.11). The heat generated by asceticism is not an outer-directed heat; it is rather an inner-directed heat. Moreover, the earlier association of tapas with vedic sacrifice is not completely lost in the Upaniṣads, because the sacrifice becomes an internal event within the ascetic instead of an external rite performed by priests; this implies that the ascetic becomes the priest, sacrificer, and sacrificial victim all in one. Thus the renouncer performs the self-sacrifice within himself by means of his own mind.

The various forms of self-sacrifice in the Upaniṣads are based on the symbolic human sacrifice (*puruṣamedha*) of the *Rig Veda* (10.90), which is discussed in the previous chapter. There are several examples of self-sacrifice in the Upaniṣads: mental sacrifice, the offering of bodily parts, sacrifice of the breaths (ChU 5.19–23), and sacrifice of the self. These examples are different forms of self-sacrifice, which represents a process of interiorization of rites from vedic sacrificial practice.

The renouncer can mentally perform a Soma sacrifice (ChU 3.16.1–5), and a horse sacrifice (*aśvamedha*). For example, after retaining an imaginary horse for an entire year in his mind, where the horse is allowed to roam free, the renouncer, mentally sacrifices the animal (BĀU 1.2.7). And by substituting the "three strands" (*guṇas*, or three subtle element that constitute primal matter) within himself as a sacrificial offering, the renouncer can perform a fire sacrifice within himself (JaU 4). There is also an internal rite that connects the offering of an oblation into a fire, which is dedicated to the breaths. This rite is performed at the beginning and at the end of the renouncer's meal.[10] Another example of mental sacrifice involves concentrating on the sound of the word *haṃsa* (swan) and having the mental attitude of "I am he, or he am I." Combined with the correct breathing exercises, this mental sacrifice enables one to become transformed into a swan, which is equivalent to union with Brahman (PBU 12, 18).

In some instances, the body of the renouncer is burnt by his practice of tapas (austerity). When this occurs there is no reason to cremate the body, because the fire of knowledge already consumes the renouncer's body, according to the *Paingala Upaniṣad* (4.7). In a historically later text with a sectarian slant, the renouncer is encouraged to burn up his body with the fire of the god Śiva in order to gain a direct perception of Brahman (BJU 19).

In addition to mental and bodily forms of sacrifice, the renouncer can sacrifice his five breaths (ChU 5.19.2–3). The renouncer can also sacrifice his breath (*prāṇa*) in speech and speech in breath. These two offerings can be performed while awake or asleep, allowing the renouncer to sacrifice continuously (KaushU 2.5). In the *Praśna Upaniṣad* (4.3–4), three of the breaths correspond to the three vedic sacrificial altars, the mind is the sacrificer, and the two oblations are the other two breaths. From a different perspective, the *Maitri Upaniṣad* (6.26) draws a connection between catching fish and sacrificing them within the fire in one's stomach, and the renouncer draws in with his breaths the syllable OM and sacrifices them in an internal fire.

Finally, there is an example of the sacrifice of the self the in the *Maitri Upaniṣad* (6.9). In the case of a person thinking that he or she possesses two selves, he or she should sacrifice to the ātman (immortal self) alone by concentrating only on it. The sacrificial offering is situated between acts of purification. After sacrificing to the ātman, the individual should then meditate on the self, which protects one from being reborn. By reading an additional line in the text of this Upaniṣad (6.10), it is possible to recognize that self-sacrifice is imagined to be like eating food. In this case, the ātman's form becomes food and the breath consists of food. Hence, the act of eating can be construed as an act of self-sacrifice.

The path of the renouncer prescribed by the *Maitri Upaniṣad* (6.18) is the sixfold path of yoga, which possesses some remarkable similarities to the classical path of yoga discussed in chapter 5. The initial step involves restraint of breathing, because ordinary breathing is agitated and unrhythmical. The aim of breath control is to master the energy released by breathing. The procedure includes a progressive deceleration of the respiratory rhythm by holding inhaled air for as long as possible in the vessel provided by the thorax. By controlling his breath, the renouncer can penetrate to higher states of consciousness, which are normally inaccessible to him due to the interference of normal respiration. This practice also makes it possible for the mind to fix its attention on a single point. The second stage of yoga is withdrawal of the senses. A metaphorical figure that can be invoked is the turtle withdrawing its extremities when it senses danger. The objective of the practitioner is to free the senses from the distraction of external objects. Once all sense activity is suspended, the yogin becomes detached from phenomena. The third step of meditation makes it possible for a person to penetrate objects. The fourth step of concentration enables one to fix one's attention on a single point in order to quiet and calm the mind. Concentration can be accomplished by focusing on an object, one's navel, the tip of one's nose or tongue, a maṇḍala (symbolic diagram), or a mantra (formula). The meditator wants to reach a point of becoming conscious of consciousness. The fifth step is contemplation, at which instant one sees Brahman. Finally, absorption (*samādhi*) refers to the unitive experience at which point one is totally withdrawn from the phenomenal world and into the true self. The meditator is now absorbed into and identical to the one true reality or Brahman.

As the renouncer progresses on the path to liberation, he also moves from lower knowledge (*apara vidyā*) to higher knowledge (*para vidyā*), according to the *Muṇḍaka Upaniṣad* (1.1.4). The former type of knowledge gives a person useful information by relying on reason and the senses. It is, however, imperfect because it is a subject-object kind of knowing that represents dualistic knowledge, whereas higher knowledge is an immediate intuitive type of knowing that represents a unity of thought and being. The second form of knowledge transcends the differentiation of subject and object, and it comes to know the absolute. By knowing the truth, the renouncer becomes the truth.

The higher form of knowledge is liberating. When this occurs the aspirant becomes a *jīvanmukti* (one who is liberated while alive). This freedom can only be attained while an aspirant is alive. In other words, liberation from the cycle of life and death is not a post-mortem occurrence. It is not analogous to dying and then going to a place like heaven. If one does not achieve liberation during one's present lifetime, one is reborn after death. In contrast to the person in bondage to the world, the liberated individual is ungraspable, undecaying, and nothing sticks to him; he is also unbound and free from fear (BĀU 4.2.4). Without sorrow or pain, the liberated person lives in the world, but such a person is not conditioned by the structure of the world. The jīvanmukti lives simultaneously in time and eternity without desires or any doubt. Once the renouncer attains liberation, he is considered among the living dead, because he is literally dead to the world.

In a later text about renunciation, a renouncer must perform nine *śrāddhas* (last rites) for oneself.[11] The performance of death rites for oneself implies that the renouncer wanders about as a dead person, having already performed the funeral rites. Overall, the act of renunciation involves the civil death of the renouncer and has dual legal consequences: renouncers may not participate in legal transactions and are released from prior legal contracts.[12] The liberated renouncer ceases to function as a social being, and the liberated person keeps his or her contact with others to a minimum.

Lifestyle of the Renouncer

After renouncing the world, the traditional renouncer (*saṃnyāsin*) lives an austere and wandering life. He is expected to live outside of villages, remain homeless, and continually wander alone from place to place (MS 6.41–42; VasDhS 10.12–15). Although the renouncer should remain homeless, he is allowed to stay in an uninhabited house if he is near such a place at the end of the day, but he must not stay there for any length of time. The only time of the year that he can reside in one residence is during the rainy season (ĀU 4). The renouncer is also allowed to sleep on the sandy banks or in temple doorways (KauU 5; SubālāU 4). This wandering by the renouncer has important consequences for the concept of time, because the ever-flowing movement of the renouncer allows him to lose all sense of the commencement and termination of his wandering.[13]

Because of expectations concerning his itinerant lifestyle, the renouncer is not allowed to cultivate a plot of land, and he needs to beg or subsist on whatever he can find for himself. Another reason for begging is related to the prohibition against having a fire (MS 6.43; ĀpDhS 1.9.21.10). There are, however, restrictions on begging given in the authoritative texts: beg once a day in a village, beg after householders have finished their meal, beg randomly, beg from all castes or only from the highest caste, beg only enough to sustain one's existence (MS 5.59; 6.59; VasDhS 10.7; BDh 2.10.69). The following question arises: Why would a householder want to feed a wandering stranger? An obvious answer is the merit earned by the householder. The *Yatidharmaprakāśa* gives an answer to the question by stating that serving a renouncer is like feeding a god. Besides begging to sustain one's life, the renouncer may also live on fruit, roots, wild rice, nuts, green sprouts, water, and air (Mbh 3.145.30–31; 5.38.7; 1.81.15–16; Rām 2.21.2–3; 2.55.5; 1.50.26–27). The practice of begging and types of food consumed give the renouncer an opportunity to advance his detachment from the world and enable him to live a wandering life.

Besides the various eating restrictions, the lifestyle of the renouncer also entails very meager clothing. Some texts mention wearing hides and upper garments of bark cloth; (the *Rāmāyaṇa* 2.89.6) and other works cite a loincloth to cover the private parts of one's anatomy (NPU 3.28; KU 13). The *Nirvāna Upaniṣad* (25) states that the loincloth indicates the nonattachment of the renouncer to the things of the world. Of course, the renouncer could decide to go clad in space, or naked, according to the *Jābāla Upaniṣad* (6). Other belongings of the renouncer are as meager as his clothing; he is allowed to possess a water pot, an alms bowl, sandals, a patched garment in addition to his loincloth, a purifying ring of sacred grass, and a sling to carry his effects (KU 13–14; NPU 3.28). By means of his unusual attire, nakedness, and meager possessions, the renouncer is fabricating a special public body by which he becomes known.

Symbols of the Renouncer

A common symbol associated with the lifestyle of the renouncer is the begging bowl. In fact, Indian religious authorities often classify renouncers according to their modes of begging. According to the *Āśrama Upaniṣad* (4), one group begs from their children (*kuṭīcakas*); another group begs from Brahmin families (*bahūdakas*); *haṃsas* (swans) wander begging, like birds; and paramahaṃsas (highest swans) beg from all four castes. The *Bhikṣuka Upaniṣad* (2–5) identifies renouncers according to the food they consume. Haṃsas subsist, for instance, on cow's urine and other bovine products, whereas paramahaṃsas subsist on eight mouthfuls of food. According to the *Yatidharmaprakāśa* of Vāsudevāśrama, there are three classes of renouncers according to their mode of begging: a renouncer using his stomach as his begging bowl (57.57); a person that uses his hands (57.54); and a person that uses a clay or wooden begging bowl (57.32).

The staff is not only another symbol of the renouncer but is also an additional means of classifying renouncers. There are two basic distinctions with respect to the type of staff carried: those that carry three staffs (*tridaṇḍin*), who are generally Vaiṣṇava renouncers, and those who carry a single staff (*ekadaṇḍin*), who usually adhere to the injunctions of one of the ten orders allegedly established by the great sage Śaṇkara.[14] According to the *Āśrama Upaniṣad* (4), the haṃsa carries a single staff, whereas the paramahaṃsa carries no staff, water pot, or water filter, although the *Nāradaparivrājaka Upaniṣad* (5.15) describes him as carrying a staff. The staff (*daṇḍa*) possesses many religious meanings within the context of Indian culture, because it is given to a student at the end of his studies by his teacher (MS 6.52), it plays a role in the vedic sacrificial cult as the name of the handle of the sacrificial ladle, the axle of the sacrificial car, the staff given to the sacrificer after the initiation rite by the priest, and the instrument to hit a king on his back during the royal consecration ceremony.[15] The staff is also associated with the deity Indra within the context of initiatory rites and the god's festival, at which a bamboo pole is planted into the ground. Moreover, the staff is also connected to adulthood and is believed to possess magical powers.[16]

For the renouncer, the staff is symbolic of his wandering lifestyle. By touching holy sites with his staff, the renouncer is said to produce significant results.[17] The triple staff even serves in a more practical way as the tripod for the water pot of the renouncer. Another useful purpose of the staff is to ward off animals and reptiles.[18] Much like the condition of the renouncer, the staff itself possesses an ambivalent nature because it functions in traditional Indian culture as an instrument of legal punishment when associated with kingship and power, while it also serves as a sacred symbol within the sphere of religion.[19]

Besides the rich cultural connections of the staff, the renouncer's hair—long, disheveled, dirty, and matted, or shaved off—possesses equally rich cultural significance. The renouncer with long hair, a location for unspent semen and spiritual power, shares a connection with death with Punjabi women, who unbind their hair to let it hang loose without washing it during a period of mourning.[20] This is because such women observe traditional customs associated with death, and the renouncer is symbolically dead to the world. Moreover, disheveled hair also signifies dissolution and chaos in the metaphoric sense of the dissolving of social bonds and the chaotic life of the wanderer.[21] Among Śaiva ascetics, matted hair is evidence that the ascetic models his behavior on that of the great, omniscient, ascetic god Śiva. Since hair is a by-product of the human body like urine, feces, nail clippings, and so forth, it is considered polluting. By belonging to a class of polluted bodily products, matted hair evokes disgust and fear in others.[22] Furthermore, it sets a person apart from others in society and isolates the individual, whereas shaving the head suggests a different kind of symbolism.

In numerous texts, the renouncer is instructed to shave his hair, with the exception of the hair under his arms or private parts (KU 12; JāU 5), although other texts advocate the removal of all hair from the underarms, private parts, and head (SubālaU 1; KaushU 5). Whatever the exact shaving procedure, the removal of bodily hair signifies a radical change in the aspiring renouncer's life, which is also evident in cultural dramas like the tonsure ceremony of a young child, when the final vestiges of birth pollution are removed. A shaving ceremony is also important within the context of student initiation, the period when a student returns to his home after his education, the royal consecration ceremony in ancient India, and the funeral ceremony, when the nails and hair of the deceased husband are removed and the wife of the deceased is shaved because of her inauspicious condition (ĀpGS 4.6.4). Because hair absorbs and retains pollution, cutting hair or shaving the head is connected to the removal of pollution, although the ambiguous status of the renouncer makes this type of connection uncertain. The examples cited allow one to understand, however, that shaving hair takes place during periods of transition, which is true alike for those passing through the life-cycle rites, within other ritual contexts, and for those renouncing the world.

Unlike the person remaining within the social context, the renouncer shaving his head represents a radical break with his line of descent and with his past social identity.[23] The topknot (*śikhā*) signifies a person's *gotra* (family, descent), and thus serves as a visible sign of one's social identity and twice-born status. There are, traditionally, fixed family customs concerning the proper manner of wearing one's hair. The topknot is grounded in a belief that the hair is the locus of a person's vital power and a lock of hair can represent the individual himself.[24] By shaving off his topknot, a renouncer is making a dramatic gesture of totally rejecting his caste status, former identity, and family tradition.

Just as matted hair, a bald head, and staffs are external symbols of the renouncer, silence is an internal symbol of his lifestyle. As the renouncer wanders from place to place, according to some texts, he must remain absolutely silent (MS 6.41; BDhS, 2.10.18.16) or remain silent except for reciting the Vedas (ĀpDhS 2.9.21.10). Silence expresses symbolically the ineffability of the reality that the renouncer seeks to realize and terminates questions about the nature of the absolute by indicating that all such inquires into the nature of reality are without meaning. Strictly speaking, silence conveys its message paradoxically because the renouncer becomes aware on his path to liberation of the inadequacy of language and the power of silence, which is always there as the ground of all expression. Along with renunciation of action and breath control, the *Bhāgavata Purāṇa* (11.18.17) includes silence as an internal control of speech that represents one of the marks of a genuine renouncer.

More than signifying control of speech, silence also represents the renouncer's death to the world and to his body. Since the dead do not speak, it is very appropriate for the living-dead to remain silent. Silence and the motif of death that it suggests implies that the renouncer dies to his physical body and the external material realm, and it suggests in turn a spiritual rebirth that enables him to transcend the flux of time. The genuine renouncer is not trapped by human existence or the world in which he lives. By means of his ability to redeem himself, the renouncer transforms life into an opportunity to transcend the cycle of rebirth.

Renouncer and Society

By setting forth on his quest for liberation, the renouncer creates a distance between himself and the society that he rejects, because his quest propels him in the opposite direction from that followed by members of the social world. The spirit of the life of the renouncer is, for instance, inimical to the caste system. In his classic study of the caste system, Louis Dumont views it as a hierarchical opposition between pure and impure and superior and inferior. Dumont goes on to argue that the renouncer becomes an individual by living outside of the world because of the confining nature of society.[25] Various scholars have criticized Dumont's theory, but this criticism need not detain us at this moment. Whatever the merits and demerits of Dumont's theory, most scholars agree that there is a tension in Indian culture between the renouncer and society.

Sometimes this tension is expressed as a bias by Brahmin authors against renouncers. If we conceive of the priests as custodians of the Indian cultural heritage, part of the reason for the tension can be traced to the replacement of sacrificial power with ascetic and meditative power, a nonsacrificial and antisocial form, in the post-vedic period, which is reflected in the general anti-ascetic attitude expressed in Hindu mythology.[26] There are also numerous stories in Hindu mythology concerning the overwhelming power gained by some demons practicing tapas (heat of asceticism), resulting in a challenge to the dominion of the gods over human beings and the world (Rām 1.15.4–5; 1.24.4–5). It is not insignificant that demons and renouncers practice asceticism in order to gain powers, in the case of the former, and as a by-product of the ascetic lifestyle, in the case of the latter. From the perspective of the Brahmin authors, demons and renouncers can be placed in the same category because they both threaten the traditional sacrificial rites, social system, and power structure. In other words, the tapas (asceticism) practiced by renouncers or mythological demons is perceived as a threat by priestly authors of the established socioreligious order and opposition to it represents an attempt by the predominant class to protect itself and its privileged position.

In contrast to the life of the householder, the status of the renouncer is ambiguous. In the *Laws of Manu*, for instance, the life of the householder is proclaimed to be superior (6.89), while renunciation is also affirmed to be the highest stage of life because the renouncer attains the highest state (6.96). From the priestly viewpoint, the renouncer potentially violates the basic duties ordained by the Vedas, such as paying the three debts during one's life that can only be paid by being initiated into the twice-born castes, having sons, and performing sacrifices (6.35–37). If renouncers stand in violation of basic duties ordained by the sacred texts, this helps to explain why some Dharmasūtras insist that a person live as a householder (BDhS 2.10.17.2–5). The priestly perspective is not totally unsympathetic to the renouncer, but because the renouncer tends to violate basic socioreligious injunctions specified in the Vedas, he acts contrary to revelation (*śruti*). In this sense, the renouncer violates a self-evident and self-explanatory truth. This did not keep priestly authors from incorporating the renouncer into the stages of life, relegating it to the end of life after one's duty as a householder has been done. Fitting the renouncer into a cultural pattern of established knowledge demonstrates a typical way for orthodox Indian society to respond to dissent and heresy.[27]

Another reason for the tension between the renouncer and society is related to the powers (*siddhas*) acquired by these figures. The power to change form, ability to see into the future, fly, suddenly disappear, cause rain to fall, and transform others into lower forms of life by means of one's curse are all examples of powers that motivate members of society to both honor and fear renouncers.

According to textual evidence, renouncers manifest negative attitudes that also contribute to the tension with members of society. The *Nāradaparivrājaka Upaniṣad* states that the renouncer is not to associate with forest-dwellers and householders (5.46, 5.57), and he is not to bow to anyone (5.21). Such injunctions suggest that the renouncer must not recognize social distinctions, must not have any substantial contact with members of society, must remain isolated, and must not adhere to the hierarchical structure of society. This tends to suggest that the renouncer represents a threatening outsider or stranger to the established social system.[28]

Another obvious dichotomy is created by the celibacy of the renouncer and the active sexual life of the laity. Although the chastity of the renouncer is a form of restraint that differentiates him from the householder, the kind of internal and unnatural heat generated by his continence is very similar to the erotic heat generated by a husband and wife during intimate moments. By withholding his semen and drawing it up to his head, the renouncer generates an internal heat that strengthens him and gives him power. Since the sexual life of the householder is much less controlled and open to excessive indulgence, it is believed that the male householder finds his power and strength being dissipated by his uncontrolled sexual behavior, whereas the renouncer gains power by restraining himself. The discipline of the renouncer reverses the flow of the body and imposes order upon it, which is accomplished in conformity with a tradition and within the public domain (even when performed in private), because the actions of the renouncer are enacted within a community and tradition that are forms of a collective memory.[29] Because of his chastity, the renouncer becomes symbolically hot, while the laity become symbolically cold, which creates another boundary between them. Moreover, the celibacy of the renouncer is injurious to the soteriological feature of marriage; he destroys the social lineage, and his sexual restraint allows him to gain power while the householder loses power because of sexual indulgence.[30]

Even though the renouncer is expected to lead a wandering lifestyle, his life is socially, politically, and economically inactive in theory, whereas the householder is active in two of these areas and is sometimes also active in the political sphere. This distinction between activity (*pravṛtti*) and inactivity (*nivṛtti*) is developed in the *Laws of Manu*, which helps us to see two distinct visions of salvation, behavior, and attitude in Indian culture. As a salvific conception, the active path is grounded in the world, ethics, and history, whereas the inactive path of the renouncer suggests transcendence of social and individual concerns.[31] These two contradictory ways of being, acting, and striving for one's ultimate goal represent an irreconcilable dichotomy in Indian culture, even though the *Laws of Manu* attempts to integrate them. This does not mean that historically the renouncer did not have social and political importance. The renouncer's autonomy stands in opposition to the limits imposed by state power and stimulated aspirations for social and economic development.[32] Nonetheless, the begging bowl reflects the renouncer's freedom from economic labor. The mundane activity of work is without value for the renouncer, because it merely promotes rebirth, further suffering, and can never be an end in itself.

Concluding Remarks

The graceful and high-flying swan is a symbol for the world renouncer and his quest to transcend the world, human existence, and society. The renouncer's quest to realize the highest truth or reality sets him apart from members of society, and it creates a tension between the two parties. When the Pāṇḍavas of the epic *Mahābhārata* are exiled from their kingdom, they become ascetics to disguise themselves in order to hide from their enemies for twelve years. This suggests that the living dead become virtually invisible human beings.

By an intuitive insight, renouncers are unified with the one universal reality. Vedic poets and priests tended to connect one thing with something else by means of resemblance, and the teaching about the identity between the self and Brahman represents the logical climax of such a process. Thus the distinctions drawn by

Vedic seers collapses in a monistic perspective grounded in an intuitive insight into the nature of reality. The direct and intuitive insight realized by the renouncer is a self-validating kind of knowledge that is absolutely certain. This experience gives him the absolute certainty and confidence to challenge the fundamental presuppositions of the established order. The liberating experience, willingness to give up everything that social life offers, and powers of renouncers inspire ordinary people to honor and also fear them.

The Hindu religious tradition attempts to incorporate renouncers into the stages of life in an artificial way in the dharma literature. The tension between the way of life of a householder and renouncer and the difference between dharma (legal and social order) and mokṣa (liberation) persists throughout Indian religious history. This can be viewed as an opposition between two distinctive dharmas.[33] It can, alternatively, be comprehended as the renouncer performing actions that defy the predominant dharma.[34] The actions of the renouncer can also be viewed as posing a threat to the dharmic order of the world because the renouncer turns his back on society, and is only concerned with release from the world.[35] The Hindu religious tradition never truly synthesizes or reconciles the dynamic tension and difference between dharma and mokṣa, even though it attempts such a reconciliation with the stages of life which are discussed in the following chapter.

The renouncer strives to become a jīvanmukti (one liberated while alive). This quest presupposes dying to the world and society. The renouncer becomes a member of the living-dead in order to defeat final death and rebirth. The householder looks into the face of the renouncer, and possibly recognizes the finality of his or her mortality and anticipates the possibility of his or her rebirth. For the householders, there is no liberation, although such people live into the future in the guise of their children, which represents a sort of biological immortality. Nonetheless, they cannot become the ultimate reality; they remain in a state of ignorance, bound to causation, and subject to the uncertainties of the cycle of life. The householder wears the mask of life and social responsibility, which hides death. The renouncer wears the face of death, which hides the reality of immortality. It is a truism that everyone must die. By following the example of dying to the world before the advent of physical death, turning within oneself, and achieving an intuitive insight into one's true nature that is nondual, a person can ascend, fly, and be absolutely free like a swan.

4

The Way and the Structure of Life

According to the *Āpastamba Dharmasūtra* (1.20.1–4), a person should not follow the law (*dharma*) to gain mundane benefits, because the law does not produce fruits when a person's intention is incorrect. But when for instance, a person plants, a mango tree for its fruit, such a person also gains shade and fragrance to enjoy. By following the laws, a person also gains additional benefits. This chapter is intended to examine what dharma (law) means, its benefits for Indian society, and how it shapes classical Indian culture.

Although the term "law" is often used to translate *dharma*, the term is not, strictly speaking, simply law, because the meaning of dharma includes both legal and religious rules. These rules include dietary rules about what foods are allowed or forbidden, hygienic rules related to proper bathing, brushing teeth, and grooming, and finally moral rules about human behavior. In fact, there is no precise equivalent to the term *dharma* in the English language, because it also suggests a way of life, a right way to do things, and a way to maintain order and balance in the cosmos. The opposite of dharma (*adharma*) disturbs the cosmic balance.[1]

When unpacking the meaning of dharma it is important to recognize that some rules have universal application, whereas other regulations depend on particular situations. Moreover, some rules apply only to members of some groups, which means that some rules are specific to a particular group, and not all rules are universally applicable to all members of society. The nonhomogenous rules are not only different for different individuals but they are also different according to diverse circumstances.

The notion of dharma is connected to the ideal of a golden age. During this perfect age, it is imagined that everyone collectively obeys the dharma without the need for coercion. This occurs when its ontological reality and imperative dimensions are harmonized.[2] After the golden age passes, there occurs a gradual degeneration of the observance of the rules, which is conceptualized as the four *yugas* (cosmic ages) by the *Manusmṛti* (Laws of Manu): kṛta, tretā, dvāpara, and kali.

Because human beings live in the final and most degenerate age, the guidelines provided by the dharma are needed more than ever.

The dharma texts fall into the literary category of Vedāṇgas (literally, limbs of the Veda), which are considered auxiliary sciences that are necessary for the proper interpretation of the Vedas. Six types of treatises dealing with these auxiliary subjects are the following: phonetics, metrics, linguistic analysis and grammar, astronomy, etymology, and finally *kalpasūtras* (literally, threads of form or fashion), which deal with rituals. Specific treatises are written in the highly condensed aphoristic form of the *sūtra* (literally thread) style. The sentences are thus brief, abstract, and intended to be memorized. Because of their brevity and abstract nature, the sentences are often unintelligible unless they are explained by a commentary composed by a master.

The kalpasūtras are subdivided into three categories: *śrautasūtras* (those that deal with great sacrifices), *gṛhyasūtras* (domestic rites), and *dharmasūtras* (duties and privileges related to social status). The dharmasūtras are frequently appendages of the śrautasūtras. Another body of texts is the *śulabasūtras*, which are intended to offer instructions for proper construction of vedic altars and the different geometric forms of the bricks. Major examples of the dharmasūtras are: *Gautama*, *Vasiṣṭha*, *Āpastamba*, *Baudhāyana*, and *Hiranyakeśin*. The last three mentioned texts are attached to a particular vedic school for which there are also śrautasūtras and gṛhyasūtras. These three texts are thus considered complete; they were composed at different times during a period ranging from 600 to 300 B.C.E. in prose and verse.

In contrast to the dharmasūtras, the *dharmaśāstras* are composed entirely in verse in the *śloka* meter (four times eight syllables to a stanza), and they cover the same subject matter as the dharmasūtras. Some of the surviving texts include the following: *Manusmṛti* (which is the oldest composition, dating from 200 B.C.E. to 200 C.E.), *Yājñavalkya*, *Nārada*, and *Parāśara*. The final three dharmasāśtras are more recent than 200 C.E.

Hindu Social Dharma

In order for any society to endure for an extended period of time, it must have some type of structure and order. It is a widely accepted cross-cultural presupposition that human beings cannot survive for long in a condition of chaos. Ancient Indians developed a social system grounded in a revealed and eternal dharma, a term that derives from a Sanskrit root word that means to maintain, to support, to be firm, or be durable. If the term *dharma* is applied to the universe, it signifies the eternal laws that maintain the world. Dharma also represents the order that is inherent to the nature of things, and the gods are its guardians.[3] In addition to the physical world, dharma also includes the moral realm. Within a moral context, dharma represents a set of personal and social obligations and duties, enduring laws that govern how a person should act according to the individual's caste and stage of life. A person's specific dharma is called *svadharma* (one's own duties). According to the *Manusmṛti*, the violations of dharma are described as exceeding the limits. This excess is expressed metaphorically by depicting dharma as an organism injured by the dart of its opposite (*adharma*).[4]

According to the so-called dharma texts, there are four sources of the law in ancient India (GautDhS 1.1–2; VasDhS 1.4–6). The most important source of the law is the divinely revealed Vedas. For ancient Hindus, all dharma is based on revelation (*śruti*). This suggests that all dharmas have a transcendent character, and thus cannot be easily altered.[5] According to the *Manusmṛti* (12.95–96), if a tradition of thought is not based on the Vedas, it is worthless because it is grounded on what is false, and it will not produce any benefit after death. The second source of the dharma is tradition, which rests on human memory (*smṛti*) or that which is remembered. In this sense, it is an indirect perception based on memory. Although grounded in vedic revelation, it is not directly heard, like revelation, which makes its authority inferior to that of the Vedas. The third source of dharma is good custom, which suggests the way that good people live (*sadācāra*). This way is equated with a religious life and the acquiring of insight. The final source of dharma is human conscience.

It is theoretically possible that these four sources of dharma could disagree on specific points. What should a person do if such a situation arises? The *Āpastamba Dharmasūtra* (1.4.8) provides an interpretive tool to reconcile discrepancies between sources. If the Vedas are revealed literature and function as the genuine sources for all rules, and one cannot find a basis for a particular practice in these texts, it can be inferred that the rule in question that one knows is located in sources based on memory (smṛti texts) is derived from a previously lost vedic text. The hermeneutical device of inferring that a practice is based on a lost text enables one to overcome the gap between that which is revealed (*śruti*) and memory (*smṛti*).

According to various dharma texts, there are four legitimate ends of human life (*puruṣārthas*). These ends of life represent a realization by ancient Indian culture that humans possess complex personalities, which seek fulfillment through four channels. These four channels include the following: a person's instincts and natural desires, a person's craving for power and property, personal anxiety associated with a need for social security and progress, and a person's urge for spiritual liberation. Thus the four ends of life represent fulfillment of these four channels of a person's personality. Despite the emphasis on renouncing the world that was discussed in chapter 3, the four ends of life are each considered honorable and legitimate goals for which a person can strive. In fact, the acceptance of the four goals of human life implies that advocates of these ends thought of humans as basically oriented toward certain goals and possessed of certain needs.[6]

The initial end of life is *artha*, which literally means thing, object, or substance. It comprises the whole range of tangible objects that a person can possess. Therefore, it connotes the attainment of wealth, riches, and worldly property. The term *artha* conveys three meanings: an object of human pursuit, the means of this pursuit, and the needs and desires motivating this pursuit. The second end of life is *kāma* (desire, pleasure, or love). The centrality of kāma is evident in the *Manusmṛti* where an action devoid of desire is considered impossible. Therefore, whatever is done is driven by desire. Kāma is later defied as a god of desire who carries a flower bow and five flower arrows that he uses to fire into the heart of an unsuspecting victim, turning that individual into an uncontrollable bundle of desire. As will be observed in chapter 12, Kāma is the arch-enemy of the ascetic deity Śiva. There are some scholars who think that the emphasis on kāma represents an attempt to correct frustrations associated with married life. Nonetheless, kāma is construed as a product of the mind rather than the body in traditional Indian culture.

The third end of life is *dharma*, which can mean in this context ritual, religion, ethics, caste rules, and civil and criminal laws. As an end of life, dharma comprises the entire range of religious and moral duties. In short, dharma is the duty or law that a person should follow in accordance with one's nature and station of life. Thus dharma defines an entire way of life. The underlying notion of dharma is related to seeking to resolve the inevitable conflict between the real and the phenomenal, the spiritual and the material, and the eternal and the temporal. The final end of life is *mokṣa*, which means liberation, release, or redemption. By including both liberation and kāma within a list of the legitimate ends of life, there seems to be an inherent contradiction built into the four ends of life. But from the perspective of the creators of the dharma texts, the four ends of life are not mutually contradictory, because they rather serve as the physical and moral basis of a person's role in the world. The initial three ends of life—artha, kāma, and dharma—are known as the three pursuits of the world (*trivarga*).

In addition to the legitimate ends of life, the dharma texts specify four stages of life (*āśramas*), which are intended to acknowledge that there are different psychophysical stages in an individual's life, each with its appropriate ethical organization of personal life. The term *āśrama* literally means exertion or the place where exertion is practiced, and it implies that the main stages in an individual's life become a planned exertion. An important factor in the construction of the four stages of life is the ethical notion of the three debts that are owed by all males upon being born into a Hindu family. The three debts are those owed to the gods, to the seers, and to the ancestors. The four stages of life are designed to enable an orthodox Hindu to meet these ethical and cultural obligations.

The four stages of life are the following: student (*brahmacārin*), householder (*gṛhastha*), forest-dweller (*vānaprastha*), and renouncer (*saṃnyāsin*). The life of a student is governed by obedience and submission to his teacher. This period of life begins for higher-caste members with the rite of initiation that occurs between the ages of eight and twelve, and it can last for a period of twelve years. It is the student's duty to focus on his studies and to learn. After successful completion of studentship, a young man is prepared to begin the life of a householder, which necessarily includes marriage.

From the more narrow focus of the life of a student, a male turns his concerns to family, his vocation, and the wider community. This stage of life is the foundation and support of all the others. Within the context of the life of a householder, a married couple performs the five great sacrifices (*pañca-mahāyajñas*) daily as advocated in the dharmaśūtras (ĀpDhS 12.13–15; 13.1; GautDhS 3.29; 5.3,9; BDhS 2.11.1–8). The sacrifice to the gods (*devayajña*) obliges a householder to make a burnt offering, or to offer milk, curds, or butter, or sprinkle some *ghī* (clarified butter) on a piece of wood and burn it. The second sacrifice, to Brahmins, represents the debt the one owes to the sages, which is repaid by meditating on a particular vedic scripture, studying it, or repeating it. The daily sacrifice to the ancestors (*pitṛyajña*) is a way to remember the deceased, which consists of the offering of libations of water or rice balls, whereas the recognition of spirits (*bhūtayajña*) is the fourth type of daily sacrifice. Finally, a householder is obligated to honor seers (*narayajña*) by offering fellowship and hospitality to others, who may be friends, guests, or beggars.

The third stage of life occurs, ideally, with advanced age and retirement from normal social duties. At this point, a person can decide to become a forest-dweller (*vānaprastha*) and to begin to ponder the meaning of life. This stage of life is poetically expressed as looking beyond the village streets and the stars to the Absolute. Although there is a certain overlap with the third stage, the fourth stage of life is that of the renouncer (*saṃnyāsin*). This stage is considered to be beyond mere retirement from the world, because it involves a dedication to achieve the goal of liberation by means of meditation. In short, the renouncer is the holy wandering beggar of India, who is free of a fixed home and the responsibilities that accompany domestic life.

Caste System

As the renowned vedic *Puruṣasūkta* hymn (RV 10.90) expresses lucidly, there are three main castes (*varṇas*). The root meaning of the term *varṇa* is associated with color, which historically reflects the darker-skinned Dravidian people and the yellow-skinned Mongols encountered by the white-skinned Aryans in their migration into the Indian subcontinent. The term "caste" is more recent, because it dates from 1563 and the work of Garcia de Orta, a Portuguese explorer. This explorer used the Portuguese term *casta* to designate breed, race, or kin that he discovered in India in 1563. This origin scenario is, however, disputed, and it is argued that the term *caste* derives from the Gothic term kasts, which means a group of animals.[7]

From the perspective of the composers of dharma literature, castes are distinct from each other, but they are not allowed to compete with one another. The dharma writers suggest that each individual possesses a specific nature fitting for a specific function in society. And it is the caste system that helps each individual achieve what is proper to him or her. This ideal way of referring to caste does not necessarily correspond to the social reality. A caste within a village or region that owns the land is, for instance, the group with the most political power and control, because it possesses a monopoly on the means of subsistence. Thus it is not necessary to belong to a high caste in order to have social and political power. It is therefore possible to view the caste system as an example of socioreligious ideology, which owes its construction to Brahmins for their benefit, although in practice they might not have the sociopolitical power in specific locations.

The four main castes are the Brahmin (priests), Kṣatriya (rulers or warriors), Vaiśya (businessmen and farmers), and Śūdra (laborers). The Brahmins ideally administer to the spiritual needs of the people. Historically, they have functioned as advisors to kings. They are considered men of knowledge in the sense of knowing the rites, sacrifices, and sacred scriptures. The term *kṣatriya* originates from a Sanskrit word that mean rule, dominion, or power. The warrior caste is expected to perform the executive functions of the state, which makes them the custodians of social and political power. The term *vaiśya* is derived from a Sanskrit root that means community, tribe, or race. They are expected to provide for the sustenance of the people, which renders them the custodians of the economic functions of the community. These initial three castes are called the twice-born (*dvija*), because of their presumed purity of blood and education. Only members of the initial three castes are allowed to enter into the initiation rite, which allows them the opportunity to wear the sacred thread. Finally, the Śūdras represent the servants of society, who are engaged in various labor and service occupations. The members of this caste are called the once-born (*eka-jāti*) because they experience a single natural birth, whereas the upper three castes are born first from their biological mother and second from their teacher during the initiation rite. Beneath the superstructure of these four castes are a multitude of so-called Untouchables, who are responsible for the removable of various kinds of human waste and dead bodies, and other occupations considered "unclean." This mass of people has been called Harijans (children of God) by Mahatma Gandhi, and more recently Dalits (oppressed), or members of the scheduled castes—a term derived from British administration. There are many subdivisions within the four major castes that are the result of changes of occupation, migration, political, economic, and social factors. As a consequence, the fourfold varṇa division of society was not equally observed in all parts of the subcontinent.[8]

The superiority of the Brahmin caste is related to their role as the lords of the sacrifice, the power that controls the cosmos in ancient vedic religion. The Brahmins are called gods on earth, because they carry the sacrifice to the gods (ŚB 1.3.4.9). Moreover, it is believed in some contexts that their power is equivalent to that of the gods. The social superiority of the Brahmins is also related to the fact that according to some myths they were created before the other castes, represent a perfect example of a human being, alone know the Veda, and control the sacrifice.[9] Their superior status not only gives them a monopoly on the priesthood but their education and knowledge give them a decided advantage over other castes in propagating their world view and social viewpoint in the literature, over which they have exercised a monopoly; this in turn enables them to maintain their superior status.

The four main castes can be grasped as a superstructure that is superimposed over the *jāti* system of village life. The term *jāti* can be translated as birth, breed, race, family, or subcaste. Jāti is the proper term for the caste system as it operates at the village level. Jātis can be viewed as hierarchically ranked descent groups, although their order lacks consistency and uniformity throughout India. In contrast to a varṇa (caste), a jāti is geographically and linguistically limited. It is comparable to a large kin group or subcaste with distinctive, customs, dress, diet, language, profession, and behavior. It is in many ways self-governing, and it is thus responsible for the behavior of its own members. It only interacts with other castes in carefully circumscribed ways. The castes are ranked hierarchically vis-à-vis one another. Ranking is important—and often disputed—because it determines who can do what with whom, and under what conditions. In a sense, the varṇa (caste) system is imposed upon this complex village social system of jāti. Therefore, the varṇa system gives the village systems a common pattern throughout India with which members of jātis typically identify.

The superstructure of the varṇa system and the prevalence of the jāti pattern do not mean that all Indians are shaped by the caste system. Groups of people that are classified now as hill people, plains dwellers, and martial pastoralists have traditionally been untouched by the varṇa-jāti system. Even more broadly, the actual cultural situation is still more fluid because of cultural and geographic diversity, and different political systems.[10] This means that for many inhabitants of India formal caste distinctions have been of limited significance. Rather than fixed social structures, the varṇa-jāti system operates more as idealized moral archetypes, whereas the actual social situation demonstrates a more fluid situation.

The caste system is arranged into a hierarchical system, as has been said, and the fundamental opposition between purity and impurity underlies the principle of hierarchy. In other words, the highest caste is more pure than the fourth caste, whereas the fourth caste is more pure than the Untouchables. If a caste holds a higher place in the hierarchy, this means that its members have a greater responsibility to maintain purity. Impurity or pollution represents a danger to oneself, one's family members, and to a lesser extent to other members of one's caste. Purity is maintained in two basic ways: performance of basic domestic sacraments and sacrifices, and following caste regulations such as dietary regulations.

In order to grasp the nature of purity, it helps to know something about the nature of pollution. In brief, pollution is dirt, which is matter out of place. Because dirt offends against order, it is never a unique, isolated event. Thus where there is dirt there is a system.[11] Dirt is a by-product of a systematic ordering and classification of matter, and ancient Hindus excelled at classifying virtually everything.[12] Dirt can be further identified as unclean. In this respect, it stands in opposition to holiness, which is exemplified by completeness and order.

Avoiding pollution requires two things: It requires that individuals or things conform to the requirements of the class to which they belong, and it requires that the different classes of things should not be confused. Therefore it is most likely to occur where lines of cosmic or social structure are not clearly defined. When an act of pollution does occur, the polluting person is always wrong, because the polluter has developed a wrong condition vis-à-vis the person polluted, or the polluter has crossed some line and unleashes danger. Pollution can be committed inadvertently or intentionally. Whatever the case, the danger of pollution strikes when form or order is attacked, which results in disorder.

Because pollution can be transmitted from one person to another, interactions between parties are circumscribed; this is especially true with respect to eating and food, due to the polluting nature of saliva. Thus in classical Hinduism there is a restriction on the transfer of food between castes routed in the distinction between pure and impure and the hierarchical structure of the caste system. The assertion that there is a restriction on the transfer of food between castes needs to be qualified to some degree, because such a transaction depends on the type of food. As a general guideline, there are no restrictions on raw food, whereas cooked food involves numerous restrictions. Imperfect food (*kaccā*) is, for instance, boiled rice or possibly wheat flour cakes cooked without fat. This type of food is considered imperfect, that is, vulnerable to impurity because it is cooked with water. Such food is reserved for relatives or members of an endogamous group and servants of an inferior caste to the householder. Perfect food (*pakkā*) gains its status because it consists of flour cakes fried in butter and vegetables fried the same way. Since butter is a product of the traditionally revered cow, it plays a protective role by sanctifying the food cooked with it. Another guideline relates to a person's caste status. The higher a person's status, the greater the restrictions placed on his or her ability to accept food from individuals of lower status.

As intimated above, there is a strong relationship between caste and profession. Although not all members of a caste follow the same profession, it is traditionally common for a son to assume the profession of his father. If your father is an administrator within a kingdom, or if he is a sweeper, you can expect to be either an administrator or a sweeper, depending on your birth. It is no secret that upper-caste members have financial resources, political and religious connections, educational advantages, and social status not enjoyed by those with lower-caste standing.

A person's profession is not simply an occupation performed to support oneself and one's family; it is also a social function. In this respect, each varṇa and profession is necessary for the maintenance of the social order, and each varṇa relies on the contributions of other social groups. If a person performs his or her profession with skill and diligence, the dharma texts promise that person can be reborn into a higher caste in the next life. At the same time, there is also a threat directed at members of higher castes that they might be reborn into a lower caste if they do not perform their necessary duties (ĀpDhS 2.5.1.10–11; GautDhS 10.29–30).

The restrictions associated with food and those associated with profession are also reflected in the social institution of marriage. The basic restriction involves endogamy, the obligation to marry within one's jāti (subcaste). An example would be a man of caste z who marries a woman of the same caste, and the children of this union belong to caste z. By prohibiting marriage outside of the social group, castes tend to separate themselves from one another.

The Indian legal experts also established guidelines for intercaste marriages. In general, there are two major categories of such marital unions: *anuloma* (literally "following the hair") and *pratiloma* (literally "against the hair"). The former type of marriage implies conformity with the natural order. These are called hypergamous marriage because the husband possesses status superior to that or the wife. The latter type of union represents a hypogamous marriage in which the husband is inferior in social status to the wife. In both instances, the children inherit an inferior status. From the perspective of legal experts, only the anuloma unions count as genuine marriages.

Another part of the caste puzzle is the clan (*gotra*), which represents an exogamous (marrying outside of the blood group) group of individuals theoretically descended from a single ancestor. Among members of the Brahmin caste, it represents descent from an individual for whom a wise man (*ṛṣi*) acted as a family priest. Thus the gotra is not actually inherited. It is, however, acquired by the twice-born castes by means of the initiation ceremony. There is a list of ancestors (*pravara*) that are believed to have served as the original founders of a particular family. This list of names is used specifically in the initiation rite and for worship of one's ancestors. This list is important for the functioning of marriage unions because it can function as an effective bar to intermarriage. For example, if there were an identity of names between two families, intermarriage would be barred. The legal texts contain a rule that prohibits marriage (*spindā*), between any two persons who possess a common ancestor within a certain number of degrees on the father's side and a smaller number of degrees on the mother's side. Another guideline for marriage indicates that no marriage could take place between two families while the memory of a previous intermarriage lasts.

Western political leaders and missionaries leveled caustic criticism against the caste system for representing a backward social system, beginning in earnest in the eighteenth century. Indigenous reformers were also very critical of a system that condemned a huge mass of people to a lifetime of poverty and degradation. In the mid-1950s, B. R. Ambedkar (1891–1956), who was the fourteenth child of Untouchable parents, a rare college graduate for his social status, and a lawyer, led, many Untouchables to convert to Buddhism. By means of social legislation, the democratically elected Indian government has attempted to correct the injustices inherent in the caste system by allocating a certain percentage of civil service jobs to the underprivileged.

Because the shortcomings of the caste system are well documented from the perspective of its external and internal cultural critics, it might prove useful to look at the ways in which it has functioned over the centuries in India. The caste system provides an individual from birth with a fixed social setting, as well as one's general occupation. An individual cannot be removed from his or her caste because he or she proves to be a social failure. One only be removed from one's caste by a violation of caste standards. To be born into a particular caste and remain a lifetime member means that a person possesses a well- defined position in society and a permanent body of social associations that control almost all behavior and social contacts.

In terms of society, the caste functions to determine the membership of a community, and it also defines to a very large extent the social status of each caste in relation to other castes or subcastes. On behalf of the state, the caste system integrates Indian society as a whole by combining into one huge social community many competing if not incompatible groups that compose it. In this way, the caste system functions as a political stabilizer. Of course, the opposite can also be true—friction caused by caste groups dissatisfied with their status may cause unrest. Finally, caste serves as a root metaphor for Vedic ritualists by providing a means to link together different elements of culture and connect various orders of things and beings as part of a cosmic web.[13]

The King and Punishment

The classical Indian king is an incarnated god, who possesses dominion over the earth, must protect it, enforce its laws, and punish violators of the social order. The *Laws of Manu* (3.87) provides an archetype for the role of the king with its notion of *lokapālas* (guardians deities), which represents the various deities that protect the world. A common arrangement of the guardian deities places the god Indra in the east, Yama in the south, Varuṇa in the west, and Kubera in the north. There are also deities guarding and situated in the intermediate directions, beginning with Agni in the southeast, and including Sūrya, Vāyu, and Soma in the other directions. The guardian deities and the directions under their control represent a sacred totality in which directional opposites are unified.[14]

In addition to being protector and savior of the earth, a king is a guardian of the social order, and it is his duty to destroy the forces of chaos that continually threaten his kingdom. It is also his duty to transform the chaos beyond his kingdom into cosmos by incorporating it into his kingdom. In order to perform these tasks, a king must survive. On the basis of lessons from Kauṭilya's *Arthaśāstra*, a guidebook for successful monarchs, a king must supplement his high moral values with ruthless efficiency supported by a strong force, intrigue, and subterfuge.

There are two ancient rites that are very informative about the nature of Indian kingship: royal consecration (*rājasūya*) and horse sacrifice (*aśvamedha*). The royal consecration combines notions of rebirth, regeneration, fertility, ascent to heaven, world conquest, and mastery of the seasons, which are accomplished by a series of rites. It originally involved a yearly ritual for cosmic regeneration and rebirth, because the world was believed to grow old as time passed, implying that the cosmos needed to be recreated yearly. Part of the ritual included the anointment (*abhiṣeka*) of the king, with the objective of supplying him with a new body. This part of the ritual process united two aspects: igneous (Agni) and aquatic principles (Soma), which transformed the king into a cosmic pillar.[15] Within the context of the sacrificial universe, Soma is king and lord of Brahmin priests attending to him at the sacrifice and the process of fertility. During the rites connected to the pressing of Soma, the king becomes identical with the king of plants. When the king drinks Soma this symbolically represents the consumption of his own self, which suggests both self-annihilation and invigoration. The act of drinking also enables the king to communicate with his people by permeating them with his own essence. In a more symbolic fashion, the king enters and diffuses himself in the womb of the people from where he will be reborn.[16]

The royal consecration ceremony includes a couple of sporting features. A chariot race is held, for instance, which is symbolically similar to the way that the sun moves around the world. By means of the chariot race, the king renews time and integrates it within himself. Moreover, the race sets the powers of fertility into a circular motion that signifies the rebirth of the king and the cosmos. Another sporting and risky element is introduced into the rite by the game of dice, which is a cosmogonic rite designed to cause the recreation of the universe and the birth of the king.[17] Thus we see an emphasis on rebirth and creation symbolism overlapping at various points in the consecration ceremony.

If the royal consecration represents the making of a king, the horse sacrifice (*aśvamedha*) is performed for an already powerful monarch, or someone intending to become powerful. From an economic perspective, the horse is a very valuable animal, and it is thus not sacrificed for an unimportant reason. The importance of the horse is evident in ritual texts that claim that it is preeminent over all animals (ŚB 13.1.6.1), it is associated with the creative and sacrificial deity Prajāpati (ŚB 13.2.2.1,13), and is connected to the god Indra (TB 2.6.13.3) and to the Kṣatriya caste (AB 4.9). It is said to have the greatest quantity of *ojas* or life-force (ŚB 13.1.2.6). When performing the horse sacrifice, a king not only demonstrates his power but also consolidates his power and expands it. The horse is allowed to wander freely for a year, guarded by armed youths. The horse wanders in a northeastern direction, which is symbolic of victory and invincibility.[18] From a symbolic perspective, the roaming horse brings territory traversed into contact with the divine power inherent in the animal. This is also a means by which a king asserts ownership of the traversed territory.[19] The purpose of the youthful guards is to protect the horse from danger and certain prohibitions such as bathing or having sexual intercourse with a mare. Like the horse, the king must also abstain from sexual intercourse for a year, which is connected to enhancing the potency of both the horse and king.[20] The primary queen anoints the horse before it is killed. Then the brahman and hotṛ priests engage in a riddle competition. After the horse is covered by a garment and slain, the queens circumambulate the animal three times counterclockwise. The chief queen then approaches the dead horse, both are covered, and she has symbolic sexual intercourse with the animal. Meanwhile, the priest, maidens, and other wives indulge in ribald dialogue. The primary kingly wives take 101 needles to mark the paths of the knife; 303 needles represent the union of the people with the royal power, the regions of space, and a bridge to heaven for the sacrificer.[21] Finally, the horse is cut up and cooked. Some scholars argue that the sexual activity between the horse and queen is strictly symbolic, whereas some scholars think that the queen takes the horse's penis and places it into her sexual organ.[22] The overall purpose of the sexual act is the promotion of fertility, and the ribald dialogue is an attempt to also capture the power released in sexual—actual and symbolic—intercourse. The overall purpose of the rite is to promote fertility throughout the kingdom, which is another responsibility of the king, because the welfare and destiny of his land and people depends on fertile land. The welfare of the people also depends on the king maintaining order within the realm.

The king does not determine dharma, but it is his duty to support it by punishing violators. The king's responsibility is to enforce justice by determining the facts of a case and imposing the penalty, which means that it is his duty to wield sanctions (*daṇḍa*) in order to maintain order or to restore it in dire circumstances. The *daṇḍa* is a staff made of *udumbara* wood that serves a dual function. As a weapon, it is an instrument of destruction, and it also embodies the king's essence, which is his ability to nourish and exercise power. The daṇḍa is thus directly connected to violence, which is not, however, raw or primordial, but rather an instrumental force that makes life in general, farming, governing, sacrificing, and marriage in particular possible and effective.[23] According to the *Dharmasūtras of Gautama* (11.28), punishment is derived from restraint, which suggests that the king must restrain those that are unrestrained. The king uses as his model the order of the original golden age of the kṛta yuga. But by being committed to the use of force, the king is also directly connected to the impure work of violence.[24]

The king's administration of justice in classical Indian culture is best grasped within a religious context, because there crime is considered a sin. The sinful violator must expiate his or her sins by receiving punishment that is inflicted by the king, who functions as a sacrificer by performing an expiatory sacrifice that purifies the kingdom. Not only is the kingdom purified by the sacrifice but the criminal is also purified. The punishment benefits the criminal by cleansing him or her of negative karmic consequences.[25]

Besides his ministers, a ruler needs a priest (*purohita*) to govern his kingdom. If a king does not have a priest, the gods do not eat his sacrificial food offerings (AB 8.24). If the gods do not accept his offerings, his kingdom at risk of dire consequences. There are other benefits associated with having a priest: he protects the kingdom, ensures that it endures a long time, enhances the king's chances for a long and full life, and contributes to the king not being reborn (AB 8.25). This cooperation between the king and priest is only part of the overall picture, because they are sometimes portrayed as competitors and not being especially fond of each other (ŚB 13.1.5.2–3), although ideally they guard and protect each other.

A typical king administers the dharma in his audience hall (*durbar*). It is in this location that the king performs the ceremonial functions of statecraft. His ministers and the royal court surround the king as he hears petitions or makes official pronouncements. The audience hall bears a close resemblance to a temple, because it is here that the king offers his subjects an opportunity for *darśana* (sight) of his iconic form seated on a royal throne. The king functions as a divine image, and his appearance is important enough for him to carefully attend to the fabrication of a body of vital energies by means of his clothing and ornamentation that serve as a visible form for others to see.[26]

In addition to his court, the king manifests the five signs of royalty: a white umbrella, fly-whisks, shoes, turban, and throne. The necessity for a white umbrella is connected to the belief that the sun should not be allowed to shine directly on a sacred person such as a king. A related notion connects the heat of the ruler with the sun, and it was said that the king's heat could be neutralized by contact with a source of power such as the sun.[27] The fly-whisks—yak-tail fans or peacock and swan feathers—are connected to the forest, whereas the shoes of the king distinguish him further from the barefoot attendants. The shoes are associated with a belief that a king should not stand on the earth barefooted. If he did stand on the earth without shoes, his power would leave him.[28] The jeweled turban is connected to the magical value attached to jewels that protects a person from danger associated with sickness and demons. Finally, the throne is similar to an altar, which functions as a seat of a deity and supports a sacred being. By means of his throne, the king occupies the center of the earth, and the elevated nature of the throne suggests the symbolic mountain that lies at that center. Additionally, the cushion of the throne is identical to *śrī* (fortune).[29] The cushion is thus an additional element associated with prosperity, which is a foundation of kingship.

There are instances when a king abandons the support and promotion of dharma, and he becomes a tyrant. In such cases, the epic texts allow for regicide. The *Mahābhārata* (13.61.33), for instance, calls upon the people to kill a tyrant. Likewise, the *Rāmāyaṇa* (3.33.16) teaches that subjects have a right to revolt against a tyrant and to even kill him. Normally, regicide is, however, also considered a great sin, according to such authoritative dharma texts as the *Gautama Dharmasūtra* (20.1).

Rites of Passage

According to the gṛhyasūtras (dated from c. 800–300 B.C.E.), which focus on domestic matters of classical Indian life, the life of a Hindu proceeds in a succession of periods that must be marked by proper rites in order to insure the safety of the individual; transitional moments are associated with danger. As a person makes the transition from one stage of life to another by means of the sacraments, one avoids danger and moves into a new realm of social reality. From another perspective, a typical Hindu is born ontologically and socially undeveloped. It is the rites of passage that provide the ritual means to full mature development.

The various classical Hindu rites of passage are called *saṃskāras*, a term that can be imperfectly translated as sacraments. If one examines the Sanskrit term etymologically, one finds that it is connected to purity or the act of purifying as well as to memory. It is thus associated with the following notions: making perfect, refining, polishing, and consecration. The term *saṃskāra* is related to verbs meaning composing, making perfect, or preparing correctly.[30] Each saṃskāra is an action that transforms the person going through the rite, and it removes defects from that person's body.[31] Although the number of such sacraments differs according to various religious authorities, there are generally sixteen recognized in classical Hinduism.[32] Some of these sacraments begin before conception of a child and end with one's death; not all of these domestic rites are observed or considered essential by all Hindus. The major sacraments that are still observed today by many Hindus are initiation, marriage, and death. A review of the traditional sacraments, however, provides a useful context in which to understand the three major rites that continue to persist.

Childhood Rites

There are three rites that traditionally occur before a person is born. The first is called the *garbhādhāna*, and it is performed by a married couple in order to promote conception. This rite is performed anytime during the fourth to sixteenth night after a wife's menstrual period ends. If the rite is performed before this time, when a wife is in a state of pollution due to her menstrual period, a husband also risks becoming polluted by contact with his wife at this inauspicious time. Moreover, if a couple were to have sexual relations during this forbidden period, the couple is technically guilty of abortion because semen is shed in vain. If a couple wants to conceive a child of a particular sex, they can engage in sexual intercourse on even days of the week for a male and odd-numbered days of the week for a female. Due to the cultural stress upon the importance of a male son to perform ancestral rites and carry on the family bloodline, a second prebirth rite is the *puṃsavana* for the procuring of a male child. Initially, this rite was performed during the third or fourth month of pregnancy, but later legal authorities recommend enacting the rite before the fetus moves in the womb. The central action of the rite involves inserting the juice of a banyan tree, in the evening, into the right nostril (the auspicious one) of the wife as sacred mantras (formulas/verses) are recited. The third prebirth rite is the *simantonnayana* (hair parting) in order to ensure the safety of the child in the womb. This rite occurs around the fourth or fifth month of pregnancy, and it is associated with the belief that the mind of the fetus begins to develop about this time. In preparation for the rite an expectant mother fasts and preliminary rites are performed. With the wife seated to the west of a sacred fire, the husband handles an even number of unripe *udumbara* fruits, three bunches of sacred grass (*darbha*), and a porcupine quill that he uses to part her hair, beginning from the front of her head. Later authorities add the practice of making a red mark on the wife to dispel evil spirits to which a pregnant woman is especially vulnerable. The rite is intended to secure safe delivery of a child, prosperity for the mother, and long life to the unborn child.

The birth sacrament (*jātakarma*) occurs after the safe delivery of the infant but before the actual cutting of the umbilical cord, and it involves a series of ritual actions to instill in the child things needed for a long and healthy life, such as breath, speech, and nourishment.[33] For the production of intelligence, a child is given honey and ghee, (clarified butter), or sometimes just ghee, with a gold spoon. Sometimes the child is given a secret name at this moment. In order to ensure the long life of the child, the father recites sacred mantras near the navel or the right (auspicious) ear of the child. The final action involves a rite for strength of the child, which includes praising the mother for bearing a male. Then the umbilical cord is severed. At around the tenth or twelfth day after birth, the name-giving (*nāsakarana*) sacrament is performed. A name identifies a child's social status, and it protects a child because he or she is also given a secret name. Besides a family and secret name, a child will be given a popular name for public use. The actual names of a child depend on their connection to celestial constellations for the secret name, the name of the deity presiding over the month of birth, and the name of the family deity. If a child belongs to a family with a long history of tragedies, a repulsive name might be given to the child to protect it. In normal circumstances, guidelines for choosing the name of a girl involves an uneven number of syllables that end in a long vowel, and is easy to pronounce, whereas a boy's name consists of two or four syllables, an initial sonant, a middle semivowel, and an unvoiced aspiration or long vowel at the end.[34]

Traditionally, there are four other sacraments associated with childhood. The first formal outing (*niskarmana*) is celebrated by making a swastika, a sign of immortality, in the courtyard of the home or near the child. The mother scatters rice, a symbol of abundance and life, and the father concludes this simple rite by holding the child as it gazes at the sun, a symbol of god. The first feeding (*annaprātana*) marks the first solid food eaten by the child. This rite is performed after the fourth month of life. The appearance of teeth also serves as a signal for this rite. Depending on the results desired by the parents for the child, the father feeds the child different kinds of food. If the parents desire a long life for their child, the father feeds it rice and honey, or curds and rice for keen senses, or a combination of rice and ghee for an intellectually brilliant child. The third sacrament in this childhood sequence is the tonsure (*chūdarsa*) ceremony performed for long life. After the head of the child is moistened with water, prayers accompany cutting the hair. The hair is usually disposed in a secret place in order to prevent harm to the child. The topknot is retained on a male's head in a particular location and style according to family tradition. A final sacrament that is later in origin is boring the ears (*karsavedha*), which probably originated for ornamental purposes, although it became connected in the popular imagination to the prevention of certain diseases. The children of the Brahmin and Kṣatriya castes use gold needles, whereas members of the Vaiśya and Śūdra castes use, respectively, silver and iron needles, although some legal authorities allow iron needles for all castes. It is permissible to combine some of these rites into a single ceremony.

Rite of Initiation

There are five sacraments connected to education for male children. A later addition to the sequence of sacraments is the *vidyārambha* (learning the Sanskrit alphabet) from one's father. Prior to the initiation (*upanayana*) rite or in combination with it, the vedārambha marks the commencement of vedic study by a young man, and the *kesānta* or *godāna* represents the shaving of the student's beard. A rite called *samāvartama*, which means returning from the home of the guru (teacher), marks the end of the period of studentship. It is also called *snāna* (bathing) to indicate the necessity of a final bath that signifies crossing an ocean of learning. The end of studentship presupposes that a student is given permission to return home by his teacher and that the student pays the instructor for services rendered. The crucial educational sacrament is, however, the upanayana (initiation) rite.

The initiation (*upanayana*) rite is limited to males of the top three castes (Brahmins, Kṣatriyas, and Vaiśyas), although distinctions based on these three different castes are stressed at different points throughout the ceremony. It is possible to see these caste distinctions reflected in the different ages for beginning the period of studentship, different types of skin used to make the loincloth (*kaupīna*), differences in the material to make the sacred thread (*vajñopavita*), and a distinction made in the material of the staff (*daṇḍa*) and its length. Thus the caste that the individual is eventually to enter after studentship is emphasized throughout the rite. Before the actual ceremony, several preparatory events occur, including propitiating the auspicious god Gaṇeśa, the elephant-headed god, and several other deities; smearing the body of the initiate with a yellow substance; tucking a silver ring into his topknot; and instruction to remain silent during the night prior to the rite. The command for the student to remain silent is suggestive, because silence is connected to what is undetermined (ŚB 7.2.2.14), which is certainly true of the status of the student at this point. The yellow substance represents a color symbolically connected to the southern direction. The southern direction is associated with the Śūdra caste, which is the status of all males at birth and before the rite of initiation is concluded.[35] The south is also the direction of Yama, Lord of death, and yellow is symbolically associated with the demonic residents of Yama's realm.[36] These preparatory practices suggest the young male's return to an embryonic state, a condition of ambiguity and paradox due to his transitional status, in preparation for his spiritual and social rebirth.

After the young man eats his final meal with his mother, he is now symbolically separated from her by a symbolic cutting of the umbilical cord. The student is now prepared for his second birth. Sitting with his teacher north of a sacred fire, the teacher sits facing eastward, while the student faces west. The teacher recites the sacred *Sāvitrī Mantra* (RV 3.62.10) in Gāyatrī verse to a Brahmin student and uses other verses for students representing other castes. The teaching of this sacred mantra (formula) signals the second birth of the child, because the teacher is regarded as the father of the student and the mantra is understood as his second mother (MS 2.170). The student is ontologically transformed by the rite and is now called twice-born (*dvija*); his initiation represents his second or spiritual rebirth from his teacher. Moreover, the student is purified of all sin and evil in his present existence and after death, and he is now fit for union with the highest reality.

Besides the giving of a sacred mantra during the rite, the teacher ties a girdle (*mekhalā*) around the student three times and invests him with a sacred thread. This girdle possesses a mystical power by means of its ability to bind.[37] And it serves as a symbolic umbilical cord connected to the rebirth of the student and protection from evil powers.[38] On a more practical level, the girdle functions as a sort of "chastity belt" that reminds a student of his vow of celibacy for the duration of his studentship.[39] The sacred thread (*yajñopavīta*) is made of cotton and is worn by all the three top castes in the social hierarchy, although distinctions are also made according to caste. The sacred thread is equal to the height of a man, which is measured in terms of ninety-six times his four fingers, which symbolize the four states of the inner essence of a person that are associated with waking, dreaming, dreamless sleep, and silence (MāU 3–7). The three folds of the sacred thread represent the three threads (*guṇas*) or three subtle elements (*sattva*, *rajas*, and *tamas*) which constitute primal matter from which the universe and everything within it evolved at the moment of creation. In order that the *sattvaguṇa* or good quality of reality might predominate in a person, the cord is twisted upward. The three threads remind a person that he must repay three debts: to his ancestors, the ancient seers, and the gods. The knot that ties the three cords is called *brahmangranthi* and symbolizes three gods: Brahmā, Viṣṇu, and Śiva. The function of the sacred thread is to implement a cosmic harmony and human unity. Moreover, the sacred thread binds a person to the source of all life that keeps one alive but also dependent. The sacred thread is usually worn over the left shoulder and crosses to the right side, but is reversed when the weaver engages in funerary or memorial rites.

After purifying the student with water and initiating him, the teacher makes the new initiate gaze at the sun. The sun represents the cosmic law that governs the entire universe, a place of immortality, and the unchanging source of all-consuming power.[40] The sun gives to the student vitality (*ojas*), physical strength (*bala*), and beauty. This act indicates that the ancient god of fire Agni, who is identified with the sun and functions as the director of the rites or the great priest, is the ultimate teacher of the student (RV 3.2.14; 8.49.1; 6.16.1; 10.7.5). In a profound sense, the student witnesses the symbol of the cosmic law by gazing at the sun, which is also connected to rebirth in Indian culture.[41]

The life of studentship (*brahmacārin*) is closely associated in the Hindu imagination with a life of asceticism (*tapas*). The student engages in such ascetic practices as fasting, observing silence for long periods of time, begging for food, remaining awake at night, sleeping on the ground, being isolated in the forest, standing for prolonged periods of time, and practicing chastity. By filling the world with his asceticism, the student protects the orthodox brahmanic way of life, according to the *Atharva Veda* (11.5). The student's connection to asceticism (*tapas*) involves the generation of heat that assists him to transcend ordinary abilities and his human condition.[42]

Besides the change in the student's ontological state, there is also a change in his social condition. From his former profane state of ignorance, inequality, and irresponsibility, the student is incorporated into a new social condition of knowledge, quality, and adult responsibility. The ceremony is not merely a passport to the literary tradition of the culture; it is also a necessity for entrance into orthodox Hindu society and marriage to an Aryan female, marking acceptance of the person as a full member of society. For those males who fail to complete the rite, there are severe social consequences. These individuals are called *vrātyas*, social outcasts excluded from the sacred vedic literature and Aryan marriage (MS 2.39–40). The noninitiate is excluded from performance of rites, keeping a domestic fire, eating with close relatives, and is unable to marry. There is some evidence that the initiation rite included women during the early part of Indian history, but women were eventually excluded from the ceremony. Thereafter, marriage served as an equivalent to the male's rite of initiation and membership into adult society for a female.

Rite of Marriage

With respect to the sacrament of marriage (*vivāha*), it is important to note that the details of the ceremony vary according to the textual authority. There are also regional differences throughout India. There are, however, some common elements in classical Hinduism. On the morning of their wedding day, the bride and groom purify themselves with a bath. The groom proceeds to the home of the bride to retrieve her. While at the home of the bride, the groom is honored by the bride's father with an offering of an auspicious drink of honey and curds. Before the bride is given away, the names of ancestors of both parties are recited. Then her father formally gives the bride to the groom, who grabs her right hand, which is symbolic of taking charge and taking responsibility for her. Then, the couple travels to the home of the groom. Sitting near a sacred fire along with a priest, the couple offers ghee and rice to the fire before they circle it, with the groom leading the bride. A highlight of the ceremony occurs when thé bride mounts a millstone, a symbol of firmness, to the north of the fire with her right foot. This act is symbolic of devotion and fidelity. Thereupon, the couple takes seven steps toward the northern direction treading on rice, which possesses a symbolic connection to fertility. After the couple is sprinkled with holy water, the husband reaches over the bride's right shoulder and touches her heart. During the evening, the couple gazes at the Pole Star, a symbol of faithfulness. The nuptial ceremony is followed by three days of continence. On the fourth night, the husband may perform the rite for conception, and this is followed by the consummation of the marriage.

Marriage goes beyond joining two families together and transforming strangers into relatives, because two descent groups are united. The groom's side gains a worker, whereas the bride's side looses an economic member and some goods and/or money in the form of a dowry. Thereby, economic goods, labor, duties, and privileges are distributed through marriage—in addition to establishing a new domestic situation, socially sanctioning sexual relationships, and producing progeny.[43]

The Final Rite of Passage

The final sacrament is the funeral (*antyeṣṭi*) of a deceased person. Although there are exceptions for young children and holy persons, the most common means of disposal of the dead is cremation. Why is this method of disposal preferred over burial? To answer such a question involves grasping the three possible fates of a body: it can be eaten as carrion, which then turns to excrement; it can be buried, and then turns into maggots; or it can be burnt and then turns to ash. Hindus tend to agree that the final possibility is preferable.[44]

Cremation is an act of creation and a sacrifice within the Indian cultural context. The symbolism of birth and parturition can be discerned in the mortuary rites. Since the microcosmic human body is symbolically identical to the macrocosmic universe, cremation symbolically resembles the destruction and revitalization of the cosmos, implying that cremation is thus a creative and regenerative activity. Moreover, cremation is a type of heat (*tapas*).[45] If every sacrifice reenacts a primordial sacrifice performed at the origin of the cosmos, when a cadaver is placed on a funeral pyre it feeds the previous fires of creation. This scenario suggests that each death and cremation conforms to a timeless archetypal model, which results in stripping away the specificity of a particular death.[46] Cremation thus becomes a reenactment of that original sacrifice performed at the origin of the cosmos.

The mortuary rite includes preparation of the deceased for the ceremony by washing his or her body, cutting the hair and nails, applying a red mark (*tīlaka*) on the forehead, wrapping the body in cloth, and garlanding it with flowers. The eldest son purifies himself by bathing for his leading role in the funeral. Men or cows carry the body on a litter to the cremation grounds. After the eldest son circumambulates the funeral pyre and sprinkles it with water, he draws three lines on the ground with an iron rod, signifying Yama (Lord of the Dead), time (Kāla, Lord of Cremation), and death. After some sesame seeds are placed into the mouth of the deceased, the body is lifted upon the funeral pyre. In some cases the wife lies beside her husband if she is alive, but her brother-in-law calls her back. Finally, the funeral pyre is set ablaze by the eldest son, an act accompanied by hymns for the departed, invocation of deceased ancestors, and a request of Yama, Lord of the Dead, to give the deceased a comfortable place in the afterworld. Additional deities are asked to help the deceased. A designated mourner, after carrying a water jug with a hole in the back of it three times around the burning funeral pyre, breaks of on the mourner's left shoulder, an inauspicious side of the body. After the body is annointed with ghī (a sacred substance made of clarified butter) and the pyre is lit, the skull of the deceased is punctured with a blunt pole in order to release the soul for its journey to the next world. After the passing of a few days, the bones of the deceased are collected, and on the tenth day after the cremation the eldest son offers a ball of rice. About a year later a commemoration rite (*sapiṇḍīnkarṇa*) takes place for the departed in order to unite the ghost of the departed with its ancestors.

From one perspective, death represents a return to the five elements that constitute a body. Because the soul is immortal, it is reborn in another body. From this perspective, a reborn person is never entirely unique or new at birth. Likewise, a person is never completely gone when dead because a person is believed to live again in a different form.[47] Therefore, nothing is completely lost at death, which represents a return to the elements of nature and a journey onward in another life.

Concluding Remarks

The varṇa (caste) system permeates Indian social culture. But it is also possible to find its influence in the ritual sphere, cosmology, divine hierarchy, and the natural world. Certain gods are more closely associated, for instance, with particular castes, such as Indra with the warrior caste and Agni with the priestly caste. In other words, the varṇa system reflects the very structure of reality for traditional Hinduism. It also represents an ideal and rationalized system of classification for a hierarchical social system. But it is not necessarily a static structure. Although it may sound strange to outsiders, caste is not a common part of the indigenous vocabulary; it is jāti (subcaste) that is more commonly used by people in everyday discourse and that determines the boundaries for social and religious interactions.

Not only are there ways to move up the jāti system by imitating the lifestyle of the Brahmin caste; the various rites of passage also enable people to perfect themselves, and indicates that life is a process of development into a full human and social being. At the end of the process into adulthood, a person is able to accept more responsibility and to past on the dharmic tradition to future generations. This is not a system designed to encourage radical or sudden change, because it provides for changes only very slowly over a long period of time. In short, it is a social system ideally suited for stability. The social system and the rites of passage that are a part of its fabric protect the members of the society from chaos and danger, which makes life possible.

Moreover, the rites of passage affect the entire person and not just his or her spiritual side. By means of these rites, an individual is shaped, refined, and perfected into an adult member of society. This is both an outer and inner process that is necessarily visible and invisible. Contemporary Hindus do not observe all the rites of passage. Generally speaking, some early childhood rites are combined or not observed, while marriage and funeral rites are more widely practiced at the present time.

5

The Experiential Nature of Hinduism

Over the course of history, many followers of different kinds of Hinduism came to accept the basic proposition that spiritual experience is indispensable for salvation. The precise nature of this experience is open to interpretation, although it does involve a modification of the content of one's consciousness, and the modification can be either intentional or nonintentional. The intentional type of modification involves an awareness of something objective that is external to one's consciousness, and it originates from interpreting or misinterpreting objective data. When one interprets such external data one utilizes concepts. By becoming aware of an object, one becomes conscious of something (this is called intentionality), the nonintentional type of modification of consciousness, on the other hand, does not depend on something external. A nonintentional mode of consciousness involves feeling, for instance feeling enigmatically sad or happy.

A spiritual experience can manifest a variety of forms that include feeling absolutely unified with the world, which is called panenhenic feeling; or a person can have a more numinous type of experience, when one experiences something as wholly other than oneself—a mysterious power that repels and a fascinating power that attracts at the same time; or a person may have a more contemplative type of experience that does not postulate an external other, but does give a feeling that the normal subject-object distinction disappears. Different types of feelings and attitudes are generated by the numinous and contemplative kinds of experiences. Fear, trembling, respect, and humility are examples of such feelings for the former, whereas the contemplative experience is more apt to produce serenity, confidence, calm, and happiness. The numinous tends to be associated with a devotional type of religiosity, while the contemplative tends to be mystical, which creates self-awareness, a sense of wisdom, and equanimity. The second part of this book focuses on the devotional type of religious experience typical of the numinous experience. In this chapter, we will concentrate on the contemplative type of spiritual experience by examining two examples, that is, Yoga and Advaita Vedānta.

Because the school of Yoga presupposes the metaphysical context of Sāṃkhya thought, it will also be necessary to include a look at this school. Thus we have an opportunity to review three of the major six schools of Indian philosophy and two distinct types of contemplative or mystical experience within the Hindu tradition.

Indian schools of philosophy are distinct from Western forms of philosophy in that each of them is conceived as a valid path to salvation. In other words, Indians do not draw the sharp distinction common in the West between philosophy and religion. The Nyāya and Vaiśeṣika schools can be generally characterized as atomistic, pluralistic, realistic, and theistic, while the Mīmāṃsā school is primarily concerned with philosophy of language and ritual. These three schools are not covered here, but they are discussed in the companion reader of primary sources that is intended to accompany this book.

The six schools are called *darśana* or viewpoint, which is a term derived from a Sanskrit root word that includes the notions of seeing, a way of seeing, or a vision. A common synonym for viewpoint is *vāda*, which means theory. It is not unusual for subschools or a particular thesis on a specific problem to be called a vāda. Each of the six Indian systems is classified as orthodox by virtue of the fact that they accept the authority of the ancient Vedas, which makes them *āstika* (affirmer). The opposite philosophical systems are called *nāstika* (nonaffirmer), which are philosophical systems that do not accept the authority of the Vedas, such as the materialistic Cārvākas, the Buddhists, and the Jains. From the perspective of the orthodox schools that accept the Vedas, such philosophies represent examples of heretical movements. The philosophical texts of the orthodox Indian schools were constructed of texts arranged according to *sūtras* (brief prose aphorisms) and *kārikās* (verses). Because of the brevity of these aphorisms and verses, it is possible to infer that they were intended to be memorized. The sūtras (literally, threads), being brief and cryptic, needed the aid of a commentary (*bhāṣya*) in order for a reader to comprehend them. In a historical sense, Indian schools of thought developed by means of commentaries upon the pithy, abstruse, and condensed aphorisms of the sūtras. These also developed commentaries on the commentaries, which were called subcommentaries (*vārttika*). Thinkers also composed glosses (*ṭikā*) that were intended to provide additional elucidation, and they attempted to interpret the original primary sources and commentarial interpretations. The subcommentaries and glosses often ventured beyond the primary texts by extrapolating, criticizing, or clarifying.

The style of these six orthodox schools is scholastic in the sense that a philosophical proposition is enunciated and then an objection is raised and answered. The author then progresses to consider another objection and replies to it in an ongoing process, which also suggests that the style of Indian philosophy is dialogical and comparative by nature. It is also economic in the sense that it seeks to explain concepts without wasted motion or effort. The various early texts endured a long process of redaction, and they were not often the work of a single author. Although particular texts are identified with a single author, it is preferable to view these texts as products of a particular community of scholars or tradition (*sampradāya*). Nonetheless, later philosophers composed independent works (*śāstras*) that explained the position of the school in a more comprehensive and systematic manner.

There are certain criteria that must be met by any Indian philosophical system. It must, for instance, be practical. This means that the purpose of philosophy was to solve the problems of human existence, which was usually understood to mean the achievement of liberation from the world. Thus each of the Indian orthodox systems of philosophy was understood as a path to liberation. The various philosophical schools not only sought the truth but also thought that practice was the primary test of truth. By insisting on practice as a test for the truth, these philosophical schools tended to stress introspection. With respect to the truth, each school insisted that all of its concepts must be accurate and embody a theory of truth. This entailed that no mutually contradictory statements be contained within the philosophical system. Finally, the philosophy must be adequate, that is, able to explain all elements that are connected to achieving liberation.

Sāṃkhya and Yoga

The history of Sāṃkhya and Yoga is very complex and open to considerable scholarly debate. According to one scholar, the origin of Yoga can be traced to a wandering group of ascetics called Vrātyas who are identified as Aryan, but who did not belong to the orthodox Brāhmaṇic priesthood.[1] They belonged to a group that worshiped a primal god known by different names. Historically, Sāṃkhya represented a later development emerging from the Yoga tradition.[2] Due to some inherent differences, they eventually developed their own systems. It is probably more accurate to look for the origins of these two movements in a variety of traditions and not attribute their origins to any one source.[3] These systems have their roots, for instance, in early vedic speculation concerning creation. There are also passages in the Brāhmaṇa texts and early Upaniṣads that have significance for the later systematic formulation of these systems of thought. In the *Kaṭha Upaniṣad* (I.3.10–11), for instance, there appears the first lucid reference to Sāṃkhya philosophy, which dates to around the fourth century B.C.E.[4] This work influenced later texts like the *Śvetasvatara Upaniṣad* (third century B.C.E.) and the *Bhagavad Gītā* (c. first century C.E.) Another early form of Sāṃkhya appeared in a late section of the epic *Mahābhārtha* called the *Mokṣadharma* (teaching of liberation). In this work the insights of Sāṃkhya are accepted by Yoga. Sāṃhkya and Yoga are not sharply distinguished in epic and popular thought.[5] The primary difference between them is associated with their different ways of gaining salvation.

According to Hindu lore, the legendary founder of the Sāṃkhya system was named Kapila. However, there is nothing definite that can be affirmed about him. Kapila is mentioned by the compiler Īśvarakrishna as handing down the tradition to other disciples. Basically, Kapila is a mythical figure. In fact, Indian texts cite an additional twenty-five teachers of whom little is known for certain. Such a list may reflect an attempt to create an ancient pedigree for the school.

It is only with the works of Īśvarakrishna and Patañjali that the initial systematic and independent systems of thought appear with the formulations, respectively, of Sāṃkhya and Yoga. The work of Īśvarakrishna is placed at the beginning of the fourth century C.E., whereas Patañjali compiled the *Yoga Sūtra* around 300 C.E. (This Patañjali must not be confused with the second-century B.C.E. grammarian of the same name.) Patañjali does not claim to be the originator of the yogic path, although he does confess to being its compiler and preserver. His compilation of the *Yoga Sūtra* is dated to the middle of the fourth century by comparing its sophisticated development to epic literature and the Yoga Upaniṣads, and considering its criticism of the Yogācāra school of Mahāyāna Buddhism.[6] There are some scholars who identify the *Yoga Sūtra* as primarily a Sāṃkhya work.[7]

Both Patañjali and Īśvarakrishna viewed themselves as compilers of an older tradition. In fact, Patañjali admits that he was merely collecting and correcting the doctrines and technical traditions (YS 1.1). Īśvarakrishna claimed to be summarizing the contents of a text called the *Ṣaṣṭitantra* (Science of Sixty Topics), which represented a stereotyped way of discussing Sāṃkhya. There has been considerable disagreement about the contents and authorship of this text. In contrast, there has been a bit more scholarly agreement about the yogic tradition and the fact that Patañjali was attempting to combine two different ways of yoga: the method of the eight-limbed yoga and the practice of suppressing mental activities.[8] Whatever the dates for the four major parts of the compiled text, it is important to be aware that the text evolved over a period of time before its final redaction.

Like other Indian philosophical schools, Sāṃkhya and Yoga gave rise to commentaries on the fundamental texts. The realism of the Sāṃkhya school in which the world is considered real and independent of our perception of it was upheld by such commentaries as the *Light of Argumentation* (*Yuktidīpikā*), around the sixth century C.E., and *The Moonlight on the Sāṃkhya Principles of Reality* by Vācaspati Miśra, in the tenth century C.E. Important commentaries on the *Yoga Sūtra* were provided by Vyāsa between the sixth and seventh centuries, and by Advaita Vedānta thinker Vācaspati Miśra (c. 850), author of the *Tattvavaiśāradī*, which was a gloss on Vyāsa's commentary. An additional subcommentary is attributed to Śaṅkara, although there is some question about the authenticity of this work. King Bhoja (eleventh century C.E.) composed his work entitled the *Royal Sun Bird* (*Rājamārtaṇḍa*). During the sixteenth century, Vijñanabhikṣu is credited with a commentary called the *Yoga-vārttika* and a shorter summary entitled *Yogasāra-saṃgraha*.

From an etymological perspective, the term *sāṃkhya* was derived from a Sanskrit root that means reckoning, summing up, or calculation.[9] The term *yoga* was probably derived from a root term that means to bind together, hold fast, or yoke.[10] From ancient times, both terms referred to a method of salvation. The path of salvation for Sāṃkhya was through knowing, whereas Yoga accomplished its goal by doing something in the sense of following a prescribed regime of practice that included meditation.

A basic presupposition shared by Sāṃkhya and Yoga is that three forms of suffering characterize human existence: personal, external, and cosmic or supernatural. Personal suffering refers to bodily and mental pain. External and cosmic sufferings are related to a person's natural environment and the forces of nature or the gods.[11] It is not sufficient simply to identify these forms of suffering, because the goal of both systems is to overcome the various forms of suffering. Therefore, universal suffering has an intrinsic positive value by stimulating the quest for liberation. For the Sāṃkhya school this quest follows a path of intuitive discrimination of the knower (*puruṣa*), the manifest world, and the unmanifest. Accepting this metaphysical background, the Yoga school specifies an eight-step path to liberation.

The Dualistic School

The term *sāṃkhya* means enumeration, calculation, or relating to numbers, and a practitioner is someone who reasons or discriminates correctly.[12] The Sāṃkhya school views existence in terms of a dualism between matter (*prakṛti*) and self or pure consciousness (*puruṣa*). Matter possesses two major dimensions: unmanifest and manifest. What becomes manifest preexisted in unmanifest matter. Consequently, nothing new is created, because the result of the creative process preexists in the cause (*satkāryavāda*). This suggests that the world is ontologically real, and implies that the term "matter" is used in two different senses: uncreated primordial matter, and created and creative matter.

However, the most important characteristics of matter are the *guṇas* (qualities or constituents), which originally possessed a cosmogonic origin and later developed a psychological function.[13] The term *guṇa* means string, cord, or thread. It describes, for instance, the strands that constitute a rope. For the Sāṃkhya school, it represents the quality or attribute of a thing, and it includes the whole range of subjective and objective reality, although a guṇa is not a thing in itself. It is also not a predisposition or a phenomenal structure. The school identifies the three qualities according to color: *sattva* (pure), *tamas* (dark), and *rajas* (red). The pure quality is characterized by pleasure and illumination; it is buoyant and shining. The tamas quality represents indifference and restraint; it is heavy and enveloping. The rajas quality is characterized by pain and actuation; it is also stimulating and moving. All three qualities exist simultaneously in every physical, biological, and psychomental phenomenon, although they exist in unequal proportion within things. This suggests that the qualities are constantly in tension with each other. When the qualities are, in a state of equilibrium there is no creation or evolution. Once this equilibrium is disturbed, the manifest world emerges. Thus the qualities possess an objective and a subjective character, in the sense that they objectively constitute the phenomena of the external world and they subjectively support psychomental life.[14] The three qualities are complementary and dynamic principles. They not only interact with and mutually rely on each other, it is possible for one of them to dominate the others. The operation of this tripartite process is compared to the way that a wick, oil, and flame of a lamp function in unison to produce light. It is probably best to conceive of the three guṇas as building blocks of mental and material phenomena. It is also significant that the qualities function for the sake of the self (*puruṣa*), much as a lamp does for a person in a dark room (SK 13).

It was noted above that the self is neither creative nor created. Therefore, it has no attributes or relations. In other words, it is not connected with the other twenty-four principles associated with matter, and it is not constituted by the three qualities. The self (*puruṣa*) is rather discriminating, subjective, specific, and conscious. The self cannot think or act because it represents a sheer contentless, nonintentional presence that is identified with consciousness, and possesses nothing in common with ordinary mental awareness. This implies that it is incapable of performing an action or intuitively knowing itself.[15] Since it is simply present, it is not ontologically involved with matter. It is a reality entirely opposite to the created order (SK 19). The self is also characterized as being a witness, possessed of isolation or freedom, indifferent, a spectator, and inactive. Thus the self is simply present in the universe and views the modifications of the world, but is not truly engaged within the world. By functioning as a witness of the world, the self appears to itself as what it is not. In other words, it appears as the world, and the world appears as if it possesses consciousness. Thus the self and matter appear as what they are not. The functioning of the self as a witness results in its negation of itself. This is not as detrimental as it might appear because the self attains what it is in fact by appearing as what it is not, as we shall see.

The *Sāṃkhyakārikā* compiled by Īśvarakrishna does not have much to say about how the self and matter come together because the text is primarily concerned with relating why and what happens when they do come together. The text asserts that there is an absolute separation between matter and the self, suggesting that they are simply co-present, and merely in proximity to each other, never in actual contact. Due to the proximity of the two principles, an interaction occurs that results in the transformation of matter. However, it should be noted that the self is not a direct cause of the appearance of the world, because the self is simply there as a witness. But the presence of the self functions as a catalyst in releasing the causal process of transformation in the primordial matter. Consequently, without the presence of the self, the world remains unmanifested. A reader could ask the following: What is the point of the interaction?

The purpose of this interaction is to bring about the release of the self. In fact, the self is not actually bound to the world; it only appears bound to it due to indiscriminate knowledge (SK 62). Matter (*prakṛti*) and self (*puruṣa*) cooperate, for example, like a blind man and a lame man, with each one benefiting from the capacities of the other (SK 21). Actually, the self is the only principle that benefits due to the fact that it is free, whereas matter functions only for the sake of the self and is able to function due to the self. (In sharp contrast to the Sāṃkhya doctrine, the *Yoga Sūtra* states that the evolution of the world was due to ignorance [*avidyā*] instead of the interaction of the self and matter [YS 2.23–27].)

According to the Sāṃkhya school, when matter is stimulated by its proximity to the self, the basic principles (*tattvas*) emerge. This is not, therefore, a creation from nothing; it is rather a progressive unfolding of what already potentially exists. The first thing to evolve from primordial matter is the intellect (*buddhi*), which gives birth to the I-maker (*ahamkāra*) At this early point, the process of evolution is vertical. With the emergence of the I-maker, evolution becomes horizontal; the group of sixteen principles that emerge include the following elements: mind (*manas*), the five senses, the five organs of action, and the five subtle elements (*tanmātras*) that gave birth to the five gross elements. It is possible to compare this process to that of a magnet and pieces of iron filings, because the former influences the filings by being merely next to them. Their proximity does not cause any change in any of them. But there is a force that pulls them toward each other.

The intellect (*buddhi*) ascertains and decides in the process of perception (SK 30). It represents the will of a person in the sense of being the source of a person's fundamental strivings or urges. This suggests that it is the locus of both suffering and salvation.[16] The I-maker (*ahamkāra*) is the organ that forms the concept of ego; it represents pure self-awareness. However, it plays a vital role in bondage because the self erroneously identifies itself with the I-maker. This means that the self views itself as the agent of actions, as one who desires, a striver for ends, and the possessor and enjoyer of ideas. The self thinks that it is seeing, hearing, being wealthy, and so forth. The I-maker at this stage is dominated by rajas guṇa because it is concerned with action. Therefore, the self indiscriminately thinks that it is part of the process of emergence that entails rebirth and suffering. In contrast to the pure consciousness of the self, intellect, I-maker (egoity), and mind combine to form an internal organ that executes intellectual awareness of the present, past, and future by means of discerning, self-awareness, and intentionality. Pure consciousness cannot know or intuit itself, and it is the intellect that is aware of consciousness and the mind that is connected to ordinary mental awareness.

For the Sāṃkhya school, salvation and freedom already exist in fact. As previously noted, the self is never really bound; it only appears to be in bondage because it appears to itself as what it is not. It appears, for instance, as unconscious, whereas matter appears as consciousness. Thus both self and matter appear as what they are not. When a person constantly meditates upon the knowledge "I am not, nothing belongs to me, I do not exist," this knowledge becomes pure, incontrovertible, and absolute and leads to liberation (SK 64). This type of procedure leads to a knowledge (*jñāna*) that recognizes the absolute separation of matter and self. This knowledge resides in the intellect (*buddhi*). It is a result of the study and analysis of the principles (*tattvas*) that constitute the manifest world. But this knowledge results from reversing our ordinary process of knowing. This eventually leads to a fundamental change in the basic orientation of a person. This entire process of knowing implies an intuitive realization or discrimination that separates pure consciousness from whatever is not consciousness. Patañjali did not share the Sāṃkhya view at this point, because he denies that simple metaphysical truth could lead one to salvation. Patañjali argues instead that there is an ancient technique that one must follow and master.

Sāṃkhya creates an instructive narrative about bondage and liberation by comparing the relation of the self and matter to that of a spectator (self) and an actress (matter). Within the context of this tale, the spectator is a calm and unmoving observer, whereas matter is active and works arduously, like an actress. Although the observer and actress exist in close proximity of one another, their essential natures are not altered by the close contact. But during the contact, the observer becomes captivated by the appearance, grace, and charm of the actress. Then, the spectator reaches a point when he becomes aware of himself as a pure spirit. At this point, he looses interest in the actress and turns away. Once the spectator turns away, the actress terminates her performance.

The spectator leaves the performance of the actress because he is able to expel everything from his consciousness with the exception of consciousness itself. Therefore, all notions of I, ego, striving, thought, and processes of ordinary existence are eliminated, which leaves a person with pure consciousness. Once this awareness has been attained a person has attained isolation (*kaivalya*). This perfect isolation is similar to a mirror devoid of dust or like a lake without a ripple on its surface. Isolation suggests pure, translucent consciousness, which is a radical type of consciousness, without any content. In other words, this consciousness is freed of intentionality because it is no longer conscious of something. This radical and unordinary type of consciousness involves transcendence of the world and the attainment of absolute freedom that is wholly apart from suffering.

The Yoga School

As stated previously, Patañjali compiled the *Yoga Sūtra* from numerous traditions, and he attempted to synthesize them. His synthesis is usually called Rāja yoga (royal yoga), whereas Haṭha yoga (yoga of force) places greater stress on self-realization by means of perfecting the body. This process of perfection involves using various bodily postures and forms of purification in order to unblock energy channels within the body. In the second chapter of the *Yoga Sūtra*, there appear outlines of two different schemes of yoga: Kriyā yoga and the eight-limbed path of Rāja yoga. The former type involves ascetic discipline, self-analysis, and devotion; it leads to the development of meditative concentration.

Based on what Patañjali inherited, we can identify two forms of meditation: *samādhi* (concentration) and *samāpattih* (unification). These forms possess different structures, and the latter form represents a method to appropriate existentially a certain belief or truth because the belief possesses no real object; it only possesses representations and ideas.[17] Although there are two forms of meditation in the text, Patañjali appears to have conceived of them as a whole, which is the way that we will treat them.

Patañjali identifies the technique of yoga as "the restriction of the fluctuation of mind-stuff" (YS 1.2). It is significant to know that the mind is in a state of flux, agitation, and distraction. The reason for this condition can be traced to two generators of mental flux: sense activity and activity of the subconscious. If we concentrate attention on the subconscious, it is possible to discern impressions (*vāsanās*) left on the mind (*citta*) through the course of prior rebirths from experiences in other modes of life. These impressions represent latencies in the subconscious that unceasingly feed the psychomental stream. This scenario suggests that life is a constant discharge of impressions that manifest themselves through the mind, and that render human existence into an unbroken actualization of subconscious experiences. Other types of impressions are those from previous mental functions (*samskāras*), which are latent deposits located in the subconscious generated by the mind, which emerge into our thoughts and actions. This forms a circuit from the mind to the impressions and from the impressions back to the mind, which is analogous to a plant and its roots. If the plant is cut, leaving its roots, the plant will grow again. A similar type of circuit exists between human consciousness and the subconscious: the psychomental states stimulate actions that give rise to other psychomental states. This pattern means that states of consciousness are the result of the actualization of subliminal latencies that feed the psychomental states. Therefore, it is essential for the yogin to sever the subconscious-conscious circuit by destroying both types of impressions.

In order to break the subconscious-conscious circuit and control the mind, one must practice concentration on a single point (*ekāgratā*). By concentrating on a single point, a person seeks to bring under control the two major generators of mental flux; namely, sense activity and activity of the subconscious. In his commentary on the text (2.54), Vyāsa compares the calming of the mind and senses to bees that follow a queen bee; they do not rest until the queen does. In order to reach the highest level of concentration, a person must master certain exercises and techniques called members or limbs (*aṇgas*). These are the eight steps of the yogic path: (1) restraints (*yama*); (2) disciplines (*niyama*); (3) bodily attitudes and postures (*āsana*); (4) rhythm of respiration (*prānāyana*); (5) emancipation of sensory activity from the domination of exterior objects (*pratyahāra*); (6) concentration (*dhāranā*); (7) yogic meditation (*dhyāna*); and (8) absorption (*samādhi*). These steps as a whole represent a path that is diametrically opposed to the way a person ordinarily behaves.

By practicing bodily postures, one makes the body stable and immobile, like the image of a person who sits in the lotus posture, forming a perfect isosceles triangle. Because physical effort is greatly reduced, meditation comes more easily and naturally (YS 2.47). Instead of having agitated and unrhythmical breathing, the yogin attempts to control his respiration. Instead of inducing a hypnotic transformation of consciousness,[18] these exercises cause relaxation and ease of mind.

They are part physiological and part psychological.[19] By suspending respiration as long as possible, the yogin can attain to states of consciousness that are not ordinarily available to a person due to the interference of normal respiration. Contrary to the ordinary way of living, the practice of breath control enables a person to achieve a state of continuous consciousness. Rather then the fluctuating mind of a common person, the yogin withdraws his or her senses to facilitate concentration (YS 2.54). This is a repetitive practice that is intended to remove obstacles to true knowledge.[20] Withdrawal of the senses is essential because Hindu thought conceives of the sense organs as reaching outward to touch objects that engage their attention. The eyes, for instance, are thought of as emitting an active beam that shines outward rather than as receiving light impressions. Withdrawal of the senses is intended to control this visual process of externalization. This is analogous to a tortoise withdrawing its extremities at the hint of danger. Therefore, by means of yogic techniques, a person strives against natural human tendencies. In a sense, the yogin follows a path that is essentially antihuman.[21] From one perspective, the yogin appears to want to destroy all that is human, all that keeps the yogin from the unconditioned, or all that retards the yogin attaining freedom. Actually, the control of breathing, body, and mind are an attempt to unify oneself and transcend the world with the attainment of absorption (*samādhi*), a state of primordial knowledge, unity, bliss, and freedom.

Samādhi is an experience of mental pacification that results in the eventual cessation of conscious fluctuations. This does not mean that a person's mind becomes a blank slate. Rather this represents a reflexive and stable awareness of consciousness. In fact, there are types of samādhi that vary, from states associated with the analysis of gross material objects to more subtle states involving reflection on refined objects.[22] Generally speaking, there are two major types of samādhi: *saṃprajñāta*, or ecstatic states connected with objects of cognition that occur externally to the realization of the self (*puruṣa*), and its opposite, *asaṃprajñāta*, or an experience devoid of objects that transcends all mental content. With the second type of samādhi, there is no recognition of the self (*puruṣa*) existing in matter (*prakṛti*). There is no longer the misidentification of matter and self, because this represents a transmental and transconceptual state of identity in which the self is alone by itself. This transformation of identity and understanding represents an awareness of an eternal identity that was previously concealed due to misidentification and misperception of the self.

Before a state of unity can be achieved, it is necessary to purify oneself. This purification includes ethical or moral practices such as the five restraints: nonviolence (*ahiṃsā*), not lying (*satya*), not stealing (*asteya*), sexual abstinence (*brahmacārya*), and nongreed (*aparigraha*). By practicing the disciplines (*niyamas*) one purifies oneself both internally and externally. Internal purification consists in washing away the impurities of the mind (YS 2.32), which helps one to attain one-pointedness of concentration. Hence, one gains control of the senses and attains fitness for knowledge of the self (YS 2.4). The practice of physical purification accompanies disgust with one's own body and detachment from it, which results in the cessation of contact with other bodies. The practice of breath control purifies the yogin of karma that obstructs discriminative knowledge. In order to distinguish karma that is operating in the present and what will come to fruition in the future, Vyāsa compares present karma to a wet cloth that is spread out flat to dry and future karma to cloth that is squeezed into a ball of cloth. Obviously, the former type of cloth (*karma*) will dry out first.[23] By the destruction of the impurity of karma, the light of knowledge is able to shine forth.

For Patañjali, the human mind is possessed of the three qualities (*guṇas*). In its original state the mind is pure. However, it is common for the rajas quality, tamas quality, or a combination of the two to predominate and thus to obstruct the mind. When the sattva quality predominates, consciousness is calm, clear, comprehensible, virtuous, whereas it is agitated, uncertain, and unstable if rajas quality is preponderate, and it is dark, confused, passionate, and bestial when the tamas quality is prevalent. Thus it is apparent that the rajas and tamas qualities are impurities that must be removed from the mind in order for the sattva quality to shine forth (YS 1.2). Moreover, the mind is benighted by karma and the impure five afflictions (*kleśas*): ignorance, egoism, attachment, aversion, and love of life. These afflictions provide the dynamic framework of the phenomenal consciousness. They urge the organism to burst into activity, to feel, to think, or to want. As the basic emotional and motivational forces they lie at the root of all misery.[24] Becoming aware of these various impurities, it is apparent that the mind must strive to return to its original condition, which consists of the steady flow of the sattva quality. If the impurities associated with the body and mind are washed away by following the path of yoga, a person becomes fit to become illuminated (YS 1.16).

It would be useful here to distinguish between ecstasy and enstacy as states achieved through yoga. Ecstasy means to stand (*stasis*) outside (*ex*) of the self, whereas samādhi (enstasy) suggests standing in (*en*) the self. Within the context of yogic practice, ecstasy is preparatory to enstasy. These two represent a continuity of yogic experience, and the process of cessation (*nirodha*) links them together. It is possible to distinguish ecstasy by its illuminating experiences of sattva (pure) consciousness, which is the original condition of the self, for the purpose of liberating the self. Enstasy is an experience that realizes the genuine nature of the self (*puruṣa*) that transcends all worldly tainted experience. In other words, there is no subjective or ego-centered consciousness that can distort the experience. The experience of the sole self represents an awareness that there is nothing left to experience.[25]

To express it somewhat differently, as the impurities of the mind are removed, the mind becomes steady, impurity is gradually destroyed, and the light of wisdom dawns (YS 2.28). When the mind becomes pure it acquires the power of thought-transformation, which represents the four stages of enstasis without support. This means that the mind, which becomes like a transparent crystal, possesses the power to assume the shape of whatever object is presented to it, whether it be the knower, the knowable, or the acts of knowing (YS 1.41). With the removal of impurities, there is an undisturbed flow of super-reflection (*nirvicāra*), which causes enlightenment (YS 1.47). In summary, when the process of purification is complete and the yogin is rid of the obscuring impurities of the five afflictions and karma, knowledge then becomes infinite (YS 4.31). There is no suggestion that the yogin reaches his or her goal by means of self-hypnosis.[26] What the yogin achieves is an introverted and reflexive flow of consciousness that turns awareness upon itself and reflects its own nature.

Non-dual Vedānta School

During the second century B.C.E., the *Vedānta Sūtras* were written by Bādarāyaṇa; they represented an early attempt to systematize the philosophy within the Upaniṣads. This work was revived by Gauḍapāda around 780 C.E. in his commentary on the *Māṇḍūkya Upaniṣad*. According to some scholars, this commentary demonstrates traces of the influence of the Yogācāra and Mādhyamika schools of Mahāyāna Buddhism,[27] while others do not agree about the influence of Buddhism because of the orthodox nature of his system and his conviction that Buddhism represented nihilism and needed to be overcome.[28] The third major figure of this school was Śaṅkara, who was a member of a very orthodox Śaiva or Śakta family of Nambūdiri Brahmins living in Malabar in southern India.[29] Śaṅkara's dates of birth and death are disputed, but he probably lived and worked in the early eighth century. He had a distinguished career as a Hindu reformer; founder of monastic centers; commentator on ancient texts, including several Upaniṣads, the *Bhagavad Gītā*, and *Vedānta Sūtras*; and author of original works such as *Vivekacūḍāmaṇi* (The Crown Jewel of Discrimination) and *Upadeśasāhasrī* (A Thousand Teachings).

These fairly reliable aspects of his life are often overwhelmed by legends that surround his person. According to hagiographical material, his birth was auspicious because the planets were aligned favorably, and it was accompanied by heavenly music and the sweet smell of flowers. The dazzling infant was brilliant with a crescent moon located on the top of his head, symbolic of the god Śiva. Other parts of his body were marked with symbols of the deity, with a trident located on the palm of the infant, an image of a coiled cobra on his chest, and a third eye on his forehead. These marks were indicative of the infant's status as an incarnation of the god. Śaṅkara could speak, read, and write Sanskrit at age two. The child prodigy was blessed with a photographic memory. His father died when he was five years old, but this tragedy did not hinder his development and ability to do extraordinary things, such as the time that he altered the course of a river for the convenience of his mother, or when he overcame being caught in the jaws of a crocodile while bathing in a river. He renounced the world at age eight, and went on a spiritual quest that culminated with his discovery of the truth of nondualism. Such is the idealized portrait of the man.

After being initiated into the *Vedānta Sūtras*, Śaṅkara attempted to purge the text of the distinctive Buddhist traits found in the commentary of Gauḍapāda. Śaṅkara wanted to construct a philosophical edifice based on a direct interpretation of the older Upaniṣad texts.[30] The term *vedānta* literally means "end of the Veda," which suggests that it represents the culmination of the ancient Vedas. The Sanskrit term for nondual is *advaita*. Although there are other forms of Vedānta philosophy, Śaṅkara's school is called Advaita Vedānta or absolute nondualism. What makes it nondual? The simple answer is that reality is one or Brahman.

Before defining Brahman more precisely and discussing its relation to the immortal self (Ātman), it helps to understand Śaṅkara's grasp of the three levels of being: reality, appearance, and the unreal. Reality is that which cannot be sublated by any other experience—that is, the intuitive realization that Brahman is the one genuine reality cannot be contradicted by any other experience. But what does sublation mean? According to Śaṅkara, sublation (*bādha*) is a mental process in which an object or content of consciousness is canceled because it is contradicted by a new experience. Thus one changes one's previous judgment because a new experience rectifies one's prior erroneous belief. This suggests that to be able to sublate something means that it possesses a lower degree of reality. The classical example of this process is to imagine that you are walking along a path at twilight at which time you spy a snake lying in your path, from which you recoil. When the snake fails to move you decide to examine it more closely. Upon closer inspection, you discover that it is not a snake, but rather a piece of rope lying in your path. Thus your erroneous notion of the snake is overcome and you see the true nature of the object. What is it that changes for you? It is your previous judgment that changes because a new experience rectifies one's prior false belief. You have now become aware of the true nature of what you encountered.

Śaṅkara applies sublation to reality and finds that it cannot be sublated. However, appearance can be sublated by other experience. There are three types of things that exist within the realm of appearance. First, real existent entity represents those aspects of experience that can be sublated by reality itself (Brahman). A person's love of a deity is, for instance, based on the distinction between self and nonself. The experience of loving a deity can be sublated by a direct experience of reality because Brahman transcends any relational distinction. The second type of entity within the realm of appearance is the existent, which involves the type of experience that can be sublated by reality or by the previous type of experience of real existents. An example of such an experience would be encountering a friend or a stranger on the street. An ordinary encounter with another person is an experience that can be sublated by experiencing Brahman. Third, appearance also may include an illusory existent, which can be sublated by all other types of experience. A good example would be a mirage in the desert.

The third level of being is the unreal, which can neither be sublated or not sublated by other experience, because it cannot be a content of human experience. Have you ever seen a square circle? Have you ever met the daughter of a virgin?

A square circle or a daughter of a virgin are unreal and can never be encountered except in a person's imagination, hallucinations, or dreams.

In addition to the notion of sublation, Śaṅkara makes a distinction between two types of knowledge: knowledge of ultimate reality (*paravidyā*) and lower knowledge (*aparavidyā*). The former is unique; it is reached immediately and intuitively. It is self-validating, which implies that any other form of knowledge (such as inference or perception) cannot refute it. When a person achieves this higher type of knowledge all other forms of knowing are viewed as compromised by ignorance (*avidyā*). The content of the lower form of knowledge is the phenomenal world. This type of knowledge is valuable, and it can be justified as a practical means of knowing. It is useful to know, for example, that by turning a faucet water will flow, or if you touch a fire, you will burn your hand. This type of knowledge is valid as long as a person does not realize the intuitive insight into the reality of Brahman. In other words, an intuitive realization of Brahman supercedes all other forms of awareness.

Śaṅkara identifies six forms of lower knowledge: perception, comparison, noncognition, inference, postulation, and testimony. Perception yields knowledge of the qualities (such as color, size, and texture) of an object and the relations that constitute an object (such as the universal aspect of a hammer), although it does not yield knowledge of law-like relations between objects. Comparison gives knowledge derived from judgments of similarity, whereas noncognition represents judgments of absence, such as a specific object being nonexistent at a particular time and place. There is, for example, no pink elephant in your room. If a pink elephant were present, you would perceive it. Inference involves a relation between what is inferred and a reason for the basis from which it is made, suggesting that inference is based on an apprehension of universal agreement between two things, while a postulation is the assumption of some fact in order to make another fact intelligible. If, for instance, a person does not eat during the daytime and continues to gain weight, one can assume that such a person eats during the evening. Finally, testimony is accepting as true information that one has received from a reliable person. These six means of knowledge presuppose a distinction between the knower and what is known. Since it is a subject/object kind of knowing, all six forms represent dualistic forms of knowledge, which are by definition lower forms of knowing for Śaṅkara. In contrast to these six forms of knowledge, the highest type of knowledge is grounded on the Vedānta understanding of pure consciousness.

Śaṅkara denies that pure consciousness is an act because an act requires differentiation. This suggests that there are no objects to contrast with the self as knower. This can be explained in part by the fact that pure consciousness does not require a relation to any object. Śaṅkara intends to claim that an objectless consciousness is possible, and he gives deep-sleep consciousness as an example. Pure consciousness persists eternally and continually shines, which implies its self-luminous character. Śaṅkara does not mean that consciousness knows itself, because he wants to insist that it is always a pure subject. However, the highest form of knowledge for consciousness is Brahman. What is knowledge of Brahman like? It is devoid of knowledge about particulars, nonfactual, and timeless in the sense that it does not include knowledge about the past, present, or future time. When the knowledge of Brahman arrives, the empirical world of multiplicity disappears from consciousness and false notions are removed. By intuitively realizing Brahman with the higher type of knowledge, there is nothing more that needs to be known because it represents the only genuine reality. In short, Brahman is the really real, which necessarily implies that all other knowledge is tainted by ignorance.

Before a person can realize the highest reality, he or she must prepare himself or herself for this intuitive breakthrough. Śaṅkara specifies four qualifications that an aspirant for knowledge of Brahman must satisfy. The initial qualification is the ability to discriminate between the real and the unreal, which is like being able to distinguish between the snake and the rope. A person must also renounce all desire to enjoy the fruit of his or her action in this world and the next. This qualification implies that a person must renounce everything that stands in the way of ultimate liberation. Third, a person must develop mental tranquillity, self-control, dispassion, endurance, intentness of mind, and faith. Finally, an aspirant must want freedom and wisdom more than anything else. Once this type of resolve is possessed, a person must dedicate oneself to its realization. Having attained these qualifications, the path of knowledge (*jñāna-yoga*) is now ready to be traversed by the seeker.

The first stage of the path of knowledge is hearing (*śravaṇa*), which involves receiving instructions from a learned teacher about the scriptures. The fundamental source for the intuitive knowledge of Brahman is the sacred Vedic literature. Śaṅkara does not think that the seeker can totally apprehend Brahman through yogic intuition, which is more akin to preparatory knowledge. The second state involves reflection (*manana*) on the philosophical principles of the school through reasoning (*tarka*). The seeker needs to become absolutely convinced of the validity of these philosophical points. Finally, the path of knowledge entails constant meditation. The seeker of knowledge can, for instance, concentrate intently on the truth of "that you are" (*tat tvam asi*) in order to intuitively realize the Absolute. This intense concentration enables one to become completely detached from the phenomenal world and all egoism. When one knows oneself to be the one true reality then notions based on distinctions disappear with this realization, and the seeker can proclaim as Śaṅkara does, "I am the Universal, I am the All, I am transcendent, the One without a second, I am absolute and infinite knowledge, I am bliss and indivisible."[31] In contrast to a gradual kind of realization, this realization is an abrupt journey from the realm of the relative to the wholly other. Moreover, once this intuitive insight dawns, a person is no longer subject to the law of causation (*karma*) and the cycle of rebirth (*saṃsāra*).

The state of liberation is not a product or the result of some process, because it is without beginning or end. The condition of liberation is without degrees. It is defined as being, knowing, and experiencing one's genuine self. This knowing is not an act that produces additional karmic residues. What knowledge does accomplish is the utter destruction of ignorance (*avidyā*) and desires. Since desires are destroyed, it is not possible for tendencies (*vāsanās*) to be carried into action. If these tendencies do not function, karmic residues cannot determine a person's future birth. But what is the state of liberation like? It is analogous to what happens to the space inside of a pot when it breaks—the space within the pot becomes united with universal space. This is a nondualistic condition.

State of Nondualism

The condition of nondualism is being united with the lone reality that is identified with Brahman. On the basis of his commentary on the Upaniṣads and the *Vedānta Sūtras*, Śaṅkara defines Brahman as being, consciousness, and bliss (*sat-cit-ānanda*).

The assertion that Brahman is being suggests that it is the sole true being, and all empirical types of being are negated by it. It is being that directs a person's mind to what is ultimately real. In other words, if Brahman alone is real, the world does not have real being. The world is essentially illusory (*māyā*). The being of a higher reality (Brahman) sublates the existence of the world, which is completely dependent on Brahman for its existence. To affirm that Brahman is being means that it could not have originated from anything else (SB 2.3.9). Actually, Brahman comprises both being and nonbeing. If a thing can only be cognized by the mind and senses of a person, and if Brahman is not an object of mental or sense perception, it thus cannot be known by empirical means. Although a person cannot impart knowledge about Brahman with the aid of sensual or mental powers, knowledge can be obtained with the assistance of traditional authority.

That Brahman is consciousness means that it cannot be the agent of knowing; otherwise, it would become delimited by the knowable and knowledge, which would mean that it could not be infinite. By partly defining Brahman as consciousness, this denies that it is nonconsciousness. Just as the heat of a fire is inherent to the nature of fire, the consciousness of Brahman is indigenous to it. The conscious nature of Brahman means that it forms the ground of all distinctions and the very core of being.

By defining Brahman in part as bliss, Śaṅkara introduces the principle of value into his definition. If a person's finitude means that he or she is in bondage to the pains of sickness, birth, old age, and death, there is no ultimate joy in such a life of bondage to suffering. In contrast, Brahman is free from all suffering. It is undoubtedly the highest bliss of being by its very nature. In other words, to realize Brahman is to know it as blissful, which is unconditionally valuable. For Śaṅkara, the only real value resides in the nondual Brahman. Those who realize the bliss that is Brahman, by concentrating on the fact that Brahman is the absolute reality, become firmly fixed in the bliss that is the supreme Brahman. In other words, the seeker becomes Brahman itself.

Being, consciousness, and bliss do represent qualities of Brahman in a positive sense because they are better grasped as aspects of the nondualistic experience.

Śaṅkara refers to the negative aspect of Brahman as *nirguṇa*, or without qualities. A second aspect of Brahman is *saguṇa*, or with qualities like those of a deity. This distinction should not be construed as two separate entities. They are rather two aspects of the same absolute.

The nirguṇa aspect of Brahman is summarized nicely by the formula "not this, not that" (*neti, neti*). This is the only legitimate way to refer to Brahman because it eliminates any possible specification, and this negative formula also serves to eliminate all differences due to limiting adjuncts like ignorance and desire. The repetitive terms of the formula refer to something without distinguishing marks. This necessarily means that name, form, action, species, and qualities are eliminated with reference to Brahman, which is devoid of any of these distinguishing marks. In the final analysis, Brahman cannot be described because human conceptual forms cannot exhaust it. The nirguṇa aspect of Brahman also means that it is without qualities, impersonal, and nonrelational. The impersonality of Brahman means that it exceeds both the finite and the infinite. It is nonrelational in the sense that it is beyond all relations and yet is the ground that sustains all relations.

In contrast to the nirguṇa aspect of Brahman, its saguṇa aspect means that it possesses qualities and attributes; it is conditioned, personal, and qualitatively describable. The saguṇa aspect is conditioned by limiting adjuncts like ignorance, which implies that it is not the object of higher knowledge. To experience the Absolute as conditioned is to know it as Īśvara (Lord), which is an object of devotion (SB I.I.II). As Īśvara, Brahman is viewed as the creator and governor of the universe, which creates through its power of illusion (*māyā*).

Beyond the illusory or unreal nature of the world, Brahman is the sole reality that is identified with the immortal self (*Ātman*). Śaṅkara defines the self as self-luminous and timeless, which implies that it is not subject to birth or death. It is rather eternal, unchanging, and without origin; it is also spaceless and unthinkable. If thinking is a process within time that objectifies that with which it comes into contact, the self is rather a state of being that underlies all subject/object distinctions.

The most important thing to know about the self is that it is nondifferent from Brahman as expressed by the formula "that you are" from the *Chāndogya Upaniṣad* (6.16.3). Śaṅkara refers to this formula as a great saying (*mahāvākya*) that denotes pure consciousness of Brahman and the pure consciousness of the self that are equivalent to each other. The great saying helps a person to focus one's attention on the eternal self, and it thus functions to shift one's focus from the ephemeral to the eternal.[32] Therefore, when one knows oneself to be the true reality (Brahman), notions based on distinctions disappear.

From the position of lower knowledge, the self is called *jīva*, which refers to the individual person existing in the world. In its essence the jīva is one with the immortal self (*Ātman*). But it is a mere reflection of the Ātman because the jīva is limited by adjuncts like ignorance and passion. Just as the appearance of the sun in a pool of water is a mere reflection and not real, the embodied and limited jīva is immersed in ignorance and thus a mere reflection of the ultimate reality, which means that the jīva is merely appearance. But when the jīva is seen as identical with the Ātman (immortal self), it is grasped as reality. This occurs when the limitations of the jīva are removed, and it becomes one with the Ātman, which is identical to Brahman.

The nature of the jīva (empirical self) comprises four states of consciousness: waking, dream, deep sleep, and transcendence. The Ātman represents the single consciousness in each of the four states. Since the essence of the Ātman is pure immediate consciousness that overcomes ordinary distinctions, this suggests that there is no separate entity termed the jīva from the standpoint of reality.

Like that of the Ātman, the relation of Brahman to the jīva is analogous to that of a whole to a part. There is no such thing as an individual soul/self different from Brahman. It is only when Brahman differentiates itself through the mind or other limiting conditions that it is referred to as an empirical self (SB 1.1.31). In ordinary life, jīva is not distinguished from its limiting adjuncts consisting of body, senses, mind, sense-objects, and feelings. The jīva is like a pure crystal that appears red or blue before the rise of discriminative knowledge. When true cognition arises the crystal is seen in its true nature as transparent and white. Thus discriminative knowledge leads to the jīva's comprehension of its true nature. Therefore, the difference between the jīva and Brahman is not in reality a fact, and any imagined difference is due merely to ignorance (SB 1.3.19). With the dawn of true knowledge, the unreal or limiting aspect of the jīva is dissolved, and its true state, which is one with Brahman, is realized. The result is a radical nondualism.

Concluding Remarks

The discussion of ecstasy and enstasy points to the experiential nature of Yoga. With the liberation of the self from matter, the mission of the intellect (*buddhi*) is accomplished because it withdraws from the self, and is reincorporated into matter. The three guṇas dissolve, enter a permanent period of rest, and their inactivity suggests that they do not evolve again. From its enlightened, stainless, and isolated condition, the self passes beyond any relation to the guṇas (qualities). Since there is nothing to energize it, karmas cease to function. For the liberated self, matter dissolves, much like a tree that withers from a lack of moisture or fertile soil. Moreover, human consciousness ceases to function because its conditioning factors are gone and its constituent elements are reabsorbed into matter. In contrast, the self (*puruṣa*) stands alone, free, and autonomous, but this liberation must not be construed as a change of condition because the state of bondage is not the genuine condition of the self. This also means that liberation is not an acquired state. Nonetheless, the yogin is now a jīvanmukti (a person liberated while alive).

In contrast to the yoga of Patañjali, for Śaṅkara thinks that yogic intuition cannot grasp Brahman because for him the Vedas are the sole source of knowledge. Śaṅkara never claims that his philosophy is based on his own experience. It is the

Vedas (revealed literature, by which he usually means the Upaniṣads) that teach about the presence of Brahman, which is transpersonal and transworldly. Therefore, the Vedas offer insight into a timeless presence. Śaṅkara accepts the Vedas as an objective self-revelation of that precise reality which is supposed to be the exact content of the culminating experience.[33]

It is, however, true that Śaṅkara refers to an integral experience (*anubhava*). Even though the experience of Brahman means the realization of oneself as the single reality, this is known from the Vedas in an ultimate sense. Integral experience is always, however, subordinate and supplementary to the revelation represented by the Vedas.[34] Thus Śaṅkara does not claim that his thought is grounded on his own experience. From his philosophical perspective, personal experiences are variable, open to various types of interpretations, and easily misunderstood. Nonetheless, there is no interval between knowing Brahman and liberation. This immediate experience gives the knower assurance and clear undoubted awareness. The state of liberation is a consciousness that is devoid of any type of individuation associated with embodiment and specific mental states, and it is unconnected to anything specific, which is identified with universal consciousness.[35] And like a snake sloughing off its skin, the liberated person discards his or her body and world. For Śaṅkara, liberation is not attained by causal techniques like the steps of yoga. Liberating knowledge implies freedom from such techniques and freedom from performing or doing something. Liberating knowledge is more akin to being open for the absolute reality that transcends the world.

The isolation of the self from matter in Yoga and Sāṃkhya and the absorption of the self into Brahman in Vedānta are two primary examples of the important role of experience in Hinduism. These experiences are ancient, as evident by their suggested appearance in the Upaniṣads. But these two types of experience do not exhaust the significance of religious experience in the Hindu religious tradition. There are different types of experience to be discovered in the devotional traditions of India that will become evident as we proceed in this book.

PART II

Nature of Devotional and Sectarian Hinduism

6

The Sensual Nature of Hinduism

When traveling around southern India it is not uncommon to see young girls dressed in colorful outfits with beautiful flowers in their hair on their way to school with friends or riding on the back of their father's motor scooter. In the countryside, the green vegetation and flowers leave a strong sensual impression on a viewer. In the stalls adjacent to temples, vendors sell multicolored flowers linked together on a string that one can purchase to offer to a deity within the interior of the temple. At nighttime, a neon commercial sign on the outskirts of Chennai (Madras) depicts the image of a twenty-five-foot-tall elephant-headed god Gaṇeśa announcing a gas station named after this ubiquitous and popular son of Śiva. As a driver took us through the back streets of Chennai (Madras) one morning, presumably to avoid heavy traffic on a journey to a sacred site, the four members of our party began to laugh as we drove through one neighborhood because of the heavy and distinct odor of hashish. I recall remarking that it must indeed be a very happy neighborhood. The grocery stores, restaurants, streets, and temples possess their own odors. A visitor hears the chanting of hymns in temple precincts, the singing of a deity's praises on public streets, or the continuous reciting of a vedic text by a group of males until the entire text is recited. The taste of the food is very different from what one is accustomed to in the West. The really spicy cuisine can turn the interior of your mouth into what feels like an inferno. What a person sees, hears, smells, tastes, or touches are all part of an assault on the senses of a visitor. What a visitor experiences is the sensual nature of Indian culture, an experience that stands in contrast to the more intuitive experience discussed in chapter 5. The sensuous and intuitive experiences are not necessarily contradictory. Certainly, there is an attempt to control the senses on the yogic path. But the path of devotion (*bhakti*) often elicits both the intuitive and sensuous aspects of human nature. This chapter functions as an introduction to the sectarian devotional aspect of the religious tradition that persists to the present time and represents the way of religion for the vast multitude of Indians.

The Nature of Bhakti

The term *bhakti* is derived from a Sanskrit root term *bhaj*, which means "to participate," "to share," "to worship," and "to be devoted to." When the term is used with persons it implies a certain communion of mind and heart. Thus it expresses a personal relationship characterized by love.[1] When the term is used within a religious context it conveys the sense of choosing, worshiping, and adoring, a deity. It is also used to refer to a person's love of a deity in the sense of family affection, and it is common to address deities as father, mother, or brother.[2]

If we examine the history of the term, we find that in the *Rig Veda* the original conception of bhakti suggested something material, in the sense that deities were worshiped for personal gain or to obtain worldly rewards.[3] The term, moreover, refers during the vedic period to participation in a rite, especially with sharing the sacrificial remains among participants.[4] An important change is marked by the *Śvetāśvatāra Upaniṣad* (6.23), where the term *bhakti* is unequivally used for the first time in the technical sense of the love of god. This change can be dated around the fifth or fourth centuries B.C.E. The epic literature uses the term *bhakti* to refer to both secular and religious love, whereas the *Bhagavad Gītā* turns it into a means of practicing a religious path and a goal of liberation, sometime between 200 B.C.E. and 100 C.E.

Within the context of the overall epic text of the *Mahābhārata*, the *Bhagavad Gītā*, which is located in the sixth book (*parvan*), the *Bhīṣma Parvan*, of the eighteen books comprising the entire epic, represents an attempt to create a dramatic climax and solution to the human dilemma created by a just yet pernicious war. The basic dilemma facing the two subjects—Arjuna and Krishna—is between worldly duty (*dharma*) and world renunciation or liberation (*mokṣa*). The *Bhagavad Gītā* does not use the term bhakti to refer to secular or sexual love, as in other parts of the epic, because bhakti is now both a means to a goal and the goal itself. In other words, devotion is the path, and love of God is the goal that brings about release from the cycle of rebirth.

The *Bhagavad Gītā* is best read as a gradual unfolding of the truth within the context of a dialogical encounter between two significant figures, with Arjuna assuming that he knows Krishna as a warrior like himself. Arjuna becomes despondent about the prospect of having to fight his relatives and former teachers over a kingdom that was unlawfully taken from him and his brothers. After Arjuna's decision to renounce the world rather than fight, Krishna counters with four reasons for fighting: the self is immortal and thus cannot be destroyed when the body dies, everything born is reborn, it is the duty of a warrior to fight, and a warrior would lose face and be accused of cowardice if he did not fight.

Chapter seven of the text marks an important turn, because it begins to discuss the path of devotion and the real nature of Krishna. Although the text is eighteen chapters long, it reaches its climax with the grand theophany in chapter eleven, for which Arjuna is given a set of celestial eyes so that he may capture the revelatory vision of Krishna—which leaves Arjuna dumbfounded. As the dialogical encounter unfolds, Arjuna learns about a self-forgetting love in which a person excludes all objects from his or her mind when thinking about god. A devotee should also view the world as a manifestation of God. The most basic requirement of this path of devotion is faith (*śraddhā*), a necessity that is tied to a willingness to surrender oneself completely to God and to become totally attached to him.

The *Bhagavad Gītā* connects the path of devotion with the path of action (*karma marga*). The latter path requires a person to act according to his or her social duties and station in life. Since it is impossible not to perform actions, a devotee needs to find a way to become free from the binding nature of the universal law of karma (cause and effect), which mandates a positive or negative result for every action. And since the path of devotion requires a person to follow the commands of God, it is important to discover a way to reconcile the inevitability of action, doing the commands of God, and avoiding their binding effect that eventually determines one's future rebirth. The solution involves performing action as a gift to God, and thus escape the inexorable consequences of the law of karma. By acting to resign the fruits of one's actions to God, one is also relying solely on God.

Ultimately, it is the grace (*prasāda*) of God that saves a devotee. In fact, Krishna claims that no devotee of his is ever lost to rebirth by means of his grace. And it is his grace by which he reveals himself to his devotees. Because it is God that gives a devotee supreme peace and salvation by means of his grace, Krishna urges his devotees to abandon all duties and to come to him alone for refuge and release from all evil. According to the text, the path of devotion does not lead to absorption in God, but it leads instead to a personal relationship with God characterized by love, even though there are some references that could lead one to believe that the ultimate goal is union with God.

The basic message of the *Bhagavad Gītā* is expanded by the historically later *Bhāgavata Purāṇa* (c. 950 C.E.), which develops a ninefold path of bhakti. The first phase consists of listening to God's names, and the second aspect is chanting God's names, forms, merits, and sportive exploits (*kīrtana*). The third phase is remembrance (*smaraṇa*), which involves constantly meditating on God so the mind experiences drowning in the divine. It is also possible to resort to God by serving at his lotus feet (*pādasevana*), which are equivalent to a holy place of pilgrimage. The following two aspects of the ninefold devotion are related to internal and external worship. The former refers to creating a mental image of God and concentrating on it, while the latter represents worshiping an external symbol. This act of devotion is associated with physical prostration (*vandana*) before the image of God, which is a way to acknowledge one's unqualified submission in recognition of God's supremacy. The final three phases of devotion manifest the devotee's relationship to the divine. These final phases begin with a devotee's servitude (*dāsya*) to God, similar to the role of a slave. This is followed by friendship (*sakya*), which involves God recognizing a devotee's humility and making a gift of himself to the devotee. Thereafter, a person completely surrenders to God, dies to one's false self, and enters the portal of immortality.

Essential Features of Bhakti

An essential feature of devotional religion in Hinduism is sectarianism. There are many different sects, orders, or traditions of which a person can be a member. The three major sects are Vaiṣṇava (centered on the deity Viṣṇu), Śaivism (focused on the deity Śiva), and Śākta (devotion to some form of the goddess). Within these major divisions, there are many different movements that we will examine in later chapters devoted to these major traditions. These various deities are generally viewed as savior figures that dispense salvific grace. The goal of salvation is often expressed as a personal relationship with the god or goddess and not necessarily union with the divine being.

Devotional Hinduism uses local languages and music to sing the praises of the deity. Distinctions based on caste, age, and gender tend to be obliterated in the more inclusive path of bhakti. Devotional Hinduism manifests an intense and overtly public emotionalism directed at the object of a person's ardent love. As we will observe in chapter 8 on the Krishna tradition, devotional religion may be explicitly erotic and highly sensual.

There is an especially large emphasis placed on sight. The technical term for seeing the sacred is *darśana*. This term possesses a twofold meaning: one sees the image of the deity, and is seen by the deity.[5] This kind of mutual seeing represents a form of communication. As such, darśana is a means of expressing one's feelings, will, and love. By seeing the image of the sacred, the viewer also participates in the essence of the object of perception. Moreover, darśana is a form of touching and knowing.[6] It would be incorrect to assume that the devotee initiates the act of seeing, because it is the deity that presents itself in its image for a devotee to witness. What does a devotee gain by seeing the divine image? The answer is simple: the blessing of the deity, good fortune, well-being, grace, and merit.

The viewing of divine images is only one form of darśana. The other two major forms of darśana occur at sacred places and when one encounters holy persons such as *sants* (saints), *sādhus* (holy persons), and *saṃnyāsins* (renouncers).

Sensual Devotional Practices

The importance of the ancient sacrificial cult is historically eclipsed by the popularity of the practice of *pūjā* (worship), even though sacrifice continues to be practiced today. Pūjā is directly connected to divine images, the temple, festivals, and a new literature. The full sensual significance of these new phenomena lies in their interconnection.

A pūjā ceremony is based on ancient Indian norms of hospitality. When a guest comes to one's home he or she is greeted by the householder with drinking water for thirst, given foot-washing water to rinse and cool the feet after the journey, offered food to satisfy hunger, and given water to rinse out the mouth and to gargle with after a meal. The guest may also be given a pot of water for a bath to wash away the dust of the journey. Moreover, the guest may be offered a fresh change of clothes, entertaining stories, and a comfortable place to sleep. Instead of a human guest, in a pūjā ceremony the image of the deity is the supreme guest within one's home or in a temple.

Pūjā represents a series of acts of service or respect. These normally consist of a sequence of sixteen attendances. Pūjā commences with the invocation or awakening of the deity. The divine image is offered a seat, water for washing his feet and hands, water for sipping and bathing, given a fresh garment and sacred thread, anointed with unguents or sandalwood paste, offered flowers, perfumes and incense, and offered a lighted lamp, food, or a gift. Homage is made to the deity, with circumambulation of the image, reciting verses of praise, and finally bidding the deity farewell or good night. This sequence of services can be performed in a so-called pūjā room by a householder or by a priest in a temple.

A distinction can be made between temple and domestic performances of pūjā. The former is performed for the benefit of the world, whereas the domestic version is for the protection of the household. Another distinction relates to the primary role of the priest in the one case and the individual layperson in the other. Within the context of the temple, the priest is the primary actor, while the layperson plays no appreciably active role.[7] When a priest performs pūjā within a temple the ritual is considered valuable with or without observers.

When a temple pūjā ceremony ends with the waving of a camphor flame, the deity and worshiper become identified. By appealing to the senses of sight and smell, the flame signifies the embodiment of the deity within the image and also its transcendent nature with the rising and disappearance of the flame. When the divine and human perceivers witness the flame at the end of the ceremony they realize an identity within the context of their shared vision. This unity is enhanced when devotees embrace the flame with their hands and touch their eyes with their fingertips. This is a way to transfer the power and grace of god onto oneself and to absorb it through one's eyes.[8]

In some locations in India, the practice of offering lamps (*ārati*) to the icon of a deity tends to eclipse pūjā. Within the context of temple worship, the lighted lamps are waved by the priests in a clockwise direction in front of the image, with the right hand. The priest begins to wave the lamps initially at the head of the icon, and he works his way to the feet of the icon. While the ārati is being performed, the left hand of the priest may simultaneously hold a small bell that is rung continuously during the ritual action. The brass lamps are decorated with sacred symbols and are filled often with vegetable oil, or preferably with ghee (clarified butter), which is considered the most auspicious fuel because it is a product of a cow. The burning lamps signify divine energy and presence, and they function as a public acknowledgment by the devotee of the superior nature of the deity. There are times when devotees use their hands to take the effluvium of the flame and apply it to their face and/or head. This devotional gesture is symbolically similar to touching the feet of a superior and is an action indicative of respect.

A devotee's sense of taste becomes involved when the pūjā ends and the gracious leftovers (*prasāda*) of the offerings made to the deity are distributed to the faithful. Including a wide range of holy substances, because of its contact with the deity to whom it is offered prasāda (literally grace) is a transformed food substance that symbolizes the power and grace of the deity.[9] When a devotee consumes the food he or she receives a taste of the deity in at least a metaphorical sense, and a devotee internalizes the divine qualities embodied in the leftovers.

Festivals and Festivity

Festivals represent a special time when ordinary duties are set aside while one celebrates a special event. Humans and deities play roles of both givers and recipients within the context of dynamic exchange. In this way, festivals reestablish a bond between devotee and deity. During festivals, caste distinctions tend to be obliterated as the normally prevailing social order is upset, although the former social order is reestablished at the conclusion of the festival. Nonetheless, participants are refreshed and renewed by the experience. Therefore, festivals create a basis for both stability and change. A good example of such a festival is the Kumbha Mela that is held every twelve years.

According to an ancient myth, the gods and demons churned the ocean of milk together in order to create an elixir of immortality. The gods agreed to share it with the demons, but absconded with it instead. They fled for twelve days, with the demons in hot pursuit. As the deities sped away with their prize, the elixir spilled from the pot at four places on earth: Allahabad (also known as Prayag), Hardwar, Ujjain, and Nasik. Every three years millions of people arrive at one of these cities that are rotated for each Kumbha Mela to bathe in the rivers in order to commemorate this event, with the hope of attaining immortality. The climax occurs when the planet Jupiter enters into the sign of Aquarius (Kumbha), and the sun enters Aries. Thus Kumbha means house of Aquarius, which is the most auspicious time to bathe in the Ganges and Jumna rivers.

Festival time is repetitive in two basic senses: it repeats the divine acts of the deities, and it is often a reenactment of the birth of the cosmos. In thus represents renewal. Another festival, Sasti, is a celebration of the victory over demons by a son of Śiva named Skanda, which saved the dharma (cosmic and social order) and ushered into existence a new age. The festival reenacts this event in order to build a new and sacred cosmos. The festival accomplishes this renewal by returning to a mythic time when evil, chaos, and disease were nonexistent. The Holi festival, associated with devotion to Krishna, represents the destruction of the secular order and its renewal. It is the destruction of a world, which became polluted during the course of a year, followed by its purification. Thereby, it represents the symbolic renewal of society.

An important aspect of many festivals is the public procession of the image of the deity, which allows the deity to manifest to his or her devotees. In short, this procession is a new theophany. During the procession, the deity is treated like a royal person taken on a journey to view his or her subjects, be greeted by them, presented with offerings, and welcomed by those living and standing along the processional streets. Some of those living along the processional route or standing on the street to watch a procession are people of low-caste status, which compromises their ability to gain entrance into temples. A public procession offers these socially handicapped people an opportunity to view the deity and to fulfill a fundamental practice of devotionalism.

A central feature of festival is excess, which means that destruction and waste accompany festivals. Dancing, singing, eating, and drinking also characterize them. In short, festive activity is a time of revelry and joy. The participants literally "live it up" and "overdo it." Overall, this type of activity provides a break from convention, and it is an affirmative celebration in the sense that festivity says "yes to life." Despite failure, sickness, suffering, and death, festivity affirms life and gaiety within a devotional context. Festivity is never an end in itself, because it most often expresses joy about something.

During festivals, things are often turned upside down or done in reverse. This suggests that festivals display dramatic contrasts. It is not merely different from everyday life, upsetting the social structure, but it also signifies a time of intense emotion and change of being for the individual. Sometimes, a festival represents a return to primordial chaos that is newly created and rediscovered.

The Hindu devotional tradition distinguishes four types of festivals (*utsavas*). The *brahma-utsava* is characterized by hoisting a banner. The *tavana-utsava* is named for an aromatic plant that is used to decorate the vehicle of the deity. The *teppam-utsava* is a floating festival in which a float is constructed and placed in a large tank (pool) that lies east of the temple in south India. The float holds the image of the deity, musicians, and priests. Oftentimes, the float is electrically illuminated while men pull the float around the tank with ropes each evening. The rationale for such a float is the enjoyment of the deity, and it also allows aquatic creatures an opportunity to worship the deity. Finally, the *vasanta-utsava* is a spring festival.

Pilgrimage

Whereas festivals are sensuous celebrations of some mythical event, the practice of pilgrimage is a sensual journey that can often become a difficult task for a specific purpose or as the fulfillment of a vow in response to a favor given by a deity. The Sanskrit term for pilgrimage is *tīrtha-yātrā*, which literally means "undertaking a journey to river fords." The term *tīrtha* is derived from a Sanskrit verb meaning to cross over. Thus a tīrtha is a place where a person crosses over to another place. A pilgrimage (*yātrā*) is both a way and a goal. It is symbolized by a ladder or a bridge, which both refer to transcendence. Places of pilgrimage are often associated with water or rivers for drinking and bathing. Water possesses both nourishing and purifying powers, which is especially true of flowing water. After a pilgrim bathes and purifies him or herself, he or she can become a tīrtha (crossing over) for others. A place of pilgrimage is a threshold that one crosses, which links this world with heaven.[10] Thus a sacred place of pilgrimage is a place where a person can launch a journey from earth to heaven. Because a tīrtha is a ford between earth and heaven, it can function to replace the performance of traditional rites and sacrifices, or it can serve as a place to perform rites that yield bountiful blessings. It is thus not unusual to find people performing ancestral and death rites at places of pilgrimage, because the sacred site operates as a ford between earth and heaven as well as a location at which one can cross beyond the boundaries created by caste and gender distinctions. Like devotional religion, pilgrimage is open and accessible to everyone without distinction. Moreover, pilgrimage sites are places for crossing beyond sins by being purified of them and receiving blessings for a positive action.

Every pilgrimage involves a journey, but this passage is not only geographical. Pilgrimage is also an interior journey that occurs within the pilgrim; it occurs within a person's heart at the same time that it is an external crossing made physically with one's feet. Since the journey bears a close resemblance to an ascetic regimen, pilgrims can be characterized as temporary world renouncers.[11] The hardships of journey, sacrifice of time and money, and separation from daily routines are suggestive of asceticism.

There are four major types of pilgrimage sites in India. *Daiva tīrthas* are sacred places that result directly from the benevolent acts of divine beings. Second, *asura tīrthas* are sacred places associated with demonic beings. The sanctity of these places is connected to the actions of the major deities that destroyed the demons, which helped to restore the social and moral orders. Third, *ārsa tīrthas* are consecrated by the actions of saints and sages through their asceticism or sacrifices. In the region of Bengal, for instance, Gauḍīya Vaiṣṇavas visit sites connected to the saint Caitanya (d. 1533), whereas another holy site north of the city of Calcutta is identified with the temple of Daksineswar because of the fame of the Bengali saint Ramakrishna (d. 1886) who lived there. Finally, *mānusa tīrthas*, which etymologically means "human sacred place," are places theoretically sanctified by the rulers of the solar and lunar dynasties.[12] These are places where Indian rulers established a temple and duly consecrated it.

Ordinary Hindus go on pilgrimage for a variety of reasons. A person might desire to become part of the sacred order that connects many parts of India. A motivating factor is an attempt to accumulate merit or good karma. A person may journey to remove sins, or for mundane and personal reasons, with the expectation of reward. Many people go on pilgrimage to perform important life-cycle rites such as initiation or funeral rites at the banks of a sacred river like the Ganges. For some castes, pilgrimage has certain social value because at some goddess shrines lower-caste members can enter the innermost precincts of the temple. Others desire to directly experience the sacred, which can result with miraculous healings of the pilgrim or beloved ones, or it may lead to an inward transformation.[13]

Sacred Waters

Many sacred destinations for pilgrims are connected to holy bodies of water. The primary such place is the sacred city of Benares (also traditionally called Vārāṇasī and Kāśī) along the banks of the Ganges River, which functions as the quintessence of all sacred waters. There are two sectarian versions of the origins of the river. In the Vaiṣṇava version, the Ganges originates from the foot of Viṣṇu. According to the mythical narrative, Viṣṇu incarnated himself as a dwarf to defeat a demon by means of his three strides. The third step pierced the vault of heaven with his toe and released the heavenly waters. According to the Śaiva tradition, the Ganges agreed to descend to earth to revive the sixty thousand sons of King Sagara, who had been burned to ashes by the heat of the sage Kapila for disturbing his meditation. The river was certain, however, that the force of her fall would shatter the earth. But Śiva promised to catch her on his head and tame her in his hair before releasing her to flow upon the earth. This is the reason that the Ganges winds her way through Śiva's hair.

This descent of the Ganges, who is called Gaṅgā in Hindu myth, is celebrated in May or early June on a day called Daśahara (birthday of the Gaṅgā). This celebration anticipates the start of the monsoon season in India. Hindus celebrate this day by taking a dip in the river, because it is believed to destroy sins. It is also believed that the flowing water absorbs and carries away pollution.

Within Hindu myth and popular imagination, the Gaṅgā is both a river and a mother figure that gives life by means of her waters, which are analogous to mother's milk and feminine power (*śakti*). Indians are like Gaṅgā's children thirsting for sustenance from their mother. And like a mother, she provides unconditional love to her children. In fact, she saves even those who are unfit for salvation. This way to salvation is a direct result of bathing in her waters, or being cremated on her banks, and having the ashes of the deceased deposited in the river. The Gaṅgā functions as the source of all sacred waters and as their archetype.[14] Although the Gaṅgā begins in the Himalaya Mountains in northern India, winds through the plains of India, and empties into the Indian Ocean, it is more than a single river because it represents all sacred waters, and other rivers are often considered equivalent by devotees.

The feel of water and bathing are important parts of the sensual nature of Hinduism, and can be classified as obligatory, occasional, or voluntary. Daily bathing and bathing before a sacred ritual are examples of obligatory bathing, whereas purification and expiation are instances of occasional bathing. On special religious occasions, voluntary bathing occurs. The visible aspect of bathing involves physical cleansing, while the transcendent aspect is the invisible part of the activity. Traditionally, the daily bath is performed at dawn and noon, which are considered transitional times of a day. While bathing, males recite vedic mantras (repetitive sacred formulas), which are prohibited for women and Śūdras, who must bathe silently. Neither males nor females are allowed to bathe naked. All bathers must don two pieces of clothing, and they must begin by washing their hands and feet before entering a sacred body of water such as the Ganges, because bathing in the river is equivalent to entering a sacred place. Facing the rising sun, the bather walks into the water and immediately submerges the entire body.[15] Then, the male bather begins to recite mantras (sacred formulas).

Within the Hindu imagination, there is a close relationship between the flowing waters of the Ganges River, the sacred city of Benares, and liberation. As the Ganges flows past Benares, because of a bend in the river it proceeds from the south (symbolic direction of death) to the north (symbolic direction of rebirth). This directional flow makes Benares an especially auspicious place, and it suggests liberation. The liberating nature of the city is illustrated in a narrative about the corpse of an evil Brahmin, who is killed by a tiger. From the remains of the corpse, a vulture scavenges a bone, which is lost in mid-flight directly over Benares when another vulture attempts to steal it. The bone falls into the Ganges. At this precise moment, the soul of the deceased is being dragged away by attendants of death. Although the soul is going to a terrible hell, the death attendants are forced to release it when the bone falls into the sacred waters, and the soul goes straight to heaven instead of hell.[16]

Role of Food

Pūjā, festivals, and pilgrimages share a feature in common: the importance of food, which is offered to divine beings, its leftovers consumed by devotees. Within the context of Hinduism, food is more than a substance to ingest in order to sustain oneself. Food is also more than a transactional commodity that one exchanges with a divine being or people. Food tends to be synonymous with life itself because it contains elements that cause physical well-being, shapes personal temperament, and influences emotional changes, longevity, and salvation. By the proper food intake, one can regulate one's mental condition, aesthetic feelings, and spiritual attainments. In the ancient *Taittirīya Upaniṣad* (2.2), it is possible to find a connection between god, life, and food, and it is also possible to find in the same text an association between the enjoyment of food and bliss (3.2). These kinds of connections with food are continued and expanded in devotional Hinduism with notions such as completeness, auspiciousness, intimacy, emotional states, and self-surrender.[17]

Within the context of devotional Hinduism, the gracious food leftovers (*prasāda*) from a pūjā ceremony contain the blessings of the deity. And it is precisely this type of food that shows the interdependence of the deity and human beings. Food also plays an important role during peak pilgrim periods, when feasts are common. A feast of love is the annual Annakūṭa feast of Krishna.[18] The festival is named for a mountain of food created by devotees in commemoration of the time the deity persuaded the cowherd residents of the region of Braj to make their annual harvest offerings to Mount Govardhana, rather than to the deity Indra, as had been the custom. After food was piled in front of the mountain, Krishna split himself in two. One half waited with other cowherders to enjoy the feast, while the other form jumped into the mountain, which sucked in the food through a crack. Since the food was originally intended for Indra, he became angry and sent a torrential downpour to punish the people, but Krishna held aloft Mount Govardhana with his fingertip, protecting the residents from the rain. In the celebration of this mythical account, the food that is prepared and offered is as plentiful as Krishna's love.

Food is often used as a metaphor in bhakti to denote, for instance, a devotee's hunger for the nectar of devotion. Or the profuse love between god and devotee is symbolized by an outpouring of milk. The overflowing milk is a signifier of *rasa* (literally juice, sap, or liquid), which includes the connotation of flavor and taste. In connection with food, rasa or flavoring is not considered an additive that enhances flavor; it is rather essential to the food. The act of adding herbs and spices is not a supplemental action but is considered an important part of the process of creation.[19]

Within the context of food offered at a pūjā ceremony, devotees believe that the image of the deity consumes the food offering with its eyes.[20] This metaphorical use of food joins together other elements of devotional religion such as perception, relationship, love, liquid, aesthetic mood, divine image, and grace of god.

Food can make humans healthy or ill, and an improper diet can place a person at risk. An unhealthy person can be restored to good health by a proper diet that creates the right kind of inner balance. It is important to maintain a controlled level of nourishment in order to promote a healthy body. Gluttony is immoral and upsets a proper bodily balance, which can be corrected by fasting. Fasting also promotes the needed dominance of the soul over the body. Within the context of such ideas, food is often distinguished into subtle/gross, pure/impure, hot/cold, boiled/fried, human/divine, good/bad, temple/home, and feasting/fasting. More attention will be paid to food transactions in chapter 13.

Indian Art and Temples

Among the essential features of Indian art is embellishment, which is a major aim of art. The purpose of Indian art is not to imitate or to accurately depict nature; it is rather to portray nature as it should be ideally. Thus the task of the artist is to render a subject in its paradigmatic or its idealized form. Another feature of Indian art is the predominance of epic themes and myth. In addition to the actions and symbols of gods and goddesses, the deeds of heroic figures also dominate sculpture, poetry, drama, dancing, and painting. There is a tendency to render concrete divine models, which also involves the presentation in tangible form of ideal worlds to which Hindus strive to journey. Thus art attempts to present heaven on earth. In order to accomplish this, the artist must mentally identify with the object or god that is being created. Artists are instructed to meditate upon the description of the deity contained in the texts. Finally, the artist reaches a point where he can perceive the deity in his mind. The artistic creation aims at enabling the viewer to experience rasa (aesthetic mood) that can culminate in a transpersonal bliss.

Indian art also attempts to convey the often subtle, complex, and sublime truths of Hindu sages. Moreover, Indian art aims at revelation by seeking to express divinity, or to enable a person to transcend human limitations. Thus it seeks to recreate heaven on earth by making the divine immediately perceptible. Part of this attempt is connected to maintaining the world (*loka-saṃgraha*) as a crucial dimension in the spiritual quest. The artist participates in an attempt to refine and perfect himself and his world in order to make it more habitable and civilized. It is possible to witness this, for instance, with temple architecture, which is an attempt to make nature perfect. In many cultures, the circle is an image of perfection and wholeness, but Hindu art rejects the circle because of its naturalness. Instead of the circle, Indian art prefers the square, which is considered a refinement of the natural; it is an ordering and perfection of space. Because Hindu temples seek to be a miniature embodiment of a perfect, divine world, the square is fundamental to its form. The symbolic significance of the square as a mark of order can be discerned in the Vedic sacrificial plot. The āhavanīya altar is square because it symbolically represents heaven, which is perfection beyond life and death.

Around the eighth century C.E., there was an increase in the number of temples built, accompanying the rapid rise of devotional religion, and they evolved into complex institutions that met religious, economic, political, and cultural needs. The temple functioned as a nexus for the exchange of goods and services by serving as landlord, rural bank, and employer. The Hindu temple also employed people from many different professions. The wealthy donors and supporters of temples made them into symbols of power and authority that legitimized the social status of the donors. Moreover, temples were the locations for village assemblies to gather and conduct their business, and they also served as educational centers.[21] Local kings benefited financially at some temples from the tax paid by pilgrims.

Although some temples exhibit a congregational style of worship at particular times, most temples do not. There is little communal worship at fixed and repetitive times during the day or week. People simply attend at any time of their preference. Instead of places to sit within a temple, visitors usually stand for a few minutes while they look at the ubiquitous divine images. Therefore, ordinary worship tends to be informal. It is also important to keep in mind that some people worship at home instead of a temple, and many do both.

Many temples (*vimanas*) are built at the location of tīrthas (sacred places of pilgrimage), which tends to give these temples an all-India importance, although many other temples have only regional, local, or neighborhood significance. But all temples are grounded on a complex pattern of squares, which represents the spatial distribution of the gods of the Hindu pantheon. That is, the basic ground plan reflects the eternal order of divine space. This plan is necessary because a temple is the earthly dwelling place of a deity, and it must conform to the deity's heavenly abode. The temple ground plan functions as a sacred geometric diagram (*maṇḍala*), which reflects the essential structure of the universe. With the squares serving as microcosmic images of the universe, the diagram reflects the world of the deities in miniature.[22] In order to construct the temple correctly, it is constructed according to a system of precise mathematical measurement, which enables it to function harmoniously with the mathematical foundation of the cosmos.

Many temples also emphasize the understanding that humans are a microcosm of the macrocosmic order. In fact, the ground plan of the temple is imagined to contain the body of a cosmic man. The spine of this figure is identified with the vertical axis of the temple. This functions symbolically as a pillar also associated with kingship and cosmic support.[23] This suggests the king's economic support for temple construction and maintenance. By economically supporting the building of temples, a king manifested his power and economic resources. Generous donations are recorded on temple walls, and many temples are decorated with military scenes that recall the glory of the victorious king.

In addition to the symbolism associated with the cosmic man, temple models also make use of other bodily symbolism. Humans are imagined to consist of sheaths or layers, such as the image in the *Taittirīya Upaniṣad* (2.1–5). The outer layer represents the physical body and the innermost layer the Ātman, universal self. When a temple is patterned on this model the outer courts are arranged concentrically around the center. The outer courts represent the outer, physical layers of the human body, whereas the innermost sanctum of the temple, which houses the image of the deity, is identified with the Ātman.

If one examines a north Indian temple (*mandir*), there are several common features that one can discover. The innermost sanctuary that contains the image or symbol of the deity is called the womb room (*garbha-gṛha*), which is associated with the germ or embryo of a temple. It is the central point from which the temple develops, and it denotes the primordial substance from which it is born.[24] Soaring above the enclosed sanctuary there is a tower called the *śikhara*. There is an entrance hall adjoining the inner sanctum, or womb room, where the officiating priest can prepare the necessary articles for worship. Devotees can gather to watch the worship in the pillared assembly hall (*maṇḍapa*) or to gain a view of the image inside the inner sanctum. In addition to an outer entrance hall, there is a processional path (*pradakṣiṇā-patha*) that is used to circumambulate the temple.

The temple in north India is constructed to face east, which is considered an auspicious direction because it is the direction of the rising sun. The ascending towers suggest that the temple is modeled on a cosmic mountain, which stands at the center of the world, and it symbolically connects heaven, earth, and the underworld. At the entrance to a temple it is not unusual to encounter images of divine beings. But as a visitor progresses toward the center of the temple, the inner sanctum, the images become fewer and light becomes weaker. This construction gives a person the sensation of penetrating deeper into a cosmic mountain. Finally, the devotee is confronted with the single image of the deity in a dark room with unadorned walls. The devotee enters a cave, which is symbolically equated with the womb room, which lies beneath the mountain and supports it. The symbolism of the cave is suggestive, because it can function as a retreat from the flux of the world, and it serves as an occasional habitation of divine beings.[25]

The door to the inner sanctum possesses symbolic importance, because an image of a deity is carved on the center of the door lintel, which implies that the deity presides over the entrance. At the lower level of the doorjambs, the gatekeepers of the deity are located. The door symbolism suggests that the door is equivalent to God, and it is through God that one enters into the presence of the supreme principle. By entering through the door, even with one's eyes, the devotee is transformed, because of the divine beings on the doorjambs. A river goddess and flowing water are carved into either side of the lintel of the door. By looking at or passing through them, the devotee takes a symbolic ritual bath that purifies him or her.[26] Therefore, the door of the womb room is equivalent to a tīrtha, a place of crossing or pilgrimage. Seeing the sacred image in the inner sanctum, the devotee sees the divine and catches a glimpse of one's essence. By recalling the soaring tower directly over the womb room, a devotee is reminded of the transcendent nature of God and oneself and of one's identity with God.

The temple in southern India creates a different impact on the devotee because of its overall conception and plan. With the main entrance facing south, the temple consists of seven rectangular walls arranged concentrically. At the four entrance points, soaring pyramidal structures called *gopurams* that are adorned with the images of deities cover each gate. Many of the scenes depicted are taken from purāṇic literature and tell stories in stone. A large lotus tank is located in many south Indian temples. These tanks are used on ceremonial occasions, when a float with the image of the deity is pulled around it. The temple also houses the offices of administrators, subsidiary temples and shrines, and shops that cater to the needs of devotees.

The seven concentric enclosing walls of the temple represent the sheaths of human beings. A visitor journeys inward toward his or her eternal nature (Ātman). After passing through the labyrinth of alleyways, a devotee arrives at the dimly lit womb room and the image of the deity, which represents the origin of the existence of the devotee and everything else.

An unusual feature of some temples of north India is the excessive erotic sculpture. The images of couples fornicating in various postures are indicative of the value of kāma (desire), which is a traditionally accepted goal of life. In addition, these images serve an auspicious function in the sense that they depict happiness and well-being along with the wish they these happenings will occur in life. The erotic sculptures also enhance fertility and abundance in the sense that the images stimulate the generative aspects of nature.[27] The images may also be intended to ward off the evil eye and serve a protective function. Finally, it may be possible that the erotic images depict aristocratic couples having sexual relations, and thus serve as portraits of donors.[28]

Overall, temples play a complex role in Indian culture. They are places of pilgrimage regardless of their location. They represent the house and body of the deity, offering the faithful an opportunity for darśana (viewing) of the divine body, which is the precise reason for visiting a temple.[29] Some temples function as educational centers; wealthy donors make endowments to temples that create colleges. Moreover, temples are economically important in that they have functioned as landlords of farmland and its produce. Because of its holy and inviolable nature, temple land is immune from military attack. In fact, a temple may serve as a fortress to protect people during periods of war.

Sacred Images

When a Hindu artist attempts to create an image he does not portray details of physical anatomy such as musculature. The artist is more concerned about the inward quality of retained breath, because breath (*prāṇa*) is identified with the essence of life. Therefore, most images show bodies that appear tautly drawn, as if containing an internal pressure.

The actual creation of a sacred wooden image involves a very secret ritual called the *navakalevana* ceremony, which has five phases: forest rites, carving, burial and purification of the old image, preparing new images, and bathing.[30] The first phase involves a search for the wood, which might involve a non-Brahmin priest receiving information, possibly in a dream, about the location of a tree. After a tree is located, Brahmin priests perform a fire sacrifice before it is cut down. The deity Viṣṇu is asked by the party through a dream whether or not the tree is acceptable. Assuming that the acceptability is affirmed, the carving of the image begins, which is considered a very dangerous activity. Any outsider observing or hearing the creation runs the risk of becoming deaf or blind. In order to protect others from the dangers of the carving, the sound of this activity is drowned out by continuous music. This phase also involves transferring the life-substance (*brahmapadārtha*) of the old image to the new one. The third phase of the rite represents the burial and purification of the old image, which is considered dead when its life-substance is removed. Burial occurs in a cemetery within the temple compound, and it also involves mourning the dead image, and the death results in a condition of ritual impurity for participants for a period of the ten days following days. The new image is prepared by infusing it with flesh and blood, which is done by applying various layers of symbolic substances such as cloth strips for skin, red yarn or cloth for blood, resin for flesh, perfumed oil for marrow, sandal paste for fat, and rice or wheat starch for semen. Once the body of the deity is created in this manner, painters apply paint to the image, with the exception of the pupils of the eyes, because Brahmins paint the eyes onto the image, which brings it to life in a solemn ceremony within the inner sanctum of the temple. Finally, the image is bathed with the intention of freeing it from contamination incurred through contact with carpenters, sculptors, and painters, who are collectively members of the lower castes.

Indian images serve several functions. By incarnating itself in an image, a divine being works to reform individuals. The beauty of an image functions to attract people to god. Or the image operates to induce people to take refuge with god. An image serves as a means to focus the concentration of a viewer, and it enables one to honor and love god. The image also serves as both the goal and the object of the devotee's enjoyment. Moreover, the divine image functions to symbolize the accessibility of the deity. Finally, it reminds devotees of their mutual relationship to god, and it brings them into a closer relationship. This relationship between devotees and god is mutually beneficial because the former depend on a divine being, and a god depends on devotees for care.

Body Symbolism of Divine Images

When a deity descends into the body of an image, it is entrusting itself to human care. The image is thus not merely a symbol of a divine being; it is the deity. This means that images must be treated as persons with the respect due to their sovereign status. The devotee can expect beneficent returns. The use of images within a devotional context provides a means for ordinary people to gain access to god and ultimately to attain transcendence.[31] The basic presupposition behind the use of images is that ordinary sensory powers are inadequate to perceive the divine. Therefore, limited humans need visual images to objectify the divine in order to see it. It is also important to recognize that any image does not represent full divinity, because it is always incomplete, inadequate, and impermanent. Images are created, live, die, and are replaced. Thus their existence is only temporary. Images that are particularly temporary are made for festivals and discarded after the event. Temple images tend to be more permanent, even though they may one day be retired to a museum. During the medieval period of Indian history, images within temples were considered valuable enough by victorious monarchs to be seized as spoils of war. The confiscation of images was not considered theft within the context of warfare.

Many images have large eyes to emphasize the significance of perception, which we previously discussed. The facial expression of images tends to be focused inward, detached, and otherworldly. A calm expression is even retained when a deity is engaged in violent action. An excellent example of this calm and detached expression is the face of the goddess Durgā as she slays the buffalo demon. The faces of male and female deities are very similar, with fish-shaped eyes, arched eye-brows, full lips, and a prominent nose.[32] In order to understand the symbolic significance of the arms and hands of the image, it needs to be noted that the right side of the body is auspicious, whereas the left side is inauspicious.

It is common to find a divine image holding a destructive weapon in its left hand, while it makes a benevolent gesture with its right hand. A feature that strikes many Westerners as strange is the multiple arms and hands of the divine image. These many arms and hands do not mean that Hindu deities are freaks; it rather suggests the various powers of a deity. Many images make hand gestures (*mudras*) in order to convey a message to the viewer by skillful use of the fingers and hands. An uplifted outward-directed palm signifies bestowing grace or "fear not," whereas a downward palm signifies submission. The hands of images hold emblems that can become items worshiped as cult objects, such as the conch shell and discus of Viṣṇu or the flute of Krishna. These various kinds of emblems also enable a viewer to distinguish deities from each other.

In addition to arms and hands and messages that they convey about the deity, postures of the body are also informative. An image might be seated in a lotus meditative posture, or it might be standing. A favorite posture employs the three bends (*tribhanga*) that occur at the neck, shoulders, and hips. The feet upon which a deity stands are important, because they are indicative of shelter and protection, even though feet are considered the lowest part of the body. The tradition in Indian culture is that a person touches the feet of superiors and protectors. By touching the feet of another person or divine image, a person is giving a signal of their submission and surrender to that being. Touching the feet of another being is also an act of humility, because one accepts from a deity or holy person what is base and impure, and one treats it as something valuable and pure. If one surrenders by touching the feet of another, this gesture implies a reciprocal obligation, because the being to which one surrenders must accept the person doing the surrendering. This act of acceptance can be acknowledged by making a gesture of blessing such as touching the head or shoulder of the other with one's hand. Moreover, beside touching or looking at the feet of a divine being, a devotee can wash them. This water is considered foot-nectar, which is a medium of beneficial power, which a person can drink. The act of drinking it is a manifestation of the drinker's humble character and adoration of the superior figure.

Music and Its Divine Connection

Festivals, processions with divine images, and other devotional activities often include music, an important aspect of the sensual nature of Hinduism. It is said that the deities are pleased by music. In Hinduism, music possesses its own patron goddess, Sarasvatī, who governs learning and the arts. This goddess is often depicted holding a stringed musical instrument in her hand called the *vina*. Due to their connection to the sacred power of the goddess, instruments are treated with great respect. In fact, musicians worship their musical instruments as the body of the goddess with offerings of fruit, incense, and flowers. A musician must not touch an instrument with his foot. If one inadvertently does so, he or she must immediately ritually touch the instrument to the eyes and forehead in a gesture of reverent homage. The respect accorded an instrument extends to not taking it into a ritually unclean room, or allowing it to have contact with one's lips or leftover food. The latter prohibitions are associated with the polluting nature of saliva.

The rhythm of music resonates with the vibrations of the universe. The fundamental importance of rhythm can be witnessed in the rhythm of walking or running animals and the rhythmic way in which the sun and planets move through the sky. The emotions and moods of humans express a rhythm.[33] By using music within a devotional context, devotees are conforming to the rhythm of the universe. This places them and their actions within the context of a universal harmony in which they can sing and dance to the eternal music of the cosmos.

The three forms of music—vocal, instrumental, and dance—are all connected to sound (*nāda*). This is explained by stating that the essence of vocal music is sound (*nāda*), instrumental music manifests sound, and dance is based on sound. As a manifestation of sound, music is a mode of access to the highest reality. Therefore, the sounds made by musicians and their instruments possess a metaphysical status in Hinduism. Sanskrit texts identify sound (*nāda*) with Brahman, the highest reality. The gods also have sound in their essence.

There are two forms of sound (*nāda*): unstruck and struck. The former sound is a vibration of ether (*ākāsa*) that permeates all space, and it cannot be perceived, although it is the basis of the perceptible universe. The struck sound is produced by a physical blow, which consists of a temporary vibration of air. Ordinary mortals can hear the struck sound, which is a manifestation of the eternal sound. A struck sound is pleasing to people, and it breaks the cycle of earthly existence, because it reveals the unstruck sound. Thereby, it brings a person into contact with ultimate reality. Its uniqueness is connected to its ability to usher in liberation painlessly and pleasurably. In the tantric tradition, *nāda* represents the reverberating tone of verbal sound that fades away with the recitation of a mantra (sacred formula) such as AUM.[34] As a manifestation of sound, music is a mode of access to the highest reality.

This metaphysical background helps one to understand that a musician is not considered an originator of his music. He is rather a transmitter and preserver: he may be considered a conduit through whom the eternal unstruck sound becomes struck and thus accessible to other humans. In short, music exists eternally. Within the context of devotional Hinduism, the musician is not precisely a conduit; he is rather a devotee. But he possesses the ability through his music to invoke the divine presence. The music created can produce ineffable joy for the listeners, it can create an inner calm, and it can create an experience of unity.

A Sensuous Literature

The mythical themes depicted on temples, expressed in music and song, and depicted in divine images, as well as devotional practices that reflect deep sensual and emotional feelings are all reflected in a type of literature that became paramount for devotional Hinduism. This new literature is called *purāṇa*, which means ancient or old. It falls within the rubric of smṛti (what is remembered), and not revelation (*śruti*). In general, there are five characteristics of a purāṇic text that reflect five distinct topics within a particular text: creation; re-creation; genealogies of gods, sages, and the Veda; an account of the ages of the world and their regents; and the genealogies of kings. There are about eighteen major purāṇic texts that include the following examples: Agni, Brahmā, Garuḍa, Padma, Skanda, Śiva, Vāmana, Liṅga, Viṣṇu, and Bhāgavata. The emphasis on the number eighteen might be an attempt to connect the major purāṇic texts with the epic *Mahābhārata* with its eighteen parvans (sections), eighteen chapters of the *Bhagavad Gītā*, eighteen days of the epic war, and the eighteen armies fighting the war.[35] In contrast to these so-called Mahāpurāṇas (great or major Purāṇas), there is also a group of texts called the Upapurāṇas (minor texts). There is less agreement about the names of the minor works, but there are only a few differences between the great and minor texts.[36] The minor texts include, for instance, more material that reflects the local context in which they developed, and these texts fail to include all five of the distinguishing characteristics of the great texts.

It is likely that the Purāṇas originated from an oral tradition of transmission. In fact, it is possible to identify a combination of dual oral sources. The ritual practices and social values embodied within the texts demonstrate the influence of the Brahmin caste, whereas heroic deeds and social values of the Kṣatriya caste are also represented. The former material originated with reciters of the Vedas, while charioteers (*sūtas*) passed on the material within warrior circles. It was the duty of the charioteer, who occupied a lower social status than the warrior, to report on the heroic actions of his master and to celebrate his victory in battle through recitations. Thus the origin of the Purāṇas is connected with the performance of an oral tradition. The Purāṇas began to be collected during the Gupta Dynasty, which is often called a Hindu renaissance, during the fourth to sixth centuries C.E.

Smārta Brahmins, which means members of the highest caste that observe smṛti (remembered tradition), preserved these texts. This was also a group of Brahmins that began to incorporate devotional practices of non-Brahmins into their own rituals. Using the various purāṇic texts, these Brahmins were able to disseminate their ideology to a wider audience; they creating a synthesis between the social norms embodied within the caste dharma and the values of the renouncer, promoted sectarian interests, absorbed local cults, spread instruction for the proper way to conduct daily life, and incorporated as many people as possible without compromising the fundamental objective of establishing a Brahmanic social order.[37]

The morality exhibited by the epic *Bhagavad Gītā* tends to predominate in the Purāṇas. This implies that social duty, which is based on one's caste and station in life, and love of god are more important than gaining release (*mokṣa*) from the world. The purāṇic texts reflect a relatively worldly attitude by recognizing the value of life on earth and not encouraging release from the world. This attitude did not mean that the texts were less important than the Vedas. In fact, the Purāṇas considered themselves equivalent to the Vedas in importance, as exemplified by the *Vāyu Purāṇa* (1.11.4.12). The Purāṇas are distinguished from an epic such as the *Mahābhārata* because the epic is a story about events (*itihāsa*), whereas Purāṇas are more concerned with mythological narratives and genealogies of kings.

The worldview of the Purāṇas is different from the ancient Vedic view. The notion of time is expressed, for instance, by the four *yugas* (ages), which is a term that is derived from the throws of dice and suggests that life is similar to a gigantic dice game. The initial age, which represents a kind of golden period, is the *kṛta yuga*, which lasts 1,728,000 years. This age of perfection is symbolically expressed by a mythical cow, which represents the dharma (social and comic order), standing on four legs. The *tretā yuga* lasts a total of 1,296,000 years, during which time the mythical cow stands on three legs. This silver age is followed by the copper age of the *dvāpara yuga*. During this age, the mythical cow stands on two legs for 864,000 years. Finally, the mythical cow stands on one leg in the present degenerate age of the *kali yuga*, which will last for 432,000 years. The one-legged cow signifies that humans are no longer able to perform good deeds. Moreover, the kali yuga is a dark age of strife, quarrel, dissension, and war. In short, the kali yuga represents an age of evil. The kali yuga is paradoxically also called a blessed age because during it, it is easier to gain salvation, even for women and members of the lowest castes.[38] According to the *Viṣṇu Purāṇa* (5.38.8), the kali yuga began with the death of Krishna. If one compares the four yugas, one notices that each yuga lasts for a diminishing length of time, because each age signifies an increasing decline in virtue. Each cycle of four yugas is called a *mahāyuga* (great age) or a *manvantara* (age of Manu). An entire mahāyuga of 4,320,000 years is equivalent to one day in the life of the god Brahmā, which is called a *kalpa* (eon). At the end of a mahāyuga, there is a minor dissolution of the world, with a return to cosmic non-differentiation, whereas there is a major dissolution at the end of a kalpa. After an unspecified period, the cosmos is created anew and the process of time begins again with the dawn of a new kṛta age.

Besides the new understanding of time, the purāṇic texts reflect a different conception of the world. The cosmos is shaped like an egg of seven concentric spheres. The initial three spheres include the earth, atmosphere, and heaven, which correspond to the ancient vedic worldview. Human beings inhabit the earth, whereas the divine beings populate four heavens. There are seven nether worlds, which are inhabited by demons and chthonic beings. The center of the cosmic egg is the earth (*bhurloka*) with Jambūdvīpa (India) its central continent, surrounded concentrically by six other circular lands. From the center of Jambūdvīpa (India), there rises Mount Meru, which is ringed by continents and oceans. This central mountain is wider at the top than at its base, because its top is identified with a city in which the divine beings dwell. Located in no particular place are hells, which are intended to provide retribution for social transgressions. These multiple hells are the domains of Yama, god of the dead, who functions as an executor. At death a person can be sent to either of two kinds of hell.

There are hells that inflict punishment upon the body by external means such as burning vats, pincers, razor-sharp leaves, flaying of skin, and crushing by mortars, while other hells cause internal pollution of the body with such punishments as being forced to eat foul and dreadful things. These various kinds of punishment are temporary, because they are succeeded by inevitable rebirth. Because the Lord of Death, Yama, is merely an executor, there is no external judging agent associated with the various hells.[39] The realms of heaven, hell, or earth are all impermanent. Overall, the purāṇic cosmos can be characterized as a universe of bhakti (devotion).[40] This claim is supported by the fact that there is a single supreme god that represents the overarching reality.

The Unity of the Sensuous Elements

In contrast to the ascetic life of the world-renouncer discussed in chapter 3 and the inward yogic and meditative path advocated by some Indian schools of thought, reviewed in chapter 5, with its emphasis on ecstatic and unitive experiences, devotional Hinduism is more focused on this world. Instead of controlling one's senses, a devotee can use his or her senses to experience the divine. In the true meaning of the term *bhakti* (devotion), a devotee participates with others, shares love of his or her deity, and worships by participating communally in rites, festivals, pilgrimage, and sharing food with the deity. Participating, sharing, worshiping, and loving are all accomplished by using one's senses.

Bhakti is also dialogical because the devotee often carries on a conversation with the deity, or the devotee sings the praises of god. A devotee is encouraged to totally surrender to god, so that a devotee feels like a slave or a child of the deity. The devotees may experience separation from god. And reunion with the object of one's devotion can take the devotee from feelings of abjection to soaring heights of ecstasy. Whether in separation or reunion, a devotee might be pushed to tears by his or her emotions. The precise theological nature of faith and the way that grace operates are defined differently in different forms of devotional Hinduism, which will become evident in the next few chapters. Nonetheless, an intimate personal relationship between the devotee and deity persists in spite of sophisticated theological reflection.

Although theological reflection is not discouraged, it is the sensual nature of devotional Hinduism that appeals to its many adherents. We have called attention to the sectarian inclusive, emotional, and perceptual aspects of the devotional path. The participatory and sharing aspects of the path are evident in the hospitality of pūjā (worship). The leftover food offerings (*prasāda*) give an ordinary devotee a rich taste of the divine.

The sensually excessive nature of bhakti can be witnessed in festivals that render participants sensually and spiritually refreshed and renewed. Everyone is invited to participate, because the invitation to devotion is universal or obliterates social distinctions. In comparison to festivals, pilgrimage is more subdued, although it can be just as physically and emotionally draining as a festival. The pilgrimage journey is both an external transit with one's feet and an internal journey within one's heart. A pilgrim feels the journey with one's feet and body, and at the tīrtha one may experience the water with one's tactile sense. Internally, a devotee may experience love and joy.

The art and architecture of temples are perceptually sensual, as are the sacred images that are housed in them. The music and songs praising god appeal to one's emotions and sense of hearing. Finally, the rich stories of the Purāṇas appeal to the senses, or at least evoke a devotee's senses, and the reader's imagination. Nonetheless, the sensual nature of Hindu devotionalism is grounded in its social dimension and its connection to specific regional languages and cultural regions.

7

Embodiment of Viṣṇu on Earth

From the perspective of the purāṇic texts, human beings are living in the darkest, most immoral, unrighteous, and degenerate age, called the kali yuga, which is the final age before the destruction of the cosmos. During this benighted and brutal period, demonic forces plague the earth and its inhabitants. Many purāṇic narratives that recount struggles of gods battling these forces for the benefit of humankind during this degenerate age preserve instances of demonic triumph or other types of worldly catastrophe. Such an instance occurred when a demon named Hiraṇyakaśipu became uncontrollable by means of his practice of asceticism (*tapas*). In order to attempt to placate the demon, the god Brahmā granted him a boon. According to the narrative of the *Śiva Purāṇa* (2.5.4–43), the demon asked the god for the following benefit: he could not be killed by day or night, by god, man, or beast, and not inside or outside of his palace. In order to defeat this even more powerful demon, a champion of divine and human beings had to become incarnated on earth to triumph over the demon and rescue the cosmos. This incarnated god is Viṣṇu, from the perspective of his mythology and devotees called Vaiṣṇavas. Within the context of this narrative, there are two versions for the rationale of the incarnation. In one version, Viṣṇu becomes incarnate because the demon inflicted cruel punishment on his son for his devotion to the God; the alternative version depicts the demon attempting to destroy the earth because Viṣṇu is responsible for the death of the demon's brother. In both versions, Viṣṇu incarnates himself on earth at twilight, within a pillar at the entrance to the palace. The time and place are chosen specifically to counteract the boon won by the demon with respect to time of the day, location, and type of god, man, or beast. As the demon steps to the threshold of his palace, Viṣṇu, incarnated as Narasiṃha, the man-lion, leaps from the pillar and tears the demon's body to shreds.

In another narrative from the *Matsya Purāṇā* (1.11–34), the problem is a world flood. After practicing asceticism (*tapas*) for a long time, Manu is given a boon by the deity Brahmā. Representing all human beings in this story, Manu asks to be made the protector of all creatures. Later Manu finds a tiny fish, and he places it in a bowl in order to save it. But the fish outgrows the bowl, and it cries to Manu to save it. Manu responds by placing the fish in a large pitcher, which the fish proceeds to outgrow. The fish repeats this pattern as it is placed into a well, then the Ganges River, and finally the ocean. Once the huge fish is placed into the ocean, Manu asks the fish about its identity. Is it a demon? Or is it a deity? This prodigious fish is Matsya, an incarnation of Viṣṇu. Once he is in the ocean, Viṣṇu warns Manu about the coming world flood, and he orders Manu to take a representative of each creature into a boat in order to be saved. When the flood actually does come Viṣṇu appears as a horned fish, and Manu ties his boat by means of a rope, which is in the form of a snake, to the horn of the fish. Thus a remnant of each species is saved from the world flood. The narratives of the flood and man-lion suggest that Viṣṇu is a deity who is close to human beings and cares about their problems, because he is willing to become embodied on earth in order to assist in a time of need. This does not, however, mean that he is not transcendent. It is just that the Vaiṣṇava religious tradition tends to stress his immanence and loving nature. In short, this is the picture of what can be called the purāṇic definition of Viṣṇu. This understanding of the nature of this god evolved through a long historical process about which we do not possess all the evidence needed to present a complete and accurate picture. It is possible, nonetheless, to compose an outline of Viṣṇu's development into one of the major deities of Hinduism.

Historical Development of Viṣṇu

The fully evolved purāṇic Viṣṇu makes his appearance sometime between the fourth and sixth centuries C.E. In order to reach this point, Viṣṇu emerges historically from a figure that appears in the Vedic literature, and this vedic Viṣṇu merges with separate deities from three other religious traditions: Nārāyaṇa, Vāsudeva-Krishna, and Saṃkarṣaṇa-Baladeva.

The vedic Viṣṇu is best known for his three strides that separate the earth from the sky (RV 1.154). He does not have a well-defined character in the Vedas, but he is a figure of great potential development. The name for this benevolent solar deity is derived from a Sanskrit verbal root *viś*, which means to enter or pervade. Thus Viṣṇu is the one that enters or pervades the universe. Viṣṇu gains for the gods their all-pervading powers, and for humans he gains ample space in which they can live. Viṣṇu's pervading power is also expressed as being instrumental in protecting the goddess Aditi's lap, which signifies the place where creation occurs. As a traversing and pervading deity, Viṣṇu creates room for a person's sacrifice to reach the domain of the gods (RV 7.99.4), and he also helps a sacrificer by bringing him wealth, providing guidance for good conduct, and a way to safety (RV 1.156.5; 6.69.1; 8.77.10).

During the ancient vedic period, Viṣṇu is closely associated with the warrior god Indra. Here he appears as the assistant and younger brother of Indra, which implies a measure of equality with respect to rank and power. Moreover, by means of his mere presence, Viṣṇu contributes to Indra's success. Viṣṇu is depicted preparing Soma for Indra. Gradually, Viṣṇu assumes Indra's position, and he becomes a great fighter for the other members of the vedic pantheon.

In his rise to preeminence, Viṣṇu absorbs elements of Indra's nature and that of the divine Prajāpati, who is a deity closely associated with sacrifice in ancient vedic religion. Viṣṇu is identified with the sacrifice (ŚB 5.2.3.6), is called protector of the sacrificial oblations (VS 1.4; 7.20), and is even identified with the sacrificer, an equation that suggests that the god can deliver whatever the sacrifice cannot convey. Moreover, Viṣṇu is considered the deity of the sacrificial stake (*yūpa*). Viṣṇu's direct connection to the sacrificial stake means that he represents the center of the world (*axis mundi*) that supports the triple cosmos (RV 1.22.19; 1.61.7; 2.22.1; 5.87.4). When a sacrificer imitates the god's actions he reaches his goal, and he acquires the powers to pervade and penetrate the cosmos.[1]

Viṣṇu is also closely associated with the energy of the sun, and like the light of the sun that shines on everyone equally, Viṣṇu demonstrates an unremitting and equal concern with the plight of all humans. Knowing such characteristics, ancient Indians attempted to gain his cooperation in annihilating destructive influences. Therefore, Viṣṇu is a deity conceived to be close to humans in their everyday struggles for survival, a characteristic especially emphasized by his incarnations at a later date.

As the vedic Viṣṇu developed a separate identity, he absorbed features of the deity Nārāyaṇa (he whose abode is the waters), a name used for Viṣṇu when he sleeps on the cosmic ocean between successive periods of the dissolution and creation of the cosmos. Nārāyaṇa's name can also be construed as meaning the resting place or goal of the gods and humans. Nārāyaṇa is described by the *Śatapatha Brāhmaṇa* (12.3.4) as having been sent forth from the place of the sacrifice, and he is asked by Prajāpati to sacrifice again within a context of being associated with the cosmic man (13.6.1). By means of the sacrifice, Nārāyaṇa places himself throughout the universe. It is possible that Nārāyaṇa originated outside the vedic pantheon, and became adopted by priestly sources. Around the fourth century B.C.E., Nārāyaṇa appears in the *Mahānārāyaṇa Upaniṣad* (201–269), where he is cited as the absolute deity who also dwells within a person's heart. Although Nārāyaṇa is identified initially with the deity Brahmā, he is finally acknowledged as Viṣṇu sometime around the fourth century C.E. In the eleventh-century text entitled *Kathāsaritsāgara* (Ocean Stream of Stories, 54.19, 21–23), the name Nārāyaṇa is used to identify Viṣṇu dwelling in his heaven where he lies on the serpent body of Śeṣa with his consort Lakṣmi reclining at his feet.

In addition to fusing with Nārāyaṇa, the vedic Viṣṇu merged with the god of an independent cult called Vāsudeva-Krishna and an ascetic deity called Saṃkarṣaṇa-Baladeva. These additional divine figures were to develop into the purāṇic Krishna and become an important incarnation of Viṣṇu. But the historical development of Krishna will be considered in the following chapter, at which time he will be treated as a deity with his own separate identity. His devotees would agree with this approach, for them he is the ultimate deity.

Incarnations of Viṣṇu

The Sanskrit term for incarnation is *avatāra*, which connotes descent. It is not unreasonable for a curious reader to ask the following question: Why does a transcendent deity incarnate himself on earth? Krishna gives to the warrior Arjuna the classical Vaiṣṇava answer in the *Bhagavad Gītā* (4.8):

> For protection of the good,
> And for destruction of evil-doers,
> To make a firm footing for the right,
> I come into being in age after age.

Thus when chaos reigns on earth, Krishna comes to restore righteousness (*dharma*). The passage also suggests that the need for an incarnation has occurred in the past and will be needed in the future.

Prior to the notion of the avatāra (incarnation), an early Vaiṣṇava sect called the Pāñcarātras worshiped four gods—Vāsudeva, Saṃkarṣaṇa, Pradyumna, and Aniruddha—that formed the *vyūhas* (successive emanations from god). The term *vyūha* implies shoving asunder. Within the context of vedic ritualism, it represented an effective arrangement of the parts to construct a coherent whole. This suggests that by pushing asunder the parts of a coherent whole one can obtain a central place that is a safe position.[2] The four emanations represent a pure creation and the highest level of the universe. Beneath this pure creation is a mixed creation that is followed by an impure or material one. Each emanation (*vyūha*) possesses a cosmological function with respect to the lower creation, which consists of categories (*tattva*) similar to those in Sāṃkhya philosophy; this scheme accounts for the way that the one and the many relate to each other and evolve.[3] The vyūha doctrine was eventually eclipsed by the notion of avatāra in the post-epic period of Vaiṣṇavism.

The standard number of incarnations is ten, many of whom were independent deities before being merged with Viṣṇu. In addition to the Fish and Man-lion incarnations discussed at the beginning of this chapter, other incarnations include the Tortoise (Kūrma), the Boar (Varāha), the Dwarf (Vāmana), Rāma with an axe (Paraśurāma), Rāma, Krishna, Buddha, and Kalkin. The Purāṇas mention other figures as well, such as Balarāma (Krishna's brother); Hayagrīva (Horse-necked), who recovered the Vedas stolen by demonic giants; and Dattātreya, who is a rustic, pleasure-seeking figure.

Besides helping humans, Viṣṇu also incarnates himself in order to assist other deities. A good example of helping divine beings is evident in the Tortoise incarnation, when he offers his back to support the churning stick of the gods and demons as they churned the ocean of milk to obtain the nectar of immortality.

Elephant-headed deity Gaṅeśa, British National Museum, London.

Śiva and his consort Pārvatī, British National Museum, London.

Viṣṇu flanked by his consorts Bhū and Devī, Indian National Museum, Madras.

Krishna holding flute in classical "three bends" style.

Gaṅeśa making "fear not" gesture with his right hand and holding a hatchet in his left hand.

Hanuman, monkey-hero of Rāmāyaṇa epic.

Śiva as Lord of Dance.

Goddess Kālī.

Icon of Śiva and his consort Pārvatī.

Śiva.

Liṅga and yoni, iconic symbol of Śiva and his consort.

Multi-armed Gaṅeśa.

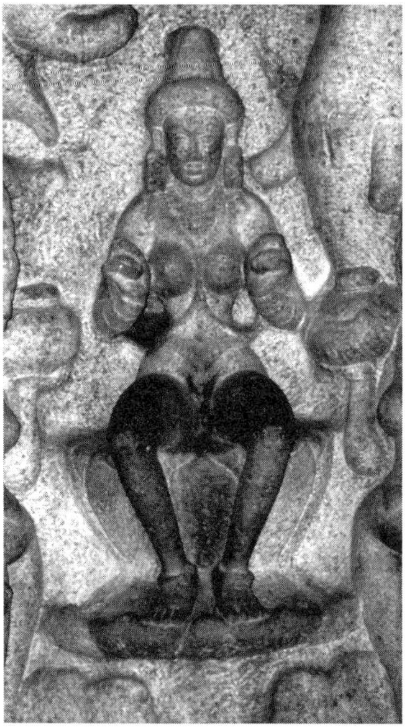

Gaja Lakṣmī, consort of Viṣṇu stone carving in temple cave at Mahabalipuram.

Viṣṇu incarnated as the boar, stone carving in rock temple at Mahabalipuram.

Goddess Durgā seated on her lion vehicle defeating buffalo demon, stone carving on wall of rock temple in Mahabalipuram.

Detail of buffalo demon, Mahiṣāsura.

Krishna on wall rock temple in Mahabalipuram.

Temple bathing tank.

One of the Five Rathas (seventh century) or miniature "temple chariots" sculped from boulders in Mahabalipuram.

Priest performing pūjā (worship) of Lakṣmī, consort of Viṣṇu.

Gopuram (gateway) to Śrī Ekamranathan Temple in Kāñchipuram.

Priests making an offering to goddess.

Entrance to Brihadishvara Temple in Thanjavur (Tanjore).

Gopuram (gateway) to Brihadishvara Temple.

Detail of gopuram to Brihadishvara Temple.

Multi-headed Gaṅeśa,
Brihadishvara Temple.

Temple tank, Brihadishvara Temple.

Gopuram (gateway) to Brihadishvara Temple.

Detail of gopuram, to Brihadishvara Temple.

Detail of temple wall,
Brihadishvara Temple.

Interior court of Brihadishvara Temple.

Gopuram (gateway) to Kapaleeswara Temple in Madras.

Carved images over entrance to building within Kapaleeswara Temple.

Carving of Śkanda, son of Śiva.

Young child feeding cow that wandered into Kapaleeswara Temple.

Shore Temple at Mahabalipuram.

Shore Temple that served Indian sailors.

Nandin, bull vehicle of Śiva, Shore Temple.

Sometimes, Viṣṇu incarnates in order to assist the earth, itself. As the Boar incarnation—an ambivalent creature because of its amphibious nature—he dives into the cosmic ocean where the earth is lost, and hooks the earth on his tusk, and returns it to the surface (ŚivaP 9.1.11.10–36). This rescue mission transforms chaos into order or cosmos. The Boar was historically at first Prajāpati.

Viṣṇu chiefly incarnates to assist humans in his other descents to earth. Recalling his three steps in vedic literature, he appears as the Dwarf to counteract the demon Bali, who gained power over the three worlds through the practice of asceticism (*tapas*). As part of his ruse, the Dwarf approaches Bali, and he asks for as much land as he can encompass with three steps. According to the *Vāyu Purāṇa* (2.36.74–86), Bali agrees to this request only to discover to his consternation that the initial step covers the entire earth, and the second step encompasses the heavens. Without a place left for the third step, Viṣṇu rests his foot on Bali's head, and pushes him into the underworld, where he now reigns. As the hero Rāma, Viṣṇu incarnates himself to defeat the demon Rāvaṇa, rescue his wife Sītā, and regain his throne. Viṣṇu incarnates as Krishna in order to defeat, among others, his evil uncle Kaṃsa.

The Paraśurāma, or Rāma with an axe, incarnation plays a role in three episodes. In one episode, he reclaims land from the sea by hurling his axe at the sea and frightening it into retreat. In another episode, blindly obeying his father's instructions, he decapitates his mother—accomplishing what his brothers could not do—and he then requests her restoration to life. Finally, he annihilates all members of the warrior caste, as a Brahmin, using an axe, in order to avenge his father's murder (BhāgP 9.15.16–41; 16.1–27).

The incarnation as the Buddha is a bit misleading and not as ecumenical as it might appear at first glance. Because the Buddha is said to lead humankind astray with false teaching, this incarnation is intended to destroy demons with an evil and erroneous teaching (ViṣṇuP 3.17.9–45). A basic Indian cultural principle behind this incarnation is that one cannot destroy a virtuous person unless one corrupts that person first. Iconographically, the Buddha appears on a Gupta-era temple called Daśavatāra temple at Deogarh, and he also is mentioned on a seventh-century Pallava inscription in south India. The Buddha incarnation might have been inspired by the final incarnation.[4]

The final incarnation will come at the end of the kali yuga as Kalkin, who will appear on a white horse (ViṣṇuP 4.24.25–29). Kalkin's purpose will be to destroy the invaders of India and exterminate all heretics, especially the Buddhists (Mbh 3.188.93). Kalkin is thus a millennial figure needed to bring the evil age to a conclusion. Although the origin of Kalkin might represent a cultural reaction to invasions during the second century B.C.E. and the second century C.E., his primary inspiration could possibly be traced to the Buddhist figure of Maitreya, a messianic figure in Buddhism expected to arrive in the future. It can be ultimately traced to Zoroastrian notions connected to a future savior.[5]

Viṣṇu is able to assume these many forms by means of his power of māyā (illusory power), which he probably inherited from his early association with

Indra. Māyā is a creative power that gives a god such as Viṣṇu the ability to change bodily forms, be creative, and deceive others with tricks, magic, and illusions. Thus māyā refers to an appearance that does not have a cause or effect. In vedic literature, māyā refers to the ability of gods to change forms, create, or extend. Like a mask, māyā is illusory because it creates a false impression that disguises something, and it is mysterious, unpredictable and bewitching.[6] The phenomenal world is created and sustained by this power. In addition to Viṣṇu, other sectarian deities also possess this power.

By the fourth century, Viṣṇu is represented iconographically with four arms, expressing his absolute power over the four directions of space, the four stages of human development, and the four aims of life. In his lower right hand, he holds a conch shell, which represents his creative tendency.[7] The conch shell, which is blown during certain religious ceremonies in the temple, is believed to produce a sound associated with the primeval sound connected to the act of creation; it thus is symbolic of the origin of existence. It possesses a symbolic association with fertility because of its aquatic origin and resemblance to a female sexual organ.[8] The conch also functions to ward off evil and destroy demons. In his upper right hand, he holds a discus, which represents a cohesive tendency. The discus also has a symbolic connection to the lotus flower, the seasons, illusion (*māyā*), and the sun. It is a fiery weapon that operates like a boomerang by returning to Viṣṇu after he throws it to cut off the head of a demon or sever ignorance from a human mind. Viṣṇu's upper left hand, which is indicative of dispersion and liberation, holds a bow and lotus. The bow symbolizes the causal power of illusion (*māyā*), which gives rise to the universe, whereas the lotus is associated with fertility and connected to the positive force of the cosmic waters. In his lower left hand, Viṣṇu caries a mace, which symbolizes primeval knowledge.

In addition to items that he holds in his hands, Viṣṇu possesses distinctive identifying marks on his body. On his chest is a jewel called the *kauṣṭubha* (treasure of the ocean), which emerged from the milky ocean after the gods churned it. There is also a whorl of golden hair (*śrivatsa*, literally beloved of Śrī) on his chest, which is symbolic of a universal monarch.[9] Viṣṇu wears a yellow cloth, which symbolizes the Vedas, around his hips, and a sacred thread whose three strands symbolize the sacred syllable AUM (OM). From his navel grows a lotus upon which sits the god Brahmā, who originates from the flower. Viṣṇu's navel represents the center of the cosmos, and it thus serves as the source of existence.

Two natural objects are associated with Viṣṇu. The black stone called the *śalagrāma* symbolizes the deity by its connection to his discus because it is similar in that it has internal spiral grooves. Some devotees wear this stone around their necks. Another natural object connected to Viṣṇu is the *tulsī* (basil) plant, whose stem is made into a necklace that is believed to destroy insects, diseases, demons, and evil spirits, and purify the atmosphere. In addition to deities residing on its leaves, the plant is said to be the meeting place of heaven and earth.[10]

As with virtually all Hindu gods, Viṣṇu possesses a vehicle (*vāhana*). In his case, he is associated with two, depending on whether or not he is awake or asleep. When he is awake Viṣṇu rides on Garuḍa, a half-eagle and half-man creature, with the head, wings, talons, and beak of an eagle and the body and limbs of a man. This creature is symbolically connected to the sun. When Viṣṇu is asleep at the end of the age of the world he reclines on the serpent called either Śeṣa (Remainder) or Ānanta (Endless). This immortal serpent floats on the cosmic waters, which represent the unevolved form of nature, and it bears the world on its enormous head. The serpent is actually identified with Viṣṇu as an animal counterpart of the sleeper.

These iconic forms of Viṣṇu are a different way for him to manifest himself, just as any of his incarnational forms is another form of embodiment. This all-pervading deity also incarnates himself within the heart of devotees and acts as their inner controller. Moreover, Viṣṇu functions as the creator, preserver, and destroyer of the world. He is credited with being the founder of all important institutions, and the guide and goal of humanity.

Consort of Viṣṇu

Sometime between the fourth and sixth centuries C.E., Viṣṇu becomes closely associated with the goddess Śrī Lakṣmī, who becomes his consort and inseparable companion. This goddess probably originated as two independent figures that merged during the period of the early Upaniṣads.[11] The term *lakṣmī* originally meant a sign or an omen of good or bad luck. During the postvedic period, she became a goddess of wealth or fortune. The term *śrī* denotes well-being, prosperity, luck, and splendor; it is associated with a complete life, offspring, the life sap, honor, glory, and dignity. Thus to lose śrī implies hunger, misfortune, and unhappiness. It is not until around 900 B.C.E. that Śrī appears as a female deity. There is textual evidence that suggests that she had a non-Aryan origin as a Yakṣinī, a semi-divine chthonic spirit, who along with male Yakṣas are guardians of wealth buried in the earth and are attendants of the god Kubera. The non-Aryan origin of Śrī is also suggested by a story in the *Mahābhārata* (12.221.60f.) that connects her to asuras (demonic beings) that she leaves because they neglect their cattle and eat meat. An earlier tale about her adoption is contained in the *Śatapatha Brāhmaṇa* (11.4.3.1–17) in which she offends the deities with her beauty and other attributes. After being dissuaded by Prajāpati from killing her because she is a female, the jealous gods confiscate her attributes in a symbolic gang rape as her initiation into the pantheon.[12]

Śrī Lakṣmī loses her independent status when she becomes the consort of Viṣṇu around the third to fourth century C.E. Her popularity among the monarchs of the Gupta Dynasty (320–540 C.E.) is evident by her appearance on their coinage, which represents the first epigraphic evidence of the union of the goddess and Viṣṇu. The conjugal union of these two figures served as an archetype of ideal married life embodied in the Purāṇic texts. Śrī Lakṣmī plays the role of the subordinate and obsequious wife, in an inferior position to her spouse that is often expressed in body symbolism. A good example is the depiction of Viṣṇu reclining on the serpent Śeṣa while the goddess massages Viṣṇu's feet like a devoted and dutiful wife. Because the body is hierarchically ordered in Hinduism, with the feet being the lowest part, Lakṣmī manifests her inferior position by massaging her spouse's feet. When the goddess appears iconographically with only two hands, she is usually at the side of her spouse, which signifies her subordinate position. When she is worshiped independently in a temple, she should have four hands.[13] The overall impression from iconography and narrative evidence is that Śrī Lakṣmī symbolizes total self-surrender and devotedness to Viṣṇu. Their relationship embodies *prema* (ideal love), which rises above mere carnal desire (*kāma*).

Śrī Lakṣmī is closely related to kingship, which is expressed in the notion of the king being wedded to her. It is believed that she selects a powerful king as her husband. Their relationship is so intimate that she is described as residing in the sovereign. In fact, the king refrains from cutting his hair, otherwise he would lose his śrī (welfare, majesty). Therefore, she is the source of the king's power. And she is very concerned about the exercise of royal virtues such as truth, generosity, austerity, strength, and dharma.[14]

Before Śrī Lakṣmī became intimately associated with Indian kingship, she was identified with the earth in the *Aitareya* (8.5.4) and *Śatapatha* (11.1.6.23) *Brāhmaṇas*. Her identification with the earth is symbolized by her association with the lotus flower. She is described as having the appearance of a lotus, which is a paradigm of beauty. In the *Mahābhārata* (12.59.131–134), she is born from the golden-colored lotus that sprang from the forehead of Viṣṇu. Because the lotus completes within itself the entire life cycle by holding within itself the new seeds and nourishing them until they develop into plants, the lotus represents a maternal womb of self-contained continuity.[15] The lotus also symbolizes both the divine transcendence and the immanent, life-giving, and life-sustaining waters; its leaf lying on the back of the waters represents the earth.[16] This vegetative symbol of the goddess is indicative of the fertility, wealth, and abundance that she offers to humankind. The fertile and aquatic associations of the goddess are evident in her appearance as Gaja Lakṣmī, which can be traced to a reference in the *Viṣṇu Purāṇa* (1.9.102). After she emerged from the ocean in this narrative, the elephants (*gaja*) of the cosmic quarters bathed her with pure water. This narrative is represented in works of art with the goddess standing or sitting on a lotus and flanked on either side by two elephants pouring water on her from two jars. It is possible to conceive of the elephants as symbolic rain clouds fertilizing the feminine earth personified by Śrī Lakṣmī.

Early Sectarian Movements

Allusion was made previously to Vaiṣṇavism as a tradition that fused together independent cults centered on deities such as Vāsudeva-Krishna, Nārāyaṇa, vedic

Viṣṇu, and Krishna-Gopāla. Probably the earliest identifiable Vaiṣṇava historical tradition was that of Bhāgavata, a term meaning "relating to the Lord (*bhāgavata*)." Early inscriptions clearly identify it, and it is promoted by aristocratic patrons. The cult included worship of Nārāyaṇa, Vāsudeva-Krishna, and often Saṃkarṣaṇa (Balarāma, Krishna's elder brother). It is not possible to determine the movement's popularity among ordinary people, although we do know that it received royal patronage by rulers of the Gupta Dynasty (320–455 C.E.). It is also difficult to know if it represented an independent tradition with established institutions.[17]

Another early sect that worshiped Nārāyaṇa was the Pāñcarātra, which means five nights. Taking into consideration their god's connection to the vedic sacrificial system, the sect might have derived its name from the "five-night sacrifice" in the *Śatapatha Brāhmaṇa* (13.6.1), where the god conceives of a sacrifice lasting five nights that would make him the highest being in the universe. Another possibility is that the term Pāñcarātra refers originally to an itinerant recluse who followed the five-nights rule of ascetics. Being eremitical seekers of enlightenment, the beliefs and practices of these ascetics were not common to vedic ritualistic sacerdotalism.[18] We previously mentioned that the sect's doctrine of emanations (*vyūhas*) eventually gave way to the doctrine of avatāra (incarnation) in the historical development of Vaiṣṇavism. As reference to these emanations makes clear in the epic *Mahābhārata* (12.337.63–64), this is the way that the absolute manifests itself.

There are some distinctive practices associated with this sect. It is common for followers to be branded with signs of the discus and conch on their shoulders or upper arms. They also recite an eight-syllable mantra that is later called the *tirumantra*.[19] The epic literature refers to the five observances of the day: (1) approaching the god with morning prayers and ablutions, (2) collection of materials for service, (3) worship, (4) textual study, and (5) meditation.[20]

Between the seventh and eighth centuries C.E., there develops a distinct body of sectarian literature that is known as the Pāñcarāta Saṃhitās, part of a larger body of literature called the Āgamas or Tantras. These texts manifest a tantric-influenced Vaiṣṇavism. Some of the more important texts are the *Pauṣkara Saṃhitā*, *Sāttvata Saṃhitā*, and the *Jakākhya Saṃhitā*, which were dubbed the "three gems." A couple of additional texts of significance are the *Ahirbudhnya Saṃhitā* and the *Lakṣmī Tantra*. These texts are the foundation for worship in south India today.

Because the meaning of terms like Pāñcarātra (also synonymous with Sāttvata) and Bhāgavata fluctuated over time and are identified with each other in some cases, it is difficult to identity specific groups precisely. They gradually establish, however, distinct identities. By the seventh century, in the *Harṣacarita* of Bāṇa, they are clearly identified as distinct groups these distinctions continue in the tenth century in literary works by the Vaikhānasa sect, which considers itself more orthodox and vedic than the Pāñcarātra sect.[21] The sect traces it historical development to the Taittirīya school of the *Black Yajur Veda*. In the fourth century C.E., the sect produced its major piece of literature, the *Vaikhānasasmārta Sūtra*, which manifests a blend of vedic and nonvedic ritual worship directed to Viṣṇu. The food offerings at *pūjā* services for Viṣṇu include vedic offerings into a fire, accompanied by the recitation of vedic and nonvedic *mantras* (repeated sacred formulas). A major theogonical notion is the "five manifestations." Beginning with the primordial Viṣṇu, the last four manifestations are functions of the God, which include Puruṣa, Satya, Acyuta, and Aniruddha. This sect made significant contributions to the growth of public temple worship in south India. In addition, the sect also possesses a separate collection of Vaikhānasa Saṃhitās.

Itinerant Poets of South India

Vaiṣṇavism penetrated into southern India around the first century C.E. Between the sixth and ninth centuries, poet saints called the Āḻvārs ("those immersed in god") appeared on the religious scene, wandering from temple to temple throughout the southern part of the country, singing praises of Viṣṇu. These mystically inclined poets, of both genders, represented a cross section of the caste system. In fact, they were very catholic in their attitude toward caste and gender, which they believed were obliterated in the path of devotion. They communicated their poetry, based on their personal experiences, by means of local languages and music.

Although the poems do not manifest a particular religious tradition, they express a territorial theology because many poems focus on the deity enshrined in a particular temple. There are allegedly 108 (a sacred number) such holy places.[22] Another related common theme in the poetry is the depiction of God as a cool village tank or pool in which devotees can bathe. This type of theme possesses erotic overtones because bathing can serve as a euphemism for sexual relations.[23] Another theme of the poems is the longing of a lovesick girl for her beloved.

The Āḻvārs sang about God as the savior and the necessity of divine grace for salvation. They also repeatedly cited the need for a guru (teacher) to guide a devotee. Moreover, they placed a strong emphasis on the need for giving up everything for God, because there was no place for insincere ways of devotion. Their poetry manifested a preference for a monistic theological position.[24]

The Āḻvārs' poems developed from an earlier Tamil poetic tradition consisting of two major themes: romantic love (*akam*) and war, heroism, and chivalry (*puṛam*). The oldest collections containing these themes are *The Eight Anthologies* (Eṭṭuokai) and *The Ten Songs* (Pattupāṭṭu), which were composed between the first and third centuries C.E. The old poems manifest five landscape settings: mountains, seaside, desert, pastoral, and agricultural. And they address situations like lovemaking, waiting for a beloved, separation, and anger over infidelity. The various landscapes symbolize particular emotional situations that form the sign system for the Āḻvārs' art of communication.

The Āḻvārs played an important role in Indian culture by harmonizing the earlier religious traditions with their own poetry, which enabled them to propagate the ancient wisdom to the common people. They thus served as social integrators of Indian culture by unifying it in terms of territory and language.[25] By giving significance to the multifarious parts of India, they demonstrate an understanding of India as holy and every language as possessing its own integrity. The poets also unified different threads of Krishna's devotion such as ecstatic religion, a literary tendency to associate Krishna with separation and a specific landscape, an earthy folk literature, and a vibrant temple cult that recognized God as transcendent.[26]

The south Indian tradition claims that there were twelve Āḻvārs, with Nammāḻvār being the most famous, along with the female Āṇṭāḷ, who is discussed more fully in chapter 11. The songs of all the Āḻvārs were collected by Nāthamuni, a theologian and founder of the Śrī Vaiṣṇava tradition, into a text known as the *Nālāyira Divyaprabandham* (Four Thousand Divine Compositions) or *Prabandham* for short. The prestige of this collection motivated commentaries on it. The most famous commentary was the *Tiruvāymoḻi* (The Ten Decads), which was eventually called the Tamil Veda. The Āḻvārs became so revered and renowned that they were regarded as incarnations of Viṣṇu, and it is not unusual to find images of them in southern temples. Their poems are considered equivalent to the Vedas.

The poems expressed love, longing, and service to a personal god. The poems evoked emotions by the way that they were sung and by their contents. The poems often evoked ecstatic experiences from the reciter and members of his or her audience, they enable God to reveal himself through the poets, who function as communicative instruments of God. Along with reverence for the Tamil poetry of the Āḻvārs, the southern Śrī Vaiṣṇava movement also reveres the Sanskrit tradition by acknowledging such works as the *Bhakti Sūtra* of Śāṇḍilya (eighth century C.E.) and the *Bhakti Sūtra* of Nārada (around the twelfth century), which stresses several degrees of emotional attachment to Krishna.

Medieval Traditions of Śrī Vaiṣṇavism

The term *sampradāya* generally means sect, order, or tradition. Many of these sects are regionally based, with membership dependent on initiation by a guru (teacher). A given teacher is often considered a member of a lineage of teachers with a common body of teachings. Being initiated into a tradition involves agreeing to adhere to the teachings and values of the sect, and it includes receiving a new name and a mantra (sacred formula) that is sacred to the tradition. Some traditions require celibacy for membership, whereas other traditions do not make such a demand and open their membership to householders.

The major influential tradition that came to be known as Śrī Vaiṣṇavism developed in the Tamil-speaking southern region of India by the end of the tenth century. The first outstanding teacher of the sect was Nāthamuni, famous for collecting the hymns of the Āḻvārs, as previously noted. By establishing this link to the Tamil Āḻvārs, Nāthamuni legitimatized his tradition. He was succeeded by his grandson Yāmuna (born in the tenth century), who defended the revelatory status of the Pāñcaratra Āgamas, while also claiming equality for the sect's ritual system to orthodox Brāhmaṇa rites. And Yāmuna was the first to introduce bhakti (devotionalism) into Vedānta as a desired goal by referring to overflowing love, a desire to serve God, and surrender to him.

The thought of Yāmuna becomes systematized by Rāmānuja (1050–1137), whose system is called qualified nondualism (*viśiṣṭādvaita*) because Brahman is not considered devoid of characteristics, but is qualified by the self (*Ātman*) and world (*prakṛti*). During his lifetime, Rāmānuja wrote the first sectarian commentary (*bhāṣya*) on the *Vedānta Sūtras*, because he viewed Śaṅkara's commentary as a threat to bhakti (devotional) religion. Besides protecting the bhakti movement, Rāmānuja was also able to reinvigorate it with his rebuttal to Śaṇkara's work. Rāmānuja's tradition became known as Śrī Vaiṣṇavism because it stresses the meditating role of the consort of the god. It is also called Ubhayavedānta because it includes both (*ubhaya*) Sanskritic Vedānta and Tamil poems of the Āḻvārs as its literary sources.

According to Rāmānuja, the self, world, and God form a unity. He argues that the self and body are interdependent. More specifically, the body is a mode of the self, sustains the self, and provides it with the means for its release.[27] The self provides the ground for the body in the sense that it animates, guides, and supports the body. Because the body is a mode of the self, they both constitute the body of God. Thus the body and self are modes of God, who in turn animates and supports them.[28] Such a position suggests that the world is real—which stands in sharp contrast to Śaṇkara's position—because Brahman encompasses the entire universe.

The essential nature of the self, which is the size of an atom, is knowledge. Rāmānuja asserts that the self is a *śeṣa* (property of, belonging entirely to) God, which means that it is subordinate and subservient to God.[29] The self is also different from God and other selves. Moreover, the self is different from the body because the former is immortal, whereas the body is a perishable entity.[30]

Rāmānuja refers to God in personal terms by calling him the Highest Person (Puruṣottama) and Nārāyaṇa. The first name is Rāmānuja's favorite metaphysical name for God, whereas the second name is the proper, personal name of God. Needless to say, Rāmānuja equates Brahman with Viṣṇu, who is the ultimate reality, the highest self, and supreme (*para*). The term "supreme" does not mean "higher than", but suggests the sense of "not other than". What Rāmānuja wants to assert is that God is the ground of all finite being because he is being itself. This position implies that all finite beings are completely dependent on God for their essential nature, continued existence, and activity, and implies that God is the inner controller of all beings and the universe. To assert that God is the inner controller expresses his personal and dynamic relation to the universe. In a more impersonal way, Rāmānuja defines Brahman as the efficient and material cause of the universe, and thus accepts the Sāṃkhya doctrine of causation.[31] To claim that God is the material cause means that he differentiates himself into self and body, whereas he is the efficient cause because he intelligently directs each new creation. Thus it is incorrect to view God as cause and the world as an effect.

Because all existent entities originated from God, they are *śeṣas* (property) of God, whereas he is their *śesin* (owner). This means that all existent entities are dependent on God, and that they constitute his body; and he is modified by them.[32] God is not, however, dependent on them. God lives in them as their inner ruler in order to save them.[33] It is important not to identify them with one another because Brahman is different from the individual self. Thus Rāmānuja disagrees with Śaṇkara's nondualist interpretation of the philosophical formula of "that you are" (*tat tvam asi*), which for the former does not convey the idea of absolute unity as it does for the latter. For Rāmānuja, the formula denotes Brahman as distinguished by difference.[34] Thus, the term "that" is intended to refer to Brahman as the universal cause, whereas the term "you" denotes Brahman as being qualified by the self, which constitutes its body.[35]

Rāmānuja also rejects Śaṇkara's interpretation of the twofold nature of Brahman by making no distinction between it with qualities (*saguṇa*) or without qualities (*nirguṇa*). For Rāmānuja, God possesses qualities that emphasize his personal nature as a merciful protector and savior. God's activity is a divine sport (*līlā*), which is a spontaneous self-expression that represents an end in itself. Therefore, God does not gain anything by his activity because sport is itself the divine purpose. Sport is for God's sake because it gives him an enjoyable experience. At the same time, sport is also for the sake of others because it gives them an opportunity to attain release. This is evident when Viṣṇu acts for the well-being of his creatures in the form of his incarnations (*avatāras*).

The self is in a state of bondage because of ignorance and karma. The root of bondage is the mistaken belief in plurality, which is based in ignorance. This ignorance conceals the true nature of Brahman.[36] In addition, karma produces the conjunction of the self with the body and the misconception that the self is the body.[37] In order to find release, Rāmānuja advocates the following path: action (*karmayoga*), knowledge (*jñānayoga*), and devotion (*bhaktiyoga*). This threefold path follows the lead of the *Bhagavad Gītā*, on which Rāmānuja wrote an important commentary.

The path of action includes disinterested activity and attributing all acts to God, who is the actual performer of them. There is an element of knowledge within the path of action because a person becomes aware that the self is distinct from the body.[38] Although action leads to knowledge, the former is superior to the latter for several reasons.

There are four degrees of the path of knowledge: (1) the overcoming of all desires by focusing the mind on the self; (2) having no desire for pleasing objects and being free from wishful thoughts, fear, and anger; (3) indifference to pleasing objects, joy, and hatred; (4) withdrawal of the senses from objects and concentration on the self.[39] Subduing the senses that disturb the mind in order to fix it on God allows one to attain these degrees of knowledge. This part of the overall path includes four degrees of awareness of the self, which culminate with one perceiving no difference between one's self and others. The path of knowledge leads to bhakti (devotion), which is the only true way of attaining God.[40]

Devotion entails both love and knowledge in a condition in which the self is completely subservient to God.[41] This means that the self must take refuge (*śaraṇāgati*) or its synonymous term surrender (*prapatti*) at the feet of the lord. The practice of refuge is equivalent to bhakti for Rāmānuja, but this does not mean that it will lead to release by itself. Rāmānuja intimates, however, that refuge provokes God's saving grace. God's grace opens the door to release by illuminating the devotee's heart.[42] When released, a devotee becomes free of all that concealed his or her true nature, and he or she experiences Brahman in his complete nature while possessed of unsurpassed bliss.[43]

Post-Rāmānuja Developments

Less than two hundred years after the death of Rāmānuja, a major schism occurred in the tradition that resulted in the growth of two subsects. The controversy that led to the split of the tradition centered on the question of human effort and divine grace. The southern school (*teṉgalai*) was called the Cat-hold School because it defined surrender (*prapatti*) as receptivity or lack of opposition to divine grace. In other words, it is like a mother cat that carries its young from one place to another, which entails no effort on the part of the kitten. This means that God takes the initiative, and he saves a person without any effort on his or her part. In this case, surrender (*prapatti*) is a frame of mind rather than a positive action.[44] In contrast, the northern school (*vaḍagalai*) was called the Monkey-hold School, because it contended that one must strive to receive God's grace by positive acts in a fashion similar to a young monkey, which clings to its mother when being transported.

The southern tradition traces its heritage to Piḷḷaṉ (d. 1161), who was a cousin and close associate of Rāmānuja. Piḷḷaṉ's works combine the Tamil and Sanskrit wings of the Śrī Vaiṣṇava tradition. He wrote a commentary on the *Tiruvāymoḷi* entitled *The Six Thousand Paṭis* (*Āṛāyīrappaṭi*), a number that represents a unit of literary measurement (*paṭi*) that is thirty-two syllables long. According to Piḷḷaṉ, auspicious qualities of God motivate a devotee to surrender immediately. He calls surrender an *upāya* (skillful means), but this must be accomplished without ulterior motive.[45] In his theology, Śrī Lakṣmī plays a role as mediator between a devotee and Viṣṇu. Moreover, he argued that caste distinctions are secondary within a devotional community. Faithful service to others was more important then caste distinctions.[46]

Another important representative of the southern tradition was Piḷḷai Lōkācārya (1250–1311), who more fully defined the relationship between Viṣṇu and Śrī Lakṣmī. He claimed that she was not equal or coeval with Viṣṇu, even though she was a goddess. This means that she possessed no independent ability to save anyone. She does, however, play a supporting role in salvation by interceding with Viṣṇu for the good of devotees.

True to the spirit of the southern tradition, Piḷḷai maintains that surrender or refuge is not a means to salvation that can be earned by any action. Since God causes all human acts, there is nothing that helpless humans can do to be saved. Saving grace is a sheer gift that is causeless and unearned by humans. The new values associated with devotion did not abrogate purity and caste regulations, in contrast to the theological position of Piḷḷa<u>n</u>.

An outstanding representative of the northern tradition was Vedānta Deśika (1268–1369), who was proclaimed the founder of the Vaṭakalai school of Śrī Vaiṣṇavism, centered in the holy city of Kāñcīpuram. He was a philosopher and poet, who was credited with producing 130 works of commentary, devotional poems, literature, and philosophical works on logic and other subjects. He defended the efficacy of rituals by developing surrender (*prapatti*) into a sixfold ritual act. In addition to the performance of sacraments, all human actions can become effect agents of salvation. By performing one's actions according to dharma, a devotee creates a pretext for the saving action of God. A basic presupposition of Deśika's thought is that God never acts arbitrarily to save a devotee. This is the reason that it is important for a devotee to create a pretext for God's saving grace, even though it may have been earned in a prior life.[47] If a devotee prays for salvation for instance, this implies that the prayer can function as a pretext for God to save that person.

For Deśika, Viṣṇu is an aesthetic deity in the sense that he manifests himself in a beauty that saves. In his poems, Deśika stresses the sensuous loveliness of the icon in the temple. The beauty of the icon creates an impact on the emotions of the viewer, which can cause an ecstatic experience. This ecstatic kind of sight becomes a divine passion. But this visual experience includes intellect and feelings.[48] It is thus both a mental and emotional vision that possesses the ability to transform the devotee.

A Tradition of Unqualified Dualism

The tradition of Mādhva (c. 1238–1317) is characterized as unqualified dualism (*dvaita*). What this means is that God, self, and world are different from one another.[49] The self and world are dependent upon God, who is the only independent reality. For Mādhva, Brahman is Viṣṇu, who releases humans by means of his grace.[50] Mādhva's school is later identified as the Brahma Sampradāya in north India. In addition to the thirty-seven works attributed to him, called the *Sarvamūlagranthāḥ* (Compendium of All the Fundamentals), Mādhva summarized his teachings in ten succinct treatises called the *Daśaprakaraṇas*. Mādhva considered the Pāñcarātra literature to be as authoritative as the vedic literature, and he often quotes the former, which he considered to be part of a single tradition.[51] Mādhva is credited by tradition with establishing eight monasteries. He also founded the Udipi Śrī Krishna temple, where he installed an idol of Krishna discovered by him encased in mud on the floor of the ocean. According to biographical accounts, he proclaimed himself to be the third incarnation of Vāyu, wind deity and son of Viṣṇu.

Mādhva believed in both the quantitative and qualitative pluralism of souls. There are no two identical souls. Even in the state of release there are differences between souls in relation to their knowledge and enjoyment of bliss.[52] A unique feature of Mādhva's thought is that some souls are damned to eternal bondage. The doctrine of eternal damnation or strict determinism is peculiar to his thought.[53] The difference between selves is true even with regard to ignorance. There is thus no single common notion of ignorance (*avidyā*) that results in bondage. The bound soul is a mere reflection of Brahman, which illustrates the dependent nature of the soul instead of Brahman's identity with it, although their relationship is eternal.

Even though liberation (*mukti*) can only be finally attained by the grace of God, a path of knowledge is presupposed. One can obtain knowledge by listening to holy texts (*śravana*), reflection (*manana*), meditation (*dhyāna*), and finally devotion (*bhakti*).[54] When a state of intense devotion is reached, God, by means of his grace, grants the self direct knowledge of himself.[55] In the state of release, the self contemplates God as bliss, intelligence, faultlessness, and master. Thus the soul's own efforts are of no avail in obtaining a direct vision of God without his grace. The soul needs the grace of God because of its limited power to act. Madhva did not believe that everyone has the ability to know Brahman and obtain liberation because he restricted those eligible for liberation to twice-born males.[56]

A Tradition of Dualistic Nondualism

The philosophical theology of Nimbārka (twelfth century) is indebted to the work of Rāmānuja. There are, however, a number of significant differences between them. While Rāmānuja's position is a qualified nondualism, Nimbārka affirms a concept of dualistic nondualism (*dvaitādvaita*), possibly better expressed as identity in difference (*bhedābheda*). In other words, he believed that both identity and difference are true. Thus Brahman is both identical with and different from the world of souls and matter. The difference between them denotes dependent existence, and identity signifies the impossibility of independent existence.[57] Therefore, the soul and matter are different from Brahman in the sense that they possess different natures and attributes. Their identity with Brahman consists of their dependence for their existence upon the absolute. Just as a part (say, a cup of sea water) is in some sense identical with the whole (ocean), for instance, so the individual self is never different from God.[58] In conclusion, whereas identity is primary for Rāmānuja, Nimbārka views identity and difference as equally real.

Nimbārka also rejects Rāmānuja's contention that the soul and matter are the body or attributes of God. For Nimbārka, God is Krishna and his consort Rādhā, and not Viṣṇu and his consort Lakṣmī, as it is for Rāmānuja. Krishna is not a mere incarnation of Brahman; he is the true reality. Even though Rādhā is not the consort of Krishna in the *Bhāgavata Purāṇa*, Nimbārka places her at Krishna's side and raises them to a universal principle.[59] It is to this divine pair that a person must direct his or her devotion in order to gain freedom.

The way to release is not through meditation. Salvation is rather attained through love and devotion.[60] A person must surrender oneself to God. Total surrender is open to everyone, including members of the lowest caste. This attitude is pleasing to God, who then engenders love (*bhakti*) in his devotees. The love of God awakens one and conducts one to a view or realization of the highest reality. From its southern base, Nimbārka's thought spread to the north and exerted considerable influence.[61] Nimbārka is credited with establishing the Nimavat tradition (*sampradāya*), whereas Madhava is given recognition for the Brahmā Sampradāya, and Rāmānuja's tradition is named after him. The establishment of the fourth major Vaiṣṇava tradition, credited to Vallabha (1479–1531), is called the Rudra Sampradāya, which will be discussed in the following chapter.

Vaiṣṇava Festivals

The Śrī Vaiṣṇava tradition expresses its joy and love of its deity in festivals such as Dīpāvali celebrated during the last two days of the month of Aṣvīnī (September–October) and the first two days of Kārttika (October–November).[62] This specific celebration actually consists of five different festivals: worship of wealth, the celebration of Viṣṇu's victory over the demon Naraka, Lakṣmī *pūjā*, the celebration of Viṣṇu's victory over the demon Bali, and the expression of brotherly and sisterly affection in celebration of Yama (the lord of the dead) dining with his sister Yamunā (or Yamī). In the first festival, the initial day commences with the participants bathing and anointing themselves with oil. Lakṣmī is worshiped by merchants after they have closed their yearly account books and cleared their shops and offices. Collecting their account books and a pile of silver coins that are smeared with turmeric and red lead, the merchants worship the giver of wealth. During the evening, lamps are lit and burn throughout the festival evenings. This same festival is called Divālī among the Jain community, although its significance is altered somewhat as a celebration of the day on which the ascetic Mahāvīra attained liberation. The presence and importance of Śrī Lakṣmī is still very evident among Jain women of the Śvetāmbara sect when they polish their jewelry and other ornaments in honor of the goddess. On the account books of Jain merchants, a priest continually writes the name of Śrī—one name on top of another—forming a pyramid, and a priest performs Lakṣmī pūjā (worship). Since many Jains are merchants, they express devotion to Lakṣmī as the goddess of wealth and the presiding deity of trade and commerce.

Different festivals are linked together to form Dīpāvali in many villages and towns.[63] Lakṣmī pūjā is celebrated by the lighting of lamps, which is intended to help the goddess find her way to one's home. The Govardhana pūjā, which celebrates Krishna's lifting of the Govardhana Hill to protect his fellow herdsmen from a violent storm, finds Lakṣmī incarnated as a cow. After cattle are driven over a replica of the mythical hill made of cow dung, the worshipers apply the cow dung to their foreheads as a gesture of profound humility before the goddess. There are many other variations on these observances.

Concluding Comments

The historical survey of the development of Vaiṣṇavism and the way that the Viṣṇu of the vedic literature merged with other divine figures to evolve into the purāṇic deity worshiped today in India testifies to the complex nature of this theistic religious tradition. An essential characteristic of Viṣṇu is his tendency to embody himself on earth when it and its inhabitants are oppressed, or when evil gains dominion over righteousness and threatens chaos. In addition, incarnations such as Krishna and Rāma evolve to the extent of creating separate and independent identities from their devotees' perspective. These examples will be considered in the following two chapters.

Even though the Vaiṣṇava tradition accepts their embodied deity, sings his praises in poetry and song, worships him at home and in temples, and celebrates festivals associated with the god, its philosophical theology manifests a wide spectrum of possibilities designed to interpret the deity and his relationship to his devotees. This impressive variety includes the qualified nondualism of Rāmānuja, the unqualified dualism of Mādhva, and the dualistic nondualism of Nimbārka. None of these philosophical theologians think that Viṣṇu is a remote and disinterested deity. Their emphasis is on his intimate relationship to humans and his concern for their welfare in the form of his incarnations and temple icons, whereas to be separated from such a deity represents a type of spiritual death for the devotees. To be closely associated with God in a loving relationship involves being spiritually alive. Thus Viṣṇu is a deity who acts in historical time and space for the benefit of his devotees. The possibilities of embodiment are endless because this pervader is eternal. Moreover, the importance of embodiment in Vaiṣṇavism—whether as a deity or a saint like Caitanya—enables us to recognize that there is no absolute distinction within this facet of Hinduism between divine and human beings.

8

Divine Play, Madness, Eroticism, and Krishna

Throughout the Indian subcontinent, in stores within towns and stalls within the walls of temples, it is possible to find lithographs depicting Krishna as the divine child with his hand in a pot of overflowing butter, walking through the woods or cavorting with local cowherd girls (*gopīs*), celebrating a victory over a demonic being, or alone with his lover Rādhā. What can be called the purāṇic Krishna possesses a spirit different from that of the figure of the *Bhagavad Gītā*, which recounts Krishna's rationale for fighting as a warrior and his divine revelation in chapter 11 to the reluctant warrior Arjuna. The Krishna of the epic *Mahābhārata* is depicted as a calculating, duplicitous, serious, and wise figure, whereas the purāṇic figure is more mirthful, mischievous, tricky, and playful. Even though the purāṇic Krishna is playful, he often drives others mad. His relationship to the gopīs (cowherd girls) and Rādhā in particular tends to be erotic, and his erotic relationship with the gopīs inspired and influenced later theologians of the movement. Because of their importance to understanding the nature of the Krishna of purāṇic literature, this chapter will focus on three themes: play, madness, and eroticism.

Historical Development of the Krishna Cult

The divine narrative of Krishna has its roots in the beliefs of the Yādava tribe. This tribe fused with another tribe called the Vṛṣṇis or Satvatas, which was devoted to a figure called Vāsudeva, who may have been a king or hero in the tribe. This tribal fusion resulted in a composite figure called Vāsudeva-Krishna. As early as the fifth or sixth centuries B.C.E., there is evidence of the worship of Vāsudeva in a book of grammar called the *Aṣṭādhyāyi* (4.3.98) composed by the famous grammarian Pāṇini. Later evidence is found in a report by Megasthenes, the Greek ambassador to the court of King Chandragupta Maurya (c. 320 B.C.E.), mentioning the worship of a god that he called Heracles, the Greek equivalent to Vāsudeva. An inscription on a column erected at Besnagar at Madhya Pradesh (c. 115 B.C.E.) by Heliodorous testifies to the deity crowned by an image of Garuḍa. Heliodorous uses the term *bhāgavata* (devotee of Vāsudeva) to describe his religious affiliation. The existence of followers of Vāsudeva is verified by a Buddhist text preserved in the Pāli language.[1] Further evidence is found in the *Mahābhāṣya* (Great Commentary 4.3.98) of the grammarian Patañjali on the earlier work of Pāṇini, in which he connects Vāsudeva with the Vṛṣṇi tribe. There is a human sage named Krishna in the *Chāndogya Upaniṣad* (3.117.6), although it is difficult to assess whether or not this figure had any connection to the later deity of the Yādava tribe. In the epic *Mahābhārata*, Krishna appears as the chief of the Yādavas. By the second century B.C.E., the fusion of Vāsudeva and Krishna is complete, and this composite figure is worshiped as a distinct deity that becomes identified with Viṣṇu in the *Mahābhārata*, as evident in passages in the *Bhagavad Gītā* (11.21, 24, 31).

The Bhāgavata tradition centered on Vāsudeva-Krishna merged further with another cult that focused on Krishna as a young man living in the town of Vṛndāvana. Moreover, the Bhāgavata tradition incorporates the tribal god of the Abhīras called Gopāla and his brother Balarāma or Saṃkarṣaṇa. These pastoral deities were associated with cowherding life, giving emergence to Gopāla-Krishna. The exploits of this deity are developed by the *Harivaṃśa*, a supplement to the *Mahābhārata* composed around the second century B.C.E., which describes the amorous adventures of a wandering young man and his brother in the forest of Vṛndāvana, where they dance and cavort with cowgirls (*gopīs*) and defeat demons. The narrative of the *Harivaṃśa* exerted a strong influence on the *Viṣṇu Purāṇa* and the later ninth-century text, the *Bhāgavata Purāṇa*, which probably originated in southern India.

In the *Bhāgavata Purāṇa*, the story of Krishna's life is recounted along with the reason for incarnating himself, which is to destroy his evil uncle King Kaṃsa, who was conceived when his mother was raped by a demon. As he grows older, Kaṃsa reveals his demonic nature by murdering children, throwing his father the king into prison, and forbidding the worship of Viṣṇu. By creating a burden for the earth, Kaṃsa motivates the earth to appeal to the gods for relief, and Viṣṇu agrees to intervene and destroy the wicked king.

Kaṃsa discovers through a prophecy that the seventh child of a couple named Vāsudeva and Devakī will be Balarāma and the eighth child will be Krishna. As Kaṃsa is about to kill Devakī, her husband agrees to yield all his sons to the evil king. The initial six sons are surrendered to the king and slaughtered. Kaṃsa also learns that divine beings are being born as cowherders, and he commands his men to slaughter every cowherd child in the area.

The leading cowherder is Nanda, who is a friend of Vāsudeva, and his wives are Yaśodā and Rohinī. When the seventh son of Devakī is conceived, Viṣṇu transfers the fetus to the womb of Rohinī, while Kaṃsa is informed of Devakī's miscarriage. With the eighth pregnancy of Devakī, the wicked king increases his vigilance and jails Vāsudeva and Devakī. When the child is born, Viṣṇu appears to Vāsudeva, instructing him to take the newborn infant to Nanda's house and substitute him for the infant daughter just born at that house. After escaping from jail with divine assistance, Vāsudeva switches the infants. The evil king tries to kill the infant girl, but she becomes a goddess and explains to the king that his rival has been born elsewhere. After the goddess vanishes, Kaṃsa orders all male children in the region to be killed.

Krishna is raised in the home of cowherders and grows into an adult. The textual narrative relates his childhood and adolescent adventures destroying demons and frolicking with his male companions and the gopīs (female cowherders). When he becomes an adult Krishna returns to the court of his uncle in Mathura, where he defeats various demons and kills his evil uncle Kaṃsa. He frees the rightful king, marries the beautiful Rukmiṇī, moves his capital to the western city of Dwaraka where he rules wisely, performs many heroic acts, and finally dies.

The Divine Player

The notion of play (*līlā*) is an important theme in devotional Hinduism. Because divine beings are complete, they need and desire nothing. They continue, however, to act. Why do they do so? The continued actions of complete divine beings can be grasped both intellectually and emotionally by the notion of līlā (play, sport, or dalliance). That the actions of divine beings represent play suggests that their actions are purposeless, spontaneous, not pragmatic—they do not act with the intention of accomplishing anything. Their actions may be seen as an aimless display that dazzles, sparkles, and sometimes terrifies us, but is always ultimately fascinating. The notion of play (*līlā*) is associated with bliss (*ānanda*), which is an attribute of divine beings. With their blissful natures, divine beings dance, laugh, play tricks, and sing. Playful, blissful, and superfluous actions are executed in total freedom and spontaneity.

When divine beings act, they do so on earth, which points to a close relationship between the world and play. In fact, the world, which functions as a stage upon which divine beings can dance and dazzle, is created in the spirit of play and represents a divine toy. The world is an ephemeral, phantasmagoric display, or magic show that entertains. At the same time, the world is delightful because it stems from the overflowing of divine bliss, and it is pervaded with the creative power of the divine. The world manifests a divine rhythm that serves as an invitation to participate in a cosmic dance. It is unnecessary to withdraw from the world within the context of devotional religion. Instead of withdrawing from the world, a devotee is invited to dance with Krishna, the divine player par excellence. Thus it is precisely the theme of play that can function as a hermeneutical key to understanding the actions of Krishna in the purāṇic literature.

Childhood Play

In his role as the child-god, Krishna expresses a pure, spontaneous play. There is the unstructured play of an infant characterized by erratic movement of arms and legs and aimless crawling. The play of the child Krishna is centered on his tricks, such as the theft of butter and sweets from his mother and other women. Why would Krishna steal butter? Within the context of Krishna devotionalism, butter is symbolic of love, and by stealing it Krishna enters into the game of love. The overflowing butter pot is symbolic of the abundance of love—and there is excitement associated with stealing it. Moreover, butter does not lose its taste when it is stolen. Love is not a commodity that can be quantified, separated, and stored in containers, as butter is. By nature, love possesses no value; it is merely simple, ample, and spontaneous.[2] It cannot be possessed like an article of clothing, because love is about relationship.

In addition to stealing butter and sweets, the child Krishna is accused of untying and setting free the cows. He teases smaller children and makes them cry. When women scold him for his bad behavior he laughs at them. He demonstrates a disdain for the property of others by biologically relieving himself in their homes. All such actions indicate that Krishna is indifferent to social convention and its rules. Instead of acting in predictable patterns, he behaves spontaneously and impetuously.[3] This suggests that the world is his playground. Krishna's play as an infant also suggests that he is intimately involved in the world, and it proposes that he is readily approachable by humans.

Krishna's pranks overlap with his conquest of demons. Disguising herself as a lovely and charming woman, the demoness Pūtanā arrives at the infant Krishna's home, and she begins to dote on him before asking the infant's mother permission to feed him from her own breasts (BhāgP 10.6.1–44). The demoness intends to kill the infant with the poisoned nipples of her breasts, but when the infant accepts her breasts and begins to nurse, the poison has no effect on him. In fact, Krishna proceeds to suck the life out of her.

The demons Tṛṇāvarta and Bakāsura are equally unsuccessful in overcoming the child Krishna. The former assumes the form of a tumultuous whirlwind, and sweeps the child into the air. Krishna makes himself very heavy, forcing the demon to drop his burden. Krishna then clings to the demon's neck, causing it to fall and kill itself. In the form of a huge crane, Bakāsura swallows the divine child, but Krishna becomes so hot inside the demon that the giant bird is forced to spit him out. Krishna then tears him to pieces.

These examples of demon conquest are violent and bloody episodes that seem superficially to have nothing in common with play (*līlā*). Within the context of Krishna mythology, this assumption would be erroneous. The demons are like children's toys, and they function as sources of amusement for the deity. Although the demons approach Krishna with the intention of killing him, he enters into combat in the spirit of play. Thus, even when it is a matter of life and death, Krishna never stops playing, and the demons become mere toys in the god's game.

Play of the Divine Lover

During an auspicious month favorable for the taking of religious vows, the cowherd women go to the Yamunā River to bathe, leaving their clothes, jewelry, and delicacies on the bank. Krishna and other cowherd boys steal the items, eat the delicacies, and pile the clothing into a heap. From the safety of a tree, Krishna announces to the women the theft of their clothing and teases them about going naked and being unable to fulfill their religious vows. The women chase after the youthful thieves and finally surround them, but the cowherd boys give the clothes to Krishna, who hangs them from the limbs of a tree. Krishna mocks the cowherd girls (*gopīs*) and instructs them to beg for their clothing (BvaiP 4.16.1–16; 25–65). In some versions of this encounter, the gopīs are reluctant to exit the water because of their nakedness, but they eventually find the courage to approach Krishna in the tree to ask for their clothing. With this type of episode, the playfulness of Krishna intersects with the erotic.

The erotic nature of the relationship between Krishna and the cowherd girls becomes even more explicit with the *rāsa līlā* dance episode (ViṣṇuP 5.13.14–62). Because he is desirous of making love with the gopīs, Krishna begins to sing. The sound of his singing causes the women to leave their homes and to travel to the source of the sound. The women sing along and call to each other that they are Krishna, whereas some women imitate his heroic exploits. The women follow footprints, but the prints disappear in the forest, making them distraught. Despairing of finding Krishna, the gopīs begin to return home, but they suddenly encounter him at the bank of the river, and they begin to dance with him by forming a circle, with the women repeatedly singing his name. The rāsa līlā (circle dance) is formed with Krishna stationed between every two gopīs by means of his power of māyā (magical power). Thus each gopī believes that Krishna is next to her.

It is often the case in Hindu mythology that dance is a metaphor for sexual intercourse. The episode of the circle dance is very instructive because it tells us that Krishna's singing excites the gopīs enough that they are willing to risk their social status to be with the singer. In some narratives, it is the flute of Krishna that excites the gopīs. The sound of the flute is anarchical because it breaks down social norms and puts an end to habitual behavior.[4] The sound of Krishna's voice or flute produces a violent, erotic, and dangerous reaction that culminates with sexual relations with god. The sensual bliss experienced by the gopīs when united with Krishna is transitory, because intimate relationship is interrupted by temporary periods of separation and finally becomes a permanent separation when Krishna leaves for the city of Mathura.[5] By surreptitiously leaving their families to be in the presence of Krishna, the gopīs risk their feminine virtue, social standing, family honor, and reputation for their mad love. Fortunately for the gopīs, their husbands never discover their unfaithfulness or become jealous because of the deluding power of Krishna's māyā (illusory power). In all this, Krishna needs the gopīs to experience supreme bliss. Krishna is already complete and needs nothing. His love making with the gopīs is intended to enable them to experience bliss.[6] Furthermore, the love of the gopīs for Krishna is a salvific love that is bereft of egoism or egocentrism.[7] This mode of love and its intensity serve as a model with theological implications for the later tradition.

From a more theological perspective, Krishna's voice or flute calls the human soul back to its creator. The call rejects moral, ethical, and social norms; it originates from another world, in which the standards of this world are invalid. The call asks for only a single response: surrender. Furthermore, the voice and flute of Krishna are expressions of his beauty, which like play is an end in itself.[8] Krishna is the essence of beauty, and his appearance transcends the mundane world. Some theologians of the tradition teach that devotees should assume the attitude of the gopī who cursed her divine creator for giving her eyelids that prevent her from constantly seeing Krishna.

A more complex and personal type of loving relationship is evident with the cowherd girl named Rādhā. In the *Bhāgavata Purāṇa*, whose origins date to approximately the ninth century, Krishna is said to have a favorite gopī (cowherd girl), but she is not identified by name. With the composition of the *Gītāgovinda* by the poet Jayadeva in 1170, the unnamed gopī is clearly identified as Rādhā. It is this poem that gives impetus to making Rādhā the consort of Krishna.

The *Gītāgovinda* gives expression to a loving relationship that is intense, passionate, violent, and erotic. Jayadeva sets the love of Rādhā and Krishna in the spring, a time of new birth and renewal. Jayadeva depicts their love as an ordeal in the sense that it is represented as a battle of sexual delight that is often violent. He writes, for instance, about the red marks of passion that stain Krishna, the tangled hair of wilted flowers, nail marks on Rādhā's breasts, and bodies moist with sweat from the ordeal. Their love is also erotic. As Krishna reaches the height of passion during sexual intercourse, Jayadeva writes that Rādhā's jewel anklets ring out an erotic sound. The couple performs eight types of sexual intercourse, and Krishna kisses her in eight mysterious ways that are not described by the poet and left to the reader's imagination. Krishna is described as assailing her with his teeth, nails, and hands. The lovers rendezvous at night, with Rādhā surreptitiously stealing out of her house during darkness, which suggests the dangerous and illicit nature of their relationship. Prying eyes are obstructed by a dark cloak that forms over the lovers. The darkness also suggests to a reader that their love takes place apart from the mundane world. In fact, it occurs in an ideal world of joy and bliss in which they play the divine game of love.

Besides the violent and erotic nature of their love, there is also a comic quality to it. After a night of blissful love making, Rādhā's speech becomes confused. At the conclusion of a sexual encounter in the dark, the couple discover each wearing the other's clothing. This suggests that their love turns the world upside down. Their love also transports them to a transcendent realm. Moreover, their sexual union obliterates time by enabling an evening to become a mere moment. Thus Jayadeva's poem expresses a very carnal relationship that is simultaneously spiritual and transcendent.

A crucial question is: Where does their love culminate? Jayadeva's answer is that it terminates in complete self-surrender, like a soul giving itself to God.

A concomitant perspective is that the sexual union of Rādhā and Krishna represents the perfect union of body, mind, and being. It is important not to lose sight of the fact that their love is divine play (*līlā*). Like many games, there is often a winner. On the one hand, Krishna is viewed as the victor when he breaks down Rādhā's defenses. On the other hand, Rādhā is depicted placing her foot on Krishna's head in a symbolic gesture of victory. Rādhā's victory is sometimes marked by her assuming the top position during sexual intercourse.

Whether Krishna is playing as an infant, a prankster adolescent, or an amorous adult, his play means that he does not act according to the laws of cause and effect. When a person acts according to the laws of cause and effect, that person is engaged in work, which is indicative of a shortcoming. In short, finite human beings work, whereas gods such as Krishna play.[9] Since Krishna is complete, he needs nothing and is free to play. The mythology recording the adventures of Krishna provides him an earthly playground in Vṛndāvana, a location that is symbolic of freedom and spontaneity.

Krishna's Playful Consort

The precise origins of Rādhā are obscure, and the exact period when she became associated with him is open to conjecture. She does appear iconically at Pahārapur in the fifth century C.E.[10] In a Prakrit literary work by Hāla that can be dated anywhere from the first to the seventh century called the *Gāhāsattasāī*, there are some references to Rādhā. In this work and some others, Rādhā appears as a fully human mistress of Krishna. A Tamil classic entitled the *Śilappadikāram* includes a female figure called Nappiṇṇai as the wife of Māyan (Krishna-Gopāla). The Āḻvār poets Āṇṭāḷ and Nāmmāḻvār also refer to Nappiṇṇai, who is an incarnation of Viṣṇu's consort. But it is difficult to ascertain with any certainty her connection to the later Rādhā. There are no explicit references to Rādhā in the epic literature or in the *Viṣṇu* or *Bhāgavata Purāṇas*, which contain stories of the birth, life, loves, and heroic exploits of Krishna. It is possible that the romance of Rādhā and Krishna originated in a folk tradition that was later adopted by Sanskrit writers.

Rādhā is, however, specifically mentioned in later purāṇic literature like the *Padma* and *Brahmavaivarta Purāṇas*. According to the *Padma Purāṇa* (composed around 900 C.E.), Rādhā's humble origin as a gopī is rationalized by explaining that she appears as the blissful energy of Krishna. She is also married to an unnamed person. Throughout the text, there are numerous traces of a developed Rādhā cult; a description of her birthday festival (*Rādhāṣṭamī*) is given, and her worshipers are glorified. The *Nāradīya Purāṇa* (c. 875–1000 C.E.) has further traces of a fully developed Rādhā cult, where she is called primal matter (*mūlaprakṛti*). The *Brahmavaivarta Purāṇa* (c. 750–1550 C.E.) represents a transition from a basically masculine-oriented theology to a feminine theology.[11] Rādhā is active as a creative, life-sustaining, loving, redemptive goddess. The text relates that while living in

Krishna's heavenly abode, Rādhā rebukes him for slighting her. Rādhā's birth as a gopī is explained as the result of a curse in order for her to suffer the torments of separation from Krishna. On earth, she is married at age twelve, experiences an earthly life, and eventually is reunited and married to Krishna in heaven at the end of her life. Although these texts make important contributions to the development of a mature portrait of Rādhā, a more profound influence was exerted by the poem of Jayadeva, Bengali Vaiṣṇavas, and other sectarian movements, as will become evident.

The Path of Grace

Centering his theology on Krishna as the herder of cows, Vallabha (1479–1531) developed his reflections and called them the "path of grace" (*puṣṭimārga*). He was allegedly a Telugu Brahmin of south India, although this is questioned by some scholars who view him as a northern figure. According to a standard tradition that is open to question, he migrated north and developed further the ideas of Viṣṇuvamin, who probably lived in the thirteenth century. Vallabha also called his system pure nondualism (Śuddhādvaita) in contrast to the impure monism of Śaṇkara. Vallabha's monism is pure because it includes bhakti (devotion) and excludes the doctrine of māyā (illusion, unreal). Vallabha is convinced that Brahman can create the world without the principle of māyā.

Vallabha equates Brahman with Krishna. Rādhā, however, plays no substantial role in his theology. Brahman is the material and efficient cause of the world. He manifests himself as the universe without changing himself; This means that the world is real. The soul (*jīva*) is both different and nondifferent from Brahman.[12] It is, more precisely, a part of Brahman. It is produced from Brahman in the sense in which sparks are produced from fire; the soul is a thus a manifestation of Brahman itself, with the attribute of bliss obscured.[13]

Vallabha believes that the way to salvation is through devotion and grace rather than ascetic practices. He is opposed to renunciation and self-mortification because in the path of devotion renunciation is not to be seen as a matter of duty—it must develop from the devotional way as a means of maintaining that path. Vallabha opposes self-mortification because he believes that the body is a temple of God.[14]

Although knowledge is useful in the path of discipline, this is not true in the path of grace (*puṣṭimārga*).[15] Vallabha intends to assert that the path of devotion (*bhakti*) is superior to that of knowledge. The home and family of a devotee are not, for instance, obstacles on the way to devotion, as they are on the path of knowledge. Action and knowledge can be a means, however, of removing obstacles.[16] The way of devotion is also superior in the sense that the knower who achieves release does not possess a body, and thus cannot experience the bliss of God. A devotee retains his or her body even after it is transfigured into its true nature of bliss. Thus a devotee can use his or her body to serve the Lord and enjoy his bliss.[17]

Mad for Krishna

In 1486, a tenth child was born into the family of Jagannāth Miśra and his wife Śachī in Bengal. The child was named Viśvambhar (literally, "he who sustains the world"). This was a bleak period of Bengal history: religious life was at a low point and the populace was ruled by Muslim conquerors. Viśvambhar was, however, to be instrumental in changing at least the religious atmosphere. His early personal life was marked by death: his father died, and his elder brother died to the world by becoming a world-renouncer. At an early age the precocious Viśvambhar started his own school in order to support himself, and was married, but his young wife died shortly afterward. Soon thereafter, he remarried.

The most profound change in Viśvambhar's life occurred about 1508 on a trip to Gayā, a place sacred to Buddhists and Vaiṣṇavas. The city was sacred for Vaiṣṇavas because the Viṣṇupad (footprint of Viṣṇu) was located there. At Gayā, Viśvambhar met Īśvara Purī, a Mādhva ascetic. Although no report exists about what occurred during this encounter, this event marks the period when Viśvambhar began to go into ecstatic trances. After returning home, he joined a group of Krishna devotees, and at times he became so absorbed in bhakti (devotion) that he was unaware of what was happening around him. He neglected personal care, ran around with his arms outstretched and his eyes full of tears. He sleep on the bare earth, did not wear ornaments or fine clothing, did not bathe himself, and did not eat regular meals. When he heard Krishna's name or sang with other devotees the praises of God, there were strange results: because he would fall into a swoon, tremble with emotion, and weep profusely. He began to attract followers, and the movement grew rapidly. He soon gave up his teaching career to devote full time to his religious vocation. In 1510, he took vows of renunciation, and was given the name Krishna Caitanya, "he who awakens consciousness of Krishna."

During Caitanya's career, a popular form of popular worship of Krishna was called *kīrtana*, which consisted of singing songs in praise of Krishna or chanting his name repeatedly. This form of worship was usually performed in small groups in private homes. Caitanya's great innovation was that he made kīrtana a public event. Devotees paraded around the streets singing and chanting praise of Krishna. The practice is associated with certainty about god's existence, and it creates internal emotional and bodily sensations such as tingling of the flesh as a response to the presence of the deity. It is possible to distinguish between different forms of kīrtana. A general term for the singing of god's praises is *sankīrtan*; *nagarkīrtan* refers to processional singing in a city (*nagar*); *līlākīrtan* are retellings of god's sportive actions; and *nāmkīrtan* is the chanting of stanzas consisting of divine names, which best characterizes the practice of Caitanya.[18]

What did this practice mean for Caitanya and his followers? Caitanya thought that in the kali yuga a person cannot gain salvation through asceticism alone. Rather a person must constantly chant Krishna's name to attain freedom. According to Caitanya, kīrtana is equivalent to a vedic sacrifice, because it purifies the soul and enables one to conquer sin. It also possesses the power to convert others. This power is illustrated by a story from the *Caitanyacaritāmṛta* (Immortal Acts of Caitanya), a hagiographical account of his life, when he stumbles on a tiger in his path while journeying through a forest. When Caitanya exclaims Krishna's name, the tiger rises and begins to dance and himself shout the god's name. In addition to its ability to convert others, kīrtana creates an atmosphere of renunciation, equality for all beings, love, seeking the highest pursuit, and total dedication. Because the devotees practicing kīrtana imitate actions of the gopīs and identify themselves with the gopīs, an atmosphere of mythical Vṛndāvana is created on earth, a place where Krishna sports with the gopīs.

Caitanya renounced the world in order to refute criticism of himself and his movement. This act stamped his movement with authority and gained it respect. During 1510 and 1512, he journeyed to south India to convert people to Krishna devotion. Caitanya's biographers describe his sojourn as a triumphant tour on which he converted many people and refuted all opponents of his theological position. During 1514, he made a pilgrimage to Vṛndāvana, a place especially sacred to Krishna, in a religiously intoxicated state. As he neared his destination, his emotional frenzy intensified, because everything that he saw reminded him of Rādhā and Krishna, which sent him into fits of ecstasy. While walking along the banks of the Yamunā River, he was overcome, for instance, by the memory of Krishna playing with Rādhā in the river, and he leapt into the water and almost drowned before being rescued by followers. When he saw the blue neck of a peacock he was reminded of his blue god, and he fell unconscious in ecstasy. Once he heard the flute of a cowherd boy, and he fell on the ground in frenzy, his breathing stopped, and he began to foam at the mouth. On his return to Puri, where he lived the rest of his life, his ecstatic devotional swoons and outbursts became increasingly frequent.

This pattern of religious behavior can be explained by two related phenomena: an experience of love in separation, and madness, which is behavior that deviates from the social norm—it is outrageous and contrary to defined patterns of thought and action. The experience of being separated from one's beloved deity causes agony. It is this experience that drove Caitanya mad. His madness manifested itself in wide mood swings and incoherent behavior. He would, for instance, laugh one moment and cry the next. He would dance, run swiftly, and suddenly faint, falling down upon the ground. Some of his physical symptoms included his limbs becoming stiff or trembling, his skin perspiring profusely and appearing to change color, his hair standing on end, his senses confused, nonsensical speech, and imagining that he saw Krishna everywhere. When he spied a mountain one day he ran toward it because he imagined that he was seeing Mount Govardhana, which was held aloft by Krishna to protect the gopīs from a tremendous storm created by the deity Indra. Others described Caitanya as a lovesick and moody girl. From one perspective, his suffering was an exact parallel to the grief suffered by the people of Vṛndāvana when they were separated from Krishna. Caitanya's madness often arose suddenly and spontaneously. In Purī, he rushed forward to embrace the icon of Jagannātha, a wide-eyed form of Krishna worshiped in the temple, and fell into an ecstatic swoon before the image. The temple custodians witnessed this event, and thought that he was mad.

Caitanya's religious madness does not mean that he was clinically insane. It can be viewed as an overflow of emotion that is impossible to contain. His madness can also be viewed as his response to the madness contained within Krishna's māyā (illusory power).[19] From this perspective, becoming mad means to be an ideal devotee (*bhakta*).

Caitanya's madness manifests five basic characteristics. It indicates his total absorption in God; his extreme infatuation and god-intoxicated state makes him appear mad to others. Second, Caitanya's madness indicates his participation in or imitation of Krishna. Like the gopīs, he is made mad with love, which is a sign of divine grace. Third, madness is indicative of Caitanya's indifference to this world, and he lives rather in a divine world. Within the context of this divine world shaped by the spirit of play (*līlā*), Caitanya is not bound by social conventions and customs, and can behave unpredictably and follow his inclinations. Fourth, madness suggests that the saint is not at home in the world, because he can see the true, impermanent, and tenuous nature of the world. Fifth, madness is symbolic of the freedom and transcendence of the saint. He is free to act contrary to social norms. He is free to act or even become mad.[20]

Cross-culturally, madness is often a characteristic of a saint. Certainly, during his lifetime, some contemporaries of Caitanya thought that he was mad. But the role of a madman does not, exhaust interpretations of Caitanya's significance by his contemporaries. Some people thought that he was an *avatāra* (incarnation) of Krishna. Other people considered him an embodiment of Rādhā and Krishna combined. This interpretation of Caitanya's nature implied that Krishna become incarnated in Caitanya in order to experience the same bliss felt by Rādhā when united with Krishna. Thus, Rādhā and Krishna united to enjoy the fruits of supreme love in the body of Caitanya, which necessarily implies the androgynous nature of the saint.

Caitanya offered a model for followers and an invitation to follow his example. In this model, the feminine attitude predominates in to a person's relation to the divine. Thus a genuine *bhakta* (devotee) should assume the behavior and attitude of a gopī (cowherd girl). This is because Krishna is the sole universal male figure, so it is only as a female that the bhakta can hope to fully experience passionate devotion to him.

Gauḍīya Vaiṣṇavism

Caitanya was not a religious thinker or organizer. The religious tradition that he inspired in Bengal, which became known as Gauḍīya Vaiṣṇavism, gives him credit for writing only eight simple Sanskrit verses called the *Śikṣāṣṭaka*. The task of theological reflection and organization was left to his disciples. The most important disciples in the immediate post-Caitanya period were the six Gosvāmins, of whom the most important were Sanātana, Rūpa, and their nephew Jīva Gosvāmī. They produced over 219 works in Sanskrit.

According to Jīva Gosvāmī, the soul is both the same as and different from (*bhedābheda*) Krishna, who is the supreme deity and not a mere incarnation. The soul is the same as God because it forms a part of the divine. The difference between the two relates to a difference in attributes and characteristics. God's relation to his devotees is characterized by pure bliss (*hlādinī*), whose essence is bhakti (devotion, love). This implies that devotion or love is present in both God and human beings. The religious experience of this lover is expressed in aesthetic terms.

Rūpa defines devotion as action, knowledge, and ultimately realization. There are two kinds of devotion (*bhakti*): *vaidhi* and *rāgānuga*. The former type arises from scriptural sources, and it also entails seeking the protection of God. Rāgānuga devotion, which is superior to vaidhi, is the deep love of God. It is more precisely a natural excess of desire by which the devotee becomes attached to God.[21] Thus this type of devotion arises spontaneously by following the emotions. For Rūpa, devotion is an absolute *rasa* (sap, essence, taste), which means dramatic sentiment within an aesthetic context. Rasa should not be confused with a passive experience, according to Rūpa, because it involves active realization. This aesthetic experience is extended to all life, which implies that the entire world becomes a stage and devotees play parts in a performance of divine play (*līlā*).[22] This type of performance occurs with kīrtana (singing the praises of God), which is an invitation to a devotee to participate bodily in an emotional realm of play.

The life of a particular devotee is characterized by five forms of pure devotion (*bhakti*): becoming aware of one's insignificance in comparison to God, considering oneself to be a slave or servant, imagining oneself as a friend, considering oneself a parent, and comprehending Krishna as a lover. In the final state, this final form of devotion is similar to the role played by Rādhā and other gopīs, which represents a state of pure erotic love that leads to joy in God. These forms of devotion are accompanied by such practices as singing God's praises, repeatedly chanting his name, worshiping temple icons, and visualizing Krishna's acts of play, especially those with the gopīs.

As the Bengal Vaiṣṇava sect developed, it divided into two factions over the interpretation of Rādhā and her relationship to Krishna—whether she was a mistress or a wife. One faction argued that Rādhā was a *svakīyā* woman, which meant that she was legally married to her husband and diligently followed the traditional social duties of her station in life. Neglecting their social duties, *parakīyā* women entered into love affairs although they belonged to another man and had no intention of marrying their illicit lover. There were two kinds of parakīyā women: married and unmarried. The former type of parakīyā women had more to lose when entering into an extramarital affair, because they risked the loss of their husband, home, and reputation.[23] Since they were willing to risk so much for their love, they were the best exemplars of pure love (*prema*). Those members of the sect who approved of the parakīyā interpretation of Rādhā won the issue, and Rādhā became the supreme example of an individual who would risk and even abandon everything for her love.

Sahajiyā Cult

The Sahajiyā cult represents a further development of the Caitanya movement. The term *sahaja* refers to what one is born with; it thus implies what is natural or easy.[24] What are natural to human beings are the senses. Since they are natural, the senses should be utilized in religion, not denied or suppressed. The term also implies a state of equilibrium between the self and the world. It is possible to recognize this state by realizing that a particular individual is a microcosm. By reaching the state of sahaja, a person is free from the cycle of rebirth, and spends eternity in the blissful place of Krishna, an eternal Vṛndāvana. This is a secret place of the "hidden moon," which represents the eternal pleasure of Rādhā and Krishna.[25]

The Sahajiyā movement does not require a guru (teacher), because one's guru is either Krishna or a released devotee, who makes no distinction between human and divine, and does not perceive a difference between kāma (desire) and prema (pure love). Human embodiment accounts for desire, which can become pure love (*prema*) by altering its motive (devotion) and object (God). The grace of Krishna plays no essential role in this movement.[26]

The historical origins of this sect are difficult to determine accurately. Some scholars trace its origins to the tantric tradition that will be discussed more fully in chapter 12. It is also possible to see a relation to an earlier Buddhist Sahajiyā, which is changed by the Rādhā-Krishna love ideal of the unconventional parakīyā type.[27] Instead of the Hindu Śiva-Śakti unity of Tantra, the Sahajiyās substituted the notion of Krishna-Rādhā. The acceptance of this divine unity leads to the belief that all males and females are physical manifestations of the principles of the divine pair. There is general scholarly agreement that this movement represented a revolt against Hindu orthodoxy.[28]

Devotional Poets

Devotion to Krishna was often expressed poetically, in part because of the strong emotions that this literary form could evoke. We have already mentioned the importance of Jayadeva's twelfth-century poem, the *Gītāgovinda*, and its broad influence. Jayadeva's poem shaped the common conceptualization of the relationship between Krishna and Rādhā. Another poem of significance was a thirteenth-century work entitled the *Krishnakarnamṛta* (Nectar of the Acts of Krishna) by Bilvamaṅgala, who was a member of the Viṣṇusvāmi sect. In northern India this sect is called Rudra Sampradāya, and its founder, named Viṣṇusvāmin, is said to have lived during the thirteenth century, but all of his works are lost. Bilvamaṅgala's work expresses adoration for Krishna by describing his body parts as reflecting features of nature, gives fragments of the Krishna narrative, expresses the soul's love and longing for God, and evokes various sentiments (*rasas*) related to devotional religion.

In the fourteenth century, the poets Caṇḍīdāsa and Vidyāpati stressed the illicit love affair between Rādhā and Krishna. They conceived of this relationship as a form of play (*līlā*). They also stressed dedicating one's soul to the service of love. Moreover, they were convinced that love was the greatest revelation. The poetry of Caṇḍīdāsa was especially autobiographical because he fell in love with a low-caste washerwoman named Rāmī. The poet publicly acknowledged his love affair, and sought to have it recognized by his fellow Brahmins. Rāmī plays the role of Rādhā in his poems, where in he expresses his own experiences.[29] Thus, the encounter of Rādhā and Krishna became a meaningful paradigm for the poet's life.

A later poet of renown was Sūrdās (born c. 1478), who was a member of the Vallabha tradition of Vaiṣṇavism. At some point during his life, he became blind, but this handicap did not obstruct his creativity. Among the six works attributed to him, one, based on the incarnation of Krishna, was entitled *Sūrsārāvalī* and another, founded on the play (*līlā*) of Krishna, was called the *Sāhityalaharī*. His most famous composition was the *Sūrsāgar*, a compendium of poems inspired by the *Bhāgavata Puraṇa* and its account of Krishna's life. Sūrdās viewed Rādhā as the legally married wife of Krishna. In fact, the couple lived as acquaintances since their childhood, according to the poet. Sūrdās's sensitive poems about Rādhā depicted her as unified mind and soul with Krishna, whereas the couple gave the appearance of being separate beings for the benefit of their devotees.

An antinomian and ecstatic group of poet-singers from the Bengal region were the Bāuls (literally mad ones). The Bāuls did not attribute their movement to any founder. Many Bāuls were from the lower castes and relatively uneducated, although there were some songwriters that were better educated. These itinerant composers and singers developed oral and written traditions. Some composers signed their works using two names: composer and guru (teacher).[30] These folk poets and singers were so named because of their unorthodox behavior and attitudes. They blurred distinctions, for instance, between castes, between genders to some extent, and between Hindu and Muslim. In fact, many Bāuls were Muslim. They criticized and rejected orthodox beliefs and practices, such as not worshiping idols or a transcendent deity, deliberately dressed in worn and ragged clothing, and wandered incessantly singing and playing a single-stringed instrument. With their embrace of strange behavior and clothing, nonvedic character, and their affinity with Tantra, the Bāuls represented a religion of rebellion.[31] They also advocated worshiping the immanent deity within each person. The Bāuls believed that God was located within a person, like a caged bird. In order to reach God, it was necessary to follow a path away from the world and to turn within oneself. Thus the Bāuls tended to emphasize personal experience in contrast to external authority. The Bāuls also manifested a concern for direct sense experience, an emphasis on the present moment, and stressed existing in the world. This empirical emphasis was opposed to more idealistic spirituality.

The Bāuls often referred to their path as a way of reverse because of its invitation to religious madness and esoteric practices called the "four moons *sādhanā*" (practice). The four moons had four colors: black, yellow, red, and white. They were called moons because of a symbolic association between the moon and bodily secretions, and a symbolic connection between the moon and water. In general, the four moons were identified with excrement, urine, blood, and semen, which are elements considered antinomian and generally evoked disgust and horror when there was any suggestion of eating or drinking them. From the Bāul perspective, these elements were nourishing and medicinal.[32] The Bāuls justified the use of these elements by claiming that it was necessary to use poison to destroy poison. By following this esoteric method, a successful aspirant became a *siddha* (perfected or realized one). The siddha transcended social norms and all worldly contexts. During one's progress, a male practitioner needed to use the services of a female partner for sexual intercourse, which was preferably practiced during her menstrual period. The practice may also include oral sex and consumption of bodily waste products. By using sexual techniques and consumption of bodily waste products, the aspirant was in a symbolic sense piercing the four moons. This type of practice will be discussed more fully in chapter 12 within the context of a discussion of Tantra.

Rādhā-Centered Movements

Rādhā eclipses Krishna in central importance in the Rādhāvallabha tradition. The alleged founder of this tradition was Śrī Hit Harivamśa (1502–1552), who was born into a rich family near Mathura. A single book in Sanskrit and two composed in Hindi are attributed to him. His son Krishnadāsa succeeded him after his death, assumed leadership of the community, and constructed a temple. The son was strongly influenced by the Caitanya tradition. He composed a poem entitled *Karnananda* in which he explored the amorous play of Rādhā and Krishna. The poem also stressed the union of the divine couple by depicting her as the legitimate wife of Krishna.

According to the theology of this tradition, Rādhā is the ground of being, the eternal power, without form or qualities, and the bestower of bliss. She is more powerful than Krishna, because he cannot control his profuse passion for her, which is an inversion of the traditional viewpoint. Rādhā's devotees are her companions or friends (*sakhīs*), who act as intermediaries for the union of Rādhā and Krishna. Devotees are instructed to contemplate this union, which leads to the emotion of joy. This experience of joy is equated with liberation.

The sakhīs are considered superior to the gopīs because the former do not experience prolonged separation like the gopīs. By sharing in the marital status of Rādhā, the sakhīs enjoy the play (*līlā*) of Krishna, and they facilitate the meeting and unitive experience of the divine couple.[33] With the advent of union, the sakhīs experience bliss. It is possible to recognize a sakhī by his or her forehead mark that consists of a curved loop that reaches the bridge of the nose with a dot in the center. The loop symbolizes Krishna, whereas the dot signifies Rādhā.

A branch of the Rādhāvallabha sect was called the Sakhībhāva tradition, or the Haridāsi tradition, founded by Haridāsa (c. 1600). For this sect also, Rādhā was the legitimate wife of Krishna. The members of the sect, who were also called friends (*sakhīs*), identified with the gopī companions of Rādhā by assuming female garb and manners in order to share the rasa (emotional mood) experienced by Rādhā in her relationship with Krishna. The members of the sect act as assistants to Rādhā in preparing for the devotional union with Krishna and serve as witnesses to the divine lovemaking. Members also identified with Rādhā in order to share her blissful experiences with Krishna.

There are two branches of the tradition: Gosvamis (householders) and sadhus (renunciants). The renouncer group cares for Haridāsa's tomb in the town of Vṛndāban, whereas the householders have custody of the image that he venerated during his life. Followers of both groups also venerate Haridāsa's poems, which have been collected into two anthologies: *Kelimal* (Garland of Divine Play) and *Ashtadas Siddhanta Pada* (Eighteen Songs of Instruction). The former collection focuses on the love of Krishna and Rādhā, in which the poet imagines himself as an attendant of Rādhā, while the latter group of poems is concerned with conversion and devotion and warns about the illusory nature of worldly life. In addition to his poems, Haridāsa made an important contribution to the development of Indian music, though we know little about his life.

The Cult of Viṭhobā

The Vaiṣṇavism of Maharashtra in central India exhibits a much less erotic and more respectable Krishna, because he is now legally married to Rukminī. Krishna is called Viṭhobā or Viṭṭhala, and is no longer referred to as the lover of Rādhā. There are two major divisions of the cult: the Mahānubhāvas (literally, "those who have a great experience") and the Vārakarīs (literally, "those who perform the tour"), which means pilgrimage to the city of Pandharpur.

The Mahānubhāvas direct their devotion to Parameśvara (the Supreme Lord) who incarnated himself five times, forming the so-called "five Krishnas." It is important to note that Krishna was not an incarnation of Viṣṇu for members of this sect. Besides the embodiment of Krishna himself, two other important incarnations of Parameśvara are Cakradhar, who was the founder of the sect, and Guṇḍam Rāül, who was Cakradhar's teacher.

Gundam Rāül was an especially fascinating figure because of his apparent madness. He was known popularly as Gosāvī. His unorthodox behavior included entering a home, breaking the storage pots, and mixing together the food. He often acted infantile, greedy, rude, excessively demanding, and petulant.[34] He frolicked in his madness by replacing, for instance, a louse that had been combed out of his hair. He also stole food and behaved in unpredictable ways, much like Krishna.

The Mahānubhāvas emphasized experience and mental exercises by which one recollected the names, deeds, and manifestations of the five incarnations. The movement combined devotional attitudes and practices with asceticism and renunciation of social ties and possessions—connecting the solitude of asceticism, for instance, with the devotional practice of recollection and painful feelings of separation.[35] On the one hand, the sect rejected traditional Brahmanic social categories and some pollution regulations. On the other hand, it was divided between lay disciples and wandering renouncers. The lay householders were called "those who have desire for God."

The Vārakarīs focus on the deity Viṭhobā. This movement traces its origin to Jñāneśvara (1275–1296 C.E.).[36] Jñāneśvara is famous for dictating the *Jñāneśvari*, an important commentary on the *Bhagavad Gītā* that gained the status of a sacred object. His childhood was made difficult by a decision by his priestly father to become an ascetic, and then reverting to the life of a householder, which caused the family to be excommunicated and persecuted. The four siblings all became religious figures, and they were considered incarnations of various gods and goddesses.

Jñāneśvara stresses the importance of the guru and the unknowable nature of god. In his commentary, he attempts to reconcile the dualistic metaphysical system of Sāṃkhya philosophy, renouncing the fruits of one's actions, the devotional path, Advaita Vedānta philosophy, classical yoga, and tantric thought. He equates, for instance, the puruṣa of Sāṃkhya thought with Brahman of Vedānta. He also refers to the awakening of the spiritual energy (*kuṇḍalinī*) of Tantra in the heart of a person, and he stresses the divine name and its power in devotionalism.

Another significant figure is the low-caste Nāmadeva (c. 1270–1350). He became a tailor like his father, but he allegedly turned to crime before being converted to the religious path of Jñāneśvara. Most of his poems were composed in the regional language of Marathi, and some have been adopted by the Sikh tradition. There is no scholarly consensus that Nāmadeva was one person or more, which causes scholars to question the authenticity of some of his poems. Nāmadeva's references to God reflect the unity and omnipresence of the deity, the importance of realizing the attributeless (*nirguṇa*) aspect of God, and the necessity of chanting his names. Nāmadeva and Jñāneśvara are usually considered part of the Sant tradition that will be discussed more fully in the following chapter.

Another notable figure is Ekanāth (c. 1535–1599), who published a reliable edition of Jñāneśvara's work. In this tradition it is not unusual to find very personal references to God as "father and mother" or mention God as a loving mother. Ekanāth started late in his life to translate the *Rāmāyaṇa* into Marathi, but before completing the task he died on the banks of the Godāvarī River, where a temple is dedicated to him. From this tradition, there emerged an ascetic follower named Rāmadāsa (1608–1681), who started his own tradition, named after him; he was the spiritual teacher of King Śivājī (d. 1680), who rebelled against Muslim rulers in Maharashtra.

Several mystic poets propagated the worship of Viṭhobā. The greatest of these poets was Tukārām (1608–1649), who came from the Śūdra caste. After his brother became a renouncer, Tukārām assumed the family business, but his life was shattered by business failure and several family deaths. He renounced the world, retired to a mountain, and eventually received a vision of Krishna, which transformed him into a madman.[37] His symptoms were very similar to those of Caitanya—erect hair, profuse sweating, and eyes full of tears. His wife and others were convinced of his madness.[38] A sense of separation from God increased his madness. Waiting for god to reveal himself, the poet barked and growled, for instance, but he continued to dance in the temple and he repeated the names of God day and night.

Tukārām thought that as it was necessary to prepare for the mystical life, and prerequisite for training was securing a good guru (teacher). It is initially necessary for an aspirant to become detached from worldly things, because such things can pollute the mystic. In order to purify oneself of various defilements, it is necessary to become indifferent to the world.[39] The aspirant must also practice certain moral precepts, such as not lusting for the wealth or wife of another man, believing in the saints, telling the truth, and not censuring others. An aspirant should only think about God, practice humility, serve others, and surrender one's life to God.[40]

Like many devotional poets, Tukārām understood the utility of kīrtana (repetitively chanting the names of God) as a way to realize the highest reality. The name of God draws the devotee near to God, and it forms a bond between the devotee and the object of his or her love. According to Tukārām, knowledge can be an obstacle to reaching God, which can only be attained by devotion. God aids the aspirant to attain his or her goal by granting divine grace, which enables one to gain union with the divine. This unitive state does not dissolve the difference between the two parties.

During the sixteenth century, another devotional poet was Dādū (1544–1604). He was born in Ahmedabad, and left home around eighteen years of age to become an itinerant ascetic, but he later married and gained employment. He composed devotional songs and religious didactic verses. A disciple named Rajjab compiled his sayings (*bani*). After the death of the master, a movement called the Dādū Panth emerged and stressed the importance of chanting God's name. This practice can lead to a nondual union with God in which one is conscious of one's complete dependence on God. The movement split into two major branches: Khalsa and Uttaradha.

Krishna on Stage and in the Streets

When discussing Krishna mythology we examined the importance of the rāsa līlā (circle dance). This dance comes to life on stage when performed by traveling actors of young boys who play male and female roles in richly colored costumes. By means of their craft, these youthful actors imitate the actions of divine figures. The rāsa līlā performed by these young boys is not merely a drama; it is also a liturgy. The drama is regularly repeated, and it entails a sacramental power, because to see it involves participation and sharing the play with others.[41] The liturgical aspect of the performance is enhanced because it begins and ends with the waving of camphor lamps (*āratī*).

A typical rāsa līlā consists of an initial dance followed by a one-act play based on any one of the multitude of Krishna's līlās, or deeds, which might be performed in the courtyard of a temple or the privacy of a wealthy Vaiṣṇava devotee's home. The dance enables the participants to meet the absolute and to keep in touch with the source of creativity. The one-act play is about the theme of play (*līlā*). The overall purpose of the play (*līlā*) is to encourage the audience to participate in whatever mood (*rasa*) is depicted by the drama.[42]

During a typical rāsa līlā performance, a person experiences the emotions of another person, which is unlike experiencing one's own emotions, in which there is no internal separation between the viewer and his or her personal emotional reaction. Being similar to empathy or sympathy, rasa enables us to feel indirectly the emotions of another person. The feeling created by a dramatic rasa upon an audience represents a mood that unifies the separate elements of a play into an integrated whole that brings together the causes of emotion, its effects, and its accompanying transitory emotions.[43] It is thus possible to witness the qualities of rasa being manifested: a sense of unity, an immediate awareness of the subject, an impersonal affective aspect, and a generalized situation that avoids partial awareness.[44] Overall, rasa combines visual, oral, and aural experiences with emotional states, and it is, moreover, connected to the essence of food.[45]

The līlās (plays) are instructive lessons about the relationship between Rādhā and Krishna. In the *Prempaniksha Līlā*, for instance, Rādhā tests Krishna's loyalty by sending a gopī to inform him that there is a girl who would like to see him. After Krishna replies that he will see no one but her, Rādhā comes to him. The gopīs warn Rādhā not to take a dancing lesson from Krishna in the *Mundariyacori Līlā* because the god is a thief. Discovering that Rādhā's ring is missing at the conclusion of the lesson, the gopīs search Krishna and find the stolen ring. Seeking revenge, the gopīs steal Krishna's flute, crown, and clock. Krishna, disguised as a lovelorn girl, approaches Rādhā hoping to retrieve his stolen goods. In an effort to console the girl, Rādhā dons the stolen property, and Krishna apprehends her. The *Vivaha Līlā* celebrates the marriage of Rādhā and Krishna. And the *Causar Līlā* depicts a chess game between the two lovers, with the loser becoming the slave of the winner. Krishna loses the game and binds himself to Rādhā as her slave.[46]

In contrast to the rāsa līlā dramas, a different type of performance is the practice of *bhajana*, a form of congregational devotional worship focused on Krishna. The origin of this form of worship dates to the seventh century near the town of Kumbakōṇam in the Tanjore district of southern India. The term *bhajana* means devotional song or prayer, and is roughly synonymous with the practice of kīrtana or sankīrtana in the north.

Six types of bhajanas are identified in southern India: private weekly meetings, monthly meetings, annually performed marriage of Rādhā and Krishna, street performance conducted in the early morning around a temple tank, independent gatherings, and the no longer commonly observed daily bhajana.[47] The participants meet to chant names of god in a manner called the necklace of names (*nāmavali*). They begin with slow repetitions; then speed up the recitation, and raise the pitch gradually; finally they lower it and slow it down, in reverse sequence. Participants in a weekly gathering sing Tamil and Sanskrit songs of the Āḻvārs, sing praises to the founding gurus, and portions of the *Gītāgovinda* each week until the entire poem is recited. The weekly service ends with an invocation for auspiciousness for Krishna and his devotees. Finally, food is distributed as prasāda (gracious offering). The monthly bhajanas use a small, lighted ritual lamp to signify Krishna's presence. Participants sit and recite the *Gopīkā Gītā*, lament the god's disappearance, beg him to return, and celebrate his return by standing, singing, and dancing. The session concludes with devotees prostrating before each other and rolling clockwise around the lamp in order to roll in the dust of other devotees. After this expression of surrender and humility, participants embrace each other.

The overall rationale of the bhajana is the belief that singing the praises of Krishna will win salvation for practitioners. Worship (*pūjā*) is also a part of the practice, along with the use of lithographs depicting the deity rather than images made of stone or metal.[48] Moreover, bhajana is a celebration of a devotee's direct love of god. Its directness and immediacy mean that there is no need for a mediator to facilitate the relationship between the worshiper and deity.

Festival Celebrations of Krishna Devotionalism

An extremely popular, widespread, and riotous festival associated with Krishna devotion is Holī, which celebrates the death of the demoness Holikā. Young boys heave dust into the air, hurl old shoes at each other (an impure activity), and race around laughing and cavorting like gopīs. The doors of homes are broken open, and inhabitants are pulled from their homes and forced to join in the revelry. Anthropologists report seeing the capture of an old victim by the celebrants, and making the old man ride a donkey seated backward.[49] A favorite activity of the festival is the throwing of colored dyes on participants and spraying each other with water. In some places women rush out of their houses to attack men with stout canes. In some areas, the beatings administered by women are a bit more organized, and the men wear head protection. The actions of the attacking women are, nonetheless, another example of things being done in reverse during the festival.

The festival is not entirely chaotic, because there is a respite for bathing. People also pay condolences to each house whose members suffered bereavement during the past year. And time is taken to enjoy the festival drink of a cool, thick green liquid, which is made of almonds, sugar, curds of milk, anise, and half a cup of *bhāng* (hashish or marijuana). This drink can make a person giddy or reduce a person to an inebriated stupor, if too much of it is consumed. This type of beverage enables devotees to lose their inhibitions and assume the role of gopīs frolicking passionately and joyfully with Krishna in a religious drama.

Another significant Krishna celebration is the swing festival (*doḷamelaṇa*), which means "the gathering or meeting of swings." The swing (*doḷa*) refers to a moveable shrine used to transport the deities (usually Krishna and Rādhā), whereas the term *meḷaṇa* means the meeting of gods.[50] The swing resembles a wooden throne in the overall shape of a small temple. This moveable sacred space contains the image of the deities on top of bamboo poles that are used to carry the images on the shoulders of devotees. Ropes are tied to two pillars on a platform that form a swing for the portable shrine. While devotees carry the palanquin with images swinging, other devotees dance, sing, and play instruments, mostly drums and cymbals.

In the eastern coastal region of Orissa, the climax of the festival is reached on the night of the full moon during the month of Phālguṇa (February/March). A regional feature unique to Orissa is the practice of one deity inviting other deities from neighboring villages to attend the festival, which transforms it into a meeting of gods. The inviting god is like a prince bestowing grace on all divine guests by receiving, feeding, and welcoming them with his sight (*darśana*), and sending them away enriched. It is the inviting god that leads the festival procession of the invited gods, which proceeds by the gods making a swinging movement—accomplished by devotees taking two steps forward and one step back. The created motion is intended to amuse the deities. The festival includes competitions for the most beautiful masks, the most skillful dances, the best drumming and singing, which adds to the popularity of the festival. For the hosting village, the festival promises prestige and economic benefits, because people from a wide area will visit the sponsoring village and spend money for food and other items.

Krishna Consciousness

The Gauḍīya Vaiṣṇava tradition has been exported to the West in the form of the International Society for Krishna Consciousness (ISKCON), which is more popularly known as the Hare Krishna movement. The movement was brought to America when Swami A. C. Bhaktivedanta Prabhupada (born Abhay Charan De in 1896 in Calcuṭta) arrived in New York in 1965; he had no money, but he managed to gather a small group around him and opened a Second Avenue storefront on the lower east side of Manhattan. His early followers were mainly recruited from counterculture youth.

Prabhupada had graduated from the University of Calcutta after studying English, philosophy, and economics. He spent much of his adult life as a married man with family responsibilities, and worked as a manager of a pharmaceutical company. In 1922, he met his guru, named Bhaktisiddhanta Saraswati Thakura, and he received formal initiation in 1933. He was entrusted with the task of taking the message of the movement to the West, but his family obligations prevented him from beginning his mission right away. He spent much of his time with the movement producing English-language literature about the message of the movement. In 1959, he entered the state of a renouncer. From 1965 until his death in 1977, he spread the message of the movement in the West. By 1970, there were twenty-one ISKCON centers in the United States, and the movement had spread to Japan, Canada, and Europe. There are currently about 350 centers around the globe.

During the 1970s and 1980s, the movement became the focus of the anti-cult movement in America. Leaders of the Hare Krishnas were accused of brainwashing and mind control of young people, which some studies have proven false. It is possible to account for converts as those fleeing freedom and choosing to surrender to a guru, who provides a direct connection to god, stability, and safety.[51] When a person converts to the movement and is initiated, he or she becomes a preaching missionary of Krishna's narrative. Converts are expected to raise money to support the movement and to convince others to join. Thus Krishna Consciousness is a missionary religion. Members consider the Vedas, *Bhagavad Gītā*, and stories about Krishna in the Purāṇas literally true. The biography of Caitanya entitled the *Caitanya Caritāmṛta* of Kṛṣṇadāsa Kavirāja is also accepted as an important piece of literature. The writings of Prabhupada have become the primary institutional embodiment of his charisma. This body of literature is held to be proof that Krishna is the supreme personal deity.

The movement holds that humans are now living in the degenerate kali yuga, and only those with Krishna consciousness will gain liberation. During this dark age, the immortal soul lies asleep in a body, and it falsely identifies itself with the body. The soul is also benighted by ordinary material consciousness, which prevents it from realizing its full potential. This potential is summarized by the magazine of the group, entitled *Back to the Godhead Magazine*. In order to return to God, certain ritual practices serve to awaken the soul and to replace its material consciousness with Krishna consciousness, which brings liberation from rebirth. This begins with lifestyle and dress. There are four simple rules of conduct: no eating of fish, meat, or eggs; no illicit sexual relations; no intoxicants; and no gambling. Adherents are required to dress in traditional Indian attire, which means a dhoti for males and sari for females. Males must cut their hair, leaving a wisp on the top of the head as a symbol of detachment. These rules reflect the belief that the human body is a temple dedicated to God.[52] The major ritual practices include mantra repetition and worship of Krishna. The mantra that one receives at initiation is repeated 1,728 times each day (sixteen rounds on a 108-bead rosary). It is believed that Krishna resides in his name, which suggests that the mantra is identical to God. The other major practice is sankīrtan, that is, devotional singing and dancing as a way of praising and honoring God. These practices are intended to fill the devotee's mind with God.

Play, Madness, and Eroticism

This chapter demonstrates that Krishna plays as a child, adolescent, and mature man. The unstructured play (*līlā*) of the infant is spontaneous, impetuous, and without pattern. The adolescent is famous for his dalliances with the gopīs in general, and in particular with his favorite Rādhā. This form of play possesses erotic overtones. Krishna's beauty, flute, and demon destruction are also forms of play with erotic overtones.

Through such activities as kīrtana and festival participation, a devotee accepts the invitation from the deity to play, and may even go mad in devotion. By taking the divine invitation, a devotee affirms life and that it is to be celebrated, a gift to be enjoyed, and experiences that life itself is sufficient. As the pilgrimage to sacred Braj (the area around Vṛndāban) suggests for devotees that participate, a pilgrim travels in a circle without end and concludes where he or she began the journey. The pilgrimage consists of ordinary activities that suggest that life itself is Krishna's play.[53] The invitation to play also suggests that it is not necessary to attempt to improve life; it is simply enough to enjoy it, to experience its many moods (*rasa*), and to taste it. Play enables a devotee to become complete and satisfied. Moreover, play allows a person to become like god in the sense of acting free, frivolous, and spontaneous.

With respect to Krishna devotionalism, this chapter enables us to witness that spiritual madness is another form of play. If play releases a devotee from work, duty, and responsibility, this is also true for the mad devotee. The emotionalism that often accompanies devotional madness serves as a force that vitalizes and inspires others. We have also called attention to a connection between madness and ecstasy. The incoherent speech, irrational behavior, and painful emotional states of Rādhā are symbolic of the highest ecstatic state.[54] The erotic practices associated with tantric-influenced forms of religiosity are connected to madness because engaging in illicit sexual relations and ingesting offensive bodily wastes are forms of religious madness from an orthodox perspective.

By viewing Krishna through the prism of play, it is possible to recognize the divine as irresistible, attractive, and overwhelmingly beautiful. As the divine player, Krishna invites us to enjoy and celebrate life. He gives the devotee an open-ended invitation to join the fun. Krishna not only reveals much about himself through play, madness, and eroticism, but he reveals, moreover, a world of transcendent joy and bliss. From this perspective, life is in fact Krishna's play (*līlā*).

The love for Krishna expressed by gopīs, madmen, and poets creates a sea of love. With tides of emotions and a sea of moods, the spiritual thirst of the devotee is quenched, and the devotee's mind melts in the salt water. This type of scenario, as many poets make clear, means that Krishna's love is a liquid love in which a devotee is invited to drown.

The various religious movements associated with Krishna devotion tend to be in general inclusive of castes and genders. The caste inclusiveness begins with the Āḻvārs and continues through the centuries. With respect to gender, a strong feminine strain runs through the various traditions. In fact, feminine behavior and symbolism play a central role in Krishna devotionalism, in which a person is invited to act like a gopī. The inclusive nature of Krishna devotionalism is evident with the Bāuls, who were both Hindu and Muslim. The contiguity and unorthodox nature of Bāul practice, for instance, contributes to producing a critique of each tradition. The phenomena of play, madness, and eroticism tend to undermine orthopraxis and orthodoxies.

9

Righteous Rāma, Untouchables, and Sants

According to the *Manava Dharmaśāstra* (7:2–9), which is more commonly known as the *Laws of Manu*, the king who has been properly consecrated has an obligation to protect the world and its inhabitants. The Lord created the king to fulfill such a role by taking eternal particles from various gods, which give the king his energy. The king can be compared to the sun in its brilliance, with the ability to burn the sight and minds of humans. Therefore, no one can bear to gaze at his brightness. By virtue of his power, he is comparable to various deities. In fact, a king is a deity in human form. This theory of the divine nature of kings is applicable to the major figures in the two major epics of India. The story of the divine Paṇḍava brothers is told in the *Mahābhārata*, and the narrative of the king Rāma is recounted in the *Rāmāyaṇa*, which is attributed by tradition to the sage Vālmīki. Rāma devotionalism is an important but often neglected aspect of Hinduism. In this chapter, we will focus on Rāma devotionalism in northern India and some of the movements and practices associated with such devotion, especially among a group of Untouchables, who often do not appear to any appreciable extent in introductory texts on Hinduism. This chapter also considers the Sants, poet-saints of northern India, even though they are a separate religious movement distinct from Rāma devotion.

In order to grasp the notion of kingship embodied in the *Rāmāyaṇa*, it makes sense to first consider the notion of kingship in the other great epic body of literature, the *Mahābhārata* and its narrative of a royal family. The *Mahābhārata* traces its origin to the sage Vyāsa (a name meaning arranger or compiler), who is probably a mythical or a composite figure. Vyāsa suddenly makes an appearance at points in the text itself, but at other times, his words or actions are recalled, by other narrators. Thus Vyāsa is not a detached compiler of the text, but is rather a direct or indirect participant in the narrative. The *Mahābhārata* is classified in Indian literature as an *itihāsa* (chronicle). The term *itihāsa* means, literally, "thus (*iti*), indeed (*ha*), it was (*āsa*)." This enormous epic is sometimes called the fifth Veda, which is an attempt to make two assertions: First, it possesses continuity with the past; and second, it is as authoritative as the sacred Vedas.[1]

Before the text finally gained its written form between 300 and 450 C.E. in northern India, it enjoyed a long period of oral transmission by *sūtas* or bards.[2] The title of the epic means the "Great narrative of the descendents of Bhārata." Its origins date to around 400 B.C.E., and it grew over a long period of its development to its present substantial size of 100,000 verses, divided into eighteen books, before achieving its written form—according to some, around the period of the Gupta Dynasty about 400 C.E.,[3] whereas dates of 400 B.C.E. to 200 C.E. have been offered by others.[4] One theory argues for composition between the mid-second century B.C.E. and the beginning of the Common Era by a group of poor Brahmins who may have enjoyed the financial support of royal or merchant patrons.[5] This would suggest a unified theory of the epic's creation and literary character. A counter argument views a gradualist model as more plausible than an organized process of composition by a committee of Brahmins working together synchronously within a relatively short period of time; a unified process of composition does not explain the variations and discontinuities of the text.[6] In addition to the eighteen books of the epic, the *Harivaṃśa* represents a supplement to the epic by forming a nineteenth book. The epic is seven times the combined size of Homer's *Iliad* and *Odyssey*. It is possible that the *Mahābhārata* evolved from a classical heroic epic, was transformed into a religious didactic epic, and also paradoxically retained some common aspects of archaic folklore.[7] The central narrative relates an apocalyptic story in the sense of uncovering a hidden divine plan for the destruction of a corrupt stratum of society. From one perspective, the narrative suggests a divine alliance of priests and divine beings, by which it becomes possible to replace the unrighteous usurpers.

Vyāsa's story is about the feuding Pāṇḍava and Kaurava families from Bhārata, a region of the upper Ganges basin around modern Delhi. In short, the Pāṇḍava family represents the coalition of priests and gods, whereas the Kauravas suggest demonic forces. The feuding families are related by blood to the two brothers named Pāṇḍu and Dhṛtarāṣṭra, who were educated by their uncle Bhīsma. Although he is forbidden to rule because of his blindness, Dhṛtarāṣṭra married Gāndhārī, who gave birth to a hundred sons called the Kauravas. In contrast to this fecundity, the ruling king Pāṇḍu does not dare to have sex with his two wives, named Kuntī and Mādrī, because of a curse directed at him that he would die if he engaged in sexual intercourse. Using a boon, Kuntī invokes various divine beings and is able to conceive three sons by them: the gods Dharma, Vāyu, and Indra help her to conceive, respectively, Yudhiṣṭhira, Bhīma, and Arjuna. Kuntī utilizes the boon further to help Mādrī conceive the twins Nakula and Sahadeva by the twin divine Aśvins. A rationale for these incarnations is provided early in the epic (Mbh 1.58), when the Earth becomes distressed and calls for help because she is being oppressed by an overpopulation of incarnated demonic beings (*asuras*).

Each of the five Pāṇḍava brothers embodies different forms of symbolic significance. Yudhiṣṭhira stands for dharma and duties of law. The impulsive Bhīma represents the energy of physical force and violence, and he stands for the protective aspect of kingship. The twins Nakula and Sahadeva symbolize abundance and multiplicity with respect to fertility and growth, which characterizes the third (Vaiśya) order of society. The fifth brother Arjuna is an image of the king as a being of light that unites the attributes of the others within himself. After Pāṇḍu attempts sexual intercourse with Mādrī and subsequently dies, Mādrī is implicated in his death, and she voluntarily commits self-immolation (*sati*) on her husband's funeral pyre. This leaves Kuntī with the responsibility of raising the five sons. After the death of Pāṇḍu, the dual sets of cousins are raised together and learn the same military skills from their uncle Droṇa. The blind Dhṛtarāṣṭra functions as the regent of the kingdom until Yudhiṣṭhira reaches the proper age to assume leadership of the kingdom.

A narrative thread that runs throughout the epic is the rivalry between the cousins and jealously of the Kauravas for the Pāṇḍavas. The five Pāṇḍavas and their mother avoid an assassination attempt by a fire started by the envious party by escaping through an underground tunnel. The rivalry is also evident when there is a contest for the hand of Draupadī, which concludes with the victory of Arjuna by means of his skill in archery. Draupadī becomes the wife of the five brothers. Draupadī represents a secret incarnation of the goddess Śrī, an embodiment of the auspiciousness and prosperity needed by any successful king. When they return home from winning Draupadī, the brothers receive half the kingdom from the blind regent, and they establish their capital of Indraprāṣṭha (Indra's station).

After successful military campaigns, Yudhiṣṭhira becomes a universal monarch by conquering enemies in the four directions. The king's victories culminate with a celebration of a *rājasūya* (royal consecration). In reaction to the success of the Pāṇḍavas, the Kauravas become increasingly jealous, and they devise a plan to undermine their cousins by challenging them to a game of dice, which is inherently connected to fate. This connection to fate associates dicing with such negative aspects as destructiveness, disintegration, crookedness, and unbalancing forces.[8] These features suggest a future war, at which time everything will be made right.

The otherwise virtuous Yudhiṣṭhira's weakness for gambling proves to be his undoing. Along with addictions to women, hunting, and drinking, the epic considers dice to be the worst vice (Mbh 3:14, 7). With the game rigged by the duplicitous Duryodhana, the king loses successively his wealth, brothers, himself, and the wife jointly shared by the brothers. Draupadī is insulted and humiliated by Duḥśāsana when she is dragged into the assembly hall by the hair, and an attempt is made to publicly strip her, but this miraculously fails as an ending flow of fabric keeps her clothed. The outraged Draupadī challenges Yudhiṣṭhira's right to stake her in the dice game. She demands to know if he had already gambled himself away before wagering her. The blind Dhṛtarāṣṭra intervenes by calling the entire match off, restores to Yudhiṣṭhira what he lost, and grants freedom to Draupadī and her five husbands. Again, Yudhiṣṭhira is challenged to gamble everything on one final throw of the dice. The agreed wager involves a period of exile, if he should lose, versus the restoration of all previous loses. After the gambling-addicted Yudhiṣṭhira loses for the last time, the brothers and their wife go into exile for twelve years in the forest, and a thirteenth year in which they must live incognito before returning to reclaim their kingdom. Their exile is told in the third book of the epic called the "Book of the Forest." Within this long part of the epic, there are numerous tales, and the importance of pilgrimage is stressed.

The fourth book of the epic recounts the final year of exile at the court of King Virāta, for whom this book of the epic is named. The Pāṇḍavas disguise themselves as humble servants at the court. Draupadī becomes, for instance, a low-caste hairdresser and maid, Yudhiṣṭhira poses as a master of dicing named Kanka (a carrion-eating and death-dealing bird), and Arjuna, who is a paragon of manhood, plays the role of a eunuch, lives in a harem, and teaches dancing to women of the palace.[9] Such disguises represent opposites of the genuine natures of the subjects. After nearly having their identity revealed at a couple of points, they finally reveal themselves, to the utter astonishment of Virāta, who offers his daughter to Arjuna. The warrior accepts the king's daughter as a wife for his son Abhimanyu.

When the Pāṇḍavas are unable to reclaim their kingdom and peace negotiations fail, the rival sides prepare for war by enlisting allies and appointing commanders. Krishna joins, for instance, the Pāṇḍavas, whereas his army is linked with the other party. The Kauravas are able to recruit such figures as Bhīṣma, Droṇa, and Karṇa. The sixth book describes the furious battle and Vyāsa's granting of a boon to Dhṛtarāṣṭra to overcome his blindness. The boon allows his charioteer Samjaya to describe in detail the battle. When the armies are prepared for battle Arjuna is suddenly afflicted by doubts, turns to his charioteer Krishna, and asks for advice. The eighteen chapters of the *Bhagavad Gītā* capture the ensuing dialogue between the warrior and his charioteer. The entire sixth book is named for the Kauravas' commander, named Bhīṣma, who becomes mortally wounded and lies on a bed of arrows. The battle continues for the next three books, which bear the names of the Kaurava commanders: Droṇa, Karṇa, and Śalya. The days of conflict are recounted in these three parts of the epic, and they relate the death of Arjuna's son, Abhimanyu, Arjuna's revenge, the duplicitous killing of Droṇa, Bhīma's revenge on Duḥśāsana for humiliating Draupadī, Arjuna's destruction of Karṇa, and the killing of the final commander-in-chief Śalya and his brother by Yudhiṣṭhira. The Kaurava army is finally led to defeat by Duryodhana, who at one point takes refuge in a lake before engaging in a mace duel with Bhīma. Duryodhana is eventually defeated after being struck in his thigh with the mace, which fulfils Bhīma's earlier vow to deliver such a devastating blow. Protests of foul play are leveled at the Pāṇḍavas and Krishna. Three remaining Kaurava warriors successfully execute a counterattack against the sleeping Pāṇḍava army, although the five brothers and Krishna are not present at the complete massacre of their army because they are at the capital. The dying Duryodhana learns of the total destruction of the army of his cousins. The theme of the eleventh book, entitled the "Book of the Women" is the lament at the carnage by the blind Dhṛtarāṣṭra and various women who survey the battlefield. Characters express recriminations and make confessions. Gāndhārī wants to curse the Pāṇḍavas for the massive carnage, but the sage Vyāsa dissuades her and she curses Krishna instead, and holds him responsible for the massive slaughter. The dead are cremated on orders of Yudhiṣṭhira, while the blind regent and others proceed to the Ganges River to make offerings to the deceased.

From one perspective, if the Pāṇḍavas represent the incarnation of divine beings and the Kauravas signify the incarnations of demonic beings, the war is an updated version of the cosmic conflict between Indra and Vṛtra in the vedic cosmogonic tale. From another perspective, the war symbolizes an all-consuming sacrificial fire. Kurukṣetra, the location of the war, is referred to as a sacrificial altar (Mbh 3.81.178). The killing that occurs at this sacrificial altar of human beings becomes an offering to the gods.[10] Moreover, the scope of the destruction suggests a cosmic dissolution (*pralaya*) that occurs at regular intervals within the context of cosmic cycles of time.[11] The presence of Krishna within the epic narrative supports this view because he is the lord of cosmic dissolution (*pralaya*), as evident in the eleventh chapter of the *Bhagavad Gītā* (11.32).

The longest book, called the "Book of the Peace," concludes the war. Yudhiṣṭhira is congratulated on his victory, but the king does not grasp the result as reason for celebration. Vyāsa persuades the victorious king to seek the advice of the dying Bhīṣma, who is still lying on his bed of arrows. Bhīṣma's advice is contained in the "Book of Instruction," which is subdivided into lessons about the duties of kings during peaceful times, the king's responsibilities during periods of conflict, the path to liberation, and the merits of giving. In order to atone for all the death and suffering, Yudhiṣṭhira decides to offer a horse sacrifice in the fourteenth book, which bears the name of this sacrifice. The fifteenth book, called "The Stay at the Hermitage," recalls the blind Dhṛtarāṣṭra's retirement to the forest along with others, and their perishing in a forest fire.

The deaths of Krishna, his brother Balarāma, and their tribes are recalled in "The Book of the Clubs." After Krishna is killed by a hunter's arrow, the ocean submerges his capital, and his soul is merged back into Viṣṇu. After learning of the death of Krishna and his tribe, the Pāṇḍavas renounce the world, leaving Arjuna's grandson as ruler. As they make their way north to the Himalayas or polar mountain toward the heavenly realm, they die one by one during the journey, with Draupadī being the first to fall. Finally, Yudhiṣṭhira is the only person left, and he continues the journey followed by his faithful dog. With the final episode called "The Book of the Ascent to Heaven," Yudhiṣṭhira enters heaven after enduring various tests that involve his refusal to abandon his dog, which is revealed as an incarnation of the god Dharma. A final test of his virtue occurs in heaven, when Yudhiṣṭhira sees only his deceased enemies there, and he is told that his brothers are in hell. He insists on joining his brothers in hell, but their location in heaven is finally revealed to him, and he passes his final test. In general, the central narrative of the epic enables a reader to grasp that the role of king is not necessarily glorious and that the burdens of the position test the fortitude of the best of men, especially those with innate character flaws.

The Righteous King

There are many similarities between the *Mahābhārata* and the *Rāmāyaṇa* of Vālmīki, which including a focus on kingship, court intrigue, deception, exile, war, destruction, death, reunion, love, jealousy, and hate. There are also many differences—the major figures, narrative, length of the narrative, and transmitter of the tale. The two epics have also been compared in the following way: "If, with regard to social norms, the *Mahābhārata* is an epic of violation, of irreducible conflicts between cultural imperatives and the subversion of them, and a brooding meditation on rupture and decay, the *Rāmāyaṇa* stands in sharp contrast to it as a paean to conformity, obedience, and as a handbook of social integration."[12] Both texts were orally transmitted over centuries before assuming their written forms. And there are regional variations of both texts. The dates for the development of the *Rāmāyaṇa* run from 500 B.C.E. to 300 C.E.[13] In comparison to the eighteen books of the *Mahābhārata*, there are seven books of the shorter *Rāmāyaṇa*, roughly 25,000 verses (which is still twice the length of Homer's two Greek epics), and it is generally agreed among scholars that the initial and last books are later additions to the main part that comprises books two to six.[14] The *Rāmāyaṇa* began as a bardic narrative, as did the *Mahābhārata*. Brahmin scholars, who inserted pieces about dharma into them and also retold the tales from a priestly perspective, reworked both epics. A cultural tension between orthodox ritualists and more autonomous ascetics spilled over into the literature. This development overlapped with the advent of devotional (*bhakti*) religion, which led to an additional reworking of the material.[15]

Indigenous traditions of India describe the Rāmāyaṇa as a work from the tretā yuga, the second of the four cycles of cosmic time. This is believed to make the author Vālmīki a contemporary of the epic hero Rāma.[16] A tradition depicts Vālmīki as beginning his life as a bandit before turning to a religious way of life. His name is derived from the word for an anthill, which grew around him while he was absorbed in meditation. Unlike the alleged author Vyāsa of the *Mahābhārata*, some scholars agree that the traditional ascription of the *Rāmāyaṇa* to a single author possesses some validity because of the uniformity of language, with its compact vocabulary and style. But there is no way to be certain that the legendary Vālmīki is that author.[17] If one examines references to Vālmīki external to the epic, it is possible to find only two allusions, one referring to an expert in vedic pronunciation and another to a mythological snake-eating bird.[18] Within the context of the epic, all the information about Vālmīki appears in the first and last books. He is described in these books as a great *muni* (ascetic), eloquent speaker, a saintly man, great-souled, and learned. This ascetic and wise author reinforces, traditional patriarchal attitudes in the text.

The first book, called the *Bālakāṇḍa*, frames the entire work by relating the birth of the hero Rāma, his early exploits, and marriage to the comely Sītā. This part of the narrative opens with a childless king named Daśaratha anxious about having an heir to inherit his kingdom. He performs a horse sacrifice and another sacrifice for sons; these sacrificial actions, along with pleas from other gods to destroy a demonic being persecuting them, prompt a response by Viṣṇu, who decides to become incarnate as the king's four sons in order to destroy Rāvaṇa, a demonic creature immune from death by any nonhuman source. Daśaratha's queens give birth to four sons: Rāma, Bharata, and the twin half-brothers Lakṣmaṇa and Śatrughna. Lakṣmaṇa becomes an unshakable shadow of Rāma and symbol of brotherly love and submissive obedience. At the age of fifteen, Rāma takes his younger brother Lakṣmaṇa on an initiatory journey, after an irascible sage Viśvāmitra demands the old king lend him his son to defend the sage's hermitage from demons. Besides defeating the demons Mārīca and Subāhu, who had been attacking the sacrifice of the sage Viśvāmitra, Rāma learns mythological lore, and is initiated into the secrets of divine weapons. Even before the defeat of these two demons, Rāma is reluctant to kill the demon Tāṭakā because she is female, but the hero nevertheless fulfils the promise that he had made to the sage Viśvāmitra. The sage takes Rāma and Lakṣmaṇa to King Janaka's sacrifice, where they learn of the miraculous birth of Sītā (literally furrow). King Janaka explains how he had been ploughing when he discovered her in a furrow, and how he reared her as his daughter. Thus Sītā had a nonhuman birth, in sharp contrast to that of Rāma. The heroes also learn from King Janaka about the existence of Śiva's bow, which no mortal can bend to string it. Rāma not only bends the bow but also breaks it. By proving his prowess, he is able to marry Sītā, Lakṣmaṇa marries her sister, while the other brothers marry her cousins.

In the second book of the epic, the aging king Daśaratha decides to appoint Rāma his heir apparent. But the old hunchback servant Mantharā convinces the king's wife Kaikeyī to supplant Rāma with her son Bharata by twisting the truth. The king is at a decisive disadvantage because he had given Kaikeyī a promise of two boons as a reward for curing him of battle wounds. Kaikeyī reminds the king of his promises and pressures him for their fulfillment. Kaikeyī's plot includes the banishment of Rāma to the forest for fourteen years. The dutiful Rāma submissively follows his father's command, and he even suggests recalling the absent Bhārata, who is totally unaware of his mother's political machinations. Without protesting the unjust nature of his exile, Rāma goes to the forest accompanied by his wife and faithful brother Lakṣmaṇa, who are both paradigms of loyalty and obedience. As the narrative unfolds, Sītā is revealed as the ideal virtuous wife (*pativratā*). On Mount Citrakūta, the trio construct a hermitage and live happily for a period of time. The king grieves for his departed son and dies soon after Rāma leaves Ayodhyā. Before the king dies he tells his wife Kausalyā, the mother of Rāma, that he is fulfilling a curse leveled against him by the blind parents of an ascetic that he accidentally killed. The king relates that he had been cursed to die when he became separated from his son.

Bhārata is recalled to Ayodhyā to assume the leadership of a kingless state, but he angrily rejects the offer and overturns his mother's devious plot. Accompanied by a huge retinue that includes three queens, Bhārata proceeds to retrieve Rāma, with the objective of placing him on the vacant throne. When the estranged brothers encounter each other, the calm demeanor of Rāma is sharply contrasted with that of the emotionally volatile Lakṣmaṇa. Rāma declines his brother's impassioned offer to return to the capital and assume the throne, and he insists on executing his father's command to live in exile for fourteen years. After returning to the capital, unable to convince Rāma to assume the role of king, Bhārata places the sandals of the hero on the throne as a symbol of his authority. Bhārata retires from the palace, but he functions as the administrative regent for his exiled brother. Then, Rāma and his companions move to an even more remote part of the Daṇḍaka forest.

This remote part of the forest is the home of hospitable sages and malevolent demons. Although he is resolved to live an ascetic lifestyle, Rāma's warrior traits become more evident because he is forced to rescue his wife from a demonic rākṣasa, and he pledges to protect the sages from demons. Rāma, his wife, and brother spend ten years among the sages, and the hero receives divine weapons from Agastya and the promise of protection from the vulture Jaṭāyus. After building a hermitage at Pañcavatī at the suggestion of Agastya, the brothers encounter a demoness named Śūrpanakhā, who makes amorous overtures to them only to be ridiculed by them. The infuriated demoness attacks Sītā, but she is mutilated by Lakṣmaṇa. After Rāma defeats the demoness's avenging brother and his horde, she concocts revenge with her brother Rāvaṇa, king of the island of Laṅkā, to abduct Sītā. The demoness Mārīca attempts to dissuade Rāvaṇa from his sinister plan. In fact, Mārīca accuses Rāvaṇa of departing from the path of righteousness (*dharma*), which becomes the demon's root problem, rather than his demonic nature. An unwilling Mārīca is disguised as a golden deer and falsely calls for assistance. In response, Sītā sends the two brothers to help. While the brothers are going to assist the distressed deer, Rāvaṇa appears at the hermitage as a holy mendicant and abducts Sītā. The vulture Jaṭāyus is mortally wounded as he attempts to stop the abduction. Rāvaṇa takes Sītā across the ocean to Laṅkā, where she rejects his lustful advances and his offer of marriage within a year or face death. Meanwhile, the brothers learn of the abduction from a dying Jaṭāyus, and Rāma despairs over his loss. The monster Kabandha gives them an element of hope by advising them about forging alliances with Sugrīva, a deposed king of the Vānaras, who are identified as monkeys, in order to rescue Sītā.

The fourth book of the epic finds the brothers in the capital of Sugrīva, and the monkey Hanumān takes them to meet the king. Rāma and Sugrīva form an alliance, and the former is shown evidence of clothes and ornaments discarded by his wife as she was being abducted. Rāma urges Sugrīva to challenge his usurping brother Vālin (who has also taken Sugrivās wife) to single combat. With the covert help of Rāma hiding behind a tree, Sugrīva is victorious, cremates his defeated brother, and assumes the kingship. Before his demise, Vālin reproaches Rāma for his deception and lack of dharmic behavior, even though his death by an instrument of the hero results in his salvation. Rāma counters Vālin by arguing that ordinary rules of chivalric combat are not applicable in his case for three reasons: the hero is an authoritative figure rightfully punishing an adulterer, the death of Vālin fulfils a promise that he made to Sugrīva, and he is a king rightfully hunting a simple beast, a monkey. With Vālin destroyed and Sugrīva secured on the throne, preparations are made to amass an army to rescue Sītā, and search parties are sent to find her. Having the most confidence of success in the search party led by Hanumān, Rāma gives the monkey a ring by which to identify himself as an emissary of the hero. Although three of the search parties return unsuccessfully, Hanumān's group encounter Sampāti, brother of the slain Jaṭāyus, who informs them of Sītā's location across the ocean.

After an account of the beauty of the island of Laṅkā, Hanumān's prodigious leap to the island is described by the text. After vainly searching for her in the palace of the demon, Hanumān finds her among a grove of trees, and he hears her reject Rāvaṇa's personal pressure and threats. Hanumān reveals himself to the incredulous Sītā. The monkey proves his identity by showing to Sītā her husband's ring, but she refuses to be rescued by Hanumān and insists that Rāma complete her rescue. Sītā gives Hanumān a jewel as a token for her heroic husband. Hanumān allows himself to be captured by Indrajit, a son of the demonic king. Vibhīṣaṇa, who is the virtuous brother of Rāvaṇa, dissuades the king from killing Hanumān because of diplomatic protocol with respect to foreign envoys. Instead the angry Rāvaṇa sets fire to the monkey's tail, which Hanumān uses to set fire to Laṅkā. Being reassured of Sītā's safety, Hanumān returns to the mainland to report his discovery to those waiting.

The sixth book of the epic recounts the battle between Rāma and Rāvaṇa. After Rāvaṇa rejects his conciliatory advice, Vibhīṣaṇa defects, is welcomed by Rāma's group, and is consecrated king of Laṅkā. A causeway is constructed to traverse the sea in order to invade the island. Meanwhile, Rāvaṇa attempts to emotionally break Sītā and get her to submit by showing her an illusion of Rāma's severed head, but she remains steadfast in her devotion to her husband. Initially, the battle goes favorably for Rāvaṇa and his army as Indrajit disables Rāma and Lakṣmaṇa, who are assisted by the half man-half eagle, the celestial bird Garuḍa. Many combatants perish as the conflict begins to swing against the demonic forces. Indrajit's use of magic and his resort to sacrifice to ensure victory prove fruitless, and Lakṣmaṇa finally kills him. The battle culminates in a duel between Rāvaṇa and Rāma, who receives divine assistance from Indra's chariot and charioteer in order to dispatch the demon. Rāma and his wife are reunited, but the hero treats her coldly by claiming that he engaged in battle for the sake of family honor and not for her benefit. As Sītā prepares to prove her virtue by self-immolation on a funeral pyre, divine beings reveal to Rāma his genuine status as an incarnation of Viṣṇu. The deity Agni restores Sītā unharmed to a delighted Rāma. The hero's deceased father appears to instruct his son to return to Ayodhyā and resume his rule. And the victors fly back to the capital using the aerial chariot of Rāvaṇa. Rāma's brother Bhārata, who had been acting as regent of the kingdom, is happy to restore the kingdom to the rightful sovereign and to participate in the installation ceremony.

The epic concludes with the seventh book called "Further Exploits." There is general agreement among some textual scholars that this book is a later addition to the epic, much as the initial book is a later addition.[19] This last book recalls the sage Agastya narrating the crimes of Rāvaṇa before his encounter with Rāma and the heroic exploits of Hanumān. The narrative then turns to the happy life and prosperous reign of Rāma and Sītā. Malicious gossip calling into question Sītā's virtue while a prisoner of Rāvaṇa disrupts their harmonious rule. Rāma is forced by public pressure to unjustly exile Sītā to Vālmīki's hermitage. While staying at the sage's hermitage, Śatrughna, a friend and constant companion of Bharata and youngest son of Daśaratha, learns of the birth of Rāma's twin sons, Kuśa and Lava. Eventually, Sītā is recalled to court from her exile. Rāma's decision to banish his wife appears to be ruthless and cruel, but his decision is based on his vision of the perfect monarch who is willing to sacrifice everything for righteousness (*dharma*). Sītā publicly reaffirms her purity. In order to prove her truthfulness, she calls upon Mother Earth to accept her, if what she swears is correct. The Earth opens to accept Sītā, and she descends into it. Rāma mourns the disappearance of his beloved, and he commemorates her loss with a golden statue. After an ideal reign of peace and prosperity, Rāma is visited by Time, which prefigures the end of his rule. His brother Lakṣmaṇa is the first to immolate himself, and Rāma and the final two brothers follow him. As Rāma's twin sons rule in his place, all the brothers are welcomed into heaven by the gods.

It is possible to identify numerous themes in the epic with sociopolitical and religious significance. There are the struggles of dharma against its opposite, along with the responsibility to fulfill one's duty. These themes are evident when the demon Vibhīṣana joins Rāma and the side of righteousness, and it is clear in the struggle to rescue Sītā. Moreover, the licentious and violent Rāvaṇa represents the precise opposite of the restraint, decorum, and righteousness of figures from the victorious group. When Bhārata places Rāma's sandals on the throne, this represents the beginning of righteous rule of the Rāmarājya. The strict adherence to dharma is emphasized throughout the epic. Queen Kaikeyī and her misshapen servant are examples of the manipulation and distortion of the truth, whereas Lakṣmaṇa is paradigm of loyalty and obedience.

The heroic conflict between Rāma and the demons (*rākṣasas*) is a cosmic and religious battle of good and evil. This gargantuan struggle suggests continuity with the earlier vedic cosmogonic conflict between Indra and Vṛtra, now represented respectively by Rāma and the demon Rāvaṇa. Of the two warrior gods, Indra becomes king of the gods, whereas Rāma becomes king of men. In the first book, the *Bālakāṇḍa*, Rāma delivers Ahalyā, wife of the cuckold ascetic Gautama, who had cursed her to become invisible after her sexual affair with Indra. When she encounters Rāma she becomes visible again, which symbolizes his power to save. Another religious theme is Rāma's forgiveness of karmic transgressions, which is prefigured by the joyful reunion of the four brothers. The salvific and forgiving power of Rāma is connected to his compassion to all beings. This is poignantly suggested by the help to the three exiles when they attempt to cross the Ganges River extended by Guha, a person of low caste embraced by Rāma. Another religious theme with environmental implications is the intimate relationship established between Rāma, humans, and nature. When the hero leaves the capital, nature mourns his departure, and the text refers to trees loving him (Rām 2.42.12). Throughout the epic, animals such as the vulture Jaṭāyus and the monkey Hanumān assist Rāma. Rāma is also hailed as a protector by, for instance, the sages of the Daṇḍaka forest (Rām 3.1.19). Finally, there is the theme of suffering at the death of his father and separation from his wife.

Development of Rāma Devotion

In books 2 to 6 of the *Rāmāyaṇa*, which constitute the earlier parts of the epic, Rāma's human nature is stressed, and he is portrayed with emotions such as joy, sorrow, and anxiety. The first and last books of the epic emphasize his status as a divine incarnation of Viṣṇu. Although Rāma is not a full divine incarnation throughout the epic, there are nevertheless passages that imply his full incarnational status (Rām 6.26.31–32; 6.105.12–28).

The influence of the *Rāmāyaṇa* spread to diverse geographical areas and different recensions of the epic developed within those locations. Among other versions of the epic are Buddhist and Jain texts. The *Daśaratha Jātaka*, a part of a larger body of narratives that relate stories about the former lives of the Buddha, is an excellent example of such a Buddhist text. In this text, the Buddha is born as Rāma, goes into exile at his father's request, and his sister Sītā and his brother Lakṣmaṇa accompany him. When the three exiles learn of the father's death, Sītā and Lakṣmaṇa grieve uncontrollably, but Rāma does not join them because he knows that all life is impermanent. Hence, Rāma acts and thinks like a Buddha. A detached Rāma uses the death of his father to teach his siblings about the transient nature of all things. There is no personified enemy in this Buddhist text. The achieved triumph is essentially spiritual, not military. The three exiles return to the kingdom of their deceased father, and Rāma rules justly.

From the medieval period, the influence of the Rāma tradition spread beyond India to places such as Laos, Cambodia, and Thailand. In such places the enactment of episodes of the Rāma tale functioned as a nonviolent substitute for animal sacrifice. The Rāma kingly paradigm captured the imagination, for instance, of the early Thai kingdom of Sukothai, as evident when the ruler adopted the name Rāmkemheng (Rāma the Strong). By the late thirteenth century, the Rāma narrative became well established in Thailand and played an important role in the culture and religion. The Thais adopted, for instance, the name Ayudhya (city of Rāma) for their capital, and several Thai kings assumed the name of Rāma.[20] The Buddha becoming Rāma in a previous lifetime provided the precedent necessary for adopting a foreign Hindu figure into Thai culture.

Two main adaptations of the Vālmīki *Rāmāyaṇa* were also made by the Jain authors Vimalalsūri and Guṇabhadra. In fact, the Jain religious tradition agreed that Rāma, his brother Lakṣmaṇa, and the demonic Rāvaṇa deserve a place among the sixty-three Jain *mahapuruṣas* (great beings); the Jains placed the heroic Rāma on a par with the other two figures.

We can trace the beginnings of Rāma devotion (*bhakti*) in India itself. At the temple of Deogadh, scenes depicting various episodes from the life of Rāma were depicted iconographically during the sixth century C.E. The first temple dedicated to Rāma dates to the Gupta dynastic era.[21] But the first real evidence of Rāma devotion is found among the Tamil Āḻvārs. Although clear references to Rāma are infrequent, the *Perumāl Tirumoḷi* text makes references to the great deeds of a son living in exile. There seems to be evidence that devotion to Rāma began in southern India, but there is no evidence of a specific community of devotees.[22]

Additional textual evidence for Rāma devotion can be found in three medieval Upaniṣads that bear his name in the title: *Rāmapūrvatāpanīya*, *Rāmottaratāpanīya*, and the *Rāmarahasyopaniṣad*. These texts contain references to worship, a specific Rāma mantra (sacred formula) and *yantra* (sacred diagram), and a Sītā mantra. Rāma is depicted metaphysically as the highest self (*puruṣa*) and Sītā is identified as the primordial matter (*mūlaprakṛti*). Another textual source is the *Yoga Vasiṣṭha*, which probably originated in the Kashmir region. Dating to between the ninth and twelfth centuries, the text recounts a philosophical dialogue between Rāma and Vasiṣṭha before the hero travels to Viśvāmitra to assist the sage. The text specifies the need for deliverance and the path to achieve it.

The first genuine evidence for a community of devotees occurs in northern India, which is the location for the origin of the *Adhyātma Rāmāyaṇa*, a sacred text for the Rāmāndin sect of holy men that can be dated to around the fifteenth century.[23] Similar to many tantric texts, the story is presented in dialogical format between Śiva and Pārvatī. Taking the purāṇic and tantric views of Rāma, the text attempts to synthesize them with its non-dual vedāntic viewpoint. This means that Rāma is not merely an incarnation of Viṣṇu but is also identified with the immanent and transcendent Brahman of the Vedānta thought. There are even references to his status as nirguṇa (without attributes) Brahman, which implies that he transcends Viṣṇu. Moreover, the hero is not one of many incarnations, but he is identified as Viṣṇu. In fact, Rāma is the source for numerous incarnations. These incarnations return to him when their tasks are completed.

And yet Sītā is the feminine energy (*śakti*) of Rāma from the tantric perspective of the work, as well as his māyā (creative illusory) power by which he creates the world. In the text, the divine Sītā informs Hanumān that Rāma is pure existence, and she is primeval matter (*prakṛti*), representing the material and instrumental cause of the universe. In short, Sītā is a creative force within this synthesis of Sāṃkhya and Advaita Vedānta philosophies. Sītā's divine status makes it improper for her to be abducted, from the perspective of the author. Therefore, Rāma instructs her to hide herself in a fire in an invisible form and to create an illusory version of herself to be abducted by the deceived demon. When she must endure the test of fire to prove her purity there is little hint that she is guilty because the true Sītā is never really abducted. More devotional themes are not, however, totally neglected in this work.

The rationale for Rāma's incarnation is to strengthen his devotion. The text stresses reading and hearing the stories of Rāma. Serving the deity and chanting his name are also emphasized. Observing his fasts and holy days, having faith in him, being devoted to his lotus feet, taking refuge with him, being protected by him, and seeking company of his devotees are mentioned in the text. These kinds of devotional activities recall typical actions among other forms of Vaiṣṇavism discussed in earlier chapters.

Movement of Rāmānanda

During the medieval period, Rāma devotion became widespread in northern India, with important centers in Janakpur, a legendary birthplace of Sītā, and Ayodhyā, a legendary birthplace and capital of Rāma's kingdom, located in the region of Uttar Pradesh. Near the Bihar border close to Nepal, Rāmānanda (c. 1360–c. 1470), who was born in Prayāg (Allahabad), founded a religious sect called either the Rāmāvat or Rāmānandī order. Unfortunately, no writings of the founder have been preserved, although some Sanskrit and Hindi works of doubtful authenticity are attributed to him. It is even possible that he never actually founded the sect, and its beginnings represent instead an imaginative action initiated by his followers.[24] According to tradition, however, Rāmānanda was a disciple of Rāghavānand, who was the fourth teacher in the line of Rāmānuja, but he broke from his teacher over criticism that he failed to observe rules of purity during a pilgrimage, which prompted him to establish his own sect. He stressed vernacular language over Sanskrit, opened his movement to all castes including Untouchables, admitted women to his order, and argued that all worshipers stand equally before God. He taught that a devotee must assume the role of a servant in relationship to God, regardless of caste or gender. The ideal servant is identified as Hanumān, who risked his life for his master. A devotee worships Rāma and his consort Sītā as the combined supreme deity, but a devotee does so without any erotic implications such as one might find associated with Krishna and Rādhā. Moreover, it is important to note that Rāmānanda identifies Rāma with the incarnation of the epic *Rāmāyaṇa*, a divine being with attributes.

Nonetheless, some male devotees don female clothing and jewelry as a way of emphasizing their indifference to common social gender distinctions. Some members add *dāsa* (slave) to their name to stress their status in relationship to God. More zealous members burn the name of Rāma into their skin. These practices are means of demonstrating one's devotion and sectarian allegiance.

In contrast to householders associated with the sect, the Rāmānandī order also allows for the practice of asceticism and renunciation. It is possible for members of all castes to be initiated into the order. In fact, new initiates reject previous caste affiliation. They are expected instead to render service to Rāma. A secondary initiation transforms a person into a renouncer, and he receives sacred ashes, obtained from a fire, which are smeared on his body twice daily. The ashes signify an ascetic's separation from the transient world.

The renouncers lead an itinerant lifestyle, although they do not wander aimlessly. They rather travel back and forth across India on an annual cycle to major Vaiṣṇava pilgrimage sites and attend festivals. The renouncers travel in groups that can be conceived of as itinerant monasteries (called *khālsā* or *jamāt*). Their wandering imitates the universal spirit. Nowadays they often travel by train, standing in the aisles at night for free because they expect the government to allow holy men to travel without financial obstruction, even though they take no vow of poverty.[25] The Rāmānandī ascetics represent one of the largest ascetic groups in India at the present time. From this religious movement, there evolved influential literary figures such as Tulsīdās and Kabīr.

The Contribution of the Poet Tulsīdās

According to traditional lore, Tulsīdās (1532–1623) was born into a family of Smārta Brahmins. While a young child, he was orphaned or abandoned because of an inauspicious conjunction of stars and allegedly raised by a holy man. He married a woman who seemed to resent his profound devotion to God rather than to her. According to the *Bhaktamāl* of Nabhadās, Tulsīdās was an incarnation of Vālmīki, born for the purpose of retelling the story of Rāma in the degenerate kali yuga and proclaiming the power of Rāmnām (name of Rām, the Hindi form of Rāma), which is intended to make salvation possible in this dark age. Although Tulsīdās was influenced by the Sant tradition of holy persons in northern India, he was also reacting to its neglect of Rāma, from his perspective. Among his compositions, he is credited with a poem on the marriage of Śiva and Pārvatī and an anthology of devotional songs to Krishna, who is actually a form of Rāma according to this text. He also wrote a work of poems to Rāma entitled *Kavitāvali*. His work the *Vinaya-patrikā* focuses on love of Rāma, but it also contains some autobiographical references to his earlier wretchedness. In one poem, he confesses to being God's slave, receives his sustenance from his deity, confesses to being bound by karma, refers to unspeakable anguish, attains liberation through the grace of God, and sings God's praises; he says that others consider him inferior, he feels obligated not to marry, does not care for caste or status, and confesses to being content with his faith in God.[26] Other poems refer more generally to the miseries of human existence, the cycle of birth and death, and the soul's estrangement from God, although devotion to Rāma can bring all this misery to an end. The dominant sentiment that must be adopted by devotees is that of slave (*dāsya*). And Hanumān is used as the ideal servant because he is active, bold, and manifests the love of a slave for his master. From another perspective, the relationship between God and the devotee is a very personal relationship in which Rāma is referred to as both father and mother of the devotee (79.3–4; 88.4). Although Tulsīdās's perspective is shaped by bhakti, he remains an independent philosophical thinker, and he combines the devotional system of Rāmānuja with the Advaita system of Śaṅkara.

His greatest work is the *Rāmcaritmānas* (The Sacred Lake of Rāma's Deeds), a Hindi-language version of the *Rāmāyaṇa*, which depicts Rāma as the supreme deity of the Indian divine pantheon with other deities in subordinate positions to him. Composition of this historically important text was begun around 1574 in Ayodhyā, which was the birthplace of Rāma and capital of his kingdom, and it was completed in the sacred city of Benares some years later. Within the context of this major work, Tulsīdās insists that the most authentic way to know god is through his finite, human actions (*līlā*).[27] During his lifetime, Tulsīdās was so revered by his contemporaries that many believed him to be an incarnation of Vālmīki, legendary author of the *Rāmāyaṇa*.

If a reader examines the *Rāmcaritmānas*, it is apparent that it is narrated by different figures who include the author, Śiva, and Bhuṣuṇḍi, who teaches the superiority of devotion over the path of knowledge and salvation by faith in Rāma. Throughout the text, Tulsīdās emphasizes the saguṇa (with attributes) aspect of God, which he considers to be superior to the nirguṇa (without attributes) form (Rām 6.110–121). This suggests less of an emphasis on Rāma as Brahman and more stress on his role as a personal deity. Even when Rāma is clearly identified as the highest reality, the text emphasizes the immanence of Brahman (Rām 1.7.3). This implies that Tulsīdās intends to stress the incarnational status of Rāma over his description of Brahman being an ocean of bliss (Rām 1.197.3). Sometimes Tulsīdās identifies Rāma with Viṣṇu, and at other points they are clearly distinguished in the text, with Rāma being superior to Viṣṇu. When Rāma's incarnation is stressed by the author, its rationale centers on the god's decision to help his devotees as a deity of mercy and love (Rām 1.121.3–4). This portrait could not be achieved by concentrating on the lack of attributes (*nirguṇa*) of the deity. Moreover, Tulsīdās's overall intention is to make a direct appeal to the emotions of his listeners and readers, and not to their intellects.

Within his text, Tulsīdās defines his version of a ninefold path of devotion, which includes keeping the company of holy men, by which he means like-minded people of devotion. The path also includes hearing the holy stories of Rāma, serving the lotus feet of a guru (teacher), singing the praises of one's deity, repetition of one's mantra with a faith-filled mind, and practicing self-control and good conduct. The constant repeating of Rāma's name is an essential practice because it represents the essence of the deity. Because the name can even be considered superior to Rāma himself, it is sometimes believed to be able to bring salvation itself for those that chant or listen to it. Embodied within its power, the name of the deity offers the promise of universal salvation. In addition, a devotee should view the world as being filled with Rāma. A poignant example of nature's love for Rāma is provided by the blind crow named Bhuṣuṇḍi who tells an eagle how fortunate he is to have received the gift of devotional grace as a mere crow. It is also important for a person to be content, not seek out the faults of others, and to be free of either enmity or envy. Finally, a devotee should abandon all duplicity in relation to others and cultivate faith in Rāma (Rām 3.35–36).

This review of the path of devotion does not do justice to the intense nature of devotion from the viewpoint of Tulsīdās. Rāma's brothers are depicted as overcome with devotional emotion. Lakṣmaṇa is described as overcome by love (Rām 2.71), whereas Bhārata utters the names of the divine couple in a condition of ecstatic love (Rām 2.203). There are also references to persons drunk with love (Rām 2.275.3) and others burning with love (Rām 2.244.2). For Tulsīdās, an authentic devotee is emotionally moved beyond oneself to the point of devotional fanaticism.

The importance of Tulsīdās for many residents of north India was matched in the nineteenth century by Tyāgarāja (1767–1847), a devotional poet and musician of south India of Telugu-speaking Brahmin parents. Tyāgarāja's compositions were famous for their melodious vowel sounds that gave his poems a naturally flowing and musical quality. During his lifetime, he was part of an artistic trio, along with two other contemporaries Muthuswami Dīkṣitar and Śyāmā Śastri. According to legend, his birth was predicted by Śiva to his parents in a dream. The parents were also informed that this son would be an incarnation of Nārada, a paradigmatic musician and devotee of Viṣṇu. The boy began composing devotional poems to his father's deity Rāma, and learned music from a court musician. After repeatedly reciting the name of Rāma countless times, Tyāgarāja had a vision of his deity, and later recitations led to further visions that he recounted in songs that eventually grew to a collection of over seven hundred. According to Tyāgarāja, music functioned as a means of spiritual liberation.[28]

Untouchables and Ramnami

Traditionally, Untouchables have been invisible in the context of books like this. Their greater visibility within Indian culture can be traced historically to Mahatma Gandhi, who championed their cause and called them harijans (children of God), and to the enactment of legal protections both under the British and since independence. Gandhi optimistically wanted to find Untouchables a place of respect within Hindu culture, whereas the more pessimistic B. R. Ambedkar, an Untouchable himself, led large numbers of his fellow citizens to mass conversions to Buddhism in the mid-1950s. After a certain percentage of some government positions were allocated to them in order to given them a chance for socioeconomic advancement, social tensions between the Untouchables and upper-caste Hindus have grown. These kinds of tensions have caused some Untouchables to keep a low social profile in order not to unnecessarily antagonize other groups.

Historically, a precise term for Untouchable appears in the dharma texts, which can be dated between the fourth and sixth centuries C.E. Within the *Viṣṇusmṛti*, for the first time, there is the term *aspṛśya* (literally, a person not to be touched), which designates both a temporary condition of pollution and a permanent state of untouchability associated with inferior caste status.[29] Before this, there is no evidence of the notion of untouchability in vedic literature. Even though a late hymn does refer to a social hierarchy (RV 10.90), it does not mention Untouchables as a generic group. Even some later texts dismiss the notion of untouchability as a fifth social category.[30] Nonetheless, the notion of untouchability is based on the religious distinction between purity and impurity, a vedic notion. This basic distinction is connected to notions of karma, decrepitude, decay, and ultimately death.[31]

Instead of the term Untouchable to refer to a group of people, the Indian constitution uses the term "Scheduled Caste," which is an adoption of former British usage. The designation "Scheduled Caste" does not have the pejorative connotations that have come to be associated with the terms Untouchable and harijan. Regarding someone as Untouchable has been illegal since prior to 1932, and the Indian Government ratified this prohibition in 1950. Article 17 of the Untouchability Offences Act XXII renewel this legal provision in 1955. Today, the preferred term chosen by Untouchables is Dalit (oppressed). The term *dalit* carries militant political implications because of its connection to protests in the 1970s. The term *dalit* also implies the explicit rejection of traditional Hindu culture. In fact, some Dalits have advanced the claim that they represent the historically original inhabitants of India that were subjugated by foreign invaders.

Over the course of its brief history, the Rāmnāmi Samāj has taken a more overt approach to social justice and religion. Parasuram, who was born in the mid-nineteenth century, founded this movement, which consists primarily of Untouchables. His parents were poor illiterate farmers, but he developed rudimentary reading skill as he grew older. During his adult years, he gained a measure of economic success, and he spent time reading and memorizing Tulsīdās's major work relating the story of Rāma. Parasuram contracted a disease (maybe leprosy) in his mid-thirties that caused other people to ostracize him. His isolation motivated him to consider the life of a renouncer. He encountered a Rāmānandī holy man by a lake, who told him that Parasuram's only disease was ignorance. The renouncer gave him instructions on Tulsīdās's text and told him that the script for the term *Rāmnām* would appear on his chest, if his faith were authentic. Just as the renouncer said it, the name appeared on his chest and his disease moreover disappeared. This miracle in combination with his teaching about the Rāmnām (name of Rām) enabled him to gather followers. Unlike many religious groups, Parasuram did not advocate adopting the socioreligious practices of the upper castes, which is a process called Sanskritizing in order to improve one's social status. In fact, Parasuram established very few rules for his followers. After a wealthy landlord hired some thugs to attack a group of Rāmnāmis for publicly practicing their religion, Parasuram filed a lawsuit against the landlord. After a lengthy court battle and delays, a judge ruled on October 12, 1912, that the group enjoyed freedom of religion and could not be prevented from worshiping. This favorable legal ruling and victory for the rights of Untouchables caused the movement to mushroom thereafter.

At the present time, the vast majority of Untouchables attempt to minimize any visible distinction between themselves and other members of Indian culture. Trying to gain acceptance, the bulk of Untouchables desire to blend into the social fabric. Instead of keeping a low profile or an even more desired social invisibility from the perspective of the upper castes, the members of the Untouchable Rāmnāmi movement call attention to themselves visually by their striking physical appearance. The major features of this distinctive appearance include tattoos, long capes and shawls, tall peacock feather hats, and sometimes a set of ankle bells.

As evident in his personal narrative, the founder Parasuram set the precedent for wearing the Rāmnām tattoo on his body. Within the context of Indian culture, body tattoos are connected to the power of sacred diagrams (*yantras*) and their widespread use among tribal groups for a combination of adornment, social status, and recognition purposes. The *ankit* (literally, mark, inscription) consists of the Hindi script letters for Rāmnām inscribed on the skin of a devotee's face, arms, torso, and legs. Some Rāmnāmis may decide to have these letters inscribed over their entire bodies. Normally, there is a cultural restriction of not tattooing below the waist because of a fear of possible contact with unclean substances. Shoes and feet are included in the ban. These types of restrictions are viewed by the Rāmnāmis as being counter to the omnipotent and transformative power of Rām's name. Thus Rāmnāmis think that no part of the human body should be prohibited from tattooing. For the Rāmnāmis, the tattoos have social and political significance with respect to their struggle against oppression by the higher castes. In addition to expressing their individuality and freedom, the tattoo serves as a visible expression of their collective service to their deity, a sign of devotion, a mark of sect membership and active participation.[32] By having the Rāmnām inscribed on their skin, Rāmnāmis are publicly giving witness to the fact that they belong to their God. In a profound sense, God signs his name on their bodies and sets them apart.

In addition to tattoos, sect members don the *ordhni* (literally, covering) ritual shawl that consists of thick white cotton cloth covered with the Rāmnām. This shawl is usually worn when chanting God's name. Similar to the tattoos, the shawl symbolizes members' devotion to God and membership in the group. When wearing the shawl members are literally wrapped in the name of God, and they are protected, purified, and empowered by it. Rāmnāmis report that the shawl is also indicative of their status as female lovers of Rām.[33] Although it is becoming more rare, some members wear ankle bells to maintain a rhythmic beat during chanting of God's name. While chanting, many members are expected to don the *mukut* (literally, crown), which is a peacock feather hat made by holy men of the sect. This practice imitates the founder, who used to wear a peacock feather.[34] The shawl and hat along with the facial and body tattoos render this Untouchable group culturally visible.

This social visibility is misleading from a theological perspective because they worship Rāma without attributes, a theological stance that includes a ban on image worship. Since their primary text is the *Rāmcaritmānas* of Tulsīdās and their devotional focus the name of God, devotees place a copy of the text in front of them when engaged in ritually chanting God's name. This practice suggests that Tulsīdās's book replaces the icon of the deity in the hearts of the devotees. Besides combining religious chanting with their holy book, many members also read other texts on devotion, such as the compositions of Kabīr.[35]

The major annual religious observance for the Rāmnāmis is their Bhajan Mela, a three-day festival that for many of them marks the beginning of the New Year. An unusual feature of this festival is that it moves to a new location every year. Villages bid for the right to hold the festival. The selection committee considers several factors when making their decision where to hold the festival. The length of time a village has been persistently requesting to host the festival is a major consideration. The location of a village along the Mahanadi River is another consideration because it must be accessible to other villagers. The selection committee examines the material capacity of a petitioning village in terms of being able to provide a large open area to accommodate the festival and the capacity to build a permanent Rāmnām *stambha* (post or pole) with Rāmnām written on it, topped with a brass ornament shaped like a stack of water pots. This permanent structure is not constructed to house any images. Another necessary criterion is unanimous approval given by the ruling body of the village (*pañcāyat*) for holding the festival within a village, including at least five initiated Rāmnāmis, who are responsible for leading the processional waving of oil lamps through the streets that commences the festival. Once a village makes a petition to hold the festival, members of the selection committee observe village members to discern their level of religiosity.[36] Villagers are motivated to hold a festival by their faith, to share festival experience with a wider group, to enhance their social status, for convenience, and for economic reasons. During the festival, villagers chant the name of Rām under canopies, and some of them remain awake the entire evening chanting. The combination of religious excitement, fatigue, and blurring of physical and mental experience gives rise to hallucinations, visions, sickness, and mentally passing out among some chanters.[37] These experiences are desirable and considered positive because they authenticate a person's religious convictions.

The Līlā (Play) of Rāma

Tulsīdās's reworking of the *Rāmāyaṇa* is not the only example of such works. The eleventh-century poet Kampan̄ composed a Tamil version of the epic entitled the *Irāmāvatāraṃ*, whereas the Telugu poet Buddharāja composed a version of the epic in the thirteenth century. In the fourteenth century, a poet name Kṛttibāsa created a Bengali version of the epic. It is probably preferable to consider each text a unique telling of the story of Rāma instead of a variant of the narrative. Since there are different versions of the epic in various regional languages and even different recensions of the Sanskrit *Rāmāyaṇa* of Vālmīki, there is no precise original text. This implies that each version of the epic narrative is unique.[38] These other versions of the epic do not always relate the full story, because shorter, episodic poems were composed that emphasize a single episode or a few connected tales. Many of these versions were semi-oral, suggesting that they were performed by being sung or recited to a group.[39]

It is also important to be aware that each telling of Rāma's story carries political messages and/or implications, even if they are not spelled out. It is possible to isolate three reasons for the story's political message: (1) the ideal of the Rāmrājya is a place of perfect justice, order, and prosperity; (2) Rāma's behavior embodies the ideal ruler and citizen; (3) the overall vision of Rāmrājya is utopian.[40] In the *Rāmāyaṇa*, the Rāmarājya represents the ideal kingdom on earth (1.1.71–73). This earthly paradise is a happy place without illness, famine, fear, or death. Within the boundaries of this paradise, religion is practiced and prosperity reigns (Rām 6.116.82–90). Certainly, conservative political forces have attempted to use this ideal of the triumph of dharma on earth to their political advantage in recent Indian history, as evident in 1992 with the destruction by an enraged mob of the Muslim Babri Masjid, which had been allegedly built over a Hindu temple honoring the birthplace of Rāma.

In a different mode, and in a pattern similar to Krishna devotion, Tulsīdās's *Rāmcaritmānas* is reenacted by young Brahmin boys annually today throughout north India. A performance of a Rāmlīlā can last from one to thirty-one days during the period of September–October. The people who attend these dramatic performances are not mere observers because they participate in the event along with the young actors. Attendees sing kīrtan (hymns chanting god's names), make offerings, receive grace (*prasāda*) from the god, and travel with the drama as it moves to different locations. People travel barefoot in order to imitate Rāma's practice during his period of exile, and to follow a common practice within the precincts of a temple, because the location of the drama is considered holy ground by means of God's presence.[41] Any demarcation between the drama and the world tends to become blurred for the participants.

A major theme of the Rāmlīlā is pilgrimage. In fact, this theme is built into Tulsīdās's text in part because of the travels of the author, after which he began to compose the text and the story of Rāma's journey. Tulsīdās suggestively compares his poem to a *mānas*, which in this context can refer to either a famous place of pilgrimage called Lake Manasarovar, to a more metaphorical "lake of the mind," or to the title of his own text. The sequence of the initial three books of Tulsīdās's composition corresponds to the journey or stages of life for an Indian student, householder, and forest dweller.[42] This theme of pilgrimage is also consistent with the outdoor nature of the performance because of a lack of a permanent, physical theater and its peripatetic method of staging.

The audience includes lay Hindus (*nemīs*), holy persons (*sādhus*), and the most devoted attendees (*nemī-premīs*). The most ardent group combines a sense of duty to attend with love of God. Audience members are free to engage in a ritual and meditative practice (*rasik*). The person who engages in such practices is referred to as a person who savors *ras* (sentiment). The practitioner does daily rituals and guided meditations in order to recreate the acts of God and enjoy the emotions evoked by the imagined practice.[43] This provides a devotee a foretaste of their religious goal of an intimate realization of God.

In addition to distinctions among devotees, there are also features between types of plays: continuous or eternal (*nitya*) and occasional (*naimittik*). The former type of play recalls God's cosmic actions; it also refers to the daily ritual pattern of eight time periods. The latter type designates specific exploits of divine incarnations.[44] From the perspective of the participants, the plays can be either earthly or spiritual. The earthly play recalls Rāma majestically acting as a model of dharma, whereas the latter possesses an erotic quality in which god expresses himself as a lover and the ultimate reality. The spiritual type of play invites an audience to contemplation.[45] Again, a practitioner enters into the spiritual type of play by passing through several initiations and meditations toward the creation of a divine body and mental service of the divine pair. And by means of a process of visualizations, the devotee can see glimpses of an authentic līlā (play) until one reaches the ability to enter into it instantly.

Besides the emotional and subjective experiential religious benefits of participating in a Rāmlīlā, a practitioner enjoys a perceptual advantage because he or she is able to receive a vision of God on a daily basis. This vision can become a source of personal power. For the local community at which the Rāmlīlā occurs, there are economic benefits. Various types of craftsmen are needed to build stages, effigies, costumes, masks, and theatrical props. Hotel and food service businesses also benefit from the performances for the services that they provide attendees. Overall, it is an economic impact on a location that can be expected on an annual basis.

The Sant Tradition and Kabīr

From approximately the thirteenth to the seventeenth centuries, there developed in northern India a religious movement that was later designated as the Sant tradition. There is no precise translated for the term Sant, although it has been translated as "good man" or "poet saint." A primary characteristic of a Sant is *ekarasa*, which is a state of being in which a person is totally immersed in devotion.[46] Nonetheless, a Sant does not renounce the world, does not usually practice yoga, possesses no secret mantras, and does not claim to have magical powers. It is impossible to identify a Sant by his or her clothing. Many Sants are detached from society, manifest strange behavior, and are contemptuous of wealth and material things. They often insist on chastity and live a life of nonviolence, which is a lifestyle not unlike other Indian holy persons. A Sant is difficult to identify because he or she is typically a layperson. The Sant ideal of holiness is thus a lay ideal that is both nonsectarian and casteless, although some Sants were founders of sects that were named after them. The true identity of a particular Sant is often not recognized because the person is a social misfit, and he or she is not recognized for saintliness until God vindicates that status.[47] Other problems associated with recognizing particular Sants may be their humble social origins, poor financial status, lack of education and even illiteracy, female gender, or use of local languages. Some Sants were even Muslims. It is important to observe for the sake of accuracy that not all Sants were gifted poets or even literary figures at all. Some Sants were merely models of humble piety, while others were more vociferous with their audacious criticism of social and religious hypocrisy.

Because the Sants were generally nonsectarian, they did not adhere to a common body of doctrine. They did share some common religious attitudes and convictions that were shaped by traditions of tantric yoga and ecstatic devotional religion. They believed that everyone could attain salvation by devotion to God. A devotee did not, however, need a sacred scripture to be saved because no scripture, including the sacred Vedas, is absolutely necessary for salvation. The Sants' failure to accept the authority of the ancient Vedas made them appear heretical from an orthodox viewpoint, as did their anti-Brahmin themes in poems, rejection of traditional sacrifices, dismissal of idol worship, denial of notions associated with pollution, and dismissal of the value of pilgrimage. Instead of these traditional forms of religiosity, the Sants stressed repeating the name of God, devotion to a guru, and keeping the company of Sants. The constant repetition of God's name assists the devotee to remember God and to become absorbed in the name of the divine. The repetition can be executed either vocally or by a silent, mental concentration on the holy name. With respect to guru devotion, the guru does not have to take a human form, because this figure can be an interiorized version on which one mentally concentrates. The guru should be comprehended as a channel of grace for ordinary devotees by being a direct link to God. If God is invisible, it is the visible and embodied guru that can lead a disciple to the formless deity. Finding and retaining the company of Sants implies attending devotional meetings (*satsang*) with other devotees to chant God's name and hear devotional poems.

There were historically two main Sant groups that are distinguished by the type of deity worshiped, language, and regional location. The southern group of Sants wrote poems in an archaic Marathi in the region of Maharashtra, and they stressed the saguṇa (with attributes) form of Viṣṇu or Krishna, whereas the northern group of Sants from the areas of the Punjab, Rajasthan, and the Gangetic valley composed poems in archaic Hindi and Punjabi and focused on the nirguṇa (without attributes or formless) aspect of God. The nirguṇa and saguṇa distinction should be used with caution, because some early poems of a figure such as Sūrdās do not stress the dichotomy; hagiographical literature composed by writers with specific sectarian associations do not use it, and early anthologies of Sant and devotional utterances also do not use it.[48]

The southern group of medieval poet-mystics consists of the so-called Varkari sect from Maharashtra and includes figures such as Gyandev (1275–1296), Nāmdev (1270–1350), Eknāth (1548–1600), and Tukarām (1598–1649). Some of these figures were discussed in chapter 8. The other group includes figures from Hindi-speaking north India, and it comprises such individuals as Kabīr, Nānak (1469–1539), Dādū Dayāl (1544–1603), and others. God is for them without shape and represents a transcendent and ineffable absolute reality, and the nirguṇa tradition has important theological implications. It rejects the notion of polytheism, dismisses the doctrine of avatāras (divine incarnations), and stresses instead the prevalence of monotheism. Even though the ultimate reality can only be expressed in negative terms within this qualityless tradition of nirguṇa, the poets emphasize experiencing the divine within one's heart and seeking a union with God. From a social perspective, because the Sant membership included women, low-caste figures, and appealed to people from the bottom of the social hierarchy, it represented a reversal of traditional religious expectations, and it served as a threat to the ideological structure of the Indian society.[49]

The yearning for God and seeking for a unitive experience of God are expressed in originally oral poems that often take the form of short utterances. The northern poets composed didactic poems (*dohās*), which are called literally "witness" (*sākhī*). A form of short rhymed poems (*pads*) including a refrain was also composed; these were often accompanied by music. The pad was intended for singing according to a musical mode. A chorus repeated the refrain between each verse. The communal singing of poems often became very emotional for the participants. Ordinary people were moved to emotional states by Sants such as Kabīr, Nānak, Mīrabāī, Raidās, Dādū, and others. The most famous, popular, and revered Sant has probably been Kabīr.

Born into a weaver family of former Muslims, Kabīr (1398–1448) refused to recognize caste distinctions and the authority of the traditional six Indian schools of philosophy, according to a hagiographical narrative of his life in the *Bhaktamālā* of the Vaiṣṇava poet Nābhāji, who lived around 1600. There is also a legend that Kabīr became a disciple of Rāmānanda by tricking the holy man into accepting a Muslim. According to the legend, Kabīr stretched himself across the stairs of a bathing ghat in the predawn darkness to cause Rāmānanda to trip over his body. Fearfully, Rāmānanda recited his mantra "Rām! Rām!" Kabīr claimed that this accidental mantra utterance functioned as a transmission and acceptance of him as a disciple.[50] The historical accuracy of this account is untrustworthy, according to some scholars, because Kabīr never received initiation by Rāmānanda and was not known to be an ascetic.[51] We do know that Kabīr composed and recited his verses orally with disciples, and listeners collected the verses. In one of his compositions, Kabīr autobiographically confesses the following:

I don't touch ink or paper,
This hand never grasped a pen.

The greatness of four ages
Kabir tells with his mouth alone.[52]

It is precisely this type of confession that makes Kabīr's poems personal.

Many legends are associated with Kabīr's life, and numerous miracles are attributed to him. According to the *Kabīr Parachai* by Anantadās, Kabīr diligently weaves cloth to sell in order to support his family, but God tests him one day by demanding more and more cloth until the weaver's supply is exhausted. Since Kabīr cannot afford to provide food for his family, he goes into hiding while they go hungry. God appears at his home with a cart full of food. After God disappears, Kabīr returns home to find the food, and he intuitively realizes the truth.[53] In another episode, Kabīr becomes overwhelmed with the demands of followers and others, and he decides to publicly associate with a prostitute, which offends people. But he does get a respite from their constant demands. Kabīr redeems himself by performing a miracle by pouring water on his feet, which actually cures a priest in a distant temple.[54] Another legend depicts Kabīr resurrecting two individuals and demonstrating his spiritual power. At the end of his life, Kabīr's Hindu and Muslim followers disagree about how his body should be disposed of. The two groups do, however, agree to send for thirty-two loads of flowers to cover his body. While devotees are singing and dancing, Kabīr attains immortality while still embodied. When his two groups of followers look for his body only the flowers remain.[55]

Among the common themes in his poems, Kabīr found it difficult to have religion without devotion. In addition, he was opposed to asceticism and practices associated with it, such as fasting and almsgiving. He was also critical of the caste system and various Hindu and Muslim religious practices and teachings. The iconoclastic poet questions image worship in a poem: "Why do you worship stones, which have never answered you?"[56] Kabīr thinks that the soul is trapped within a world subject to a combination of time, death, and illusion. It is of the utmost importance for the soul to return to God. He poetically urges others to "plunge into Rām! There: No Hindu. No Turk."[57] In other words, within God everyone becomes one. This can be achieved by devotedly repeating the name of God that enables one to perceive the light of God, by the grace of the guru. Kabīr makes his position absolutely clear when he writes, "The Name of Rām is the essence of Reality."[58] While humans are on earth they should be exposed to the truth and honesty. He imagines, for instance, death standing above one's head, which forces one to urgently face life and become honest. The message of death is that we do not have forever to correct our lives and overcome our situation.

It is necessary to call attention to the uniqueness of Kabīr's poetry. In some of his poems, he employs an upside-down language that is often absurd, crazy, paradoxical, and difficult to penetrate. How is it possible to make sense of a buffalo smoking a pipe, leeches coughing, a jolly woman consuming a neighbor for breakfast, a cow drinking milk from a calf, a son born from a sterile womb, a snake guarding a frog, a fish hunting in a forest, or a lion swimming in the sea? These poetic images are ludicrous, ironical, paradoxical, incongruous, and humorous. When attempting to discern their meaning it is possible to feel foolish. If this upside-down language is difficult, problematic, and confusing, one can take refuge with the name of Rām and concentrate on it until one is aware of nothing besides that sacred name. In a sense, Kabīr reverses time by using his upside-down language to overturn the common idea of time.[59] For Kabīr, Rāma is not the anthropomorphic deity of the *Rāmāyaṇa* epic, but he is rather without qualities, invisible, and the all-pervading Brahman that ultimately transcends all distinctions.

The originally oral poems of Kabīr eventually gave birth to a collection of his poetry called the *Bijak*, which literally means seed. It is the tiny seed in which the entire tree is originally contained. The term *bijak* is also connected to finance and business, where it suggests an invoice, a list of goods, or a list of valuables. Moreover, the term is associated with a guide to hidden treasure, the identity of the treasure, and its owner.[60] The *Bijak* became the scripture of the Kabīr Panth.

The term *panth* means the lineage of the solitary Sant. Three phases of its development can be identified. The initial phase centers on the lone, independent figure who is distinguished from ordinary people by his or her piety, poetry, or odd behavior. The solitary guru is recognized by others who become disciples within the development of the second phase of a specific Sant tradition (*paramparā*). The disciples become like the Sants. The disciples also sing about the grace of Sants and their power to transform lives. Finally, the third phase of a Sant lineage is designated by the term *panth*. By this point, the tradition formed by disciples has become a sectarian institution, implying that a panth disseminates the teachings and spiritual power of a past Sant.[61]

In light of Kabīr's fierce opposition to the notion of an avatāra (incarnation) it is somewhat ironical to find members of the Kabīr Panth transforming him into an incarnation from the mid-seventeenth century on. Members imagine Kabīr to be endowed with *sattva guṇa* (pure quality), divine form, and attributes. Kabīr's incarnation is identified as Satyapuruṣa (true self), which is a reference to the descending of the ultimate reality. In comparison to this incarnation, other manifestations are inferior.[62]

Kabīr's influence extends beyond his own panth. His songs and verses can also be found in the anthologies of the Dādūpanth entitled the *Kabīr Granthāvali* and in the *Ādi Granth* or *Guru Granth Sāhib* of the Sikhs. The Sikhs developed their own separate identity distinct from Hinduism, whereas Dādū Dayāl was another poet-saint of north India who composed intensely personal poetry in Hindi about the God beyond qualities in a way similar to Kabīr. He is discussed briefly in chapter 8.

The Kabīr Panth uses Kabīr's social and religious teachings about dissent to rally marginal social groups such as low-caste Śūdras, Untouchables, and tribals for the purpose of social and political protest. Kabīr's teachings have been used as a precedent to reject aspects of caste ideology and to promote assimilation of such groups within society.[63] In overtly courting low-caste Indians, the Kabīr Panth offered them a devotional form of Hinduism with the social restrictions of traditional Brahman religion. Sometimes, they developed groups with their own identity. An excellent example of such a movement is the Satnāmīs, whose name derives from Kabīr's reference to God as *sat nām* or *satya nām* (true name). An Untouchable named Ghasidās (1756–1850) founded the movement in the 1820s. He is credited with yogic power and divine insight from an early age. Besides advocating worship of one true God by means of chanting his name and abolishing image worship, he preached that everyone was created equal regardless of current social status. Ghasidās also instituted a process of Sanskritizing, which involves copying the social and religious practices of higher castes, by instructing followers not to consume meat, alcohol, or foods that resembled flesh in color; to use brass utensils suitable for reuse in cooking and eating, refrain from smoking or chewing tobacco, and cease working with leather and carcasses of animals; he also forbad use of cows for cultivating land. He instructed members to wear a necklace of tulsī beads and holy persons to wear all white, a color that signifies truth because it is untainted by the things within the world.[64]

In 1928, the movement convinced the national government to pass a law making it illegal to label anyone that works with leather as Chamar, which had been a traditional designation for such persons. Instead the name of the caste was changed to Satnāmi. The movement became heavily involved in local, state, and national politics. External events and the new impetus of the group tended to transform it into a sociopolitical movement rather than an originally religious organization.[65]

Within the region of the Punjab in the twentieth century, an organization called Adi Dharm worked to publicize the oppressive conditions of Untouchables. This group used the traditional popular veneration of Ravidās (or Raidās, c. 1450–1520) to connect with the lower-class masses. A loose connection of shrines and pilgrimage centers function to keep alive the memory of this Sant and former Untouchable shoemaker. At some centers considered sacred to Untouchables, Ravidās assumes the status of a deity.[66] During his lifetime, Ravidās criticized the caste system and asserted that there was nothing fundamental about it. He claimed that the absence of love in a person's life makes one an Untouchable, and not an accident of birth. In fact, in relation to God everyone is an Untouchable because of God's very nature.

Numerous legends grew to illustrate Ravidās's superiority over Brahmins. In order to settle a dispute, for instance, the king of Benares gathered Brahmins and Ravidās to the palace, where the king announced that he would favor the party that could demonstrate to which side God was inclined. Standing before an image of God, Brahmins chanted vedic sacred hymns, but these verses appeared to have no effect. In turn, Ravidās began to sing some of his poems, and he asked God to reveal himself as the one whose nature is to rescue the fallen. In response, the divine image jumped directly into the poet's lap. In another legend, Brahmins challenged Ravidās's right to preach publicly. The two sides agreed to allow the river goddess—the Ganges—to decide the case by throwing something into the river. The Brahmins tossed a piece of wood into the river, but it sank like a stone, whereas Ravidās threw a stone into the river, and it miraculously floated on the surface. In his oral poems, Ravidās stressed the irrelevance of caste for someone seeking salvation. Other recurring themes of his poetry are humility and confession. Such themes are indicative of the ecumenical and socially subversive aspects Ravidās's life and work.

The Radhasoami Faith

The Radhasoami sect of north India is a tradition that is historically connected to the Sant leaders Kabīr and Nānak.[67] There are two major branches of the tradition: Agra and Punjab. The Agra branch is divided into two primary subbranches: Soami Bagh (Garden of the Master) and Dayal Bagh (Garden of the Merciful). These headquarters of these two subbranches are directly across the street from each other. Shiv Dayal Singh, who later became known as Soamiji Maharaj, founded the movement. Formerly a follower of the Sikh leader Nānak, he was born in August 1818 in Agra to a father who earned his living as a moneylender. After his father's death, he dissolved the family's moneylending business, and he never sought employment again during his life. Although he married at a young age, he and his wife never had any children. The different divisions of the sect disagree about whether Soamiji was a founder or heir to a long line of Sants. According to the Agra view, he was spiritually autonomous, because he neither had nor needed a master.

According to the genealogy of the Agra group, Rai Saligram, known by the name Huzur Maharaj to the tradition, succeeded Soamiji. This college-educated man was born in 1829, worked for the postal department, and met Soamiji in 1858. After he joined the group, Soamiji revealed the highest truth to him, that the Supreme Being was Radhasoami. This decisive revelation shaped the faith of the group and distinguished it from other religious groups. Huzur also recognized Soamiji as an incarnation of the Supreme Being. In addition to writing four volumes of poetry, Huzur functioned as the great consolidator of the faith.

In 1885, Huzur met Brahma Shankar Mishra, who became known as Maharaj Saheb and was the second successor of Soamiji. Born in 1861 to a Brahmin family in Benares whose father was a professor of Sanskrit, Maharaj Saheb earned a master's degree in English literature and taught at Bareilly College. He would later write in English a work entitled *Discourse on Radhasoami Faith*, and he began construction of the great *samādhi* (resting place of the physical remains of the founder) at Soami Bagh in 1904. Maharaj Saheb is important historically in part because he banned the ochre robe of sadhus (holy people), attempted to regulate their movements, and encouraged them to gain employment. He was motivated by his desire to retain the original impetus of the movement as a householder's path. He also established the Central Administrative Council in 1902 in order to curtail schismatic factions within the movement and protect the movement's property. After his death in 1907, another crisis challenged the movement when a small group collected around Buaji Saheba, an older sister of Maharaj Saheb, because they conceived of her as the rightful successor to her brother. Because she spent her entire life in seclusion, she could not deliver speeches or act publicly for the movement. Her group never flourished because of a lack of direct contact; she died in 1913.

From the perspective of the Radhasoami faithful, previous Sants were merely forerunners of Soamiji, who represent an appearance of the Supreme Being in history. This momentous event altered the possibility of redemption for everyone in the world by offering genuine salvation for the first time in history. This notion of salvation history also embodies a messianic perspective because it is believed that Soamiji will be reborn into a royal family and that his son will be an incarnation of his earlier historical successor Huzur Maharaj, who will complete his father's work. Until this messianic moment occurs, human beings should attach themselves to a living *satguru* (true master) for guidance about the path to salvation.

In order to understand the path to salvation, it is necessary to grasp the cosmology and how the self fits into this view of the world. Without going into great detail, the world was created by the Supreme Being by means of his delight (*mauj*, a term that also contains the notions of pleasure, whim, or wave). The creative act assumes the form of a current of sound energy that is like a fluid substance that flows downward. As it descends, there occurs a process of discrimination and increasing differentiation in a downward flow of coarser elements. Finally, the cosmos assumes the form of many stratified layers, with the human soul imprisoned in the third region, and it is human desire that keeps the self imprisoned within this region. Desire is imagined to be like a surging wave that flows from the human body and engages in the desired act or object. Desire operates by pulling the self downward into the body and motivating it to flow into the external world. It is essential to reverse these downward and outward flows and to get the self to withdraw from the world and ascend to its original transcendent home.

The world is thus an alien place in which the self is hidden within a cover of body and mind, in which the self forgets its true nature and former lives. An important enemy of the self is time, assisted by delusion, which spreads a web of attachments for the entanglement of the self. When time is not entangling the self it is devouring it by death. In order to extricate the self from the world and time, it is imperative for the self to enter into a guru-disciple relationship.

Within the context of a relationship with one's guru, it is possible to nurture a path that will lead to a direct experience of reality. This profound experience is cultivated by special spiritual and secret practices that are taught only upon initiation into the group. The basic elements of the spiritual discipline involve repetition of God's name, and contemplation on his form as the Sant satguru. The fulfillment of the technique is reached by bhajan, a mental repetition of the name of *rādhāsvāmi nām* (name of Rādhāsvāmi or highest reality), which represents an oral-auditory realization of the underlying and unifying principle of the cosmos and a redeeming power that draws the self upward. These methods can be practiced within the context of external or internal satsangs (religious gatherings). The former type involves being in the company of the Sant satguru or congregational observances. Devotees make offerings to the guru, touch his feet with their hands or foreheads, and the guru often blesses the devotees by placing his hands on their heads. Such practices are intended to cultivate guru devotion and destroy the devotee's egoism, especially if the devotee consumes the body fluids of the guru. External satsang prepares the self for internal realization by keeping inward company of the current of sound energy emanating from the Supreme Being, which is the authentic form of the guru.

Concluding Remarks

The two epics discussed in this chapter manifest continuity with the vedic Indra-Vṛtra myth. The forces of goodness, righteousness, or dharma are victorious over the forces of evil, wickedness, and adharma in both epics. The victory is not ultimately definitive because the forces of evil are never completely vanquished. It is true that the hero restores righteousness, but the danger that unrighteousness could again gain supremacy always lurks in the shadows of time. Within the context of a threat to return to unrighteousness, a righteous ruler is absolutely essential to protect the people and to dispense justice for those that might try to disrupt social harmony.

There is something special about the story of Rāma that appeals to a broad audience throughout South Asia and that transcends the national borders of India. It does not seem to matter whether one stresses the human aspect of the hero or his divine status. In fact, the story of Rāma became a missionary agent for Indian culture throughout the region. Part of the reason of this broad appeal seems to reside with fact that the narrative connects with the emotions of listeners and not their intellects. It is also popular within cultures in which kingship played an essential role in the societies. Moreover, listening to the tale of Rāma is not conceived as a passive process. Listeners can get engaged in the story and participate in it. Thus, there is a strong experiential aspect that people of South Asia have found attractive about this type of devotional religion.

There is also something essentially disruptive about bhakti (devotional) religion. The devotional emphasis of the Sants calls into question the traditional social hierarchy and its domination by the priestly caste. Not only does Rāma have the power to save human beings but he also embraces people among the lowest rungs of the social ladder. This willingness and promise to save everyone has revolutionary political and social implications. If devotional religion is open to everyone regardless of caste status, this type of religion undermines and threatens the social hierarchy. Upper-caste leaders have been aware of this possibility, and they have attempted to harness the potential threat by assuming leadership roles in devotional religion where it is possible. The political and social implications are apparent with the Kabīr Panth and the poetical message that inspires it. The Kabīr Panth, Rāmānandīa movement, Rāmnāmis; Satnāmis, and Ravidās Panth are examples of religious movements that have become rallying points for the disaffected, oppressed, and disenfranchised.

From another perspective, it is somewhat ironical that a kingly figure such as Rāma would become the chosen deity of some Untouchables, a group of people far removed from the upper strata of society. This phenomenon can be partly explained by examples of Rāma coming to the aid of oppressed people. Another factor is the influence exerted by figures such as Kabīr and Ravidās, who originated from the lowest rung of the social hierarchy and still composed poems praising God. Such gifted and revered poets established a model of devotion to be imitated by others.

An awareness of the wide variety of devotional Hinduism is evident in this chapter. The Sants manifest disagreements, for instance, with traditional devotional religion. From the perspective of the qualityless (*nirguṇa*) type, the Sant's love is offered directly to a supreme deity and not to an incarnation. The monotheism of the Sants rejects conceiving of God in anthropomorphic terms. God is manifested through his immanence in his creation and his indwelling within the human soul. It is within the human soul that God reveals himself by means of his grace. The proper human response to this gift of grace is love that is expressed through meditation on the divine name.

The devotional religion discussed in this chapter places a great importance on the guru, who can take the form of a human teacher and/or an inner voice of God. The prevalence of guru adoration in north India connects this form of devotionalism to vedic religion and its emphasis on the teacher-student relationship. It is the guru that makes this type of religion intimate and personal, even if the deity is impersonal and abstract.

10

Dance of the Ascetic Deity Śiva

As a visitor to the Chidambaram temple in a town of the same name in southern India moves through the *gopuram* (tower-like structure at the four compass points to the entrances of the inner precincts of the temple), one notices on the inner walls carved images of dancers that stretch from the ground level of the gopuram to the top of the structure. As one stands gazing at these carvings of dancers and compares them, one notices that the dancers are each depicted in a different dance pose. Each of these poses represents a dance posture from classical Indian dance that can be identified in a handbook of classical dance, the *Nāṭya Śāstra* of the alleged author Bhārata. This classic work on the arts (compiled between c. 500 B.C.E. – 200 C.E.) describes in chapter 8 thirteen poses of the head, thirty-six kinds of glances, nine different movements of the eyes, nine different actions of the eyelids, seven types of nose movements, and various kinds of cheek, lower lip, chin, and mouth postures. In chapter nine, the work describes the numerous hand gestures with one hand and two hands. In addition, the text describes various arm, feet, and combined gestures. Besides various poses of the body and its parts, the author discusses vocal expressions, costumes, ornamentation, mental states and their expressions, and movement. Bhārata explains, for instance, that in order to express jealousy and envy one slightly bends at the waist and makes a hand gesture in which the forefinger is bent like a bow, thumb is bent, and other fingers are stretched upward. The dancer places her hands on the thigh and then on the back of the thigh. Then, another hand gesture is performed, after which the dancer lowers her hands down to her thighs with outward-turned palms and wrists slightly bent. Each of these movements has a specific name. The important thing to stress for a novice of the subject is that the dancer uses her entire body to convey meaning. Moreover, dance permeates all facets of Indian life, although its major function is to render abstract and subtle religious notions into symbolic expression and to make them more accessible to ordinary people.[1]

As a visitor moves through the gopuram, one eventually encounters the hall of a thousand pillars, on which dancers are also carved and depicted in various dance positions. It is possible to witness dancing *gaṇas*, who are pot-bellied, neckless, short, round, and deformed figures with a human appearance and animal heads, whose fame is connected to their work as attendants of Śiva. A further journey into the inner precincts of the temple takes one to the Hall of Consciousness (*cit sabhā*) where Śiva is enshrined as Naṭarāja (Lord of Dance). If prior doubts existed, they are now dispelled by the conviction that one has entered a realm of dance. On a raised platform, Śiva strikes his dance pose with his left foot raised. To the right of the dancing deity is the rahasya (secret) on the wall hidden behind a curtain in the form of a yantra (sacred diagram) depicting Śiva and his consort named Śivakāmasundarī in the center of the diagram.[2] The dancing deity suggests gracefulness, the source of grace, and the raised foot suggests a channel for the salvific grace of the god. This emphasis on dance is intended to convey rasa (sentiment) that is the result of the awakening of latent psychological states or emotions (*sthāyī-bhāvas*), which is exactly what the dancer attempts to evoke from the viewer in a classical dance performance.

And according to southern Indian folklore, Śiva performed the Ānanda Tāṇḍava (dance of bliss) at Chidambaram, or Tillai, another name for the same location. Thus it is only appropriate that Śiva is enshrined as the Lord of Dance in the temple. By means of the Ānanda Tāṇḍava, Śiva reveals joyfulness and perfection. The dance also represents the centering of the cosmos, a place where kings and sages desire to be located in order for their status and work to have a transcendent legitimacy identical with the location of the dance.[3] In some texts, Śiva dances the Tāṇḍava in order to save the world at the end of time by dancing the world out of existence.[4] While the great yogin dances, white ashes fall off his body as he laughs wildly. This type of dance allows us to witness the close connection between dance and death, in which this frenzied dance marks the periodic destruction of the cosmos. Nonetheless, the mythology of Śiva also reveals the erotic aspects of the dancing of the great god.

Sometimes, Śiva is depicted dancing erotically before the wives of the sages of the Pine Forest. In some versions of the myth, he seduces the wives of the sages after he drives them mad with his dancing. Both scenarios suggest a close connection between sexuality, seduction, and dance. There are also episodes in which dance is intimately connected to death. According to a myth in the *Kūrma Purāṇa* (1.15.121–218), the demon Andhaka (literally "blind")—whose origin resulted from the playful blinding of Śiva's eyes and binding of his hands by his mischievous spouse and the inadvertent shedding of the ascetic god's seed or drop of sweat—attempts to abduct the comely Pārvatī, but Śiva intervenes, impales the hapless demon on the tip of his trident, and begins to dance, which causes the demon to lose its sins and gain salvific knowledge.

An even more dramatic connection between dance and death is evident in a myth from the *Liṅga Purāṇa* (106.2–28) in which the demon Dāruka gains great powers by practicing austerities (*tapas*) before proceeding to destroy both gods and Brahmins. Since only a woman could kill the demon, various gods go disguised as women to further their purpose, but they are defeated. Then, the gods ask Śiva for assistance, and he recruits his spouse for this challenging adventure. She enters the body of her husband, and she creates for herself another body from the poison in Śiva's throat, which he contracted by drinking the poisonous venom that resulted from the churning of the cosmic ocean by the gods. When Śiva emits the goddess from his throat, she appears as the terrifying Kālī along with *siddhas* (perfected yogic beings) and ghoulish *piśācas*. Pārvatī commands the terrible black goddess to destroy the demon, but the earth becomes sick from the fever of the goddess's rage. With the earth suffering and everything out of control, Śiva assumes the form of a crying child in a ghost-filled cremation ground in order to quell her anger. Pārvatī, appearing as Kālī, is fooled by the māyā (illusory trick) of her spouse, and she offers the infant milk from her own breasts. This affords Śiva an opportunity to drink the anger from her body. At twilight Śiva begins to perform a frenzied Ūrdhva Tāṇḍava dance accompanied by numerous ghosts and goblins in order to win the favor of the goddess. In response to Śiva's dance, the goddess dances with him.

According to the *Tiruvālaṅkāṭṭu Purāṇa*, because Kālī is unable to defeat Śiva in battle, she decides to challenge him to a dance contest. When the god begins to dance Kālī imitates him until he begins to get tired, to her gleeful satisfaction. Anticipating victory over her weakening rival, Kālī agrees with the god's suggestion to perform a fierce dance called the *pāṇaraṅkan*. With one foot planted on the ground, Śiva lifts the other leg straight up to the heavens and thereby exposes his masculinity in a very dramatic way. In response, the goddess falls to the earth in a faint and admits defeat, but she regains her power by contact with the earth. It is possible to see a number of messages in this narrative: the affirmation of the chthonic character of the goddess, dance as a form of marriage and male domination (Kālī loses the dance contest because of her feminine nature), the dangerous and destructive nature of the dance, and restoration of peace by male domination over dangerous female sexuality.[5] But sometimes the folk tradition conflicts with the textual tradition. A short distant from the image of the Lord of Dance in the Chidambaram temple is a silver-covered image of the goddess Kālī with its leg sticking straight up, and a priest informed me that this icon of the goddess commemorates her dance victory over Śiva. The version told to me by the temple priest contradicts the textual tradition and it ironically takes place precisely in a temple in which the god is enshrined as the Naṭarāja (Lord of Dance).[6] Therefore, it is not only possible to have several versions of a narrative about the god but also possible to have contradictory oral and written traditions.

Besides its connection to death and destruction, the dance of Śiva can also express the creative aspect of the deity, a feature that can be discerned by the symbolism of Śiva's iconic form as Naṭarāja (Lord of Dance). This beautiful icon depicts the god with his right leg raised and his left foot standing and crushing the demon-dwarf named Muyalaka, which is symbolic of the god's ability to destroy evil in the world and within the heart of a person. The rhythm of the dance is timed by the drum that he holds in his upper right hand, reflecting also the tempo of the cosmos, the coursing of the planets, the repetition of the ages (*yugas*), and the primal sound vibrating in space that is connected to the initial forms of existence and the first stirrings of revelation and truth. As the god dances, his hair flows freely, with the symbols of the sun, crescent moon, Ganges River, and plant life adorning it. Wearing a faint intoxicated smile, the face of the deity reflects the bliss of being mentally absorbed in himself. His earrings symbolize the androgynous nature of Śiva because he wears a masculine earring on one ear and a female earring in the other. The symbolism of his upper right hand, with the drum, represents the opposite of that of his upper left hand, which holds a flame, representing destruction or the final cremation fire at the end of time. The lower right hand displays the fear-not gesture in order to counterbalance the destructive threat from the upper left hand. The lower left hand informs the viewer how one can be saved from potential destruction: it points to the raised foot, and it invites the viewer to take refuge under the feet of God and gain salvation. Overall, the image of Śiva as Naṭarāja provides a symbolic summary of his five major activities: creation, maintenance of the cosmos, destruction, refuge, and divine favor or release. The icon also summarizes the dualities and paradoxes within the nature of the deity, and it demonstrates the complementary nature of these opposites and their fundamental unity.

Development of the Dancing God

The fully developed deity, or what can be called the purāṇic Śiva, that is worshiped by many Hindus throughout India today appears during the vedic period (c. 1800 B.C.E.) as the figure Rudra, who is called the "roarer" or "howler." Although it is by no means certain, it is possible that Rudra may have his roots in the ancient Indus Valley civilization, where seals discovered by archeologists depict figures seated in a meditation posture and surrounded by animals along with images of phallic design, which are all features that eventually become associated with the fully evolved Śiva. Contrary to this traditional connection, a more recent scholar argues that the so-called proto-Śiva seal is actually a seated bull and not the figure of Śiva.[7] Rudra is described in the vedic texts as brown-skinned, with a black-colored belly, a red back, and wearing an animal skin. In the Rig Veda hymn of praise (1.114), Rudra is asked to leave the petitioner alone, not to harm the requester's children or grandchildren, and not to kill his cattle and horses, reflecting the petitioner's obvious fear of this deity. Other vedic-period hymns (2.33, 7.46) refer to a more benign Rudra who is a great physician, bestower of health, and remover of sorrow.

As the narrative of the vedic period unfolds, Rudra inherits attributes of other deities through close association with them. Rudra's connection to the Maruts, storm gods, brings him into contact with the warrior god Indra and an opportunity to share the god's attributes of destruction and healing. Rudra also shares Indra's phallic nature and the close connection to fertility, and they share adulterous proclivities and the ability to change forms from male to female. Both Rudra and Indra are described as possessing a thousand eyes, an attribute with implications for the power of perception, both in a potentially moral sense due to their ability to see violators of legal standards, and in an immoral sense because the many eyes have erotic connotations due to their ability to spy many beautiful women. Rudra shares in the attributes of other important vedic deities besides Indra. He shares his androgynous nature with the vedic god Brahmā. And Rudra inherits the vedic god of fire Agni's connection to tapas (heat generated by ascetic practices) and kāma (heat created by sexual excitement). The tendency to seduce women and commit adultery also connects Rudra and Agni.

A hymn to the hundred names of Rudra appears in the so-called black (*Taittirīya Saṁhitā* 4.5.1) and the white (*Vajasaneyi Saṁhitā* 16.1–66) recensions of the *Yajur Veda*. This hymn is called the *śatarudriya*, and Śaiva sects and their worshipers use it in their daily devotion at the present time. The hymn refers to the paradoxical nature of Rudra as possessing an auspicious (*śiva*) form contrasted to his malignant nature. Rudra is a healer due to his association with medicinal herbs; he is lord of cattle (Paśupati), inhabits dangerous and haunted locations, and lives apart from human communities. All this suggests the possible non-vedic (non-Aryan) origins of Rudra. An especially informative body of evidence for the non-vedic origins of Rudra appears in the Brāhmaṇic literature of ancient India.

In a sacrificial narrative from the *Śatapatha Brāhmaṇa* (9.1.1.6), the god Prajāpati is dismembered. All deities leave the scene with the exception of Manyu (Fury), upon whom the tears of Prajāpati fall and he becomes Rudra, who frightens the gods by his appearance. In another narrative from the *Kauṣītaka Brāhmaṇa* (6.2–9), Prajāpati creates offspring by means of the power of his austerities (*tapas*). The progeny are four brothers and the goddess Uṣas (dawn), who assumes the form of a beautiful celestial nymph (*apsaras*). Overwhelmed by her beauty, the four brothers shed their seed, which is collected into a golden cup by Prajāpati. From the contents of this cup of semen, there arises Rudra. These narratives are indicative of the strange origins of Rudra. A different type of scenario is evident in the *Aitareya Brāhmaṇa* (3.33) when Prajāpati commits incest with his daughter in the form of a male antelope. Putting together their most terrible parts, the gods produce Rudra in order to punish Prajāpati for his transgression of the cosmic law pertaining to proper family conduct. The gods reward Rudra for his efforts with control over domestic animals. However, the most revealing narrative about the non-vedic origins of Rudra and his attempt to gain admission into the vedic pantheon is his exclusion from the sacrifice. Angry over not obtaining a share of the sacrifice, Rudra pursues and threatens the niggardly deities. Being fearful of the power of Rudra, the gods acquiesce to his demands and reserve the final offering of the sacrifice for Rudra. This initial denial of the sacrifice and eventual inclusion into the sacrificial cult is repeated at a later historical period when Śiva is denied access to the sacrifice of Dakṣa in the purāṇic literature. These kinds of narratives are probably indicative of the original alien nature of Rudra with respect to orthodox vedic religion. Being depicted as a marginal social figure, a stranger to vedic religion, and an intruder in the texts, scholars have tended to imagine Rudra's origins within the pale of some mountain or forest tribe of indigenous Dravidian sources.

Embodying features of Rudra, Agni, Brahmā, and Indra from the vedic period of Indian history, Śiva appears in the *Śvetāsvatara Upaniṣad* (composed around the fifth or fourth centuries B.C.E.), which manifests the continuation of his rise to prominence within Indian culture. This strongly theistic text stands in contrast to earlier monistic types of upaniṣadic texts. It begins with a series of questions about the origins of the world and human beings, which are answered by identifying Rudra as the supreme being and cause of the cosmos that he also maintains by his power. Rudra is not merely transcendent but also immanent by dwelling with human hearts. Liberation from the cycle of rebirth may be achieved by yogic efforts and the grace (*prasāda*) of Rudra. At the final verse (6.23) of the text, there is a reference stressing the importance of loving (*bhakti*) God and one's guru (teacher). In fact, it is only such a person who can understand the message of the text.

The epic literature identifies features of Śiva that become standard by the historical period of the purāṇic texts (which began to be composed around the fourth century C.E.). In the epic *Mahābhārata* (7.78.39), the great god is described as carrying a trident, having matted locks and a thousand eyes, and being clad in bark and animal skins. Later in this epic (13.17) he is described additionally as having a serpent form, being a lunatic, ithyphallic, four-faced, and skull carrier. There is also the odd story of that he initiated Krishna and that the dark god is a lifelong devotee of Śiva. The epic also refers to the existence of Śaiva ascetics as the Pāśupatas (9.349.64). The other major epic tale of India, the *Rāmāyaṇa*, contains numerous myths associated with the exploits of the deity such as Dakṣa's sacrifice, Śiva's marriage, drinking of poison, killing the demon Andhaka, destroying the triple city, and other tales. These developments set the stage for the fully defined deity of the purāṇic texts. Within the Purāṇic texts, Śiva appears in many roles such as the ascetic, married householder, destroyer of demons, androgynous being, and dancer. All of these roles exemplify important features of the deity and have connections to other features of Śaiva devotion. There is also a reference to Śiva worshipers in the grammarian Patañjali's commentary on the Sanskrit grammar of Pāṇini (*Aṣṭādhyāyi*, 5.2.76).

In his rise to preeminence, Śiva is consistently hailed as the great ascetic. His appearance reflects his status as an ascetic; he is depicted as white in color due to the ashes that cover his body, his hair is matted with the Ganges River flowing through it, a tiger skin adorns his waist, or he is simply naked. Snakes serve as his sacred thread, bracelets, necklace, bowstring, and at times clothing, and they function to emphasize the phallic character of the god. The overt male sexuality, immodesty, and poverty are evident in his ascetic role. The ashes of corpses that cover his body are his life-blood and symbolize his antierotic nature as an ascetic. In the *Skanda Purāṇa* (5.2.2.2–37), the sage Maṅkaṇaka, having performed asceticism for many years, cut his finger on a blade of grass, and he witnessed vegetable sap flow from the cut. When he responded by dancing for joy, his dance disturbed the universe. In order to discern the source of the cosmic disturbance, the gods sent the ascetic Śiva disguised as a Brahmin, to whom the joyous sage explained the motivation behind his dance. Upon hearing the story of the sage, the great god laughed, and he struck his thumbs against one another, causing snow-colored ashes to flow from his wound. Upon witnessing this astonishing event, the sage was ashamed at his pretentious behavior. By his action, Śiva demonstrated that ashes are his life force. The ashes of the God are also a remedy for the fever associated with love, a point that suggests the past sexual excesses of the ascetic deity.

As the primal ascetic, Śiva stands in opposition to the god Kāma, a figure of desire. In the *Vāmana Purāṇa* (6.25, 58–77), Kāma strikes Śiva with a flower arrow and drives him mad, a condition that sends him wandering throughout the countryside, causing him to have erotic dreams, and enflaming the deity even more from a second arrow of desire. During his wandering, Śiva begs from the Pine Forest sages and their wives, only to be followed by the love-struck wives. Due to the erotic behavior of their wives, the sages curse Śiva with the intended effect that his phallus falls to the ground. When the phallus of the ascetic god falls it splits the Earth and causes her to suffer. When Kāma appears for a third time to insert desire into the heart of the ascetic god, Śiva uses his third eye to reduce the deity of desire to ashes. In some versions of the myth, the wife of Kāma begs Śiva to restore her husband, which allows the deity an opportunity to demonstrate not only his destructive aspects but also his creative and salvific powers.

Even though Śiva destroys Kāma in many narratives, this does not mean that the chastity associated with asceticism and sexuality represent polar opposites. Chastity and sexuality are symbiotic, which implies that the chaste ascetic is procreative by virtue of his chastity.[8] Thus the asceticism of Śiva complements his role as a householder and head of a family. His family consists of his early wife Satī, later spouse Pārvatī (also called Umā in some texts), and two sons named Gaṇeśa and Kārttikeya (literally son of the Kṛttikas or Pleiades), who is also called Skanda, Guha, Kumāran, Shaṇmukha, Subrahmaṇ, or Murugaṉ.

Śiva's two sons are not linked to him in the ordinary way. In the *Śiva Purāṇa* (*Rudra* 13.15–37; 17.3–59), Pārvatī becomes aggravated when her husband interrupts her bath, and she decides that she needs a guardian to protect her privacy. Therefore, she creates from her own bodily dirt the body of a strong, valorous, handsome, young man who is made door guardian and chief of the *gaṇas* (demonic figures), and names him Gaṇeśa. The next time Śiva attempts to gain admittance to his wife's personal quarters the entrance is blocked by her guardian, who is unaware of the identity of the intruder. Śiva becomes infuriated when a stick strikes him. Eventually a battle occurs between the two armies of gaṇas, until Śiva's forces win the conflict. The final episode of this conflict results in the beheading of Gaṇeśa by Śiva using his trident. Pārvatī is furious to find her son dead, and she is unsatisfied with Śiva's sorrowful response. She creates a vast army of *śakti*s (female powers) to annihilate the world and the gods; the remaining gods beg Pārvatī for compassion, but she only agrees to stop if her son can be revived. The gods vow to collect the head from the first animal that they encounter during their northern journey, which happens to be a single-tusked elephant. This severed head is attached to the inert body along with holy water, mantras, and *tejas* (energy) of the combined gods in order to revive the inert body and restore it to life. In a different version of the story from the *Bṛhaddharma Purāṇa* (2.60.1–4, 7–97), it is Śiva who secures the head of the elephant named Airāvata, a vehicle of the deity Indra. Gaṇeśa is given a tiger skin by Śiva, a sacred thread by the deity Bṛhaspati, and a rat for a vehicle by the goddess Earth. He is given various names including Lord of Obstacles, which means that anyone undertaking a journey or a new endeavor should remember Gaṇeśa for a successful outcome. Gaṇeśa is an extremely popular divine figure, especially in southern India—remember the twenty-foot neon sign in the form of the deity advertising a Gaṇeśa gas station on a major road in the city of Chennai (Madras) with which we began the book. With his rat vehicle and elephant-headed appearance, the overall impression manifested by Gaṇeśa is comic, but this does not affect his popularity with ordinary people.[9]

In contrast to Gaṇeśa, Kārttikeya is born from the semen of Śiva. According to the *Vāmana Purāṇa* (27.1–62), Fire drinks the semen of Śiva, but he cannot bear it so he gives it to the goddess Kuṭilā to carry in her waters. After carrying the embryo for five thousand years without giving birth, the goddess is instructed by Brahmā to cast the embryo onto a wide mountain plain. Releasing the embryo through her mouth, the goddess abandons the child, returns to Brahmā, and becomes entirely water. When the child is born it cries for care. Six goddesses, the Kṛtikkās, find the crying child and proceed to argue over who will nurse it. In order to placate the goddesses, the infant produces six faces, and each is given loving care by each of the six goddesses. As the child grows, Fire learns of its existence and argues with Kuṭilā over its parentage. In order to settle this dispute, they decide with Śiva's blessing to let the child choose its parent. Thereupon, the six-faced infant becomes four bodies, and he divides himself among the interested parties, with Kumāra becoming the son of Śiva. The spouse of the ascetic god accepts this son.

Pārvatī represents the second wife of Śiva, and she is regarded as a reincarnation of the goddess Satī, who committed suicide to protest an insult to her husband by her father. Śiva is attracted to Satī because of her beauty and practice of asceticism. After their marriage, they retire to enjoy each other in their mountain paradise. Because of Śiva's asceticism and appearance, Dakṣa, father of Satī, never really fully embraces his son-in-law, and there is always a tension between the two males figures. According to the *Kūrma Purāṇa* (1.14.4–97), Dakṣa makes arrangements for a grand sacrifice to which he invites all the gods with the exception of Śiva; this does not affect the deity. His wife, however, is very upset with her father at what she interprets as an insult to her husband. She angrily chastises her father for the insult, but he rebuffs her, which motivates her to commit suicide by burning herself by means of her yogic power. With a horde of demonic beings, an enraged Śiva destroys Dakṣa's sacrifice and decapitates his father-in-law, transforming Dakṣa into the sacrificial victim. After Śiva resuscitates everything that was destroyed by his vengeful actions, the sacrifice continues smoothly, with the inclusion of Śiva. In another version of the mythical narrative from the *Bṛhaddharma Purāṇa* (2.40.18–54), Śiva picks up the inert body of his dead wife, and in a frenzy of necrophilia and sorrow he begins to dance, balancing the dead body on his head. The earth begins to tremble and suffer, but the mad god continues to dance wildly. In order to calm Śiva and protect the earth, Viṣṇu hurls his discus at the dead body, cutting it into pieces. While Śiva continues to dance, the body on his head becomes lighter until he realizes that all the limbs have been severed, and he ceases to dance. When the pieces of the dead body of the goddess fall to the earth they become sacred places of pilgrimage. In still another twist to the narrative in the *Bṛhaddharma Purāṇa* (2.6–10), Śiva finds the yoni (female generative organ) of Satī at Kāmarūpa in the region of Assam and plunges into her as the *liṅga* (male generative organ), remaining conjoined forever. According to some versions of the narrative, Satī is incarnated as Pārvatī, the second wife of the ascetic God.

Pārvatī, as her name implies, is associated with the mountains. She is born to Menā and Himavat in order to lure the ascetic deity into marriage and worldly life. She is called Kālī (dark one) because of her dark complexion. After her husband calls her Kālī, she takes umbrage at her husband's denigration of her appearance, and she practices austerities to transform her dark color into a golden one; thereafter she is called Gaurī (bright). From one perspective, Pārvatī complements her husband because she symbolizes Soma, which represents the primordial waters from which the cosmos is reborn, whereas Śiva symbolizes the final fire that destroys the cosmos at the end of the creative cycle. She also stands for domesticity, distraction of her spouse's asceticism, and taming of his sexual excesses. Moreover, she becomes the śakti (feminine, active, creative principle) of the god that he needs to express himself in the world, and she represents the prakṛti (primal matter) necessary for creation. These masculine and feminine principles often compete against and complement each other. An excellent example of this competition is the dice game between the pair.

In one version of the dice game narrative in the *Skanda Purāṇa* (1.32.7–112), Śiva wages his crescent moon and earrings against his spouse's pearls and golden ornaments. When he loses he proves to be a poor sport and does not pay her, because he claims to be invincible. In turn, she mocks him. But a servant reminds her that since she is female she cannot understand Śiva's ascetic and invincible natures. The matrimonial discord between the pair is sometimes due to Pārvatī's anti-ascetic stance (even though there are instances when she practices asceticism herself), or Śiva's fondness for drugs (usually opium and/or bhang). In other episodes of the dice game, such as that in the *Skanda Purāṇa* (1.1.34.130–39), Pārvatī wins his loincloth, and Śiva threatens her with his third eye, but he finally leaves for the forest without fulfilling his threat. According to a version of the dice game in the *Kāñchīmāhātmya* (23.1–35), Śiva wins at dice and proceeds to laugh at his spouse for losing, who grows angry and accuses him of cheating by using loaded dice. She continues by reprimanding him and criticizing his appearance. In response, Śiva curses his wife to have three eyes and turn a black color. After she begs his forgiveness, Śiva instructs her how she can become free of the curse, and she becomes Kāmākṣī (having the eyes of Kāma, desire) and patron goddess of the city of Kāñchīpuram. Although episodes of the dice game expose the tensions between the pair, there are other aspects that manifest their complementary natures.[10]

As the śakti (feminine energy) of her husband, Pārvatī helps to emphasize the androgynous nature of Śiva. Iconic symbols of this condition are the liṅga and yoni, in which the former rises from the latter instead of entering or penetrating the yoni. The *Bṛhaddharma Purāṇa* (1.3.16–36) relates the mythical origin of the liṅga and yoni. While Śiva is absorbed in a yogic trance, the goddess is unable to awaken him from his meditation. After she takes the shape of a foul-smelling corpse, Śiva notices her presence, and he returns to his trance condition and assumes the form of a liṅga. When the goddess recognizes this she takes the shape of a yoni, and she places the liṅga within her, plunging into the cosmic waters to create progeny. This myth not only emphasizes the active role played by the goddess. It also indicates that the liṅga represents a cosmic substance that reflects the many potential possibilities for prakṛti (primal matter). It is possible to view the liṅga and yoni as a paradoxical visual symbol because, without entering or penetrating it, the liṅga rises out of the yoni.[11]

The anonymous sages cited by the *Śiva Purāṇa* (2.18.76–77) interpret the name Śiva as androgynous: the syllable 's' represents bliss, 'i' stands for the masculine principle, and the syllable 'va' denotes Śakti or the feminine energy. The devotee is encouraged to make his or her soul harmonious like that of the androgynous Śiva. There is thus a mutual dependence between Śiva and Śakti. They cannot exist separately, just as the sun neither exists without its light nor can light exist without the sun (ŚivaP 9.214.11–12). Śakti assumes the form of *cit* (consciousness), which depends on Śiva and is the means by which the deity bestows worldly pleasures and salvation (ŚivaP 9.2.4.13–14). This implies that the source of the universe is masculine and feminine, which means necessarily that the macrocosm and microcosm are also androgynous. In other words, earthy beings embody the androgynous nature of their creator (ŚivaP 1.5.29). When Śiva appears in his androgynous form he is referred to as *ardhanarīśvara*. According to the *Liṅga Purāṇa* (1.70.325), this can be portrayed as the female form in one half of his body, through an act of self-will by the deity.

A south Indian folk tale reflects a situation in which not everyone is pleased to worship Śiva in his androgynous form. As a fanatical devotee of Śiva, Bhṛṅgin refuses to worship the female aspect of the androgynous nature of the god. The devotee becomes a bee or beetle, and burrows straight through the middle of the androgynous body, which allows him to circumambulate only the male aspect on the right. Becoming angry at this slight to her nature, the goddess curses him to lose his flesh and blood (that is, the female parts of his body), reducing him to a ghoulish skeleton that could barely stand on its own. Taking pity upon the poor devotee, Śiva grants him a third leg that grows from the empty space between the other two leg bones (an obvious male phallic gift from his father).[12] In his mutilated, emasculated, emaciated form, Bhṛṅgin becomes the adopted son of Śiva and Pārvatī, and he is assimilated to the ranks of the deformed gaṇas of the god, much like Gaṇeśa. It is possible to see in this unbalanced, hideous, and comic figure a caricature of the yogic and ithyphallic Śiva, a manifestation of death, and the frightening aspect of the great god.

Śaiva mythology embodies many tales about the liṅga as a sign proving its superior nature, the existence of Śiva, and as something that represents the subtle essence of the deity. An excellent example appears in the *Kūrma Purāṇa* (1.25.64–95). During a period of cosmic dissolution, at which time there is only a single ocean, Śiva appears in order to awaken the gods Brahmā and Viṣṇu, who are arguing over who is the genuine creator of the world. While the argument is occurring, a bright burning liṅga appears to the two argumentative deities. Brahmā proposes that he go up and that Viṣṇu go down the liṅga in order to discover its limits. Since neither god can find its limits after searching for a hundred years, the two amazed and frightened deities stand confused by the illusion of Śiva, and they proceed to praise it. Thereupon, Śiva reveals himself to the two gods, and he tells them not to fear—he, the greatest god, will protect them. The liṅga represents the pillar form of the god in temples, like the sixteen-foot-tall icon at the Bṛhadīśvara temple in Thanjavur (Tanjore) in southern India, and it ironically symbolizes the retention of seed rather than sexual arousal.

A frequent narrative about the liṅga revolves around the theme of castration. According to the *Śiva Purāṇa* (Dharmasaṁhita 49.35–86), since the gods get tired of waiting for Śiva to create the world, Brahmā performs the deed, to the eventual displeasure of Śiva who angrily responds by castrating himself, an act symbolic of his refusal to create. The liṅga pervades the earth and sky, and the myth concludes with the other gods worshiping the liṅga and having their desires satisfied. In contrast to this creative type of myth, there are other narratives about castration that end with chaos. A good example is the curse of the sages of the Pine Forest in response to the licentious and/or seductive activity of Śiva directed toward their wives. After Śiva allows the curse to take effect, the fallen liṅga causes the cosmos to return to chaos. Once chaos occurs the frightened sages turn to the ascetic god and worship him in his liṅga form. It is important to note that castration tends to be a cyclic event and never a final act. When the liṅga falls to earth there is always a suggestion of fertility.[13] Śiva's phallic character is enhanced and further emphasized by his vehicle (*vahana*) Nandi, the bull, a symbol of masculine sexual power.

It is possible to become confused by the intention behind the phallic nature of Śiva. The phallic nature of numerous Śaiva myths and its iconography is not simply about raw masculine sexual potency. By remembering that Śiva is an ascetic deity, it is possible to understand his erect phallus to be more about control of his senses, sexual drive, and seminal retention. As the great yogin, Śiva does nothing less than dramatically transform the primal sexual urge. Rather than direct the sexual drive toward pleasure and procreation like ordinary beings, Śiva redirects it toward intuitive wisdom.[14]

The Paradigm of the Ascetic

In several places within the corpus of the epic *Mahābhārata* (1.157.11; 3.41.25; 5.189.8), Śiva is called the great ascetic. By serving as the archetypical model for an ascetic, Śiva's ascetic character functions as an inspiration for his devotees on which they can model their own behavior and lifestyle. It is possible to witness the ascetic deity functioning as a paradigm among such ascetic groups as the Pāśupatas, Lakulīśas, Kālāmukhas, Kāpālikas, and the Nātha-Yogins. These ascetic groups were less concerned with Śiva as the Lord of Dance than as the great ascetic.

As suggested by their chosen name, the Pāśupatas were worshipers of Śiva as the Lord of Beasts (*paśupati*), whose initial reference can be traced to the *Atharva Veda* (2.34.1; 11.2.1,28; 11.6.9). It was possible that they were Brahmanical theists getting their inspiration from the *Śvetāśvatara Upaniṣad*. In their theology, Śiva was pati (lord) who created and protected paśus (creatures, animals). The paśu was bound to the world by the fetter (*pāśa*) of ignorance. Since pāśa also means cause and effect, it also referred to the notion of time (*kāla*), representing a state of bondage that was beginningless.[15] The goal of the paśu was to escape this bondage characterized by illusion, pain, unrighteousness, attachment, ignorance, and hopelessness.

The path of liberation was similar to other yoga-like disciplines: celibacy, detachment from worldly objects, withdrawal of the senses, and concentration. There were, however, some features that were unique to this movement. The paśu lived ideally in a cremation ground, and he or she bathed three times a day in ashes gathered from this area, which was considered a form of purification. It was necessary for the ascetic to purify his or her body, thought, and self.[16] This purification was necessary in order for the ascetic to rid himself or herself of evil karma in preparation for the acquisition of good karma, which was essential for the construction of a superhuman body that eventually equated the ascetic with Śiva.[17] The ascetic was also advised to go naked or clothed in a single cloth. At a later stage of spiritual development, the ascetic was instructed to act mad or ridiculous, thereby incurring the censure of others. This was called subjecting oneself to dishonor (*avamāna*). This was often done by acting as if asleep when one was not, making amorous gestures toward women, uttering senseless words, walking as if crippled, and generally acting like a beast. The ascetic's intention was to be transformed into a beast of god and finally to become the Lord of Beasts.

The behavior of the Pāśupatas was prefigured by the antics of Śiva in Śaiva mythology. The *Brahmāṇḍa Purāṇa* (1.2.27.1–64) provides an excellent example when Śiva goes to the Pine Forest to bestow his grace upon the sages for their ascetic practices. Besides being naked, covered in ashes, red-eyed, and with disheveled hair, Śiva is described as having his penis and testicles colored red, with the tip of his penis ornamented with black and white chalk. He appears to be mad as he dances erotically, laughs, sings, and smiles at the bewitched wives of the sages. From out of his mouth with pointed teeth, he roars like a bull and bellows like an ass. His appearance and behavior are contrary to the behavior of householders and traditional ascetics. But he represents a new paradigm of the ascetic for ascetic groups like the Pāśupatas and others.

A subsect of the Pāśupatas was the Lakulīśas, a group named for their founder, who probably lived sometime before the third century C.E. One scholar has speculated that this founder Lakulīśa, was derived from a term meaning club.[18] According to his followers, Lakulīśa was an embodiment of Śiva, who by means of the god's yogic powers entered a dead body left in a cremation ground and became this ascetic. Lakulīśa was depicted as possessing two arms, carrying a short club, naked, and with an erect penis. The erect penis symbolized priapism and chastity, and it had little to do with sexual arousal. From one perspective, it signified that the penis was alive, even though the body was dead. As noted previously with Śiva, the erect penis of the ascetic figure pointed to the withholding of semen. In a sense the ascetic attempted to store up semen in order to gain tapas (thermal energy) and thus power.

Two even more extreme forms of Śaiva ascetics were the Kālāmukhas and the Kāpālikas. The former group followed the thought of the Pāśupatas. Unfortunately, since these groups left no scriptures, information about them is limited to temple inscriptions and often-critical remarks made by opponents. The Kālāmukhas inhabited the Karnātaka region of India from the eleventh to the thirteenth centuries. The name of the sect was probably related to the practice of marking their foreheads with a black streak. They bathed in ashes, like the Pāśupatas, and carried a staff (*laguda*). The Vīraśaiva movement gradually absorbed them. Their unorthodox practices included worshiping their deity in a vessel filled with alcohol, a favorite liquid of their deity. The Kāpālikas, on the other hand, were probably incorporated into the Kānphaṭas and the Aghorī Śaiva tantric sects, and they virtually disappeared around the fourteenth century. The Kāpālikas were noted for carrying a human skull with them from which they ate their meals, which was a practice traceable to the decapitation of the god Brahmā by Śiva with his thumbnail, making the ascetic deity guilty of Brahminicide. Śiva was condemned to atone for his transgression by wandering homeless, begging for alms, and carrying Brahmā's skull. When he reached Benares the skull fell off his hand. This scenario served as a paradigm in a dharmic text, the *Manusmṛti* (II.73), for killing a Brahmin, because the penalty for this crime included living a solitary lifestyle in a forest hut apart from society and carrying the skull of the victim for twelve years to atone for the transgression of the legal code. The Kāpālikas smeared their bodies with ashes and carried a trident (*khaṭvaṅga*). They also used wine in their worship, a very unorthodox practice, and detractors alleged that they engaged in human sacrifice. Although this might not be historically accurate, they appeared, to have practiced extreme forms of self-mutilation by cutting off pieces of their flesh and using these pieces as sacrificial oblations. Nonetheless, the foundation of their worship was devotion (*bhakti*). They attempted to obtain two fundamental rewards: suprahuman magical powers and final liberation, viewed as residing in a heavenly realm of perpetual sexual bliss.[19]

Unlike the Kāpālikas, the Nātha-Yogins believed in a tradition of eighty-four *siddhas*, immortal demigods or teachers of the sect who resided in the Himalayan region of India. The number eighty-four has dubious historical significance, although it has a pronounced mystical importance for the sect because it most likely represented completeness or totality. Therefore, the eighty-four siddhas signified the totality of the revelation.[20] The movement of the Nātha-Yogins can be traced to ancient pre-Hindu and pre-Buddhist views and practices. It combined tantric elements, common yogic practices, and popular philosophical views with different Hindu and Buddhist aims.[21] The leader of this Śaiva sect was Gorakhnāṭh, who was instructed in the secrets of the cult by Matsyendranāṭh, who is also considered a Buddhist saint. Gorakhnāṭh lived probably not later than 1200 C.E. The sect that he founded was also known as the Kānphaṭa Yogins because of their practice of having their ears split for the insertion of huge earrings; it was believed that the splitting of the ear cartilage assisted in the acquisition of yogic powers. This Śaiva sect was essentially a yoga cult following the practice of Haṭha yoga. There was a close historical association with the Rasāyana school, which practiced alchemy to attain perfection.[22]

Since the Nātha-Yogins conceived of the body in a way very similar to Tantra, we will review that position in a subsequent chapter and not at this point. It seems useful, however, to mention their path to liberation. As in classical yogic practice, the ascetic practiced certain postures, breath control, sense withdrawal, concentration of the mind on a single point, meditation, and identification of the self with the object of meditation. By means of these six stages of yoga, the yogin attempted to manipulate his or her bodily functions by means of physical exercises and mental concentration that was called *kāya-sādhana* (culture of the body), whose aim was to achieve perfection of the body (*kāya-siddhi*).[23] This practice was also referred to as a regressive process. Ordinarily, a person's biological and psychological processes work in a downward manner. The aim of the yogin was to reverse this downward motion and to have these processes move upward. From another perspective, the yogic sādhana (practice) was also regressive in the sense that it strove to lead the yogin to his original divine body and away from the common process of becoming and decay. In a sense this regression or process of reversal was analogous to smoking a pipe. The correct way to smoke was to draw the smoke up the pipe stem. But sometimes the inside of the stem gets clogged with some kind of obstruction, a smoker can then clear the stem and get rid of the obstruction by reversing the process.

Tamil Poetic and Theological Expressions

While some Śaiva faithful were emphasizing the ascetic nature of their god, there was a group of remarkable poet-saints that expressed their faith by means of their poetry as they traveled throughout southern India singing the praises of their god. The spirit of Śaiva devotion was spread throughout southern India by the poetic singing of sixty-three Nāyanārs, who like the Vaiṣṇava Āḻvārs made no distinctions based on caste, age, or sex. The hymns of the sixty-three Nāyaṉārs were preserved in the *Tirumurai*, an anthology arranged in eleven books. These hymns are used in worship services at the present time in temples throughout southern India. The poetry of three of the earliest and most prominent Śaiva poets, namely, Appar (seventh century), Campantar (seventh century and pronounced Samban'dar), and Cuntarar (ninth century and pronounced Sun'darar), were collected into a work entitled the *Tēvāram* that consists of 796 hymns. These hymns demonstrate the creativity of the poets who "combined the basic metrical patterns of Tamil verse with prosodic principles largely new to Tamil poetry, creating a large number of new 'musical' meters, as well as a new song form, the *patikam*, with its ten stanzas and refrain, eminently suited to the spirit and themes of the new religion of *bhakti*."[24]

Besides their poetic contributions to Tamil religiosity, these poet-saints became significant to the religiosity of ordinary people. Icons of the poet-saints became a vital part of temple devotion, and the recitation of their poetic creations became an important aspect of the ritual performances in the temples. Because of their itinerant lifestyles, these poet-saints unified many sacred places of southern India and connected many of them directly to their god, creating a Śaiva sacred geography.[25] The particular locations visited by the saints became known as "a place sung by the saints."[26] Thereby, the Nāyaṉārs enhanced the prestige of particular locations and contributed to making the temple the center of Tamil culture. These poets used the first-person singular voice to express their love of God, suggesting the personal nature of their experience. If praise of Śiva represented the content of their compositions, it was pilgrimage to various locations that formed the context of their devotional songs.[27] They wanted to visit all the sacred abodes of their beloved deity in order to experience his different personas and different manifestations associated with each location.[28] Following the example set by previous kings in their employment of singers to recite the hymns of the Nāyaṉārs, and their construction of impressive temples, the Cōḻa kings (in the eleventh and twelfth centuries) expanded these kinds of religious practices, rebuilt Śaiva shrines, and constructed grand stone temples. Hagiographical narratives of the poet-saints were preserved in the *Periya Purāṇam* (Great Tradition), which many scholars date to around 1135 C.E., during the reign of Kulōttunga II (c. 1133–1150).[29]

Let us concentrate on the three poets already mentioned. We learn that Appar though born into a Śaiva Vellala (farmer) family in the town of Tiruvāmūr, converted to Jainism as a young man; he rose to the position of head of a Digambara Jain monastery. As an adult, he was afflicted with acute colitis, and he found help from his sister, a devout Śaiva. By following his sister's advice to take refuge with Śiva, Appar was cured of his medical adversity, and he converted back to the religious path of his sister and family religious tradition. Turning to the composition of melodious hymns praising his god, he was allegedly persecuted or tortured by the Jains, but he survived his hardships to convert the Pallava king to Śaivism.

The biography of Campantar was considerably different from Appar's, although they were friends. Campantar was born into a Brahmin family in Cīrkāḻi, a coastal town located in the vicinity of Chidambaram near the Kaveri River. His popular name is a shortened version of Naṉacampantar or Tiruāṉcampantar (He who is related to the Lord through divine wisdom), which reflected his status as a child prodigy and creator of poetry at a very young age. By around three years of age, he received the divine gift of poetry, in which he referred to defeating Buddhist and Jain monks in debate. This gift was bestowed, according to legend, by a revelation of Śiva and his wife, while his father bathed during a trip to the local temple. The crying child was given milk from the breast of the goddess in a golden cup, and thereby received the milk of wisdom. Besides being credited with many miracles like curing a friend of fever, curing a woman of epilepsy, and reviving a dead person, he was given credit for reconverting the Pandyan king of Madurai to Śaivism. He also converted many others to Śaivism, and helped to eclipse Buddhism and Jainism in the south. His hagiography relates his union with Śiva, his spouse, and attendants on the wedding day of the god.

The hagiographical accounts of the life of Cuntarar, also named Cuntaramūrtti (the handsome lord), depicted him as an incarnation of Ālālacuntarar, an attendant of Śiva in retreat at Kailāsa. A transformative experience occurred to Cuntarar when he was about to be married to the temple dancer named Paravai. An old man interrupted the ceremony, declaring that the poet-saint was his bonded slave, and produced documentation to support his contention. After the old man vanished, Cuntarar was transformed and declared his bondage to God. While on a visit to another town, he fell in love with a pious woman named Caṅkili, a weaver of floral garlands at a local shrine, and he received assistance from God, who appeared to the woman in a dream in order to get her to agree to the marriage. After becoming nostalgic for his home and first wife, he decided to leave Caṅkili and was forced to break an oath that he would remain with her after their marriage. When he left her, Cuntarar was struck blind. He proceeded to protest the severity of his punishment and asked for God's help. In a slow progression of steps while the poet-saint composed poems of divine praise and journeyed to various locations, Śiva finally restored his complete sight and helped to reconcile Cuntarar with his first wife. Like other saints, Cuntarar was credited with various miracles by hagiographers, such as saving a boy from an attack by a crocodile, quelling a flood, and defeating robbers in a remote forest. Finally, he ascended to heaven on a white elephant with his friend the king Cēramāṉ Perumāḷ, ruler of one of three ancient Tamil kingdoms.

Before the lifetimes of these three poets, Tamilnadu was ruled by three major kingdoms: Pāṇḍiya; an earlier Cōḷa dynasty; and Cēra. The dominance of these kingdoms ended around the third century C.E. The next major development occurred three centuries later with the rise of the Pallavas, a dynasty devoid of Tamil heritage that ruled from the city of Kāñcīpuram. After the period called the Caṅkam classical age, Buddhism and Jainism flourished in southern India during the so-called Kalabhra Interregnum around the sixth century. In fact, these religions made major contributions to Tamil culture. The author of the Tamil national epic entitled *Cilappatikāram*, for instance, was a Jain monk named Ilaṅkōvṭikal. He depicted the three major religions as coexisting harmoniously, whereas the *Tēvāram* hymns painted a more competitive picture of the historical period, with the different religions vying for royal support.

The poets used their poems to reflect the tensions between the major religions, to express personal religious experiences, make their poetry more public and personal, to create a beautiful visual image of God which others can then imagine or see for themselves, to motivate listeners to devotion and protest, and to bestow their poetry as gifts to the public. Their poetry broke out of the genre of the classical Caṅkam poetry, with its division into interior (*akam*) and exterior (puṟam), in order to create something less impersonal. Nevertheless, the poet-saints alluded to and evoked Tamil culture in their poetry, which promoted a self-conscious affection for this culture and the sacredness of its language and music, while at the same time uniting the population and land in a common religious viewpoint. The pilgrimages of the poets to various locations and identification of these places in their poems represented a geographical unity, and everyone was united personally with everyone else as a servant (*aṭiyār*, literally, "one who resides at the feet") of Śiva. The devotee's relationship to God was expressed even more strongly by becoming the slave (*toṇṭar*) of God, which was a freely chosen inferior status. By adopting this voluntary, inferior, and even abject status, the devotee was choosing to marginalize other kinds of social relationships characterized by exchange and obligation.[30]

These poet-saints composed poems about the dancing deity. Appar referred, for instance, to "the sweet golden foot raised up in dance," and Campantar composed poems about the Naṭarāja "holding a blazing fire in the hollow of his hand" and "the skullbearer who dances in the burning-ground for the dead."[31] But these poets also depicted God as father and mother, as did Appar; the mad love of God for his devotees, according to Cuntarar; and the unitive experience expressed in terms of conjugal love, as sung by Campantar. These poets expressed the importance of a single-minded love of God, the self-sacrificial nature of love, love as a gift from God, love as a means of release, and the necessity of total loving surrender to God. Cuntarar imagined himself as a woman in love with her husband Śiva, Appar imagined himself as a bride, and Campantar depicted himself as a lovesick woman who expressed her love by bestowing flowers, an external sign of love and respect. By expressing the relationship between the soul and God in terms of conjugal love, these poets revealed the divine androgynous condition.

Māṇikkavācakar (ninth century) in his beloved work entitled *Tiruvāśagam* continued to evoke Śiva's androgynous nature when he conceived of the soul as male and God as its ladylove.[32] By means of Śiva's grace, the soul is released. The grace of Śiva calms, purifies and elevates the soul.[33] The result of Śiva's grace is union with a personal deity characterized by love and symbolized by conjugal love. By losing itself in God, the self of the devotee is not totally annihilated, but it rather represents the death of the phenomenal self and attaining the form of Śiva. When the soul gains the form of Śiva, the poet intimates that it becomes androgynous due to the androgynous nature of God cited by the poet. The life and work of Māṇikkavākar marked the last of the great Tamil Śaivite poets. During his life, he served as a prime minister for a Pāṇḍiya king named Arimarttaṉār, but he eventually renounced his position to devote his creative energies to composing poetry and singing the praises of God. Besides miracles that were attributed to him, much like the other poet-saints, his greatest gift to the people of Tamilnadu was the *Tiruvāśagam*, that has been recited in homes and temples for centuries up to the present time.

The poems of the four major poet-saints were to be complemented by more systematic thinkers such as Tirumūlar (c. 800) and his devotional treatise entitled *Tirumantiran*, a work in which he identified God with love. This position suggested that God was only accessible to those whose heart possessed love or melted in love. In contrast to the fettered heart of stone, the melting or liquefied soul was docile, pliable, and could more easily receive the gift of divine grace. As the soul was melted by God and poured forth in response to God's grace, Śiva poured out his love for the devotee in a mutual exchange of love that led to knowing God in an intimate way; this suggested a total lack of opposition between love (*bhakti*) and knowledge. Tirumūlar was important for rendering into Tamil the Śaiva doctrine as it was found in the twenty-eight Sanskrit Śaiva Āgamas. He also may have been the first to use the terms *patti* (Tamil form of *bhakti*) and aṉpu (love, devotion), terms that referred not only to love of God but were also used to describe union with God.[34] The state of union with God was one of love, wherein God did not absorb the devotee's individuality.

Even more systematic thinkers followed Tirumūlar several centuries later. The work of these thinkers came to be known as Śaiva Siddhānta (culmination of the knowledge of Śiva). Aruḻnandi composed the *Śivañāṉa Cittiyār* around 1253 and the *Irupāvirupatu*, a poetic eulogy for this teacher, around 1254. Intending to focus on the truth, in 1255 Maṉavācakar Kaṭantār composed the *Uṇmaiviḷakkam* in the form of a dialogue between him and his teacher. Fifty years later, the *Śivap Pirakācam* was written by Umāpati, a convert from Vaiṣṇavism after hearing the words of poet-saint Campantar in the city of Chidambaram, around 1306.

Owing a considerable debt to the Śaiva Āgamas and the hymns of the Nāyaṉārs, Meykaṇda (he who has seen the truth) Tēvar composed the first truly systematic rendition of Tamil Śaiva theology around 1221, entitled the *Śivajñānabōdam*. It is this last work that can serve to elucidate Śaiva Siddhānta tradition of theology for our purposes. According to Meykaṇda, God is not different from the soul, but the soul is not God. In other words, God and the soul are distinct, but God lives in the world with the souls. Just as oil exists in the sesame seed so that it can be separated from the seed, so God lives in the world, and yet God is separable from it. Although God is immanent in the world, the soul cannot know God by means of its own power because God has caused the soul to be in a state of bondage.[35] The soul is entangled in the three *malams* (impurities): *ānava*, māyā, and karma. The ānava malam reduces the power of the soul, which suggests that it restricts the soul's powers of doing, desiring, and knowing. Although karma and māyā also prevent the realization of God, ānava is the ultimate hindrance to true knowledge because it is a natural impurity. Depending on the number of malams that the soul possesses, it is classified accordingly, which indicates that Śiva reveals himself differently to each class of souls. In the final analysis, the soul can only rid itself of its fetters and come to know God through his grace (*aruḷ*).[36]

The path to God is through bhakti (devotion), of which there are three degrees: *caryā* (a virtuous way of life), *kriyā* (ritual action), and yoga. These practices entail a progressive revelation of God and the undoing of that which conceals the soul's vision of God. They lead to a state of *iruvinaippu* (literally, equality of the two deeds).[37] This means that the soul regards good and evil deeds with equanimity. This results in the crushing of the power of malam (*malaparipāka*). These practices do not result in release by themselves; they only make it possible. In the final analysis it is only by the assistance of God's grace that the devotee can be freed. God comes to a person as a guru and manifests himself in different degrees, depending upon the number of malams that a person possesses at the time. After Śiva reveals himself, the soul realizes its unity with God. This is similar to iron that is placed into a fire. Eventually, the nature of the iron disappears, and it assumes the form of the fire.[38]

After the malams (impurities) are removed, the soul comes to know Śiva. This knowledge is penetrated by bhakti (devotion). The Śaiva theologian Umāpati likewise argues that knowledge is a gift of the grace of Śiva.[39] The soul and Śiva become united, possessing the same form. The soul is still, however, the servant of God. Thus union is to be understood as a unity in duality. This final state is characterized by love (*aṉpu*). In short, liberation (*mukti*) is the state of bhakti, according to Umāpati.

Within the context of the Tamil Śaiva devotional tradition, there developed the *cittar* (siddha, perfected one) movement of which the already-mentioned Tirumūlar was a forerunner. This exponent of yoga defines the cittars as those who have experienced divine light (*oḷi*) and power (*catti*) through yogic concentration.[40] This movement had a number of significant leaders; some of the earlier leaders were named Civavākkiyan, Pattirakiriyar, Pāmpāṭṭi, Cittar, Itaikkāṭṭucittar, and Paṭṭiṉattār. These individuals flourished between the tenth and fifteenth centuries. They had a profound interest in medicine and alchemy, especially as it related to the health of the body. Their goal was immortality through the perfection of the body by means of physiological yogic techniques and knowledge. They held that is necessary to protect and perfect the body because it is the seat of the life-force or soul (*vyir*).[41] The soul and the body were interdependent because without one the other could not exist. The cittars were opposed to the bhakti (devotional) movement in Tamilnadu. They also exhibited an anti-ritualism and anti-ceremonialism in their religious path, although they stressed ethical principles and a quest for knowledge. Furthermore, the cittars protested against the caste system. In short, they were opposed to religious practices that hindered the attainment of magical powers and perfection. The Śaiva cittars looked to the paradigm of the yogic Śiva for their religious inspiration.

The cittar development within the Tamil Śaiva tradition is an example of a stream or line of transmission of texts and practices being passed from one generation of teachers and followers to another. Sometimes, Śaiva traditions of textual transmissions and teachings were classified according to the four directions or the five mouths of Śiva. Whereas Tamil Śaivism represents a southern transmission of the tradition, its northern transmission is represented historically by Kashmir Śaivism.

Kashmir Expressions of Śaivism

As a student of Śaivism, imagine yourself lying in an open field gazing at the stars when suddenly you spy Śiva performing his cosmic dance. As the divine yogin dances, he gives off a vibration that moves throughout the entire cosmos like waves of sound or the ripples created when a stone is thrown into a still body of water. Now try to image yourself hearing and feeling a cosmic vibration of sound that fills your ears with a mysterious reverberation that permeates and penetrates your skin and flesh until it finally makes your bones tingle. The result of the experience is that you are now shaking and tingling from the tips of your toes to the hair on the top of your head. What you are experiencing is the flow of Śiva throughout the universe in a divine act of overflowing and creation. When you can feel such a vibration you have entered into the world of Kashmir Śaivism.

Kashmir was an ancient center for diverse Brahmanic and Buddhist groups that adhered to various forms of classical Hindu philosophy or Buddhist schools of thought such as the Vaibhāṣika, Sautrāntika, Yogācāra, and Mādhyamika. The Kashmir theological and philosophical expression of Śaivism began around the ninth century with a line of outstanding teachers originated with a teacher named Vasugupta (c. 875–925), who is credited with having taught the *Śiva Sūtras*. Somānanda (c. 900–950) was most likely a student of Vasugupta, and he articulated a nondualistic Śaiva theological position for probably the first time. In turn, Somānanda passed on the tradition to Utpaladeva (c. 925–975). However, the most distinguished, erudite, and prolific writer of the school was Abhinavagupta (c. 975–1025), who passed on his teachings to Kṣemarāja (who lived in the eleventh century). Abhinavagupta was born into a wealthy and noble Brahmin family that lived in Śrīnagar, but his mother died when he was young. After receiving a liberal education that included teaching by Buddhist and Jain instructors, he went to Jālandhara and encountered a teacher named Śambhunātha, who taught him the fundamentals of tantric practice associated with the Kaula tradition (from the term *kula* meaning families associated with goddesses or *yoginīs*). Abhinavagupta never married because he preferred to devote his life to renunciation, scholarship, and writing more than forty works. Some of these works made important contributions to Indian aesthetic theory.

The complex religious and philosophical environment of Kashmir encompassed at least three major traditions of Śaivism: a nondualist tantric tradition, a dualist and very conservative Śaiva Siddhānta tradition, and a movement between these two traditions that centered around the cult of Svacchandabhairava, a frightening and terrible form of Śiva. The Bhairava Tantras are a body of texts that concentrate on Śiva as the ferocious Bhairava. This form of the deity originated with ascetic groups that congregated near cremation grounds. An excellent example of such a Śaiva ascetic group is the already-mentioned Kāpālikas. They were called "skull-men" both because of the skull-topped staff that they carried with them and because they ate from a skull.[42] In addition to the ferocious Bhairava, there were also three goddesses called Parā, Parāparā, and Aparā. These terrible goddesses were placated with offerings that consisted of blood and alcohol, followed by ordinary offerings of flowers and incense. On the more esoteric levels of worship, deities demanded other impure substances and liquid, such as feces, phlegm, semen, urine, and menstrual blood. Foods such as garlic and onions that are normally polluting to Brahmins were also used.[43]

In order to make better sense of a complex religious tradition, we will focus our attention on the contributions of Abhinavagupta. This Kashmiri thinker understood Kashmir Śaivism as representing three distinct branches of thought: Krama, Kaula, and Pratyabhijñā. The term *trika* was frequently used for the entire system or to designate the Pratyabhijñā system. Trika points to the major authority of the triad of Āgamic texts, on which the entire system of thought is founded. It is important to affirm that the distinctions and dividing lines between the different Śiva groups were not rigidly maintained, and there seems to have been considerable overlap and interpenetration.[44]

The Krama system is essentially a path of knowledge in which ritual plays an important part, whereas Kaulism is described as the path of liberation through enjoyment (*bhoga*) and liberation (*mokṣa*).[45] In other words, the aspirant uses worldly pleasures to attain spiritual goals. It is a path toward unity in the sense that it believed in an essential unity of knower, known, and knowing. From a slightly different viewpoint, it is an attempt to unite the universal masculine (Śiva) and feminine (Śakti) principles. Śiva is nondual (*akula*) Being, whereas Śakti is the totality of universal existence (*kula*). The goal is to unite these two masculine and feminine elements and realize Anuttara, the perfect unity of Śiva and Śakti.[46] This union of spiritual bliss is attained by means of sexual union (*maithuna*) between two partners. The objective is not the satisfaction of finite carnal pleasure; it is rather a means to the end, of spiritual bliss. More time will be devoted to this esoteric subject in a later chapter on the tantric movement. But for the present purposes, one should be aware of the obvious androgynous symbolism.

From another perspective, Abhinavagupta thinks that it is possible to find evidence of the existence of God because God created the thirty-six categories that constitute the universe, which also consists of a universal creative vibration (*sāmānya spanda*) grounded in Śiva's pure consciousness, identical with the pure consciousness of the self.[47] It is thus possible to find evidence of God within the world and oneself. By means of gaining enlightenment, one gains certainty about

God. Abhinavagupta understands God as a dynamic reality, that is, God is continually contracting and expanding. In other words, Śiva is in a state of perpetual movement or vibration (*spanda*).[48] An important implication for such a philosophical position is that Śiva is identical with the universe because the latter shares with God the light of consciousness. Even though Śiva projects his various manifestations through the process of vibration (*spanda*) in which there are appearances of differences, there is a total absence of difference within the highest consciousness.[49] Moreover, by its participation in the light of pure consciousness that is free from the influence of illusion (*māyā*), the self is identical with Śiva, pure consciousness with pure consciousness. Abhinavagupta also defines the ultimate as both different and nondifferent (*bhedābheda*). This means that what appear to be different things that we perceive in the world are really identical. From one perspective, it is the experience of difference that makes unity meaningful, which is possible because all things are a manifestation of the single pure consciousness (*saṃvid*) identical to Śiva. This abstract thought should not obscure the fact that, from the perspective of Abhinavagupta, Śiva is a personal god.

Looking at the situation from the human perspective, Abhinavagupta perceives the self in a state of bondage due to ignorance (*ānavamala*), an impurity that covers the self. The other two impurities (*malams*) are karma and māyā. The impurity of ignorance is beginningless, and it functions to conceal the real nature of the self; it is, however, destructible. The impurity of ignorance is to be distinguished from intellectual ignorance because it is independent of a person's connection with the body, whereas intellectual ignorance is not. The impurity of ignorance is also independent of the other two major impurities, which implies that the impurity of ignorance continues to exist even if the others are destroyed. However, if the impurity of ignorance is destroyed, the other impurities will disappear. Abhinavagupta portrays an even more complicated situation because the self is also obscured by the covers of illusion (*māyā*) called the five *kañcukas* (sheaths): finite determination that limits one's actions, limited knowledge, attachment of passion, limits of necessity or natural law, and the power of time. Along with illusion, the five sheaths constitute the impure principles of the universe that are opposed by the five pure universal principles connected to the śakti (creative energy) of Śiva. A fundamental difference between the pure and impure principles is that the latter are characterized by duality. Therefore, the bondage of the self entails the three impurities and the false sense of duality.

This problematic situation cannot be overcome by a person's own efforts. The grace (*anugraha*) of Śiva is necessary to purify the intelligence in order for the self to progress toward perfection, just as a face is revealed in a mirror free of impurity.[50] If we understand that everything originates with Śiva in a process of a descending vibration, the path to liberation can be grasped as an ascent of the person to an enlightened condition in which one is coequal with Śiva.

This ascent involves seven states (*sapta-pramātṛs*) that begin in the realm of dualistic reality to culminate with a nondualistic state. The lowest stage (*sakala*) finds the self captive to the three impurities and the five sheaths. By overcoming karma due to a dissolution of perception (*pralayākala*), the self is freed from rebirth and experiences an emptiness devoid of perception, although one is still in bondage to the other two major impurities. With the next stage (*vijñānākala*), only the very subtlest of impurities remain as one experiences distinct alternations between external awareness and a meditative internal awareness. Emerging from the realm of contradiction, one enters the pure path of mantra (word formula). With the expansion of a person's self-consciousness, it is possible to describe this condition as "I am I and this is this." Here one lucidly experiences Śiva, whereas experience of the world becomes lost to a person because one experiences the world as false and illusory as one approaches the threshold of liberation. Further awareness and insight enable one to grasp the world as an expansion of universal consciousness and not as false or illusory. This occurs at the fifth stage, called *mantreśvara* (lord of the mantras), because the objective universe is no longer obscured by the realization of the freed self, and one is able to state "this I am." The next stage of *mantra-maheśvara* (great lord of mantra) enables one to reach and experience the *sadāśiva tattva* and to find consciousness moving, vibrating, and sparkling within every object within the world. This suggests that the objective universe is gradually being experienced as consciousness. Finally, a person ascends to the level of *Śiva-tattva*, an experience of the limitless totality of God. A person's individual consciousness is now reunited with Śiva and devoid of any contraction, duality, or limitation. By means of such an experience, a person is now able to legitimately state "I am Śiva" as the objective world slips away, and one is assimilated into the consciousness of Śiva. At this point, a person's consciousness is free from all disturbances, and one attains a state of perfect purity of consciousness.[51] Even though one is still united to one's body, one is free from bondage and is a free jīvanmukti (one liberated while alive).

A Heroic Expression of Śaivism

According to the *Basava Purāṇa* of Pālkuriki Somanātha (c. thirteenth century), Basaveśvara (c. 1105–1167) was credited with founding the Vīraśaiva sect (literally, heroic Śaivas), who were also known as the Liṅgāyats (literally, wearers of the liṅga). A considerable body of hagiographical literature developed around the author Somanātha. But prior to that development, the *Basava Purāṇa* represented a hagiographical account of the life of Basaveśvara (also named Basava for short, or Basavaṇṇa) and the early followers of the movement. According to this account, Basava was an incarnation of Nandikeśvara, who the text insists was identical to Śiva and the vehicle of the god. The reason for the incarnation was the necessity of purifying the world.[52] As a young man, Basava refused the traditional Brahmanic initiation ceremony, an action that reflected the anti-Brahmanic position of the sect and an emphasis by the sect on interacting only with sect members.

Much in this hagiographical account is historically inaccurate, because the sect was already in existence before Basava appeared on the scene. The reliable information that we possess about Basava reflects his position as an officer of the treasury and his marriage to two women. We also know that he condemned in his preaching such things as magic, astrology, caste, untouchability, occupational inequalities, and superstition. Although there is no knowledge about the sect before the twelfth century, its theology and metaphysics suggest that it is a very ancient tradition.[53] Even though the religious system preexisted Basava, he used his political position and influence to aid the sect in its rise to prominence and to disseminate its doctrine.[54] Besides Basava, other members of the movement of importance were Prabudeva, who was also known as Allama Prabhu, and Cennabasava, a nephew of Basava. An important female saint was named Mahādēviyakka, a younger contemporary of Basava, who allegedly married a king only to eventually leave this mortal husband for her true love, Śiva. She wandered around naked except only for her hair that covered parts of her body, although she did claim to be clothed by the light of Śiva. Her writings reflect her pain at being separated from God, whom she called "lord white as jasmine," her erotic feelings toward God, and how her love for God drives her mad. Many legends also surrounded her life and the lives of the male saints of the movement.

Besides inspiration provided by the Śaiva poet-saints, the Āgamic texts, and narratives like the *Basava Purāṇa*, a primary text for this movement was the *Śūnyasaṁpādane* (fifteenth century).[55] The compositions in this text were called *vacanas* (what is said). These poetic creations embodied the dynamism stressed by the movement because they were opposed to the distinction between śruti (revelation or what is heard) and smṛti (what is received or remembered tradition) of classical Hinduism. These compositions stressed an active mode in contrast to the historically prior more static revelation and tradition.[56] The emphasis on the active mode of communication focused attention on an experience in the present moment; the Vīraśaivas were convinced that religion was not a spectator activity where one can passively watch what happens. Their way of religion involved an active participation by all members, which sometimes reached extreme expressions.

Many of the tales about sect members in the *Basava Purāṇa* manifest a proclivity toward violence that was directed toward outsiders, fellow devotees, and oneself. An early member of the movement named Allama Prabhu appeared before Basava in the form of a household deity. After the proper bows, Basava prepared a sumptuous meal that the deity consumed in a brief time. Undismayed by the voracious appetite of his guest, Basava offered himself as food to the deity.[57] Other Vīraśaiva devotees offered their heads or other bodily parts as sacrificial gifts to God in other episodes of heroic devotion.[58] This early emphasis generating and legitimizing violence places the sect within a long historical tradition of actual or symbolic violent activity in Hinduism, and it represents an attempt to organize the sect into a closed religious cult. But its early militancy waned at a later period, giving way to a validation of caste identities and the superiority of the Brahmin caste. Nonetheless, this expression of Śaivism represents a sectarian protest movement embodying elements of anticlericalism, anticonism, antiritualism, rejection of the notions of rebirth and caste, egalitarianism in spirit and emphasis on a strong work ethic.[59]

In their everyday religious practices, the Vīraśaivas disapprove of worship of what they call the *sthāvaraliṅga* or the liṅga consecrated in temples. They approve, however, of the *iṣṭaliṅga*, which is given to a devotee by his teacher (*guru*) at initiation. When a guru initiates each Vīraśaiva, regardless of sex or caste, he places the palm of his hand upon the head of the devotee. This is believed to impart the energy of Śiva into the body of the initiate, who is therefore believed to be reborn from the palm of the guru, who is now regarded as the father of the devotee. As part of the initiation, the guru also gives the devotee a liṅga that the devotee must carry around his or her neck all the time—except for five times a day, when the devotee takes the object and places it in the palm of the hand and worships it.

The basic reason for this distinction between the personal liṅga and that in the temple is that the sthāvaraliṅga is said to be the static form of the symbol of Śiva, whereas the iṣṭaliṅga is the dynamic aspect of it. Since the iṣṭaliṅga represents Śiva directly, it is the only form in which he is to be worshiped. Besides representing Śiva, the liṅga also symbolizes the devotee's soul, which is nondifferent from the divine. Moreover, the devotee must wear the iṣṭaliṅga as a public manifestation of his or her faith. The Vīraśaivas also believe in wearing *rudrākṣa* seeds, which also serve the purpose of counting beads during prayer. These seeds are believed to have originated from the eyes of Śiva.

As suggested by their distinction between different kinds of liṅgas, an important concept in the Vīraśaiva system is the opposition between standing (*sthāvara*) and moving (*jaṅgama*). The former describes an inanimate thing like a piece of property that does not move. The latter term describes a moving object, one that is not fixed to one place. Within the Vīraśaiva context, jaṅgama is applied to a person of a religious order, who is continually traveling and preaching. The jaṅgama is a religious mendicant who is free from worldly attachments, limiting adjuncts (*upādhis*), and the influence of impurities (*malams*). The sect makes no distinction between guru, liṅga, and jaṅgama.

Because the soul is subject to finite limitations, it does not recognize that it is the supreme being. This lack of awareness is due to the three impurities (*malams*). The Vīraśaiva notion of impurity is very different from that of orthodox Brahmanic Hinduism because the sect does not recognize forms of pollution associated with birth, female menstruation, death, saliva, defecation, and so forth. The first of the malams is built into the cosmos in a natural way (*ānava*) for the Vīraśaivas, suggesting its universal nature. It functions to reduce the power of the soul, so a person tends to experience objects as distinct from the self. The second impurity is māyā in the sense of perceiving differences between objects and not being able to discern their common features. It is also all-pervasive because the entire material and mental worlds originated from it. The Vīraśaiva notion of māyā represents a complex mixture of many elements: six instruments, six enemies (such as lust, avarice, delusion, envy), six misconceptions, six changes, six waves (such as hunger, thirst, sorrow, delusion, old age, death), ten objects, eight conceits, seven sources of attraction, five sources of pain, five sheaths, eight bonds, and three distresses.[60] A major consequence of this impurity is that the soul is limited in knowledge and tends to be deluded in its perception of external objects. The final impurity is karma (action), meaning that any action that we perform is tainted by this impurity. Overall, these impurities place limits on the power of the soul and keep it in a state of bondage.

For the soul to be liberated from these limitations, it must follow the six *sthalas*, a Sanskrit term meaning "place" or "ground."[61] Within the Vīraśaiva context the term refers to the stages or steps of devotion (*bhakti*), and there are many subsections to each of them. Before one can begin, there is a preliminary step to the path that involves belief in the distinctiveness of the soul from God, who is viewed as a personal deity. Once the initial step is taken, the belief in a personal God vanishes, although the conviction in the distinction between the soul and God is maintained.

The initial step is *bhaktasthala* or devotion to Śiva by means of supplicating the *ācāraliṇga*, an aspect of the liṅga, and greeting his saints. The next step is *mahēsvarasthala*, which is a move toward discipline. At this point the devotee dedicates all his or her deeds to Śiva. In the *prasādisthala* stage, the Vīraśaiva strictly observes all moral codes, and all the devotee's acts become actions of devotion to God. Once a devotee possesses a firm faith in Śiva enhanced by the initial two steps, that person is ready to received the gift of grace, which often manifests itself in a personal way by self-surrender and in the social realm by shared labor.[62] The devotee moves next to experience *prānaliṇgisthala*, which means to experience Śiva in all things. An excellent expression of this is the following poetic statement:

Everywhere you will find Him:
In minutest particles of dust,
  In the hard wood,
  Or tender blade of grass.
Everywhere He is![63]

Now, the soul of the devotee is purified of egoism, the five afflictions (*pañca-kleśas*, that is, ignorance, egoism, attachment to sense objects, passion, and hatred), and passions. The devotee's heart is also purified, one's senses are controlled, one is filled with compassion, and one begins to see the light of Śiva within oneself. At this point, the devotee surrenders to Śiva, in the *saranasthala* stage. Surrender manifests itself for the devotee in the loss of memory and awareness as well as the end of motion. With the manifestation of a condition analogous to death and the destruction of all symbols, the mind of the devotee is now lost in the liṅga. At this point, the devotee is unaware of the distinction between himself or herself and God. Finally, the devotee reaches the final step of complete unity (*aikkyasthala*). The devotee realizes at this point that he or she is the ultimate principle, having merged into the universal liṅga. With a process that began with the preliminary distinction between the soul and God, it ends with unity, which is known as the void (*bayalu*), being encompassed entirely by Śiva.

This path to liberation is also integrated with the everyday life of Vīraśaivas and their occupation. It is not necessary to renounce the world, from the perspective of the Vīraśaivas, because it is possible to attain liberation while one works within the world. This attitude is embodied in their notion of *kāyaka* (performance, work, labor, practice), which can be either ritual or occupational. The notion of kāyaka (labor) involves five central injunctions (*pañcācāras*), of which two are ritual and three are occupational. The initial ritual injunction is called *liṅgācāra*, which involves wearing and worshiping only one's personal liṅga (*iṣṭaliṅga*) that was given by one's guru at initiation. The second ritual injunction is to worship only Śiva (*śivācāra*) to the exclusion of all other divine beings. Since Śiva is real and forms the basis of the world, the world itself is real and not illusory, as in some branches of Hinduism. These two ritual injunctions represent a complete unity of belief and practice with respect to God. The final three injunctions are connected to the occupation of the devotee. By acting as a servant to one's society and fellow believers, the devotee serves God and community in a spirit of humility. Working, serving, and even fighting to defend the community of believers (*ganācāra*), because one believes that oneself and the members of the community are suffused with the power of Śiva, represent actions related to the second of the occupational injunctions. Finally, the devotee's dedicated labor in a chosen profession (*sadācāra*) represents the third occupational injunction. This injunction forbids such immoral and unethical acts as stealing, killing, lying, and anger, and it includes tolerance of others. These three occupational injunctions suggest that work is akin to a religious calling, but it presupposes that one chose an occupation that is morally and ethically proper. From the perspective of the Vīraśaiva community, work possesses both an individual dimension in the sense of being one's livelihood, but it also involves a social dimension that expresses itself in community projects and cooperation. Unlike the world renouncer of classical Hinduism, the work performed by a Vīraśaiva helps that person attain a blessed condition after death. The work that one performs in everyday life is not divorced from the religious path, and it can be enhanced by other aids that are readily accessible to all Vīraśaivas. Even though the Vīraśaiva movement represents a protest movement that is anticlerical, anticonist, anti-ritualistic, and a significant socioreligious change, its emphasis on the importance of work possesses continuity with the importance of action and duty at least from the time of the composition of the *Bhagavad Gītā*.

Besides such aids to faith as the guru, liṅga, moving religious figures (*jaṅgama*) who are teaching, and preaching the faith to others (although today these teachers tend to be priestly figures who are more stationary), the individual Vīraśaiva can also use other resources such as drinking the holy water (*pādodaka*) made sacred from contact with the feet or other bodily part of the guru, in order to purify body and mind. Another aid to faith is consecrated food (*prasāda*). This is food a devotee initially offers to a guru, who returns it to the devotee after touching it and thereby making it holy by his touch. In addition to wearing the personal liṅga (*iṣṭaliṅga*), a devotee can wear the rudrākṣa seeds or beads sacred to God around different parts of the anatomy. They can serve a double purpose by functioning as beads by which to keep track of one's prayers, similar to a Roman Catholic rosary or string of Tibetan Buddhist prayer beads. Another item that one can wear is sacred ash (*vibhūti*), whose connection to and importance for Śiva has been discussed. A final aid to faith is the sacred five-syllable mantra: "Śivāya nāmaḥ," called the six-lettered mantra (*ṣaḍakṣara*) when the syllable OM is added to it.[64]

A Vīraśaiva named Śrīpati in his work the *Śrīkara Bhāṣya*, which is a commentary on the classical *Vedānta Sūtras*, developed a theological system more akin to the Vedānta school. The author argues that there is no difference between Śiva and the self, although each is qualified by Śakti. Consequently, the individual soul (*jīva*) is the body of God in a system called Śaktiviśiṣṭādvaita, a qualified nondualism of Śakti, and a creative principle residing in the eternal Śiva. This system is more akin in spirit and position to the system of Rāmānuja than that of Śaṅkara. In a line of argument reminiscent of the Kashmir Śaiva school, everything issues forth from Śakti at the dawn of creation and returns to it at the end of time. In his system, Śrīpati identifies devotion (*bhakti*) with the Śakti of Śiva. This theological system has not won wide spread acceptance within the Vīraśaiva community, which is heavily concentrated in the Indian state of Karnataka. Overall, the Vīraśaiva movement can be viewed as a blending of the Kannada regional elements of *marga* (an elitist, minority cultural pattern) with *desi* (a localized, popular cultural pattern) along with a selective tension between these two traditions.[65] Thus the movement manifests abstract philosophy/theology with an emphasis on such notions as human freedom, equality, rationality, and brotherhood.

Ritual and Festive Expressions of Śaivism

We started this chapter by passing through the gopuram of the Chidambaram temple and witnessing the figures in various dancing postures on the inner walls. But we mentioned nothing about the daily ritual that takes place within this temple or many others. There is a rhythm to the ritual practices akin to the dance of Śiva and the time kept by the drum in his upper right hand.

The Hindu year is divided into two parts: an auspicious and inauspicious division. The initial half of the year begins with the winter solstice called the *uttarāyaṇa*, which is referred to as the God's day. The second division begins with the summer solstice, and it is called the *dakṣiṇāyana* or God's night. Since Āti, for instance, is the first month of the inauspicious half of the year, no happy or auspicious events like marriages or life-cycle rituals should be performed then. New ventures should not be started because they will probably have negative consequences. But time is more complicated than indicated by this simple division. There are also lunar and solar distinctions of time along, with ages (*yugas*), days of the week, and times of the day. Thus a single cycle of time operates within another and alongside other cycles of time, a system that can be called "concentric cyclicality."[66] Within the context of daily worship in many Śaiva temples, there are periods of time that are considered sacred and other times that are considered dangerous. The latter period falls at night, which symbolizes cosmic darkness, and is generally a period of inactivity. The sacred time begins after midnight and before the predawn hours. Dawn (between 4:00 to 6:00 A.M.) marks a very significant period because it is associated with the initial pūjā (worship) of the day and the awakening of the sleeping deity. This is followed by four additional daytime periods that are intended to flow according to the dynamic nature of the cosmos. These are daybreak (approximately 6:30 to 7:15 A.M.), middle time (7:30 to 9:00 A.M.), mid-morning (10:00 A.M.) and noon, which represents the zenith of the daily time periods and ritual observances. The three evening time periods are evening (4:30 to 6:30 P.M.), junction (7:30 to 9:30 P.M.) and half-night (9:45 to 10:30 P.M.). The ritual of the bedchamber, at which time the deity is put to rest, marks the final evening time period, and the ritual day ends.[67] Rituals must be punctually performed during the various appropriate time periods.

In the Chidambaram temple, for instance, the day begins with an elaborate pūjā (worship) ceremony announced by reed horns and drums. An image of the feet of the deity is removed from a room where it spent the night with an image of the goddess. The image of the feet is tied and taken on a palanquin to the eastern side of the Cit Sabhā (hall of consciousness) section of the temple complex. After the doors are closed, a priest offers a breakfast of milk. Later a fire sacrifice takes place at around 8:00 A.M., and at 9:00 A.M. bathing of the crystal liṅga begins. The waving of camphor lamps before the deity follows this. After a second bathing of the crystal liṅga, the four-inch-high ruby Naṭarāja is bathed with water, honey, and sandal paste water. The camphor light is shown five times in such a way that light shines through the red stone. The evening set of rites begins around 7:00 P.M., which is marked by the highlight of singing poems of the Tēvāram saints.[68]

This pattern of worship presumes certain cosmological notions to which the ritual conforms, and there are specific preliminary actions that must be executed by the performer of the rite. The basic cosmological presupposition based on their philosophical and theological position is that the Śaiva universe oscillates by emerging and disappearing. The cosmos oscillates between periods of creation and destruction, evolution and involution, and expansion and contraction.[69] As evident in the pattern of daily ritual, there are moments of activity and others of quietude. As a Śaiva performs his or her daily worship, he or she reenacts these cosmic motions and becomes involved in a creative action similar to the animation of the cosmos by Śiva. Just as the cosmos is ever in flux between the rhythms of emission from God and reabsorption into God, the worship follows the flow of this divine rhythm, much like a cosmic dance. The former rhythm moves from unity to differentiation, whereas the latter reintegrates the many, gross, and different into a unity.

But before one can take part in this oscillating dance of the cosmos, the worshiper must purify oneself by directing mantras (sacred utterances) onto one's hands and rubbing them together to consume their impurities in order to transform them into the hands of Śiva. The fundamental symbolism revolves around the worshiper becoming God, because in Śaiva theology a person must become God in order to worship him. In other words, it is a basic belief that only Śiva can truly worship Śiva. This is made possible by the power of the holy mantras that are not only effective instruments by which God acts in the world but are also considered the body of Śiva. By means of the mantras, the worshiper purifies his or her gross and subtle bodies, and assumes a divine body created by the power inherent with the mantras.[70] The worshiper is now ready to perform a series of services connected to a typical pūjā ceremony. While the worshiper takes on the body of god, Śiva assumes the body of the liṅga for the purposes of worship. Needless to say, only a person in a purified condition may approach the liṅga.

A purified worshiper is categorized as a *mumukṣu* (a person who seeks liberation), whereas the Āgamic texts classify a nonpurified worshiper as *bubhukṣu* (a person who desires worldly enjoyments). The goal of the first type of person is liberation (*mokṣa*) or a going to Śiva, while the goal of the second type of person is worldly enjoyment (*bhoga*) or a going forth from Śiva, which reflects the cosmic oscillation between absorption and emission. It is only the first type of person who can approach the consecrated liṅga in the temple, whereas anyone can approach the anthropomorphic image of Śiva on the temple walls or pillars. Again, we can witness another basic distinction between the gross images of the god around the outside of the temple and the more pure and subtle image enclosed within the inner sanctum or garbhagṛha (womb-room). This distinction between inner and outer parts of the temple suggests that the temple itself represents the oscillation of emission from and reabsorption back into Śiva that we noted with the flow of daily ritual. In a sense, when one enters the temple one is being absorbed into Śiva, according to the symbolism of the Āgamic texts and Śaiva Siddhānta theology.

Within his temple, Śiva resides with his consort as a royal couple. On festival occasions, they journey forth into the public realm in order to give their subjects an opportunity to view them and for them to see their loyal subjects. The most auspicious religious festival on the Śaiva religious calendar is the Śivarātri (Śiva's night) that is celebrated on the fourteenth lunar day during the dark half of the month of Phālguṇa (February–March), representing the last month of the lunar year and point of mediation between the years. With the moon waning (symbolically dying), this is a transition period that links to the rebirth of the moon. There is a legend associated with the festival that tells of a hunter of evil character who mocked and imitated some Śaiva devotees performing worship. By uttering God's name, some of his sins were removed. Since his hunting exploits were unsuccessful that day, this lack of success resulted in his involuntary fast. At night, he climbed a tree sacred to Śiva to protect himself from carnivorous animals, but he was unable to sleep and kept an involuntary vigil. While sitting in the tree, he accidentally dislodged some wet *bel* leaves that fell on a liṅga. This series of involuntary actions released him from his negative karmic past and enabled him to enter Kailāsa, the heavenly abode of Śiva.[71] The major religious activities of the festival at the present time include fasting during the entire day, holding a vigil, worshiping the liṅga with offerings of flowers and bel leaves during the night, a purifying bath for the devotee, reciting mantras, and reciting Śiva's many names. All of these actions have symbolic significance that reflects the legend connected to the festival.

The nighttime is especially sacred to Śiva because it is a time in which he comes into the world for the purposes of worship and to dance with ghoulish figures. The night-time possesses spiritual significance for the devotee in the sense that it represents a time to withdraw the senses, withdraw the mind into the soul, and surrender the soul to God. The vigil is symbolic of the cultivation by the devotee of one's inner wakefulness, which includes an opening of the mind to the descent of God into the human being, while fasting promotes control of the senses.[72] These symbolic features point to liberation of the devotee and union with Śiva on his sacred mountain. But the religious practices associated with the festival can also lead to reaching mundane goals during one's lifetime. In some areas of India, Śivarātri is less of a festival and manifests more the features of a religious vow (*vrata*) or duty.[73] Another Śaiva festival commemorates the destruction of the triple city of demons by Śiva with a single arrow in mythical time. This festival is called the Tripurī Pūrṇimā, and it is observed on the full moon of the month of Kārttika (October–November). Besides bathing, this festival includes giving gifts of lamps to Brahmins. At sunset, the lamps are lighted in homes and temples to burn through the night.

Tiruvadirai, a festival recalling Śiva's adventures in the Pine Forest and his seduction of the wives of the sages, who were convinced that they had conquered their lustfulness only to become madly infatuated with the naked ascetic-deity, is widely celebrated throughout Tamilnadu during the month of Mārkaḻi (December–January). Because this is the time of the winter solstice, when the sun reaches its greatest distance from the earth, it is widely considered a dangerous time. A major feature of this festival that is popular among unmarried Brahmin females is the worship of Naṭarāja in order to win him as their husband.[74] Besides a flag-raising ceremony that signifies the kingship of the deity, a unique feature of this festival is the public procession of a beautiful image of Śiva as the Beggar (Piṭcāṭnaṉ) on the eighth day at the middle of the afternoon. On the morning of the ninth day, the genuine images of the divine consorts are taken from the inner sanctum of the Chidambaram temple, instead of a substitute festival image (*utsava mūrti*), and pulled by many on a chariot through the streets. The final day concludes with what is for many devotees the most holy moment of the year when the images are elaborately bathed after 4:00 A.M. with ten golden pots of different substances. This culminates with water from the Ganges River that is poured over the images, a bath akin to a royal coronation.[75]

A different type of regional cult observance is called Vīrabhadrudi sambaram (the nocturnal procession of Vīrabhadrudi, a terrifying deity born from Śiva's rage), in the coastal region of Andhra Pradesh. The focus of this religious observance is a pilgrimage of disgruntled dead that have died in infancy or childhood. It is "a defiant dance of death, a boisterous overnight pilgrimage, and a solemn celebration of renewal by a wider family that includes deceased children among its vital and active members."[76] This rite can be performed in conjunction with the Śivarātri festival. The procession includes red cloth banners (a favorite color of Śiva) to add beauty. A young male hero (*vīra*) is dressed, usually, in bright red or olive green, carries a trident, gyrates, and imitates a cobra. As the groups march, the bodies of the marchers become vehicles for departed spirits that can communicate through the marchers by possessing them and expressing their wishes or states of mind. Those who are possessed by the departed spirits of children become *gaṇacārīs*, parts of Śiva's ghoulish entourage. As some of the marchers are possessed, they experience an ascent and become uncontrollable. In order to bring them down to earth, ritualists use incense, drum beats, and fresh lime juice that is poured on the head of the possessed in order to cool them of the heat associated with their condition. After the cooling lime juice is used, the halves of the severed lime are thrown away in opposite directions. The procession proceeds toward a river where family members bathe, in addition to washing and then drying ash-fruits, which are symbolic of the deceased child. These ash-fruits are made of the ashes of cow-dung mixed with acacia gum and pressed by members of the potter caste into molded cones with rounded tops; they represent the remnants of a previous existence and seeds of new creation. In the final action of the ritual, yellow turmeric powder is applied to three of the ash fruits.[77]

Change and Continuity

The themes of dance, asceticism, and androgyny run throughout the narrative associated with the mythological biography of Śiva. These themes are also reflected in the religious behavior, hagiographical literature, and symbolism connected to Śaiva ascetics, saints, religious thinkers, and ordinary devotees. Śaiva ascetics imitate and enact in their lives their vision of the ascetic Śiva. This is a way for them to participate in God. The poet-saints used the emotions evoked by their personal experience and poetry to evoke the notion of participating in Śiva, whereas the various sectarian and theological/philosophical movements use their creative emotional outpourings and intellectual constructions to participate in Śiva. It is also possible to witness this type of active participation in Śaiva temples, ritual, and festive activity. These features of their religiosity give worshipers an opportunity to emotionally experience God, see God, and re-enact in festivals mythical events associated with the deity and to thus share in the narrative of Śiva.

By tracing many of the highlights of the mythology of Śiva and the god's connection to earlier divine figures, it was possible to demonstrate the development of this deity and his continuity with vedic figures. Asceticism is an ancient form of practice in India that predates the rise of sectarian Śaivism as it is known today.

Śaiva ascetics continue the use of this ancient practice, but they alter it to conform to the paradigm of their own deity. The poet-saints and various Śaiva sectarian movements embodied the spirit of asceticism to varying degrees with their emphasis on wandering, pilgrimage, and paths to liberation. The practices of purification and fasting associated with rituals and festivals performed by priests and ordinary devotees echo the spirit of asceticism connected to Śaivism. The same can be said to a degree about the theme of dance. The pilgrimages of the poet-saints represent a kind of dance. The oscillating universe of Śaiva Siddhānta thinkers and ritual practitioners, the vibrating universe of Kashmir Śaivas, and the emphasis on motion in Vīraśaivism are all evidence of the rhythmic motion associated with dance. Moreover, Śaiva festivals are a time for the life-affirming action of dance.

And since Śiva is an androgynous deity, it is to be expected that we would find this an important theme among his devotees. The Nātha-Yogins view the human body as a microcosm of the androgynous macrocosm, which means that human beings are essentially androgynous. It is yogic practice that transforms a fragmented condition and potentiality of completeness into a reality and an awareness of the true nature of the macrocosm (Śiva/Śakti). This is also true for Kashmir Śaivas and to a lesser extent for Vīraśaivas. Moreover, the poet-saints often viewed their personal relationship to Śiva in terms of a potentially androgynous condition in which the feminine soul seeks union with the male principle. Once this occurs, the soul, which is often conceived as a bride seeking a bridegroom, becomes complete and androgynous.

In retrospect, the development of devotional religion in India represented an important change with respect to language because the move from classical Sanskrit to such regional languages as Tamil and Kannada (evident among the Vīraśaivas), opened the door for common people to have access to the literary tradition to a greater extent than possible in the Sanskrit tradition dominated by an educated clergy. But the theological works of the Śaiva Siddhānta, Kashmir Śaiva, and Vīraśaiva thinkers returned to Sanskrit and maintained a connection to a more prestigious tradition through the language.

11

Feminine Thread

Like other major world religions, Hinduism has been hierarchical and male-dominated from ancient times. Ironically, there has also been a strong presence of female deities from ancient times to the present. Although many of these goddesses are mentioned in books of this kind women are often neglected and treated as if they never existed. And although males have dominated the written tradition of the religion, women have always played an important and even essential role in the religion. Women have been ordinary practitioners, teachers, religious leaders, and even saints revered by both genders. By examining temple inscriptions from the Cōḻa period (850–1300 C.E.) in the Tamil area of south India, for instance, it is possible to find evidence that wealthy women gave money to endow the temples and patronize rituals.[1] Thus support for religious institutions and activities was not simply a male prerogative.

The Tradition of Goddesses

In some sense the feminine thread that runs throughout the Hindu religious tradition begins in the vedic period. There is a tendency among some scholars and Hindus to claim that all goddesses are manifestations of a single underlying feminine principle or a single great Goddess. But any review and comparison of their mythical biographies can cause a reader to conclude that they are really very different from each other. In comparison to male figures, goddesses played minor roles in vedic religion. Nonetheless, the role of goddesses is not without significance even then, and they certainly played an important role as consorts of male figures and as more independent deities within the context of sectarian Hinduism. As we trace the thread of goddesses in this chapter, we will not include a discussion of goddesses that play an important role in major sectarian movements because those goddesses were already discussed or will be examined in the following chapters.

During the vedic period, there were three goddesses renowned for the speed of their actions: Saraṇyū, Saramā, and Sarasvatī. Saraṇyū was the daughter of Tvaṣṭṛ, a god famous for fashioning the cosmos and all living beings. Rushing from her father into creation, she hurried forth and married Vivasvat, the Radiant (RV 10.17.1) with whom she conceived twins named Yama and Yamī. She also gave birth to the Aśvins, who were savior figures on the earth and in heaven. Saraṇyū had a brother with three heads who functioned as her opposite. He retained power for himself, did not communicate, did not create, and deprived the cosmos of sustenance for its existence (RV 10.8.8–9). Eventually, Indra defeated the brother.

In contrast to Saraṇyū, Saramā is described very differently as the mother of the Sarameyas, two dogs of varied color. Thus Saramā became known as the bitch of the gods. She functions as a messenger of Indra, and she is credited with finding the cows and light of the primeval fire priests, the Angirases, that were stolen by the Paṇis, demonic robbers. She is able to find the cave where the precious items are hidden by crossing the formidable Rasā, a river that flows around the heavenly sphere (RV 9.41.6), by following the path of cosmic order (*ṛta*). By restoring light to the world and showing Indra the location of the cows, Saramā functions as a savior figure. Her two sons, who are messengers of Yama, Lord of the Dead, represent the dangerous side of this goddess because these four-eyed sons steal life (RV 10.14.10–12).

A third swift goddess is Sarasvatī, who is identified as one of the seven sisters (RV 6.36.10) and one of the seven celestial rivers that course through the triple cosmos (RV 6.61.10). In addition, she is a river on earth, which is invoked to give intuitive insight, over which she rules (RV 1.3.12).

Pṛthivī and Aditi are more clearly maternal in nature. The former is identified with the earth, and she is mostly connected in the vedic hymns with Dyaus, sky god. Together they function as universal parents of the world and the divine beings (1.159, 185). Pṛthivī is described as firm and as the support of all things (RV 1.185). There is a hymn dedicated to her in the *Atharva Veda* (12.1), where she appears as the consort of Indra, and the veda stresses her fertility as a source for plants, crops, and her nursing of all living things. Pṛthivī shares motherhood with Aditi, who is mother to the Ādityas, a group of seven or eight deities (RV 2.27.1) and of Indra. She is associated with or identified as a cow that provides nourishment. As the cosmic cow, her milk is akin to Soma (RV 1.153.3). Moreover, she is called boundless, free, and remover of hindrances for humans. Conversely, she also binds people. Within her lap are located being and nonbeing (RV 10.5.7).

Another vedic goddess is Vāc, whose name means speech, voice, or word. She inspires the vedic seers and bestows vision. She proves to be indispensable within the context of ritual and cult because of her powers to enable people to hear, see, understand, and verbally express things. In addition, she is given credit for sustaining Soma (RV 10.125).

In contrast to the visionary powers of Vāc, there are two goddesses that are symbolically associated with darkness: Nirṛti and Rātrī. The former is equated with death, bad luck, and destruction (RV 10.59). The generally more benign Rātrī is mostly associated with the night. Due to this association with darkness, people ask her for comfort, security, and give her thanks for providing rest for all creatures.

The darkness connected to these goddesses is countered by Uṣas, who is identified with the dawn. This virgin daughter of heaven is depicted as a young maiden who is pulled by a hundred chariots (RV 1.48). When she arrives each morning she drives away darkness (RV 6.64). She is also connected to the cosmic law (*ṛta*), like Saramā, and like Aditi she is compared to a cow and called mother of cows (RV 3.58). She also functions as the eye of the gods because she can see the actions of people (RV 7.75). But there is also a darker side to her nature, as the skilled huntress and mistress of time. In this role, she wastes away the lives of people, and she awakens the living, although she lets the dead sleep.

In contrast to these vedic goddesses and later ones that are closely identified with male deities such as Śrī Lakṣmī, Rādhā, and Pārvatī, the goddess Durgā begins to emerge around the fourth century; images of her killing the buffalo demon appear around the sixth century. She probably originated among indigenous, non-Aryan cultures of India because there is nothing similar to her in vedic literature.[2] The best known of several mythical accounts of her origin depicts her defeating the demon Mahiṣa, who had received a boon that he would be invincible to all opponents, with the exception of a woman. In order to defeat the victorious demon, the gods created a mass of light that became a beautiful woman and armed her with weapons. Once on the battlefield, Durgā creates ferocious helpers like Kālī and the seven Mātṛkās (Mothers). Although Durgā's beauty is seductive and fools the demon into believing that he can easily defeat her, her appearance is not intended to attract a male. It rather serves to entice the demon into a fatal encounter in which she is victorious; her power is not compromised by drinking wine to such an excessive extent that her eyes turn red and she laughs uncontrollably. Her military actions are part of the periodic destruction of the cosmos, which she also creates and maintains, according to the *Devimāhātmya* (12.33–35). Her beauty is offset by her ferocious nature, symbolized by the lion that functions as her vehicle and combat assistant.

Another goddess depicted riding a lion is Śerānvālī from northwest India. She is said to assume the form of wind when she possesses women. Although possession by an evil spirit is viewed as an affliction or punishment, possession by the goddess is perceived as a gift of grace.[3] When the goddess enters a woman her hair flies freely, her eyes become glazed, her voice changes, and her head whirls, tossing her around wildly as if taken by the wind. A woman must be pure to become a vehicle of the goddess by not eating meat, drinking liquor, or being unchaste. Ordinary people interpret the possession of a woman as a form of play by which the goddess speaks through a person in order to assist devotees and reveal her power (*śakti*), the fruit of karma, mental impressions from a previous life, or a devotional reward.[4]

Other modern goddesses reign over a specific location, as Kāmākṣī does over the city of Kāñcipuram, which is considered one of India's seven sacred cities and the only one of the group that is located in the southern part of the country. According to the *Brahmānda Purāṇa* (4.5.40.10–16), Śiva sends Pārvatī to the city of Kāñci to propitiate Kāmākṣī for an unintended transgression involving closing his eyes, which plunges the cosmos into darkness. In another myth, Kāmākṣī assists Śiva rid himself of the curse of brahminicide connected to his beheading of the god Brahmā with his fingernail, to which the god's head becomes stuck (4.5.40.52–86). In addition to her association to Śiva, Kāmākṣī is also connected to the arch protagonist of the deity in the form of Kāma, god of desire and arch-enemy of the ascetic Śiva—she restores Kāma to life after he is reduced to ashes by Śiva (4.4.30.35–55). Kāma therefore acknowledges himself as the son of the goddess. By means of her close association with Kāma, she acquires some of his attributes, which can be witnessed by her icon in her temple in Kāñcipuram that depicts her holding a sugarcane bow and five flower-arrows, respectively, in her lower left and right hands, whereas she holds, respectively, a noose and goad in her upper left and right hands.

While Kāmākṣī still reigns today over her city, other goddesses continue to come into existence. An excellent example of such a figure is Santoṣī Mā, whose worship spread rapidly in northern India in the 1960s as temples were dedicated to her. In 1975, her cult received a large impetus with the release of the Hindi film *Jay Santoṣī Mā*. Information about her comes from popular pamphlets that inform a reader that she is the daughter of the elephant-headed god Gaṇeśa and his wife Riddhi-Siddhi. Being benevolent when pleased and fierce and destructive when displeased, she is the center of rituals connected to fasts and vows (*vrats*) performed on Fridays. Her rapid rise to prominence in the popular imagination is a good example of continuity within the Hindu goddess tradition.

What many of these goddess figures share in common is the feminine power of śakti. In many cases, male deities need the feminine power of śakti in order to become effective, empowered, and energetic. As we will see shortly, the large number of goddess figures in the Hindu religious tradition does not mean that the lives of ordinary women is exalted in terms of cultural influence and prestige. Some goddesses are subservient to male figures, whereas other goddesses are independent. Of the goddesses discussed in this chapter, Durgā is a perfect example that violates the feminine model for an ordinary Hindu woman because she lacks submissiveness, is not subordinate to a male, and does not perform household chores. She instead excels at a male occupation of being a warrior. As we will see, Durgā thus presents a model of the feminine that challenges the stereotypical view of women.[5] Of course, other goddesses serve as models for the subservient and submissive spouse, such as Śrī Lakṣmī, Pārvatī, or Sītā. As evident from some of the examples of goddesses in ancient vedic culture, some goddesses identified as mothers are equated with the cow. The cow-mother becomes a cultural ideal of the feminine because she plays the role of the giver of milk and functions in a nonerotic, nonthreatening way.[6]

Women during the Ancient Period

The social characteristics of the vedic period include its patriarchal nature, its ethnic emphasis, its family-oriented society, and its life-affirming aspect. The goals of life revolved around personal desires for progeny, prosperity, and longevity, and the preservation of male dominance and Aryan identity. As wives and mothers, women played an import role in meeting these goals. Thus a woman's role was directly related to the maintenance of the social and cosmic order.

Vedic hymns included praise for a maiden's youthful beauty, appealing adornment, sweet odor, ample hips, and broad thighs. Such references suggest an interest in feminine sensuality and childbearing capacity. A *Rig Veda* text (10.85ff.) includes a prayer to Viśvāvasu, who protected the transfer of virgins from the natal family to that of the new marital family, where the bride is called fortunate and auspicious. Besides mention of the bride's ornaments, prayers are recited for the couple's good fortune, the attainment of old age together, prosperity, progeny, and unity of hearts. The bride is given practical advice, such as refraining from anger or not being hostile to her husband. Other sage advice included being tender, amiable, a mother of males, devoted to the gods, and bestower of happiness.

From ancient times, domestic and public rituals emphasized the co-presence of husband and wife. In short, they formed a ritual team. Since vedic priests presupposed that deities were receptive to families, they believed that the presence of a wife was necessary for the presence of gods at a rite. Likewise, a home was considered auspicious only with the presence of a husband and wife. There were, however, sacrifices performed only by women, like the Rudrabali performed to insure the fertility of cattle, the Rudrayaya sacrifice to secure good husbands for their daughters, and the Sītā harvest festival. In addition, women trained in music sang *Sāma Veda* hymns. Some vedic hymns described women engaged in priestly activities. The woman Ghosā invoked the twin sun gods on behalf of the people (RV 10.39), whereas Apālā was depicted harvesting the Soma plant, pressing it, and offering it to Indra (RV 8.80). When conducting a ceremony herself, Viśavavārā invoked and offered a sacrifice to Agni (RV 5.28).

The ritual actions of such women can be understood within the context of the necessity for the presence and participation of a wife that was required of all solemn ritual because a wife was called the "back half of the ritual" (ŚB 1.3.1.12). Another ancient text stated that a wife is half of a man (BŚS 29.9). From the location of the householder's fire at a sacrifice, this is called the navel of the wife, home base of the ritual, and the place to which it returns at the conclusion. From this place, the wife recites mantras (sacred formulas). Previous to these recitations, she undergoes a symbolic initiation similar to that of her husband. An especially important role played by a wife is her injection of sexuality into the ritual cosmos.[7]

In comparison to her husband, a wife's ritual activities were circumscribed. If a wife was menstruating, she would be excluded from a rite due to fear associated with pollution directly connected with blood. Generally speaking, independent female ritual action was forbidden. However, some domestic ritual texts allow a wife to offer daily offerings in the domestic fire, whereas other authorities prohibit it. But the important thing was that women were ritually necessary partners.

Although there were a few exceptions, with some women composing Rig Vedic hymns, women were not granted extensive education. Moreover, the lack of female educational opportunities led to increasing differentiation of sexual roles. Even though this pattern was to increase over time, a few female exceptions were scholars, poets, and teachers. In fact, upper-class women could partake of the rite of initiation (*upanayana*) during the formative stages of Indian culture.

The Upaniṣads present evidence of learned women. The sage Yājñavalkya had, for instance, two wives. The first is described as possessing the inferior knowledge of a woman, whereas the second wife, named Maitreyī, gives discourses on the knowledge of the highest reality. When the sage renounces the world he agrees to split his wealth between his two wives, but the second, wiser one rejects his offer because she wants to attain immortality (BĀU 2.4.2–3), serving as a paradigm for those seeking the highest goal and detachment from the traps of the world. Later in the same text, the sage Yājñavalkya encounters a self-confident woman named Gārgī (BĀU 3.6, 8), who persistently presses the sage for a perspicacious definition of reality. It is unusual to discover a woman challenging an authoritative male sage over issues of knowledge, where males are traditionally depicted as the preeminent custodians of knowledge in the culture.

Importance of Marriage

Marriage was such an important social institution that the early vedic deity Aryaman, a guardian of custom and culture, protected it. In the *Laws of Manu* (3.27–34), eight types of marriage are identified. When a father gives a daughter as a gift to a groom, this is called the Brāhma rite. The gift of a daughter to a priest represented the Daiva rite, whereas the gift of a maiden upon receipt from the groom of two oxen was the Ārṣa rite. The Prājāpatya rule involved the gift of a maiden with a verbal agreement to practice the dharma together. If a maiden is voluntarily given to someone who has given wealth to her relatives and the maiden, this transaction is called an Āsura rite. A Gāndharva rite involved a mutual union based on desire of two people. The Rākṣasa rule represented a forcible abduction of a maiden, while the Paiśāca rule reflected a man approaching a woman secretly when she was asleep, intoxicated, or inattentive. Each of these types of marriage was indicative of a type of exchange in ancient India, and it meant that a woman was a piece of property.

Traditionally, Hindus have identified three basic goals of marriage. The first was related to dharma (religious duty). Marriage was considered a sacrament, and it became by default the initiation ceremony for women into adulthood. The second goal of marriage was the creation of progeny. This was essentially tied to the necessity of a male heir to perform the funeral riles that ensured the salvation of the parents. Finally, the last (and least important) goal of marriage is pleasure (*rati*). Thus religious reasons took precedent over personal reasons for marriage. In short, marriage was a religious duty.

A player who was often neglected with respect to marriage in ancient India was the father. After the menarche of his daughter, a father had from three months to three years to find her a husband. Since the daughter was menstruating and not having her eggs fertilized, the father was technically guilty of embryo murder (BDhS 4.1.11) Moreover, each wasted menstrual period of a virgin represented the loss of a potential son.[8]

After the wedding ceremony, a man and a woman formed a religious team because they acted in unison during domestic religious rites. Thereby, they received their religious rewards together, although a wife could not act independently of her husband in the realm of ritual action. The team-like nature of a marriage was evident with respect to the three debts of every man. These three cultural debts and their means of payment were the following: a debt to the sages, paid by studentship; a debt to the gods, paid by performing sacrifices; and a debt to the fathers (ancestors), paid by having sons. What was important for women about these three debts was that they were absolutely necessary if a man was to repay two of these debts: to the gods and fathers. Therefore, the goal of a woman's life was to get married and to have sons—becoming a wife was the dharmic duty and destiny of a woman.

Within the context of the ritual practices of vedic culture, a wife played an essential role because she dynamically completed her husband; only married males could perform sacrifices and aspire to heavenly immortality. An unmarried male was an incomplete religious person, and male became a full ritual person after his marriage, which was a status that he owed to his wife. Because they were ritual partners and actors, women became elevated in status. Nonetheless, the heavenly aspirations of women were tied to their status as wives of their heaven-destined husbands. This interconnected spousal destiny was symbolized within the context of the Soma sacrifice, when the husband and wife symbolically climbed the sacrificial post that connected heaven and earth. In summary, women were not independent ritual actors. But it was not impossible for them to attain heaven as wives.

A vital cultural role played by women was in the quest for immortality (*amṛta*). It can also mean the quest for vitality or vital energy, as well as referring to things that sustain and promote a full and prosperous life, including such items as food, drink, cattle, and medicine.[9] There is a close connection between the quest for immortality and a long and full life (*āyus*). The *Śatapata Brāhmaṇa* (10.2.6.7–9) views long life as a visible sign that a person is destined to become immortal, with the sentiment that a life of a hundred years makes for heaven.

The major means for a wife to serve as an instrument of immortality was to give her husband sons. Members of vedic culture were convinced that a son was a physical and ritual continuation of the father and served as the father's biological immortality. A vedic hymn (RV 4.4.10) asked the god Agni for children in order to attain immortality. Thus, despite the inevitable death of the male parent, the father and his biological family line of descent continued into the future. The son replaced the deceased father as the ritual and economic head of the family. In this way, the father survived biologically through his son and thus survived his own death. For her essential role in this scenario, a wife was called the completion of her husband.

From the perspective of sexuality, a husband engaged in sexual congress with his wife in order to be born again from her in the form of the son. Within the context of this sexual pattern, a husband could correctly view his wife as both the mother of his son and his own mother because she gave birth to the husband in the form of her son. This pattern can be explained partially by ancient speculation about the nature of semen and its equation of father and son. Since a man's sperm represented his essence, a man literally replicated himself by means of his production of sperm. It was as if the sperm represented an embryonic form of the male that he carried within himself. By depositing his semen into the womb of his wife, a husband experienced his first birth by giving birth to himself. The second birth occurred when a wife gave birth to a son. The husband's sexual act of ejaculation of semen is accompanied by an experience of bliss, whereas his wife plays a passive and instrumental role by serving as the symbolic fertile field in which the seed is planted.

In the north Indian village of Pahansu and elsewhere in this region, marriage is conceived as the "gift of a virgin." This gift removes evil (*pāp* and danger, *sankat*) from the family of the donor. If a daughter remains in the house of her parents after she begins to menstruate, this creates a dangerous situation that could lead to misfortune and inauspiciousness. By bestowing the gift of a virgin on another family, the wife-giver transfers inauspiciousness to the home of the groom.[10] We will consider other implications of the transfer of a virgin shortly.

Women and the Legal Tradition

Upper-caste women enjoyed a higher status in the vedic period than they did afterward. The period that saw the advent of legal texts like the *Manusmṛti* (Laws of Manu) witnessed the lowering of the status of women and restriction of their creative freedom. Women were forbidden, for instance, the right to study vedic literature, which rendered sacred knowledge the sole possession of men. From a religious perspective, a woman was considered equivalent to a member of the Śūdra caste. The cultural context for this low-caste status for women was tied to their monthly menstrual cycle, which rendered them polluted, making them untouchable during four days of every month. Increasingly, women were viewed as in general impure due to the polluting nature of blood associated with menstruation and also pregnancy.[11] This low social status had important social consequences for a woman; for example, she could not eat with her husband due to her polluting condition. In fact, it was considered meritorious if she ate only his leftovers after the meal. During her menstrual period, a woman could not cook, bathe, decorate her body, or have sexual relations with her husband. The lower social status of women also had religious consequences because they were excluded from the initiation ceremony and reciting of sacred mantras. The lower status of a woman was reflected in the cultural expectation that she was to be subordinate throughout her life. As a young girl she was under the control of her parents, as a wife she was subordinate to her husband, and as a widow she deferred to her sons.

This dramatic change in social status for women was actually foreshadowed and shaped by negative attitudes toward women even in the vedic literature. The mind of a woman was described as uncontrollable (RV 8.33.7). Since women have hearts of hyenas, it was said, it was impossible to have a friendship with them (ŚB 11.5.1.7). In another passage, a woman, a Śūdra, a dog, and a crow were equated with untruth, sin, and darkness (ŚB 14.1.1.31), each of these creatures was considered unclean and polluting. Other texts asserted the wickedness of women, their poisonous and snakelike nature, their dangerous character, and their immorality.

Due to the low status of and pervasive negative attitudes toward women, the *Laws of Manu* (11.67) asserted that killing a woman was a minor offence, comparable to with having sexual relations with a woman that drinks or steals grain, metals, or livestock. Although the negative attitudes toward women and legal penalities imposed for transgressions are harsh according to contemporary sensibilities, there is no evidence that a text such as the *Laws of Manu* was ever adopted by any king or made the legal code of any kingdom. The text represents social attitudes and legal guidelines suggested by a conservative, orthodox, elite religious group and reflects the opinion of a small, although influential social group, and was not necessarily indicative of the entire subcontinent. Such a text does not accurately inform us about how women were treated in ordinary social situations. Thus it is wise to maintain a skeptical attitude when considering the attitudes toward women expressed in the text.

In contrast to such examples of negative attitudes toward women, some texts defended them. In the sixth century C.E., the *Varāhamihira* referred to women as the goddess Lakṣmī of the house who should be honored and given wealth. Women embodied a high status in Indian culture as mothers. Even the *Laws of Manu* (2.145) state that a mother exceeds a thousand times a father's claim to honor on the part of a child as its parent and educator. According to the *Mahābhārata*; due to her role as a child's educator, a mother excels a child's father in greatness (12.105.14–15).

Overall, women were captive to a patriarchal social system that kept them subordinate throughout their lives to a series of male figures: father, husband, and eldest son after the death of a husband. Females were not, however, the only captives to the system, because young males, which included brothers and other male relatives of the dominant male householder, were also subject to his authority. Of course, young males eventually became leaders of a household and by definition dominant figures, whereas women did not theoretically assume such a role, although they could exercise considerable power and influence within the home and over their husbands by the force of personality, the nature of the characters involved, and interpersonal dynamics. It is possible to understand patriarchical authority in Indian culture as analogous to monarchical power because of an obvious parallel between the authority of a husband and that of a monarch over his subjects.

The Ideal Wife

In spite of many negative cultural attitudes toward women, the ideal wife was called a *pativrata*, which means literally devoted to her husband, or a woman that has taken a vow (*vrat*) to protect her husband (*pati*). This ideal entails unquestioning loyalty to her husband, along with unassertiveness and submissiveness. The foremost duty of a wife was to obey her husband and to honor him as a god. The *Laws of Manu* (5.154) provide a perfect summation of this aspect of the ideal: "A virtuous wife should constantly serve her husband like a god, even if he behaves badly, freely indulges his lust, and is devoid of any good qualities." The epic *Rāmāyaṇa* (2.24.26–27) echoed this attitude: "The husband is the god and master of the wife, while she is alive, and she obtains the highest heaven by serving her husband." The other epic saga—the *Mahābhārata* (3.196.6)—described the ideal wife as restrained and possessing a controlled mind, speech, and body, which was a description with ascetic connotations.

This ideal of womanhood embodied other social expectations. The ideal woman arose in the morning before her husband, and she rubbed his feet when her husband was weary. Moreover, she was expected to eat after him and went to sleep after him. In addition, she was expected to occupy a seat lower than that of her husband and elders. In the public domain, she walked slowly behind her husband. These types of expectations functioned to emphasize her inferior and subservient social status. Whether in public or private, she should conduct herself in a decent manner. This was described as getting permission to exit the house from her husband or elders, and not speaking with an unrelated male, although exceptions were made for a renouncer, an old man, or a physician. Decency for a woman included her attire and style of dress. She should not, for instance, allow her navel to be seen; she should wear her garment or sari in such a way that it reached down to her ankles, make certain that her clothing did not expose her breasts, and she should not laugh loudly without covering her mouth.

If a woman were able to live according to this type of ideal of single-minded devotion to her husband, what would be her reward? The *Laws of Manu* (5.166) provide a direct answer to such a question: "The woman who restrains her mind-and-heart, speech, and body through this behavior wins the foremost renown here on earth and her husband's world in the hereafter." If this was the reward for a virtuous wife, what was the punishment for an unvirtuous wife? Again, The *Laws of Manu* (5.164) answer: "A woman who is unfaithful to her husband is an object of reproach in this world; (then) she is reborn in the womb of a jackal and is tormented by the diseases born of her evil."

The pativrata ideal presupposed virginity at marriage. This expectation had important social consequences, one of the most important being that strict precautions were taken to protect a young girl from sexual transgressions. This included guarding her reputation from any rumor of sexual immodesty that might eventually impair her marriage chances. Precautions involved, for instance, never allowing her to be unattended in public; a chaperon was always present when an unmarried girl was in the company of a male. From a practical perspective, this resulted in a young girl growing up exclusively in a world of other females. The second major consequence of the necessity of virginity was early marriage. In other words, virginity at marriage could be insured if females were married before they reached puberty or soon afterward. A corollary of this was that girls were denied educational opportunities in traditional India. Also, since parents arranged their marriages, girls did not have much input into the decision. A third consequence was that parents developed a special affection and solicitude toward their daughters because a young girl was viewed as a temporary family member. A girl's future fate was locked into the alien household and joint family of her husband that she would join at some time. A final consequence of the insistence upon virginity and the necessity for early marriage was a large number of child widows. Widowhood in traditional Indian was not an enviable way of life due to its hardships for many women, which will be addressed shortly.

Other members of society not only held the ideal virtuous wife (*pativrata*) in high esteem, but such a woman was believed to possess real power, for which Indian literature provides testimony. In epic literature, a hunter cursed Draupadī, who was the polyandrous wife of the five Paṇḍava brothers, for her faithfulness to her husbands. Due to her power and faithfulness, the hunter fell dead. Another example from epic literature was Savitrī, who rescued her husband from the realm of the dead. It was reported in the *Mahābhārata* that Gandhārī possessed the power to burn the entire cosmos. Although she did not use this potential power, she stopped the movements of the sun and moon.

Whether or not a wife was considered ideal, she possessed certain fundamental rights in classical Indian society. A wife had the right of residence, for instance, in her husband's house. The authorities could fine any husband who abandoned his wife. A husband was expected to guard his wife from evil and not to physically abuse her. With respect to property rights, women were allowed some personal property. When a wife died her property passed to her sons and not her husband, although a husband could sell her property in a dire emergency. A big benefit for women was not being obligated to pay taxes.

During the colonial period, the ideal Hindu woman of virtue and chaste body assumed political consequences because she was seen as different from foreign women, and it was believed that in spite of foreign rule she maintained her uniqueness. In comparison to the Hindu male, whose body had been marked by and worn down by the burden of colonialism and represented loss, surrender and defeat, the female body was unmarked, pure, and loyal, although subservient to the legal code and social tradition. The female body promised healing and possible redemption, unlike the male body. For Hindu nationalists, the Hindu ideal woman became a paradigm for strength and power.[12] It is curious, however, that critics of those advocating woman's education equated a desire for education with sexual immorality on the part of a woman.

Female Sexuality and Its Consequences

The legal literature tends to connect female sexuality with the amoral inclinations of women. The *Laws of Manu* (9.14), for instance, affirm that women will have sex with even ugly men, and they are depicted running after men like whores due to their fickle minds (9.15). Women cannot be trusted because it is part of their innate nature to corrupt men with their sexuality (2.213). Other texts express similar sentiments about the sexuality of women. The dangers associated with female sexuality can, however, be controlled by the social institution of marriage, which tames sexual proclivities by a process of domestication. This social process neutralizes a woman as a threat to the social and moral fabric of the culture.[13]

On the one hand, a wife ideally could not refuse the sexual advances of her husband. If she refused his sexual inclinations, the husband could resort to social pressure by publicly proclaiming the attitude of his wife in the village. Then, the wife could be further humiliated by being driven from the house. On the other hand, a woman's sexuality represented a powerful force. As a consequence of the dangers associated with this force and the greater requirement for sexual satisfaction on the part of women in comparison to men, it was commonly believed that only strict control and satisfaction within the context of marriage could suppress a woman's dangerous sexual instincts. At the same time, women were believed to be a constant temptation to men. Therefore, women were potentially dangerous to men because of both the allure of sexual temptation that could divert men from the spiritual path and the necessity of meeting the insatiable sexual appetites of women, who could assume the form of witches if their sexual desires were not satisfied. In comparison to this cultural stereotype, a virtuous woman was portrayed as modest and chaste. The importance of female chastity was for the benefit of men and not women, because it served to protect males from the uncontrollable sexual drives of women.

Even though women were at the mercy of their personal, tumultuous, sexual drives, the inability to have children was considered a curse. Barren women were avoided by others in the society and even subjected to humiliation. Moreover, barren women were required to avoid contact with crops, female animals, and other women. There was a cultural fear that these cursed women could contaminate others and make them sterile.

In cases of sexual transgressions of social norms, classical Hindu society treated cases of adultery with a degree of tolerance, although the context of the actors involved in the social violation was also important. If a wife was caught in an act of adultery, a husband had no absolute right of abandonment. Adultery was considered a minor transgression that could be atoned for by performing penance. In the legal text of the *Nāradasmṛti* (12.91), the penalty for adultery involved shaving a transgressive female's head along with requirements that she sleep on a low bed, and receive inferior food and clothing. In short, these practices represented her penance. However, if a woman committed adultery with a low-caste male, her punishment was much more severe. According to the *Laws of Manu* (8.371), the king could punish her by decreeing that dogs devour her. This particular violation was extreme because it was viewed by priestly and noble castes that controlled the society as a direct attack on the social fabric. In the case of a rape, Indian social norms were more tolerant because the violated women could not be abandoned. She was merely considered impure until her next menstrual period. Although her impure status involved avoidance of other members of society, at the end of her menstrual cycle, she could purify herself by bathing and assume her former social role.

These incidences of adultery and rape need to be comprehended within the context of attitudes toward marriage and divorce. In classical Hinduism, marriage is a sacrament that is considered indissoluble. The *Laws of Manu* (9.101–102) express the lifelong commitment of marriage lucidly: "Let there be absence of infidelity until death; this should be known as the supreme duty of a man and a woman, in a nutshell. A man and woman who have performed the [wedding] ritual should always try not to become separated and unfaithful to one another." What occurred when a woman could not have children? In such a case, a husband was permitted to practice polygamy. But this practice needs to be placed in the cultural context and the emphasis on the importance of sons for helping a man meet certain social debts.

When a woman married she left the comfort and familiarity of her parental home and entered the joint family of her husband. This transit from her childhood home to that of strangers involved important consequences. She had to learn to love and respect the groom, whom she may not ever have met. She must accept his family, customs, traditions, and gods. Although she might have personal problems accepting the new deities of her new family, she could find ways of incorporating these new deities by reconceiving her natal god as her personal deity, identify her old and new deities with a Sanskrit goddess, or retaining her old deity by giving it a less observable status in the new home with respect to image, location, and ritual.[14]

A newly married women was not only under the control of a husband but also came under the authority of her mother-in-law. If the married woman was strong willed and had an independent tendency, she could have a difficult relationship with her mother-in-law. Therefore, a mother-in-law sought a daughter-in-law who would be deferential, loyal, work hard, and serve well. If the mother-in-law was successful, the relationship between the two women could be very loving and tender. It is important to note that a wife entered a joint family to serve her mother-in-law and to bear children.[15] Even though the mother/son relationship might be very strong, it was not uncommon for the wife to replace the mother-in-law as the nurturer and most intimate companion of the son.

By entering a joint family, the young woman joined a social situation in which there was a little physical privacy, which militated against observable displays of affection between spouses. This absence of visual expressions of affection was even more evident in public, where there was a cultural injunction against such displays. This had important consequences for a female, whose need for love, solicitude, and succor went unsatisfied in the joint family. A young bride attempted to compensate for the situation by sentimentalizing the love and affection that she received from her own family. It was common for her to contrast her life with her mother with that of her new life under the authority of her mother-in-law. In a study of a village in the Bengal region, a critical part of the wedding ceremony includes a moment when the mother symbolically offers her breast to her daughter for the final time. In turn, the daughter offers her mother earth obtained from a mouse hole, and she places it into a fold of the mother's sari three times. Since the earth is considered a form of wealth, this gesture is symbolic of attempting to compensate her mother for expenditures incurred during their lives together. Although it is a common social opinion that a child can never repay her mother, this act represents a formal act of erasing the debt owed by a daughter to her mother.[16]

In upper-caste households, some families practiced seclusion (*purdah*) of females. The practice of seclusion involves the location of women in a particular part of a home that is set apart for female use and from which ordinary males are excluded. Although this practice is implied in the *Laws of Manu*, it was not adopted in India until the arrival of Islam between the twelfth and thirteenth centuries, with the intention of protecting women. In comparison to upper castes that practiced seclusion, there was more equality between the sexes among the lower castes and in southern India, where the Muslim influence was negligible and various goddess cults were common.

Female Empowerment through Religious Vows

If women have assumed an inferior and subservient position in Indian culture, they have also discovered ways to empower themselves. Besides using educational opportunities to enhance their status, women use vows (*vratas*) as a means of empowering themselves and gaining a degree of personal autonomy, which occurs within a social context in which women frequently lack control and self-determination. Vows represent a voluntary personal promise to do something. They involve a rite that is performed on a regular basis to achieve particular objectives that are normally instrumental in nature, because the performer expects a response. If a vow is directed to a deity, a woman expects the deity to respond to her vow. A woman can perform a vow for virtually any purpose, although it is usually done for personal benefit or for the well-being of another person such as her children or for the health and long life of her husband. An unmarried woman might perform a vow, for instance, with the hope of obtaining a husband. With few exceptions, a vow is never observed for the purpose of harming someone.[17]

Although most vows are rooted in domestic life, they are evidence of women exercising action and gaining a measure of control over their lives. For instance, a vow can provide women control over their own bodies because they can legitimately refuse sexual activity with their husbands while adhering to a vow.[18] Since vows are performed for the benefit of male family members, there is little protest from men. In fact, husbands are known to brag to others about the piety of their wives who perform vows for their benefit.

When a woman performs a vow her action is often accompanied by fasting. Women use the vows to express spiritual yearning, gain peace of mind, receive a sense of accomplishment, and exercise control over their bodies and certain aspects of their lives to some degree. Vows also promote mental purity, whereas eating and sexual relations are usually considered polluting. The curtailing and even total abstinence from these types of action are considered physically purifying. In addition, a woman practices self-control, which can be a means of asserting herself, and gains auspiciousness, purity, and peace of mind.[19] Most important, she gains power to achieve her goal and get control of her life. As a woman fasts during the period of her vow, she increases her feminine power (*śakti*). This transformative and creative energy is transferred to her husband for his benefit. Overall, there is a transparent connection between vows and ascetic activity.

Besides its connection to power, there is a direct connection between vows and ritual art. Along with performing a vow, women also create decorative and symbolic designs at the threshold of their homes. These designs tend to be abstract forms of art with intricate geometric lines and space that use ephemeral substances such as powered rice, wheat flour, rust-colored chalk, and turmeric. Sometimes these threshold paintings are performed daily in order to invite auspiciousness into the house.[20] In addition, these folk paintings by women demarcate a sacred space. The threshold art and vows are often considered expressions of devotion that have a connection to faith and the desire to become closer to a deity.

Widowhood and Sati

When she becomes a widow, a woman enters an unhappy stage of life in which she is considered unfortunate and inauspicious. The *Skanda Purāṇa* (29.22) refers to the inauspicious nature of a widow because she is no longer considered legitimately sexually active. Therefore, she is unable to produce sons and convey well-being to the family. In fact, a greater social stigma surrounded widowhood in the sense that a woman was considered responsible for the death of her husband. A widow was compared to an ogress with karmic jaws that devoured her husband over a period of time.

The status of widowhood was accompanied by a dramatic body symbolism: a widow's head was shaved as part of her mourning. The shaving of her head implied an act of severing social connections and renunciation. In addition, her forehead showed lines of misfortune—she could no longer wear a red dot (*tilaka*) mark on her forehead that normally signified a married woman. Widows were forbidden to wear jewels or adorn their nose and ears with rings or earrings; they could wear no bangles on their wrists, and no rings on their toes. A widow was expected to walk barefoot. By accepting the life of a widow, a woman continued to play the role of the devoted and ideal wife.

The overall lifestyle of a widow was analogous to that of an ascetic. And like an ascetic, a widow reduced her needs and consumption to a bare minimum at the physical and social levels. Although she could enjoy her grandchildren and the company of her children, her central hope was to be united with her husband in the next life. Because the wife of a widow could be a bleak and joyless existence of despair, some widows choose to commit *sati*, which means immolation on her husband's funeral pyre.

The practice of sati began after 500 C.E. as a custom among the warrior caste. The *Rig Veda* (10.18.8) and *Atharva Veda* (18.3.1) instruct a wife to arise from her husband's side at death and to resume her place in the world. The *Gṛhyasūtras* and their description of daily family ritual do not mention sati, nor do the *Laws of Manu* provide directions for its performance. Although it was mentioned in the fourth century B.C.E. in northwestern India and began to be extolled after 700 C.E., it was not validated by religious law until the early eighth century C.E. Historically, there was probably a connection between this practice and the defeat of men on the battlefield. Since widows faced a future of enslavement by the conquerors, some of them choose self-immolation on their husband's cremation fire. During the period of the fourteenth and fifteenth centuries in the region of Rajasthan in northwest India, a custom of suicide by poison and burning grew among the warrior caste, connected to their martial lifestyle and the dangers associated with defeat when women could be faced with slavery, rape, or slaughter.[21] Culturally, a widow suffered under the belief that she was culpable in the death of her husband due to possible insufficient or insincere wifely devotion to her spouse, even though the death might have occurred on the battlefield. By taking a vow of sati, a widow could escape any suspicion of unfaithfulness to her husband, as is reflected in the term itself, which literally means "good woman" in addition to an act of suicide.

The practice of sati involved a specific procedure to be followed. Theoretically, a widow made a decision to commit sati immediately upon learning of the death of her husband, a decision ideally made of her free will and without deliberation. If sati was in theory voluntary, this did not always reflect the fact, because social and family pressure sometimes made it virtually obligatory on high-caste widows.

Once the widow declared her intention she could not recant, even though she had a right to do so by means of a ritual expiation.[22] From an Indian perspective, the declaration to commit sati was an act of truth.

Once a widow made her decision, she donned her bridal sari for the event. She proceeded to bless those present, and she prostrated herself before her elders and asked for their blessings. Then the elders prostrated themselves to her in return, partly because she now was considered an incarnation of the Goddess. The widow led a procession to the cremation ground where witnesses to the event joined her. Before proceeding to the cremation area, the sati pressed the vermilion- or *kuṃkum*-smeared palm of her right hand against the walls or doorways of her house, or against the monumental gates of the palace or city, if she came from royalty. In the area of Rajasthan, sati stones represented relief carvings of a woman's hand that functioned as a symbol of her act. On these stones, when the open palm of the hand was flanked by the sun and moon this was a reminder to others to remember this act as long as the sun and moon exist. Other symbols like the swastika, which was a symbol of good fortune, and the lemon, which dispels evil and protects the living, were sometimes added.[23] The overall symbolism suggested the auspicious and fruitful aspects of the sacrifice.

With folded hands, the widow climbed a ladder onto the funeral pyre of wood. When doing this with the body of her husband she took his head on her lap, or reclined beside him, while others lit the fire. The igniting of the funeral pyre also had theoretical and symbolic aspects. When a woman was a devoted wife during her life with her husband she created a moral heat. After the death of her husband, this moral heat began to consume her to such an extent that it was believed that she was too hot even to touch. Thus, when she mounted her husband's funeral pyre, her body theoretically and symbolically exploded into flames. In this ideal sense, fire represented her essence. As the flames consumed the bodies, the witnesses acclaimed her as a good wife. The cremation of the body of the deceased husband and living wife was a mirror image of the wedding ceremony, with the funeral pyre symbolizing the marital bed on which the couple was united for the first time.[24]

Survivors viewed this act as courageous, and it possessed important consequences. By committing sati, a widow was instrumental in purifying her husband of bad karma. Her death by immolation on her husband's funeral pyre functioned to validate her status as an ideal wife (*pativrata*). A wife who committed sati was viewed as a very powerful figure. In fact, it was believed that she possessed special powers related to the power of her ability to curse and establish prohibitions. After she took a vow of sati, she might prohibit surviving women from wearing particular colors, types of jewelry, or using baby cradles of certain types. Another consequence of sati was that the act insured that the widow would be reunited with her husband in heaven, and be expected to dwell there for as many years as there are hairs on her body. The intermingling ashes of the two bodies from the cremation dramatically and romantically symbolized the union of the couple.

Upon completion of the cremation, the widow earned the name of *satimata*. The term *mata* means mother, whereas satimata was a goddess into which the wife has been transformed. Not only did she remain eternally married to her husband but she also functioned as a powerful, transcendent being with the power to protect and cure surviving family members from illness and misfortune. Some people believed that it was possible for the sati to transfer some of her merit to her husband in order to improve his chances for a higher form of rebirth or even residence in a heavenly realm.[25] Moreover, it was not uncommon for her to appear to others in dreams and visions. In summary, a wife may not have been very powerful during life, but her status was transformed by her decision and dramatic action of vowing to commit sati.

Liminal Women

A liminal woman can be defined as someone with an ill-defined status or as someone on the fringe of normal society with an ambiguous social position. It could be argued that a widow could fit this description, along with a courtesan or prostitute (*veśyā*). Courtesans possessed expertise in music and dance in order to entertain. A king could become famous if he had beautiful women in his harem. Since a major function of a king was to insure prosperity for his kingdom, having auspicious prostitutes could enhance its prosperity and fertility. The liminal status of courtesans was evident by the fact that they were not bound by rules and social restrictions pertaining to ordinary women. Due to the clientele that they encountered, many high-caste prostitutes were better educated than ordinary housewives. Courtesans also enjoyed the protection and supervision of the state. Like Western monarchs, Indian kings often enlisted courtesans as spies to protect a kingdom from potential enemies.

Indian kings surrounded themselves with courtesans within the confines of their palace, and they also indirectly supervised temple females called *devadāsis*, which literally means female servant of the deity. In the eastern Indian city of Puri, they referred to themselves as earthly *apsaras*es (celestial nymphs associated with water), who are female dancers and singers within the heavenly court of the god Indra. These women did not marry mortal men. However, their dedication to temple service was regarded as constituting a marriage with the principal deity of the temple. They were called auspicious women, and they sang auspicious songs. Paradoxically, due to their liminal status, the impurity associated with sex, and lack of rank or caste status, they were never allowed into the inner sanctum of the temple.[26] However, they did represent a paradigmatic marital status because they were married to a god. This meant that they could never become widows like ordinary married women. Why was it necessary for temples to employ such females? The rationale was reflected in the belief that the temple represented the royal palace of the god on earth. And as in the palace of an earthly king, courtesans should also surround the god within his temple.

The vocation of devadāsi was related to a well-defined social process. Before reaching puberty, it was common for young girls to be dedicated to temple service. This dedication constituted a marriage to the god of the temple in a ceremony called *sādhi* (a cloth associated with the image of the deity) *bandhana* (tying).[27] Thus a young girl was literally tied to the god. A more formal wedding took place at a later time when the girl reached puberty. Either the king or a priest formally associated with the temple consummated the marriage between the courtesan and god. In order to be dedicated, a female had to meet certain prerequisites. She had to embody wholeness, which meant that she could not be lame, deaf, blind, or have wounds on her body. She also could not come from a caste that could not dispense water to Brahmins. Thus she would be excluded if she were an Untouchable. Parental petitioning of the court was also involved in the basic prerequisites of the position.

Moreover, the courtesan was formally initiated. This ceremony included ritual bathing, application of turmeric powder, fasting, and donning of new clothes and jewelry. The application of turmeric to a woman's skin was symbolically akin to pregnancy, and its temporary yellowing effect evoked notions of beauty, luminescence, appeal, and physical-moral benefits. The yellow color suggested gold and the sun, and metaphorical associations with purity, illustriousness, and prosperity.[28] The female candidate received an initiatory mantra (sacred formula) from her teacher (*guru*). After receiving a mantra, she proceeded to the temple, where her sari would be tied outside the inner sanctum of the deity, a cloth tied around her head, and a sandalpaste mark drawn on her nose; finally she circumambulated the temple.

Due to the fact that sexual intercourse was considered polluting, a devadāsi had to refrain from sexual activity when it was her turn of duty in the temple. Without this prohibition, her sexual activity would pollute the temple. The sexual relationships of temple courtesans were a private affair to the extent of being secret relationships. Unlike common prostitutes, a devadāsi did not sell her services for money.[29] Thus she was not dependent on her lovers for maintenance. Although it was permissible to receive gifts, the devadāsi was not receiving the gift for services rendered.

The lifestyle and receiving of gifts has to be placed within the context of the worldview of the devadāsi. From her perspective, she and her colleagues were analogous to heavenly courtesans who adorned the court of a godly king like Indra. With a curtain drawn in front of the inner sanctum of the temple, the devadāsi danced outside of it. This dance performance took place when food was offered to the deity at specific times during the day. Such activity can be understood to reflect a close connection between dance, food, and sexually. From a mythical context, a god could only be fed in the presence of a sexually active courtesan. From this type of context, being a courtesan became synonymous with dancing, as the devadāsi also symbolized the living embodiment of the god's consort.

There was also an intimate connection between dancing and the sexual fluids of the courtesan. As the devadāsi danced, she was believed to secrete a sexual fluid from her vagina that was a direct result of her dance movements. This sexual fluid was called the nectar of *kula*. The dancing and sexual fluids were symbolically equivalent to food and fertility.[30] The dripping sexual fluid prompted worshipers to roll in the dirt and fluid on the temple floor in order to share in the sacred liquid.

Sati, Courtesans, and the Modern Period

Between the eighteenth and twentieth centuries, Christian missionaries, the British Raj, and Hindu reformers criticized Indian culture over various women's issues such as sati; temple service that was perceived by outsiders as a form of prostitution; child marriage; exorbitant dowries; and problems associated with inheritance, divorce, remarriage, and female infanticide. In addition to external calls to reform the social system, internal social reformers provided an impetus for reform from within the tradition. Reform-minded Indians like Ram Mohan Roy condemned polygamy and campaigned vigorously against sati, which was criminalized in 1829. Dayānanda and his reform movement, the Ārya Samāj, called for women's education and actively opposed child marriage. In 1891, the government passed the Age of Consent Act to control child marriage, and to prohibit cohabitation with a wife under twelve years of age. In 1929 and 1934, the respective provincial legislatures of Madras and Bombay passed laws designed to phase out the practice of temple service because it appeared too much like prostitution. Other regions of India followed the lead of these cities. When India gained independence in 1947, the rights of women were guaranteed by the new constitution, and sexual discrimination was prohibited.

Educational efforts were also instituted. Subbalakshmi (b. 1886), for instance, married at age eleven. Her husband died soon afterward, and she was forced into a life of abuse and discrimination. She started a school for Untouchables in 1932. In 1944, a former student of Subbalakshmi started Queen Mary's College in Madras. By the turn of the twentieth century, there were other women exerting themselves for women's causes. Ramabai (1858–1922) publicized the plight of widows, whereas a Bengali woman named Swarnakumari Devi (1856–1932) started Sakhi Samiti in 1887 to assist widows and destitute women. Independence in 1947 brought changes in legal status for women that initiated their enfranchisement with the rights and privileges of citizens.

The legal changes were begun with the Hindu Marriage Validating Act of 1949, which removed intercaste barriers to marriage. In 1955, the Hindu Succession Act gave women equal rights with men with respect to inheriting and holding property. The Hindu Marriage Act the following year provided a legal basis for monogamy, divorce with alimony, and maintenance. This act also increased the minimum age of marriage to fifteen years for females and eighteen for males. The Hindu Succession Act of 1956 equalized inheritance claims of females with males. And later that year the Adoption and Maintenance Act allowed women to adopt children. These were precisely the types of changes advocated by Indian reformers in the nineteenth century.

Female Saints

During the course of Hindu religious history, some women assumed especially prominent religious positions. Many of them can be correctly called saints. Even though the term "saint" has many Christian overtones, I am using the term in the sense of holy person with special powers and charisma to help and influence others. Within the Hindu cultural context, saints were born and not made, because it was not a status that one could achieve. In a sense, sainthood was a status that the holy person revealed to others during her lifetime as her true identity.[31] Many of these female saints were associated with various devotional movements. This section will review a selection of these female saints from different locations and time periods.

A couple of the earliest female saints are Kāraikkālammaiyār (literally, the Lady of Kāraikkāl) and Āṇṭāḻ (literally, the Lady; her real name was Kōtai, meaning She of the fragrant tresses). The former figure was a sixth-century south Indian saint who was considered one of the sixty-three Nāyaṉār poets of the Śaiva tradition. She married, but she also spent her adult life absorbed in Śiva, and she devoted her poems to expressing her profuse love of God. She expressed a love without any hope of reward, and she referred to God as Father and Lord. She was convinced that as her love of God grew greater it would be matched equally by God's grace.[32] Āṇṭāḻ was the only female of the twelve Āḻvār poets of the Vaiṣṇava tradition, who were considered secondary incarnations of Viṣṇu. She wrote two works: *Tiruppāvai* of thirty verses, and a set of fourteen hymns of 143 verses called the *Nācciyār Tirumoḻi*. The former text was arranged according to the *pāvai* vow that was taken by young unmarried girls who bathed at dawn in the cold waters of a river or pond for a month. This practice was done to secure the blessing for a happy married life.[33] Some of her poems depicted gopīs (cowherd girls) totally surrendering as brides to Krishna as the only true groom. At the end of her life she surrendered to her deity by merging with the image of Viṣṇu, after the deity had arranged a bridal procession to the local temple, according to her hagiographical narrative.

A major female saint of the Vīraśaiva tradition during the twelfth century was Mahādēviyakka. She probably married against her will, because she claimed that Śiva was her true husband. When her human husband jealously attempted to prevent her worship of God, she left him to become a wandering naked ascetic. She let her hair grow long to cover part of her nakedness, although she referred to wearing the light of God in some of her poems. Her poems expressed themes of forbidden amorous feelings, love in separation, and unitive love. In some poems she stated that Śiva was her only legitimate husband, whereas other poems referred to the illicit nature of their relationship. She referred often to Śiva as the "Lord White as Jasmine," whose love slew and drove the poetess mad.

In contrast to the south Indian roots of Mahādēviyakka, the region of Maharashtra was the home of Janābāī, a disciple of the saint Nāmadeva of the Sant tradition of the Vārkarī Pantha during the thirteenth century. This tradition stressed a pilgrimage to Pandharpur twice a year, during August and September. The individual *vārkarī* (pilgrim) was a devotee of the deity Viṭṭhal, who represented an incarnation of Viṣṇu/Krishna. The sacred tulsī beads worn around his or her neck and the constant chanting of God's name helped to identify such a devotee.

It would not be unusual in Maharashtra to encounter women in the villages singing Janābāī's devotional songs in the morning as they grind grain. Janābāī was a neighbor of the younger Nāmadeva, and she was present at his birth and naming ceremony, which made her six or seven years older than the saint. According to her biography, her father was a tailor whose wife could not have children until her father prayed to the deity Viṭṭhal (Viṭhobā). The deity appeared to him in a dream with the prediction that his daughter would become a renowned follower of a saint. Soon after giving birth, her mother died, and her father died when she was five or six years old. The mother of Nāmadeva adopted her. She stayed within this family until her death.

Unlike some other female devotees, Janābāī did not renounce the world. She rather remained in the world as a helpless, low-caste female. Like the village women that sing her devotional songs, she was lonely and overburdened by daily chores. Nonetheless, she followed the spiritual path as the maid of the saint Nāmadeva, trying to reach God by means of this path until she reached the goal of union. She overcame her low-caste status to transcend her social limitations in order to find a meaningful relationship to God, who she transformed into a female. Janābāī was able to accomplish this by means of her own power and her ability to tolerate suffering.[34] She also referred to God in her poems in a personal way as mother, father, friend, husband, and child.

Another low-caste female saint was Chokhāmeḷā of the fourteenth century in western India. This Marathi-speaking Untouchable was a member of the Mahār caste, with the responsibility of removing dead animals and supplying fuel for funeral pyres. This poet-saint vehemently protested the notions of purity and pollution that kept her socially subjugated. According to legend, the deity Viṭhobā disguised himself as a Brahmin, and he begged fruit from her mother. After tasting a mango, he claimed that it was sour, and returned it to her. The mother set out to deliver the rest of the mangoes in her possession, only to discover that the bitten mango had become a baby—Chokhāmeḷā—within the folds of her sari. Members of her caste that are devotees call themselves Chokhāmeḷās in honor of the saint.[35]

During the sixteenth century in northwestern Rajasthan, an especially interesting female saint appeared as a Rajput princess, according to her hagiography. From early childhood, Mīrabāī was absorbed in the love of Krishna, and she comprehended herself as his bride. When she matured into a comely young woman she was married to the heir apparent of Mewar. Although she was pressured by her new family not to worship Krishna, she persisted to compose love songs and dance for her deity at a local temple. Denigrating her marriage by speaking of Krishna as her genuine husband, she also avoided sexual contact with her husband, whom she regarded as her brother, and neglected her household duties. When her husband died young, his younger brother resented Mīrabāī's unfaithful attitude and her unwillingness to behave as a proper widow. The new king attempted to have her poisoned, but Krishna rendered the substance harmless. Mīrabāī also escaped another attempt on her life when a cobra was hidden within a basket of fruit. After this incident, she decided to leave and assume a life of an ascetic. By traveling alone or associating with male ascetics, she gave members of society the impression of that she was a harlot, but she traveled, danced, and sang songs for Krishna. Due to the declining fortunes of the royal family and the widespread fame of Mīrabāī, her former mother-in-law sent a party to retrieve her. When the party went to the temple they discovered her sari draped upon the icon of Krishna. Apparently, Mīrabāī had merged into the icon of Krishna, and her sari testified to this event. In summary, her hagiography depicted her as the persecuted and ardently devoted devotee of Krishna, but there is no way to know for certain how much of her hagiography might be based on her actual life.

Within the context of the royal Rajput society, the actions of Mīrabāī were extremely provocative and radical. She violated, for instance, the accepted practice of seclusion by singing and dancing in public at the temple. She also assumed a male rôle by becoming an ascetic and communing with male ascetics. Moreover, she was an unsupervised woman, which in conservative Rajput culture was equivalent to becoming a woman of questionable morals, a whore, or a prostitute. Finally, her poems were expressive of an adulterous relationship with Krishna. From a socially conservative perspective, her life was a scandal, but from the viewpoint of devotional religion her life expressed total absorption in God.

Another Vaiṣṇava saint was Bahinabāī of the seventeenth-century Maharashtra region in western central India. She was a member of the Brahmin caste, but she flouted caste regulations by accepting a Śūdra as her instructor. This unorthodox decision did not stop her from instructing women to obey their husbands, control their sexual desires, and perform household chores.

Female Hindu saints have continued to appear into the twentieth century. An excellent example is the illiterate Bengali woman named Ānandamayī Mā (1896–1982; literally, Bliss-filled Mother), born in the tiny village of Kheora in East Bengal into an orthodox Vaiṣṇava family. Muslim families surrounded her family, and she often visited their homes. She functioned as a teacher, and some of her followers viewed her as an incarnation of the goddess Kālī. As a child, she communed with animals and trees, and she often fell into trance states. She married at twelve years of age in 1908 to a Brahmin later named Bholānāth, but she was not willing or able to function as a virtuous wife. Allegedly, she never had sexual relations with her husband. When her husband attempted to touch her he received a violent electric shock. She withdrew from everyday activities, and attracted followers as she fell into frequent trance states. She would also sit in a yogic posture and repeat the names of God, and it was not unusual for her to assume intricate yogic postures and hand movements that were coordinated with the rhythm of her breathing.[36] Moreover, she displayed yogic powers such as the ability to cure illness and enable women to have children.

At one point of her career, she performed a self-initiation that was followed by a three-year period of silence. In 1926, she asked her husband to perform Kālī pūjā, and she allowed herself to be worshiped as the goddess. During this year, she ceased feeding herself, and her husband assumed this duty. In 1928, her husband became her disciple, having become convinced that she was an incarnation of the goddess, and they traveled around the country. In 1938, her husband died of smallpox. But she continued to attract followers who included devoted Muslim disciples and members of the Nehru family, including Indira Gandhi, later prime minister of India.

Ānandamāyi stressed the equality of all religious paths, which placed her in direct opposition to the exclusive claims of Christianity. Within the context of this tolerant view, she was convinced that all religious paths would eventually emerge into one. The most viable path for the vast majority of householders was a life of karma yoga and mantra yoga because these practices could be integrated into everyday life. In addition, she urged disciples to spend at least a few minutes each day in meditation (*dhyāna yoga*).[37] Although she welcomed people of all castes, races, and religions, she continued to allow the observance of strict caste regulations in her twenty-one ashrams (monasteries) located in northern and central India.

Overall, the lives of these female saints manifest an identifiable pattern that begins with an early dedication to a deity.[38] If a particular deity is her first love, the saint does not need to convert to a specific path of religion. If the future saint marries, she can escape her marriage by attaining God through love, winning God by extreme forms of worship and sacrifice, become a courtesan of God, become transformed into a male, wait for old age, or simply renounce or deny her marriage. The female saint may leave her husband, terrify him with her miracles and strange behavior, become a widow and refuse to commit sati or follow the course of life expected by society for someone of her social status. Many of these female saints defy social norms by rebuking men for their sexual advances, defying caste hierarchy, or becoming renouncers. Some female saints neglect initiation, others have initiated themselves, or been initiated by male figures. Finally, many women marry or merge into God.

Concluding Remarks

Goddesses of the Hindu religious tradition are figures of power, even though they may be depicted as inferior to male divine beings. Sometimes this inferior status of goddess figures reflects the subservient role of women within Indian society, and some goddesses function as models for female human behavior. There are examples of successful and unsuccessful attempts by women to gain power or to empower themselves by playing the role of a virtuous wife, taking vows for the benefit of their husbands, or committing sati and achieving immortality. Overall, female sexuality is a powerful and ambivalent force because it can serve potentially as either creative or destructive, much like ancient notions of fire discussed in chapter 2.

In addition to attempts to empower themselves, another theme of this chapter on women is the prevalence of asceticism, even though women are traditionally confined to the household mode of existence. The taking of vows is, for instance, a form of asceticism. The food that women consume during periods of vows is analogous to ascetic food. Fasting women consume fruit, wild rice, or vegetables because they are considered pure foods and conducive to spirituality. These types of pure foods are also considered cool because they dampen a person's passions, whereas hotter foods come from crops cultivated by ploughing the earth. The life of a widow with its diet, head shaving, wearing of coarse clothing, and sleeping on the floor is essentially an arduous ascetic lifestyle. Furthermore, the voluntary immolation of a widow on her deceased husband's funeral pyre is similar in form (if not substance) to the practice of yogic discipline and control.

Women are unlike male ascetics, however, in the way that they increase their power by letting their body fluids like milk flow freely, whereas ascetics withhold or draw up their seed. The milk-secreting female and the semen-retaining male ascetic are two very different models for human perfection. The former is rooted in social interaction and well-being, whereas the ascetic model is antisocial and gazes beyond the confines of society and the world to something more permanent. Women are also unlike ascetics because the latter have no exchange value. Ascetics are essentially noneconomic entities, whereas women serve as tokens of economic exchange.

Another theme that traditionally runs throughout the lifespan of women is sacrifice. A woman is expected to sacrifice nobly for her children and husband. The adoption of vows embodies a sacrificial motif. Moreover, at the end of her life some women were traditionally expected to climb onto their husband's funeral pyre and sacrifice themselves. In a sense, the widow's body functions as her sacrificial oblation, the purity of her life as a model wife operates as the sacrificial fire, and her feminine power (*śakti*), which was developed over her lifetime, makes the sacrifice effective.

If the lives of Hindu males represent temporal continuity in Indian culture, the lives of women stand for discontinuity because their bodily substance becomes altered at marriage, and they are transformed into half of their husband's body. From the hierarchical perspective of patriarchal Hindu culture, women are inferior to men. And yet, women are directly connected to auspiciousness and power (*śakti*) as the creators of life, nurturers of life, providers of well-being, and sources of pleasure and comfort. In summary, the feminine thread in Hinduism is rich and complex.

12

Desire Transformed: Tantra and Śāktism

During the colonial period of Indian history that began in the eighteenth century and ended with India's independence in 1947, the British colonial establishment imagined a connection between gangs of deceivers and murders called Thugs, the horrendous goddess Kālī, pervasive criminal activity, and Tantra. It was alleged that the Thugs kidnapped unsuspecting victims and sacrificed them to the bloodthirsty Kālī. British colonial officials used this type of imaginative association as a justification to prove that Indians were not prepared to govern themselves because they lived in a lawless and perverse society that condoned murder of innocent people. The colonized people of India took the imaginative construct of the colonial rulers and used it as a parody to mock them, in some instances, and more subversively to invert such images to promote social and political resistance toward the occupiers.[1] Within the exuberant imagination of the colonial powers, Tantra was an example of a perverse, degenerate, and demonic form of religion that appealed to baser human instincts and demanded deviant and psychotic sexual behavior that resulted in illicit sexual license, ritual murder, and cannibalism.

Present-day practitioners in the West have transformed this negative view of Tantra, which summarized the very worst about Indian culture, into a cult of ecstasy that represents an ideal synthesis of sexuality and spirituality. Whereas the colonial British viewed Tantra suspiciously and Indians responded to the imaginative construct of the British by viewing Tantra as frightening, dangerous, and weirdly alluring, the current view of Tantra as a "cult of ecstasy" represents a major shift in imagination as it becomes a part of the strange blend of New Age religion in the West, with its blend of Eastern thought, occult and psychic phenomena, pagan religions, magic, and superstition. Within the New Age religious context, Tantra is not viewed as so dangerous and secretive, because it is now perceived as healthy, pleasurable, and liberating. It is now something that can be consumed and practiced by the contemporary masses, like other self-help methods.[2] If one reviews the obscure history of Tantra in India, its contemporary constructed fantasy as a "cult of ecstasy" and the degenerate religion depicted in colonial India both miss the mark. Tantra is a complex notion, which this chapter is intended to begin to unpack without claiming to be exhaustive in its treatment of an obscure, diffuse, complex, fragmentary, esoteric, and heterogeneous notion.

Origins and Development of Tantra

According to the text of the *Tantrarāja Tantra*, the teaching of Tantra was originally revealed by Śiva to feminine Śakti at the commencement of the cosmos. After this, Tantra was transmitted through a succession of nine Nāthas (perfected yogic masters), who descended from the heaven of Śiva to the earth. These yogic masters then revealed its teachings to humankind.[3] This myth of its origin suggests a close relationship between Śiva, the goddess Śakti, ascetics, and Tantra. Since chapter 10 discussed Śiva and his cult, these topics will not be repeated. And as is often the case, there is an overlap within Hinduism of devotion to the goddess and Tantra, along with Vaiṣṇavism, which was touched on when we discussed Krishna. This chapter will deal with other aspects of these themes, and then will focus on the goddess, Kālī, her cult, and some devotional followers.

The term *tantra* comes from a Sanskrit root *tan* meaning "to stretch," or to weave a thread on a loom, according to the famous Indian grammarian Pāṇiṇi.[4] The second part of the term is *tra* meaning "to save." If one looks at the term metaphorically, it suggests being able to espouse, to explain, or to lay out, as the body of the cosmic Puruṣa is divided and laid out to form the cosmos in the famous vedic hymn (RV 10.90). A different type of image is evoked by the metaphor of the spider weaving its threads that appears in the Upaniṣads (BĀU 2.1.20). By the period of the Brāhmaṇa texts (c. 1200–900 B.C.E.), the word *tantra* refers to something more abstract by indicating the essential aspect of something. By the time of the epic literature (c. 200 B.C.E.–200 C.E.), *tantra* refers to a rule, theory, or scientific work (Mbh 13.48.6). By the ninth century C.E., it is possible to find the first tantric texts; the oldest such texts are of Buddhist origin, namely, the *Guhyasāmaja Tantra* and the *Hevajra Tantra*. It is not until the nineteenth century that it is possible to discern a clear reference to Tantrism as a distinct tradition. Therefore, the term *tantra* represents an historical development of earlier theories and practices.[5] It is not a coherent or unified religious tradition, although elements of ancient vedic and Brāhmaṇa culture such as complex ritual, micro-macrocosmic correlations, and the importance of feminine energy later became a part of Tantrism. It is probably more accurate to view Tantrism as various religious traditions focused on particular texts and practices that suggest something changing and fluid.[6]

It is likely that by the sixth to seventh centuries, Tantra had become established in India. The Gangdhar stone inscription (424 C.E.) suggests the worship of tantric deities as early as the fifth century, although its most productive textual and artistic period occurred from around the eighth to the fourteenth centuries in areas located on the frontier, such as Bengal and Assam in the northeast, Kerala in the south, and

Madhya Pradesh and Orissa, where temples to yoginīs were located. Early practitioners of Tantra represented a clan (*kula*) that originated from those such as Kāpālika ascetics that practiced their religiosity around cremation grounds and focused on the worship of Śiva Bhairava (the terrible form of the deity). This practice also included worship of the consort of the god, yoginīs, and the horrific goddess Kālī. Around the ninth century, there was a reformation of the movement by an unknown figure who rejected certain mortuary features of the movement. The reformer emphasized instead the erotic elements of the yoginī cults and created a new organizational system represented by such clan groups as the Siddha Kaula, Yoginī Kaula, the Krama cult of Kālī, and the Trika cult centered on three goddesses named Parā (transcendent), Parapara (transcendent and material), and Aparā (material), which we have discussed in chapter 10.

The Kaula tradition divided itself into four transmissions named after the four directions. The eastern transmission represented worship of Kuleśvara (Śiva) and Kuleśvarī (Śakti), whereas the western transmission focused on the hunch-backed crone Kubjikā. The northern transmission directed devotion to Guhyakālī, while the southern transmission concentrated its worship on Kāmeśvarī or Tripurasundarī (Three Cities), who is erotic and beautiful. From the eastern transmission of the Kaula, the Trika branch of Kashmir Śaivism developed, whereas the northern and southern transmissions gave impetus, respectively, to the Krama movement that worships a series (*krama*) of ferocious deities, and the Śrī Vidyā tradition. In summary, the inspiration and material for the historical development of Tantra originates in Śaiva sources, but its overall religious culture also includes Buddhist elements.[7]

As Tantra developed historically, it evolved from the teaching of inspired yogis and focused on particular texts that tended toward sectarianism. Some worshipers followed Viṣṇu, Śiva, or one of many goddess figures, making them Śaktas. It was often difficult to differentiate between Śaivas and Śaktas because Śiva and his female counterpart were so intertwined metaphysically. In addition, there were examples of Tantra within Buddhism and Jainism. The principal example of Tantra within Vaiṣṇavism was the group called the Pāñcarātras, but Sahajiyās with their erotic mysticism and the poetic Bāuls would also be included as Tantric-shaped movements. Śaiva tantric groups included the Gāṇapatyas (worshipers of elephant-headed Gaṇeśa), Kālālikas, Kalamukhas, Nāthas, and Kula or Kaula. Distinctions between Śiva and Śakta were also made on the basis of right, left, or accepted currents, doctrinal differences, methods of worship, geographical divisions, and modes of conduct. This portrait was at times made more confusing by sectarian exclusivity and hostility between groups. There was also no common doctrine among the sects, which could be dualistic, semidualistic, or nondualistic.

This complex portrait of Tantra does not mean that it is impossible to isolate some general characteristics. Tantric texts and traditions are not considered part of the corpus of vedic scriptures. Tantric scriptures are secret and esoteric; they are composed in a code language intended to conceal their teachings and to prevent the unqualified from gaining entrance to its secrets. Its terminology is polysemic, which means that word and statement imply a spectrum of other meanings.[8] Tantric teachers developed a unique form of yoga that is often called *kuṇḍalinī*, which will be examined later in this chapter. Tantra involves an extensive use of rituals accompanied by mantras (repetitive sacred utterances), speculations on the nature of sounds, and mudras (hand gestures), with the intention of producing mundane goals or spiritual liberation. These mundane goals can be associated with astrology, medicine, and magic in the sense of securing knowledge of the future, cures for illness, and a means to manipulate life. The proper reciting of mantras such as OM, Svahā, or Hum enables the adept to enter into a universal energy. This is possible because mantras are phonematic embodiments of divine beings and their energies. Tantric practitioners are also aided by diagrammatic representations in the forms of yantras, maṇḍalas, and cakras (representations of bodily centers).

There is a close connection between maṇḍalas and the power of kingship. A maṇḍala is an idealized kingdom that fits somewhere between an actual geographical and political entity on earth and a heavenly kingdom governed by gods. Since the king is a god on earth, he represents the microcosm of a heavenly deity. The king is also related in the Indian religious imagination with goddesses. And like the goddess, the king plays the motherly role of progenitor of the kingdom and the part of the fearsome female warrior at its periphery.[9]

Many followers of the path of Tantra conceive of their texts as a revelation superior to the Vedas. These texts are considered to be of divine origins, revealed by Śākta, Śiva, or Viṣṇu, transmitted by sages to the world. The texts often have a narrative structure, with a dialogue between Śiva or another god acting as the teacher and the goddess playing the role of the student by asking questions. These texts often include such topics as doctrine, ritual, yoga, and discipline. The basic dialogical narrative of the texts emphasizes the important role of the teacher (*guru*).

Any person aspiring to become a follower of Tantra must find a guru, because this person ritually initiates an adept into the power that he embodies, the energy that pervades the universe, the secrets of the teaching, and its esoteric rites. The guru is thus the linchpin of Tantra. Secrecy is absolutely essential because Śakti (feminine energy) is fluid, dynamic, ever-changing, volatile, and dangerous.[10] The guru possesses the ability to empower and guide the initiate. The path of Tantra is dangerous, and it is essential for the adept to have a guru to help master its secrets. With the assistance of the guru, ritual, mantras, and related means, an initiate attempts to manipulate cosmic power for himself or herself.

In contrast to the more conservative right-handed type of Tantra, its more radical left-handed variety is excessive and transgressive. The left-right symbolism in Indian culture suggests unorthodox versus orthodox, inauspicious versus auspicious, excess versus moderation, anti-hierarchy versus hierarchy, hedonistic versus forbidden, impure versus pure, and so forth. The left-handed type of Tantra uses prohibited substances called the five Ms: wine (*madya*), meat (*mamsa*), fish (*matsya*), parched grain (*mudrā*)—which was probably an intoxicant, and sex (*maithuna*).

By using substances prohibited to orthodox religionists such as Brahmins, and engaging in illicit sex outside the boundaries of accepted social institutions such as marriage, Tantrics intentionally violate religious and social norms to tap into their energy and to hasten the path to liberation by means of such transgressions. Instead of conquering desire, Tantra embraces desire and puts it in the service of liberation. In other words, Tantrics harness lower human impulses and instincts and use them for a higher purpose. In a literal sense, when Tantric aspirants engage in sexual relations they are merely imitating the divine copulating couple. By following such a transgressive path, Tantrics want to use the mundane to reach something profoundly higher. They believe that since Śakti pervades the entire universe, it is possible to tap into this energy at the ordinary level of existence and to manipulate it for one's purposes. Tantra also violates the hierarchical structure of traditional Indian social structure by admitting impure (lower-caste) people into its fold as initiates, and calls into question the underlying assumptions and principles of the predominant social order.

A final characteristic of Tantra is its symbolic identification of microcosmic and macrocosmic elements, a bipolar symbolism that is used in ritual contexts and meditative practices. This type of symbolic correlation implies that everything that exists in the macrocosmic universe is also contained in the microcosmic individual. Just as the macrocosm is male (Śiva) and female (Śakti), a person is a miniature model of this universal androgynous condition. The fundamental human problem is that this androgynous condition exists only potentially in human beings, but following the tantric path can actualize it.

Microcosmic Human Body

Many tantric texts make a distinction between the gross body and the subtle body. The former is what is accessible to our sense perception; it includes the material mass formed by flesh, skeleton, muscles, and so forth. This gross body changes over the course of a person's life, and is different from one person to another. These differences are due to impressions accumulated in past modes of existence according to the inexorable law of karma.

In contrast to the gross body, the subtle body is not accessible to a person's senses, although it does coexist with the gross body; it is invisible and superior to the material body. The subtle body contains all the elements in the gross body, but they are multiplied to their maximum power in the subtle body. Moreover, the subtle body is the model from which the gross body is derived, which implies that the latter is inferior in quality to the former. Remaining unchanged in all humans, the subtle body is identical in everyone and devoid of imperfections. Furthermore, the subtle body is analogous to the universe, which makes it a perfect microcosm. This necessarily implies that the same elements that constitute the universe are also contained in the subtle body. Examples of some of these macrocosmic elements would be the earth, water, fire, stars, sun, planets, and rivers.

The subtle body is divided into five main sections, with each related to a cosmic element. Each of these sections is governed by a principal element that is arranged in a hierarchy. Located between the feet and knees is the element earth, while water is found between the knees and anus. Fire is situated between the anus and heart, whereas air is positioned between the heart and the eyebrows. Finally, the element ether is located between the eyebrows and the top of the head.

In addition to the distinction between the gross and subtle bodies, a human being consists of innumerable channels of breath that form an intricate network, a weblike configuration that serves as the structure of the subtle body. This structure is analogous to the veins and arteries of the gross body. The intricate network of channels makes possible the inner circulation of the breath within the subtle body. Tantric texts identify three major channels (*nāḍīs*) that originate in the area of the human head: *suṣumnā*, *iḍā*, and *piṅgalā*. The central channel is the suṣumnā, with the other two situated on each side of the central channel. The top of the iḍā and piṅgalā are located at the level of the nose, with the iḍā starting in the left nostril and the piṅgalā originating in the right nostril. The top of the suṣumnā channel is situated at the top of the skull. The path of breath normally operates by the inhaled air traveling through the iḍā to the base of the body and then returning via the piṅgalā. More specifically, the iḍā channel is located on the left, symbolizes the feminine, and the moon, is described as wet and cool, is colored a pale yellow, and is geographically associated with the Ganges River. In contrast, the piṅgalā is located on the right, symbolizes the masculine principle, is dry, represents heat and sun, is colored red, and is geographically analogous to the Yamunā River, a tributary of the Ganges. In comparison to these feminine and masculine channels, the suṣumnā transcends these opposites, is transparent, and is geographically connected to the Sarasvatī River, which is believed to flow into the other rivers subterraneously.

The human body also is constituted by seven centers (*cakras*, literally wheels) or lotuses located along the spinal column. The identify of the centers differs among schools and teachers, although the six-center configuration was initially developed within the Kubjikā Kaula sect as a fixed coherent system.[11] At the base of the spinal column is the *mūlādhāra* (literally, root) center, which is described as a circle containing a square with a downward pointing triangle (yoni, female organ). It also consists of a four-petaled lotus, is yellow in color, is inscribed with the mantra syllable *lam*, and it symbolizes the element earth. The second center is located at the level of a person's sexual organ. It is described as a circle containing a crescent moon, and it is believed to travel at night. When the moon is new it is believed to fertilize the waters. There is also a symbolic connection between the moon deity and its presence when two people are having sexual intercourse. It is the function of the moon deity to deposit a drop of semen into the womb. It is described as a six-petaled lotus with a white color, inscribed with the syllable *vam* mantra. Its cosmic element is water. The third center is the *manipurā* (literally, jewel city), located on the level of the navel. It assumes the form of a circle enclosing a downward-pointing triangle. It is also characterized as a ten-petaled lotus, red in color, inscribed with the mantra *ram*; it symbolizes the cosmic element fire, which suggests a connection to digestion and the destruction of food by an inner fire. The fourth center is the *anāhata*, situated at the level of the heart. It is represented as two superimposed triangles in a circle with one pointing up (masculine) and one pointing down (feminine). It represents a twelve-petaled lotus with gray color, inscribed with the *yam* mantra, and symbolizing the cosmic element air. The fifth center is called *visuddha* (purity), which is designed as a circle containing a downward-pointing triangle enclosing a smaller circle. This symbolism of the smaller circle suggests the moon, whereas the triangle within it represents the female sexual organ (*yoni*). A sixteen-petaled lotus with a brilliant white appearance surrounds it; it is inscribed with the syllable *ham* mantra, and it is connected to the cosmic element ether. Located at the level of the forehead and between the eyebrows is situated the sixth center, called *ājñā*. It appears as a circle containing a downward-pointing triangle and surrounded by a two-petaled lotus. Its color is white, its mantra is OM, and it is associated with the cosmic element *mahant* (majesty, greatness), which transcends the other elements and represents the world-soul or universal intelligence. This center is symbolic of the origin of all things. Finally, the seventh center is the *sahasrāra*, which is described as a circle radiating splendor; it is surrounded by a thousand-petaled lotus and possesses no color, sound, or cosmic element. It is associated with no specific symbolism and is considered beyond all quality, and it is located above the top of the head.

This survey of the features of the human body suggests that it represents a miniature rendition of the universe. Whatever truth exists in the macrocosmic universe is also contained within the microcosmic human body. If one examines closely the various parts of the body, it is possible to conclude that it is essentially androgynous, at least in a potential sense. But a person's androgynous nature is fragmented within one's subtle body. The objective of tantric practice is to unite the masculine and feminine principles that are already present and to become whole. Once a person is able to accomplish this wholeness and realize one's true androgynous nature a person is liberated. Such a person awakens to the true nature of oneself and of the macrocosmic universe. There is a definite method to follow in order to achieve this awakening.

Tantric Meditation

A unique feature of the human body is the kuṇḍalinī, which assumes the form of a snake and represents the chaotic. It is located in the root center (*mūlādhāra*) at the base of the spinal cord, and symbolically represents the Goddess and her energy (*śakti*), who is described as sleeping, blocking the door of Brahmā with her mouth. When she is sleeping she is considered to represent inertia. The kuṇḍalinī is ambivalent because she represents poison when asleep, but she manifests nectar when rising through the channels of the body. The sleeping kuṇḍalinī is also identified with the fire of time that cooks people and makes them ready for death by means of the aging process, but she also possesses the potential for reversing the cooking process by means of the heat created by yoga with a fire that destroys the fire of time for the practitioner.[12]

The yogin's objective is thus to awaken the kuṇḍalinī. When she is awakened this causes an intense heat at the base of the spinal cord. The yogin's objective is to get her to rise up the spinal column through the central channel to the top of the head at the *sahasrāra* center, which is considered the abode of Śiva. When the kuṇḍalinī (feminine principle) rises up the central breath channel and finally unites with the male principle, that symbolically represents the union of Śiva and Śakti.

The union of these two principles is made possible by a process of meditation and breath control. The aspirant meditates, for instance, on the existence of the element earth and becomes cognizant of its location in the subtle body. By means of breath control, the yogin suspends the breathing, and directs the breath down to that part of the body belonging to the element earth. Then, a yogin acquires an intuitive knowledge of that element, and it is possible to see that it is a yellow square with the syllable *yam* inscribed on it. Now, the yogin tries to make the syllable sound there. If the yogin succeeds, he or she receives a revelation of the deity that presides over the element, which in this case is the god Brahmā. By meditating on this deity, one acquires mastery over the cosmic force symbolized by the earth, which is earthly death, and one need not fear it any longer. This progress is accompanied by the acquisition of certain powers. This method presupposes that to know something is to take possession of it and become master of it. A similar procedure is repeated for each of the other six centers and its cosmic elements.

It is important to be aware that breath control involves guiding the breath toward some specific area inside the body. Thus it is the internal circulation of the breath that determines the success of meditation. It is only when the breath reaches the selected area that the yogin acquires the intuitive knowledge necessary for progress toward liberation. Within this meditative scenario, breath is the motive force of spiritual progress. In other words, it is the breath passing through the various channels that triggers an alchemical process by which one can become a genuine yogin.

As the yogin meditates, controls his breathing by directing it through the channels, and stimulates the rise of the kuṇḍalinī through the central channel, it is possible to measure the heat created as it rises up the spinal cord. Once the kuṇḍalinī (feminine principle) reaches the center at the top of the head, the feminine Śakti unites with the masculine principle personified by Śiva. The yogin now is transformed into an androgynous being, implying that the yogin finally achieves his true nature and identity.

The so-called left-handed form of Tantra believes that the sleeping kuṇḍalinī can be awakened and motivated to rise faster by taking five polluting things (*pañca tattva*), the five Ms, already discussed, within a ritualistic context. Wine and parched grains are intoxicating, and meat and fish are forbidden from an orthodox dietary perspective. In addition, illicit sexual relations are scandalous and a violation of social norms. The rationale for this type of ritual and its forbidden items must be grasped within the context of the tantric conviction that everything in the universe is pervaded by Śiva and Śakti. It is this androgynous energy that affirms the basic sanctity of the five Ms. Normally, human beings perceive the world as fragmented and compartmentalized, and they do not recognize the underlying energy of the universe due to being bound by ignorance. The ignorant and fragmented nature of human knowledge means that we view things as either/or. We see things, for instance, as sacred or profane, ethical or unethical, and true or false. Tantra strives to dissolve prejudices and distinction between holy and profane, and get us to see things as they really are in fact.

Tantric Worship

Assuming that a guru (teacher) initiates a person, tantric worship (*pūjā*) involves internal and external aspects. The internal aspect begins with a worshiper being transformed into a deity, because it is presupposed that only a god can properly worship another god. Using a combination of meditation, mantra utterance, placing the letters of the name of the deity mentally on each limb of one's body (*nyāsa*), and hand gestures (*mudrā*), an adept transforms the body into a divine entity. This process also includes purification of the elements of which one is composed, and replacing the finite, limited self with that of the deity. Finally, the internal phase of the worship culminates with an inner sacrifice that enables the adept to experience the deity inwardly. The external part of the worship can utilize an image or, preferably, a sacred diagram (*maṇḍala*) that is drawn according to prescribed ritual procedures. After the deity and its attendants are visualized, they are placed mentally on the diagram. Then the diagram is instilled with breath that brings it alive, and it is now fit for devotion.

In the more radical left-handed type of Tantra, the five Ms would be used. The most radical of the five Ms is sexual intercourse within a ritualistic context. This ritualistic type of sexual congress is also ascetic, because it must be performed with detachment. It is even possible that the sexual rite could assume the form of a collective rite that is called "worship in a circle" (*cakrapūjā*). Sitting in pairs of male and female, the couples form a circle. This extremely secret rite is reserved for advanced initiates.

According to the Kashmiri Tantric Abhinavagupta, it is important for the male adept to find a woman (*dūtī*) of any caste, irrespective of her appearance, and a mind free of doubt and uncertainty. Among some tantric schools, women of the lower castes are preferred as partners because acting with such a women is a more radical social violation of norms. This secret ritual is called the *kulācārya* practice, and part of it involves the couple engaging in mutual worship. A couple with the intention of generating universal bliss rather than mere pleasure performs the essential part of the rite simultaneously.[13]

Among practitioners of the Kaula sect, ingesting sexual fluids and their power can occur in two basic ways: sexual intercourse or through a method called urethral suction (*vajrolī mudrā*). The latter method operates like a fountain pen by drawing through the penis the discharge female fluid of the partner. This fluid is then circulated within the body of the male partner. It is likely that this type of procedure was historically preceded by an oral method of ingestion of female sexual fluids. In fact, the initiate becomes sometimes doubly inseminated. Before ingesting the fluids of his ritual consort, the initiate ingests a drop of semen from his guru. This sometimes twofold insemination from his guru and consort transformed the initiate and made him a son of the tantric clan (*kula-putra*). From an historical perspective, tantric sexual practice seems to have evolved from the pleasure of sexual orgasm to the experience of bliss. From this point, it developed in a more psychological direction with the emphasis on the bliss of expanding consciousness.[14]

It is possible to worship a woman as symbolic of the goddess with or without engaging in sexual intercourse, a rite that is often called kumārīpūjā or yonipūjā, representing the direct worship of the sexual organ (*yoni*) of the woman. This female sexual organ is equated with a Vedic sacrificial altar. In order to make it a genuine sacrifice, the male adept offers his semen at the altar of the female organ. From another perspective, worship of the female sexual organ (*yonipūjā*) involves the consumption of the discharged fluid from the female organ by the male counterpart.[15] According to the *Hevajra Tantra* text of Indo-Buddhist fame, the male practitioner must consume any female waste product from the eyes, ears, nose, vagina, and anus. In fact, licking these bodily parts for their waste is part of the exercise. To the uninitiated this type of worship is disgusting, but to a Tantric adept worship of the female organ and consumption of its fluid makes perfect sense, because the object of one's devotion is not an ordinary female; she is the goddess. And what the goddess discharges is nectar and not carnal waste. Moreover, the adept is imitating Śiva enjoying a brew of female discharge that is located in the sixth center of the body (*ājñā cakra*) located in the cranial region at eye level. This is the nectar of immortality. Symbolically, the third eye on the forehead of Śiva represents the female vulva, which connects it to the sixth center of the body where the deity is in sexual union with his consort.[16] It is also important to keep in mind that the vulva possesses ambivalence for Tantra because it is a dangerous organ of great power, and it is also a site of potential great pleasure for a practitioner.[17]

According to the Yonitantra text, which probably originated in the region of Cooch Bihar, a practitioner can perform the worship (*pūjā*) of the female organ (*yoni*) with any of nine acceptable women, who are mostly from the lower strata of society, with the exception of a Brahmin woman. The other women include an actress, an ascetic, a prostitute, a washerwoman, and daughters of a Śūdra caste member, a barber, a cowherder, or garlandmaker (2.3, 4). The two most important criteria are that she be unmarried and not a virgin (3.25–26). Thus the text promotes choosing a sexually experienced and wanton woman. However, it is never acceptable to choose one's mother (2.5), although it is permissible to perform the rite with one's wife or the spouse of another person. A broad age range is given for the woman, although other tantric texts advocate a range between thirteen and twenty-five. In contrast to the śakti, there are few restrictions on the male, who is allowed to eat and drink anything and accept food from anyone. The male figure is described as an ascetic with dirty skin, nude, and unbound hair (2.18). The only real restriction on a male is that he must not perform the worship for the purpose of sensual pleasure.

The most favorable time for the rite is at night (2.17). The male practitioner places his partner in the center of a sacred diagram (*maṇḍala*), and he gives her a narcotic such as hashish to consume. He then places her on his left thigh (inauspicious part of the body), and he should honor her unshaven yoni. The significance of the woman's pubic hair can be traced to the *Bṛhadāraṇyaka Upaniṣad* (6.4, 3) where female pubic hair is identified with the sacred kuśa grass in vedic ritual. Next, the male anoints the yoni with sandal paste with the purpose of transforming it into a beautiful flower. The male gives his partner wine to consume, paints a sacred sign on her forehead with vermilion, places his hands on her breasts and recites a *yonibīja* (seed mantra) possibly 108 times, kisses her, and fondles her breasts. Before the final step of the worship, the female partner anoints the liṅga (phallus) of the male with sandalpaste and saffron (*kumkum*). The worship reaches its dramatic climax with the male reciting to the yoni 108 or a thousand times a sacred seed mantra and finally a full mantra. This recitation accompanies the simultaneous insertion of the liṅga into the yoni with the objective of producing the female fluid called the sublime essence, clan nectar, or clan fluid, which is based on the *bindu* (a drop that encapsulates the being, energy, and pure consciousness of the divine), which consists of pale white semen and red menstrual blood. The latter is equivalent to Soma juice of vedic ritual. The worship concludes with the male paying his respects to the yoni maṇḍala and his guru, and he verbally expresses what he has accomplished. The various elements of this rite are intended to arouse desire and to use this desire to further transcend ordinary desire.

Śākta Tradition

The Śākta tradition refers to followers of some manifestation of the goddess. Its name is derived from feminine power (*śakti*), and the term Śāktas denotes the devotees of the goddess. The goddess is personally addressed as Mother; in the Hindi-speaking north she is called Mata or Mataji, whereas she is called Amma in the Dravidian languages of the southern part of the country. The Śākta tradition is often intermixed with various tantric traditions, and it is difficult to differentiate between them because they have mutually influenced each other. There is early evidence for Śākta Tantrism prior to the eleventh century, originating from a southern Kaula transmission. Kaulism can be grasped as developing within Yoginī cults and later trying to reform them. The term *kula* means body and the totality of the body of power (*śakti*), which refers to a cosmic body formed by the eight families of the Mothers. Kaulism developed into four major systems that were transmitted in the four directions, as previously mentioned. The three major traditions associated with the Kālī cult are the Mata, Krama, and cult of Guhyakālī.

By following the path of the Mata tradition, a seeker reaches a point of worshiping the twelve Kālīs, who are depicted with multiple animal faces. Possession is a part of the cult, because the twelve Kālīs possess the consciousness of a copulating couple during sexual union. This form of possession is considered positive because it destroys the binding conscious structures that cause dualistic experiences. The cult of Guhyakālī dates to around the tenth century, with a text called the *Kālīkulakramārcana* of Vimalaprabodha. In part, this cult manifests a concretization process based on the Krama system. This means that the deity is given concrete form by means of its iconic representation.[18]

The Krama tradition probably originated in the northern areas of India before the ninth century, within the context of the cremation-ground religiosity of the Kāpālika ascetics, as vividly depicted by the *Jayadrathayāmala* text; it exerted an influence on the Trika and Śrīvidyā movements. Within this text, Kālī appears as the black-faced, twenty-five armed, and blood-dripping goddess trampling the body of time (*kāla*). As the Krama tradition developed, it adopted some aspects of Kaulism that functioned to reform it. Its most authoritative text is the *Devīpañcaśataka*, which refers to worshiping sets of deities in a fixed sequence, connected with the phases (*krama*) of the cyclical operation of cognition. These phases culminate with the achievement of an all-pervading consciousness.[19] Therefore, the macrocosmic sequence of divine powers manifests itself within the microcosm of individual cognition by convincing a particular consciousness that it is part of the spontaneous play of macrocosmic powers identified with the goddess. During the course of its historical development, the Krama tradition was influenced by the thought of the Kashmirian Pratyabhijñā school, and it eventually spread to southern Śaiva centers of influence.

The earliest texts of the Śākta Tantrism are split into the Tantras of the Śrīkula or the family of the Auspicious Goddess, who is depicted as benevolent and gentle, and the Tantras of the Kālīkula or the family of the Black Goddess, who is a ferocious and horrifying figure. The tradition that developed from Śrīkula texts became known as Śrīvidyā, which was focused on a beautiful and benevolent goddess named Lalitā Tripurasundarī or simply by her second name, which means Beautiful Goddess of the Three Cities; she is a tantric example of the goddess Śrī Lakṣmī. This goddess is worshiped in the form of a yantra (sacred diagram) with nine intersecting triangles along with a fifteen-syllable mantra. The former is called the *śrīcakra* and the latter mantra is known as the *śrīvidyā*. Bhāskararāya, a major theologian of Śrīvidyā, identified three main manifestations of the goddess: a physical or iconic form, a subtle or mantra form, and a supreme form, which is represented by her diagrammatic (*yantra*) form, the śrīcakra.

This more conservative movement associated itself with orthoprax Brahmanical values and with Vedānta philosophy. The movement's concern with external rituals and their magical effects can be found in an early text called *The Ocean of the Tradition of the Sixteen Nityā Goddesses* (Nityāṣodaśikārṇava). In comparison, another text entitled *The Heart of the Yoginī* (*Yoginīhṛdaya*) focuses on more esoteric subjects such as the expanding and contracting cosmos symbolized by the śrīcakra sacred diagram. The four upward-pointing triangles of the diagram represent the masculine principle, whereas the five downward-pointing triangles symbolize the feminine principle of the goddess. The intention of tantric practice is for the seeker to realize this symbolic union of Śiva and the goddess within his or her body. Although the goddess transcends the cosmos, it is a manifestation of her that she unfolds and contracts in perpetual cycles of emanation and reabsorption. In southern India, the Śrīvidyā tradition was embraced by the Daśanāmi monastic order attached to the Vedānta school founded by Śaṅkara in the cities of Śṛngeri and Kāñcīpuram.

In contrast, the Kālīkula tradition, which is also called Kālīkrama, aligned itself with more unorthodox Kālī cults that deliberately embraced impure substances and practices. It is not unusual to find, for instance, evidence of macabre rites that are designed to take place in cremation grounds. A good example is the rite of offering to jackals, which function as canine manifestations of Kālī.

A western transmission of the Kaula tradition is associated with the goddess Kubjikā (Crooked One). Its principal text is the *Tantra of the Teachings of the Crooked Goddess* (*Kujikāmata Tantra*), which depicts the goddess as pure consciousness.[20] According to the *Kularatnoddyota* (1.75–76), she received her name because she huddled over from shame caused by Śiva's declaration of love for her. Some scholars view her name as an oblique reference to the coiled form of the sleeping serpent (*kuṇḍalini*) that lies at the base of the lowest center of the tantric conception of the human body.[21] The Kaula tradition portrays her as a goddess of a royal court in northern India. There is historical evidence for this cult at the beginning of the twelfth century, although it may have originated earlier. The cult ceased to exist around the fifteenth or sixteenth centuries.

The Mad Goddess

We will now focus on the history of the goddess Kālī, symbolism associated with her image, her connection to a goddess collective called the Mahāvidyā, a dedicated poet, and a saintly devotee of hers. The madness of the goddess will be stressed because of its impact upon saintly devotees.

The only early ancient references to Kālī are of dubious historical value because these references do not seem to refer to the goddess of later times. In the *Atharva Veda*, the word Kālī appears, and it also appears in the *Kāṭhaka Gṛhya Sūtra* (19.7). In the *Muṇḍaka Upaniṣad* (1.2.4), it appears as a name of one of the seven tongues of the vedic god of fire Agni. There are some prototypes of Kālī in early vedic literature, like Rātrīdevī, a goddess of night, and Nirṛti, a demon personifying death, destruction, and sorrow. The first manifestation of Kālī as a wild, bloodthirsty, and frightening goddess appears in the epic *Mahābhārata* (10.8.64), where she is depicted with a bloody mouth, disheveled hair, holding a noose, and associated with a group of goddesses called the Mātṛkās or Mothers.

It is not until the text of the *Devī-Mahātmya* portion of the *Mārkaṇḍeya Purāṇa* (87.5–8, 9–10, 12; 88.9.56) that there is a narrative about Kālī's origin. During a terrible, bloody battle with demonic beings, the goddess Ambikā's face grew dark with anger, and suddenly Kālī issued forth from her forehead. With a terrible and frightening appearance, Kālī began to throw the demons, their elephants, and their chariots into her mouth, and killed them by grinding them with her sharp teeth. She proceeded to seize and decapitate the two leaders of the demon army while howling and laughing. Among other exploits, there is the defeat of Raktabīja, a demon endowed with a magical power associated with its blood. Whenever a drop of the demon's blood fell to the earth it created an instantaneous replica of itself. Whenever the goddess Candikā inflicted a wound on the demon she made her plight even worse. In order to defeat the demon's powers of self-duplication, Candikā commanded Kālī to extend her mouth to drink its blood. By quaffing the demon's blood, Kālī thereby devoured him, and she took delight in its destruction and death.

With the composition of the *Bhagavata Purāṇa* (5.9.12–20) around the ninth century, Kālī appears as the patron goddess of a band of thieves. In this narrative, the robber chieftain wants to have a son, and he decides to sacrifice a human victim to the goddess. After his subordinates have captured a saintly man to sacrifice, the chieftain takes his sword to behead the victim before the image of Kālī. Recognizing the saintly nature of the intended victim, Kālī emerged suddenly from the icon. In a rage, she cuts off the head of all the thieves with the chief's sword. Then, she drinks the hot, intoxicating blood streaming from their severed necks. Becoming inebriated from the blood, Kālī and her attendants, while singing and dancing, play catch with the heads.

There are numerous references to Kālī's dancing, and she is often depicted dancing with her consort Śiva. When Kālī dances, this normally represents the pulsating of the universe and even contains the seeds of new creation. But when her dancing becomes uncontrolled it threatens the destruction of the universe. Besides its connections to creation and possible destruction of the universe, Kālī's dancing can also be interpreted as divine play (*līlā*), which possesses no purpose beyond itself.

From a historical perspective, Kālī is a non-vedic divine being with origins probably within the many tribal cultures outside of the orthodox culture, which is also true of aspects of the numerous tantric traditions. As Kālī grows in popularity, she becomes more closely associated with Śiva and finally becomes his spouse, and she represents his energy, strength, and potency (*śakti*). The fact that Kālī is the active, creative principle in their relationship is evident in the image of her dancing on his nude and prostrate body. As she dances on his prone body, her energy flows into him and brings him to life. Śiva opens his eyes, lifts his head, and his phallus rises in response to the feminine energy infused into his inert, corpse-like body. The rising phallus of the great god signifies the beginning of creation, and the dancing

Kālī is the active, creative principle that will received the divine seed and give birth to the universe. There are other images with Kālī sitting on top of Śiva in a position of reverse intercourse. Whether dancing or sitting on the body of Śiva, this body symbolism and the energy of the goddess point to the superiority of Kālī. Such representations also suggest the sexually aggressive nature of Kālī, as evident by her assuming the superior sexual position.

In many of these images, Kālī appears as a terrible crone with a dark complexion, which why she is called the "Black One." When she is depicted as the ugly crone she is called Dakṣiṇakālikā. The term *dakṣiṇa* (south) represents the sacrificial altar in ancient vedic religion, which is located in the southern direction and is used for offerings to deceased ancestors. Moreover, the south is the direction of death and evil.[22] Kālī's symbolic association with death and the southern direction are enforced when she is depicted riding on a ghost. The similar term dakṣiṇā (with a long vowel at the end) means sacrificial gift.[23] With respect to Kālī the term represents death, danger, darkness, and dread, and yet it also suggests that underlying these dismal features the goddess is a bestower of gifts.

Kālī's overall appearance is full of symbolic significance. Besides her dark color, she is depicted as naked and immodest, standing on a corpse in a cremation ground, and surrounded by jackals, snakes, and ghosts, which places her on the fringes of society. According to the *Kālikā Purāṇa* (63.94), the goddess holds a club with a skull at its end in one of her left hands, a scimitar (a curved sword) in one of her right hands, a hide in her lower right hand, and a noose in her lower left hand. Around her neck hangs a garland of human heads; newly cut human hands dangle from her waist, and two dead infants form her earrings. These ornaments are all intended to enhance her frightening appearance, with her sunken belly, sagging breasts, disheveled hair, large fangs, sunken, reddish eyes, and protruding tongue.

The raised and bloodied sword of Kālī symbolizes death and destruction. The threatening sword also directly identifies her as the mistress of death, which enables her to grant release from the cycle of rebirth. The promise of release is evident in her upper right hand, which makes the sign (*mudrā*) of "fear not" and the lower right hand that signifies the hand gesture of granting boons.

Kālī's blood-stained mouth with protruding, sharp fangs represents the devouring cavity of her body, which stands in sharp contrast to her lower cavity or womb that gives life. Her orgy of eating flesh and drinking blood is closely associated with sexual activity, because the symbolism of feeding is intimately connected to sexuality in Indian consciousness.[24] Thus, the devouring mouth of Kālī is symbolically akin to a *vagina dentata*, a vagina with teeth that consumes penetrating penis flesh and blood. Her lolling tongue is often depicted lapping up the spilt blood of her victims or just protruding. Some scholars claim that the protruding tongue of Kālī reflects her shame at consuming blood and a sign of "horror and fear."[25] Within the context of her tantric-influenced cult, it is difficult to imagine Kālī becoming ashamed of anything. It is, however possible that when she sticks out her tongue that she is reflecting the feminine Bengali cultural habit of doing the same thing when embarrassed.[26] Within the context of tantric thought, the mouth and tongue of the goddess function, respectively, as a sexual orifice and instrument of pleasure, with the lolling tongue being connected to sexual pleasure or arousal.[27] Moreover, the lolling tongue associates her with time and its ability to consume all things. As mistress of time, Kālī makes no distinctions between upper and lower castes, rich or poor, success or failure.

The disheveled hair of Kālī is a predominant feature of her image. Within the context of Indian culture, hair is associated with an invigorating and auspicious vital force (*śrī*). The *Laws of Manu* (11.49) also equate hair with skin, which helps to explain why hair, a dead and impure form of skin, is removed before one can perform a sacrifice. Since hair is located at the margin of a human or divine body, the disheveled hair of Kālī also suggests her marginal and extreme nature. If the cutting, care, and styles of hair manifest social control over females and males in Indian society,[28] Kālī's long, disheveled hair represents her freedom, transcendence, and unrestrained sexuality. Moreover, the disheveled hair of mortal women is connected with death, an impure and polluting condition, in Indian culture, which throws further light on the hair of Kālī and reinforces her association with death.

The ominous picture of Kālī with her sagging, flabby breasts of an old crone suggests an inability to lactate any longer. This seems to point to an inability to sustain life, but such a conclusion would be too simple. According to the *Liṅga Purāṇa* (2.106.19–23), Kālī kills the demon Dāruka at the request of Pārvatī, consort of Śiva. The universe becomes disturbed from the turmoil caused by the profuse and overflowing anger of Kālī directly related to her destruction of the demon. In order to calm Kālī, the ascetic Śiva assumes the guise of a young boy by means of his illusory power (*māyā*), stations himself within a cremation ground full of corpses and ghosts, and cries to draw the attention and pity of the goddess. Kālī takes the young boy in her arms, kisses him on his head, and suckles him at her breasts. Thereby, the disguised Śiva is able to delude the angry goddess and demon killer and drink the intertwined wrath and milk from her breasts. The mixture of wrath and nourishment as a product of Kālī's breasts reflect the many contradictions that unite in her nature.

In narratives and images associated with her, Kālī is closely connected to blood, and she even gets inebriated from drinking it. When Kālī is depicted as an old crone with sagging breasts, this is intended to signify that they do not produce much milk, but she does generate a considerable flow of blood, which often forms her gracious offerings (*prasāda*) for her devotees. After the decapitation of sacrificial animals and the offering of their blood to the goddess, it is reported that devotees dip their fingers in the blood and then apply this liquid to their foreheads or lips, absorbing the blood like the sacrificial leftovers (*prasāda*) of the goddess.[29] A similar practice is followed after the Pāthābali (male goat sacrifice) in Calcutta, where the blood of the victim is believed to confer immortality.[30]

It is common for devotees of Kālī to make blood offerings to her because of the belief that she subsists on the blood of her victims. According to the some purāṇic texts, she receives a month's pleasure from the blood of some animals, but she receives satisfaction for a thousand years by a human sacrifice. In fact, a victim benefits from being offered to the goddess because the human or animal gains her love, their blood turns to nectar, and they attain the status of a divine ruler for many years. Her close connection with blood associates her with strength, vigor, and life. Kālī's demand and thirst for a continuous flow of blood suggests two related phenomena: she gives life due to the flow of blood to her, and she subsists on blood to sustain her creative efforts.

In her appearance and actions, the bizarre Kālī behaves mad — she acts outrageously, unpredictably, tumultuously, and wildly. Her incomprehensible behavior threatens the world, and it appears to lack any apparent intention. But it is important to recognize that Kālī is the mad mistress of a world that is itself mad because it is a magical creation (*māyā*) of the divine that is insanely self-intoxicated and moving toward its own inevitable destruction. By means of her madness, Kālī urges her devotees to look beyond this mad world toward something more permanent and eternal. This message points to Kālī's freedom, transcendence, and her detachment from the impermanent and ephemeral world. If the world owes its existence to a mad goddess, it lacks harmony, stability, and predictability. The world is best understood as an insignificant plaything of the gods that is created in the spirit of her madness, a form of divine play (*līlā*).

An emphasis on the feminine nature of the transcendent is stressed in many tantric texts. According to the *Śakti-saṃgama Tantra* (1.2.22–45), Śiva needs Kālī, otherwise he becomes despondent and confused. It is her energy that removes his condition, motivates him to create, and instills him with knowledge, teaches him the method of tantric yoga, and bestows him with a consort. All this is indicative of the overlapping of Śākta and tantric literature.

Kālī and the Mahāvidyās

In Hindu mythology and sectarian practice, Kālī may stand on her own, or she is sometimes associated as one of the ten Mahāvidyās, a group of mostly fierce goddesses known since the tenth century. This group can be interpreted to represent a single goddess with numerous manifestations. The term *vidyā* (knowledge) refers to perfect knowledge, which represents the pure awareness that causes release. In a tantric context, it is also connected to a śakti-empowered formula that gives power and release. According to the *Bṛhaddharma Purāṇa* (2.6.65–89, 128–52), Kālī created the Mahāvidyās to block any escape route for Śiva after he became frightened at seeing the terrifying aspect of the beautiful Satī, daughter of Dakṣa. In this account, Satī is secretly Kālī, who blocks the fleeing Śiva in every direction.

The Mahāvidyās tend to call into question the ideal woman of Indian culture, with her virtue, chastity, self-effacing nature, subordinate position, and willingness to be obedient. These antisocial, marginal, and polluting figures are related to inauspiciousness and death, which makes them antimodels.[31] Although they can bestow liberation and powers, these sexually powerful and polluted goddesses have very few temples dedicated to them. Since Kālī has already been considered, this section will concentrate on the nine other figures.

The goddess Tārā is more famous within the Buddhist tradition of Tibet, and she probably entered Hinduism by way of Buddhist tantric influence. According to an origin narrative, she came from a tear shed by the bodhisattva Avalokiteśvara. Tārā is renowned for her compassionate nature and beauty, although she lacks this virtue and appearance in Hinduism, where her fierce and horrifying features are emphasized, such as an association with blood, a pot belly, ascetic-like hair and large, full breasts. By means of her scissors and sword, she is able to help people sever ignorance and self-delusion.

In contrast to Tārā's horrific features in Hindu Tantra, Tripurasundarī is auspicious, beautiful, and erotically inclined because of her close association with desire. She is iconographically represented seated on a lotus that lies on the supine body of Śiva. This image rests upon a throne with legs symbolizing four major deities: Brahmā, Viṣṇu, Śiva, and Rudra. Her cult is associated with devotion directed to and meditation on her mantra (sacred formula), which is identified as the Śrīvidyā, and her yantra (symbolic diagram used for meditation purposes) called the Śrīcakra.

Some Mahāvidyās are closely connected with either creation or destruction. Bhuvaneśvarī represents creation in general and is more specifically identified with the earth, which she protects and nourishes. Likewise, Kamalā is associated with the fertility of the earth, and like the goddess Lakṣmī she is depicted seated on a lotus flower. Mātangī, who is depicted seated on a corpse clothed in red garments and ornaments and wearing a garland of seeds, counters these creative goddesses. This young female with full breasts is also represented holding a sword and a skull. On ritual occasions, she is offered leftovers that are considered very polluting because of their association with saliva. Her polluting status directly connects her with lower castes. The goddess Bhairavī, who eats forbidden food and drinks liquor, embodies the principle of destruction. She is described as seated on a corpse and wearing a garland of freshly severed hands that drip blood over her exposed breasts.

If these four goddesses are primarily connected with creation and destruction, another goddess symbolizes the plight of widows. Ugly, with gray and disheveled hair and wrinkled facial skin; unsteady, angry, with sagging breasts, trembling hands, and long teeth and nose—these are terms that describe the widow goddess Dhūmāvatī. In addition, she is always hungry, thirsty, and unsatisfied. Her geographical location is the south, the direction of death. She often rides in a chariot with a banner decorated with a crow, another sign of death, or she is depicted sitting in a chariot without any horses to pull it. Like a luckless, unattractive, and inauspicious widow, she is going nowhere. In addition to wearing a garland of skulls, this fierce and frightening figure holds a winnowing basket in one hand and offers boons with her other hand. She originates from the smoke of the burning body of Satī, a spouse of Śiva, on her father's sacrificial fire, in one myth. Or she originates from a curse uttered by Śiva after being swallowed by his wife for not feeding her.

An especially bizarre Mahāvidyā is Chinnamastā, she is depicted holding her own severed head in one hand and a sword in the other, and she drinks the blood gushing from her headless, naked torso. While standing on Kāma and Ratī joined in sexual intercourse, she is also flanked by the yoginīs Varṇinī on her right and Ḍākinī on her left, holding swords and drinking blood gushing upward from her headless body. Although the severed head is a polluted object, the goddess decapitates herself to nourish her devotees, which makes her action a selfless deed. The copulating couple beneath her feet signifies the awakening kuṇḍalinī. The goddess and the two yoginīs symbolize the three principal channels, with the former standing for the central channel and its upward flowing of nectar.

The yoginīs are appropriate figures to be conjoined with the headless Chinnamastā, a symbol of transcendent consciousness, because they are devouring semidivine beings, embodied in ordinary women with whom men can interact sexually. At a cremation ground or an isolated place, yoginīs descend from the sky to meet earthly male consorts waiting to have sexual relations with them. Their ability to fly is made possible by a diet rich in human and animal flesh. They are able to share the power of flight with their devotees. During their sexual congress, males gain access to and are inseminated by a "clan fluid" carried by the yoginīs that provides them membership in the cult. Yoginī temples are circular and roofless constructions, in order to make it possible for them to fly to earth, land, and later ascend. An ithyphallic image of Śiva or Bhairava forms the center of the temple, with sculptured yoginīs on its inner walls. Similar to the cult of Kālī, the yoginī cult is intimately connection to the blood of sacrificial victims, and with menstrual and sexual emissions.

The final example of a Mahāvidyā is Bagalamukhī, seated on a lion throne, with a yellow complexion and wearing a yellow dress, ornaments, and garland. Her iconographic representation depicts her holding the tongue of a demon in her left hand and a raised club in the other. She possesses the ability to paralyze and attract others. Sometimes, she is represented seated on a corpse, which can serve as a significant object in tantric ritual in the so-called practice of using a corpse (*śava sādhanā*). The actual rite involves a practitioner selecting the correct location and corpse, which must be intact and a member of a low caste. The ideal corpse committed suicide, drowned, or was murdered. The ritual includes taking the corpse to the place of ritual and purifying it by means of mantras (repetitive sacred utterances). After offering the corpse a flower, the practitioner pays obeisance to it, bathes it with perfumed water, creates a bed of sacred grass (*kuśa*), and places the head of the corpse in an easterly direction. After putting betel nut into the mouth of the cadaver, he turns it over and smears sandal paste on it and draws a sacred design (*yantra*) on its back with an eight-petaled lotus and four gates, which is covered by a woolen cloth. The practitioner is allowed to spit on the corpse if it moves. Then, he makes offerings to the guardian of the directions and the yoginīs. Thereafter, he sits on the corpse and worships it, expresses his purpose for performing the rite, and ties the hair of the corpse into a knot. Offerings that he makes to the deities are placed in the mouth of the corpse, which is followed by meditation, breath control, repeating of mantras, and dispersing mustard and sesame seeds in all directions. Finally, he bathes and disposes of the corpse.

Kālī and Theatrical Performance

In the southern state of Kerala, there is a theatrical performance concerning Kālī that consists of seven scenes recounting her birth, battle with demons, and decapitation of the demonic Dārika, which is accomplished by removing his headgear. This play is called Muṭiyēttu (literally, carrying of the headgear). The term *muṭi* means head-dress, crown, or hair. Within Kerala, it also refers to the heavy bundle of harvested rice paddy carried on the head by agricultural workers at harvest time.[32] A male actor, who is usually over fifty years of age, always plays the goddess. When the actor dons the costume of the goddess, he ceases to be human and is transformed into the goddess. In fact, he identifies himself mentally with her. Thereby, he becomes taboo for ordinary humans: his transformed status means that he must not be touched, and he must not talk to anyone. The role is very demanding because it requires strength, maturity, and total mastery of the many technical aspects.

The Muṭiyēttu performance is a form of theater with complex music, art, and staging. It must be performed in the dead of night, between midnight and dawn. This is an especially dangerous time. It is ideally performed on a Tuesday or a Friday because these days are sacred to the goddess. These two days are directly connected with death as well as with the hunger and needs of the spirits of the dead. The actual performance is preceded by a series of elaborate rituals. These rituals include the drawing of a *kaḷam*, an artistic drawing on the floor of the inner sanctum of the temple devised with different colored powders. The preliminary activities include singing, drumming, offering of lights and food items, and waving of lamps. Most of these actions are done to exorcize evil spirits. Finally, the artist destroys the kaḷam, and the colored powders are given to the faithful as gracious leftovers (*prasāda*).

The most dramatic aspect of the performance occurs when Kālī, who appears as an unmarried, beautiful, virgin girl named Bhadrakāḷi in Kerala, possesses the actor playing the goddess. The virgin goddess is hot and dangerous. Her heat can be traced to her virgin condition, which is symbolic of the hot earth at harvest time. The goddess is hot with desire and anger, which makes her thirst for male body fluids. This forms the cultural context for her possession of the male actor, whose spiritual experience is profound.

Kālī and Poetry

Rāmprasād Sen (c. 1718–1755) worked as an office clerk who composed devotional poetry to Kālī. His biographers present him as a Śākta version of the Vaiṣṇava saint

Caitanya. And like Caitanya he was unable to work due to divine madness. Thus Rāmprasād devoted full time to his religious vocation of composing and singing devotional songs about the goddess. Some people claimed that he was the incarnated son of the goddess. According to traditional accounts, he died singing a song and became immersed in the holy Ganges River. Probably his major contribution to Śāktism was his ability to synthesis classical purāṇic views of the goddess, the folk tradition of local goddesses, including folk beliefs about Śiva, and elements of the esoteric and secret tantric tradition.[33] After his life, Rāmprasād became a new model for the saint/singer.

Besides identifying Kālī with Brahman and the essence of the soul, Rāmprasād gives expression to the goddess as the supreme saving power in the universe and its mother. Like a loving mother, Kālī is always forgiving her children. How does the poet reconcile this image with her terrible, frightening features? Behind the ugliness of her appearance, the poet discovers a surprising beauty, comparing her dark complexion to the brilliance of dark blue clouds; her face is like the autumn moon, her sparking teeth like white flowers, and the blood flowing down her thighs is like flashes of lightning in dark rain clouds. Rāmprasād juxtaposes the grotesque and the graceful, ugliness and beauty to suggest that Kālī's beauty transcends earthly norms. He also depicts her as an erotic female warrior who shamelessly flaunts her nakedness.

Moreover, Rāmprasād juxtaposes the world as a lunatic asylum with the madness of Kālī, whose condition can be traced to the madness of the divine love with which she is intoxicated. The poet often claims in his compositions that Kālī forgets about the world and her worshipers, which make her appear uncaring and merciless, and yet she cares for them like a mother. Thus Rāmprasād tends to stress the benevolence of the goddess and not her destructive aspects.

During his lifetime, Rāmprasād was controversial, the butt of humor, and skilled at extemporaneous versifying, according to his biographer, who depicted the poet as an heir to insights of the regions Śākta tantric personages.[34] Even though the overall knowledge about Rāmprasād is scare today in the region of Bengal, his biography is enacted by the Rāmprasād Līlākīrtan Samiti (Rāmprasād Dramatics Society) founded in 1952. Another such group is the Āndul Kālī-Kīrtan Samiti, which consists of married men who don wigs to impersonate renouncers in order to inspire both themselves and their audience into a meditative mood as they sing poetry. There are also stand-up poets called Kabioyālas that jointly sing poems to the goddess while a small orchestra accompanies them. Sometimes rival troupes stage public contests to test their cleverness and ability to create extemporaneous poems. Another kind of performance is the open-air play (*yātra*) that enjoyed popularity during the mid-1800s in Bengal. These public plays included mimicry, dance, orchestral music, singing by a chorus, and improvised dialogue during interludes between songs. There were also farcical pantomimes that were performed with singing, dancing, and floats. Finally, there were also poetic contests (*tarjās*) that were rather ribald.[35]

The Mad Goddess and Mad Saint

The mother of Rāmakrishna (1836–1886) heard voices and had visions before his birth, and she experienced a light emanating from an icon of Śiva enter her body. This birth story implies a divine conception, but not with a virgin because she had had an older son in 1805. Rāmakrishna's father died when he was seven years old. Rāmakrishna's traumatic childhood led to bisexual confusion and identity consciousness in later life.[36] In 1852, he became a temple assistant to his older brother Rāmkumar at a Kālī temple in Dakshineswar, a town north of the city of Calcutta, built by a wealthy widow of low caste named Rani Rasmani. Because the widow could not find an orthodox Brahmin priest to officiate at a temple she wanted to build, due to her low-caste status, Rāmkumar devised a solution that involved making a gift of the temple to a Brahmin and endowing it with ample funds. Although the solution was heretical, this did not stop the construction of the temple.

After Rāmakrishna became a priest of this temple, his strange behavior began to manifest itself. Many episodes of his life and sayings were preserved over a four-year period by a teacher named Mahendranath Gupta, who was also known simply as M. This work was to be translated in an abridged edition entitled *The Gospel of Sri Ramakrishna*. After his strange behavior began, his mother became concerned for his mental well-being, and arranged a marriage in 1859 with a five-year-old girl named Saradā Devī, who became the mother of the religious movement inspired by her husband after his death. The couple did not live together until she reached thirteen years of age, and the marriage was allegedly never consummated. In 1881, Rāmakrishna encountered a young man named Narendranath Dutt, who was later to be known as Swami Vivekananda. When Vivekananda touched the foot of the saint he was sent into an ecstatic trance state. Vivekananda would later establish the Ramakrishna Math and Mission, the Vedanta Society, and represented Hinduism at the World's Parliament of Religions in Chicago in 1893. Vivekananda was the first person to transform Hinduism into a missionary religion to all parts of the world. Another important figure in Rāmakrishna's life was Keshab Chandra Sen (1838–1884), who became the leader of the reform movement called the Brahmo Samāj and editor of a newspaper that publicized the teachings of Rāmakrishna and spread his fame.

From one perspective, Rāmakrishna's life was a series of religious experiments. In 1861, he practiced Tantra, tried devotional religion focused on the deity Rāma in 1864, studied Advaita Vedānta in 1864, received a vision of the prophet Muhammad in 1866, and gained a vision of Jesus in 1874. It is possible to view these religious experiences as artificially structured within his biography in order to culminate with the nondualist experience of Advaita Vedānta.[37] Rāmakrishna's ecstatic trances, visions, and teachings need to be grasped within a tantric context, even though he failed to complete the path with its heterosexual assumptions, perhaps due to his own conflicted sexual identity.[38] These various religious experiences led to a catholic attitude toward other religions, which led Rāmakrishna to the conclusion that all religions are true. This did not mean that all religions are identical, but it did mean that they are truthfully equivalent. These various religious experiments did not lead to a genuine synthesis because Advaita Vedānta was used to explain his various experiments, and Rāmakrishna remained a devotee of the goddess Kālī throughout his life. Moreover, Rāmakrishna viewed Hinduism as the eternal religion (*sanātana dharma*), and the truth embodied by this eternal religion was that Kālī was identical to ultimate reality.

Like some other saints, Rāmakrishna was odd; he acted like a child throughout his life, created his own society of mirth within the confines of his room, played the role of divine beings, fell into trance states, and mimicked women by donning their clothing and mannerisms. Among examples of his odd behavior are the following: sitting inert for long periods of time, wide mood swings, acting like a demented person, crying profusely, conversing with the image of Kālī, singing and dancing with the image of the goddess, feeding the image, and loosing track of time. Contemporary Hindus thought that he was insane because of certain unorthodox practices like offering flowers to Kālī after touching his own feet with them, eating offerings made to the image of the goddess, lying in her bed, and performing impure acts like playing with his own body waste. Even his primary disciple Vivekananda thought that he was insane. After one group singing session (*kīrtana*) of devotional songs, Rāmakrishna took Vivekananda aside and suddenly grasped his hand and cried profusely. With tears of joy running down his cheeks, the master stood, folded his palms, paid homage to his disciple, and told Vivekananda that he was in reality an incarnation of the ancient sage named Nara, a part of Viṣṇu. Vivekananda reported to be shocked and convinced that Rāmakrishna was insane.[39]

Rāmakrishna was often confused about his own identity. During one episode, he acted like the monkey god Hanumān by eating only fruits and roots, living in trees, jumping from one place to another instead of walking, and he tied a cloth around his waist and let it hang down to form a tail. He proudly reported that his coccyx enlarged by about an inch. Rāmakrishna also worshiped his own penis as a substitute for the liṅga of Śiva. From his devotion to Krishna, Rāmakrishna experienced some strange physiological results like a burning sensation in his body, an oozing of blood from the pores of his body, a loosening of bodily joints, and a cessation of his sense faculties and physiological functions. Being concerned about his apparent madness, his employer concluded that his problem might be due to sexual continence. Rani hired two prostitutes to provide the necessary cure, but when they entered Rāmakrishna's room he ran to seek shelter at the feet of the icon of Kālī in the temple.

Not only was Rāmakrishna aware of his own madness but he also thought that it was necessary in order to realize the divine. At an early point of his priestly career, he felt separated from Kālī. In a distraught state of mind, he took the sword from the image of the goddess in order to commit suicide. Suddenly, he had a vision of her. In another episode, Rāmakrishna fed food intended for the goddess to a cat, and he justified his action by saying that the goddess was everywhere. In such an incident, madness allowed him to gain insight into reality. If the world was a madhouse, a person must be mad to survive. But a person must not be mad for the impermanent things of the world; he or she must become mad for Kālī, which suggests becoming mad for what is permanent. Thus madness is a divine gift, and it is grounded in the madness of Kālī. This madness is an aspect of divine play (*līlā*) that allowed Rāmakrishna an opportunity to play in turn with his followers in complete freedom.[40]

Concluding Remarks

Tantra has had a pervasive influence on Indian culture and on other religious developments beyond the confines of Hinduism. It advocates ritual practices, yoga, repetitive recitation of sacred formulas (*mantras*), sacred hand gestures (*mudrās*), and purification. The revered teacher (*guru*) represents an embodiment of Śiva. In order to actualize one's inherent androgynous condition and become like the macrocosmic pair of Śiva-Śakti, some tantric movements advocate a path of radical transgressions that intentionally violate orthodox cultural norms. Partaking of impure substances and illicit sexual relations are not hedonistic ends in themselves. They are rather an attempt to speed progress toward the attainment of a person's real androgynous nature, precisely, like that of Śiva. This path is very dangerous and secretive. Instead of culminating with an enlightening realization of androgyny, it could just as easily end with madness for the aspirant.

The close connection between blood, death, sex, madness, and time has been highlighted with respect to Kālī, who serves as a dramatic representation of the Śakta tradition in Hinduism. Within the many-colored rainbow that functions as a metaphor for Hinduism, Kālī can represent the color black for her skin color and connection to death, or she can represent the color red for her connection to blood, the sap of life. Her appearance and actions manifest the holy as frightening, awesome, and terrible. At the same time, Kālī is grounded in the reality of life with her connection to sex, birth, growth, decay, death, and the madness of the world. Her strangeness is intended to shock people into rejecting this ephemeral world, and motivate them to embrace a mad goddess who cannot be circumscribed or truly understood.

It is certainly true that the symbolism associated with Kālī provides humans with a view of the darker aspect of existence. Kālī appears as an old crone to frighten us from our attachment to the world, thereby intending to help her devotees. For those that respond to her with love, she appears as a mother, but for those that reject her, she manifests herself as the terrible shrew. To a poet and devotee like Rāmprasad she appears as a mother with saving power. Instead of seeing the frightening appearance of Kālī, Rāmprasad perceives a loving and forgiving mother, a goddess of beauty, and a mistress of mad divine love for her children.

This chapter ends by calling attention to the Bengali saint Rāmakrishna and his role as a mad mental and social misfit, whose radical freedom breaks down all order and points to the absurdities of conventional social life. Rāmakrishna's madness did not deter people from visiting him. In fact, his madness acted as a magnet for others and as a unifying force. Overall, the madness of the saint is a form of play of the goddess. And due to the nature of the degenerate kali yuga, it is necessary for the goddess to communicate through a madman.

PART III

Issues in Modern and Contemporary Hinduism

13

The World of the Goddess: Village Hinduism

Touring or living in an Indian village can be an awakening experience. A typical rural village home is made of mud with a thatched roof. There is often no door to cover the entrance. As one walks into the first room, one encounters a table that takes up much of the room. Behind the table, there might be another room used as a bedroom. Both rooms have a dirt floor and no windows. There are no pipes, sink, or toilet facilities. The bed might be a mat on the floor or a simple wooden framed bed. Some kitchen items may be stored in a corner of the outer room. There might not be any electricity, and simplicity is the overall impression that a visitor has of these homes. The better homes in the village might, however, be built of brick, include doors and widows, and be equipped with electricity.

From ancient times to the present, a vast number of Indians have lived in villages of various sizes all over the subcontinent. A village (*grāma*) consists of several families that share the same habitation. It is possible that the term *grāma* originated among nomadic groups and referred to the members of a group and their vehicles. When the nomads stopped, they would form a ring of wagons for protection. The meeting of two or more *grāma* is suggested by the term *samgrāma* (*sam* meaning together), which contextually probably referred to a conflict. With the adoption of a settled lifestyle, grāma referred to a village instead a train of vehicles.[1]

Villages are not identical, because their specific ethnic, linguistic, and caste constitution determine each of them. Villages are also not isolated social entities and self-sufficient social unities, because they are connected with the broader society of other villages, towns, and cities by ties created by marriage, caste, trade, religion, and politics.[2] Although villages lack complete autonomy and independence because of their socioeconomic and religious interconnections throughout a broad territorial spread, a village council (*pañchāyat*) governs each village, which gives it relative independence and autonomy in its domestic affairs.[3] In addition, each village is guided by local and regional social traditions that determine how inhabitants dress, speak, and behave.

Indian villages have maintained old traditions for long periods of time, but they have also slowly changed and adapted to new influences of various kinds. Therefore, villages are not static social entities that are timeless and thus not subject to change. Considering Hinduism on the village level will give this study a more balanced view of the religious tradition and provide a further glimpse into its complex nature.

General Characteristics of Village Hinduism

With more than 70 percent of the Indian population living in villages in the 1990s, understanding village life is essential to gaining an appreciation of the diversity of Hindu religion and life. The village consists of at least four features: a physical location, a place that nurtures humans, the physical relation of residents to their village, and an intersection of actions among members. People are intimately connected to the land as farmers regardless of caste, and their homes are packed into a small space surrounded by the fields. The soil of the fields connects the villages with the fields by nurturing the crops and eventually the inhabitants. The villagers will prosper, assuming that the soil and humans are compatible. A lack of such compatibility leads to suffering and ultimately death by starvation. The intersection of human actions results in individual and collective accumulation of sin and merit.[4] Do villagers have any recourse when there is an accumulation of sins that poses a danger to the group? In some locations, there is a ritual called *khāppar*, which begins with a group of men collecting offerings from all the homes of the village. During the evening, members worship the village goddess at her shrine, and some may become possessed by her. In the middle of the night, a male dresses as the goddess, and other men take a pot (*khāppar*) around the village with which they enter each home to collect its inauspiciousness and sins. Then, the men take the pot to the village boundary and toss away the sins contained in it.[5]

Religion on the village level of Indian culture is extremely elastic in the sense that there is a considerable degree of regional and local variation with respect to beliefs and practices. The common attitude among villagers is shaped by resignation toward what are perceived to be predestined facts constructed by the doctrine of karma. In fact, this common fatalistic attitude is shaped by a synthesis of the notions of karma and fate.[6] This attitude is combined into a practical precept: a person's present life is predestined on the basis of one's acts in a past life. The belief in fate also functions as a way to rationalize disappointments associated with life, because it is not a person's fault now that he or she committed misdeeds in previous lives. A person is merely a victim at the present time of what happened in a previous mode of existence. Nevertheless, by acting rightly in this life, a person can influence the course of one's life after death. Villagers accept the inexorability of the doctrine of karma, but they do not, generally speaking, have a lucid notion of liberation (*mokṣa*). Of course, acceptance of the law of karma implies recognizing the related notion of rebirth.

In addition to the notion of karma, the concept of dharma plays an important role in village life. The notion of dharma covers all phases of the human life-cycle. By following dharma, it is believed that one can shape one's personal destiny. Notions of sin (*pāp*), merit (*punya*), and pollution are fundamental to the wider concept of dharma.[7]

There is a nearly universal belief in village Hinduism in such phenomena as the existence of ghosts and spirits of various kinds. There are sixty-four varieties of malevolent ghosts (*bhuta-pretas*). For the most part, ghosts are former humans who have met untimely or bad deaths, which includes murder, suicide, accidental injury, snakebite, various types of disease, and deaths connected to pregnancy. There are, for instance, three major types of female ghosts: spirits of young virgins (*bhavani*); spirits of barren women or those females dying during pregnancy or childbirth (*churail*); and especially malicious Untouchable female spirits (*mari*). Villagers most susceptible to ghosts are pregnant and menstruating women, and attacks upon them usually result in problems with fertility or gynecology.[8] Ghostly attacks are also more likely to occur during transitional states and times during a person's life and dangerous periods of the day, week, or month.

In addition to a belief in ghosts, witchcraft beliefs are common, and particular people are suspected of practicing it. In the village of Chhattisgarh in central India, for instance, the witch possesses distinct feminine associations with heightened powers of perception and movement. A witch can rely on ghosts or food poison to inflict harm upon her victims. The Baiga, a type of priest-exorcist, who specializes in diagnosing and healing victims and worshiping village deities, counters the witch. The village Baiga possesses knowledge of special mantras that give him power over certain benevolent and malevolent spirits.[9] During a typical performance, a Baiga intones mantras while blowing cowdung ash onto the patient. A different kind of religious expert is used in the Kerala region of southern India, where temples dedicated to the goddess Bhagavati require the permanent presence of an oracle, who embodies the goddess during daily worship. The oracle is believed to share the substance of the goddess when she possesses him. Even though the goddess communicates through the oracle, he is not permitted to enter the inner sanctum of her temple. When temple priests hand the oracle the goddess's sword, her spirit enters into him.[10] In the northern village of Sirkanda, a shaman acts as the medium of a particular deity, invites the deity to possess him, and enables the deity to speak through him and to inform the clients about their troubles, the cause for their problems, and what action can be taken to alleviate the trouble.[11]

With the occupation of farming playing such a vital role in village life, it is not surprising that festivals that generally follow the agricultural cycle mark the yearly religious calendar. In the north Indian village of Shanti Nagar, there is a festival called "The Cooking Pot of the Goddess" that is celebrated in mid-April in the midst of the wheat harvest, which is known by various names in other villages. Cleaning the house is part of the festival. Other aspects include fasting, lighting a lamp for the goddess on the eve of the festival, and may include pilgrimage to her shrine.[12]

Another festival in the same village is called the "Protection Tie" or "Charm Tying" that is celebrated on the full moon of July-August. The dominant theme of the festival is interaction and the exchange of presents consisting of protective charms and money between relatives. A sister, for instance, ties protective string-charms around her brother's wrist and receives a gift in return.[13] Other examples of festivals connected to the agricultural cycle can be discovered in other parts of the country.

Another important characteristic of village life is that each village represents a miniature world. The little world is largely self-sufficient, largely self-governing, and with its own social structure based on the interdependence of its specific local castes. This small world is intertwined into a single whole of economics, government, social interaction, and religion. This does not imply that villages are isolated islands of disconnected inhabitants; they are, rather, interconnected by members of a given caste who intermarry with members of other villages from the same caste. Therefore, kinship and marriage associations create regional caste units that are often called subcastes.[14]

Villages are very dependent for their well-being upon their deities, who contend with demonic forces that desire to transform the cosmos of the village into chaos. This struggle to maintain cosmos and avoid being transformed into chaos or being overcome by chaotic forces is a continual struggle. The possibilities of success with this struggle are enhanced by the role played by goddesses that serve as guardian deities for villages. In short, the village is the domain of the goddess, and villagers are her children. There are also other deities that preside over ordinary, significant, and defining events such as marriage, conception, or childbirth. Not surprisingly, some divine figures are concerned with agriculture, fertility, wells, and animals.

Village Pantheon

There are three main classes of supernatural beings within village culture. The high or great deities of the Sanskritic tradition constitute the first class. Local deities represent the second major group. And the third group consists of spirits of various kinds.[15] In the north Indian village of Sirkanda, for instance, villagers make a distinction between gods indigenous to the village that are considered household gods or family gods, and village deities. Members of a specific family worship household gods consistently, whereas nearly all members of a village at a central shrine worship village gods. This is not a rigid distinction, because some household gods become village deities.[16]

The great gods like Viṣṇu, Śiva, Krishna, Rāma, or goddesses directly associated with these male figures are part of the Sanskrit tradition. These are divine figures that create, control, and maintain the cosmos and the fate of individual humans. These divine beings are considered mostly pure and vegetarian. Although these divine beings are all-powerful and omnipresent, ordinary villagers often think of these beings as remote and inaccessible, without caring about the everyday struggles and concerns of average people. Due to the stature of these great gods, villagers cannot worship them directly and independently. A priestly intermediator is necessary to communicate with them. It is considered presumptuous for a villager to request that a god change the order of earthly events, so the power of these divine beings does not mean that they will assist an individual. In fact, villagers tend to believe that gods with a narrower sphere of influence are more likely to help a person, because the great gods can neither be manipulated nor forced to comply with one's wishes. At the same time, these great deities are not generally considered to cause misfortune to a particular villager. Although a villager may not be able to coerce or influence an omnipotent deity, he or she worships such a figure in order to obtain merit (*punya*), which is believed to affect a person's karmic destiny. Due to their exalted stature, the Sanskrit deities are housed in temples or shrines in private homes.

The local deities (*devatas*) are impure compared to the deities of the Sanskrit tradition. Their impure nature is exemplified by their tendency to consume meat. These figures, who are rarely represented by icons, are both benevolent and malevolent, although villagers tend to believe that they are more concerned with a person's daily affairs.

These local deities fall into three categories. There are those that protect a specific social group and its property. These figures guard the village, and they are called *grāma devatas*. A good example of such a figure is Māriamma, goddess of smallpox, cholera, and plague. A stone or a tree represents the residence of such a deity. In some villages such goddesses are collectively called the Seven Sisters, and they include the following figures: Śitala Mātā (smallpox goddess); Kalka Mātā (goddess of cremation grounds); Khamera Mātā (goddess of measles); Khasra Mātā (goddess of itches, scabies, and similar skin maladies); Marsal Mātā (goddess of mumps); Phul Ki Mātā (the Flower Mother, who is a goddess of boils and other skin eruptions); and Kanti Mātā (goddess of typhoid).[17] These village goddesses are not linked with pan-Hindu figures.

Another category of these divine figures comprises the family or lineage (*chowdi*) deities, which tend to possess and speak through a shaman. The final category of local deities includes those that cause illness by possessing a victim, due to the deity's desire for food or worship, or because of having fallen in love with the possessed person. Such deities cause afflictions such as fever, abdominal pains, diarrhea, skin lesions, and broken bones.

The final class of village supernatural beings is spirits (*devvas*). These figures have no permanent residence because they are conceived as free-floating and marauding beings. These malicious and destructive figures are always hungry and seek opportunities to cause illness, but they speak very rarely. They tend to prey on the weaker members of village society such as domestic animals, women, children, and non-Brahmin males.

The Goddess and Her Village

The goddess is the local tutelary deity of the village. Because the village is her domain, its destiny is in her hands. This necessarily means that the inhabitants of the village are her people.[18] A shrine that is sometimes located at the base of a communal tree marks her presence, or she is identified with a navel stone. Either way, she represents the center of the village. Her power extends from the center to the outer boundaries of the village and no farther, although this does not mean that the area beyond the village is unimportant. In fact, the outlying territory represents a threat to village welfare, with the greatest threat being epidemic disease that is imagined as coming from beyond the sphere of the village and attacking it. Any disease or enemy of the village is also a foe of the goddess, against whom she will fight to defend the general welfare of the people.

An excellent example of a village goddess is Śitala, a goddess of smallpox. She is conceived as a hot, angry, capricious, and deadly mother, although her name ironically means "the cool one." Villagers can take steps to protect themselves from the goddess. A person can make ritual offerings to her, and make gestures of obeisance to her by uttering, for instance, her name at the moment of the birth of a child. A householder can protect a child by having it wear charm necklaces that include a coin for the goddess. Another method of protecting oneself is to place pots of water and sugar candies on rooftops. The underlying notion of this practice is for the goddess to cool herself. In northern India, women observe a festival called the Cold Seventh on the seventh day of the month of Chaitra (March-April). This is strictly a married women's festival, observed for the benefit of children and protection against the illness-causing goddess.[19]

In the case of Śitala, she is illness itself. When a person catches smallpox villagers believe that she possesses the victim. In fact, she manifests herself in the rash and pustules on the skin of the victim. These pustules are called pearls and viewed as her teeth that literally devour a stricken victim. It is commonly believed that victims of smallpox possess oracular powers.[20] When a person contracts smallpox, that person's sickroom becomes a temple to the goddess. In addition to the performance of a pūjā ceremony, a clay pot of water is placed under the patient's cot, and another pot of water and sugar is placed near the door, so that the goddess may cool herself. Being fed cooling foods like fruits of various kinds helps the patient. It is also important to maintain purity within the victim's room because impurity will cause the goddess to become angry if she is polluted.

The role of the guardian goddess within village religion is paradoxical because on the one hand she keeps away demons that might cause disease, with her power ensuring their expulsion. On other hand, she is said to inflict an epidemic on inhabitants as punishment for her people. When she possesses some people with an affliction, the experience of the disease represents an immediate manifestation of her presence. At the same time, there are expressions of her also being the victim of the disease. In summary, this scenario suggests that an epidemic disease is something that the goddess suffers, something that she inflicts on her people, and something that she combats for the benefit of her people. During normal periods without the anxiety and suffering associated with disease, the goddess receives little attention from villagers. However, once a crisis arises, the villagers will hold a festival to attempt to placate the goddess.

In south India, it is not uncommon for a figure to be placed before the village goddess, functioning as her watchman. Such a figure is the popular Telugu god Pōtu Rāju (Buffalo King), who is represented by a small wooden post of varying height that is erected in front of a sanctuary or beneath a tree and made of wood from a *śamī* tree. In his human form, he assumes the role of a warrior wearing a diadem headdress, holding a sword in his right hand and a severed head in his left.[21] Besides symbolizing the buffalo demon and a stylized form of the vedic sacrificial post, Pōtu Rāju also represents the goddess. By means of her grace, the goddess transforms him from a buffalo demon into her devotee and guardian.[22] This village guardian is, moreover, associated with the ancient vedic fire cult because of the wood from which he is constructed.

Village Festivals

Villagers throughout India celebrate festivals connected to the Sanskritic deities, much like city dwellers. Many of these festivals bring villagers and city dwellers into contact for a particular celebration. A good example of such interaction is the Citrā festival to celebrate the marriage of the goddess Mīnākṣī to Sundareśvara, a south Indian manifestation of Śiva. The name Mīnākṣī means "fish-eyed" goddess. Within the Indian cultural context, to be called "fish-eyed' is a compliment because large, unblinking eyes with dark pupils are considered a mark of human beauty.[23] Moreover, unblinking eyes are a characteristic of a deity. The name has theological implications because it suggests metaphorically that a mother fish (goddess) watches over her young offspring (people). The Citrā festival is celebrated annually during a month of the same name (from late April to the initial weeks of May).

According to the narrative behind the festival, Śiva's consort Pārvatī incarnates herself as Mīnākṣī, the offspring of a previously childless king, who is born with three breasts. The king is depressed that his daughter is a freak because of her extra breast. But the celestial voice of Śiva informs the king that his daughter's third breast will disappear when she meets her true husband. After her father's death, Mīnākṣī rules as a just and beneficent monarch, even though she is unmarried, which is unusual according to Indian cultural expectations for female leaders. She sets out to conquer the world by battling the gods for control of it. Besieging Mount Kailāsa, a place sacred to Śiva, she confronts and defeats an army commanded by Nandin, Śiva's bull vehicle. The routed Nandin appeals for help to Śiva. When Mīnākṣī sees Śiva her third breast disappears, which can be interpreted as a change from an androgynous being to a female.[24] The sister of the goddess calls this miraculous event to the attention of everyone. Śiva instructs Mīnākṣī to return to Madurai, where he will marry her. When she returns to the city a great celebration occurs. In the meantime, Śiva makes his way to Madurai with an impressive entourage, and the god is welcomed as he arrives in the city. Some especially buxom women are driven mad with lust when they spy the handsome deity. A series of ceremonies take place. Finally, as women sing, Śiva leads his bride into the marriage chamber where the wedding occurs. After bestowing lavish gifts on the guests, Śiva assumes the throne of Madurai. Having incarnated himself and become king in an act of grace, Śiva obtains a kingdom on earth and the city becomes great.

The festival is a twelve-day affair that includes a flag-raising ceremony at the temple on the first day, after a ceremony to repel evil or inauspicious influences. The entire festival involves seventeen formal processions outside of the temple. Each procession of images travels on vehicles with specific iconographic and mythological associations. Mīnākṣī is enshrined in an image made of green stone, standing in the bent-leg posture with two arms, holding in her right hand a lotus bud on which sits her green parrot, while her left arm hangs by her side. On the eighth day of the festival, Mīnākṣī is crowned Pāṇḍyan queen of Madurai, and she is defeated in battle by Śiva on that night, which differs from the mythological narrative in which she surrenders to the god instead of being conquered. The tenth day marks the actual wedding. But prior to the actual wedding, images of the god and goddess are taken to the temple and placed on a lover's swing before being taken to the marriage hall. Lamp-waving rituals honor the images, colored cord is tied around the right wrists of the images, and they are garlanded with flowers. A priest ties a series of silken scarves on the images along with a marriage necklace (*tāli*). With the marriage concluded, guests file by, honoring the images. The repetitious, yearly nature of the marriage ceremony is explained by claiming that someone sneezes or performs another inauspicious act during the ceremony. During the evening, the images of the newly married couple are taken in public procession through the streets. The Cart Festival occurs the next morning, with more public processions.

During the course of a typical day in the temple, the goddess and god are separate. They are, however, united at night. In fact, the image of the god is brought to the bedchamber of the goddess and placed on her bed, to the right. After evening worship is concluded, the bedchamber doors are closed until early the next morning, when the images are awakened and separated for the day. The daily pūjā rites symbolize the sexual relations of the deities, which have important cosmic implications because their relationship is necessary for the preservation of the universe. Even though the goddess is considered the inferior party when united with her husband, they complement each other because she represents his creative energy (*śakti*). Mīnākṣī's regular sexual relations are linked to her normal peaceful nature, whereas completely independent goddesses tend to be fierce, bloodthirsty, angry, and aggressive. If the goddess's sexual power represents a dangerous force, it is the male figure that functions to control this power within the context of marriage and regular sexual release. And yet, Minākṣī can be worshiped alone, but her spouse can only be worshiped in conjunction with her.

A separate nine-day festival during the month of Citrā occurs when Viṣṇu, who is known as the Beautiful One (Aḷakar), travels to the city of Madurai. This festival commemorates the freeing of a holy man from a curse to become a frog after praying to Viṣṇu for help. Many Hindus connect this festival with the marriage of Minākṣī and Śiva by explaining that Viṣṇu, as Aḷakar, is the brother of Minākṣī, but he does not arrive on time for the actual wedding. When told by another divine form of himself that the wedding has already taken place, Viṣṇu becomes angry, although there are several versions of this scenario. It is possible to view the juxtaposition of these festivals as Minākṣī standing "at the center of the temporary ritual alliance between Śaivas and Vaiṣṇavas which the festival and the sacred marriage represent."[25] It is also interesting to note that inauspiciousness is linked with the independence of the goddess Minākṣī that occurs in festivals in which she is worshiped alone, whereas her auspiciousness is directly linked to her union with the male figure.[26] Moreover, the superiority of the male deity is emphasized by the myth and the fact that he is taken to her bedchamber nightly in a form called the Cŏkkar, a pair of feet embossed on a metal stool, which suggests that the spouse gets to sleep with the lowest part of the god's body. Overall, the Citrā festival possesses a strong regional importance for Madurai, although it does attract Hindus from distant places and thus also possesses significant economic consequences for the city.

The Importance of a Village House

A home in south India is similar to a human being in the sense that it possesses a life. In short, a house is not an inert structure. It is a living being with a horoscope, dispositions, and feelings.[27] It is also like a child in the sense that it is conceived, develops, is born, changes, and eventually dies when it is abandoned. A house is thus a substance in constant flux. In fact, it mixes and changes according to the substances that come in contact with it.

In the southern Tamil region, houses are built very close to one another because Tamils feel cozy and comfortable when in a crowd. Tamil fear being left alone, and their ultimate fear is to die alone. They also demonstrate a fear of unknown substances invading their space. In the northern Indian village of Sirkanda, a new house and its occupants are protected from hostile alien spirits by a ceremony called "house pot." This all-night rite involves sealing into the wall of the home a pot containing sacred items. It is believed to protect the house from disease, accident, violence, death, economic misfortune, and crop failure.[28]

When building a house in a southern village in India, certain guidelines must be followed. It is essential that a site be chosen that is unoccupied by another house, and it must not contain the remains of any dead things. Another useful guideline is that there should be no creatures destructive to building material like white ants or wood beetles. Moreover, it is important to look for favorable signs such as a garden lizard, tree frog, or a crab that would indicate that the soil is virgin. Earthworms are also auspicious because they indicate the presence of water.

Once an appropriate piece of land is selected, it is time to conceive the house. This occurs when a corner post is placed into a hole dug in the southwest corner of the site. The actual birth of the house occurs when the life breath of the owner and his wife enter the house. Likewise, when the last living person abandons a house it dies. While the house and its inhabitants are alive, the initial inhabitant influences the disposition of a house. When an inhabitant and a house are incompatible, this situation can cause serious problems for each party. Assuming that compatibility exists between the house and its inhabitants, the house reaches maturity when it attains a stable nature and interacts in predictable ways with its occupants and other houses.

There is also a connection between the house and the caste of the inhabitant, which means that a house assumes the rank of the *jātī* (subcaste) of it occupants. This entails a house observing the rules of status and propriety associated with the specific subcaste to which the inhabitants belong by birth. Nonetheless, it is also possible for a house to have a nature that is independent of its owner. For the most part, a house and its inhabitants are made of similar substances that they share and exchange.

There is an especially intimate connection between a house and its inhabitants in Kerala. A person's initial name is the same as the house name, which is also the family name.[29] Among the higher-caste homes of Kerala, many consist of a four-sided structure centered around an atrium, which is a sacred place for festivals, a place for growing flowers, and a location at which members can enter into social agreements. Divine images are located in the western part of the house, and a person enters from the east. In the northeastern part of the house, there is a place to bathe, whereas the northwest is the direction for defecation. The western end of the house is where birth occurs, and the east end is the location of the kitchen. The south is where matchmaking, marriage, worship, and feasts occur. There is also a diagonal that runs from the southwest to the northeast corner where there are finger-size holes in the wall that facilitate the flow of air through the house. It is imagined that the foundation of the house is built upon a demonic (*asura*) being with a human form. As a visitor moves toward the private areas of the home the rooms close and become smaller to provide for privacy, security, and seclusion. The homes are not static entities because they are believed to expand toward the east, and the east-west dimension of the house enables blending and its opposite to occur. Moreover, the actions of the residents are believed to affect the house.[30] Therefore, these upper-caste homes are always changing and naturally expanding dwellings that interact with the residents, share features with a temple, and serve as a miniature cosmos for its residents.

Among the Coorgs of Mysore state, the lamp in the home symbolizes the unity of the joint family, whereas the kitchen stove signifies domestic solidarity and strength. The sudden extinction of the lamp suggests decay and death.[31] When a member of the joint family dies, the funeral pyre is lit by fire from the kitchen stove.

Human Body Symbolism

By understanding the way that villagers conceive of the human body, it is easier to grasp the distinction between pure and impure in everyday life. The human body is hierarchically ordered in Hinduism, with the head considered the highest part and the feet the lowest part of the body. In addition to the vertical contrast between the head and feet, there is a distinction between the exterior and interior of the body. Furthermore, the right and left side of the body and the front and back aspects of the body stand in opposition to each other.

The head is the highest and most noble part of the body. During periods of illness, it is the initial part of the body to be protected, by wrapping it with towels. In contrast to the head, the feet are far inferior.[32] They are not merely the lowest part of the body, but they are also the part of the body that often comes into contact with dirt, refuse, or impure things. If one extends the feet toward a person, shrine, or an image of a deity, this gesture is considered an insult. An even worst insult is to kick another person or beat them with a shoe. Conversely, to extend or bow one's head is a compliment and an act of respect. To lower one's head to the level of the feet of another person and to touch them with one's head or hands represents an act of submission and surrender to the other person. It is a common custom to touch the feet of figures that are superior, those that function as one's protector such as parents, or represent a politically or religiously powerful person such as a king, guru, or deity. This humble gesture suggests, however, a reciprocal obligation for the person to whom one surrenders. In other words, the person who accepts one's act of surrender is obligated to accept the gesture and its implications for reciprocity.[33]

By touching the feet of another person, the initiator of the gesture is fundamentally taking the purest and most noble part of his or her anatomy and communicating that it is the same or less than the basest and most polluted part of another party. This social act is a ritual gesture that is an integral part of ordinary village life. It is common for a villager, for instance, passing a shrine of a deity to slightly incline the head forward toward the shrine and to bring both hands together at the level of the face.[34]

The right and left sides of the human body are significant. The right hand, for instance, is connected with correctness, purity, and auspiciousness, whereas the left hand represents the exact opposite. The right hand is used for important acts such as eating and accepting gifts. The left hand is used for impure acts such as cleaning oneself after defecating. It is not uncommon to witness the left hand of a villager hanging limply at his or her side or tucked behind the back in order to be out of the way.

The front and the back of the body are equally significant. By directly facing something or someone, a person demonstrates respect. When a villager encounters an acquaintance he or she will place his or her palms together before the face and say "namaste." If one turns one's back on another person, this is considered an affront. It is socially permissible, however, to turn one's back on a low or polluting thing.

The final bodily distinction is between inside and outside. In short, the inside must be protected from its external surroundings because of the dangers associated with ingesting polluting items. What enters the body from the outside must meet a higher standard of purity than what one might simply touch with a hand. Careful scrutiny must be paid to what one eats and its source of preparation. Interior bodily waste such as urine, feces, spittle, earwax, nail and hair clippings, nose mucus, semen, and blood are all considered inferior and polluting. Thus the margins of the human body are considered dangerous because one encounters polluting items there and one gives off polluting things at the edge of one's body. If one accepts the leftover food of another person that has been contaminated by contact with a person's saliva, this is considered an act of profound humility, more even than touching the feet of another person.

Bodily Possession

Being possessed violates the integrity of the body. A villager can become possessed by three main sources: sorcery, demons, and the goddess. Redressive action may call for the services of a priest or exorcist.

In south India a possessed villager can counteract sorcery by employing an exorcist to perform the *kaḷippu* (removal, casting out, rejection) ritual. The rite begins exactly at midnight, with the person afflicted facing east and sitting cross-legged. The countermeasure used by the exorcist involves the creation of a seven-inch anthropomorphic effigy of the victim made of rice or wheat dough, dung, clay, or ashes from a funeral ground. The effigy shares the bodily features of the possessing demon: protruding tongue, bulging eyes, and exaggerated sexual organs. The effigy is given birth by being placed on a winnowing fan, which distinguishes between pure and impure, and having charcoal paste applied to it to "open its eyes," which gives it life. The exorcist offers it delicacies preferred by demons such as cigars, liquor, and puffed rice. He then proceeds to destroy the effigy before a stone image of Kālī. The rite ends with the death of the effigy, which functions to neutralize the spell. A small lamp is lit near the effigy that is reminiscent of ordinary funeral practice.[35]

In the same village, there is also a ritual designed to drive away demons (*pēy*s), who tend to represent the malevolent spirits of failed lovers who were driven to suicide. These demons have a different personality from sorcery demons because they possess proper names, have a clearly defined identity, and are motivated by love and lust. This type of demonic possession is more apt to occur among women. These demonic spirits cause serious psychic disorders and incite women to reject their husbands. The demon enters the female victim through a lock of hair. Then the demon elopes with her by forcing her to separate mentally and physically from her husband and community. After entering the victim, the demon sexually enjoys her and prevents her from resuming relations with her husband. The major countermeasure employed is to entice the demon/victim to dance and speak. This involves the exorcist pulling the victim's hair and whipping her with leather straps.[36] It is possible to view these lustful demons as a class of cultural symbols that express deep psychological conflicts. From a practical perspective, it is also a way for women to express and manage their personal problems.[37]

In addition to demons, it is also possible for a person to be possessed by a goddess—for example, by Māriyamman in the village of Samayapuram near the south Indian city of Tirucirapaḷḷi.[38] During the second week of April, a festival occurs and follows a familiar pattern that begins with a worshiper taking a vow some months prior to the festival to worship the goddess in a particular way in response to a personal crisis. Not to fulfill the vow would involve a severe penalty inflicted by the goddess. The vow involves months of fasting and sexual abstinence, shaving the head, donning bright yellow clothes, taking an exhausting walk to the temple area, and finally dramatically dancing along the road to the temple. The dance can take many different forms. Some dancers insert sharp metal objects through their tongue or cheeks. Other dancers carry on their backs a shrine-like structure that is anchored to them by wires. The most heroic dancers are considered the "hook swingers," who come along the road suspended from a long boom, held by a hook through a muscle in their backs. It is common for parents to give the hook swinger their child to hold, because this brings blessing upon the child. After worshipers make offerings at the temple, they leave by a back door to discern the type of power given to them by the goddess. This phase involves the trance of possession. There is often a feeling that a dancer obtains an answer, becomes healed, or is freed from his or her personal crisis. It is also common for those who are possessed to be used by other people who want answers to their own problems.

In northwest India, the goddess may possess a woman in what locals call "wind form" and "playing." What this means is that the goddess assumes the form of the wind, enters a woman, and plays with her. This possession gives a woman a vision of the goddess that is accompanied by a sensation of wind. The vision of the goddess presupposes the preexistence of faith in the devotee. An observer witnesses the possessed person's voice change, her eyes becoming glazed, a constant whirling of her head, and the accompanying freely flying hair. The possessed person is designated a vehicle because the goddess rides on or inhabits her. Once a woman is possessed, the goddess can speak through her in order to help her devotees and reveal her power (*śakti*).[39]

Toward the end of some goddesses' festivals such as those of Draupadī and Māriyamman, devotees who have made vows to the goddess perform fire walking. The firewalkers bathe before walking on the hot coals and don new yellow dhotis for the occasion, while they hold margosa leaves in either hand. The fire is lit, using the fire from an earlier marriage ceremony. It is possible to interpret this type of devotional action as a form of torture to which devotees willingly agree to commit themselves. It is also possible to view the practice as resembling the fire that would consume everything at the end of the world.[40] Hence, firewalking can be viewed from at least two perspectives: a personal act or an eschatological one that symbolizes the total destruction of the world.

Oppositions in Village Culture

There are numerous oppositions within village culture that are in tension with each other, although similar types of opposition can also be encountered in the Sanskrit and regional traditions. These oppositions include such distinctions as hot and cold, auspicious and inauspicious, and pure and impure. The opposition between hot and cold can be seen with respect to food, colors, and ritual.

Hot and cold are relative concepts that depend on locality, caste, individual, and time. They are in constant contention with each other, because heat is essential for life, whereas cold implies something that is inanimate and inert. If heat is uncontrolled, it can be dangerous. It is heat that animates a substance.[41] A menstruating woman is, for instance, considered physically and emotionally hot.[42] In order to cool themselves in Kerala, menstruating women apply coconut oil to their head, hair, and entire body, and they use fresh turmeric on their faces and bodies as an additional coolant and cosmetic.[43] Hot and cold are distinctions used to differentiate two forms of a goddess: an iconic cool form within a shrine or temple and an aniconic hot form located outside of a shrine such as, ironically, a pot of water.

An important distinction is made between hot and cold foods. Foreign foods are, for instance, without exception hot. Ice cream is, for example, very hot. Thus the distinction between hot and cold have little to do with temperature.[44] It is possible to understand this distinction by noting that heat is associated with transformation, whereas cold is connected to that which is stable, sterile, and nonprocreative. However, it is still difficult to construct general rules. It is easier to understand the distinction by living within the context of Indian culture. Therefore, citrus fruits and cow products are cooling, as are oils and spices, while grains and strong liquors are hot.

The opposition between hot and cold applies to illness, too. Generally speaking, heat is connected with the buildup of blood. Since erotic desire is associated with the increase of blood, this situation can lead, for instance, to the outbreak of facial pimples. The cure for such skin problems is marriage and frequent sexual activity to cool oneself down.

There are also hot and cold colors. The colors green and white are considered cool, whereas the color red is a hot and auspicious color with respect to marriage in general and fertility, procreation, and motherhood in particular. Since white is a cool, infertile, and nonpassionate color that is associated with widowhood, marginality, and lack of social interest, married women refrain from wearing garments of such a color.[45] It is possible, however, to find an exception in Kerala, where white is the preferred color of dress for both genders. This preference can possibly be attributed to a perceived need to compensate for the natural female redness.[46] It is also possible to understand the use of color in Indian ritual as originating primarily from assumptions about the nature of heat.[47]

There is also a connection between auspicious events and hot and cold colors. It is considered important to begin and end an auspicious event with white or coolness and to have heat occur in the middle of an event. Betel leaf and areca nut are, for instance, commonly served to guests when they arrive at one's house and when they depart. These are considered cooling substances. It is believed that these delicacies leave a guest in a cool and auspicious condition.

As mentioned previously, heat and color play a role in a ritual context, where heat is associated with life and fertility. Heat is something that can either activate or nullify life, which points to its dangerous aspects. Thus, heat must be focused and controlled in order to become a source of power. Within the context of ritual, cooling things must encompass heat. South Indian rituals follow a sequence of three stages, with an initial cool state symbolized by white which gives way to a transitional stage that is a hot and red, which finally leads to coolness or white again.[48] The color white is auspicious, for instance, in a situation in which stability, well-being, and absence of evil are primary concerns, whereas the color red is desirable when innovation is sought.

Colors and heat also play a role in ritual purification. The intention of a ritual bath is to move a person from a condition of lesser to greater purity. This proceeds with a fully dressed person squatting with a kin or priest who pours a pot of freshly drawn water over his or her head and body. The water is poured in stages, and interspersed with small balls of cooked rice that a priest waves in front of the person. When this action is performed for the first or third time the rice is white. The second action involves rice that is reddened by the addition of a dye. It is believed that there is a reaction between the rice and additive that produces heat, that is, warmth is believed to accompany this change of color. Therefore, the white rice balls remain cool and stable, while the red ball of rice is heated and unstable.

Within the context of Indian culture, auspiciousness is an absolute value that is manifested as a quality of events in the lives of persons. With respect to time, this notion means that certain days are auspicious and others are inauspicious because of the planets with which they are connected. Auspicious days and their astrological associations are: Sunday (sun) Monday (moon), Wednesday (Mercury), Thursday (Jupiter), and Friday (Venus). The inauspicious group is: Tuesday (Mars) and Saturday (Saturn). A female villager, for instance, smears her floors with cow dung on Tuesday, and Saturday because they are considered inauspicious days. Sunday or Tuesday are, for instance, auspicious days for beginning the wheat harvest, whereas Tuesday is an auspicious day for traveling but Saturday is considered inauspicious. The sources of inauspiciousness can be traced to astrological conditions. This means that the conjunction of times and activities are important because certain periods bring inauspiciousness, when particular activities are undertaken. Another factor is the conjunction in a person's horoscope, which refers to particular configurations of heavenly bodies. Unless a person is careful, it is possible to make an inappropriate matching of persons and places. It is also important to avoid inappropriate conjunctions of spaces and times. For instance, auspicious lunar days are the second, third, fifth, seventh, tenth, and thirteenth, and fifteenth of each half of the month, whereas auspicious solar days include Sunday, Monday, Wednesday, Thursday, or Friday. The lunar month is divided into the light half (auspicious), reflecting the waxing of the moon, and the dark half (inauspicious), when the woon wanes.

It is important to be aware that inauspiciousness circulates spontaneously among related persons. Thus bodily connections serve as channels.[49] And these connections are created at certain crucial points of life such as marriage, death, and birth. The culturally approved method of getting rid of inauspiciousness is giving, which is a gift that another person is obliged to accept, but does not have a right to claim. This ritual form of giving involves a gift bestowed upon a designated recipient. There are two cultural functions of this type of giving: it enables a god to appropriate the offering, and it transfers the negative qualities and substances of inauspiciousness from the donor to the recipient. By the transferal of inauspiciousness, its opposite is ensured, because the gift removes the danger, affliction, sin, or evil from the donor to the recipient.

The various oppositions between hot and cold, auspicious and inauspicious, and pure and impure that characterize village culture are not rigid forms of antagonism. These kinds of oppositions should be understood as complementary. They also do not represent breaks in cultural continuity with the past.[50]

Purity and Pollution

Due to the importance of purity and impurity for Brahmins in particular and village society in general, we will examine them separately from other forms of oppositions in village culture. We will review the significance of this distinction for members of the Brahmin caste in this section and its implications for members of the lower castes in the next section. We will also examine the stages of purity, its implications for food and eating, and sources of pollution mostly with evidence borrowed from southern India.

There are three stages of ritual purity for members of the Brahmin caste: ritually pure (*maḍi*), ritually impure (*muṭṭucheṭṭu*), and normal ritual status (*mailigē*).[51] The first is obtained by ritual bathing; it is a relative concept. The second stage occurs when a ritually pure person eats, sleeps, or touches another person. These activities compromise one's ritual purity. Normal ritual status involves a person that is impure relative to a person in ritual purity. This occurs when one contacts objects of extreme impurity. Such an example would be a Brahmin male coming into contact with a member of the Untouchable caste or a menstruating woman. This type of severe pollution can be removed by doing the following: bathing, changing one's sacred thread, changing clothes, and eating the five sacred products of a cow. Bathing and changing clothes can rectify less severe types of pollution.

If one is ritually pure, one can lose purity by being touched by someone in a lesser condition of purity, not necessarily a member of a lower caste or a menstruating woman. A pure person can lose purity by touching a piece of cloth that is not ritually pure (*maḍi*). Due to such possibilities, a person can take certain protective measures, such as wearing silk while ritually pure because this fabric does not readily transmit pollution. In fact, silk remains ritually pure for one week. A person wishing to remain ritually pure can also take protective measures when traveling. Travelers can, for instance, carry a vessel of pure water to protect their ritual purity, and purify the ground in front of them by sprinkling it with water. Protective measures can also be exercised against another person because a person can, for instance, talk to another person through a third party. If one is alone, one can simply pick up a stick and talk to it and thus avoid direct contact with another person.

In order to maintain purity, a person must be careful about eating habits and food. In order to maintain ritual purity, only vegetarian food is permissible for a member of the Brahmin caste. Such strong foods as onions and garlic are considered inappropriate to Brahmin status. This is also true of foods that resemble meat in color like pumpkins, tomatoes, radishes, and carrots. Alcoholic beverages are also prohibited. There are certain Brahmin groups that do not accepted cooked food from any other caste, whereas uncooked foods can be received or handled by members of any caste.

It must also be noted that the process of eating is potentially polluting because saliva is extremely defiling. Moreover, the manner of eating determines the amount of pollution. If, for instance, a Brahmin male inadvertently touches his fingers to his lips, he should bathe or change his clothes. Saliva pollution can also be transmitted through some material substance. The practical result of such beliefs is that one must drink water, for instance, by pouring it into one's mouth instead of putting one's lips on the edge of a cup, or one smokes cigarettes through the hand so that the cigarettes never touch one's lips.

For religiously observant Brahmins, there are two types of meals: *ūṭa* (whose basis is boiled rice) and *tiṇḍi* (which consists of fruits, fried foods, sweets, and dishes cooked in water). A person eats correctly by using the right hand because the left hand is used for unclean practices associated with excretion and urination. When one eats, this action conveys polluting saliva to the body and to the leaf or dish from which it is eaten. The second type of meal is not as defiling because it can be tossed into the mouth. The practice of biting or chewing food is symbolic of conveying saliva pollution to the body. The *tiṇḍi* type of meal is prepared using metal pots, which can be cleaned. In contrast, the pottery vessels can never be purified after they become polluted. The female serving the meal remains in a state of *maḍi* (ritual purity) until others have finished eating. Then she serves herself.

Once she begins to eat, she should not touch cooking vessels because her status changes when she begins to eat and generates saliva. Due to her inferior and subservient status in comparison to her husband, a wife is expected to eat her husband's leftovers, while the husband is expect to leave a small amount of food for his wife as a mark of affection.

In addition to the pollution associated with eating and saliva, a major source of pollution is menstruation. Menstruating women are highly visible in Indian villages, and talk about their identity is commonplace. When a woman begins to menstruate she leaves the house and remains outside, for example, on the back or front verandas of the home. Such a woman does not change her clothes, refrains from combing her hair, does not bathe or wear the red dot on her forehead (a mark of beauty and married status) for five days. In terms of her normal household chores, she can sweep or clean the exterior area of the house. She can also clean rice, milk cows, and bring vegetables home, but she cannot cut them. If a woman is a mother with very young children, they can stay with her, while children over two years of age must avoid their mother. While a woman observes her menstrual period, a husband is forced to assume some female duties like cooking and serving meals to the children, caring for the children, drawing water for cooking and bathing, and caring for the livestock. By doing this work, the husband gives his wife what is ordinarily agreed to be a "menstrual vacation" by the community. At the conclusion of her menstrual period, a woman takes a ritual bath to regain her full purity and resume her normal life.

The discrimination normally exercised against menstruating women is absent at Mel Maruvattur, a village about fifty miles from Madras at the temple of Ādiparāśakti. Based on a revelation made to a village member, the land associated with the village is a location in which the goddess resides. The young male recipient of the revelation from the goddess instructs all pilgrims to wear red clothes, which is symbolic of the blood that unites them in spite of different skin shades. This basic equality extends to everyone, of any gender, caste, or race. In addition, menstruating women are allowed to worship in the temple, in sharp contrast to orthodox temples, because they are not polluted according to the villagers.[52]

In addition to pollution associated with blood, death pollution is another major form; the body of the deceased is impure and the surviving kinfolk are also infected. Thus death pollution is transmitted by genealogical linkage. Pollution is greater the more closely related a person is to the deceased. A close kin is impure for a period of eleven days. If a nonrelative comes into contact with someone polluted by death, that person becomes polluted. Bathing and changing clothes can remove the impurity. During periods of death pollution, members of a family can neither perform any ceremonies nor conduct religious rites.

A so-called happy form of pollution is associated with birth and is also transmitted through kinship, with the exception that birth involves a smaller group of kinsfolk. For example, a new mother's parents are defiled for a period of three days. But if a daughter gives birth in the home of her parents, they are defiled for eleven days. Due to the pollution associated with the blood of birth, a midwife from the washerman caste assists with the delivery and is paid for her services. After giving birth, a mother is polluted for a period of three months, while her husband is defiled for eleven days.

In addition to pollution connected to blood and death, other types of pollution are connected to bodily emissions, such as that from the blood or pus associated with a wound. Another type of bodily emission is urine, which should not be splashed on an individual. In order to prevent splashing of urine and defiling someone, there is a traditional prohibition against a male urinating while standing: It is preferable to squat. After defecating, it is preferable to use water to cleanse oneself instead of paper, which causes a person to remain in a state of impurity. Accidentally stepping on dog, goat, sheep, or chicken waste is considered polluting. Crow waste and spit are especially defiling and should be avoided at all cost. Another general source of impurity is contact with leather. Thus it is important not to touch leather sandals with one's hands or to be hit with leather sandals by an angry person. Sexual relations, shaving, cutting of hair or nails by a barber—these are all activities that cause impurity. A person can also become impure after a solar or lunar eclipse because these are considered inauspicious times.

A final major category of defilement is respect pollution. Unlike many of the instances of the other categories of defilement, respect pollution is intentional; it is done to show deference and respect. By doing that which under normal circumstances would be defiling, one expresses one's inferior position. Such an instance would be a wife eating from her husband's leaf or plate. Another appropriate illustration is worship of the feet (*pāda pūjā*) that is done by person in an inferior or subservient social position. Such worship occurs when a dutiful wife washes the feet of her husband, or when ordinary people wash the feet of their guru (teacher) and possibly drink the so-called foot nectar. A less dramatic example is for an inferior person to touch the feet of a superior. This would include touching the feet of a teacher, father, or mother.

This review of major categories of pollution makes it evident that purity is a relative and not an absolute state. The Sanskrit deities are, for instance, more pure than local divine beings, vegetarian deities are more pure than nonvegetarian figures, gods are more pure than Brahmins, whereas Brahmins are more pure than members of the lower castes. It is probably best to think of fields of purity like islands within a sea of impurity. This metaphor suggests that purity is artificially created and specially maintained; it also suggests that purity is a ritual state of being that is temporary. Within this context, it is incorrect to view purity and impurity as simply opposites, because only some beings can become pure; a group such as the Untouchables is condemned to an absolute and permanent condition of impurity. As we have noticed, pollution can flow either through a conductor or from one being to another, whereas purity cannot flow. Purity is an impermanent state that can be lost but not transferred. From all that has been said, it is obvious that being a member of the Brahmin caste and attempting to maintain one's ritual purity is a constant and considerable burden, although the Brahmin caste is aided in their religious struggle by the lower castes.

Lower-Caste Ritual Specialists

There is no single caste that is self-sufficient because each caste requires the services of other groups within the socioeconomic context, with certain castes holding a monopoly over particular crafts and professions. These different craft and professional castes are interdependent. Thus Indian village life manifests a system of cooperative labor that is based on a pattern of intercaste relationships governed by tradition.[53] The result is that each family is attached socially and economically to other village families with different occupational specializations. Although exchange of cash payments does occur, most economic dealings involve exchanges of services or farm products.

An essential specialist is the potter, who represents the middle rank in the village caste system. Potters make pots and other earthenware items for everyday use. They also supply vessels for ritual occasions. Since a potter's vessels are used for purification, he plays a crucial role in the management of ritual pollution.[54] In addition, they sacrifice sheep or goats at some village goddess festivals. They may also serve as a priest (*pūjāri*) in certain contexts, such as the shrines of the Untouchable caste. Potters also perform funeral rites for other castes.

Village ritual specialists also include barbers and washers as experts in impurity. Their work renders them among the lowest caste because they deal directly with defiling bodily emissions like hair, fingernails, and toenails. Moreover, washers deal with various types of bodily fluids that soil clothing. Barbers and washers deal with pollution by taking it upon themselves, and they serve others by freeing them from defilement. They also perform nonpurifying services. Washermen notify relatives, for instance, of births and first menstruations, whereas barbers are traditional mediators in marriage negotiations. In addition, barbers are commonly the village surgeons and often serve as general physicians and exorcists. Moreover, women of the barber and washerman caste are usually village midwives. Both barbers and washermen serve in the village goddess cult by sacrificing animals. Sometimes the potter presides over the sacrifices, while the barber and washerman do the actual killing.[55] It is also not unusual to witness the washerman carrying the image of the goddess in procession during a festival celebration.

The single social group that removes the most pollution is the Untouchables. Their traditional responsibilities include village sanitation, scavenging, disposing of the carcasses of dead animals, and leatherwork. The Untouchable subcaste called the Mādigas play a social role as drummers (they are Untouchable because of the connection of this musical instrument and leather) and work as musicians at religious ceremonies and at the head of funeral processions. It is easy to miss the irony of this situation, with the most defiled members of the village community leading the remainder of the community in a festival procession. Some Untouchables specialize in telling and dramatizing narratives from the epic literature, purāṇic literature, and local legends. Female members of the Mādigas also serve as community prostitutes, while males function to slay the buffalo sacrificial victim at the festival of the goddess. Thus lower-caste members play a vital social role protecting the highest caste from pollution. In a sense, the lower castes enable the Brahmins to follow their lifestyle and fulfill the demands of their religion.

Concluding Remarks

The typical Hindu village is the domain of the goddess. The destiny of its inhabitants is in her hands. Although she represents the symbolic center of the village and her power only extends to its boundary, she usually receives little attention. This changes drastically when a crisis arises. The typical response to a crisis is to hold a festival. As evident by the complex festival for Mināksī, villages share a cultural continuity with cities by sharing common mythological themes and festival observances. The pattern of village life suggests that the answers to the critical problems of life are essentially religious in nature.

The binary oppositions common to village religious life are grounded in the symbolism of the human body. The opposition between head and feet, right and left, interior and exterior, front and back are directly connected to common village oppositions associated with hot and cold, auspicious and inauspicious, and purity and impurity. These binary opposites are not mutually exclusive. Therefore, they do not need to be kept separate.

The various binary oppositions do not suggest that village life is divided or fragmented. The typical village is a socioreligious whole that is arranged according to caste and is territorially grounded. Its various servant castes provide everyday services, and they function to facilitate the orderly flow of polluting items in particular and village life in general. During times of crisis, potters, barbers, washermen, and Untouchables play vital religious roles. These impurity experts know how to remove it for the maintenance of purity and order. Therefore, the upper castes are dependent upon their expertise for continuing their way of life.

14

Reformers, Missionaries, and Gurus in Modern Hinduism

Suffering under the yoke of colonialism; criticized for their religious beliefs, practices, and hierarchical social system by foreign Christian missionaries intent on converting Indians to the true path of salvation; encountering hundreds of years of Western thought in a short period of time; and being exposed to Western science and technology—all these functioned as a culture shock to Indians during the eighteenth and nineteenth centuries. Christian missionaries openly criticized what they perceived to be a hopelessly benighted and backward culture with many barbarian customs. The only hope for Indians, they said, was for them to be converted into Christians. It is ironic that the attempt to convert Hindus into Christians resulted in the conversion of "heathens" into reformist Hindus: "The challenge of orthodox Christianity in India stimulated the Hindu intelligentsia to rediscover the sources of their own religious tradition and to reform their religion according to their new image of the remote past."[1] Some Indians reacted to the Western challenge by becoming social, religious, and political reformers. Adopting Western practices, some Indians became missionaries, whereas others became leaders of their own religious movements that were centered on a deified guru (teacher). Modern Hinduism is characterized by the words and actions of these reformers, missionaries, and deified leaders.

Hindu Reformers

Arguably the greatest reformer was Rammohan Roy (1772–1833), who worked as a revenue officer for the East India Company until 1814. He founded the Brāhmo Sabhā in 1928, which was a monotheistic form of Hinduism devoid of images, financially supported by the wealthy Dwarkanath Tagore. This movement later became the Brāhmo Samāj (Society) in 1843, when it was revitalized by Debendranath Tagore (1817–1905), the father of the creative literary figure Rabindranath Tagore (1861–1941), who won the Nobel Prize for literature in 1913 for his work entitled

Gitanjali. The purpose of the organization was to restore the ancient tradition of dharma to India and to worship the single, supreme, eternal god. The latter intention of the organization was influenced by European deism and Unitarianism, which also motivated Roy to deny the role of prophets and the uniqueness of the notion of the Son of God.

A member of the Brahmin caste and son of a landowner, Roy studied the Upaniṣads and Vedānta philosophy, and he used the former texts to argue that its rationality should be used to judge social institutions and practices. Roy argued that the Upaniṣads embodied a pure theism that excluded image worship, and did recognize human rights. Grounded in his appeal to India's glorious past and a deistic type of theism, Roy rejected many traditional Hindu notions such as rebirth, karma, meditation, idolatry, sacrifice, and caste. Convicted of the unity of God from his study of Hindu sources and the influence of Unitarianism, he repudiated all myths, miracles, magic, and image worship that might compromise the unity of God. His belief in the unity of God also motivated him to reject the Christian doctrine of the trinity, virgin birth, and vicarious atonement. He initiated a vigorous campaign against compulsory widow immolation (*sati*) on the funeral pyre of a husband. While a young man, Roy was motivated by the forced immolation of his beloved sister-in-law. He argued that sati was not a part of the original dharma of the tradition. His campaign against widow immolation was a contributing factor that eventually led to a change of public opinion that made it possible to pass legislation making it illegal in 1829. Roy also criticized the practice of child marriage, worked to establish English-speaking schools, and established the first Bengali newspaper. His social reforms were based on his call for a return to Indian sources and away from blind adherence to custom and prejudice. Roy, in other words, was making an appeal to reason and common sense.[2] For his many reformist efforts, the Mughal emperor—who still held the title, if not much power—conferred upon him the title of Rāja, although orthodox Hindus excommunicated him.

The Brāhmo Samāj split in 1866 into the more conservative, original group lead by Debendranath Tagore, who created a Bengali newspaper and a school to train Brāhmo missionaries to counteract the spread of Christian missions, and the newer, more liberal Bhāratvarshīya Brāhmo Samāj of India lead by Keshab Chandra Sen (1838–1884) that emphasized a universal brotherhood under God the Father. The original group became known as the Adi Brāhmo Samāj, whereas Keshab led the new Brāhmo Samāj. The original reform movement was essentially religious under the leadership of Tagore, whereas the newer movement was more concerned with social issues, such as widow remarriage, after Keshab joined in 1857. Keshab also raised funds for victims of floods and famines, advocated schools for boys and girls, fought for literacy, criticized child marriage, encouraged intercaste marriage, and pleaded for widow remarriage. The particular issue that split the movement occurred over Keshab's insistence that members reject their sacred threads. The reform movement did experience success with the passage of the Native Marriage Act III in 1872, which established minimum age limits for marriage. This legislative success was to further split the reform movement, when Keshab blatantly disregarded the law and married his daughter to the Maharaja of Cooch Behar in 1878. Many members of Keshab's movement seceded to form Sādhāran (General) Brāhmo Samāj, whereas Keshab formed his own new organization that reflected his personal religiosity, called the Church of the New Dispensation in 1879.

The New Dispensation (Naba Bidhan) was an effort to synthesize Hinduism, Islam, and Christianity, which led to some eclectic elements that included twelve disciples, advocacy of the motherhood of God, revival of waving (*āratī*) of camphor lamps, *homa* (fire oblation) ceremonies, the Durgā festival, and religious chanting like that of Caitanya. The organization intended to harmonize all sacred scriptures and religions within a message of love, allowing direct worship of God without a mediator.

The schism of the Brāhmo movement ushered in important internal changes that prevented a particular person (such as Keshab) or a family (such as the Tagores) from controlling the affairs of the organization by establishing definite rules and procedures for its operation. In comparison to Keshab's organization, the rational Sādhārans were liberal minded with respect to the possibility of social and political change. In addition to opposing mysticism and sentimentalism, the Sādhārans believed in a personal deity, the usefulness of congregational prayer, and the benefit of social action. Convinced of the brotherhood of human beings, they opposed caste distinctions and oppression of women. With a belief in the freedom of conscience, they envisioned working to create the moral and spiritual regeneration of humankind.

In contrast to the Sādhārans, Keshab began to believe that a Western solution to the problem of modernism in India was not possible. Keshab was attracted to Rāmakrishna's religious experiments and his claim to have direct contact with major religious figures (such as Buddha, Jesus, and Muhammad) by means of intuition, which made the Bengali saint appear to be more of a universalist than Brāhmo members. After his encounter with Rāmakrishna and learning about the importance of the goddess Kālī in the religiosity of the saint, Keshab utilized Śāktism for his own purposes, and he became intrigued by the "Motherhood of God," which he began to think might be a more effective symbol of the divine than was the father. He also began to recognize the figure of Christ as a vehicle of imperialism, which caused him to totally withdrawal from the social gospel advocated by Unitarianism in India.[3] Historically, Keshab made a contribution to the Rāmakrishna movement, because he was instrumental in spreading the fame of the Bengali saint through his newspaper.

In the region of Maharashtra, there emerged a reform movement called the Prārthana Samāj in 1867, which was led by Justice M. G. Ranade (1842–1901). He was one of the originators of the Indian National Congress (1885), the Indian National Social Conference (1887), and the Industrial Association of India (1890). These institutions reflect his broad interests in religion, politics, and economic reform. Many of the positions of the Prārthana Samāj were similar to those of the Brāhmo

Samāj, with special emphasis on improving the status of women and Untouchables. Another social reform it advocated was the elimination of caste restrictions. Unlike the Brāhmo Samāj, it grounded its worship in the devotional poems of the Vārkarī Panth and the compositions of the saint Tukārām.

In sharp contrast to the direction of the Brāhmo Samāj, the Ārya Samāj looked to India's past for its inspiration. Swāmi Dayānanda Sarasvatī (1824–1883) founded it in 1875 with the intention of restoring dignity to Indian culture. While a young boy, he witnessed rats climbing up the image of Śiva during a night vigil with his father. This sight perplexed him because the deity did not respond to this sacrilege, and he wandered for twelve years from one teacher to another seeking spiritual assistance. Finally, he met the blind teacher Swāmi Virājānanada Sarasvatī of Mathura, who addressed the young man's restless spirit. Dayānanda perceived a need to return to the Vedas and to use them as his guideline, which involved rejecting everything after the Vedas as superstition. When returning to the vedic hymns, Dayānanda interpreted them through a yogic perspective, devoid of any Western intellectual influences. He denied the polytheism of the Vedas, and he claimed that there was a single god behind all the divine names. He did, however, accept the notions of karma and rebirth, and he thought that the caste system was a social institution and nothing religious. For Dayānanda, the Vedas had a universal significance, although he remained an ethnically centered thinker by using the old concept of ārya, which is a notion of "nobility" shaped by ethnicity and geographical location.[4] Dayānanda conceived of the Vedas as the source of all human wisdom, including even the natural sciences. He also advocated the liberation of women and the end of caste abuses.

Dayānanda was concerned about conversions to Islam and Christianity. In order to counter conversions of low-caste Hindus, he established training institutions (*gurukulas*) for children to give them a vedic education. For those who had converted and wanted to return to the Hindu fold, he advocated a rite of purification for readmission. He thought that Hinduism had a mission to perform for the world. Because of his polemical style, he made numerous enemies, and it was rumored that he was fatally poisoned.

These reform movements appealed most strongly to younger Indians during the 1860s. By joining these reform movements, many of these young people lost social standing when they were excommunicated from their castes and ostracized by their families. With their new and often marginal social identity, these young people became the vanguard for modern India.[5]

Convinced that Brāhmo heritage could function as an antidote for Bengali social and political malaise, Rabindranath Tagore assumed leadership of the Adi Brāhmo Samāj as well the editorship of its journal, the *Tattvabodhini Patrika*, in 1911. Retaining pure theism and piety, he wanted to focus on the need for an internal vitality by means of self-discipline and meditation. He proceeded to condemn factionalism, sectarianism, communalism, and Brāhmo nationalism because these things lead to division rather than unity. In 1913, Rabindranath criticized religious figures that took their message to the West for giving a false impression of Hinduism.[6] This did not mean that he thought that India's problems with modernization could be solved by Westernization. He viewed the problems associated with modernization in India as social. Toward the end of his life, he established an educational institution called Shantiniketan, which was an attempt to recapture the spirit of the ancient Indian forest hermitage and its personal learning environment.

By the 1930s, the optimism ushered into India by Brāhmo ideology turned into disillusionment and despair. Worldwide economic depression, the rise of fascism, and new imperialist wars contributed to a change in attitude. The political struggle against colonialism continued, led by a religious figure, Gandhi, and a secularist, Nehru, among many others.

In contrast to both Gandhi and Nehru, another reform movement, the Rashtriya Swayamsevak Sangh (RSS) combined an ideology of healing, health, and yogic training with a political ideology that was anti-Western, anti-Christian, anti-Muslim, and opposed to secularism, corruption, and self-centered consumerism. The RSS, still active today, represents an attempt by Hindu fundamentalist forces to initiate a moral and cultural reform movement that would eventually culminate in national unity, with the establishment of a pure Hindu society. By means of discipline, yogic training, and good organization, the RSS attempts to cleanse Indian society of all impurities embodied by those things to which it is opposed. Its brand of religious nationalism is based on an "emotional bond between Hindu men and the idea of Bhārat Mātā, Mother India."[7] The ultimate goal of the RSS is the creation of a modern and strong Hindu nation, devoid of foreign influence, that is recognized as a world leader and military power.

Theosophy and Its Messiah

The Theosophical Society was founded in 1875 in New York by two fascinating figures named Henry Steel Olcott and Helena Petrovna Blavatsky (1831–1891). The former was born in Orange, New Jersey, in 1832, studied agriculture, wrote a book on sorghum, established a farm school, worked as a writer on agriculture for the *New York Tribune*, fought in the Civil War as a signals officer, and attained the rank of colonel, which is a title that he used throughout his life. After the Civil War, Olcott became a lawyer, married, fathered three children, and later divorced because he enjoyed the lifestyle of a playboy. Blavatsky was an eccentric Russian woman born in the Ukraine. She abandoned her first husband, had a long-term affair with an opera singer, is alleged to have given birth to one or more illegitimate children, entered into a short-lived bigamist relationship with a second husband while not divorced from her first spouse, and served as a spiritual medium.

While working for a newspaper, Olcott was sent to investigate some spiritual phenomena in a farmhouse in Vermont. After his published article made a positive impression, he was sent back to do a more complete investigation. The twice-weekly essays of Olcott were read by Blavatsky, who was motivated to visit the house in

Vermont and become acquainted with Olcott. On March 9, 1875, Olcott was invited by letter to join an occult group called the Brotherhood of Luxor. Another letter from Blavatsky claimed that she was to serve as Olcott's teacher in esoteric instruction. These activities lead to séances, spiritual investigations, and meetings of occultists that culminated in the founding of the Theosophical Society in the fall of 1875, with Olcott elected president and Blavatsky serving as corresponding secretary.

Blavatsky became famous for her writings, namely, the two-volume *Isis Unveiled* (published in 1877) and the two-volume *The Secret Doctrine* (published in 1888). Blavatsky claimed to have studied with Masters in Tibet, and they allegedly sent her to America with ancient esoteric knowledge that they dictated to her. Blavatsky was accused of plagiarism by spiritualists such as William Emmette Coleman, and by the Pali Text Society and other scholarly organizations. Her work claims that all faiths originated from a single source, an ancient universal religion. Therefore, all religions are based on a single true and secret doctrine. The book also promotes a view of the human spirit devolving into matter before it slowly ascends to its source. Blavatsky's second two-volume work was her masterpiece. The book claims to be based on the "stanzas of Dzyan," a mysterious ancient religious text unknown to scholarship. *The Secret Doctrine* depicts the creation of the universe, history of the earth, and the evolution of humankind. The book rests on three fundamental principles: existence of one absolute reality, the appearance and disappearance of cycles of the universe, and the identity of all souls with the single universal soul.[8]

The Theosophical Society made significant contributions to Indian culture in the nineteenth century, after the founders traveled to India in December 1878. A year after they arrived in India, they established a magazine entitled *The Theosophist* to promote their cause. The society formed a bond with the Ārya Samāj, although they never merged into a single entity. The society also made contributions to the Indian National Congress—the political movement that spearheaded the nationalist cause—and influenced a revival of Buddhism in Sri Lanka, where Olcott published a *Buddhist Catechism*, which went through forty editions in his lifetime. By 1880, the two leaders were in conflict, but the conflict ended with Blavatsky's death four years later. Thereupon, Olcott and William Quan Judge engaged in a struggle for power within the society, resulting in a schism. Finding herself in the middle of this struggle, Annie Besant, who became second president of the society, eventually supported Olcott.

Besant (d. 1933) led the Adyar Theosophists in India, and she became involved in the independence movement in India. She also adopted the cause of Indian education, and she was instrumental in establishing Central Hindu College, which later became Benares Hindu University. During a six-month tour of America in 1897, she established twenty-three new branches of the Theosophical Society. Besides promoting social work in India, she became involved with Indian Home Rule, and she served in the honorary position as president of the Indian National Congress in 1917. When she became an apologist for the British after the Amritsar massacre she was declared an unsympathetic foreigner.

An important associate of Besant was Charles W. Leadbeater, who was born in England in 1847 and ordained a minister of the Church of England, only to later publicly proclaim himself a Buddhist. He was considered a gifted clairvoyant and able to converse with the Masters, but he embarrassed the society when it was discovered that he was a pedophile. Besant defended him at first, but she later turned against him, and he was forced to resign. After Leadbeater was readmitted to the society, this led to a schism with the society in Australia.

Leadbeater discovered a gifted young Brahmin boy whose father was a member of and secretary within the society. The father was convinced by Besant to relinquish guardianship of his son, named Jiddu Krishnamurti (1895–1986) and his brother Nityananda, and allow them to move into Adyar (near Madras, now Chennai) to live. Besant and Leadbeater proclaimed fourteen-year-old Krishnamurti to be the next appearance of the World Teacher, which was equivalent to acclaiming him a messiah. This event occurred under the influence of the Budhists' expectation that the *bodhisattva* Maitreya would appear on earth. Leadbeater supervised Krishnamurti's training for his religious role and initiated him. Leadbeater also published a series of essays about the former lives of Krishnamurti in *The Theosophist*. Besant and Leadbeater started an organization called the Order of the Star in the East (later shortened to Order of the Star) to sponsor and promote Krishnamurti, who was taken to England in 1911 to be educated. After he was unable to gain entry to Oxford University, he attacked intellectualism and stressed his own unfettered mind.

At a Star Congress in 1925, Krishnamurti dramatically admitted to the audience that he was the expected World Teacher. In 1929, he made a complete turnaround by giving a speech dissolving the Order of the Star, renouncing all claims to divine status, and renouncing disciples. He thought that his status as the World Teacher was incompatible with his new convictions about the pathless and limitless nature of the truth that he had discovered for himself. He now argued that the truth can only be gained by complete self-awareness and self-knowledge achieved through meditation. Krishnamurti also resigned from the Theosophical Society the following year, which caused the society to lose a third of its membership. Thereupon, he began a career as an author, lecturer, and teacher unattached to any religion or sect. In addition, he rejected the role of a traditional guru, because he did not want people to become attached to him. He rather wanted people to become free by transforming their psyches.

Missionary Hinduism

The first genuine mission to the West was conducted unintentionally by Swami Vivekananda, who traveled to America for the World Parliament of Religions held in September of 1893 in conjunction with the Chicago World Fair, in order to represent Hinduism and raise funds for relief work in India. After postponing his address to the Parliament several times, he finally felt prepared to give his speech, which he began by saying "Sisters and Brothers of America." This personal approach received a very positive response from those listening. After the conclusion of the Parliament, he remained in America to raise money, lecture, and establish the Vedanta Society in America. Vivekananda's success in the West stirred deep patriotic feelings among Indians, and the public made him a national hero upon his return to India in 1896.

After his return to India, he created the Ramakrishna Mission in 1897, with the intention of establishing monastic institutions throughout the country. Between 1897 and 1899, Vivekananda established three periodicals to convey his message: *Brahmavadin* and *Prabuddha Bharata* published in English and the *Udbodhan* in Bengali. These organizations and publications would be the foundation for a worldwide mission and enable India to play a significant role in the development of human civilization. Vivekananda was convinced that India represented a treasury of religion and spirituality that it needed to share in order to save the materialistic West from moral and spiritual bankruptcy. Therefore, India had a duty and destiny to share her spiritual treasures with the West. When he returned to America in 1899, he established a second Vedanta Society in San Francisco. He left America in 1900, and he never returned due to physical debilities caused by diabetes; he died in 1902 on the fourth of July.

Vivekananda was a disciple of the Bengali saint Rāmakrishna, although the young man was originally convinced that the saint was insane, as was described in chapter 12. Earlier in his career, Vivekananda was a well-educated person from an upper-class family and a member of the Brāhmo Samāj. During his earlier years, he did not exhibit any mystical or spiritual inclinations, but he was a very complex person with intellectual strengths and personal failings throughout his life.[9] Similar to other reformers with sympathies for the Brāhmo Samāj, Vivekananda's reformist social agenda was critical of the privileges of Brahmins, because their social advantages functioned as an obstacle to his nationalist political aims. There was also a political aspect to his foreign missions, because they assumed that Advaita Vedānta arrived whenever religion disappeared. Vivekananda used indigenous cultural categories to argue his case by asserting that the West possessed an abundance of *rajas* qualities that gave it strength, energy, and vitality, whereas India had the superior *sattva* quality that gave it spirituality, light, and freedom.[10] From an economic and technological perspective, the West was dominant, but India possessed richer religious and spiritual resources.

Vivekananda's archetype for Hindu spirituality was a reinterpreted Advaita Vedānta that he characterized as practical, by which he meant Vedānta with a social conscience and this-worldly perspective. This is partially manifested as service to humanity. Although it is difficult to maintain that Vivekananda was a Vedāntin in the tradition of Śaṅkara because of the discontinuities between their philosophies,[11] he reinterpreted the tradition and utilized it in a way that he thought would appeal to a Western audience. Nonetheless, by stressing the practical aspect of his version of Vedānta, Vivekananda intended to call attention to the dynamic nature of his brand of universal religion that blended together action and compassion. Besides the practical side of his religion, Vivekananda emphasized experience (*anubhava*), which he perceived as blissful and self-validating. His notion of experience served as a key to his religious hermeneutic that allowed him to select truths from various world religions and gave his thought an eclectic character.[12] Within the context of this apparently tolerant selective process of interpretation, Vedānta philosophy was always Vivekananda's measure of fitness, which rendered other religious systems subordinate to it. In fact, Vedānta represents the culmination of all religions, because there is a single reality (Brahman) with which the universe and all souls will eventually merge. Rejecting the Christian notion of original sin, the official position of the movement is that everyone can attain liberation and everyone possesses a place within Hinduism, which is deemed identical with Vedānta philosophy.

These types of convictions and Vivekananda's influence on the movement were reflected in the movement's interpretation of the life of Rāmakrishna, whose religious experiments are interpreted as culminating in Advaita Vedānta. Scholars have called this official portrait of Rāmakrishna into question.[13] In his writings, Vivekananda confesses that a Western audience would never respond positively to a mad saint that worshiped a horrific goddess figure and practiced Tantra to some extent.[14]

Along with its universal message and emphasis on Advaita Vedānta as genuine Hinduism, the movement promotes a cult focused on Rāmakrishna and his wife Saradā Devī, the Holy Mother. For the most part, the early movement, during the initial decades of its development, ignored her. Followers rediscovered her after they reflected on an episode in the life of Rāmakrishna. This incident occurred in 1872, with the master in an ecstatic trance state. While in this condition, Rāmakrishna seated his wife on a chair and began to worship her as an incarnation of the goddess Kālī. Devoted followers interpreted this episode to mean that the master intended that his wife should be accepted as divine.

Revolutionary Mystic

After fourteen years of education in England, Aurobindo Ghose (1872–1950) returned to India and joined state service in Baroda. After the partition of Bengal in 1905, he joined the nationalist movement, and he became a leader of Bengali terrorists. In 1908, he was arrested for a bomb plot and incarcerated for sedition. While in prison, he underwent a religious experience that transformed his life and motivated him to abandon political activism. Before Aurobindo's imprisonment, Bankim Chandra Chatterjee (1838–1894), a religious nationalist famous for his fictional work entitled *Ānanda Math*, influenced him. This influential book contained the poem "Vande Mataram," (I Praise the Mother), which was a devotional hymn to the goddess Kālī. This poem was to be adopted by members of the nationalist movement as a national anthem for India. In 1910, Aurobindo traveled secretly to Pondicherry, a French settlement south of the city of Chennai (Madras). It was here that he established a monastery and the seclusion necessary to develop his own philosophy called Integral Yoga. He adopted the spiritual nationalism of Vivekananda, but Aurobindo transformed it into revolutionary action, simultaneously, transforming nationalism into something religious, akin to a political Vedāntism, which dramatically changed the notion of salvation (*mokṣa*).[15]

On the basis of his personal experience, Aurobindo developed a philosophy with several goals. A primary goal of his thought was to know, possess, and become a divine being, or what he called a superman. This involved a transformation of one's mentality into a supramental illumination. Another goal of his teaching was to build peace and bliss, to establish infinite freedom, and to discover and realize immortal life within our body. The highest goal of a person was to manifest the divine within oneself and realize God internally and externally.[16] Finally, his thought was intended to establish a unity that was both horizontal and vertical, which involved a unity that was singularly transcendent and included the many on the cosmic level. He also envisioned the aim of humankind as the realization of God within and without oneself. Moreover, Aurobindo envisioned himself following a middle path between materialism and spiritual monism.

Aurobindo viewed everything as originating from the absolute Brahman and eventually returning to it. Although he accepted spirit and matter as real, this position did not mean that the universe possessed an independent reality, because it existed for an observing consciousness.[17] Aurobindo perceived a purposeful force operating in the world, and he also thought that there was an impulse within human nature toward self-realization. Moreover, he envisioned a spiritual evolution operating within the universe.

The alpha and omega of the evolutionary process is Brahman, which is considered integral because it unifies many states of consciousness. The integral nature of Brahman challenges individuals to become likewise in order to manifest the nature of the absolute.[18] The absolute is defined as sat (being), cit (consciousness), and ānanda (bliss). The dynamic aspect of the absolute is supermind, a perfect unity and diversity, which Aurobindo calls supermind integral consciousness because it comprehends data of perception as inseparably interrelated parts of a cosmic whole. This is a nondual type of thinking that sees things as whole, and it is also nondichotomous when it intuitively grasps the ultimate unifying principle of creative freedom. The supermind, which represents a union of being and consciousness, functions as an intermediary link between the absolute and the world. As a self-extension of the absolute into space and time, supermind dwells in all things, but humans cannot see it because it is veiled. Moreover, Aurobindo referred to the supermind as the ecstatic śakti (feminine force) dimension of Brahman. By the power of the supermind, being-consciousness-bliss involve and evolve, descend and ascend, and the supermind thereby fulfills the process of evolution.

The next phases of the spiritual evolutionary process are the overmind and mind. The former is a delegate of supermind that functions as a mediating plane between supermind and individual mind. This makes it a sort of inferior supermind, but it does not possess the power to transform the natural order or the integral quality of the supramental truth. Overmind is aware of the essential truth of things, but it is unconcerned with absolutes. It does, however, possess the power to transform an individual, and it can bring one close to supermind.[19] In contrast to the overmind, the mind is an instrument of analysis and synthesis, but it is not an instrument of essential knowledge. It participates in the supermind in a limited way because it cannot see the whole. The mind is divided by ignorance, which separates it from the supermind.

The final three aspects of spiritual evolution are soul or psyche, life, and matter. The soul is the immortal principle within an individual. By life, Aurobindo means a cosmic energy supported by a conscious force that creates, maintains, and modifies things. Matter represents the nonconscious, which is a creation of consciousness and also identified with Brahman. Aurobindo's thought emphasizes that there is nothing stable because everything is in motion. In fact, the notion of stability is merely a human construct.[20]

The impetus for the process of evolution is līlā (creative play), which is a way by which consciousness liberates itself. An inner law of necessity directs it. From Aurobindo's perspective, karma is an instrument in evolution by becoming part of the rhythm of freedom. The impetus of this entire process is twofold: a primordial starting point of involution and a reverse process of evolution. Involution is similar to a pressure from above, which calls the lower forms to evolve out of their limitedness and to break through to a new stage of consciousness. A key aspect of this process is that the divine descends through supermind. In short, involution makes evolution possible. Although evolution presupposes involution, evolution is a self-unfolding of the supreme spirit from matter to being-consciousness-bliss. This is made possible because spirit is presently involved in matter. But when will supermind descend? Aurobindo's answer is that it will descend when humans have evolved to the point where they can utilize it. In the meantime, overmind functions as a bridge. How can the gulf between mind and supermind be bridged? Aurobindo responds by asserting a combination of human effort (*yoga*) and divine involution, which points to an eventual triple transformation that is a psychic change; a spiritual change occurs with the descent of light, knowledge, and power, which is due to the descent of the overmind and a supramental transformation (ascent to supermind). From an historical perspective, the spiritual change was first accomplished on the "Day of Siddhi" (day of Aurobindo's spiritual accomplishment) on November 24, 1926. From this day, Aurobindo asserted that the descent of the supermind was a certainty. With respect to the supramental transformation, the Mother of the ashram announced in April of 1956 that the manifestation of the supramental was a living fact that ushered in a new light on the earth, birth of a new world, and the fulfillment of what was promised.

In the final analysis, it is yoga that works to effect the triple transformation. Aurobindo rejects traditional forms of yoga because they fail to invest the finite and infinite worlds with equal reality and value. Aurobindo proposes what he calls integral yoga, because it uses the ideas and practices of the other forms of yoga, although it is new with respect to its aims, standpoint, and method. Without getting into specifics, it can be asserted that it represents the liberation of the soul and achievement of perfect union in the sense of a total integrated change of consciousness and nature. The feminine force of śakti plays an important role in integral yoga by liberating a meditator from the forces of lower nature and bringing one to an actualization of one's higher nature. Liberation includes perfection, unity, and a communal aspect that is characterized by love, justice, and equality.

During Aurobindo's later life, Mira Richard, a collaborator and disciple, was designated an incarnation called the Divine Mother. Followers credited her with the inspiration for the city of Auroville in a dream in 1956. Located five miles north of the former French colonial city of Pondicherry, Auroville (the City of Dawn) was intended to be a harmonious utopian society modeled on the philosophy of its inspiration. It was intended to be a place where inhabitants could naturally evolve toward human perfection. Features of the Mother's community included no compulsory education for children, an emphasis on individual patterns of growth, cooperative work, respect for others, no monetary rewards, and mutual sharing of goods and services. This would be a spiritually centered city that would enable individuals to move toward perfection and unity of humankind. The city was designed as an integrative *maṇḍala* (sacred diagram), but its unity has been thwarted in actuality by human self-centeredness, persistent fragmentation, and disunity. This scenario can be traced in part to a failure to institutionalize the Mother's charisma.[21]

A Guru-Centric Reform Movement

The Swaminarayan movement, beginning in the early nineteenth century in Gujarat eventually established temples in the West in the late twentieth century. Instead of proselytizing Western followers, the movement directs its efforts to serving Indians living in the West by focusing devotional attention on its founder. He was born into a Brahmin family on April 3, 1781, in the village of Chhapia, and he was named Ghanashyam, which is a childhood name of Krishna. After his parents died when he was eleven years old, he renounced the world and wandered India for seven years under the name of Neelkanth. After studying yoga and practicing celibacy, he eventually adopted the modified nondualism of Rāmānuja. Around 1800, he was initiated as a Vaiṣṇava ascetic, and he received a new name of Sahajanand Swami by his guru Ramananda, who publicly appointed him his successor. Some followers would not accept the authority of the new leader after the death of Ramananda. Other followers also disagreed with the strict separation of the sexes imposed by the new leader, who had been anointed with the new name of Narayan. Followers of Narayan used his name as a mantra (repetitive sacred formula) in their personal devotion, and he donned a red turban as a symbol of his authority along with a golden staff and umbrella, which are items with an historical connection to royalty in India. The movement split schismatically into two major branches: Vadtal and Ahmedabad. A new school of the movement developed with the Akshar Purushottam Sanstha. Representing an institutional division and doctrinal split, this event was caused by the departure of Swami Yagnapurushdas (1865–1951) from the Vadtal temple in 1906 because of his criticism of lax ascetic behavior. An additional split occurred in 1966 when two brothers left to form a separate organization called the Yogi Divine Society.

The movement promulgated a message of social and religious reform, in which the ascetic members performed useful labor. They opposed social practices such as infanticide and immolation of widows. The movement stressed nonviolence, and devotees took five vows: not to steal, not to commit adultery, not to eat meat, not to drink intoxicants, and not to accept food from a member of a lower caste, although disciples were recruited from all castes with the exception of the Untouchables. Some members believed that Swaminarayan was an incarnation of Krishna, while others thought that he was a manifestation of the Purushottam, or supreme person himself. In his work entitled *Vachanamṛtam*, which followers believe to be a divinely revealed text, Swaminarayan argues that god does not appear to humans in his absolute divine form because humans could not cope with such an encounter. Therefore, god intentionally suppresses his divine form and appears as a human being, although he is also simultaneously living in his divine abode.[22] By assuming human form, god enables humans to approach him and develop love for him.

Swaminarayan expounds a path to salvation that differs from that of Rāmānuja in terminology, although not in essence. For Swaminarayan, the goal of life is the development of a path to salvation, which is defined as including dharma, detachment (*vairagya*), knowledge, and devotion.[23] To practice dharma means to observe nonviolence, celibacy, and caste and stage-of-life duties,[24] which curbs the senses and enables one to conquer desire even if one does not achieve detachment from sense objects which include all worldly things or the evolutes of primal matter. In short, in detachment a person rejects everything except God. A devotee can develop detachment by listening to the recitation of scriptures and the discourses of a saint.[25] By knowledge, Swaminarayan means awareness of one's ātman (self). Once this awareness dawns, the aspirant discards the consciousness of his physical body. Having realized that the body is separate from the ātman and ultimately perishable, a devotee attains freedom from the power of the evil guṇas (strands, qualities). If a person falters in the initial three steps, it is still possible to be saved by devotion (*bhakti*). Devotion includes hearing about the exploits of Krishna and chanting his name. Beyond an all-consuming emotional love of God, devotion also entails doing the will of god.[26] The highest form of devotion is, however, taking refuge in God, which involves the following: an indomitable faith in God, loving attachment to God, and knowing the negative and positive forms of God.[27] By following this path of salvation, a devotee earns the grace of God. Although a devotee can make a contribution to his or her salvation, Swaminarayan affirms that a devotee is saved by God's grace in the final analysis and attains the state of absorption or deep concentration (*samādhi*). The unitive state does not entail losing one's identity in the single reality; it implies rather losing oneself in devotion to Krishna.[28]

Operating in India and the West, the Swaminarayan movement has functioned effectively to preserve ethnic and linguistic identity.[29] During the 1950s, the movement spread to Great Britain, where it became one of the largest Indian religions. Its large temple in London has become a center for pilgrimage.

Proselytizing Movements

What Vivekananda began in the late nineteenth century with his mission to the West provided the inspiration for other Hindu religious leaders. Since the International Society for Krishna Consciousness and its founder Bhaktivedanta Swami Prabhupada were discussed in an earlier chapter, it will not be included here. Like the Hare Krishna movement, several movements in the twentieth century were led by charismatic and often deified gurus (teachers). These figures include Yogananda and the Self-Realization Fellowship, Maharishi Mahesh Yogi and Transcendental Meditation, Satya Sai Baba and the Satya Sai Federation, Guru Maharaj Ji and the Divine Light Mission, Bhagwan Shree Rajneesh, Swami Satchidananda, and Gurumayi and the Siddha Yoga Movement. Generally speaking, followers of these gurus owed them complete obedience, usually practiced some form of meditation, asserted that all religions are fundamentally valid, and manifested a tendency to deemphasize social work and political involvement. Assuming that a follower has been properly initiated, ethnic identity is inconsequential for practice of the religion.[30]

Yogananda (1890–1952) was born in northeastern India into a family of eight children of Bengali parents of the Kṣatriya caste. When he was eight years old he became very ill with cholera, but he was cured after viewing a photograph of a holy man named Lahiri Mahasaya. Yogananda reported seeing a blinding light that enveloped his body and the entire room as he gazed at the photograph. He attended Scottish Church College in Calcutta, and he eventually graduated from Serampore College. He arrived in Boston on October 6, 1920, to attend a conference sponsored by the Unitarian Church. He stayed after the conference to teach Americans yoga, which he called the "science of religion," and he eventually established the Yogada Satsang, which evolved into the better-known Realization Fellowship in California in 1925. He composed his autobiography, entitled *Autobiography of a Yogi*, in 1946, and it has been reprinted many times. In this work he discusses acquired powers, defeating a tiger with his bare hands, receiving telepathic messages from his teacher, and acquiring various forms of power to heal.

The type of yoga taught by Yogananda was called Kriya-yoga because it was a form based on practical efforts. For Yogananda, it was essential for religion to be based in and confirmed by personal experience. He thought that religion and science shared a common emphasis on the necessity for their views to be tested through experiment and experience. His emphasis on self-realization stands in contrast to other Indian spiritual leaders who stressed god-realization or the attainment of a state of absorption with the one real principle of the universe. Being grounded in yogic practice, Yogananda's message made an appeal for personal experience and the universal nature of the practice, which found a positive reception from Americans during the 1930s through the 1970s. The organization created a mail-order self-study course of 180 lessons that a person could practice at home. A practitioner could also receive personal guidance by attending a convention.

Transcendental Meditation

Beginning as a method discovered by Maharishi Mahesh Yogi, Transcendental Meditation (TM) became an international movement that was presented as a scientific response and practical remedy to the various problems of modern life. This was stressed even more when its founder and teachers denied that the movement was a religion. Instead they argued that it was an easy technique that could be mastered by anyone. By using this method, a person could overcome ordinary problems by alleviating mental and emotional stress, reducing high blood pressure, producing relaxation, gaining greater physical energy and mental clarity, and achieving more advanced stages of consciousness. In spite of its many modern benefits, this new method of yoga claimed to be part of an ancient Hindu spiritual lineage.

Maharishi Mahesh Yogi, who was born Mahesh Prasad Varma on October 18, 1911, in Uttar Kashi, traced his spiritual heritage to the great Advaita Vedānta thinker Śaṅkara (c. 788–820) and beyond him to ancient vedic literature. Maharishi studied for fourteen years with Swami Brahmananda Saraswati at the Jyotimath located high in the Himalayan mountains, although he was never appointed successor to his own teacher. Before his student apprenticeship, Maharishi earned a college-level degree in physics and mathematics at Allahabad University. His educational background helps to partially explain his tendency to wrap his message in scientific jargon and to stress the scientific advantages of his method. The Science of Creative Intelligence (SCI) is, for instance, the official name of his belief system, which is conceived as dynamic because of its ever-expanding nature.

The use of scientific language to convey a religious message accomplishes at least two objectives: it gives the belief system legitimacy, and it forms a cognitive connection to the contemporary Western worldview that is dominated by science. Transcendental Meditation operates from the basic presupposition that there is compatibility between Advaita Vedānta, the Vedas, and Western science. Since 1988, Transcendental Meditation has, for instance, worked intensively to demonstrate the parallels between quantum physics and its own method. The connection made between science and yogic practices reflects intellectual influences of the colonial era, with an emphasis on health, morality, and science. The linking of science and yogic practices is also seen in a sustained association with the acquisition of power and knowledge by practitioners.[31]

Maharishi arrived in America in 1959 and lectured on yoga in San Francisco, with additional trips to Los Angles, New York, London, and Germany. His initial movement began as the Spiritual Regeneration Movement, which was later to become the adult branch of the movement. The other wing of the movement was named the Students International Meditation Society (SIMS), established in 1964 in Germany. An early emphasis of the movement focused on its mission to college campuses, which was given a huge impetus in the mid-1960s when the British rock group, the Beatles, studied with the Maharishi in India. This event generated worldwide publicity for his movement. After his estrangement from the Beatles, the Maharishi initiated, instructed, and toured with the Beach Boys. He used his celebrity status with members of popular culture to endear himself to the youth culture. By the 1970s, student centers could be found at over a thousand campuses. The movement estimated that 1.5 million people had practiced Transcendental Meditation with a teacher. The college campus focus of the movement culminated with the establishment of Maharishi International University in Fairfield, Iowa, in 1974 on the campus of the bankrupted Parsons College.

Pushing the margins of science, Maharishi established the Maharishi European Research University in 1975 at two lakeside hotels on Lake Lucerne in Switzerland. The purpose of the university was to research the effects of Transcendental Meditation and to determine the existence of higher states of consciousness. During the following year, Maharishi envisioned his own world government with the ancient Indian Vedas as the basis of its constitution. He appointed ministers to various positions with titles like the Development of Consciousness, Prosperity and Fulfillment, and Health and Immortality. During the 1980s, Maharishi began a program called TM-Sidhi with the purpose of teaching students to achieve yogic powers like the ability to fly or levitate. There was a public demonstration before 120 journalists in Washington, D.C., on July 9, 1986, which did not correspond to the media hype for the event, and it resulted in media ridicule of the movement.

The meditative technique of the Maharishi is grounded in a neo-Vedānta metaphysical philosophy in which an unchanging reality is opposed to an ever-changing phenomenal world. A book entitled *Science of Being and Art of Living: Transcendental Meditation* expresses his basic philosophical position. In it, unchanging reality is equated with Being, which represents a state of pure existence that is omnipresent, unmanifested, and transcendental. Not only is Being beyond time, space, causation, and ever-changing phenomena, it remains unrecognized by human beings because their minds do not realize their essential identity with Being, since minds are captive to the outward projecting senses. The essential nature of Being is further identified with absolute blissful consciousness, which radiates from Being. Maharishi compares Being to the ocean upon which there are many waves. These waves are like the field of continually changing phenomena. What is really important for Maharishi is for human beings to realize Being, because without this realization a person's life is without foundation, meaningless, and fruitless; this realization is within the capabilities of everyone by means of transcendental meditation.

This form of meditation is intimately connected to a person's breath (*prāna*), which is an expression of the latent power of Being within a person. As the nature of Being, breath plays a role as the motivating force of creation and evolution. The breath can be harnessed and used to help the mind of a person realize Being directly. This is accomplished by transcendental meditation, which enables one to extricate oneself from a state of relative experience, transcend ordinary thinking, and gain the permanent state of Being, implying that a particular mind loses its individuality and becomes instead a cosmic mind that is omnipresent, pure, and eternal.

The human mind before achieving this cosmic state of mind is compared to a seed that produces a tree. What this analogy attempts to show is the interdependent nature of the mind and karma (action). It is impossible for action to occur without a mind. In turn, it is karma that produces the mind that in turn creates more karma. This suggests that karma owes its existence to the mind and in turn creates the mind. By means of karma, the original pure consciousness of Being is transformed into conscious mind. If karma represents what is temporary and perishable, Being is the exact opposite of it because it represents eternal unity, whereas karma creates diversity within the unity of Being.

Within the context of this metaphysical edifice, the technique of transcendental meditation involves saturating the mind with Being by harnessing one's breath and making it harmonious with the rhythm of nature and cosmic life. The Maharishi emphasizes the naturalness of his technique. Moreover, the technique is a simple, easy, and direct way to develop one's mental capabilities and latent potentialities. Unlike ancient ascetic traditions of India, it is not necessary to renounce the world or withdraw from one's family. This is an ascetic practice that can be performed within the context of the ordinary activities of the world.

Instruction in the technique of meditation stresses that it is an easy and natural process. Students are instructed to devote twenty minutes each day to practice that is ideally performed in the morning and early evening. At the beginning stage, a student does not have to be convinced that the method will work. What is important is the correct practice. If a student performs the technique properly, positive results will follow automatically. The proper technique involves seven steps. The initial step involves attending an introductory lecture that is intended to prepare a person for what is to follow. The theory of transcendental meditation is given in the second step, with a preparatory talk. The third step involves an interview with the teacher, at which time a student is given a scared mantra (repetitive formula), personally fitted to that person, which one is not to reveal to others. By focusing on the mantra, one is able to concentrate one's attention on it. The final steps involve periodic verification and validation of one's experiences by returning to and checking with a teacher. Maharishi identifies seven levels of consciousness, with the final state culminating in a state of unity. The fifth state represents cosmic consciousness, an awareness of Being even after the cessation of meditation, whereas the fourth stage stands for the transcendental state, which is a state of pure consciousness described as beyond the previous states of waking, dream, and deep-sleep consciousness The sixth state is called God consciousness.

Traditional yogic postures are unnecessary. A person can simply sit upright and comfortably on a chair with eyes closed. The movement tends to stress that anyone can learn this simple, effortless, and easy mental technique. This yogic technique and neo-Vedānta metaphysical edifice do not represent a form of Hinduism, from the perspective of the founder. In fact, Transcendental Meditation is not a religion at all. By deemphasizing its Hindu roots, stressing its nonreligious nature, and focusing on the scientifically demonstrable value of the technique, Transcendental Meditation created a successful message that was embraced by many spiritual seekers and a scientifically minded audience. The movement used scientific means to demonstrate how the technique calmed the mind, increased awareness, relaxed the body, and lowered metabolism.

When the Maharishi initially arrived in America he stated at a press conference his rationale for coming. He confessed that he had learned a secret, swift, deep form of meditation that he was motivated to share now with the world for the spiritual regeneration of its inhabitants. A few years later, he established the Spiritual Regeneration Movement of Great Britain, located in northern London. In 1975, the Maharishi announced the "Dawn of the Age of Enlightenment." This bold and optimistic pronouncement suggested the commencement of a period during which humans can reach their fullest potential, which will be characterized by boundless happiness, harmony, peace, and personal fulfillment. This new dawn will also represent a period when science will verify and validate the teachings of the Maharishi. Moreover, even those who did not mediate would enjoy the benefits of this new age. The Maharishi took this message on tour to various countries. The impetus for such millennial hope continued in July 1985 when he created the Taste of Utopia Assembly, which was staged in several nations. The purpose of this organization was to unite vedic wisdom and the practice of TM-Sidhi program. Their fusion would usher into existence a utopian age of peace and prosperity. This vision represented a fuller expression of a utopian hope embodied within the movement from its earliest moments.

The Transcendental Meditation movement promised both a transformation of the individual and society by means of an expansion of consciousness to unimagined states. In short, Transcendental Meditation aimed to create a perfect society inhabited by perfect individuals. The movement offered a realized eschatology for a transformed mode of living in the present moment that promised a horizon of economic well-being, psychological and somatic healing, good health, peace, and mental comfort. The movement also intersected with New Age spiritualities with respect to organic and vegetarian dietary practices and alternative forms of medicine. In 1985, the Maharishi launched, for instance, the "World Plan for Perfect Health" along with a world center for Ayurveda medicine.

Other Guru-Centric Movements

Even though he never referred to himself as a guru, a good example of a guru-centric movement was Ramana Maharshi (1879–1950), who was born in a small village approximately twenty miles south of the city of Madurai in south India. His father, a pleader at the local court, died when he was twelve years old, and his mother moved the family to the city. At the American Mission School, he learned English, but he was an uninterested and uninspired student with a gifted memory. After he encountered a copy of the *Periya Purāṇa*, a twelfth-century biography of sixty-three Śaiva saints from the southern region, reading it sparked a religious spirit in the young man. During 1896, he had a profound religious experience, and he became obsessed with death to the point of imagining his own demise. This experience destroyed his sense of self and individuality, and it gave him a new religious identity. He secretly renounced the world and his social ties, and he traveled 120 miles southwest to Arunachala, a favorite haunt of renouncers. Within an underground shrine at the temple, he meditated and remained silent. He slowly began to attract disciples, who learned his identity after one threatened to fast unto death. Even though his fame spread, he refused to leave Arunachala even at the request of his mother, who eventually joined him many years later. Ramana lived in a cave from 1900 to 1916, and he maintained his silence.[32] By means of gestures and writing, he gave wordless instruction to his disciples in his nondualistic philosophy of Vedānta, with his direct experience functioning as his source of authority. The focus of his teaching was to encourage others to discover for themselves the nature of their true identity, which was theoretically possible for everyone.

Ramana's simplicity tends to be overshadowed by more flamboyant gurus such as Satya Sai Baba, who was born on November 23, 1926, in a small village in south India. At the age of thirteen, he experienced fainting spells, bouts of laughter, crying, singing, and scripture recitation. He announced to his father his identity as a reincarnation of a holy man called Sai Baba from the town of Shirdi in the region of Maharashtra, who died in 1918. He proved his status by performing miracles, materializing sweets and flowers, healing, and teaching. In 1963, he fell into a coma for several days, but he recovered before a crowd of devotees. Thereupon, he announced that he was an incarnation of Śiva and Śakti, initiating the second incarnation of the movement. His androgynous condition is expressed by his name Sai (divine mother) and Baba (divine father). After Sai Baba dies at age ninety-eight, it is said, there will be a third, future incarnation called Prem Sai who is destined to be born in the state of Karnataka, complete the work of Sai Baba, and manifest himself as God to the world.

Along with seeing and touching the guru, miracles are crucial to the cult of Sai Baba because they confirm his divinity to his followers.[33] He is believed to be able to leave his body and travel to distant places to help others; he can cure illness, read minds, be in two places simultaneously, and transform or materialize objects and substances. His most famous miracle is his ability to produce sacred ash (*vibhūti*), which is given to devotees for purposes of self-application. These various kinds of miracles are considered divine sports (*līlās*). He teaches the necessity of the repetition of God's name, meditation on God's form, a moderate vegetarian diet, and no alcohol or smoking. It is possible for a follower to remove the effects of karma and to directly experience genuine reality within.[34] Overall, his message combines universalism and nonuniversalism in the sense that he embraces all religions while also asserting that all knowledge and wisdom originated in India.

In 1936, Swami Sivananda Saraswati (1887–1963) founded the Divine Life Society, and he would also establish monasteries, a hospital, and a university. Sivananda began his adult career as a medical doctor before renouncing the world and wandering around India. He claimed, like the Ramakrishna Mission, that Advaita Vedānta was the truth that formed the basis for all religions. He compared the superior spirituality possessed by Indian culture to the materialism of the West. This implies that India has a leading international religious role to play by setting a spiritual example for the West. To prepare disciples for their missionary role they are educated in English. The movement asserts that it is nonsectarian and tolerant. At the same time, it also claims to pursue national goals and complements the efforts of the Indian government.[35] Before the death of the founder, Swami Vishnu-Devananda (born 1927) established yoga centers in America, and large campuses located in Quebec and the Bahamas. In order to improve the world, he founded a movement called True Word Order to advance the practice of yoga and interpret experience from a Vedānta perspective.

Some gurus made relatively brief appearances in America, such as Guru Mahraj Ji and Bhagwan Shree Rajneesh. The former was a young teenage guru when he arrived in America to lead an organization founded by his father in 1960 called the Divine Light Mission. The movement stresses vegetarianism, renouncing drugs, and refraining from consuming alcohol. New followers are initiated by an authoritative person appointed by the guru, introduced to chanting praises of God, religious discourses, and knowledge that leads to the realization of God. Followers are called "premies" (lovers of God). The movement teaches that religious figures such as Buddha, Jesus, Krishna, Muhammad, and others have essentially taught the same message: Knowledge based on meditation techniques is the key to liberation. This knowledge was passed from one master to another, and it now rests in the person of Guru Maharaj Ji, who is the current primordial guru.

In an event that was publicized as the most significant event in human history, the organization rented the Houston Astrodome to promote their movement in 1973, but the event was poorly attended. This left the organization deeply in debt, and motivated it to retrench and reorganize. The movement split after Guru Maharaj Ji married his American secretary and broke his vow of celibacy. The guru's mother departed for India with her other sons. After his mother, Mata Ji, appointed the eldest son to be the new leader of the organization, a court case gave this son control of the organization in India, whereas Guru Maharaj Ji retained control of the international movement.

Bhagwan Shree Rajneesh (1931–1990) was the son of a Jain father, and he followed an academic vocation until 1966, when he began his religious career and founded a movement with various names, such as Orange People (for the colored robes worn by followers), Rajneeshees, or followers of Bhagwan. Adolescents from America and Europe were attracted to his movement when he moved to Pune in the mid-1970s, in large part because he taught a method of tantric meditation with many practices involving group sex. In 1981, Rajneesh appeared on the west coast of America, and he established a monastery community in the small town of Antelope, Oregon. After the town council refused to grant the community building permits, members of the movement got themselves elected to the local council, and they changed the name of the town to Rajneeshpuram, City of Rajneesh. The guru purchased a fleet of Rolls Royces in which he would ride to survey his community, with followers bowing as he drove past them. Because Rajneesh took a vow of silence until 1984, his personal assistant, Ma Anand Sheela, ran the community until she disappeared from the premises in 1985 and was later arrested. The community disintegrated in 1985 because of legal controversies and internal dissent. Thereupon, Rajneesh was expelled from the country, returned to India, and changed his name to Osho.

Rajneesh taught that there was a single source of bioenergy. His practices were designed to tap into this force or to unblock passages of energy within the human body. Becoming aware of oneself is essential to reaching one's goal. Whether a person renounces sexual relations or engages in them, one can reach one's goal as long as one is keenly aware of what one is doing. Rajneesh also taught that the power of Śakti can be transmitted ritually by touch or glance in order to resolve internal conflicts and unblock obstructed passages of energy. Rajneesh's spiritual message combined sexual enjoyment, transcendence, and pursuit of wealth, an unusual association that appealed to many people.

Another advocate of tantric yogic practices was Swami Muktananda (1908–1982), who taught siddha yoga. Although he traced his spiritual lineage back to Kashmir Śaivism, he was personally initiated (*śaktipat*) by Bhagawan Nityananda, which caused his spiritual energy (*kuṇḍalinī*) to awaken. The śaktipat should be comprehended as a descent of grace that functions as a trigger to awaken dormant spiritual energy within a person. It is taught that one can awaken to divine consciousness within oneself and others. Muktananda has been accused of taking sexual liberties with some of his followers in India. After Muktananda's death and his appointment of a brother and sister as successors, a period of turmoil followed when the brother, Swami Nityananda, resigned over a sexual scandal three years later. His sister, Swami Chidvilasananda (Bliss of the Play of Pure Consciousness), who is popularly known as Gurumayi Ji (b. 1955), assumed sole leadership of the movement. As a daughter named Malti of a Bombay restaurateur, she received śaktipat initiation at age fourteen. In 1980, her guru gave her the responsibility of delivering public talks on Sunday, and the following year she became the executive vice president of SYDA Foundation. At age twenty-six, in April of 1982, she officially received initiation into the status of renouncer. She established the Siddha Yoga Dham Ashram in South Fallsburg, in the northern region of the state of New York. From her position of leadership, she provides a gender model.[36] The movement has reached out to and attracted members of the academic community in America, which has given the organization external legitimacy.

In contrast to the guru-centric movements of recent time, a more prophetic type of movement is represented by the Brahmā Kumārīs (Daughters of Brahmā) founded by Dada Lekhraj (1876–1969), who was a wealthy jeweler. He began to have visions when he was around sixty years old, and he discovered that he was chosen to be a medium by Śiva. His visions informed him about the coming end of the world and that a paradise would be established on earth. Advocating abstaining from tobacco, alcohol, and sexual relations, this women's movement advocated yoga because it induces peace of mind and other benefits, whereas sexual relations weaken the human body. Women, who operate the educational organization with the goal of liberating women, often run the movement's yoga centers. The movement traces the inequality of women to the advent of sexual intercourse and body consciousness, which helps to explain the emphasis on celibacy.

The movement teaches that whereas the world was transformed into a kind of hell by sexual relations, ignorance and forgetfulness help to account for the soul identifying itself with the body and failing to recognize its real nature as immortal and plural. Moreover, the human soul is captive to a constantly changing material nature within a cosmic dualism that operates historically in a series of endlessly repeating cycles of creation, degeneration, and destruction. It is necessary for the soul to escape from this cycle of history and return to its forgotten home in the world of Brahmā.[37]

Concluding Remarks

Modern and contemporary movements within Hinduism have produced some inspiring and fascinating figures. These various religious leaders have infused Hinduism with new energy, and they have transformed a culturally insular religion into a missionary religion with a presence throughout the world. Developments in modern Hinduism have demonstrated its remarkable resiliency, with reformers seeking to correct what they perceived to be injustices within the culture and others seeking continuity with the past.

Some movements have experienced growing pains due to internal schisms over doctrine and/or practice. The problems with some movements have been exposed by scandals, often of a sexual nature. An organization such as the Vedanta Society, for instance, never captured a wider audience for its message because its organizational structure never became a unified national body in America. Instead, individual centers receive their leadership from its headquarters in Calcutta.[38] Nonetheless, such Hindu religious movements now mark the religious landscape of nations in the West. There are also other organizations such as the

Infinity Foundation and the Dharam Hindujia Institute of Indic Research established at the University of Cambridge that promote Indian culture by financially supporting certain projects or institutions.

Some of the modern movements within Hinduism associated with thinkers such as Aurobindo, Maharishi Mahesh Yogi and his Transcendental Meditation, Rajneesh, Divine Life Society, and other guru-centered movements have become associated with New Age religion in America. The so-called New Age is not a movement, because it is a fluid phenomenon that embodies a wide diversity of ideas and practices that are a "highly optimistic, celebratory, utopian, and spiritual form of humanism."[39] From another perspective, it also represents a combination of pagan religions, Eastern thought, and occult-psychic phenomena.[40] With its popular ideology, it envisions that humanity is on the threshold of a "New Age," representing a major cultural shift.

When some of these Hindu movements gained a wider audience in America, young people were experimenting with drugs like LSD to induce altered states of consciousness and bliss. Within the context of the drug culture and New Age religion, movements such as Transcendental Meditation appeared to ordinary people to be offering similar results. Thus, numerous practitioners of various forms of New Age religion and former drug experimenters were attracted to such movements. People were also attracted to the holistic view of life offered by some of these movements, promise of extricating oneself from the dichotomy of body and mind, promise of better health, a transformation of society and the individual, economic well-being, psychological and somatic healing, peace, and mental comfort.

These new movements add more colors to the cultural rainbow of India. This book began with a journey to India in order to explore its many metaphorical colors of religion, and a person can only be impressed by the many colors of the Hindu cultural rainbow. As we end the journey to India, we might be tempted to sing the words to the song "Vande Mātaram" (We Bow down to the Mother) composed by Bankim Chandra Chatterji in his novel *Ānanda Math* of the nineteenth century. Many radio stations in India play the opening bars of this nationalist song every morning when they begin their daily transmissions. As students of Hinduism, we can join the praise of Mother India out of respect for the richness of her rainbow.

CHRONOLOGY

Western Dates	Major Events
c. 2600–1700 B.C.E.	Harappa culture
2000–1500 B.C.E.	Decline of Indus Valley civilization
c. 1500–500 B.C.E.	Creation and compilation of vedic hymns
c. 1000–800 B.C.E.	Development Brāmaṇic literature and early Śrauta Sūtras
c. 900–600 B.C.E.	Composition of Āraṇyakas and early Upaniṣads
c. 600–200 B.C.E.	Composition of later Upaniṣads and Dharma Sūtra literature
563–483 B.C.E.	Life of Siddhārtha Gautama, the Buddha
c. 468 B.C.E.	Death of Mahāvīra, twenty-fourth sage of Jainism
c. 362–321 B.C.E.	Nanda Dynasty
327–325 B.C.E.	Alexander of Macedonia in India
321 B.C.E.	Chandragupta establishes Mauryan Dynasty
300 B.C.E.–300 C.E.	Composition of the *Mahābhārata*
268–231 B.C.E.	Reign of Aśoka
200 B.C.E.–200 C.E.	Composition of epic *Rāmāyaṇa*
185 B.C.E.	Beginning of Śunga Dynasty
c. 166–150 B.C.E.	Reign of Menander, Indo-Greek king
50–200 C.E.	Kushana Dynasty in northwest India and central Asia
c. 150–300 C.E.	Composition of early Dharma texts
c. 250–325	Composition of *Sāṅkhya Kārikā* Īśvarakṛṣṇa
c. 300–500	Composition of early purāṇic literature
c. 320–500	Gupta Dynasty
c. 400–500	Composition of *Kāma Sūtra* of Vatsyāyana
402–411	Fa-hsien, Chinese Buddhist pilgrim, visits India
c. 450	Composition of Tamil epic *Cilappatikaram*
c. 455	Hunas invade north India
c. 500	Compilation of *Yoga Sūtra* by Patañjali
c. 500–700	Composition of early tantric literature
c. 550–750	Chalukya Dynasty of south India
c. 574–560	Ascent of Pallava Dynasty
630–643	Hsüan Tsang, Chinese Buddhist pilgrim, visits India
711–715	Arab Muslims invade northwest India

788–820	Life of Śaṅkara, Advaita Vedānta philosopher
1000–1026	Mahmud of Ghazni raids northwest India
c. 1056–1137	Life of philosopher Rāmānuja
1110	Rise of Hoysala Kingdom
1206	Delhi Sultanate established
c. 1238–1317	Madhva, founder of Dvaita school of Vedānta
c. 1333	Ibn Battūta travels in India
c. 1440–1518	Life of Kabīr, devotional poet
c. 1469–1539	Life of Guru Nānak, founder of Sikhism
c. 1479–1531	Life of Vallabha, religious thinker and devotee of Krishna
c. 1485–1533	Life of Caitanya, Bengali devotional saint
1498	Vasco da Gama lands on west coast of India
c. 1498–1546	Life of Mīrābāī, devotional poetess of Rajasthan region
c. 1500–1600	Life of Sūrdās, north Indian devotional poet writing in Hindi
1510	Portuguese occupy Goa
1526–1707	Mugal Empire reigns in north India
c. 1532–1623	Life of Tulsīdās, author of Hindi *Rāmāyaṇa*
c. 1542	Francis Xavier, Jesuit missionary, lands in Goa
c. 1608–1649	Life of Tukārām, poet-saint of Maharashtra
1651	East India Company opens first factory in Bengal
1664	Śivajī becomes king of Maharashra
1675	French found colony at Pondichéry
1784	Founding of Asiatic Society of Bengal by Sir William Jones
1772–1833	Life of Ram Mohan Roy, founder of the Brāhmo Samāj
1824–1883	Life of Dāyānanda Sarasvatī, founder of Ārya Samāj
1836–1886	Life of Rāmākrishna, Bengali saint
1858	British Crown begins to administer India, replacing East India Company
1863–1902	Life of Swami Vivekananda, founder of Ramakrishna Math and Mission
1869–1948	Life of Mohandas K. Gandhi
1861–1941	Life of Rabindranath Tagore, won Nobel Prize for literature in 1913
1872–1950	Life of Aurobindo Ghose, philosopher and founder of religious center in Pondichéry
1879–1951	Life of Ramana Maharshi, south Indian mystic
1893	Vivekananda attends and speaks at World Parliament of Religions in Chicago
1896–1977	Life of A. C. Bhaktivedanta, founder of International Society for Krishna Consciousness
1926	Birth of Satya Sai Baba, Hindu holy man
1930–1934	Civil Disobedience movement
1947	India gains independence

1948	Gandhi assassinated
1950	India becomes a republic
1962	China invades north India
1964	Death of Jawaharlal Nehru, prime minister of India
1971	East Pakistan becomes Bangladesh
1975	Indira Gandhi wins general election
1984	Indian government evicts Sikh extremists from Golden Temple, and Indira Gandhi is assassinated
1985	Rajiv Gandhi, oldest son of Indira, elected to lead government
1991	Rajiv Gandhi assassinated by Tamil extremist
1992	Destruction of Babri Masjid by Hindu mob, and communal riots in cities

ABBREVIATIONS

AB	Aitareya Brāhmaṇa
ĀpDhS	Āpastamba Dharma Sūtra
ĀpGS	Āpastamba Gṛhya Sūtra
ĀpŚS	Āpastambiya Śrauta Sūtra
ĀU	Āruṇi Upaniṣad
AV	Atharvaveda Saṃhitā
BĀU	Bṛhadāranyaka Upaniṣad
BDhS	Baudhāyana Dharma Sūtra
BGS	Baudhāyana Gṛhya Sūtra
BhāgP	Bhāgavata Purāṇa
BhG	Bhagavad Gītā
BJU	Bṛhajjabala Upaniṣad
BŚS	Baudhāyana Śrauta Sūtra
BSU	Bhikśuka Upaniṣad
BvaiP	Brahmavaivarta Purāṇa
ChU	Chāndogya Upaniṣad
DMU	Dakṣiṇāmurtya Upaniṣad
GautDhS	Gautama Dharma Sūtra
GGS	Gobhila Gṛhya Sūtra
JaU	Jābāla Upaniṣad
JB	Jaiminīya Brāhmaṇa
KaiU	Kaivalya Upaniṣad
KathU	Kaṭha Upaniṣad
KauU	Kauṣītaki Upaniṣad
KB	Kauṣītaki Brāhmaṇa
KeU	Kena Upaniṣad
KS	Kaśyapa Saṃhitā
KŚS	Katyayana Śrauta Sūtra
KU	Kuṇḍika Upaniṣad
KurmaP	Kurma Purāṇa
LingaP	Liṅga Purāṇa
MaitU	Maitri Upaniṣad
MārkP	Mārkandeya Purāṇa

MatsyaP	Matsya Purāṇa
MaU	Māṇḍūkya Upaniṣad
Mbh	Mahābhārata
MNU	Mahānārāyaṇa Upaniṣad
MS	Manu Smṛti
MuU	Muṇḍaka Upaniṣad
NPU	Nāradaparivrājaka Upaniṣad
PainU	Paiṅgala Upaniṣad
PAU	Prāṇāgnihotra Upaniṣad
PB	Pañcaviṁśati Brāhmaṇa
PBU	Pañcabrahma Upaniṣad
PHU	Paramahaṁsa Upaniṣad
PrasU	Praśna Upaniṣad
Rām	Rāmāyaṇa
RV	Ṛg Veda Saṃhitā
SB	Śaṅkara Bhāṣya on the Vedānta Sūtras
ŚB	Śatapatha Brāhmaṇa
ŚivaP	Śiva Purāṇa
SK	Sāṃkhyakārikā of Īśvarakrishna
ŚŚS	Śaṅkhyana Śrauta Sūtra
SubālāU	Subālā Upaniṣad
ŚvetU	Śvetāśvatara Upaniṣad
TB	Taittirīya Brāhmaṇa
TS	Taittirīya Saṃhitā
TU	Taittirīya Upaniṣad
VamanaP	Vamana Purāṇa
VasDhS	Vasiṣṭha Dharma Sūtra
VisnuP	Viṣṇu Purāṇa
VS	Vaitana Sūtra
YS	Yoga Sūtra of Patañjali
YSU	Yogaśikha Upaniṣad

NOTES

CHAPTER 1 A JOURNEY TO MOTHER INDIA

1. See Bruce Lincoln, "The Indo-European Cattle-Raiding Myth," *History of Religions* 16/1 (1976): 42–65.
2. Wendy Doniger O' Flaherty, "Sacred Cows and Profane Mares in Indian Mythology," *History of Religions* 19/1 (1979): 11.
3. W. Norman Brown, *Man in the Universe: Some Continuities in Indian Thought* (Berkeley: University of California Press, 1970), 59, 64.
4. Julius Lipner, *Hindus: Their Religious Beliefs and Practices* (London: Routledge, 1994), 9.
5. Romila Thapar, *Interpreting Early India* (Delhi: Oxford University Press, 1993), 79.
6. See Joseph T. O'Connell, "The Word 'Hindu' in Gauḍīya Vaiṣṇava Texts," *Journal of the American Oriental Society* 93/3 (1973): 340–344. In response to those who claim that Hinduism was invented or constructed by European colonizers after 1800, David N. Lorenzen argues that the evidence suggests that Hindus began to identify themselves in contrast to Muslims sometime between 1200 and 1500, and Hindus formed their common identity on loose family resemblances grounded in certain beliefs and practices, which he traces back to 300–600 C.E. in the early Purāṇas; see "Who Invented Hinduism?" *Comparative Studies in Society and History* 41/4 (1999): 630–659. For scholars who agree in spirit with Lorenzen, see: Will Sweetman, "Unity and Plurality: Hinduism and the Religions of India in Early European Scholarship," *Religion* 31 (2001): 209–224; and Robert Eric Frykenberg, "Constructions of Hinduism at the Nexus of History and Religion," *Journal of Interdisciplinary History* 23/3 (1993): 523–550.
7. Sharada Sugirtharajah, *Imagining Hinduism: A Postcolonial Perspective* (London: Routledge, 2003), x.
8. David Kopf, "Hermeneutics versus History," *Journal of Asian Studies* 39/3 (1980): 502.
9. Sugirtharajah, *Imagining Hinduism*, xi.
10. Richard King, *Orientalism and Religion: Postcolonial Theory, India, and "The Mystic East"* (London: Routledge, 1999), 103–107.
11. Brian K. Pennington, *Was Hinduism Invented?: Britons, Indians, and the Colonial Construction of Religion* (Oxford: Oxford University Press, 2005), 4–5.
12. Heinrich von Stietencron, "Hinduism: On the Proper Use of a Deceptive Term," in *Hinduism Reconsidered*, edited by Günther D. Sontheimer and Hermann Kulke (New Delhi: Manohar Publications, 1989), 20.
13. Brian K. Smith, *Reflections on Resemblance, Ritual, and Religion* (New York: Oxford University Press, 1989), 26.
14. Axel Michaels, *Hinduism: Past and Present*, translated by Barbara Harshav (Princeton: Princeton University Press, 2004), 18.

15. Ibid., 19.
16. Julius Lipner, "Ancient Banyan: An Inquiry into the Meaning of 'Hinduism,'" *Religious Studies* 32 (1996): 124.
17. Lipner, *Hindus*, 6. In contrast, King (*Orientalism and Religion*, 108) argues that Lipner's position—in which there are microcosmically many religions and an overarching macrocosmic unity—can lead to misunderstanding. King supports his position by stating that a good example of such confusion is evident in the inclusive nature of neo-Vedānta and the absolute character of Hindu political nationalism. King disagrees with Lipner's appeal of polycentricism and perspectivism as features of Indian thought because it fails to admit any kind of unity in Indian culture within the context of its relativistic perspective. Contrary to King, Lipner argues that there are many substantial features of Hinduism (for example, beliefs, practices, myths, symbols, and artifacts). Moreover, it is important to be careful of ideology and to draw responsible conclusions instead of allowing any kind of interpretation. Lipner thinks that we need functional terminology and pragmatic descriptions, even though Hinduism is a constructed notion.
18. F. Max Müller, *Chips from a German Workshop: Essays on the Science of Religion*, volume 1 (London: Longmans, Green, 1867), 27ff.
19. Michaels, *Hinduism*, 27.
20. Wendy Doniger O'Flaherty, *Women, Androgynes, and Other Mythical Beasts* (Chicago: University of Chicago Press, 1980), 6.
21. Hermann Kulke and Dietmar Rothermund, *A History of India*, fourth edition (London: Routledge, 2004), 29.
22. Romila Thapar, *Early India: From Origins to AD 1300* (Berkeley: University of California Press, 2002), 105.
23. Sir John Marshall, *Mohenjo-Daro and the Indus Civilization*, 2 volumes (London: Arthur Probstain, 1930, 1931), I: 111.
24. Edwin Bryant, *The Quest for the Origins of Vedic Culture: The Indo-Aryan Migration Debate* (Oxford: Oxford University Press, 2001), 174.
25. Thapar, *Early India*, 83, 107.
26. F. R. Allchin, "The Legacy of the Indus Civilization," in *Harappan Civilization*, edited by Gregory Possehl (New Delhi: Oxford University Press, 1993), 388.
27. Bryant, *Quest for the Origins*, 190.
28. Michael Witzel, "Vedas and Upaniṣads," in *The Blackwell Companion to Hinduism*, edited by Gavin Flood (Oxford: Blackwell Publishing, 2003), 70.
29. Thapar, *Early India*, 130.
30. Ibid., 48.
31. James W. Laine, "The dharma of Islam and the dīn of Hinduism: Hindu and Muslims in the Age of Śivājī," in *Surprising Bedfellows: Hindus and Muslims in Medieval and Early Modern India*, edited by Sushil Mittal (Lanham, md.: Lexington Books, 2003), 102.
32. Peter van der Veer, *Imperial Encounters: Religion and Modernity in India and Britain* (Princeton: Princeton University Press, 2001), 42.
33. Pennington. *Was Hinduism Invented?*, 59.
34. Van der Veer, *Imperial Encounters*, 41.
35. Stanley Wolpert, *New History of India*, sixth edition (Oxford: Oxford University Press, 2000), 231.
36. Percival Spear, *A History of India*, volume 2 (Hammondsworth: Penguin 1964; reprint 1978), 145.

37. Susanne Hoeber Rudolph and Lloyd I. Rudolph, *Gandhi: The Traditional Roots of Charisma* (Chicago: University of Chicago Press, 1967; reprint 1983), 5, 39.

38. Judith M. Brown, *Gandhi: Prisoner of Hope* (New Haven: Yale University Press, 1989), 386.

39. Stanley Wolpert, *Nehru: A Tryst with Destiny* (New York: Oxford University Press, 1996), 410.

40. Ibid., 69.

41. Ved Mehta, *The New India* (New York: Viking, 1978), 39.

42. Dom Moraes, *Indira Gandhi* (Boston: Little, Brown, 1980), 224.

43. Robert Frykenberg, "Accounting for Fundamentalism in South Asia: Ideologies and Institutions in Historical Perspective," in *Accounting for Fundamentalism: The Dynamic Character of Movements*, edited by M. E. Marty and R. S. Appleby (Chicago: University of Chicago Press, 1994), 596.

CHAPTER 2 TONGUES OF FIRE OF THE VEDIC SACRIFICIAL CULT

1. J. C. Heesterman, *The Broken World of Sacrifice: An Essay in Ancient Indian Ritual* (Chicago: University of Chicago Press, 1993), 86, 215.

2. Ibid., 24.

3. Ibid., 25.

4. J. Gonda, *Vedic Ritual: The Non-Solmn Rites* (Leiden: E. J. Brill, 1980), 164.

5. J. Gonda, *Notes on Names and the Name of God in Ancient India* (Amsterdam: North-Holland, 1970), 14, 24.

6. J. Gonda, *Some Observations on the Relations between "Gods" and "Powers" in the Veda, A Propos of the Phrase Sunuḥ Sahasaḥ* (The Hague: Mouton, 1957), 17–18.

7. For a more complete discussion of the world, see J. Gonda, *Loka: World and Heaven in the Veda* (Amsterdam: N. V. Noord-Hollandsche Uitgevers Maatschappiji, 1966).

8. Louis Renou, *Religions of Ancient India* (New York: Schocken Books, 1968), 20.

9. Sukumari Bhattacharji, *The Indian Theogony: A Comparative Study of Indian Mythology from the Vedas to the Purāṇas* (Cambridge: Cambridge University Press, 1970), 13.

10. Brian K. Smith, *Classifying the Universe: The Ancient Indian Varṇa System and the Origins of Caste* (New York: Oxford University Press, 1994), 89–90.

11. J. Gonda, "The Popular Prajāpati," *History of Religions* 22/2 (1982): 129–149; J. Gonda, *Prajāpati's Rise to Higher Rank* (Leiden: E. J. Brill, 1986).

12. Charles Malamoud, *Cooking the World: Ritual Thought in Ancient India*, translated by David White (Delhi: Oxford University Press, 1998), 2.

13. Ellison Banks Findly, "Mantra kaviśasta: Speech as Performative in the Ṛgveda," in *Mantra*, edited by Harvey P. Alper (Albany: State University of New York Press, 1989), 15–47. Laurie L. Patton, *Bringing the Gods to Mind: Mantra and Ritual in Early Indian Sacrifice* (Berkeley: University of California Press, 2005), 2.

14. William K. Mahony, *The Artful Universe: An Introduction to the Vedic Religious Imagination* (Albany: State University of New York Press, 1998), 8.

15. J. Gonda, *Notes on Brahman* (Utrecht: J. L. Beyers, 1950), 43.

16. Malamoud, *Cooking the World*, 46.

17. Heesterman, *Broken World*, 144.

18. Ibid., 150.

19. Madeleine Biardeau, *Stories about Posts: Vedic Variations around the Hindu Goddess*, translated by Alf Hiltebeitel, Marie-Louise Reiniche, and James Walker (Chicago: University of Chicago Press, 2004), 37.

20. Madeleine Biardeau, *Histoires de poteaux: Variations védiques autour de la déese hindoue* (Paris: École Française d'Extrème-Orient, 1989), 43.

21. Mircea Eliade, *The Sacred and the Profane*, translated by Willard R. Trask (New York: Harcourt, Brace, 1959), 37.

22. Pandurang Vaman Kane, *History of Dharmaśāstra*, 5 volumes (Poona: Bhandarkar Research Institute, 1953–1973), II: 1134.

23. Ibid., II: 1247, 1249.

24. Ganesh Umakant Thite, "Animal-Sacrifice in the Brāhmaṇa Texts," *Numen* 17/2 (1970): 154.

25. Brian K. Smith, *Reflections on Resemblance, Ritual, and Religion* (New York: Oxford University Press, 1989), 41; J. C. Heesterman, *The Inner Conflict of Tradition: Essays in Indian Ritual, Kingship, and Society* (Chicago: University of Chicago Press, 1985), 91.

26. Charles Malamoud, *Cuire le monde: Rite et pensée dans l'Inde ancienne* (Paris: Editions la Découverte, 1989), 101.

27. Alf Hiltelbeitel, *The Cult of Draupadī: On Hindu Ritual and the Goddess*, Volume 2 (Chicago: University of Chicago Press, 1991), II: 138.

28. Malamoud, *Cooking the World*, 35.

29. Jan Gonda, *Die Religionen Indiens I: Veda und älterer Hinduismus* (Stuttgart: W. Kohlhammer, 1960), 42.

30. Kane, *History of Dharmaśāstra*, II: 847, 849.

31. Herman Oldenberg, *Die Religion des Veda* (Stuttgart: J. G. Cotta 'Sche, 1923), 362; Arthur Berriedale Keith, *The Religion and Philosophy of the Veda and Upanishads*, 2 volumes, Harvard Oriental Series volumes 31, 32 (Delhi: Motilal Banarsidass, 1970), II: 347; A Weber, "Ueber Menschenopfer bei den Indern der vedischen Zeit," *Zeitschrift der Deutschen Morgenlandischen Gesellshaft* 18 (1864): 269–270; Louis Renou and Jean Filliozat, *L'Inde classique*, 2 volumes (Paris: L'Imprimerie Nationale, 1953, 1957), I: 727. For a contrary viewpoint, see Willibard Kirfel, "Der Aśvamedha und der Puruṣamedha," in *Beiträge zue indischen Philogie und Altertumskunde, Walter Schubring zum 70. Geburtstag dargebracht von der deutschen Indologie* (Hamburg: Cram, 1951), 44, 46f. Those scholars arguing for the actual sacrifice of victims include the following: A. Barth, *The Religions of India*, translated by J. Wood (Delhi: S. Chand, 1969), 58–59; A. L. Basham, *The Wonder That Was India* (London: Sidgwick & Jackson, 1969), 339; Dieter Schlingloff, "Menschenopfer in Kausambī," *Indo-Iranian Journal*, II (1969): 184ff.

32. Alfred Hillebrant, *Ritual-Litterature Vedische Opfer und Zauber* (Strassburg: Karl J. Trubner, 1897), 153.

33. W. Caland, trans., *Das Śrautasūtra des Āpastamba* (Amsterdam: Utigave van de Koninklijke Akademic, 1928), 20.24.3.

34. Abel Bergaigne, *La Religion vedique d'après les hymnes du Rigveda*, 4 volumes (Paris: Librairie Honore Champion, 1963), II: 156. Willibald Kirfel, *Symbolik des Hinduismus und des Jinismus* (Stuttgart: Anton Hiersemann, 1959), 99.

35. Madeleine Biardeau and Charles Malamoud, *Le Sacrifice dans l' Inde ancienne*, Bibliothèque de l'École des Hautes Études, Sciences religieuses 79 (Paris: Presses Universitaires de France, 1976), 16.

36. J. C. Heesterman, *The Ancient Indian Royal Consecration* (The Hague: Mouton, 1957), 13f.

37. P. E. Dumont, *L'aśvamedha: Description du sacrifice solennel du cheval dans le culte védique* (Paris: Paul Geuthner, 1927), xi.
38. Sylvain Lévi, *La doctrine du sacrifice dans les Brāhmaṇas* (Paris: Ernest Leroux Editeur, 1898), 131–132, 81.
39. Bhattacharji, *Indian Theogony*, 54.

CHAPTER 3 THE SWAN, WORLD RENUNCIATION, AND UPANISADS

1. Joachim Friedrich Sprockhoff, *Quellenstudien sur Askese im Hinduismus*, Abhandlungen für Die Kunde Morgenlandes 42/1 (Wiesbaden: Kommissionverlag Franz Steiner GMBH, 1976), 82–86.
2. Heinrich Zimmer, *Myths and Symbols in Indian Art and Civilization*, edited by Joseph Campbell (New York: Pantheon Books, 1963), 48.
3. For a discussion of the swan (or goose): in Indian epic literature, see Jean Philippe Vogel, *The Goose in Indian Literature and Art*, Memoirs of the Kern Institute No. 2 (Leiden: E. J. Brill, 1962), 17–29.
4. Patrick Olivelle, "Contributions to the Semantic History of Samnyāsa," *Journal of the American Oriental Society*, 10/3 (1981): 273–274.
5. Thomas J. Hopkins, *The Hindu Religious Tradition* (Encino, Calo: Dickenson, 1971), 49; A. L. Basham, *The Wonder That Was India* (London: Sidgwick & Jackson, 1969), 246; J. C. Heesterman, "Householder and Wanderer," in *Way of Life: King, Householder, Renouncer*, edited by T. N. Madan (New York: Vikas, 1982), 253.
6. Biardeau and Malamoud, *Le Sacrifice dans l'Inde ancienne* (Paris: Presses Universitaires de France, 1976), 73.
7. Patrick Olivelle, *The Aśrama System: The History and Hermeneutics of a Religious Institution* (New York: Oxford University Press, 1993), 115.
8. Wendy Doniger O'Flaherty, *Dreams, Illusion, and Other Realities* (Chicago: University of Chicago Press, 1984), 16, 18.
9. Wendy Doniger O'Flaherty, *The Origins of Evil in Hindu Mythology* (Berkeley: University of California Press, 1980), 14.
10. Jean Varenne, trans., *La Mahā Nārāyaṇa Upaniṣad*, 2 Volumes (Paris: Éditions E. de Boccard, 1960), II: 99.
11. Patrick Olivelle, ed. and trans., *Vāsudevāśrama Yatidharmaprakāśa: A Treatise on World Renunciation*, 2 volumes (Vienna: Publications of the de Nobili Research Library 4, 1976, 1977), 7.1–61; 21.3–35.
12. Olivelle, *The Āśrama System*, 115.
13. Richard Burghart, "Wandering Ascetics of the Rāmānd Sect," *History of Religions*, 22/4 (1983): 362.
14. Patrick Olivelle, *Renunciation in Hinduism: A Medieval Debate*, 2 Volumes (Vienna: Publications of the De Nobili Research Library; 1986, 1987), I: 37.
15. Ariel Glucklich, "The Royal Scepter (Daṇḍa) as Legal Punishment and Sacred Symbol," *History of Religions* 28/2 (1988): 109.
16. Olivelle, *Renunciation*, I: 37.
17. Ibid., I: 41.
18. Olivelle, *Yatidharmaprakāśa*, 4.93.
19. Glucklich, "Royal Scepter," 108–110.
20. Paul Hershman, "Hair, Sex, and Dirt," *Man* 9 (1974): 283.

21. Alf Hiltebeitel, "Draupadī's Hair," in *Autour de la déesse hindoue Purusārtha* 5 (Paris: Éditions de l'École des Hautes Études en Sciences Sociales, 1981), 207–208.
22. Gananath Obeyeskere, *Medusa's Hair: An Essay on Personal Symbols and Religious Experience* (Chicago: University of Chicago Press, 1981), 36.
23. Alfred Hillebrant, *Ritual-Litterature Vedische Opfer und Zauber* (Strassburg: Karl J. Trubner, 1897), 50; Sprockhoff, *Quellenstudien*, 115.
24. Gonda, *Vedic Ritual: The Non-Solemn Rites* (Leiden: E. J. Brill, 1980), 95.
25. Louis Dumont, *Homo Hierarchicus: An Essay on the Caste System*, translated by Mark Sainsbury (Chicago: University of Chicago Press, 1970), 46.
26. O'Flaherty, *Origins of Evil*, 79–80.
27. J. C. Heesterman, " 'Orthodox' and 'Heterodox' Law: Some Remarks on Customary Law and the State," in *Orthodoxy, Heterodoxy and Dissent in India*, edited by S. N. Eisenstadt, Reuven Kahane, and David Shulman (Berlin: Mouton, 1984), 149.
28. Carl Olson, *The Indian Renouncer and Postmodern Poison: A Cross-Cultural Encounter* (New York: Peter Lang, 1997), 47–71.
29. Gavin Flood, *The Ascetic Self: Subjectivity, Memory and Tradition* (Cambridge: Cambridge University Press, 2004), 4–9.
30. William P. Harman, *The Sacred Marriage of a Hindu Goddess* (Bloomington: Indiana University Press, 1989), 134.
31. Ariel Glucklich, *Religious Jurisprudence in the Dharmaśāstra* (New York: Macmillan, 1988), 4.
32. J. Gonda, *Die Religionen Indiens II: Der jüngere hinduismus* (Stuttgart: W. Kohlhammer, 1963), 288.
33. Veena Das, *Structure and Cognition: Aspects of Hindu Caste and Ritual*, second edition (Delhi: Oxford University Press, 1982), 334.
34. Jean Varenne, *Yoga and the Hindu Tradition*, translated by Derek Coltman (Chicago: University of Chicago Press, 1976), 134.
35. J. C. Heesterman, "Householder and Wanderer," in *Way of Life: King, Householder, Renouncer*, edited by T. N. Madan (New Delhi: Vikas, 1982), 251.

CHAPTER 4 THE WAY AND THE STRUCTURE OF LIFE

1. Ludo Rocher, "The Dharmaśāstras," in *The Blackwell Companion to Hinduism*, edited by Gavin Flood (Oxford: Blackwell Publishing, 2003), 102.
2. Ariel Glucklich, *Religious Jurisprudence in the Dharmaśāstras* (New York: Macmillan, 1988), 11.
3. Robert Lingat, *The Classical Law of India*, translated by J. Duncan M. Derrett (Berkeley: University of California Press, 1973), 3.
4. Ariel Glucklich, *The Sense of Adharma* (New York: Oxford University Press, 1994), 116.
5. Lingat, *Classical Law*, 8.
6. Hartmut Scharfe, "Artha," in *The Hindu World*, edited by Sushil Mittal and Gene Thursby (New York: Routledge, 2004), 258.
7. Julian Pitt-Rivers, "On the Word 'Caste,'" in *The Translation of Culture: Essays to E. E. Evan-Pritchard*, edited by T. O. Beidelman (London: Tavistock Publications, 1971), 161.
8. Romila Thapar, *Early India: From Origins to AD 1300* (Berkeley: University of California Press, 2002), 125.

9. Brian K. Smith, *Classifying the Universe: The Ancient Indian Varṇa System and the Origins of Caste* (New York: Oxford University Press, 1994), 32.
10. Susan Bayly, *The New Cambridge History of India IV: 3: Caste, Society and Politics in India from the Eighteenth Century to the Modern Age* (Cambridge: Cambridge University Press, 1999), 25.
11. This discussion is informed by the work of Mary Douglas, *Purity and Danger: An Analysis of Concepts of Pollution and Taboo* (New York: Praeger, 1966).
12. See Smith, *Classifying the Universe.*
13. Ibid., 12.
14. Glucklich, *Religious Jurisprudence*, 32.
15. J. C. Heesterman, *The Ancient Indian Royal Consecration: The Rājasūya Described According to the Yajus Texts and Annotated* (The Hague: Mouton, 1957), 118, 122.
16. Ibid., 192, 194.
17. Ibid., 136, 139, 149, 153.
18. J. Gonda, *Ancient Indian Kingship from the Religious Point of View* (Leiden: E. J. Brill, 1969), 110.
19. Herman Oldenberg, *Die Religion des Veda* (Stuttgart: J. G. Cotta 'Sche, 1923), 474; Gonda agrees with him in *Ancient Indian Kingship*, 114.
20. Alfred Hillebrandt, *Ritual-Litterature Vedische Opfer und Zauber* (Strassburg: Karl J. Trubner, 1897), 149.
21. P. E. Dumont, "The Horse-sacrifice in the Taittirīya-Brāhmaṇa," *Proceedings of the American Philosophical Society* 92/6 (1948): 483.
22. J. Puhvel, "Aspects of Equine Functionality," in *Myth and Law among the Indo-Europeans*, edited by J. Puhvel (Berkeley: University of California Press, 1970): 159–172, views it as a symbolic act, whereas Stephanie W. Jamison interprets the sexual act literally in *Sacrificed Wife/Sacrificer's Wife: Women, Ritual, and Hospitality in Ancient India* (New York: Oxford University Press, 1996), 65, 68.
23. Glucklich, *Sense of Adharma*, 224, 234.
24. Madeleine Biardeau, *Hinduism: The Anthropology of a Civilization*, translated by Richard Nice (Delhi: Oxford University Press, 1989), 64.
25. Glucklich, *Sense of Adharma*, 13.
26. Joanne Punzo Waghorne, *The Raja's Magic Clothes: Re-Visioning Kingship and Divinity in England's India* (University Park: Pennsylvania State University Press, 1994), 215, 232.
27. Jan Gonda, *Ancient Indian Kingship*, 37.
28. Ibid., 21.
29. Ibid., 45.
30. Jan Gonda, *Vedic Ritual: The Non-Solemn Rites*, (Leiden: E. J. Brill, 1980), 364.
31. Ronald B. Inden and Ralph W. Nicholas, *Kinship in Bengali Culture* (Chicago: University of Chicago Press, 1977), 37.
32. The best single source for a discussion of these sacraments is Raj Bali Pandey, *Hindu Saṃskāras* (Delhi: Motilal Banarsidass, 1969).
33. Mary McGee, "Saṃskāra," in *The Hindu World*, edited by Sushil Mittal and Gene Thursby (New York: Routeldge, 2004), 342.
34. Ibid.
35. Willibald Kirfel, *Symbolik des Hinduismus und des Jinismus* (Stuttgart: Anton Hiersemann, 1959), 100–101.

36. Arthur Berriedale Keith, *The Religion and Philosophy of the Veda and Upanishads*, 2 volumes (Delhi: Motilal Banarsidass, 1970), I: 237.
37. See note 2 in Oldenberg, *Die Religion des Veda*, 465.
38. Jan Gonda, *Die Religionen Indiens I: Veda and älterer Hinduismas* (Stuttgart: W. Kohlhammer, 1960), 119.
39. McGee, "Saṃskāra," 346.
40. Heinrich Zimmer, "Death and Rebirth in the Light of India," in *Man and Transformation: Papers from the Eranos Yearboks*, edited by Joseph Campbell (New York: Pantheon Books, 1964), 329.
41. Jan Gonda, *Change and Continuity in Indian Religion* (The Hague: Mouton, 1965), 366.
42. Ibid., 294.
43. Axel Michaels, *Hinduism: Past and Present*, translated by Barbara Harshav (Princeton: Princeton University Press, 2004), 111.
44. Jonathan P. Parry, *Death in Benares* (Cambridge: Cambridge University Press, 1994), 172.
45. David Knipe, *In the Image of Fire* (Delhi: Motilal Banarsidass, 1975), 132.
46. Parry, *Death in Benares*, 6.
47. Ibid., 172.

CHAPTER 5 THE EXPERIENTIAL NATURE OF HINDUISM

1. J. W. Hauer, *Der Yoga: Ein Indischer weg zum Selbst* (Stuttgart: W. Kohlhammer, 1958), 91.
2. Ibid., 208–209.
3. J.A.B. van Buitenen, "Studies in Sāṃkhya," *Journal of the American Oriental Society*, I, 76 (1956); II, 77 (1957); III (1957): 101–102.
4. E. M. Johnston, *Early Sāṃkhya: An Essay on Its Historical Development According to the Texts* (London: Royal Asiatic Society, 1937), 20.
5. John Brockington, "Yoga in the Mahābhārta," in *Yoga: The Indian Tradition*, edited by Ian Whicher and David Carpenter (London: Routledge Curzon, 2003), 14–15.
6. J. N. Farquhar, *An Outline of the Religious Literature of India* (Delhi: Motilal Banarsidass, 1967), 132.
7. Yohanan Grinshpon, *Silence Unheard: Deathly Otherness in Patañjala-Yoga* (Albany: State University of New York Press, 2002), 55.
8. Erich Frauwallner, *Geschichte der Indischen Philosophie*, 2 volumes (Salzburg: Otto Muller Verlag, 1953, 1956), I: 438.
9. Gerald James Larson, *Classical Sāṃkhya: An Interpretation of Its History and Meaning* (Delhi: Motilal Banarsidass, 1969), 2.
10. Mircea Eliade, *Yoga: Immortality and Freedom*, translated by Willard R. Trask (Princeton: Princeton University Press, 1969), 10.
11. Larson, *Classical Sāṃkhya*, 167.
12. Gerald James Larson, "Introduction to the Philosophy of Sāṃkhya," in *Sāṃkhya: A Dualist Tradition in Indian Philosophy*, edited by Gerald James Larson and Ram Shankar Bhattacharya, Encyclopedia of Indian Philosophies (Princeton: Princeton University Press, 1987), 3.
13. Van Buitenen, "Studies in Sāṃkhya," III: 93.
14. Eliade, *Yoga*, 19–20.
15. Larson, "Introduction," 80.

16. Larson, *Classical Sāṃkhya*, 199.
17. Gerhard Oberhammer, "Meditation und Mystik des Patañjali," in *Weiner Zeitschrift für die Kunde Sud-und Ostasiens und Archiv für Indische Philosophie*, edited by E. Frauwallner and G. Oberhammer, volume 9 (Leiden: E. J. Brill, 1965), 113–114.
18. Sigurd Lindquist, *Die Methoden des Yoga* (Lund: Ohlsson, 1932), 57.
19. J. W. Hauer, *Der Yoga: Ein Indischer Weq zum Selbst* (Stuttgart: W. Kohlhammer, 1958), 319.
20. David Carpenter, "Practice Makes Perfect: The Role of Practice (*abhyāsa*) in Patañjali Yoga," in *Yoga: The Indian Tradition*, edited by Ian Whicher and David Carpenter (London: Routledge Curzon, 2003), 27.
21. Eliade, *Yoga*, 95.
22. Ian Whicher, *The Integrity of the Yoga Darśana: A Reconsideration of Classical Yoga* (Albany: State University of New York Press, 1998), 37.
23. Cited by Grinshpon, *Silence Unheard*, 43.
24. Georg Feuerstein, *The Philosophy of Classical Yoga* (New York: St. Martin's Press, 1980), 65.
25. Whicher, *Integrity of the Yoga Darśana*, 183.
26. This type of erroneous claim is made by Linquist, *Die Methoden des Yoga*, 201.
27. S. Radhakrishnan, *Indian Philosophy*, 2 volumes (London: George Allen and Unwin, 1966), II: 464.
28. Natalia Isayeva, *Shankara and Indian Philosophy* (Albany: State University of New York Press, 1993), 145; Sengaku Mayeda, "Śankara and Buddhism," in *New Perspectives on Advaita Vedānta: Essays in Commemoration of Professor Richard De Smet, S.J.*, edited by Bradley J. Malkovsky (Leiden: E. J. Brill, 2000), 18–29.
29. J. Gonda, *Die Religionen Indiens II: Der jüngere Hinduismus* (Stuttgart: W. Kohlhammer, 1963), 83.
30. Surendranath Dasgupta, *A History of Indian Philosophy*, 5 Volumes (Cambridge: Cambridge University Press, 1962–1969), I: 437.
31. Śaṅkara, *Vivekachudamani of Shri Shankaracharya*, translated by Swami Madhavananda (Calcutta: Advaita Ashram, 1966), 516.
32. Carl Olson, *Indian Philosophers and Postmodern Thinkers: Dialogues on the Margins of Culture* (New Delhi: Oxford University Press, 2002), 40.
33. Wilhem Halbfass, *India and Europe: An Essay in Understanding* (Albany: State University of New York Press, 1988), 391.
34. K. Satchidananda Murty, *Revelation and Reason in Advaita Vedanta* (Waltair: Andhra University, 1959), 112; Anantanand Rambachan, *Accomplishing the Accomplished: The Vedas as a Source of Valid Knowledge in Śankara*, Monographs of the Society for Asian and Comparative Philosophy 10 (Honolulu: University of Hawaii Press), 114.
35. Chakravarthi Ram-Prasad, *Knowledge and Liberation in Classical Indian Thought* (Houndsmills: Palgrave, 2001), 191.

CHAPTER 6 THE SENSUAL NATURE OF HINDUISM

1. Mariasusai Dhavamony, *Love of God According to Śaiva Siddhānta: A Study in the Mysticism and Theology of Śaivism* (Oxford: Oxford University Press, 1971), 14, 43.
2. Suvira Jaiswal, *The Origin and Development of Vaiṣṇavism* (Delhi: Munshiram Manoharlal, 1967), 111.
3. Dhavamony, *Love of God*, 55.

4. Louis Renou, *Religions of Ancient India* (New York: Schocken Books, 1968), 42.
5. Diana L. Eck, *Darśan: Seeing the Divine Image in India* (Chambersburg, Pa.: Anima Publications, 1981), 5.
6. J. Gonda, *Eye and Gaze in the Veda* (Amsterdam: North-Holland Publishing, 1969), 19.
7. C. J. Fuller, *The Camphor Flame: Popular Hinduism and Society in India* (Princeton: Princeton University Press, 1992), 62–63.
8. Ibid., 73.
9. Ibid., 74.
10. Diana L. Eck, *Banaras: City of Light* (New York: Alfred A. Knopf, 1982), 34; Eck, "India's Tīrthas: 'Crossings' in Sacred Geography," *History of Religions* 20 (1981): 323–344.
11. Ann Grodzins Gold, *Fruitful Journeys: The Ways of Rajasthani Pilgrims* (Berkeley: University of California Press, 1988), 5; E. Alan Morinis, *Pilgrimage in the Hindu Tradition: A Case Study of West Bengal* (Delhi: Oxford University Press, 1984), 64.
12. Surinder Mohan Bhardwaj, *Hindu Places of Pilgrimage in India* (Berkeley: University of California Press, 1973), 97–98.
13. Ibid., 148–153; Morinis, *Pilgrimage*, 268.
14. Diana L. Eck, "Gangā: The Goddess Ganges in Hindu Sacred Geography," in *Devī: Goddesses of India*, edited by John S. Hawley and Donna M. Wulff (Berkeley: University of California Press, 1996), 138.
15. Ariel Glucklich, *The Sense of Adharma* (New York: Oxford University Press, 1994), 72–73.
16. This narrative is cited by Jonathan Parry, *Death in Benares* (Cambridge: Cambridge University Press, 1994), 27.
17. R. S. Khare, "Food with Saints: An Aspect of Hindu Gastrosemantics," in *The Eternal Food: Gastronomic Ideas and Experiences of Hindus and Buddhists*, edited by R. S. Khare (Albany: State University of New York Press, 1992), 43.
18. Paul M. Toomey, "Mountain of Food, Mountain of Love: Ritual Inversion in the *Annakūta* Feast at Mount Govardhan," in *The Eternal Food: Gastronomic Ideas and Experiences of Hindus and Buddhists*, edited by R. S. Khare (Albany: State University of New York Press, 1992), 117–145.
19. Susan Schwartz, *Rasa: Performing the Divine in India* (New York: Columbia University Press, 2004), 9.
20. Paul M. Toomey, "Krishna's Consuming Passions: Food as Metaphor and Metonym for Emotion at Mount Govardhan," in *Divine Passions: The Social Construction of Emotion in India*, edited by Owen M. Lynch (Berkeley: University of California Press, 1990), 163.
21. Romila Thapar, *Early India: From Origins to AD 1300* (Berkeley: University of California Press, 2002), 360, 387.
22. George Michell, *The Hindu Temple: An Introduction to Its Meaning and Forms* (New York: Harper & Row, 1977), 71.
23. Ibid.
24. Stella Kramrisch, *The Hindu Temple*, 2 volumes (Calcutta: University of Calcutta, 1946; reprint Delhi: Motilal Banarsidass, 1976), I: 163.
25. Michell, *Hindu Temple*, 69.
26. Kramrisch, *Hindu Temple*, II: 313–315.
27. Devangama Desai, *Erotic Sculpture of India: A Socio-cultural Study* (New Delhi: Tata McGraw-Hill, 1975), 105.
28. Ibid., 34.

29. Kramrisch, *Hindu Temple*, I: 133, 143.
30. James J. Preston, "Creation of the Sacred Image: Apotheosis and Destruction in Hinduism," in *Gods of Flesh Gods of Stone: The Embodiment of Divinity in India*, edited by Joanne Punzo Waghorne and Norman Cutler (Chambersburg, Pa.: Anima Publications, 1985), 9–30.
31. Richard H. Davis, *Lives of Indian Images* (Princeton: Princeton University Press, 1997), 31.
32. Michell, *Hindu Temple*, 38.
33. Glucklich, *Sense of Adharma*, 57.
34. Guy L. Beck, *Sonic Theology: Hinduism and Sacred Sound* (Columbia: University of South Carolina Press, 1993), 82.
35. Freda Matchett, "The Purāṇas," in *The Blackwell Companion to Hinduism*, edited by Gavin Flood (Oxford: Blackwell Publishing, 2003), 134.
36. Ludo Rocher, *The Purāṇas: A History of Indian Literature*, volume 2.3 (Wiesbaden: Otto Harrassowitz, 1986), 69.
37. Matchett, "Purāṇas," 131. Kural Chakrabarti, *Religious Process: The Purāṇas and the Making of a Regional Tradition* (New Delhi: Oxford University Press, 2001), 52.
38. Biardeau, *Hinduism: The Anthropology of a Civilization*, translated by Richard Nire (Delhi: Oxford University Press, 1989), 105.
39. Cornelia Dimmitt and J.A.B. van Buitenen, "The Purāṇas: An Introduction," in *Classical Hindu Mythology: A Reader in the Sanskrit Purāṇas* (Philadelphia: Temple University Press, 1978), 27.
40. Biardeau, *Hinduism*, 149, 172.

CHAPTER 7 EMBODIMENT OF VIṢṆU ON EARTH

1. J. Gonda, *Aspects of Early Viṣṇuism* (Delhi: Motilal Banarsidass, 1969), 173.
2. F. Otto Schrader, *Introduction to the Pāñcaratra and the Abhirbuddnya Saṃhitā* (Madras: Adyar Library, 916), 24. J. Gonda, *Viṣṇuism and Śivaism: A Comparison* (London: Athlone Press, 1970), 50.
3. Gonda, *Viṣṇuism and Śivaism*, 49.
4. John Brockington, *The Sanskrit Epics* (Leiden: E. J. Brill, 1998), 287.
5. Ibid.
6. David R. Kinsley, *The Divine Player: A Study of Kṛṣṇa Līlā* (Delhi: Motilal Banarsidass, 1979), 12–13.
7. Alain Daniélou, *Hindu Polytheism*, Bollingen Series 73 (New York: Pantheon Books, 1964), 155.
8. Gonda, *Aspects of Early Viṣṇuism*, 100–101.
9. Ibid., 100.
10. Gonda, *Viṣṇuism and Śivaism*, 111.
11. Gerda Hartmann, "Beiträge zur Geschichte der Göttin Lakṣmī" Ph.D. dissertation, Christian Albrechts Universität zu Kiel, 1933.
12. Carl Olson, "Śrī Laksmī Rādhā: The Obsequious Wife and the Lustful Lover," in *The Book of the Goddess Past and Present: An Introduction to Her Religion*, edited by Carl Olson (New York: Crossroad, 1983), 127.
13. T. A. Gopinath Rao, *Elements of Hindu Iconography*, 2 volumes, second edition (Delhi: Motilal Banarsidass, 1968), I: 89–90, 259.

14. For a more complete discussion, see Alf Hiltebeitel, *The Ritual of Battle: Krishna in the Mahābhārata* (Ithaca: Cornell University Press, 1976), 148–166.

15. Stella Kramrisch, "The Indian Great Goddess," *History of Religions*, 14/4 (1975): 252.

16. Ananda K. Coomaraswamy, *Yakṣas*, 2 parts (Washington, D.C.: Smithsonian Institute, 1929–1931; reprint edition New Delhi: Munshiram Manoharlal, 1971), I: 22; II: 56. Heinrich Zimmer, *The Art of Indian Asia: Its Mythology and Transformation*, edited by Joseph Campbell, Bollingen Series 39 (New York: Pantheon Books, 1960), 175.

17. Gérard Colas, "History of Vaiṣṇava Traditions: An Esquisse," in *The Blackwell Companion to Hinduism*, edited by Gavin Flood (Oxford: Blackwell Publishing, 2003), 232.

18. The first option is espoused by Schrader, *Introduction to the Pāñcarātra*, 24. The second position with respect to an ascetic origin of the term is that of J.A.B. van Buitenen, "The Name 'Pāñcarātra,'" *History of Religions* 1/2 (1962): 296–299.

19. Vasudha Narayanan, *The Way and the Goal: Expressions of Devotion in the Early Śrī Vaiṣṇava Tradition* (Washington, D.C.: Institute for Vaishnava Studies and Center for the Study of World Religions, Harvard University, 1987), 11.

20. J. Gonda, *Medieval Religious Literature in Sanskrit* (Wiesbaden: Otto Harrasowtiz, 1977), 72.

21. Colas, "History of Vaiṣṇava Traditions," 239.

22. Narayanan, *The Way and the Goal*, 33.

23. Steven Paul Hopkins, *Singing the Body of God: The Hymns of Vedāntadeśika in Their South Indian Tradition* (Oxford: Oxford University Press, 2002), 203.

24. V. Raghavan, *The Great Integrators: The Saint-Singers of India* (Delhi: Patiala House, 1969), 32.

25. Ibid., 45, 47.

26. F. Hardy, *Viraha-bhakti: The Early History of Kṛṣṇa Devotion in South India* (Delhi: Oxford University Press, 1983), 128.

27. Rāmānuja, *The Vedānta Sūtras with the Commentary of Rāmānuja*, translated by George Thibaut, Sacred Books of the East, Volume 48 (Delhi: Motilal Banarsidass, 1971), 2.1.10.

28. Rāmānuja, *Vedārthasaṃgraha of Rāmānuja*, translated by J.A.B. van Buitenen (Poona: Deccan College, 1959), 2.17.

29. John Braisted Carman, *The Theology of Rāmānuja* (New Haven: Yale University Press, 1974), 147.

30. Rāmānuja, *Rāmānuja on the Bhagavadgītā*, translated by J.A.B. van Buitenen (Delhi: Motilal Banarsidass, 1968), 2.12, 2.16.

31. Rāmānuja, *Vedāntasāra of Rāmānuja*, edited and translated by M. B. Narasimha Ayyangar (Madras: Adyar Library, 1953), 1.1.2.

32. Rāmānuja, *Bhagavadgītā*, 9.4.

33. Rāmānuja, *Vedāntasāra*, 1.2.8.

34. Rāmānuja, *Vedānta Sūtras*, 1.1.1.

35. Rāmānuja, *Vedārthasaṃgraha*, 3.65.

36. Rāmānuja, *Vedānta Sūtras*, 1.1.1.

37. Rāmānuja, *Bhagavadgītā*, 5.15.

38. Ibid., 4.18.

39. Ibid., 2.55–58.

40. Ibid., 2.72.

41. Rāmānuja, *Vedārthasaṃgraha*, 3.141.

42. Rāmānuja, *Bhagavadgītā*, 4.2.16.
43. Ibid., 4.4.17.
44. R. G. Bhandarkar, *Vaiṣṇavism, Śaivism and Minor Religious Systems* (Banaras: Indological Book House, 1965), 56.
45. Narayanan, *The Way and the Goal*, 123.
46. See Patricia Y. Mumme, *The Śrīvaiṣṇava Theological Dispute: Manavāḷamāuni and Vedānta Deśika* (Madras: New Era, 1988), 163.
47. Hopkins, *Singing the Body of God*, 87.
48. Ibid., 130, 195, 209.
49. Mādhva, *The Vedānta Sūtras with the Commentary of Śrī Mādhvacharya*, translated by S. Subha Rau (Madras: Minerva Press, 1904), 2.3.38.
50. Ibid., 1.1.7.
51. Suzanne Siauve, *La doctrine de Madhva: Dvaita-Vedānta*, Publications de l'Institut Français d'Indologie 38 (Pondicherry: Institut Français d'Indologie, 1968), 16.
52. Mādhva, *Vedānta Sūtras*, 1.1.1.
53. Surendranath Dasgupta, *A History of Indian Philosophy*, 5 volumes (Cambridge: Cambridge University Press, 1962–1969), IV: 58. Deepak Sarma, *An Introduction to Mādhva Vedānta* (Aldershot: Ashgate, 2003), 80.
54. Mādhva, *Vedānta Sūtra*, 1.1.1.
55. Ibid., 3.2.22.
56. Sarma, *Introduction*, 81.
57. S. Radhakrishnan, *Indian Philosophy*, 2 volumes, second edition (London: George Allen & Unwin, 1966), II: 753.
58. Dasgupta, *History*, III: 413–414.
59. Helmuth von Glasenapp, *Die Philosophie der Inder: Eine Einfuhrung in ihre Geschichte und ihre Lehren* (Stuttgart: Alfred Kroner, 1958), 189.
60. Gonda, *Die Religionen Indiens*, II: 157.
61. Helmuth von Glasenapp, *Der Hinduismus: Religion und Gesellschaft im Heutigen Indien* (Munchen: Kurt Wolff Verlag, 1922), 387.
62. M. M. Underhill, *The Hindu Religious Year* (Calcutta: Association Press, 1921), 59–63.
63. Lawrence A. Babb, *The Divine Hierarchy: Popular Hinduism in Central India* (New York: Columbia University Press, 1975), 164.

CHAPTER 8 DIVINE PLAY, MADNESS, EROTICISM, AND KRISHNA

1. *Mahaniddesa*, volume I, edited by Louis de la Vallée Poussin (London: Pail Text Society, 1916), 89, 92.
2. John S. Hawley, "Thief of Butter, Thief of Love," *History of Religions* 18/3 (1979): 206.
3. David R. Kinsley, *The Divine Player: A Study of Kṛṣṇa Līlā* (Delhi: Motilal Banarsidass, 1979), 67.
4. David R. Kinsley, *The Sword and the Flute: Kālī and Kṛṣṇa, Dark Visions of the Terrible and the Sublime in Hindu Mythology* (Berkeley: University of California Press, 1975), 34.
5. F. Hardy, *Viraha-Bhakti: The Early History of Kṛṣṇa Devotion in South India* (Delhi: Oxford University Press, 1983), 101.
6. Freda Matchett, *Kṛṣṇa: Lord or Avatāra? The Relationship between Kṛṣṇa and Viṣṇu* (Surrey: Curzon Press, 2001), 138.

7. Madeleine Biardeau, *Hinduism: The Anthropology of a Civilization*, translated by Richard Nice (Delhi: Oxford University Press, 1989), 145.

8. Kinsley, *Divine Player*, 95.

9. Kinsley, *Sword and Flute*, 73.

10. The following works are good resources for the historical development of Rādhā: Barbara Stoler Miller, "Rādhā: Consort of Kṛṣṇa's Venal Passion," *Journal of the American Oriental Society* 95/4 (1975): 655–671; Sadashuva L. Katre, "Kṛṣṇa, Gopas, and Rādhā," in *Professor P. K. Gode Commemoration Volume*, edited by H. L. Hairyappa and M. M. Patkar (Poona: Oriental Book Agency, 1960), 83–92; Asoke Kumar Majumdar, "A Note on the Development of the Rādhā Cult," *Annals of the Bhandankar Oriental Research Institute* 75 (1955): 231–257; Charlotte Vaudeville, "Evolution of Love-Symbolism in Bhagavatism," *Journal of the American Oriental Society* 82 (1962): 31–40.

11. Cheever Mackenzie Brown, *God as Mother: A Feminine Theology in India* (Hartford, V.: Claude Stark, 1974), 1.

12. Vallabha, *Anubhasya with Balabodhini*, edited by S. T. Pathak (Bombay: Sanskrit Prakrit Series 77, 81, 1921–1926), 2.3.43–53.

13. Ibid., 2.3.43.

14. S. Radhakrishnan, *Indian Philosophy*, 2 volumes, second edition (London: George Alien of Unwin, 1966), II: 760.

15. Vallabha, *Anubhasya*, 2.3.29.

16. Ibid., 3.4.25.

17. Ibid., 3.4.38.

18. Norvin J. Hein, "Caitanya's Ecstasies and the Theology of the Name," in *Hinduism: New Essays in the History of Religions*, edited by Bardwell L. Smith (Leiden: E. J. Brill, 1982), 21, 24.

19. Hardy, *Viraha-Bhakti*, 434.

20. David R. Kinsley, "'Through the Looking Glass': Divine Madness in the Hindu Religious Tradition," *History of Religions* 13/3 (1974): 271–286.

21. Sushil Kumar De, *Early History of the Vaiṣṇava Faith and Movement in Bengal* (Calcutta: Firma K. L. Mukhopadhyay, 1961), 373.

22. David L. Haberman, *Acting as a Way of Salvation: Study of Rāgānugā Bhakti Sādhana* (Oxford: Oxford University Press, 1988), 36–37.

23. Edward C. Dimock, Jr., *The Place of the Hidden Moon: Erotic Mysticism in the Vaiṣṇava-Sahajiyā Cult of Bengal* (Chicago: University of Chicago Press, 1966), 16–17.

24. Ibid., 35.

25. Ibid., 42, 168.

26. Ibid., 137.

27. Shashibhusan Dasgupta, *Obscure Religious Cults* (Calcutta: Firma K. L. Mukhopadyay, 1969), 116, 119.

28. Manindra Mohan Bose, "An Introduction to the Study of the Post-Chaitanya Sahajia Cult," *Journal of the Department of Letters, University of Calcutta* 16 (1927): 1.

29. Friedhelm Hardy, *The Religious Culture of India: Power, Love and Wisdom* (Cambridge: Cambridge University Press, 1994), 326.

30. See John Stratton Hawley, "Author and Authority in the *Bhakti* Poetry of North India," *Journal of Asian Studies*, 47/2 (1988): 269–290.

31. June McDaniel, *The Madness of the Saints: Ecstatic Religion in Bengal* (Chicago and London: University of Chicago Press, 1989), 160.
32. Jeanne Openshaw, *Seeking the Bāuls of Bengal* (Cambridge: Cambridge University Press, 2002), 228–229.
33. Charles S. J. White, *The Caurāsī Pad of Śrī Hit Harivaṃś*, Asian Studies at Hawaii 16 (Honolulu: University Press of Hawaii, 1977), 29.
34. Anne Feldhaus, trans., *The Deeds of God in Ṛddhipur* (Oxford: Oxford University Press, 1984), 278.
35. Anne Feldhaus and Shankar Gopal Tulpule, *In the Absence of God: The Early Years of an Indian Sect* (Honolulu: University of Hawaii Press, 1992), 19.
36. C. Vaudeville, "The Slaiva-Vaishnava Synthesis in Maharashtrian Santism," in *The Sants: Studies in a Devotional Tradition of India*, edited by Karine Schomer and W. H. McLeod (Berkeley: Berkeley Religious Studies and Motilal Banarsidass, 1987), 218, n. 9.
37. R. D. Ranade, *Mysticism in India: The Poet-Saints of Maharastra* (Albany: State University of New York Press, 1983), 303.
38. Justin E. Abbott, trans., *Life of Tukaram, translation from Mahipati's Bhaktalilamrita, Chapter 25 to 40* ([1930] Delhi: Motilal Banarsidass, 1980), 28; 30.88; 31.64; 33.81.
39. Tukarama, *The Poems of Tukarama*, 3 volumes, edited and translated by J. Nelson Fraser and K. B. Marathe (Madras: Chrisitian Literature Society, 1909, 1913, 1915), hymn. 83.
40. Ibid., hymn. 1439.
41. John Stratton Hawley, *At Play with Krishna: Pilgrimage Drama from Brindavan* (Princeton: Princeton University Press, 1981), 16.
42. Ibid., 107.
43. McDaniel, *Madness of the Saints*, 81.
44. Edwin Gerow, "Rasa as a Category of Literary Criticism," in *Sanskrit Drama in Performance*, edited by Rachel Baumer and James R. Brandom (Honolulu: University Press of Hawaii, 1981), 250–251.
45. Susan L. Schwartz, *Rasa: Performing the Divine in India* (New York: Columbia University Press, 2004).
46. Norvin Hein, *The Miracle Plays of Mathura* (Delhi: Oxford University Press, 1972), 169–177.
47. Milton Singer, "The Rādhā-Krishna *Bhajanas* of Madras City," in *Krishna: Myths, Rites and Attitudes*, edited by Milton Singer (Honolulu: East-West Center Press, 1966), 91–101.
48. Ibid., 92.
49. McKim Marriott, "The Feast of Love," in *Krishna: Myths, Rites and Attitudes*, edited by Milton Singer (Honolulu: East-West Center Press, 1966), 202.
50. Heinrich von Stietencron, "A Congregation of Gods: The Doḷamelaṇa Festival in Orissa," in *Jagannath Revisited: Studying Society, Religion and State in Orissa*, edited by Herman Kulke and Burkhard Schnepel (New Delhi: Manohar, 2001), 364–376.
51. Larry D. Shinn, *The Dark Lord: Cult Images and the Hare Krishnas in America* (Philadelphia: Westminster, 1987), 71.
52. Mikael Rothstein, *Belief Transformations: Some Aspects of the Relation between Science and Religion in Transcendental Meditation (TM) and the International Society for Krishna Consciousness (ISKCON)* (Aarhus: Aarhus University Press, 1996), 110–111.
53. David L. Haberman, *Journey through the Twelve Forests: An Encounter with Krishna* (Oxford: Oxford University Press, 1994), 73–74.
54. McDaniel, Madness of the Saints, 29.

CHAPTER 9 RIGHTEOUS RAMA, UNTOUCHABLES, AND SANTS

1. John Brockington, *The Sanskrit Epics* (Leiden: E.J. Brill, 1998), 26.
2. James L. Fitzgerald, "India's Fifth Veda: The *Mahābhārata's* Presentation of Itself," *Journal of South Asian Literature* 20/1 (1985): 126–128.
3. Brockington, *The Sanskrit Epics*, 34.
4. Jan Gonda, *Die Religionen Indiens I: Veda und älterer Hinduismus* (Stuttgart: W. Kohlhammer, 1960), 220.
5. Alf Hiltebeitel, *Rethinking the Mahābhārata: A Reader's Guide to the Education of the Dharma King* (Chicago: University of Chicago Press, 2001), 18–19.
6. James L. Fitzgerald, "The Many Voices of the *Mahābhārata*," *Journal of the American Oriental Society* 123/4 (2003): 811.
7. Yaroslav Vassilkov, "The *Mahābhārata's* Typological Definition Reconsidered," *Indo-Iranian Journal* 38/3 (1995): 255.
8. David Dean Shulman, "Devana and Daiva," in *Ritual, State, and History in South Asia: Essays in Honour of J. C. Heesterman*, edited by D.H.A. Kloff and M. S. Oort (Leiden: E. J. Brill, 1992), 359.
9. Alf Hiltebeitel, "Śiva, the Goddess, and the Disguises of the Pāṇḍavas and Draupadī," *History of Religions* 12/1–2 (1980): 147–174.
10. Alf Hiltebeitel, *The Ritual of Battle: Krishna in the Mahābhārata* (Ithaca: Cornell University Press, 1976), 318.
11. Madeleine Biardeau, "Études de mythologie hindoue (I–V)," *Bulletin de l'École Française d'Extrême-Orient* 54 (1968): 19–45; 55 (1969): 59–105; 58 (1971): 17–89; 63 (1976): 111–263; 65 (1978): 87–238.
12. Robert P. Goldman, "Resisting Rāma: Dharmic Debates on Gender and Hierarchy and the Work of the Vālmīki Rāmāyaṇa," in *The Rāmāyaṇa Revisited*, edited by Mandakranta Bose (Oxford: Oxford University Press, 2004), 21.
13. Brockington, *Sanskrit Epics*, 34.
14. Frank Whaling, *The Rise of the Religious Significance of Rāma* (Delhi: Motilal Banarsidass, 1980), 36.
15. J. L. Brockington, *Righteous Rāma: The Evolution of an Epic* (Delhi: Oxford University Press, 1985), 94–95.
16. Robert P. Goldman and Sally J. Sutherland Goldman, "Rāmāyaṇa," in *The Hindu World*, edited by Sushil Mittal and Gene Thursby (New York: Routledge, 2004), 76.
17. Brockington, *Righteous Rāma*, 10.
18. Julia Leslie, *Authority and Meaning in Indian Religions: Hinduism and the Case of Vālmīki* (Aldeershot: Ashgate, 2003), 80–94.
19. Whaling, *Rise of the Religious Significance*, 31, note 2.
20. Frank E. Reynolds, "*Rāmāyana, Rāma Jātaka*, and *Ramakien*: A Comparative Study of Hindu and Buddhist Traditions," in *Many Rāmāyaṇas: The Diversity of a Narrative Tradition in South Asia*, edited by Paula Richman (Berkeley: University of California Press, 1991), 50–55.
21. G. S. Ghurye, *Gods and Men* (Bombay: Popular Book Depot, 1962), 190.
22. Whaling, *Rise of the Religious Significance*, 101.
23. Ibid., 113.
24. Richard Burghart, "The Founding of the Rāmānandī Sect," in *Religious Movements in South Asia 600–1800*, edited by David N. Lorenzen (Delhi: Oxford University Press, 2004), 247.

25. Richard Burghart, "Wandering Ascetics of the Rāmānandī Sect," *History of Religions* 22/4 (1983): 363, 367.

26. F. R. Allchin, trans., *Tulsī Dās, The Petition to Rām* (London: George Allen & Unwin, 1966), 76.

27. Linda Hess, "Rām Līlā: The Audience Experience," in *Bhakti in Current Research 1979–1982*, edited by Monika Thiel-Horstmann (Berlin: Dietrich Reimer Verlag, 1983), 183.

28. See William Jackson, *Tyāgarāja—Life and Lyrics*, fourth edition (New Delhi: Oxford University Press, 2002).

29. See Mikael Aktor, "Untouchables, Women and Territories: Rituals of Lordship in the Parāśara Smṛti," in *Invented Identities: The Interplay of Gender, Religion and Politics in India*, edited by Julia Leslie and Mary McGee (New Delhi: Oxford University Press, 2000), 135–140.

30. Pandurang Vaman Kane, *History of Dharmaśāstra*, 5 volumes (Poona: Bhandarkar Research Institute, 1953–1973), II. 1, 167–168.

31. Mark Juergensmeyer, *Religion as Social Vision: The Movement against Untouchability in 20th Century Punjab* (Berkeley: University of California Press, 1982), 11.

32. Ramdas Lamb, *Rapt in the Name: The Ramnamis, Ramnam, and Untouchable Religion in Central India* (Albany: State University of New York Press, 2002), 82–89.

33. Ibid., 90–91.

34. Ibid., 90–91, 94.

35. This information was shared with me in a private correspondence with Ramdas Lamb of the Univerisity of Hawaii.

36. Lamb, *Rapt*, 99–103.

37. Ibid., 110.

38. A. K. Ramanujan, "Three Hundred Rāmāyaṇas: Five Examples and Three Thoughts on Translation," in *Many Rāmāyaṇas: The Diversity of a Narrative Tradition in South Asia*, edited by Paula Richman (Berkeley: University of California Press, 1991), 46.

39. William L. Smith, "Rāmāyaṇa Textual Traditions in Eastern India," in *The Rāmāyaṇa Revisited*, edited by Mandakranta Bose (Oxford: Oxford University Press, 2004), 88.

40. Paula Richman, "Questioning and Multiplicity within the Ramayana Tradition," in *Questioning Ramayanas: A South Asian Tradition*, edited by Paula Richman (Berkeley: Univeristy of California Press, 2001), 5–6.

41. Hess, "Rām Līlā," 174.

42. William S. Sax, "The Ramnagar Rāmlīlā: Text, Performance," *History of Religions* 30/2 (1990): 140–141.

43. Philip Lutgendorf, *The Life of a Text: Performing the Rāmacaritmānas of Tulsidas* (Berkeley: University of California Press, 1991), 311.

44. Ibid., 250.

45. Ibid., 316–317.

46. Vaudeville, "The Shaiva-Vaishnava Synthesis in Maharashtrian Santism," 215.

47. Charlotte Vaudeville, "Sant Mat: Santism as the Universal Path to Sanctity," in *The Sants: Studies in a Devotional Tradition of India*, edited by Karine Schomer and W. H. McLeod (Berkeley: Berkeley Religious Studies and Motilal Banarsidass, 1987), 37.

48. John Stratton Hawley, "The Nirguṇ/Saguṇ Distinction in Early Manuscript Anthologies of Hindi Devotion," in *Bhakti Religion in North India: Community Identity and Political Action*, edited by David N. Lorenzen (Albany: State University of New York Press, 1995), 162–165.

49. David N. Lorenzen, "The Lives of the Nirguṇī Saints," in *Bhakti Religion in North India: Community Identity and Political Action*, edited by David N. Lorenzen (Albany: State University of New York Press, 1995), 192.
50. Linda Hess and Shukdeo Singh, trans., *The Bijak of Kabir* (Oxford: Oxford University Press, 2002), 3.
51. Charlotte Vaudeville, "Introduction," in Vauleville, *Kabir*, volume 1 (Oxford: Oxford University Press, 1974), p. 110.
52. Hess and Singh, *Bijak*, poem pp. 111–112.
53. David N. Lorenzen, *Kabir Legends and Ananta-Das's Kabir Parachai* (Albany: State University of New York Press, 1991), 2.2–15.
54. Ibid., 4.9–5.1.
55. Ibid., 13.2–5.
56. Vaudeville, *Kabir*, 26.8d.
57. Hess and Singh, *Bijak*, sā. 75.
58. Vaudeville, *Kabir*, 3.13d.
59. Linda Hess, "The Cow Is Sucking at the Calf's Teat: Kabir's Upside-Down Language," *History of Religions* 22/4 (1983): 314, 336.
60. Hess and Singh, "Introduction," in *Bijak*, 27.
61. Dan Gold, *The Lord as Guru: Hindi Sants in North Indian Tradition* (Oxford: Oxford University Press, 1987), 85, 88.
62. Uma Thurkal, "The Avatar Doctrine in the Kabīr Panth," in *Bhakti in North India: Community Identity and Political Action*, edited by David N. Lorenzen (Albany: State University of New York Press, 1995), 222.
63. David N. Lorenzen, "The Kabir-Panth and Social Protest," in *The Sants: Studies in a Devotional Tradition of India*, edited by Karine Schomer and W. H. Mcleod (Berkeley: Berkeley Religious Studies Series and Motilal Banarsidass, 1987), 283.
64. Lamb, *Rapt*, 53–56.
65. Ibid., 59.
66. Juergensmeyer, *Religion as Social Vision*, 84.
67. Two informative discussions of this movement are: Lawrence A. Babb, *Redemptive Encounters: Three Modern Styles in the Hindu Tradition* (Berkeley: University of California Press, 1986), 15–89, and Mark Juergensmeyer, *Radhasoami Reality: The Logic of Modern Faith* (Princeton: Princeton University Press, 1991).

CHAPTER 10 DANCE OF THE ASCETIC DEITY ŚIVA

1. Anne-Marie Gaston, *Śiva in Dance, Myth and Iconography* (Delhi: Oxford University Press, 1990), 6.
2. David Smith, *The Dance of Śiva: Religion, Art and Poetry in South India* (Cambridge: Cambridge University Press, 1996), 83.
3. Paul Younger, *The Home of Dancing Śivan* (Oxford: Oxford University Press, 1995), 183.
4. There are two good examples of this phenomenon: *Haravijaya of Rājānaka Ratnākara with the Commentary of Rājānaka Alaka*, edited by Durgāprasād and Kāśināth Pāṇḍurang Parab (Bombay, 1890), 1.46; *Mahimnastava or Praise of Śiva's Greatness*, translated and edited by W. Norman Brown (Poona: American Institute of Indian Studies Publication, 1965), 16.
5. See David Dean Shulman, *Tamil Temple Myths: Sacrifice and Divine Marriage in the South Indian Śaiva Tradition* (Princeton: Princeton University Press, 1980), 216, 223;

Wendy Doniger O'Flaherty, *Women, Androgynes, and Other Mythical Beasts* (Chicago: University of Chicago Press, 1980), 141–42.

6. See discussion by Ananda K. Coomaraswamy, *The Dance of Shiva: Fourteen Indian Essays*, revised edition (New Delhi: Sagar Publications, 1971), 66–86; Heinrich Zimmer, *Myths and Symbols in Indian Art and Civilization*, edited by Joseph Campbell, Bollingen Series 6 (New York: Pantheon Books, 1946), 151–175.

7. Asko Parpola, *Deciphering the Indus Script* (Cambridge: Cambridge University Press, 1994), 248–250.

8. See Wendy Doniger O'Flaherty, *Asceticism and Eroticism in the Mythology of Śiva* (London: Oxford University Press, 1973).

9. See Paul B. Courtright, *Ganeśa: Lord of Obstacles, Lord of Beginnings* (Oxford: Oxford University Press, 1985); John A. Grimes, *Ganapati: Song of the Self* (Albany: State University of New York Press, 1995); Robert L. Brown, ed., *Ganesh: Studies of an Asian God* (Albany: State University of New York Press, 1991).

10. For a more complete discussion of the dice motif in the mythology of Śiva, see Don Handelman and David Shulman, *God Inside Out: Śiva's Game of Dice* (Oxford: Oxford University Press, 1997).

11. Stella Kramrisch, *The Presence of Śiva* (Princeton: Princeton University Press, 1981), 242–243.

12. T. A. Gopinatha Rao, *Elements of Hindu Inconography*, 2 volumes, second edition (Delhi: Motilal Banarsidass, 1968), 2.1, 322–323.

13. O'Flaherty, *Asceticism and Eroticism*, 135.

14. Agehananda Bharati, *The Tantric Tradition* (New York: Doubleday, 1970), 296.

15. *Pasupata Sutram* with Panchartha-Bhasya of Kaudinya, translated by Haripada Chakraborti (Calcutta: Academic Publishers, 1970), 1.1.

16. Ibid., 5.3; 1.2; 1.9.

17. Daniel H. H. Ingalls, "Cynics and Pāśupatas: The Seeking of Dishonor," *Harvard Theological Review* 55 (1962): 291–292.

18. David N. Lorenzen, *The Kāpālikas and Kālāmukhas: Two Lost Śaivite Sects* (Berkeley: University of California Press, 1972), 175.

19. Ibid., 87, 83.

20. Mircea Eliade, *Yoga: Immortality and Freedom*, translated by Willard R. Trask (Princeton: Princeton University Press, 1969), 304.

21. Jan Gonda, *Die Religionen Indiens II: Der jüngere Hinduismus* (Stuttgart: W. Kohlhammer, 1963), 221.

22. George Weston Briggs, *Gorakhnath and the Kanphata Yogis* (Delhi: Motilal Banarsidass, 1973), 250.

23. *The Goraksa Śataka*, translated by George Weston Briggs in *Gorakhnath and the Kanpahata Yogis*, 7.

24. Indira Viswananatha Peterson, *Poems to Śiva: The Hymns of the Tamil Saints* (Princeton: Princeton University Press, 1989), 23.

25. See George W. Spencer, "The Sacred Geography of the Tamil Shaivite Hymns," *Numen* 17 (1970): 232–244.

26. See Indira V. Peterson, "Singing of a Place: Pilgrimage as Metaphor and Motif with Tēvāram Hymns of the Tamil Śaivite Saints," *Journal of the American Oriental Society* 102/1/ (1982): 62–90.

27. Karen Pechilis Prentiss, *The Embodiment of Bhakti* (Oxford: Oxford University Press, 1999), 44.
28. Indira Viswanathan Peterson, "Lives of the Wandering Singers: Pilgrimage and Poetry in Tamil Śaivite Hagiography," *History of Religions* 22/4 (1983): 354.
29. Kamil V. Zvelebil, *Tamil Literature*, Handbuch der Orientalistik (Leiden: E. J. Brill, 1975), 178–181.
30. Prentiss, *Embodiment of Bliss*, 63–64.
31. Peterson, *Poems to Śiva*, 118–119.
32. Kamil V. Zvelebil, *The Smile of Murugan: On Tamil Literature of South India* (Leiden: E. J. Brill, 1973), 198.
33. Māṇikkavācakar, *The Tiruvāsagam of Mānikka-Vāsagar*, translated by G. U. Pope (Oxford: Clarendon Press, 1900), 10.23.
34. Mariasusai Dhavamony, *Love of God According to Śaiva Siddhānta: A Study in the Mysticism and Theology of Śaivism* (Oxford: Oxford University Press, 1971), 127–128.
35. Meykanta, *Siva-gnana-pothan*, translated by Henry R. Hoisington, *Journal of the American Oriental Society* 4 (1853–1854), 2.7.
36. Ibid., 6.1; 9.9.
37. Violet Paranjoti, *Saiva Siddhanta in the Meykanda Sastra* (London: Luzac and Company, 1938), 180.
38. Meykanta, *Siva-gnana-pothan*, 9.7.
39. Umapati, *Siva Pirakasam*, translated by Henry R. Hoisington, *Journal of the American Oriental Society* 4 (1853–1854): 75.
40. Kamil V. Zvelebil, *The Poets of the Powers* (London: Rider, 1973), 27.
41. Kamil V. Zvelebil, *Smile of Murugan*, 228.
42. Alexis Sanderson, "Purity and Power among the Brahmanas of Kashmir," in *The Category of the Person: Anthropology, Philosophy, History*, edited by Michael Carrithers, Steven Collins, and Steven Lukas (Cambridge: Cambridge University Press, 1985), 200–202.
43. Alexis Sanderson, "Meaning in Tantric Ritual," in *Essais sur le rituel III*, 15–95, edited by Anne-Marie Blondeau and Kristofer Schipper (Louvain: Peeters, 1995), 82.
44. See Harvey P. Alper, "The Cosmos as Śiva's Language-Game: 'Mantra' According to Ksemarāja's *Śivasūtravimarśinī*," in *Mantra*, edited by Harvey P. Alper (Albany: State University of New York Press, 1989), 249–294. Alexis Sanderson provides a good historical introduction to the complex subject in "Śaivism and the Tantric Traditions," in *The World's Religions*, edited by Stewart Sutherland et al. (London: Routledge, 1988), 660–704. Some of the more recent studies of Kashmir Śaivism of note are the following: Paul Eduardo Muller-Ortega, *The Triadic Heart of Śiva: Kaula Tantricism of Abhinavagupta in the Non-dual Shaivism of Kashmir* (Albany: State University of New York Press, 1989); and Mark S. G. Dyczkowski, *The Doctrine of Vibration: An Analysis of the Doctrine and Practices of Kashmir Shaivism* (Albany: State University of New York Press, 1987).
45. *Kularnava-tantra*, edited by Tarantha Vidyaratna (London: Tantrik Texts, Vol. 4, 1917), 3.23.
46. Abhinavagupta, *The Tantraloka of Abhinava Gupta with Jayarath's Commentary*, 12 volumes, edited by Mukunda Rama Sastri and M. S. Kaul. Kashmir Series of Texts and Studies. (Allahabad: Indian Press, 1918–1938), 5.356.
47. Abhinavagupta, *A Trident of Wisdom: Translation of Parātrīsikā-Vivarana*, translated by Jaideva Singh (Albany: State University of New York Press, 1989), 77.

48. Abhinavagupta, *Tantraloka*, 4.181–193.
49. Abhinavagupta, *Trident of Wisdom*, 120.
50. Abhinavagupta, *Paramarthasara of Abhinavagupta*, edited and translated by L. D. Barnett, *Journal of the Royal Asiatic Society, London* (1900), 9.
51. Abhinavagupta, *Tantraloka*, 4.3–7.
52. Velcheru Narayana Rao, trans., *Śiva's Warriors: The Basava Purāṇa of Pālkuriki Somanātha* (Princeton: Princeton University Press, 1990), 50.
53. S. C. Nandimath, *A Handbook of Vīraśaivism* (Dharwar: Lingayat Education Association, 1953), 3.
54. R.G. Bhandarkar, *Vaiṣṇavism, Śaivism and Minor Religious Systems* (Banaras: Indological Book House, 1965), 28.
55. For a useful English translation of the text, see *Sūnyasaṁpādane*, 5 volumes, translated by S. C. Nandimath, L.M.A. Menezes, and R. C. Hiremath (Dharwar: Karnatak University, 1965). For a textual study of the work, see R. Blake Michael, *The Origins of Vīraśaiva Sects: A Typological Analysis of Ritual and Associated Patterns in the Śūnyasaṁpādane* (Delhi: Motilal Banarsidass, 1992).
56. A. K. Ramanujan, "Introduction," in his *Speaking of Śiva* (Baltimore: Penguin Books, 1973), 37.
57. Narayana Rao, *Śiva's Warriors*, 74–75.
58. For a fuller discussion, see Carl Olson, *The Indian Renouncer and Postmodern Poison: A Cross-Cultural Encounter* (New York: Peter Lang, 1997), 128–188.
59. For a discussion of this sect as a protest movement, see K. Ishwaran, "Bhakti Tradition and Modernization: The Case of Lingayatism," in *Tradition and Modernity in Bhakti Movements*, edited by Jayant Lele, International Studies in Sociology and Social Anthropology 31 (Leiden: E. J. Brill, 1981), and R. Blake Michael, "Work in Virashaiva Tradition," *Journal of the American Academy of Religion*, 50/4 (1982): 605–619.
60. Nandimath, *Handbook of Vīraśaivism*, 118–119.
61. Ibid., 164.
62. K. Ishwaran, *Religion and Society among the Lingayats of South India* (Leiden: E. J. Brill, 1983), p. 101.
63. *Śūnyasaṁpādane*, 1.56.
64. Nandimath, *Handbook of Vīraśaivism*, 32–39.
65. Ishwaran, *Religion and Society*, 5.
66. Fred W. Clothey, "Chronometry, Cosmology, and the Festival Calendar in the Murukan Cult," in *Religious Festival in South India and Sri Lanka*, edited by Guy R. Welbon and Glenn E. Yocum (New Delhi: Manohar, 1982), 180.
67. Ibid., 159–160.
68. Younger, *Home of Dancing Śivan*, 24–25.
69. See Richard R. Davis, *Ritual in an Oscillating Universe: Worshiping Śiva in Medieval India* (Princeton: Princeton University Press, 1991), 42–111.
70. Ibid., 48–49.
71. M. M. Underhill, *The Hindu Religious Year* (Calcutta: Association Press, 1921), 93.
72. J. Bruce Long, "Mahāśivarātri: The Śiva Festival of Repentance," in *Religious Festivals in South India and Sri Lanka*, edited by Guy R. Welbon and Glenn E. Yocum (New Delhi: Manohar, 1982), 212.
73. Ibid., 190.

74. C.J. Fuller, *The Camphor Flame: Popular Hinduism and Society in India* (Princeton: Princeton University Press, 1992), 197.

75. Younger, *Home of Dancing Śivan*, 54–56.

76. David M. Knipe, "Night of the Growing Dead: A Cult of Vīrabhadra in Coastal Andra," in *Criminal Gods and Demon Devotees: Essays on the Guardians of Popular Hinduism*, edited by Alf Hiltebeitel (Albany: State University of New York Press, 1989), 125.

77. Ibid., 130–132.

CHAPTER 11 FEMININE THREAD

1. Leslie C. Orr, *Donors, Devotees, and Daughters of God: Temple Women in Medieval Tamilnadu* (Oxford: Oxford University Press, 2000), 161–162.

2. David Kinsley, *The Goddesses' Mirror: Visions of the Divine from East and West* (Albany: State University of New York Press, 1989), 4.

3. Kathleen M. Erndl, *Victory to the Mother: The Hindu Goddess of Northwest India in Myth, Ritual, and Symbol* (New York: Oxford University Press, 1993), 106.

4. Ibid., 112.

5. Kinsley, *Goddesses' Mirror*, 5, 8.

6. Wendy Doniger O'Flaherty, *Women, Androgynes, and Other Mythical Beasts* (Chicago: University of Chicago Press, 1980), 111.

7. Stephanie W. Jamison, *Sacrificed Wife Sacrificer's Wife: Women, Ritual and Hospitality in Ancient India* (Oxford: Oxford University Press, 1996), 41, 53.

8. Ibid., 253.

9. See Patrick Olivelle, "Amṛtā: Women and Indian Technologies of Immortality," *Journal of Indian Philosophy* 25 (1997): 427–449.

10. Gloria Goodwin Raheja, *The Poison in the Gift: Ritual, Prestation, and the Dominant Caste in a North Indian Village* (Chicago: University of Chicago Press, 1988), 134.

11. Pandurang Vaman Kane, *History of Dharmaśāstra*, 5 volumes (Poona: Bhandarkar Research Institute, 1953–1973), II: 803.

12. Tanika Sarkar, *Hindu Wife, Hindu Nation: Community, Religion, and Cultural Nationalism* (Bloomington: Indiana Univeristy Press, 2001), 202–203.

13. Ellison Banks Findly, "The Housemistress at the Door: Vedic and Buddhist Perspectives on the Mendicant Encounter," in *Jewels of Authority: Women and Textual Tradition in Hindu India*, edited by Laurie L. Patton (Oxford: Oxford University Press, 2002), 25.

14. Linsey Harlan, *Religion and Rajput Women: The Ethic of Protection in Contemporary Narratives* (Berkeley: Univeristy of California Press, 1992), 95–96.

15. Sarah Lamb, *White Saris and Sweet Mangoes: Aging, Gender, and Body in North India* (Berkeley: University of California Press, 2000), 55.

16. Ibid.

17. Anne Mackenzie Pearson, *"Because It Gives Me Peace of Mind:" Ritual Fasts in the Lives of Hindu Women* (Albany: State University of New York Press, 1996), 5.

18. Ibid., 10.

19. Ibid., 203.

20. Ibid., 155–157.

21. Mandakranta Bose, "Sati: The Event and the Idealogy," in *Faces of the Feminine in Ancient, Medieval, and Modern India*, edited by Mandakranta Bose (Oxford: Oxford University Press, 2000), 26.

22. Catherine Weinberger-Thomas, *Ashes of Immortality: Widow-Burning in India*, translated by Jeffrey Mehlman and David Gordon White (Chicago: University of Chicago Press, 1999), 37.

23. Ibid., 52–53, 68, 77; Harlan, *Religion and Rajput Women*, 113.

24. Weinberger-Thomas, *Ashes of Immortality*, 217.

25. Lindsey Harlan, "Sati: The Story of Godāvarī," in *Devī: Goddesses of India*, edited by John S. Hawley and Donna M. Wulff (Berkeley: University of California Press, 1996), 233.

26. Frédérique Apffel Marglin, *Wives of the God-King: The Rituals of the Devadasis of Puri* (Delhi: Oxford University Press, 1985), 10, 18–20.

27. Ibid., 67.

28. Mary Hancock, *Womanhood in the Making: Domestic Ritual and Public Culture in Urban South India* (Boulder: Westview, 1999), 131, 133.

29. Marglin, *Wives*, 90.

30. Ibid., 240.

31. O'Flaherty, *Women, Androgynes and Other Mythical Beasts*, 68.

32. Mariasusai Dhavamony, *Love of God According to Śaiva Siddhānta: A Study in the Mysticism and Theology of Śaivism* (Oxford: Oxford University Press, 1971), 136–137.

33. Vidya Dehejia, *Āṇṭāl and Her Path of Love: Poems of a Woman Saint from South India* (Albany: State University of New York Press, 1990), 17.

34. Rajeshwari V. Pandharipanda, "Janābāī: A Woman Saint of India," in *Women Saints in World Religions*, edited by Arvind Sharma (Albany: State University of New York Press, 2000), 146.

35. Eleanor Zelliot, "Chokāmeḷā Piety and Protest," in *Bhakti Religion in North India: Community Identity & Political Action*, edited by David N. Lorenzen (Albany: State University of New York Press, 1995), 212–217.

36. Lisa Lassell Hallstrom, *Mother of Bliss: Ānandamayī Mā (1896–1982)* (Oxford: Oxford University Press, 1999), 36.

37. Alexander Lipski, "Some Aspects of the Life and Teachings of the East Bengali Saint Ānandamayī Mā," *History of Religions* 19/1 (1969): 71.

38. For a fuller discussion of this pattern, see A. K. Ramanujan, "On Women Saints" in *The Divine Consort: Rādhā and the Goddesses of India*, edited by John Stratton Hawley and Donna Marie Wulff (Berkeley: Berkeley Religious Studies Series, 1982), 316–324.

CHAPTER 12 DESIRE TRANSFORMED: TANTRA AND ŚĀKTISM

1. Hugh B. Urban, *Tantra: Sex, Secrecy, Politics, and Power in the Study of Religion* (Berkeley: University of California Press, 2003), 83, 88. See also Cynthia Ann Humes, "Wrestling with Kālī: South Asian and British Constructions of the Dark Goddess," in *Encountering Kālī: In the Margins, at the Center, in the West*, edited by Rachel Fell McDermott and Jeffrey J. Kripal (Berkeley: University of California Press, 2003), 155–161.

2. Urban, *Tantra*, 205.

3. André Padoux, *Le Coeur de la Yoginī: Yoginīhṛdaya avec le commentaire Dīpikā d'Amṛtānanda* (Paris: Diffusion de Boccard, 1994), 1.

4. Sumitra M. Katre, trans., *Aṣṭādhyāyī of Pāṇini* (Austin: University of Texas Press, 1987), 5.2.70, 7.2.9.

5. Alexis Sanderson, "Meaning in Tantric Ritual," in *Essais sur le rituel*, volume 3, Colloque du Centenaire de la Section des Sciences Religieuses de l'École Pratique des Hautes Études, edited by Anne-Marie Blondeau and Kristofer Schipper (Louvain: Peeters, 1995), 79.
6. Urban, *Tantra*, 43.
7. See David Snellgrove, *Indo-Tibetan Buddhism: Indian Buddhists and Their Tibetan Successors* (London: Serinda Publications, 1987), 152–160.
8. Ronald M. Davidson, *Indian Esoteric Buddhism: A Social History of the Tantric Movement* (New York: Columbia University Press, 2002), 262.
9. David Gordon White, *Kiss of the Yoginī: "Tantric Sex" in Its South Asian Contexts* (Chicago: University of Chicago Press, 2003), 124.
10. Douglas Renfrew Brooks, *The Secret of the Three Cities: An Introduction to Hindu Śākta Tantrism* (Chicago: University of Chicago Press, 1990), 65.
11. Mark S. G. Dyczkowski, "Kubjikā the Erotic Goddess: Sexual Potency, Transformation and Reversal in Heterodox Theophanies of the Kubjikā Tantras," *Indologica Taurinensia*, 21–22 (1995–1996): 139.
12. David Gordon White, *The Alchemical Body: Siddha Traditions in Medieval India* (Chicago: University of Chicago Press, 1996), 232.
13. Abhinavagupta, *The Tantrāloka of Abhinava Gupta with Jayaratha's Commentary*, 12 volumes, edited by Mukunda Rama Sastri and M. S. Kaul, Kashmir Series of Texts and Studies (Allahabad: Indian Press, 1918–1938), 29. 101, 105, 115–116.
14. Alexis Sanderson, "Śaivism and the Tantric Traditions," in *The World's Religions*, edited by Stewart Sutherland, Leslie Houlden, Peter Clarke, and Friedhelm Hardy (London: Routledge, 1988), 678–680.
15. J. A. Schoterman, ed., *The Yonitantra* (New Delhi: Manohar, 1980), 2.22–24.
16. White, *Kiss of the Yoginī*, 101.
17. White, *Alchemical Body*, 234–235.
18. Sanderson, "Śaivism and the Tantric Traditions," 683.
19. Ibid.
20. Mark S. G. Dyczkowski, *The Canon of the Śaivāgama and the Kubjikā Tantra of the Western Kaula Tradition* (Albany: State University of New York Press, 1988), 87–92.
21. J. A. Schoterman, trans., *The Satsāhasrasaṃhitā, Chapters 1–5* (Leiden: E. J. Brill, 1982), 11; and Teun Gourdiaan, "The Wedding of Śiva and the Goddess in the Kulālikāmnāya," in *Tantra in Practice*, edited by David Gordon White (Princeton: Princeton University Press, 2000), 188.
22. Jan Gonda, *Die Religionen Indiens I, Veda and älterer Hinduismus* (Stuttgart: W. Kohlhammer, 1960), 140–141.
23. Jan Gonda, *Change and Continuity in Indian Religion*, (The Hague: Mouton, 1965), 198–228.
24. Sudhir Kakar, *Intimate Relations: Exploring Indian Sexuality* (Chicago: University of Chicago Press, 1989), 91.
25. Jeffrey J. Kripal, *Kālī's Child: The Mystical and Erotic in the Life and Teachings of Ramakrishna* (Chicago: University of Chicago Press, 1995), 249.
26. Rachel Fell McDermott, "Kālī's Tongue: Historical Re-interpretations of the Blood-lusting Goddess," paper delivered at the Mid-Atlantic Regional Conference of the American Academy of Religion, Barnard College, New York, March 21, 1991. S. C. Banerji, *Tantra in Bengal: A Study in Its Origins, Development and Influence* (New Delhi: Manohar, 1978; second edition, 1992), 181.

27. Kripal, *Kālī's Child*, 249.
28. C. R. Hallpike, "Social Hair," *Man* (NS) 4 (1969): 260–261.
29. E. Alan Morinis, *Pilgrimage in the Hindu Tradition: A Case Study of West Bengal* (Delhi: Oxford University Press, 1984), 34.
30. Suchitra Samanta, "The 'Self-Animal' and Divine Digestion: Goat Sacrifice to the Goddess Kālī in Bengal," *Journal of Asian Studies* 53/3 (1994): 790.
31. David Kinsley, *Tantric Visions of the Divine Feminine: The Ten Mahāvidyās* (Berkeley: University of California Press, 1997), 6.
32. I have relied on the description provided by Sarah Caldwell, *Oh Terrifying Mother: Sexuality, Violence and Worship of the Goddess Kāli* (Delhi: Oxford University Press, 1999), 43–44, 107, 132–135.
33. Malcom McLean, *Devoted to the Goddess: The Life and Work of Ramprasad* (Albany: State University of New York Press, 1998), 58.
34. Rachel Fell McDermott, *Mother of My Heart, Daughter of My Dreams: Kālī and Umā in the Devotional Poetry of Bengal* (New York: Oxford: Oxford University Press, 2001), 46–47.
35. Ibid., 134.
36. Narasingha P. Sil, *Rāmakṛṣṇa: A Psychological Profile* (Leiden: E. J. Brill, 1991), 29.
37. Walter G. Neevel, Jr., "The Transformation of Śrī Rāmakrishna," in *Hinduism: New Essays in the History of Religions*, edited by Bardwell L. Smith (Leiden: E. J. Brill, 1982), 53–97.
38. Kripal, *Kālī's Child*, 2.
39. Swami Saradananda, *Sri Ramakrishna The Great Master*, 2 volumes, translated by Swami Jagadananda, fifth edition (Madras: Sri Ramakrishna Math, 1978, 1997), II: 825.
40. The themes of madness and play are explored more fully in Carl Olson, *The Mysterious Play of Kālī: An Interpretive Study of Rāmakrishna* (Atlanta: Scholars Press, 1990).

CHAPTER 13 THE WORLD OF THE GODDESS: VILLAGE HINDUISM

1. Wilhelm Rau, *Staat und Gesellschaft im alten Indien nach den Brahmana-Texten dargestellt* (Wiesbaden: F. Steiner Verlag, 1957).
2. Milton Singer, *When a Great Tradition Modernizes: An Anthropological Approach to Indian Civilization* (New York: Praeger, 1972), 268.
3. S. C. Dube, *Indian Village* (London: Routledge and Kegan Paul, 1955), 5.
4. Susan S. Wadley, "Grāma," in *The Hindu World*, edited by Sushil Mittal and Gene Thursby (New York: Routledge, 2004), 431.
5. See William Henricks Wiser, *The Hindu Jajmani System: A Socio-Economic System Inter-relating Members of a Hindu Community in Services* (Lucknow: Lucknow Publishing, 1958).
6. Dube, *Indian Village*, 90. Gerald D. Berreman, *Hindus of the Himalayas: Ethnography and Change* (Berkeley: University of California Press, 1972), 84.
7. Dube, *Indian Village*, 92–93.
8. Jonathan P. Parry, *Death in Benares* (Cambridge: Cambridge University Press, 1994), 230.
9. Lawence A. Babb, *The Divine Hierarchy: Popular Hinduism in Central India* (New York: Columbia University Press, 1975), 197–198.
10. Sarah Caldwell, *Oh Terrifying Mother: Sexuality, Violence, and Worship of the Goddess Kāli* (New Delhi: Oxford University Press, 1999), 11.
11. Berreman, *Hindus of the Himalayas*, 89.

12. Stanley A. Freed and Ruth S. Freed, *Hindu Festival in a North Indian Village*, Anthropological Papers of the American Museum of Natural History 81 (Seattle: University of Washington Press, 1998), 37.
13. Ibid., 250–251.
14. Murry Milner, Jr., *Status and Sacredness: A General Theory of Status Relations and an Analysis of Indian Culture* (New York: Oxford University Press, 1994), 47.
15. See Edward B. Harper, "A Hindu Village Pantheon," *Southwestern Journal of Anthropology* 15/3 (1959): 227–234.
16. Berreman, *Hindus of the Himalayas*, 95–96.
17. Freed and Freed; *Hindu Festival*, 124–125.
18. Richard L. Brubaker, "The Untamed Goddess of Village India," in *The Book of the Goddess Past and Present: An Introduction to Her Religion*, edited by Carl Olson (New York: Crossroad, 1983), 145–160.
19. Freed and Freed, *Hindu Festival*, 122.
20. Babb, *Divine Hierarchy*, 130.
21. Biardeau, *Stories about Posts: Vedic Variations around the Hindu Goddess*, translated by Alf Hiltebeitel, Marie-Louise Reiniche, and James Walker (Chicago: University of Chicago Press, 2004) 6–8.
22. Ibid., 74–75.
23. William P. Harman, *The Sacred Marriage of a Hindu Goddess* (Bloomington: Indiana University Press, 1989), 24.
24. David Dean Shulman views the loss of the third breast as a change from androgynous to female in *Tamil Temple Myths: Sacrifice and Divine Marriage in the South Indian Śaiva Tradition* (Princeton: Princeton University Press, 1980), 209–211.
25. Harman, *Sacred Marriage*, 97.
26. C. J. Fuller, "The Divine Couple's Relationship in a South Indian Temple: Mīnākṣī and Sundareśvara at Madurai," *History of Religions* 19/4 (1980): 333–334.
27. See E. Valentine Daniel, *Fluid Signs: Being a Person the Tamil Way* (Berkeley: University of California, 1984), 109–139, 149.
28. Berreman, *Hindus of the Himalayas*, 98.
29. Caldwell, *On Terrifying Mother*, 35.
30. Melinda A. Moore, "The Kerala House as a Hindu Cosmos," in *India through Hindu Categories*, edited by McKim Marriott (New Delhi: Sage, 1990), 169–202.
31. M. N. Srinavas, *Religion and Society among the Coorgs of South India* (Calcutta: Asia Publishing House, 1952; reprint 1965), 89–90.
32. See the discussion by Brenda E. F. Beck, "The Symbolic Merger of Body, Space, and Cosmos in Hindu Tamil Nadu," *Contributions of Indian Sociology* (NS) 10/2 (1976): 218–219.
33. Lawrence A. Babb, "Glancing: Visual Interaction in Hinduism," *Journal of Anthropological Research* 37 (1981): 395.
34. Babb, *Divine Hierarchy*, 51–53.
35. Isabelle Nabokov, *Religion against the Self: An Ethnography of Tamil Rituals* (Oxford: Oxford University Press, 2000).
36. Ibid., 70–85.
37. Gananath Obeyesekere, *Medusa's Hair: An Essay on Personal Symbols and Religious Experience* (Chicago: University of Chicago Press, 1981), 115–122.

38. Paul Younger, *Playing Host to Deity: Festival Religion in the South Indian Tradition* (Oxford: Oxford University Press, 2002), 96–101.
39. Kathleen M. Erndl, *Victory to the Mother: The Hindu Goddess of Northwest Indian in Myth, Ritual and Symbol* (New York: Oxford University Press, 1993), 105–134.
40. Biardeau, *Stories about Posts*, 275, 281, 283.
41. Babb, *Divine Hierarchy*, 236.
42. See Daniel, *Fluid Signs*, 189, and Susan S. Wadley, ed., *The Powers of Tamil Women* (New York: Maxwell School of Citizenship and Public Affairs, Syracuse University, 1980), 164.
43. Caldwell, *Oh Terrifying Mother*, 119.
44. Daniel, *Fluid Signs*, 185.
45. Ibid., 189–190.
46. Caldwell, *Oh Terrifying Mother*, 121.
47. Brenda E. F. Beck, "Colour and Heat in South Indian Ritual," *Man* 4/4 (1969): 553–572.
48. Ibid., 553.
49. For a fuller discussion of the distinction between auspiciousness and inauspiciousness, see T. N. Madan, "Concerning the Categories *śubha* and *śuddha* in Hindu Culture: An Exploratory Essay" (11–29) and Frédérique Apffel Marglin, "Types of Oppositions in Hindu Culture" (65–83) in *Purity and Auspiciousness in Indian Society*, edited by John B. Carman and Frédérique A. Marglin (Leiden: E. J. Brill, 1985).
50. Biardeau, *Stories about Posts*, 308.
51. Much of the material for this section relies on Srinavas, *Religion and Society*, 102–112, and Edward B. Harper, "Ritual Pollution as an Integrator of Caste and Religion," in *Religion in South Asia*, edited by Edward R. Harper (Seattle: University of Washington Press, 1964), 151–196.
52. Vasudha Narayanan, "Ālaya," in *The Hindu World*, edited by Sushil Mittal and Gene Thursby (New York: Routledge, 2004), 450.
53. Dube, *Indian Village*, 7.
54. See the informative essay by Richard L. Brubacker, "Barbers, Washermen, and Other Priests: Servants of the South Indian Village and Its Goddess," *History of Religions* 19/2 (1979): 128–152.
55. Dube, *Indian Village*, 114–115.

CHAPTER 14 REFORMERS, MISSIONARIES, AND GURUS IN MODERN HINDUISM

1. David Kopf, *The Brahmo Samaj and the Shaping of the Modern Indian Mind* (Princeton: Princeton University Press, 1979), 157.
2. Wilhelm Halbfass, *India and Europe: An Essay in Understanding* (Albany: State University of New York Press, 1988), 206.
3. Kopf, *Brahmo Samaj*, 268.
4. Halbfass, *India and Europe*, 245.
5. Kopf, *Brahmo Samaj*, 102.
6. Ibid., 300–303.
7. Joseph S. Alter, *Yoga in Modern India: The Body between Science and Philosophy* (Princeton: Princeton University Press, 2004), 171–172.
8. Bruce F. Campbell, *Ancient Wisdom Revised: A History of the Theosophical Movement* (Berkeley: University of California Press, 1980), 42.

9. Narasingha P. Sil, *Swami Vivekananda: A Reassessment* (Selinsgrove: Susquehanna University Press, 1977), 152.

10. Torkel Brekke, *Makers of Modern Indian Religion in the Late Nineteenth Century* (Oxford: Oxford University Press, 2003), 41, 48–49.

11. A. Rambachan, "Is Karmayoga an Indirect and Independent Means to Moksha? An Evaluation of Vivekananda's Arguments," *Religion* 15 (1985): 53–65.

12. Brian A. Hatcher, *Eclecticism and Modern Hindu Discourse* (Oxford: Oxford University Press, 1999), 117.

13. Gwilym Beckerlegge, *The Ramakrishna Mission: The Making of a Modern Hindu Movement* (Delhi: Oxford Univeristy Press, 2000); Jeffrey J. Kripal, *Kālī's Child: The Mystical and Erotic Life and Teachings of Ramakrishna* (Chicago: University of Chicago Press, 1995), and Carl Olson, *Mysterious Play of Kālī: An Interpretive Study of Rāmakrishna* (Atlanta: Scholars Press, 1990).

14. Swami Vivekananda, *The Complete Works of Swami Vivekananda*, 8 volumes, seventeenth edition (Calcutta: Advaita Ashrama, 1986), V: 75, 81.

15. Halbfass, *India and Europe*, 249.

16. Sri Aurobindo, *The Life Divine*, sixth edition (Pondicherry: Sri Aurobindo Ashram, 1970), 4.

17. Ibid., 22.

18. Ibid., 32, 36.

19. Ibid., 278.

20. Ibid., 73.

21. Larry D. Shinn, "Auroville: Visionary Images and Social Consequences in a South Indian Utopian Community," *Religious Studies* 20/2 (1984): 247, 252.

22. H. T. Dave, trans., *Shree Swaminarayan's Vachanamritam* (Bombay: Bharatiya Vidya Bhavam, 1977), Penchala 4, 335.

23. Ibid., Loya 6.

24. Ibid., Gadhada I.47.

25. Ibid., Kariyani, 7.

26. Manilal C. Parekh, *Shri Swaminarayan* (Bombay: Bharatiya Vidya Bhavan, 1980), 176.

27. *Vachanamritam*, Gadhada I.47; II.9.

28. Ibid., Gadhada, II.8, 38.

29. Raymond Brady Williams, *An Introduction to Swaminarayan Hinduism* (Cambridge: Cambridge University Press, 2001), 233.

30. Gerald James Larson, *India's Agony over Religion* (Albany: State University of New York Press, 1995), 14.

31. Alter, *Yoga in Modern India*, 26, 33.

32. Peter Schreiner, "Sri Ramakrishna und Ramana Maharshi als Vertreter moderner indischer Mystik," in *Raush-Ekstase-Mystik: Grenzformen religiöser Erhafrung*, edited by Hubert Cancik (Düsseldorg: Patmos Verlag, 1978): 59–77.

33. Lawrence A. Babb, *Redemptive Encounters: Three Modern Styles in the Hindu Tradition* (Berkeley: University of California Press, 1986), 179.

34. Ibid., 171.

35. Lise McKean, *Divine Enterprise: Gurus and the Hindu Nationalist Movement* (Chicago: University of Chicago Press, 1996), 168.

36. Karen Pechilis, "Gurumayi, the Play of Shakti and Guru," in *The Graceful Guru: Hindu Female Gurus in India and the United States*, edited by Karen Pechilis (Oxford: Oxford University Press, 2004), 223.

37. See Babb, *Redemptive Encounters*, 93–155.

38. Diana L. Eck, *A New Religious America: How a "Christian Country" Has Now Become the World's Most Religiously Diverse Nation* (New York: Harper San Francisco, 2001), 104.

39. Paul Heelas, *The New Age Movement* (Oxford: Blackwell, 1996), 28.

40. Michael York, *The Emerging Network: A Sociology of the New Age and Neo-Pagan Movements* (Lanham, Md.: Rowman and Littlefield, 1995), 34.

INDEX

Dharmasūtras; of of *Āpastamba*, 14, 82; of *Baudhāyana*, 82; of *Gautama*, 82, 92–93; of *Jaimini*, 82; of *Vasiṣṭha*, 82; *Hiranyakeśn*, 82
dhi (insight), 59
dhimmis (protected people of the book), 21
Dhṛtarāṣṭra, 188
dhyāna (meditation), 109
Digambara Jainas, 16, 231
Dignāga, 18
dīkṣā (consecration), 53
Dīkṣitar, Muthuswami, 202
dirt, 87–88
discus, 150, 153
Dīvāli/Dīpāvali (the festival of lights), 161
Divine Light Missions, 337, 343
dohās (powers), 209
doḷamelaṇa (swing festival), 183
Draupadī, 189–191, 260, 315
Dravidian culture, 4, 11, 17, 85, 222
Droṇa, 189–190
dualism of consciousness and materiality (*puruṣa* and *prakṛti),* 159
Duhśāsana, 189–190
Dumont, L., 77
durbar (audience hall), 92
Durgā, 33, 252–253, 326
Duryodhana, 189
dūtī, 283
Dutt, N., 296
Dvaita Vedānta school, 160
Dvāpara Yuga, 81, 146
Dyaus, the sky god, 42, 251
Dyer, General, 29

earth, 41, 152, 188, 196, 219, 223–224, 251, 263
east, 50
East India Company, 23–24, 26, 324
ecstasy, 111, 118, 296
eighteen, 141
ekāgratā (concentration on one point), 109
Ekanātha, 179–180, 209
ekarasa (immersed in devotion), 207
Ellora, 20
enstasy, 111, 118
Epics, 142, 187, 215, 276
equitheism, 8
Eschatology, Vedic, 57–59
Eṭṭuokai (The Eight Anthologies), 154
evil, 219
exorcism, 168–169, 185–186, 240, 277

festivals, 128–129, 305–306, 323; Krishna, 182–183; Vaiṣṇava, 161–163; village, 309–311
Firdausī, 21
fire, 37–47, 225, 266, 282, 316, 326
fire-sacrifices (*homā*), 57–59, 72
firewalkers, 315–316
flute, 168
food, 49, 55, 88, 132–133, 268, 274, 308, 319–320
funerary process, death and cremation, 99–100

Gaja Lakṣmī, 152
gāna, 13
gaṇas (deformed figures), 218, 223
gancārīs, 248
Gānapatyas, 277
Gandhāra school, 17
Gāndhārī, 188, 191
Gandhi, Indira, 32–33, 273
Gandhi, M. K. (Mahatma), 27–33, 86, 202, 328
Gandhi, Rajiv, 33–34
Gaṇeśa, 1, 96, 123, 223–224, 227, 253, 277
Ganges, 11, 128, 131–132, 146, 188, 191, 220, 222, 247, 280, 295
garbhādhāna, 94
garbha-gṛha (womb room), 135
Gārgī, 255
gārhapatya fire, 50–51
Garuḍa, 18, 151, 164, 195
Gauḍapāda, 112–113
Gauḍīya Vaiṣṇava tradition, 130, 173–175
Gauri, 225
Gautama, 197
Gāyatrī-mantra, 96
gazing, 48
gift, 48, 55, 125, 159, 234, 247, 257, 268, 289
Gītā Govinda (of Jayadeva), 168, 175, 182
Gitanjali (of R. Tagore), 325
godāna (shaving head), 96
Godāvarī River, 179
goddess/es, 250–253, 273, 284, 303–323
gods (*devas*), 47, 55, 63, 156–157, 159–160, 176, 180, 200, 208–210, 221, 223–224, 232–235, 242–244, 256, 306–307, 325, 327, 343
Gokhale, G. K., 27
Gopāla, 164
Gopīkā Gītā, 182
gopīs, 161, 164–170, 171–173, 177, 182–183, 185, 270
gopuram (temple pyramids), 244
Gosvāmī, Jīva, 174
Gosvāmī, Rūpa, 174
gotra (family descent), 76, 89
Govardhana, Mount, 133, 161, 172
Govardhana *pūjā*, 161
Government of India Act, 26
grace, 158–160, 170, 208, 211, 233–236, 238, 270, 310
Granth Sahib, 23
Greeks, 5, 7
gṛhastha (stage of the householder), 84
gṛhya (domestic), 51, 84
Gṛhyasutras, 82, 265
Guha, 197
Guhyakālī, 277
Guhyasāmaja Tantra, 276
guilds (*shreni*), 17
Guṇabhadva, 198
guṇas (strands), 72, 97, 105–106, 111, 118, 336
Gupta dynasty, 17–19, 141, 151, 153, 188, 198
Gupta, M., 246
Gurjara-Pratīhāras, 20
guru, 154–155, 175, 179–180, 201, 208, 211, 214–215, 222, 241, 243, 268, 278, 282, 284, 298, 321, 324, 330, 335–345
Guru Gobind, 23
Gurukulas (training institutions), 327
Guru Maharaj Ji, 337, 343
Gurumayi, 337, 344
Guru Tegh Bahadur, 23
Gyandev, 209

hair of renouncer, 76
Hanumān, 194–196, 199, 201, 297
Hardāsi, 178
Haridāsa, 178
Harijan (children of god), 31, 86, 203
Harivaṃśa, 164
Harṣa, 19–20
hartal, 29
Hastings, Warren, 24
Haṭha yoga, 108, 230
haviryajñas sacrifice, 52
hearing (*śravaṇa*), 115
Hedgewar K. B., 35
Helidorous, 164
hell, 142–143
Hevaja Tantra, 276
Hind Swaraj (Indian Home rule), 28
Hindu, as a term, 5–9
Hindu Marriage Act, 269
Hindu Marriage Validating Act, 269
Hindu Succession Act, 269
Hindutva, 6–7
Hiraṇyakaśipu, 145
hlādinī (pure bliss), 174
Holi festival, 128–129, 182
Homer, 188, 192
horse, 3, 11, 91–92
horse sacrifice, 19, 55, 91–92
hotṛ priest, 48, 91
Hsüan Tsang, 20
Hūṇas, 18–19

Ibn 'Arabi, 21
inauspiciousness, 76, 257–258, 304
India/n, 4–5, 44, 346
Indian history, 15–35
Indian Opinion, 28
Indian National Congress, 329
Indo-Aryan, 4, 9–13, 15
Indra, 3, 39–40, 42–43, 52, 57, 59, 65–66, 75, 90–91, 100, 133, 146–147, 188, 191, 196–197, 220–222, 224, 251, 268
Indrajit, 195
Indraprāṣṭha, 184
Industrial Revolution, 26
Indus Valley civilization, 5, 9–11
initiation (*dikṣā*), 46–47
integral experience (*anubhava*), 119
Integral yoga, 333, 335
International Society for Krishna Consciousness 183–184, 337
Irāmāvatāram (of Kampaṅ), 205
Irupāvirupatu (of Aruḻnandi), 234
iruvinaippu (equality of two deeds), 235
Irwin, Lord, 30
Islam, 8–9, 327
iṣṭaliṅga (personal *liṅga*), 241, 243–244
iṣṭis (class of ritual), 52
Īśvara, 117
Īśvarakrishna, 103–104, 106
Īśa Upaniṣad, 14

Jābāla Upaniṣad, 62, 74
Jagannatha temple in Puri, 172
Jahangir, 22
Jaimini, 102
Jaiminīya Brāhmaṇa, 13
Jainas (Jains), 161, 197–198, 232, 236
Jainism, 4, 16, 18, 28
Jakākya Saṃhitā, 153
Jallianwalla Bagh, 29
Jambūdvipa, 142
Janābāī, 271
Janata Morcha, 33
jaṅgama (moving), 241, 243
jatakarma (birth rite), 95
Jaṭāyus, 194, 197
jātis (subcastes), 87, 312
jātis and *varṇa*, 87, 100
Jesus, 296, 343
Jinnah, M. A., 31
jīva (self, soul), 118, 170, 244
Jīva Gosvāmī, 174
jīvanmukti (liberated while alive), 73, 80
jñāna, 71, 107
Jñāneśvara or Jñānadeva, 179–180
Jones, Sir William, 25
Judaism, 9
Jumna River, 128
jyotirśāstra (science of astrology), 14
Jyotisa (astronomy), 49

Kabīr, 5, 21, 200, 205, 209–211, 213, 216
Kabīr Panth, 216
Kabīr Parachai (of Anantadās), 210
kaccā (imperfect food), 83
Kailāsa, Mount, 232, 247, 309
Kailāsanātha, 20
Kailasa temple, 20
kaivalya (isolation), 108
kāla (time), 57, 67–68, 99, 228
Kalabhra Interregnum, 232
kaḷam (drawing), 294
Kālamukha sect, 228–229, 277
Kālī, 219, 225, 252, 272–273, 275, 277, 286–298, 314, 326, 332
Kālidāsa, 18
Kālikā Purāṇa, 289
Kālīkulakramārcana (of Vimalaprabudha), 286
Kālīukla tradition, 287
kali yuga, 81–82, 142, 145, 149, 171, 184, 200
Kalkin, 148–149
kalpa, 14, 142
Kalpasūtras, 82
kāma (desire), 84, 136, 152, 175, 221
Kāma or Kāmadeva, 223, 253, 293
Kāmākṣī, 226, 253
Kameśvarī, 277
Kaṃsa, 149, 164–165
Kāñcimāhātmya, 225–226
Kāñcīpuram, 20, 159, 226, 232, 253
Kaniṣka, 17
Kanka, 190
Kānphaṭaṣ, 229–230
Kāpālika Śaivism, 228–230, 237, 277, 286
Kapila, 103, 131
Kāraikkālammaiyār, 270
kārikās (verses), 102

ABOUT THE AUTHOR

PROFESSOR CARL OLSON has taught at Allegheny College since 1981. The college has appointed him to the National Endowment for the Humanities Chair (1991–1994), Teacher-Scholar Professorship of the Humanities (2000–2003), and chairperson. During 2002, he was appointed to a Visiting Fellowship at Clare Hall, University of Cambridge, and was elected a Permanent Fellow of Clare Hall by its board of trustees.

Professor Olson has published over two hundred articles and reviews for various journals. He has served as review editor for the *International Journal of Hindu Studies* since 1996. He has also published the following books: *The Book of the Goddess Past and Present: An Introduction of Her Religion* (1983); *The Mysterious Play of Kali: An Interpretive Study of Ramakrishna* (1990); *The Theology and Philosophy of Eliade: A Search for the Centre* (1992); *The Indian Renouncer and Postmodern Poison: A Cross-Cultural Encounter* (1997); *Zen and the Art of Postmodern Philosophy: Two Paths of Liberation from the Representational Mode of Thinking* (2000); and *Indian Philosophers and Postmodern Thinkers: Dialogues on the Margins of Culture* (2002); *The Different Paths of Buddhism: A Narrative – Historical Introduction* (2005); *Original Buddhist Sources: A Reader* (2005).